TOLSTOY'S DIARIES
VOLUME II

Tolstoy's Diaries

Volume II: 1895–1910

Edited and translated by
R. F. CHRISTIAN

FABER & FABER

This edition first published in 2015
by Faber & Faber Ltd
Bloomsbury House, 74–77 Great Russell Street
London WC1B 3DA

Printed by Books on Demand GmbH, Norderstedt

All rights reserved
Selection, English translation and editorial matter © R. F. Christian, 1985
Preface © Rosamund Bartlett, 2010

The right of R. F. Christian to be identified
as author of this work has been asserted in accordance
with Section 77 of the Copyright, Designs and Patents Act 1988

This book is sold subject to the condition that it shall not, by way of
trade or otherwise, be lent, resold, hired out or otherwise circulated
without the publisher's prior consent in any form of binding or cover other than
that in which it is published and without a similar condition including this
condition being imposed on the subsequent purchaser

A CIP record for this book is available from the British Library

ISBN 978–0–571–32405–7

Our authorised representative in the EU for product safety is
Easy Access System Europe, Mustamäe tee 50, 10621 Tallinn, Estonia
gpsr.requests@easproject.com

Contents

Preface to the 2015 Edition   vii
The Diaries
1895–1902   397
1903–1910   505
Notes   689
Index   741

Preface to the 2015 Edition

Tolstoy's literary activities famously began in the venereal diseases clinic of Kazan University in the spring of 1847, when he was eighteen years old. During the month that he spent in the clinic, in almost complete isolation, he started keeping a diary. To begin with, Tolstoy regarded his diary as a record of his hopelessly optimistic self-improvement programme. Later it became an outlet for his creative and philosophical reflections, and as such comprises an indispensable companion to his published writings, both fictional and otherwise.

Keeping a diary, for Tolstoy, was not the deeply private affair it is for most people, even if it started out that way. In the all-too-brief week between Tolstoy's proposal and marriage to Sonya Behrs in September 1862, he felt it incumbent upon him to give his young fiancée his diaries to read. The vivid realism which is the hallmark of Tolstoy's fiction is matched by the frankness of his diary entries, but he did not feel he should conceal anything in his past from his future bride.

As an innocent and inexperienced eighteen-year-old girl, who had seen little of life, Sonya was deeply shocked and upset by what she later termed his 'excessive conscientiousness', particularly when it came to reading about his sexual history with peasant girls. Nevertheless, she went ahead with the marriage and before long she and her husband were regularly and sometimes frenetically reading each other's diaries. It was a habit kept up until the very last months of Tolstoy's long life in the summer and autumn of 1910, when his deteriorating relations with Sonya led him to try for the first time to keep a diary for 'himself alone'.

Tolstoy did not keep a diary regularly throughout his life, for sometimes he transferred his exploration and articulation of psychological processes to his fictional works. Since his diaries span his entire adult life, however, they are indispensable reading for anyone seeking to look behind the scenes of the great novels and become better acquainted with their creator.

The same is true of Tolstoy's letters, and his epistolary output was, as one might expect, equally prodigious – there are 8,500 letters published in the Russian edition of his *Complete Collected Works*. Tolstoy wrote thousands of letters, to all manner of people, from persecuted peasant sectarians exiled to Siberia to the Romanovs, eventually addressing both *muzhik* and Tsar as 'Dear brother'.

The most touching letters Tolstoy wrote were to his immediate family – his wife Sonya, his children, his 'aunt' and surrogate mother Tatyana Alexandrovna ('Toinette'), his sister and brothers. The most important letters he wrote were to his closest friends. First there was his distant relative Alexandra Andreyevna, a lady-in-waiting at Court, for whom he had the deepest respect and affection until his defection from the Orthodox Church. Then there was the shy and retiring Nikolay Strakhov, who worked at the Imperial Library in St Petersburg, but the most frequent recipient of Tolstoy's letters was the aristocratic Vladimir Chertkov, his devoted follower. Chertkov was instrumental in disseminating Tolstoy's religious ideas in translation, and thousands of people, from a dizzying array of faiths, felt compelled after reading them to write to the 'Sage of Yasnaya Polyana' for his advice on how to live their lives. Tolstoy tried to reply to them all.

It will be a long time before we have full English editions of the fourteen volumes of Tolstoy's diaries and the twenty-five volumes of his letters in the *Complete Collected Works*. In the meantime, we can be eternally grateful to R. F. Christian, doyen of Anglophone Tolstoy studies, for doing all the hard work for us. The result of Professor Christian's scrupulous work is four manageable volumes containing faithful translations of the most important of Tolstoy's diary entries and letters. Rendered into supple English, they are enhanced by judicious and helpful annotations, and introductions which draw on Professor Christian's deep knowledge, the fruit of a distinguished career of studying and writing about Tolstoy. It is hard to see how these invaluable editions can be surpassed.

Rosamund Bartlett

Rosamund Bartlett is the author of Tolstoy: A Russian Life (*Profile Books*).

R. F. Christian's four volumes of Tolstoy's Diaries *and* Letters *are all available in Faber Finds.*

1895–1902

Much of Tolstoy's energy in the last years of the nineteenth century was concentrated on his vigorous campaign on behalf of the Dukhobors, victims of religious persecution in the south of Russia, many of whom were eventually resettled in Canada thanks largely to his efforts and the financial proceeds of *Father Sergey* and *Resurrection*. *Father Sergey* is often linked with *The Devil* and *The Kreutzer Sonata* because of their common theme of sexual passion and its evil potential, although Tolstoy was concerned to show that the struggle against pride and worldly fame was even more difficult to wage than the struggle against lust. His wide-ranging, if artistically flawed, major novel *Resurrection* was in effect a vast synthesis of all his social, political and religious ideas. To the same period belong the short story *Master and Man* with its theme of an eleventh-hour act of unselfishness in the face of death, and the stimulating, irritating and iconoclastic treatise *What is Art?* All these works were written when Tolstoy was approaching seventy, and they were written against a background of an unsettled family life, complicated by his absurd jealousy of his wife's platonic friendship with the composer Taneyev, his puritanical disapproval of his son's disorderly behaviour and his anxiety over his daughters' matrimonial intentions.

In his seventieth year Tolstoy was busy organising aid for the starving peasants of the Tula province. Three years later he was excommunicated from the Orthodox Church for his heretical beliefs and writings, and retaliated with *A Reply to the Holy Synod's Edict*. Shortly afterwards he became seriously ill, and was persuaded to move to the Black Sea coast of the Crimea to the luxurious house of the wealthy Countess Panina near Yalta, where he and his wife lived for nearly a year until he was well enough to return to Yasnaya Polyana in the summer of 1902. Despite his serious illness he continued to work as and when he could, his most important essay being *What is Religion and What is its Essential Nature?* While convalescing in the Crimea he also wrote a long letter to Nicholas II appealing to him among other things to abolish the private ownership of land. Not surprisingly there was no reply. Despite his advancing years and erratic health, Tolstoy's energy remained formidable. If his enthusiasm for bicycling and tennis waned, he continued to ride and walk long distances and he kept up an extensive correspondence. He published no more works of fiction in his life-time, but his posthumous publications show that his creative energy was by no means exhausted. In 1902 he was still working on his late masterpiece *Hadji Murat* (eventually finished, but not published, in 1904), the theme of which took him back to his days as a soldier in the Caucasus, and seemed to accord ill with his belief in the doctrine of non- resistance to evil by force. He also returned intermittently to his drama *The Light Shineth in Darkness*, which Shaw believed was his greatest play, and in which Tolstoy appeared to be mocking all his most cherished ideas and to be hinting at the disastrous results likely to follow from becoming a 'Tolstoyan'!

1895

3 January, Nikolskoye The Olsufyevs'.[1] We set off as planned on the 1st. I worked on *Master and Man* till the last hour. It's now respectable artistically, but still weak in content. The business about the photograph is very sad. They are all offended. I wrote a letter to Chertkov.[2] Even before that I felt unwell, and I was unwell and weak when I set off. We arrived in good shape. The next day and today I did nothing – read, walked and slept. Yesterday there was a lively argument about Orthodoxy. All the confusion of understanding is due to the fact that people don't acknowledge that to live is to be part of the process of improving oneself and improving life. *Be better and make life better*. I've made no notes these last days. It's now gone 8 in the evening – I'm sleepy.

Today is 6 January, Nikolskoye I'm quite well and have begun work again on *The Catechism*: yesterday and today. It interests me very much and is very near to my heart, but I still can't find the right form and am dissatisfied. Read my story[3] the day before yesterday evening. It's not good. Both lack character. Now I know what to do. Twice argued with Dmitry Adamovich.[4] He has organised for himself a form of practical service to the people in a Slavophile spirit, i.e. a feather-bed on which to lie, and not work. The point is that they regard life as static and not fluid. Thought about something very important yesterday and forgot it. Mikhail Adamovich[5] is obviously afraid of Tanya. It's a great shame. And she's thin and pale. Received many pleasant letters: from Kenworthy, Sergeyenko[6] and Stadling. Did some thinking. [. . .]

It's now 6 o'clock in the evening. I'll go for a walk and also see the Christmas tree. Went to the hospital today and was present at an operation.

29 January, Moscow Haven't written my diary for more than three weeks. Had a good time at the Olsufyevs'. Was mainly busy with the story. And I still haven't finished it, although it's in proof. An important event which, I'm afraid, won't be without consequence for me is the Tsar's audacious speech.[7] We went to Shakovskoy's meeting. We shouldn't have done so. It's all stupid, and it's obvious that an organisation paralyses the powers of individual people. [. . .][8]

Today is 7 February, 11 o'clock in the morning, Moscow [. . .] More than a week has passed. During this time I wrote a short foreword to the biography of Drozhzhin and continued revising my story. An unfortunate story. It was the cause of a terrible storm on Sonya's part that broke out yesterday. She was unwell, weak and exhausted after dear Vanechka's illness, and I've been unwell these last few days. It began with her beginning to copy out the proofs. When I asked why . . . [A page of the diary has been torn out here.]

Help me not to desert Thee, not to forget who I am, or what and why I am. Help me.

Thought during this time: [. . .]
(4) The situation of the majority of people educated in true brotherly love and now oppressed by the deceit and cunning of those who wield power and who force this majority to ruin their own lives – this situation is terrible and seems to offer no way out. Only two ways out present themselves and both are barred: one is to break violence by violence, terror, dynamite bombs and daggers as our nihilists and anarchists did, to smash the conspiracy of governments against peoples, without our participation; the other is to enter into agreement with the government, make concessions to it and, by taking part in it, gradually unravel the net which holds the people fast and free it. Both ways out are barred.

Dynamite and daggers, as experience shows us, only provoke reaction and destroy the most valuable power, the only power in our control – public opinion; the other way out is barred by the fact that governments have already come to know how far to tolerate the participation of people who want to reform them. They only tolerate what doesn't destroy the essentials, and are very sensitive about what is harmful to them, sensitive because it concerns their very existence. They do tolerate people who don't agree with them and want to reform the government, not only in order to satisfy the demands of these people, but also for their own sakes, for the sake of the government. These people would be dangerous for governments if they remained outside these governments and rose up against them; they would strengthen the one weapon which is stronger than governments – public opinion – and so they need to make these people safe, win them over by means of concessions made by the government, render them harmless like microbe cultures – and then use them to serve the aims of governments, i.e. the oppression and exploitation of the people.

Both ways out are firmly and impenetrably barred. What then remains? You can't break violence by violence – you increase reaction; nor can you join the ranks of government – you become an instrument of government. Only one thing remains: to fight the government with weapons of thought, word and way of life, not making concessions to it, not joining its ranks, not increasing its power oneself. That's the one thing necessary, and it will probably be successful. And this is what God wants and this is what Christ taught.

(5) Looking at what goes on in all assemblies, at what goes on in society with its conventional proprieties and entertainments, I was struck very vividly by the thought which, I think, had never occurred to me before, that only evil is done by a group, or crowd or an assembly. Good is done only by each individual person separately. [. . .]

15 February God has helped me; helped me in that He has manifested Himself in me, though weakly, through love – love for those who do us evil, i.e. the only true love. And once this feeling had manifested itself, it first of all overwhelmed and inflamed me, and then those near to me as well, and everything disappeared, i.e. the suffering disappeared.

The following days things got worse. She was decidedly close to madness and to suicide. The children followed her on foot and by vehicle, and brought her back home. She was suffering terribly. It was the devil of jealousy, insane, groundless jealousy. I had only to love her again for me to understand her motives, and having understood her motives, it wasn't a question of forgiving her, but there being nothing to forgive. Sent the story to the *Northern Herald*, and it's being printed here by her and also in *The Intermediary*.⁹ I finished three fables and sent them off.¹⁰

15 February, Moscow Got up tired in the morning and couldn't do any work. Ivan Ivanovich¹¹ and Goltsev came. I refused to sign the petition about legalising freedom of the press.¹² [. . .]

Today, I think, is 21 February, Moscow. These five days I've been revising the fables, revising *Master and Man*, and thinking about – I can't say writing – the *Catechism*. Sonya's health is fully restored. Snegiryov came and explained that it was the menopause which comes with old age. How good to grow old and free.

An event which astonished me very much during this time was the drunkenness and rowdyism of the Petersburg students.¹³ It's terrible. This is what they have reduced the young to – by they, I mean not only the government, but also the liberals and revolutionaries, the ringleaders with no basis. Another thing: Škarvan's refusal to serve, the demand by Alyokhin and others in Nalchik to pay allegiance without swearing an oath, and Posha's fine all seem to me to be the start of a direct conflict with the government.¹⁴ I very much want to write about this, and several times have had clear ideas about it. Clear ideas how to describe the lies amid which we live and what supports them, and to include at the same time that simple philosophy which I express in the *Catechism*.

Thought: [. . .] (4) Further clarified my ideas during this time in a conversation with the young Goryushin, a friend of Pavel Petrovich,¹⁵ about a subject I never cease to think about – the state: we have reached the point where a merely good and reasonable man cannot take part in the affairs of state, i.e. cannot be in sympathy with it – I'm not speaking about our own Russia, but cannot be in sympathy in England with the ownership of land and exploitation by factory owners and capitalists, or with the extermination of peoples in Africa, the preparations for wars and wars themselves. And the firm ground on which a man says: 'I don't know what the state is or how it works, and I don't want to know, but I do know that I can't live contrary to my conscience' – this point of view is unshakeable, and the people of our time must adopt it in order to further the progress of life. I know what my conscience bids me, and you people who are concerned with the state, you organise it as you like, as long as it conforms with the demands of the conscience of the people of our time. But meanwhile people are abandoning this unshakeable ground and adopting the point of view that state forms must be amended and improved, and they are thereby losing their ground by acknowledging the need for the state, and so departing from their unshakeable point of view. Not clear, but I think I'll write about this theme. It seems very important to me.

It's now 12 o'clock. I'm going to send the proofs to Petersburg, and Sonya is very agitated. Poor woman. I'm sorry for her and love her, the more so now that I know about her illness.

Yesterday Ogranovich helped me to be more fair towards Lyova.¹⁶ He explained to me that it's a latent form of malaria. And I began to understand his condition and to feel sorry for him, but I still can't summon up any vital feeling of love for him.

Today is the 26th night-time, Moscow We've buried Vanechka.[17] A terrible – no, not a terrible, but a great spiritual event. I thank Thee, Father. I thank Thee.

Today is 12 March, Moscow So much has been felt, thought, and lived through during this time that I don't know what to write. The death of Vanechka was for me, like the death of Nikolenka – no, to a far greater degree – a manifestation of God, a drawing of me towards Him. And so not only can I not say that it was a sad, painful event but I can say outright that it was a joyful one – not joyful, that's a bad word – but a merciful event, coming from God, disentangling the lies of life, and bringing me closer to Him.

Sonya can't see it that way. For her the pain – almost physical – of separation conceals the spiritual importance of the event. But she astonished me. The pain of separation immediately released her from all that was darkening her soul. It was as if doors had been thrown open and the divine essence of love which constitutes our soul had been uncovered. She astonished me during the first days by her amazing power of love: everything that in any way destroyed love, that was a condemnation of anyone or anything, even a gesture of ill-will – all this offended her, made her suffer and caused a painful contraction of the newly exposed shoot of love. But time passes, and that shoot is hidden once more, and her suffering ceases to find satisfaction, *vent*, [relief], in universal love, and is becoming unrelievedly painful. She suffers particularly because the object of her love has gone from her, and she thinks that her happiness was in that object and not in the love itself. She can't separate the one from the other; she can't take a religious view of life in general or of her own. She can't clearly understand and feel that there are only two alternatives: either there is death, which hangs over all of us, has power over us and can separate us and deprive us of the happiness of love, or else there is no death, but only a series of changes which happen to all of us, among which one of the most important is death, and that these changes come over all of us like waves, in different combinations, some earlier, others later.

I try to help her, but I can see that I haven't helped her so far. But I love her, and to be with her is both painful and good for me. She is still weak physically: no periods for two months, and she sometimes thinks she is pregnant. Poor dear Tanya is also very weak. We are all very close to one another, as D.[18] put it very well: just as when one leaf falls, the others soon bunch closer together. I feel very weak physically and can't write anything. Worked a bit on the *Catechism*. But only in thought. Wrote a letter to Schmitt with a programme for an international *Intermediary*.[19] During this time *Master and Man* came out, and I hear praises on all sides and I don't like it, but despite that, I feel a petty, vain satisfaction.

Felt like writing something literary today. Tried to remember what things of mine were unfinished. It would be good to finish them all, namely:
(1) Koni's story, (2) *Who is Right?*, (3) *Father Sergey*, (4) *The Devil in Hell*, (5) *The Coupon*, (6) *Notes of a Mother*, (7) *Alexander I*, (8) the drama, (9) The settlers and the Bashkirs.[20] At the same time I must finish the Catechism. And now having planned all this – enough work for about eight years at least – I may die tomorrow. And that's good.

Thought during this time: [...]
(3) The death of children from an objective point of view: nature tried to give forth her best, and when she sees the world isn't ready for them, she takes them back again. But she has to try, in order to advance. It's an experiment. And like swallows which fly in too early, they die of cold. But they must fly in all the same. So with Vanechka. But this is an objective, foolish argument. A sensible argument is that he did the work of God: the establishment of the kingdom of God through the increase of love – more so than many people who lived for half a century and more.
(4) Sonya often said: 'He saved me from evil. Mine is a bad and harsh nature; he softened it by his love, and brought me closer to God.' As if he isn't doing so now! [...]
(6) Yes, one must always live as though a favourite child is dying in a room nearby. He is always dying. And I am always dying. [...]
(8) A few days after Vanechka's death when love began to grow weaker within me (what God gave me through Vanechka's life and death will never be destroyed), I thought that it would be good to sustain that love in myself by seeing all people as children – imagining them as they were at the age of seven. I can do that. And it's good.
(9) The joy of life without temptation is the subject of art.
(10) Understood with a new special force that my life and that of all people is only service, and has no end in itself.
(11) Read a bad article by Solovyov against non-resistance.[21] Every practical moral injunction contains the possibility of contradicting that injunction by another one deriving from the same principle. Abstinence: well, should we stop eating, and become incapable of serving mankind? Don't kill animals: well, should we let them eat each other? Don't drink alcohol. Well, should we not take communion, or use alcohol for medicinal purposes? Don't resist evil by violence. Well, should we let a man kill himself and others?

Trying to look for these contradictions only shows that a person who spends his time at it doesn't want to follow the moral rule. It's always the same story: because of one person who needs alcohol for medicinal purposes, drunkenness is not resisted. Because of one imaginary aggressor, people kill, execute and imprison. [...]

Today is the 18th   Morning. Five days have passed. I've done nothing. In the mornings I've thought about the *Catechism*. Once I wrote a little more of *Father Sergey*, but it wasn't good. Masha has gone to Ilya's. Sonya is moving into a new stage of life, with painful suffering. Help her, Lord. All this time I've had headaches and felt great weakness. In the evenings there have been many visitors. And they depress me very much.

Writing, especially works of fiction, is frankly harmful to me morally. When I was writing *Master and Man* I succumbed to the desire for fame. And the praise and the success of it are a sure indication that it was a bad thing to do. Today I seem to have woken up a little morally. [...]

Today is 27 March, Moscow   During this time I've written, or rather revised, letters to Schmitt and Kenworthy and somebody else. And apart from that, to my shame,

I've done nothing. I don't like the letters to Kenworthy and Schmitt with the plan for a European edition. A voice in the bottom of my heart seems to say that it isn't good. And I don't think it is. I've written nothing; I'm not dissatisfied with myself. The love of God has not deserted me.

With Seryozha I feel well and at ease. And I don't remember any unkind feeling towards anyone in all this time. Since I don't hear all the criticisms, but only the praise for *Master and Man*, I have the impression of a lot of fuss, and remember the anecdote about the preacher who stopped at a burst of applause which drowned a phrase of his and asked: 'Did I say something stupid?' I feel the same and know I've done something stupid: spending time on the artistic revision of a shallow story. The idea itself is unclear and laboured – not simple. The story is bad. And I would like to write an anonymous criticism of it if I had the time and it didn't mean bothering about something that isn't worth it.

During this time I've visited Izyumchenko in prison and Khokhlov in hospital.[22] Izyumchenko is very simple and cheerful. Khokhlov is very pitiable. I'd also like to write about the cruelty of this form of violence. Sonya is still suffering and can't raise herself to a religious height. Probably she needs this suffering, and it's doing its work within her. I'm sorry for her. But I believe it's necessary – necessary in order to feel the action of the hand of God, to recognise it and to love it. I was thinking yesterday about Leskov's will,[23] and thought I ought to write a similar one. I keep putting it off as though it were still far away, but whatever I do it's close at hand. It's good and necessary, not only because it saves one's nearest and dearest from doubts and uncertainties about what to do with the body, but also because a voice from beyond the grave is especially audible. And if one has anything to say to one's nearest and dearest, and to anybody else, it's good to say it in these first moments. *My will would be roughly as follows. Until I write another one it will be entirely as follows.*[24]

(1) Bury me in the place where I die, in the cheapest cemetery if it should be in town, and in the cheapest grave – as paupers are buried. Lay no flowers or wreaths, and make no speeches. If possible, bury me without a priest and a burial service. But if that should be unpleasant for those who bury me, let them do so in the usual manner with a burial service, but as cheaply and simply as possible.

(2) Do not announce my death in the newspapers and do not write any obituaries.

(3) Give all my papers to be looked through and sorted out to my wife, V. G. Chertkov, Strakhov, (and my daughers Tanya and Masha) (what is crossed out I crossed out myself. My daughters need not bother about this), – to those of these people who are still alive. My sons I exclude from this commission, not because I have not loved them (I have loved them more and more in recent times, thank God), and I know that they love me, but they are not fully aware of my thoughts, have not followed their course, and might have their own particular views about things, as a result of which they might keep what ought not to be kept, and throw out what ought to be kept. The diaries of my former bachelor life I ask you to destroy, after selecting from them what is worth it, and in the diaries of my married life I ask you to destroy everything which, if published, might be unpleasant for anybody. Chertkov has promised to do this for me while I am still alive. And given his great love for me which I have not deserved and his great moral sensitiveness, I am sure that he will do

it very well. The diaries of my bachelor life I ask you to destroy, not because I would like to conceal from people my own bad life – my life was the usual life of unprincipled young men, worthless from the point of view of the world – but because these diaries, in which I only wrote down what tormented me through the awareness of my sins, produce a falsely one-sided impression and are . . .

But no, let my diaries stay as they are. At least they will show that despite all the triviality and worthlessness of my youth, I was still not abandoned by God, and, if only in my old age, began to understand Him a little and love Him.

Of my other papers, I ask those who will be sorting them out not to print everything, but only what might be useful to people.

I write all this, not because I ascribe great, or indeed any importance to my papers, but because I know in advance that in the early days after my death my works will be printed and discussed, and importance will be ascribed to them. If that is the case, then let my writings not cause any harm to people.

(4) The right to publish my earlier works: the ten volumes and the *Primers* I ask my heirs to make over to the public, i.e. to renounce copyright. But I only ask this, and I don't will it. If you do it, it will be good. It will be good for you too. If you don't do it, that's your own affair. That means you were not able to do it. The fact that my works have been sold these last ten years has been the most depressing thing of my life.

(5) Furthermore, and in particular, I ask all people near and far not to praise me (I know they will do so because they have done so in my lifetime in the most unseemly way), but if they want to study my writings, let them look carefully at those passages in them in which I know the power of God spoke through me, and make use of them for their own lives. There have been times when I felt I was becoming the bearer of God's will. I have often been so impure, so full of personal passions, that the light of this truth has been obscured by my own darkness, but nevertheless this truth has sometimes passed through me, and these have been the happiest moments of my life. God grant that these truths should not have been defiled in passing through me, and that people might feed on them, despite the superficial and impure form which I have given to them.

In this alone lies the importance of my writings. And so I can only be reproved for them, not praised at all. That is all. [. . .]

Today is 6 April, Moscow There have been no particularly interesting visits or letters. [. . .] I'm very oppressed by this bad, idle, luxurious town life. I think I'm being useful to Sonya in her weakness. But it's unforgivable that I'm not writing, if I can't do anything else apart from that.

The only justification is that I've been physically very weak all this time. I've grown ten years older. My inclination to love is weaker. But, thank God, I haven't yet forsaken the state of universal love. In that respect I feel well – in so far as a parasite that is aware of its parasitism can feel well. During this time I've written a few letters, one to Vengerov with a foreword for Bondarev,[25] and have read Ruskin's splendid *Birthday Book* and made notes in it.[26]

Thought during this time: [. . .]

(6) A mother suffers over the loss of a child and can't be comforted. And she can't be

comforted until she understands that her life is not in the vessel which is broken, but in the contents which spilled over and lost their shape, but have not vanished. [. . .]
(13) The greatest number of sufferings which arise from the association of men and women are due to the complete misunderstanding of one sex by the other. Few men understand what children mean to women, what place they occupy in their lives, and even fewer women understand what duty to society, or to religion means to men. [. . .]

10 April, Moscow All this time – all Easter Week – I continue to be unusually weak: I'm doing nothing and thinking little: only rarely do islands of thought suddenly emerge from the darkness and mist, and probably for that reason they seem particularly important. Sonya is still ill. She had almost recovered and unfortunately had started to adopt her former irritable and domineering tone – I was so sorry to see the loss of that loving mood which was apparent after Vanechka's death – but the day before yesterday she began to have a headache and a temperature again, though not a high one, and acute apathy and weakness. Help me, Father, to do and feel what I should.

Yesterday I walked along the streets and looked at people's faces: there were few which were not disfigured by alcohol, nicotine or syphilis. Their feebleness is terribly pitiful and offensive, when the road to salvation is so clear. Sheep jump into the water and you stand and wave them back, but they go on jumping in, and you get the impression they are doing what they should be doing, and you are getting in their way. I'm terribly tempted to write about the relationship of society to the Tsar,[27] explaining it by the false attitude towards what is old, but Sonya's illness and weakness hold me up.

Thought during this time:
(1) The natural course of life is as follows: at first, as a child and a youth, a person merely acts, and then through acting, making mistakes and acquiring experience, gets to know things, and then when he has learned the main thing a person can know, – what is good – he begins to love that good: to act, to get to know, to love. His subsequent life (like our present life which is a continuation of a previous one) is first of all activity in the name of what you love, then getting to know what is new and worthy of love, and, finally, love of this new thing, worthy of love. This constitutes the circular movement of all life.
(2) A man is considered to be disgraced if he lets himself be beaten, or if he is accused of robbery, brawling or not paying card debts, etc., but not if he signs a death sentence, takes part in an execution, reads other people's letters, separates fathers and husbands and wives from their families, confiscates people's last resources or puts them in prison. But surely that is worse. [. . .]

Today is 14 April, Moscow Thought further: Continue to be idle and bad. No thoughts or feelings. Mental lethargy. And if any feelings emerge, they are the basest, most egotistical ones: the bicycle, freedom from family ties, etc. Am I tired after what I have experienced recently, or am I experiencing a new stage in life, having entered upon a pure old age which I have long desired? I don't know, but I'm asleep. In the mornings I don't even read, but play patience. Sonya's health is not improving, rather it is getting worse. [...] Thought during this time:

(1) I was walking beside the Alexandrovsky Gardens when suddenly, with astonishing vividness and delight, I imagined to myself a novel – how an educated man of our circle ran away from his wife to join the settlers, and took his son and his son's nurse with him. He lived a clean, hard-working life and brought his son up there. And then the son went back to his mother who had sent for him, and who lived the completely luxurious, dissipated urban life of our gentry. I could write it wonderfully well.[28] At least it seemed so to me. [...]

(3) I've been reading a journal with articles by M. Kovalevsky, Pypin and Solovyov, a story by Orzeszkowa and something by Bourget, etc.,[29] and recalled what my brother Seryozha demanded of literature. There is the work of the heart and the spirit, clothed in thought. This is real, and this is what Seryozha and I and all understanding people love. And there is the work of the intellect without the heart, and with stuffing in place of the heart, and this is what journals and books are full of.

During this time I've been to court.[30] It was dreadful. I never expected such incredible stupidity. I've been busy with Khokhlov. I never expected such baseness and cruelty by doctors. And Sonya's illness. I'm very sorry for her and love her. [...]

25 April, Moscow Yesterday Sonya left for Kiev with Tanya[31] who came to fetch her. Her health is a bit better – she has picked up, but is quite jaded and still can't find any moral point of support. A mother's position is terribly tragic: nature has endowed her above all with irresistible desire (she has similarly endowed man, but with a man it doesn't have the same fateful consequences – the birth of children), as a result of which children appear, for whom she is endowed with an even stronger love, a physical love, since carrying, and bearing and nursing and looking after children is a physical thing. A woman, a good woman, gives her entire soul to her children, devotes herself entirely to them, acquires the habit in her soul of living only for them and by them (a most terrible temptation, especially since everybody not merely approves, but praises it highly); the years go by and these children begin to depart – into life or death – in the first case slowly, paying back love with anger, as against someone who had been a millstone round their necks, interfering with their lives; in the second case – through death – which momentarily causes terrible pain and leaves behind emptiness. The woman must live, but there is nothing to live by. She lacks the habit of, lacks even the strength for a spiritual life, because all her strength has been expended on her children, who are no longer there. That's what I must write about in a novel about a mother.

During this time I began learning to ride a bicycle in the riding-school. It's very strange why I should be drawn to do this. Yevgeny Ivanovich[32] tried to dissuade me, and was distressed at my riding, but I'm not ashamed. On the contrary, I feel that it's a natural folly, that it's all the same to me what people think, and that it's quite harmless and amuses me in a childish way.

Sonya's spiritual condition is not good – she can't raise herself above personal interests, in her case family ones, and find meaning in a spiritual life. Masha[33] has gone to Kiev. Poor girl, she is thin and weak. Something is happening between

Seryozha and Manya.³⁴ It will be difficult for him, and he will need to change himself in many ways. If he does so, he will be all right. The treatment is continuing twice a week. I think I'll stop at No. 20.

All this time I've felt a lack of energy and initiative of thought. Only occasionally are there flashes of thought – and especially vividly, artistic images – and not only artistic images, but whole tasks and plans for works of art.

Thought during this time: [...]

(2) I went to the theatre with the girls³⁵ – Sasha and N. Martynova – and on the way back they began to talk about the sort of material progress there would soon be, such as electricity, etc. And I grew sorry for them, and began to say to them that I was waiting for and dreaming about – and not only dreaming about but trying to work for – another sort of progress, the only important one – not electricity or flying in the air, but progress in brotherhood, unity, love and the establishment of the Kingdom of God on earth. They understood, and I said to them that life only consists in serving to bring nearer and to realise this Kingdom of God. They understood and believed me. Children are serious people – 'theirs is the Kingdom of God'. Read today some more dreams by an American about how well streets and roads, etc. will be made in the year 2000, and yet these foolish scientists have no idea what progress is. Not even a hint. But they say that war will be done away with only because it interferes with material progress.

It's now 11 o'clock, 26 April, Moscow [...] Yesterday I rode my bicycle in the riding-school. Then walked to Sergey Nikolayevich's.³⁶ He's terribly out of spirits, and all his family are suffering. Then I wanted to sit alone at home, but Ivan Mikhaylovich came.³⁷ I think I was useful to him. Wrote a letter to Sonya. Went to bed feeling depressed at heart for no reason, and woke up today with the same feeling. Sat down just now at my desk, wanted to get on with Koni's story, but I definitely can't. So I took up my diary. I'll write some letters at least. Saw my photograph yesterday, and was astonished how old I looked. There's not much time left. Father, help me to use it to do Thy work. It's terrible that as you get older, you feel that the life force within you becomes more valuable (in the sense of its influence on the world), and it's terrible not to expend it on what it was intended for. It's as if life has been brewing and brewing (in youth one can spill it – it hasn't yet brewed), and towards the end it is all one thick brew. [...]

28 April, Moscow Yesterday morning I went to see Khokhlov. He's virtually at liberty, but says he's confused. 'I really have gone mad.' I don't know how to help him. Probably it's all to do with sexual desire. Having known women in his youth, he couldn't control himself any longer, and put everything he had into the struggle against desire. He was left with the conclusions of Christian teaching, but not the teaching itself. He became an egoist as a result of this intense struggle with himself, just as a man who is drowning or falling thinks only of himself.

The question is: what's to be done? Ivan Mikhaylovich suffers from the same thing. What's to be done? What should one say to one's son who is entering the age of struggle? I talked about it yesterday with Sinitsyn. All life is a struggle between the flesh and the spirit, and gradually the flesh triumphs over the spirit.

The sexual struggle is the most intense, but on the other hand it always ends with the victory of the spirit. One should say to one's son that this struggle is not a casual or exceptional phenomenon, but the business of one's whole life, that one should know about and prepare for this struggle – like athletes; one should always be on guard, not despair or lose heart when beaten, but pick oneself up and prepare for the struggle anew. There is the casual fall, the fall with women who don't want to tie their lives to one person, and there is the fall of marriage which may last, like mine, for thirty-two years, but a fall is still a fall, and still one mustn't lose heart, but wait for the release which will come and which, I think, has come to me. [. . .]

Thought yesterday: [. . .]

(2) There are three methods of relieving the situation of workers and establishing brotherhood between people: (1) Don't make people work for you, don't demand work from them either directly or indirectly – do without the need for work which requires excessive labour: all objects of luxury. (2) Do for yourself (and, if you can, for other people) work which is hard and unpleasant, and (3) not actually a method, but the result of applying the second method: study the laws of nature and invent devices for making work easier: machines, steam, electricity. You will only invent what is really necessary and not something superfluous when you invent something to make *your own* work easier – or at least work which you have personally experienced.

But people are busy applying the third method only, and that wrongly, because they are renouncing the second method, and are not only unwilling to use the real methods 1 and 2, but are even unwilling to hear about them. [. . .]

4 May, Moscow   Still the same apathy and laziness. I'm doing no work. The bicycle. Lyova came, and left with Andryusha for Hangö. He [one word erased] a difficult ordeal. I'm trying hard and seeking, not with the confidence of success which brings either success or failure, but not without hope either; but rather like water which is constant, and which changes its shape but not its force. Thank God I can't see spring yet, and I've no wish to. I seem to be ready to do God's work, but am still not doing it. Help me, Father. Sonya returned from Kiev no better. If only one could contrive not to get angry about mental aberrations and deformities as one can about physical ones, but not to disregard them either, and if one can't cure them, at least patiently help people either to gain relief from them or live with them. Dushkin came. Had a long talk with him.

One thing: one shouldn't, after entering into certain practical arrangements with people, suddenly disregard these conditions in the name of a Christian renunciation of life. Began to expound these thoughts, without success. [. . .]

13 May, Moscow   Medical treatment and the bicycle, and the collapse of my spiritual life. Was even angry the other day because the bicycle wasn't ready, and was rude to the man. I don't remember such depression for a long time. I've withdrawn into myself, and sit and wait. Just as little of the egotistical as of the godly.

Today is 15 May, Moscow   Everything just the same. My head is a bit clearer and more alert. Slept only four hours during the night. Was tired on the bicycle yesterday. Went for a ride with Strakhov. Even my enthusiasm for the bicycle is waning. Tomorrow we're expecting Manya from London. I think Seryozha's marriage will take place. That's good, as a school for Seryozha and a distraction for Sonya. I want to finish my treatment today and go to the Olsufyevs' tomorrow.

Thought during this time: [. . .]
(2) One mustn't confuse vanity with love of fame, still less with the desire for love – love of love. The first is the desire to be distinguished from other people by worthless, sometimes even bad actions, the second – the desire to be praised for something useful and good, the third – the desire to be loved.

The first: to be able to dance well; the second – to have the reputation among people of being good and clever; the third – to see the expression of people's love. The first is bad; the second is better, despite everything; the third is legitimate [. . .]
(4) Sonya began to talk last night about the fact that Vanechka's death was a very great misfortune and suffering, and that his death was the work of God. People often talk about the evil which God does to people. And when they speak and think like that, people imagine that they believe in God, and pray to Him. God do evil! If God were to do evil, He would not be good, would not be love, and if He is not good he is not God. [. . .]

Today, I think, is 18 May, Moscow Life is very depressing. Still no desire to work or write, still the same gloomy mood. The day before yesterday Andryusha said some very rude things to me for no reason at all. I couldn't forgive him. First I didn't want to say hello to him, then I started to reprimand him, but he began again to say even worse things and I couldn't stand it and went out, saying he was alien to me. All this is bad. I must forgive him, forgive him entirely and then help him. [. . .]

Probably 20 May, Nikolskoye, at the Olsufyevs'.[38] Seryozha and Manya were getting ready to leave yesterday. I talked to them. Seryozha is touching; life itself has made him take a strict moral attitude towards himself. Sonya is better. A dull journey. I probably have a fever. Melancholy. Today is the same, I can't do anything. Yesterday I only wrote a few letters. The newspaper I received yesterday with the article about the libels and stupidities of Seuron's book distressed me, to my shame.[39] But not much. The journalist proposes I should refute them. I've made no statements about myself and so there is nothing for me to refute. I am what I am. And what I am, only I know and God. Never do recollections manifest themselves with such force as when one is in a mentally weak condition, as I am now. Thought of writing at the Olsufyevs', but it's 12 o'clock and I haven't sat down yet.

Today is 26 May, Nikolskoye Wrote that same evening. Then fell ill with a fever. Didn't write during the day, and then wrote in the evening again, and quite a lot, so that more than half has been sketched out. It's turning out in a strange way: Nekhlyudov must be a follower of Henry George and must bring this in, and he must weaken as he pits his strength against the daughter of the refined lady lying there (Mary Urusova).[40] Sonya has been here. She was very excited as a result of the quinine. Thank God, all ended well and amicably. She left early this morning. I'm better today. Anna Mikhaylovna[41] is cleverer and far kinder than I thought.

Thought:
In a pleasure ground they erect masts to climb up and win prizes. Such a form of entertainment which attracts a person for hours on end (even though he ruins his health), or else a sack race which we enjoy watching, could only have arisen with the division of people into masters and servants. All our forms of life have only taken the shape they have because there has been this division: acrobats, waiters in inns, chamber pots, the manufacture of mirrors and visiting cards, all factories – all these things could only have arisen the way they have done because there has been a division into masters and men. And we want to lead a brotherly life while retaining these servile forms of life. [. . .]

Today is 29 May, Nikolskoye The day before yesterday I began to feel better. No fever today either, and were it not for my leg which has not quite healed up yet, I would consider myself quite well. Only wrote a little today and wrote badly – no energy. But I got a clear picture of Nekhlyudov while committing the crime. He should have wanted to marry and simplify his life. I'm only afraid *que cela n'impiète sur le drame* [that it will be to the detriment of the drama]. I'll decide when I feel stronger. I've just been for a ride, on horseback and on my bicycle. I'm reading Poltoratsky the whole time. I love these memoirs.[42] Relations with Sonya are not cordial, and this hurts me. Nothing stimulating in my letters or outward life. Thought: [. . .]
(3) Today we have the kingdom of materialism, i.e. of women and doctors. There's much that could and should be understood about this.
(4) They say: 'She[43] can't understand.' But if she can't understand, why doesn't she listen to others? As it is, without understanding life or knowing that this life is to be condemned, she wants to dominate it. [. . .]

4 June, Moscow Had an operation in Nikolskoye on Tuesday, and by mistake Pyotr Vasilyevich used oil with a 3 per cent solution, so that I . . . became ill. Left the next evening, however. I was quite ill. Arrived in Moscow, and found Tanya, Seryozha and Manya there. The same evening I had a bad attack of gall stones. During the attacks I couldn't think of anything except to wish that the pain would stop. The cause of the pain, probably, was getting too hot in the sun the day before. Since then, I've been ill for five days and done nothing but read. Read Castellion's wonderful book.[44] He was a true Christian of the sixteenth century. Also a translation of Matthew Arnold.[45] Then I saw visitors. Dekhtyarev is interesting, he was here today.

I feel like writing – clarified something of importance for Koni's story, namely duality of mood – two people: one timid, lonely, striving to improve himself, a timid reformer; and the other a worshipper of tradition, living by inertia and poeticising it.

Despite almost enforced idleness my life is not bad – there is progress I would venture to say – I love people more, love is becoming more natural and lack of love more painful. Poor Andryusha has been; I tried to help him, but without much success.

I suddenly felt sorry for Seryozha and Manya. Both want to extricate themselves and get on to the right road, and they are getting more and more entangled and further from the road. Read yesterday about Ibsen[46] that he says that if you renounce carnal love you grow cold, that carnal love will lead to true love. What a delusion! Only if you renounce it, or as long as you don't know it, can you know the true tenderness of love.

Oh, how well Koni's story could turn out. How I think about it sometimes. It will have two extremes of true love with a false middle.

Thought: (1) About the fact that the structure of our life is based on slavery, and that to think that the maintenance of this structure can be reconciled with brotherhood, or even with equality and freedom, is like thinking that the Egyptian pyramids could have been built by a community of brethren.

Today must be 7 June, Yasnaya Polyana Arrived the day before yesterday. Travelled with Boulanger in a separate carriage. Very unpleasant. I'm very weak both physically and spiritually: couldn't suppress an unkind feeling in me . . .

Did nothing all day yesterday. Started to write letters, but couldn't. Yesterday I felt the awakening of sexual desire, and was horrified. Help me, Father.

I've just been playing patience and thinking about my catechism. [. . .]

Moscow in summer: unpolished windows, covers on the chairs, freedom for the yardmen and those left behind in the house and their children, tight summer clothes – thighs tightly covered by old white trousers – and houses with wonderful gardens empty, and on the streets, on boiling hot paving stones, road workers covered in dust. And outings with cigarettes and oranges, and drunken and dissolute laughter. [. . .]

Today must be 12 June, Yasnaya Polyana The days are getting shorter. Was seriously ill for two days. Had a temperature of 40.1°. My daughters, dear things, were very frightened. What a pity that by my death I shall almost inevitably be the cause of grief to them – short-lived and good, but still grief. Read the whole time. Sometimes *The Week*, sometimes *Russian Thought*. All interesting, but all unnecessary. In the Transcaspian region only those settlements flourish which run their economy like suburban ones. Isn't it the same throughout Russia? But where does the money come from in the towns? From taxes, from the people, from trade, and again from the people. Wouldn't it be simpler to refrain from stealing this money? But there would be no army, no civil servants, no factories, no circulation of goods. That's true, but if there was no slavery, those who till the land would no longer be slaves. Those who administer the army, the civil servants, the factories and trade would be dependent on them, and not the other way round, as at present. [. . .]

13 June, Yasnaya Polyana Health still bad. I'm weak. Bile fills my stomach and makes me feel sick. I'm afraid I'm beginning to get preoccupied with my medical condition and with treating myself and observing myself, the very thing I condemned so much in Lyova. Yesterday Seryozha and Manya came. They are very much in love, but I'm afraid that now they are married they are doing what people sometimes do when, let's say, a key doesn't open a door or the door is stuck: turn it and push it in the opposite direction. The comparison isn't accurate, but I mean to say that people may not and cannot live their lives by going their own separate ways; we must try to live by joining forces. God grant this may be a false prediction. Read an excellent article about mathematics in *Russian Thought*.⁴⁷ [...] Thought. [...] (2) The concrete sciences, as opposed to the abstract ones, become less exact the nearer their subject approaches human life: (*a*) mathematics, (*b*) astronomy, (*c*) chemistry, (*d*) physics, (*e*) biology (here inexactitude begins), anthropology (the inexactitude is greater), sociology (the inexactitude reaches limits where the science itself is destroyed). [...]

17 June, Yasnaya Polyana Still the same stomach ailment, and hence a mood of depression and great weakness. Yesterday was a depressing day. Sonya was out of sorts. And she only spoke about what hurt me: my works and the revenue from them, the distribution of the property, theft, vegetarianism. I was outwardly restrained, but inwardly I couldn't summon up in myself the feeling of pity for her which I ought to have done, because life has been so difficult for her. I remembered moreover that all my relations with people are relations with Him – but weaker than in the early days. I don't want to weaken, I want to think and feel like this until the end. [...]

18 June, Yasnaya Polyana Yesterday a military judge came to ask for money for a school. I had a long talk with him – bad, unconvincing and unnecessary. I'm beginning to forget my attitude to God in my associations with people. Yesterday I also received a newspaper cutting from Dunayev to say that nine Dukhobor soldiers had refused to do military service and a few reservists had returned their military passports. Surprisingly, it doesn't make me glad. The reasons for that later. I wasn't kind to Sonya and Misha. Walked to Kozlovka. In the evening I went for a ride. Read Herron's *Christian State*⁴⁸ – untalented, cold and imprecise. Ilyusha and the boys went back home. Health just the same – weakness. I must adapt myself to weakness. Thought:
(1) Read Herbert Spencer's reply to Balfour.⁴⁹ A profession of agnosticism, as atheism is now called. I say that agnosticism, although it tries to be something different from atheism in advancing the alleged impossibility of knowing, is essentially the same as atheism because the root of it all is the refusal to acknowledge God. This is how I read Spencer, who says not that I *wish* to overthrow belief in God, but I *must* do so. [...]

Today is 28 June, Yasnaya Polyana [...] Thought during this time: [...]
(2) So that there should be order in political life, that people should not give way to their passions and to arbitrariness, should not fight, but should sort out their affairs according to law – for these reasons government was established. Such government consists in constitutional countries of representatives, or deputies. And now these very deputies, elected to save people from arbitrariness, are resolving disagreements among themselves by fighting. It was so in the French, and then the English parliaments, and now the same thing has happened in the Italian parliament.

(3) *June 20*; it rained the night before. There were heavy, ragged, low, dark clouds in the sky. Their shadow raced after me across road and field. The shadow caught

me up, and it grew chilly and at the same time, ahead of me, the shadow lifted from the waving rye which had seemed almost black, and the rye became bright green. But only for a moment. The light caught up with me again, and the shadow of the cloud fell on the rye once more.
(4) Science and art are well and good – only given the brotherhood of man they will be different. But it is more important for the brotherhood of man to come than for science and art to remain the same as they are now.
(5) Love is only real when its object is unattractive.

Today is 4 July, Yasnaya Polyana   During these last days I've had a couple of good spells of writing. And I can say that I've now finished touching up Koni's story. Wrote letters yesterday and the day before – wrote more than ten, including one in English in which I said what I now think.⁵⁰ Went mowing twice. Went to Tula yesterday on my bicycle. Seryozha has been. And I didn't get on well with him. My decision always to observe my relationship to God in my relationship with people is beginning to weaken. Still I'm trying, and it sometimes helps me. Thought during this time:
(1) Good which exposes evil in other people is quite genuinely taken by them for evil. As a result, charity, humility, even love seems to them to be something offensive and shocking. Nothing argues more clearly than this phenomenon that a man's main activity – self-improvement – consists in trying to understand his own consciousness. [. . .]
(3) Read an amusing academic dispute between Elpe and some professor: scientific arguments lead to diametrically opposite conclusions.⁵¹

Just received a telegram to say Strakhov is coming.

12 July, Yasnaya Polyana   Strakhov has arrived in the meanwhile. I was very glad to see him. I wrote to Veselitskaya that when we know that a man is condemned to death we are kind to him – we love him. And how can we not love anybody, when we know that we are all condemned. He – surprisingly enough – doesn't know his condition.⁵² I'm writing almost every day. Things are progressing. Just as you get to know people by living with them, so you get to know your poetic characters by living with them. I've also done quite a lot of work – although I feel I've grown weak with age. I've been to see Davydov, and he's been here. Took notes from him about trial procedure.⁵³ Constant guests are a burden. No peace and quiet, no summer seclusion. [. . .]

5 August, Yasnaya Polyana   Haven't written my diary for almost a month.
This month hasn't been spent badly. I worked a little in the fields. Once mowed the rye. Wrote quite a lot of Koni's story. It's making progress. During this time I read Kidd's *Social Evolution*⁵⁴ and articles about myself in *Wahrheit* and elsewhere.⁵⁵ When you read about yourself, it might seem that what you are occupied with, the whole world is also occupied with, but that's not true. A letter from Khilkov with a description of the persecutions of the Dukhobors. I wrote a letter to the English newspapers. It's being translated now.⁵⁶ [. . .]

Things have got worse with Sonya. I went for a ride and was held up in the rain; she hurt me with her sarcasm and I was offended – the old wounds. Today she demanded that I should give her the diaries to copy. I refused, saying that this always caused unpleasantness. I did wrong not to pity her. She is exhausted, mentally ill, and it's a sin to argue with her. How sorry I am for her that she is never aware of her mistakes. However, that's not my business. I need to be aware of my own, and not to compare my mistakes with hers. Everyone sins in proportion to the light that is in him. Also during this time the boys have upset me. Especially Andryusha. He is quite out of hand and has gone mad. He doesn't see or hear a thing, as though he were perpetually drunk. Thought and noted during this time: [. . .]

(2) Thought as I read Kidd's book: what is progress? Progress, in my opinion, consists in the greater and greater predominance of reason over the animal law of struggle, but in the evolutionists' opinion in the triumph of animal struggle over reason, since only as a result of this animal struggle, in their understanding, can progress take place.

(3) Another thing that I thought as I read Kidd's book is that science is only science when it investigates what should be. But according to the teaching of the evolutionists, science should investigate what has been and what is, and explain why what is is good. This is how all evolutionists regard science. And so they conclude that struggle is a necessary condition of progress, and therefore good.

(4) According to Weismann,[57] the explanation of heredity consists in the fact that in every embryo there are biophors, and biophors form themselves into ids and ids into idants. What a splendid idea for a comedy.

(5) According to Weismann again, mortal creatures have continued to exist because all those which were not mortal failed to survive in the struggle against the mortals, i.e. – *the immortal ones died*. Surely I can manage to make use of this splendid idea.

(6) Kidd concludes that the main motive force in human progress is religion, but religion is an unreasonable instinct which shouldn't therefore be studied. And so he doesn't study what the main motive force in human progress consists of. But I consider that this – religion – is precisely what needs to be studied, i.e. the thing that is the basis of human progress; but I don't reject the study of struggle as well. [. . .]

(7) We had a talk about family life. I said that a good family life is only possible given the conviction, consciously fostered in women, of the need for constant submission to their husbands (in everything, of course, except questions of the soul – religious questions). I said that this is proved by the fact that it has been so for as long as we have known human life, and the fact that family life with children is a crossing on an unseaworthy boat, which is only possible when those on board submit to one person. And this one person has always been recognised to be the man, because, since he doesn't carry or nurse children, he can be a better guide to his wife, than a wife to her husband. But is a woman always inferior to a man? Not at all; as long as they are both virgins they are equal. But what is the meaning of the fact that wives now demand not only equality, but supremacy? Only that the family is evolving, and therefore its previous form is disintegrating. The relations between the sexes are seeking a new form, and the old form is breaking down. What this new form will be it is impossible to know, although there are many possibilities. Possibly more people will remain

chaste; marriages might be temporary and come to an end after the birth of children, so that both spouses, having produced children, will separate and be chaste in future; children might be brought up by society. It's impossible to foresee the new form. But there's no doubt that the old one is breaking down, and that its continued existence is only possible given the submission of the wife to the husband, as has always been the case everywhere, and as it now is where the family still holds together. [. . .]

[7 September] Haven't written my diary for more than a month. Today is 7 September, Yasnaya Polyana. During this time I've suffered because of the bad life of the boys: Andryusha and Misha. I've tried to help them. I've been riding my bicycle and getting on with my *Resurrection*. Read it to Olsufyeva, Taneyev and Chekhov,[58] but it was a waste of time. I'm very dissatisfied with it now, and either want to give it up or revise it. These last few days I've been walking through the woods, selecting trees for the peasants. Thought during this time:

I've recently felt death very close. My material life seems to be hanging by a thread, and must very soon break off. I'm getting more and more used to this and beginning to feel – not pleasure, but the interest of expectation, of hope – as I do with the progress of *this* life.

During this time I wrote a contribution for the English newspapers about the Dukhobors, but didn't send it, and Posha went to the Caucasus[59] and ought to have come back on the 1st, but it's now the 7th and he's still not here. Also read an interesting letter from a Pole about patriotism and drafted a reply to him.[60] The day before yesterday a Frenchman came from Ertel's.[61] He believes in matter, but not in God. I told him that that was a mental epidemic. My sister Masha is staying with us, Tanya and Sasha are at Seryozha's, Masha and Misha in Moscow. They are coming tomorrow. Thought during this time: [. . .]

(2) The material world is subject to the law of the struggle for existence, and we, as material creatures, are subject to it too. But, apart from our material existence, we are conscious in ourselves of another principle, not only independent of the law of struggle, but opposed to it – the principle of love. The manifestation in us of this principle is what we call free will. [. . .]

Today is 22 September, Yasnaya Polyana During this time I've written some letters – to the Pole and Menshikov[62] – and have worked again on my article about the persecutions of the Dukhobors. Posha returned and brought some information, but less detailed than I would have liked. My article isn't bad. But perhaps I'm mistaken. Sent everything off today to Kenworthy.[63]

Sonya has been to Moscow and returned. She is very pitiful, and dearer than ever to me. I can see her whole character more clearly. Andryusha worries me because I can't work out a proper relationship towards him. Tanya is dear, quiet and good. Masha is in Moscow. Gastev has been, and Andrey Butkevich came yesterday. He is alien to me, as always. Tregubov left today. I always get on well with him. I've been unwell, and still haven't quite recovered, but am quite fresh in the head. I can see new aspects and very important ones in my story which I had almost overlooked. I mean the joy of breaking all accepted laws and customs, and the consciousness of one's own good life.[64] Thought a lot during this time, and have forgotten a lot.

(1) Yes, love is a real magician. One has only to love, and what one loves becomes beautiful. [. . .]

(2) Recalled how often I used to argue with religious dogmatists: Orthodox, Evangelical and others. How absurd. Can one seriously reason with a person who maintains that he believes that there is only one correct view of the world and of our attitude to it, the one which was expressed 1,500 years ago by the bishops assembled by Constantine at Nicaea – the view by which God is a Trinity and sent His son into a Virgin 1,890 years ago in order to redeem the world, etc. You can't reason with such people, you can only be indulgent to them, pity them, try to cure them, but you must regard them as mentally ill, and not argue with them.

(3) Dissatisfaction with oneself is friction, the sign of movement.

(4) There is not a single believer who has not had moments of doubt, doubt about the existence of God. And these doubts are not harmful; on the contrary, they lead to a higher understanding of God. The God you know becomes a habit and you don't believe in Him any more. You only fully believe in God when He is revealed to you anew. And He is revealed to you from a new side when you seek Him with all your soul. [. . .]

24 September Spent the day well yesterday, but did little work. Wrote a letter to Masha. Thought:

I went out for a walk round the garden before breakfast and saw on a lime tree a fresh, newly grown mushroom. I knocked it off with my stick, and thought: it's alive. The right conditions for its existence occurred, and it appeared on the scene and is alive. And I thought about everything that lives in the infinite world according to the same laws. And I marvelled at the wisdom – the reasonableness – of the organisation of the world. And then I collected myself and realised that I was marvelling, not at the great wisdom of the organisation of the world, but at the great wisdom of my own reason which sees everything so very wisely. Surely it's just the same as marvelling at the regularity of the hemisphere I see in the sky, or of a circle drawn around me. Surely it's only the law of my vision. And in the other case it's the laws of my reason which have invested everything that exists with this regularity at which I marvel. [. . .]

Evening of 25 September Got on with Koni's story in the morning; began revising it from the beginning. It's quite good. At least I'm not disgusted by it. Kept thinking about living for God, only forgot twice, with regard to Andryusha. In the morning, when I heard him getting up, I didn't go in to see him, and again in the evening when he came back. He hadn't been home for two days, and must have been depressed himself. The nastier he is, the more I need to love him. And that's just what I haven't done. After dinner I went off with Gastev to fell trees for Filipp and Andriyan, and then for a ride on my bicycle. [. . .]

26 September A depressing day. Woke up early, couldn't sleep, and did some thinking. After breakfast I waited for Andryusha to get up. Worried about whether to go in or not. I went in, he had his head under the bedclothes; eventually I saw he wasn't asleep and began to speak to him. I spoke gently and kindly, but unconvincingly; felt shy and suffered anguish. He remained silent. Not a sound. I went out to work and before an hour had passed I heard the incessant noise of an accordion in the kitchen. I couldn't believe my ears, and looked through the kitchen window. He moved away. I couldn't bear it and said: 'You're worse than Khokhlov.' At dinner he didn't answer me and went off in a rage. I was ashamed that I couldn't control myself. Very ashamed. In an egotistical fashion I was distressed that my words had had no effect, and forgot that one can and must live only for God. Had no success with my writing either. Made too many changes and got muddled. And I felt ashamed to write down all these fabrications. Bodyansky[65] is right when he says that it's no good writing literary allegories. I always feel this, and I'm only at ease when I am writing at full stretch what I know and think. [. . .]

Today is 29 September, Yasnaya Polyana 8 o'clock in the evening. The day before yesterday I came across Andryusha at tea and made an effort to talk to him. And I was rewarded. He was contented enough, and willing to talk to me, but yesterday he came home to dinner with his breath smelling of alcohol, and I couldn't suppress a feeling of annoyance – I said nothing. Yesterday and the day before I got on with Koni's story. Yesterday I cycled to Tula and talked with Mme Kern, not sufficiently seriously – I forgot why I'm alive. [. . .]

Thought about two things: (1) Gastev said a wonderful word to me. We were talking about the impression made on the peasants by books. It's difficult to please them, because their life is *very serious*. That's the important word. If only more people of our world understood it! (2) I dreamed today that I had been struck in the face, and was ashamed that I hadn't challenged the person to a duel, and then I realised that I needn't challenge him, since that would prove the consistency of my non-resistance. Generally speaking, thoughts that occur in dreams are only of the lowest kind. When one is dreaming the mind is active, but reason, the force behind moral progress, is missing.

Today is 6 October, Yasnaya Polyana I've had letters from Popov, Posha, Chertkov, Schmitt and Kenworthy. Yesterday I answered them all. Wrote some long letters: to Bodyansky and Menshikov. Gastev was here. The girls teased and offended him. He's gone now. A good fellow. Ilya has been. There's little of the spiritual in him. Andryusha has arrived. I can see him soon getting consumption and dying. An American came, a worker who had got rich – a Finn by birth, a socialist and communist.[66] Very unprepossessing, but he told me a lot of interesting things, far more so than refined Americans. The main thing he told me was that in the United States only six million out of sixty million people work with their hands, that's to say 10 per cent, whereas with us, I think, it's 50 per cent or more; that over there one man ploughs with eighteen horses, and the ploughs cut furrows an *arshin* wide, and one man works ten acres a day and gets from two to four or more dollars a day. What does this mean? Where is it all leading? It's extraordinarily important, but I still haven't clarified for myself the meaning of it all. The labour problem is being solved this way. Fewer working hours, more pay, lighter work. The only question is what work to do? The thought occurs to me that it's all a question of making the work and the life of the workers pleasant, *travail attrayant* [attractive work]. It all seems to be a question of that. Then the capitalists will want to be workers. But how to make work attractive? The conditions for it must be pleasant, and there must be no necessity for it. I feel there is much that is new and important here, but I still don't know how to express it. God willing I'll think about it. My writing has become repugnant to me. [. . .]

Today, I think, is the 9th Nothing to copy out of my notebook. Sergeyenko has been, and was unpleasantly flattering. I've written fairly well for two days. Cycled to Tula and got overtired. Tanya has gone to Moscow. I felt depressed with Sonya. But of course I'm to blame. I'm reading the Gospels in Italian, wrote letters to Edwards[67] and another one to Schmitt. A pleasant autumnal feeling. Went for a walk and thought about the duality of Nekhlyudov. I must express it more clearly.

12 October, Yasnaya Polyana I'm alone with Sonya and Sasha. I'm reading Italian. Andryusha distresses me. Talked with him a lot yesterday. I feel it's in vain. Marya Alexandrovna[68] is here. Arsenyev has been. I've received an Italian book. It's about the teaching of Christianity in school.[69] An excellent thought that the teaching of religion is coercion – that corruption of children which Christ spoke about. What right have we to teach what is disputed by the enormous majority of people? The Trinity, the miracles of Buddha, Mohammed, Christ? The one thing that we can and must teach is moral instruction. An excellent thought. Just now as I was playing patience I thought how Nekhlyudov must take a touching farewell of Sonya.[70]

13 October All these last days I've seen that something has been distressing Sonya. I caught her writing a letter. She said she would speak to me later. This morning came the explanation. She had read my angry words about her, written at moments of exasperation. I had got exasperated about something, and immediately wrote it down and forgot it. I felt in the bottom of my heart that I had done something wrong. And now she has read it. And, poor woman, she suffered terribly, and, dear woman, instead of being angry with me she wrote me this letter.[71] Never before have I felt so guilty and so full of emotion. Oh, if only this were to bring us still closer together. If only she could rid herself of her belief in trivialities and come to believe in her own soul, her own reason.

When reading through my diary I found a passage – there were several of them – where *I repudiate those angry words which I wrote about her. These words were written at moments of exasperation. I now repeat this once more for the sake of everybody who should come across these diaries.* I was often exasperated with her because of her hasty, inconsiderate temper, but, as Fet used to say, every husband gets the wife he needs. She was – and I can see now in what way – the wife I needed. She was the ideal wife in a pagan sense – in the sense of loyalty, domesticity, self-denial, love of family – pagan love – and she has the potential to become a Christian friend. I saw this after Vanechka's death. Will this be realised in her? Help her, Father. What happened today really made me glad. She has seen, and will see the power of love – of her love for me. [. . .]

24 October I've missed many days. Sonya has been to Petersburg and come back. Relations continue to be better than good. *The Power of Darkness* is a success.[72] Thank God, it doesn't make me glad. 'Seek that your names may be written in Heaven.' Wrote a letter to Andryusha who distressed me very much. And fortunately this letter had at least some effect. Wrote a letter to Misha – long and too rationalising.[73] Took up *Resurrection* again, and was convinced that it's all bad, that the centre of gravity is not where it ought to be, that the land question is a distraction and a weakness, and will turn out to be weak itself. I think I'll give it up. And if I do go on writing, I'll begin it all again from the beginning. [. . .]

Yesterday was 24, today is 25 October, Yasnaya Polyana Sonya and Sasha have just left. As she sat in the coach I felt terribly sorry for her; not because she was leaving, but sorry for her, for her soul. And now I'm so sorry, that it's an effort to hold back my tears. I'm sorry that she's depressed, sad and lonely. I'm the only person she has to hold on to, and at the bottom of her heart she's afraid I don't love her, don't love her as much as I can, with all my heart, and that the reason for this is the difference in our views of life. And she thinks that I don't love her because she hasn't come to me. Don't think that. I love you still more, I quite understand you, and know you couldn't, couldn't come to me, and so are left alone. But you aren't alone. I'm with you, just as you are, I love you, love you to the very end with a love that could not be greater.
I'm continuing what I didn't finish writing yesterday. Thought: [. . .]
(4) Doing nothing is more important than people think – than I used to think myself. In moments of depression don't force yourself to do something. It only makes it worse: you will spoil what you did before, and interfere with what you might do afterwards. [. . .]
(7) I've often been struck by the assured, beautiful and impressive tones of people who are talking nonsense. Now I know that the more impressive and imposing sounds and sights are, the more empty and insignificant they are. [. . .]

28 October, Yasnaya Polyana [. . .] There's only a short time left for me to live, and there's so much I terribly want to speak about: I want to speak about what we can, must, and are bound to believe in, and about the cruelty of the deception which people subject themselves to – economic, political and religious deception – and about the temptation to stupefy themselves with alcohol, and with tobacco which is considered so innocent, and about marriage and about education. And about the horrors of autocracy. Everything has come to a head, and I want to speak. And so there's no time to go on turning out that literary nonsense which I had begun to do in *Resurrection*. But I immediately asked myself: can I write when I know nobody will read it? And I felt a sort of disappointment – but only for a while – that I can: that means there was something of the desire for fame in me, but also the important thing – the need to serve God. I've received a wonderful letter from Sonya. Help me,

Father, to follow the same path of love. I thank Thee. Everything comes from Thee. Wrote a letter to Misha yesterday. Rode to Tula. I've been thinking during this time. What I thought I'll write down in the next exercise book. [. . .]

5 November, Yasnaya Polyana I've missed six days. I don't think I've done much during that time: wrote a little, chopped some wood and felt ill, but I've lived through a lot. And I've lived through a lot because in fulfilment of a promise to Sonya I read through all my diaries for seven years.[74] I seem to be approaching a clear and simple expression of what I live by. How good that I didn't finish the *Catechism*. Probably I'll write it differently and better. If the Father wills it so. I understand why it's impossible to say these things quickly. If they could be said all at once, what would one live by in the realm of thought? This task is the most I can undertake just now.

I've just been for a walk and clearly understood why I'm not getting on with *Resurrection*. The beginning was wrong. I understood this as I thought about my story about children – *Who is Right?*; I understood that I should have begun with the life of the peasants, that they are the subject, the positive element, while the rest is shadow, the negative element. And I understand the same about *Resurrection*. I must begin with her.[75] I want to begin now. [. . .]

7 November, Yasnaya Polyana Got on a bit these last two days with the new *Resurrection*. I'm ashamed to recall how banal it was to have begun with him. So far I'm glad when I think of how I've begun the work now. Chopped some wood. Went to Ovsyannikovo, had a good chat with Marya Alexandrovna and Ivan Ivanovich.[76] Walz's[77] assistant was here, and a Frenchman with a poem – a stupid man. A cheerful letter from Sonya. Will there really be *complete* spiritual unity? Help me, Father.

Today is 15 November, Yasnaya Polyana I've been so weak the whole time that I couldn't write anything except a few letters. A letter to Škarvan. Dunayev, Posha and Marya Vasilyevna[78] have been. They left yesterday, and yesterday I went to see Marya Alexandrovna.[79] She is ill. Aunt Tanya and Sonya came back today. I didn't sleep all night and so couldn't work. But I made some notes for Koni's story and some entries in my diary. I'm reading Schopenhauer's aphorisms.[80] Very good. Only put service to God in place of the knowledge of the vanity of life, and we would agree. [. . .]

7 December, Moscow Haven't written my diary for almost a month. During this time we moved to Moscow. The weakness has passed off a little, and I'm working hard, although with little success, on an exposition of religious belief. Yesterday I wrote a short article on flogging.[81] I lay down to sleep during the day and had just dozed off when someone seemed to push me, and I got up and began to think about flogging and wrote the article. During this time I've been to the theatre for rehearsals of *The Power of Darkness*. Art both began as play and continues to be a plaything, and a criminal plaything, of adults. This is confirmed by music, of which I have heard a lot. It exerts no influence. On the contrary it distracts one, if one ascribes to it the inappropriate importance which is usually ascribed. Realism, moreover, weakens its meaning.

The boys are all behaving badly, they keep disappearing and are obtuse. Suller[82] has refused to do military service. I visited him. Filosofov has died.[83] Sonya is enduring her critical period well. Wrote a few insignificant letters.

Thought a lot – in terms of importance – during this time. Much of it I can't make sense of and have forgotten.
(1) I often wanted to suffer, wanted to be persecuted. This means that I was lazy and didn't want to work, but wanted others to work for me, thereby causing me distress, while I only had to endure it. [. . .]
(6) Beautiful women smile, and we think that because they smile, what they say when they smile is true and good. But a smile often seasons something that has quite gone off.
(7) Education. One has only to be involved in education to see all one's own shortcomings. And having seen them you begin to corrrect them. And self-correction is also the best means of educating one's own and other people's children and grown-ups.

I've just read a letter from Škarvan, who says that medical aid doesn't seem to him a good thing, and that the prolonging of many empty lives for many hundreds of years is far less important than the weakest fanning – *blowing*, as he writes – of the spark of divine love in another person's heart. It's just in this *blowing* that the whole art of education lies. And in order to kindle the spark in others, you must kindle it in yourself. [. . .]

[23 December] Masha is at Ilya's, a nice letter from her today. Today is 23 December, Moscow. Haven't written my diary for a long time. During this time the Chertkovs arrived. It's two days since Kenworthy arrived. He's very pleasant. My son Seryozha has arrived – sad and thinner. He talked about his theory today. I'm glad that I only felt sorry for him. I got on well with him. Andryusha has joined the army. Today the soldier came home. He's good-natured and unaffected. Continued to write my exposition[84] – I'm making progress. I think on and off about a drama.[85] It went round and round in my head all last night. I'm unwell – a heavy cold, influenza. Apropos of a letter to me from an Englishman I also began a letter about the conflict between England and America.[86] [. . .]

24 December, Moscow I.I.A Yesterday I received an open letter to the papers from the socialist Spielhagen on behalf of Drozhzhin.[87]

1896

23 January, Moscow   Haven't written my diary for exactly a month. During this time I've written a letter on patriotism[1] and a letter to Crosby, and for about two weeks now I've been writing a drama.[2] I've written three acts very badly. I'm thinking of sketching it out in rough, to give it a *charpente* [framework]. Haven't much hope of success. The Chertkovs and Kenworthy left on the 7th. Sonya has gone to Tver to see Andryushka. Nagornov died today. I'm rather unwell again. Noted down during this time:
(1) A true work of art – an infectious one – is only produced when the artist seeks and strives towards a goal. This passion in poetry for depicting what is, stems from the fact that the artist hopes that by seeing clearly and pinning down what is, he will understand the meaning of what is.
(2) In every art there are two aberrations: triviality and artificiality. Between the two there is only a narrow path. And this narrow path is defined by inner drive. Given inner drive and direction, you avoid both dangers. Of the two, the more terrible is artificiality.
(3) It's impossible to force the mind to understand and comprehend what the heart doesn't want.
(4) It's bad when the mind wants to attribute virtuous significance to egotistical strivings.
   Kudinenko[3] was here, a remarkable man. Suller took the oath and is serving.[4] A letter from Makovitsky with an article about the Nazarenes.[5]

25 January, Moscow   The main event of the last two days was the death of Nagornov – death is always new and significant. Thought: they represent death in the theatre. Does it make one ten-thousandth of the impression which the proximity of real death makes?
   I'm continuing to write the drama. I've written the fourth act. It's all bad. But it's beginning to resemble something real.

26 January, Moscow I.I.A   I'm alive, but not living. Strakhov. Heard the news of his death today. They buried Nagornov today – and now this news. I lay down to sleep, but couldn't sleep, and a clear picture came to me of an understanding of life whereby we might feel ourselves to be travellers. Ahead of us lies one and the same station in one and the same, familiar conditions. How can we travel past that station otherwise than eagerly and joyfully, in a friendly and cooperative spirit, without lamenting the fact that we ourselves are going, or that others are going ahead of us, to the place where we shall all be together again, even more so than before?
   Today I wrote a post-script to the letter to Crosby. A good letter from Kenworthy. Unpleasantness with Manson.[6] He's a journalist.

[*13 February*] Haven't written my diary for almost a month. Today is 13 February, Moscow. Wanted to go to the Olsufyevs'. Sonya wasn't pleased. I stayed here. There's a lot of fuss here, and it takes up a lot of time. I settle down late to work and so don't write much. Managed somehow to finish the fifth act of the drama and took up *Resurrection* again. I've got eleven chapters done and am making a bit of progress. Revised the letter to Crosby. An important event was Strakhov's death, and as well as that – Davydov's conversation with the Tsar.[7] To my shame I feel glad about this. Ertel's article about the usefulness of flirting with liberalism and Spielhagen's letter about the same thing irritate me.[8] But I shouldn't and musn't write – there's no time. Letters from Sopotsko and Zdziechowski about Orthodoxy and Catholicism irritate me from a different aspect, but I probably won't write.[9] And then yesterday there was a letter from Grinevich's mother about the religious education of children.[10] Something must be done about it. At least, I must make every effort to do something. A great deal of music – useless. The girls – especially Masha – are weak. Will she manage to get over it somehow? I don't give them enough guidance. They need to be helped. The boys are alien to me. With regard to religion, I've been very cold all this time. Thought during this time:
[...]
(3) The possibility of killing oneself is a freedom given to people. God didn't want slaves in this life, but free workers. If you stay on in this life, it means that conditions are favourable for you. If they are favourable – then work. But if you want to escape from the conditions here and kill yourself, you will be offered the same conditions again in the next life. So there is nowhere to escape to. It would be good to write a story about the experiences in this life of a man who had killed himself in a previous one: how, when running up against the same demands made on him in the other life, he comes to the realisation that he must fulfil them. And in this life he would be more intelligent than other people, remembering the lesson he had had. [...]

Today is 27 February, Nikolskoye I'm getting on with the drama. It's going very sluggishly. I don't even know whether I'm making any progress. Some moderately discontented letters from Sonya in Moscow. But I feel very well here – the main thing is the quietness. I've been reading *Trilby*[11] – poor. Wrote letters to Chertkov, Schmitt and Kenworthy. Read Corneille.[12] Edifying. I've been thinking:
(1) I once noted that there are two kinds of art. I've been thinking about it now and can find no clear way of expressing my idea. At that time I used to think that there is an art, as it has rightly been defined, which derives from play, from the need of every creature to play. The play of a calf is jumping, the play of a man – a symphony, picture, poem or novel. This is one kind of art – the art of playing and inventing new games, performing old ones and making up new ones. This is a good, useful and valuable thing because it increases the joys of man. But understandably one can only engage in play when one is well fed. Likewise society can only engage in art when all its members are well fed. And until its members are well fed, there can be no real art. But there will be an art of the overfed, a misshapen one, and an art of the hungry – crude and pitiful – as is the case now.

And so with this first kind of art – play – only that art is valuable which is accessible to all, and increases the joys of all. If this is so, it is not a bad thing, especially if it does not require an increase of the labour of the oppressed, as happens now. (*This could and should be better expressed.*)[13]

But there is another kind of art also which *evokes in people better and higher feelings*.

I've just written what I've said many times, and I think it's not true.

There is only one kind of art, and it consists in increasing innocent joys, common and accessible to all – the good of man. A fine building, a gay picture, a song or a story produces a little good; the awakening of a religious feeling of love of the good brought about by a drama, a painting or singing produces a great good. (2) What I also thought about art is that nowhere else is conservatism so harmful as in art.

Art is one of the manifestations of man's spiritual life, and so, just as if an animal is alive, it breathes and secretes the products of its breathing, so, if mankind is alive, it manifests the activity of art. And so at any given moment it must be contemporary – art of our time. One only needs to know whereabouts it is (it isn't in the music, poetry and novels of the Decadents). But it must be sought not in the past, but in the present. People who wish to show themselves to be connoisseurs of art and who therefore praise the art of the past – classical art – and abuse the contemporary, only show by this that they have no feeling for art. [. . .]

(7) Today at dinner there was talk about a boy with vicious inclinations who had been expelled from school, and about how good it would be to commit him to a reformatory. This is exactly what a man does who has lived a bad life, injurious to his health, and who, when sickness overtakes him, turns to a doctor to be cured, never thinking that his sickness is a beneficial indication to him that his whole life is bad and that he ought to change it. It's the same with the sickness of our society. All the sick members of this society fail to remind us that the whole life of our society is wrong and ought to be changed, but we think that for every such sick member, there is or ought to be an institution ridding us of this member or even reforming him. Nothing hinders the progress of mankind so much as this false belief. The more sick society is, the more institutions there are for treating the symptoms, and the less concern for changing its entire life. [. . .]

Today is 2 May, Yasnaya Polyana Haven't written my diary for nearly two months. I was living in Moscow all that time. Important events: a closer acquaintance with the scribe Novikov[14] who changed his life as a result of my books which his brother, a man-servant, received from his mistress abroad. A spirited young man. Then his other brother, a worker, asked for *What I Believe*, and Tanya sent it to Kholevinskaya. Kholevinskaya was taken to prison. The prosecutor said they ought to have laid hands on me. All this taken together made me write letters to the ministers of Internal Affairs and Justice, asking them to direct their persecutions towards me instead. All this time I've been getting on with my exposition of religious belief.[15] Made little progress. Chertkov has been. Posha has been and gone. Relations with people have been good. I've given up riding my bicycle. I'm surprised how I could have been so infatuated. Heard Wagner's *Siegfried*.[16] Many thoughts about this and other things. Noted down twenty in all in my notebook.

Another important event – the work of Afrikan Spir.[17] I've just read through what I wrote in the beginning of this exercise book: essentially nothing but a brief exposition of Spir's whole philosophy, which I not only hadn't read then, but of which I hadn't even the slightest notion. It's astonishing how this work illuminated from various sides and confirmed my thoughts about the meaning of life. The essence of his teaching is that there are no things, only our impressions, which appear to us as objects in our conception of them. Our conception (*Vorstellung*) has the faculty of believing in the existence of objects. This derives from the fact that the faculty of thinking consists in ascribing to impressions an objectivity, a substance and a projection of them in space.

5 May Andryusha and Misha are in the village again. There's the same general mood of despair. And I'm sad. The only reason is: a high moral demand is made. In its name, everything beneath it is rejected. But it isn't followed. Fifteen years ago I offered to give away the greater part of my property and to live in four rooms. Then they would have had an ideal. Now they have none. They see that the one their mother proposes – being *comme il faut* – won't stand up to criticism, and mine is made fun of in front of them – and they are glad. The only thing left is pleasure. That's what they live for. It's impossible to live without an ideal – even a very low ambitious one, even a selfish ideal.

Rode past Gill's today, and thought: no undertaking is profitable with only a little capital. The more capital, the more profitable; the fewer expenses. But it doesn't follow at all from that that, as Marx says, capitalism leads to socialism. Perhaps it will do, but only to socialism by force. The workers will be compelled to work together and they will work less and their pay will be more, but there will be the same slavery. It's necessary that people should work together in freedom, should learn to work for one another, but capitalism doesn't teach them that. On the contrary, it teaches them envy, greed – egoism. And so, while the material condition of the workers can be improved through forcible association brought about by capitalism, their contentment certainly cannot be guaranteed. Contentment can only be guaranteed through the free association of workers. And for that, it's necessary to learn, to try to come together, to improve oneself morally – to serve people willingly without being offended at getting no reward. And this certainly can't be learned under a capitalist, competitive system, but only under a completely different one.

I'm sleeping alone downstairs.

Today is 9 May, Yasnaya Polyana [. . .] The family have gone away, some to the coronation, some to Sweden.[18] We are alone – Masha and I. She has a sore throat. I'm well.

Today is 16 May already, Yasnaya Polyana Morning. I can't get on with my exposition of religious belief. It's unclear, too philosophical; and I'm spoiling the good things that were in it. I'm thinking of starting it all over again or making a break and working on the story or the drama.[19] N. N. Ivanov[20] has been. It was a difficult examination in love. I only got through it on the surface, and badly at that. If the examiner had put me through it well and truly, I would have failed shamefully. A splendid article by Menshikov, 'The Mistakes of Fear'.[21] What joy. I could almost die – indeed I could die. And yet it always seems there is still something more that needs doing. Do it, and it will be seen in the next world, and if you are no longer fit for work, you will be replaced and another person sent, and you will be sent to do some other work. If only one could keep on advancing in one's work. Sonya has gone to Moscow to see about her tooth. It's difficult for her to find any life without the children. The main thing is that I get in her way. [. . .]

17 May, Yasnaya Polyana [. . .] I'll now write out the twenty-one points from my notebook: [. . .]
(2) Read about Granovsky.[22] In our literature it's customary to say that in the reign of Nicholas, conditions were such that great thoughts could not arise (Granovsky complains about this, and others too). But in fact there were no real thoughts. It's all self-deceit. If all the Granovskys, Belinskys and others had had anything to say, they would have said it, despite all the obstacles. Herzen is the proof of that. He went abroad. And despite his enormous talent, what did he say that was new or necessary?

All these Granovskys, Belinskys, Chernyshevskys and Dobrolyubovs who have been promoted to the stature of great men ought to thank the government and the censorship, without which they would have been the most insignificant feuilletonists. Perhaps there actually was something real in them, in Belinsky, Granovsky and others unknown, but they suppressed it all because they imagined that they had to serve society within the forms of social life, and not serve God by professing the truth and preaching it without any concern for the forms of social life. Given the content, the forms will come about of themselves. People who act like this, i.e. who accommodate their striving for truth to existing forms of society, are like a creature which has been given wings to fly, unconscious of all obstacles, and which uses these wings to help itself to walk. Such a creature would not reach its goal – any obstacle would stop it and damage its wings. And then the creature would complain that it had been held back, and would say sadly (like Granovsky) that it would have gone far if it hadn't been held back by obstacles. The qualities of true spiritual activity are such that it cannot be held back. If it is, it means that it isn't real. [. . .]
(7) Christian truth, they say, can't be proved, it must be believed; as if it were easier to be convinced of the truthfulness of the nonsensical than of the reasonable. Why deprive Christianity of the power to convince? Why? [. . .]
(14) The article about art[23] must begin with a discussion of the fact that, say, for a picture which cost the artist 1,000 working days, people pay 40,000 working days: for an opera or a novel even more. And some people say of these works that they are splendid, others that they are no good at all. And there is no indisputable criterion. There is no such disagreement about water, food, or good deeds. Why is that? [. . .]
(2) The chief purpose of art, if there is art and if it has a purpose, is to manifest and express the truth about man's soul, to express those secrets which can't be expressed

in simple words. That is the origin of art. Art is a microscope which the artist fixes on the secrets of his soul, and shows to people these secrets which are common to all. [. . .]
(27) Katyusha, even after her resurrection, has periods when she smiles in a sly or idle manner, as though she has forgotten all she previously considered true, and is simply happy and wants to live.[24] [. . .]
(31) Read about the coronation and was horrified at the deliberate deceiving of people.[25] In particular the regalia. [. . .]

28 May, Yasnaya Polyana 12 o'clock noon. For several days I've been struggling with my work and making no progress. I'm asleep. I wanted to finish it off somehow in rough,[26] but I just can't. I'm in a bad frame of mind, aggravated by the emptiness, the barren, self-satisfied, cold emptiness of the life around me. I've been to Pirogovo during this time. A most joyful impression: my brother Sergey has undoubtedly had a spiritual transformation. He has himself formulated the essence of my faith (and evidently recognises it as true for himself): to exalt in ourselves the spiritual essence and subordinate to it the animal. He has a miracle-working icon, and has been troubled by his uncertain attitude towards it. The girls are very good – they take life seriously. Masha has been infected by them. Then Salomon was here. Also Taneyev, who disgusts me with his self-satisfied, moral and, ridiculous to say, aesthetic (real, not outward) obtuseness and his *coq du village* situation in our house. It's an examination for me. I'm trying not to fail.[27]

A terrible event in Moscow – the death of 3,000.[28] I somehow can't respond to it as I should. I'm still unwell – getting weaker. In Pirogovo there was a harness-maker, an intelligent man. Yesterday there was a worker from Tula, intelligent, and, I think, a revolutionary. Today a pathetic seminarist. Work is making very, very slow progress. Letters, rather boring because they require polite answers. Wrote to Bondarev, Posha and someone else. Yes, an officer, Dunin-Barkovsky, has also been. I think I was useful to him.[29] Wonderful notes by Škarvan.[30] A letter yesterday from poor Suller whom they have driven away to the Persian frontier in the hope that he will die there. Help him, God. And don't forget me. Give me life, life – i.e. let me serve Thee consciously and joyfully. Thought during this time:
(1) It's surprising how many people see some insoluble problem in evil. I've never seen any problem in it. It's completely clear to me now that what we call evil is the good whose effect we can't yet see.
(2) The poetry of Mallarmé[31] and others. We, who don't understand it, say boldly that it's nonsense, that it's poetry which has wandered off into a blind alley. But why, when we listen to music which is incomprehensible and equally nonsensical, don't we boldly say the same thing, instead of timidly saying: yes, maybe. It needs to be understood, one must prepare oneself, etc. That's nonsense. Any work of art is only a work of art when it's comprehensible – I don't say to everyone, but to people on a certain level of education, the level of a man who reads poetry and judges it. This reasoning brought me to the quite definite conclusion that music lost its way and wandered off into a blind alley sooner than other arts (decadence in poetry and symbolism, etc. in painting). And the person who made it lose its way

was the brilliant musician Beethoven. Very important: the authorities and the people devoid of aesthetic feeling who judge art. Goethe? Shakespeare? Everything that goes under their names is bound to be good, and *on se bât les flancs* [does one's uttermost] in order to find something beautiful in the stupid and unsuccessful, and taste is completely perverted. But all these great talents – the Goethes, Shakespeares, Beethovens, Michelangelos produced side by side with beautiful things not merely mediocre, but repulsive ones as well. Mediocre artists produce mediocre quality work, and never anything very bad. But recognised geniuses produce either really great works, or absolute rubbish: Shakespeare, Goethe, Beethoven, Bach, etc. [. . .]

I think it's 6 June, Yasnaya Polyana The main thing: during this time I've made progress in my work, and am still progressing. I'm writing about sins,[32] and the whole work is clear to me right to the end. Finished reading Spir. Splendid. Three methods for the economic progress of mankind: the abolition of the ownership of land according to Henry George; a tax on inheritance, which would hand over accumulated wealth to society, if not in the first generation, then in the second; and a similar tax on wealth, on an excess of income over 1,000 roubles a family, or 200 roubles a person.

The Chertkovs came today. Galya is very nice.[33] The day before yesterday there was a police-spy here who admitted that he had been sent to keep an eye on me. It was both pleasant and nasty.[34] [. . .]

Today is 9 June, Yasnaya Polyana [. . .] This is the people's religion: There is a God, and there are gods and saints (Christ came to earth, as a peasant said to me today, to teach people how to pray and to whom). The gods and the saints work miracles, have power over the flesh and do heroic deeds and good works. But people only need to know how to pray and to whom. People can't do good works, they can only pray. That is their whole faith. [. . .]

19 June, Yasnaya Polyana All this time I've been feeling weak and sleeping badly. Yesterday Posha came. He spoke well about Khodynka, but wrote badly about it.[35] Our very idle, luxurious life oppresses me. Zlinchenko[36] came. He's alien to me. He's young, and doesn't understand in the same way as I do what he understands, but agrees with me about everything. Finished the rough draft on 13 June.[37] I've been revising it now, but am working very little. Seryozha is here, and is pitiful and depressing. Twice struggled with myself, and successfully. If only it were always so!

I went out one evening beyond the Zakaz wood and wept with joyful gratitude – for life. I have very vivid pictures of life in Samara: the steppe, the struggle between the nomadic patriarchal way of life and the civilised, agricultural one. It draws me very much. Koni's story wasn't born inside me. That's why it's going so slowly. Thought: (1) Something very important about art: What is beauty? Beauty is what we love. *I don't love him because he's beautiful, but he's beautiful because I love him.* That's just the problem: why is he loved? Why do we love? To say that we love a thing because it's beautiful is just the same as saying that we breathe because the air is pleasant. We find the air pleasant because we have to breathe. And similarly we discover beauty because we have to love: and the person who can't see spiritual beauty, at least sees physical beauty and loves it.

19 July, Pirogovo   Today is 19 July. I'm at Pirogovo. Arrived the day before yesterday with Tanya and Chertkov. A spiritual revolution has certainly taken place in Seryozha; he admits it himself, saying that he was born a few months ago. I'm very glad to be with him. I've endured much hardship at home during this time. Lord, Father, release me from my vile body. [. . .]

During this time I've made progress with *The Exposition of Religious Belief*. It's far from what is needed and what I want, and is quite inaccessible to the ordinary person and the child, but still it expresses everything I know coherently and logically. During this time I also wrote a foreword to the reading of the Gospels[38] and marked off passages in the Gospels. Had some visitors: Englishmen, Americans, no one of importance.

I'll write out what I noted down:

(1) Yesterday I walked through a black-earth, fallow field which had been ploughed up again. As far as the eye could see there was nothing but black earth – not one green blade of grass. And there on the edge of the dusty grey road was a Tatar thistle (burdock) with three shoots: one was broken, and a dirty white flower hung from it; the second was also broken and spattered with mud, black and with a cracked and dirty stem; the third shoot stuck out to the side, also black, but still alive and red in the middle. It reminded me of Hadji Murat. I'd like to write about it. It fights for life till the end and, alone in the middle of the whole field, somehow manages to win the fight.[39]

(2) He's good at languages and mathematics, quick to understand and to answer, can sing, draw accurately and beautifully and write similarly, but he has no moral or artistic feeling and therefore nothing of his own. [. . .]

(8) Yesterday I looked through the novels, stories and poems of Fet. I remembered our incessant piano music for four hands at Yasnaya Polyana, and it became so clear to me that all this – novels, poems, and music – was not art in the sense of something important and necessary to people generally, but the wanton play of robbers and parasites who have nothing in common with life: novels and stories about nasty love affairs, poems about the same thing, or about people dying of boredom. And also music about the same thing. But life, the whole of life, is seething with its own problems about food, accommodation, work, belief, relations between people . . . It's shameful and vile. Help me, Father, to serve Thee by showing up this lie.

(9) I was coming back from the Chertkovs on 5 July. Evening time and beauty, happiness, and goodness in everything. But in the world of men? Greed, malice, envy, cruelty, lust, dissipation. [Five or six words erased.] When will it be with men as it is with nature. In nature there is struggle, but it's honest, simple and beautiful. But with men it's base. I know it and hate it because I am a man myself. (It's no good.) [. . .]

26 July, Yasnaya Polyana Morning. Didn't sleep all night. My heart aches incessantly. I continue to suffer and can't surrender myself to God. One thing: I've overcome lust, but – what is worse – I haven't overcome pride and indignation, and my heart aches incessantly.⁴⁰ One thing comforts me . . . I'm not alone, but with God, and therefore, however painful it is, I feel that something is being achieved. Help me, Father.

Yesterday I walked to Baburino and couldn't help meeting (I rather tried to avoid than sought to meet) eighty-year-old Akim ploughing, Yaremich's old woman who hasn't a fur coat in her house, and only one caftan, and then Marya whose husband died of cold and who has nobody to cart the rye away and whose child is dying of hunger. And Trofim and Khalyavka, husband and wife, are dying and their children too. And we discuss Beethoven. And I prayed that He would release me from this life. And I pray again, and cry with pain. I've lost my way, I'm stuck, I can't do anything, but I hate myself and my life.

30 July, Yasnaya Polyana I've suffered and struggled a lot more, and still haven't overcome either the one thing or the other.⁴¹ But it's better. Annenkova was here and expressed it well: [Five words erased.] They have spoiled my diary too; I write with an eye to the possibility of its being read by people still alive. Only the awareness that one must have pity, that she is suffering and there is no end to my guilt made me feel better. Just now the talk upstairs turned to the Gospels, and Taneyev began to argue *en ricanant* [with a sneer] that Christ advised castration. I was angry – and ashamed.

A couple of days ago I went to visit the fire victims, had no dinner and was tired, but it was good. Tanya has left. I gave her some advice and feel sorry for her. Yesterday I was at a lawyer's who wanted to take a hundred roubles off a poor woman to decorate his own house with. It's the same everywhere. During this time I've been to Pirogovo; my brother Seryozha has come over to our side completely. Had an enjoyable journey with Tanya and Chertkov. Took leave today of a dying peasant in Demenka. I'm making good progress with my writing. [. . .]
(17) Aesthetic pleasure is pleasure of a lower order. And so the highest aesthetic pleasure leaves us dissatisfied. Indeed, the higher the aesthetic pleasure, the more dissatisfied it leaves us. We keep wanting something more. And there is no end to it. Complete satisfaction only comes from moral good. Therein lies complete satisfaction – nothing further is wanted or needed.
(18) Lying to other people is far less important and harmful than lying to oneself. Lying to other people is often an innocent game, the satisfaction of vanity; but lying to oneself is always a distortion of the truth, a retreat from the demands of life. [. . .]

31 July Alive. It's now evening, it's gone 4. I'm lying down and can't sleep. My heart aches. I'm exhausted. Through the window I can hear them playing tennis and laughing. Sonya has gone to the Shenshins'. Everyone is well, but I feel depressed and can't control myself. It's like the feeling I had when St Thomas locked me in and from my dungeon I could hear everyone enjoying themselves and laughing.⁴² But I don't want to. I must endure humiliation and be good. I can. [. . .]

[14 September] It's terrible to think how much time has passed: a month and a half. Today is 14 September, Yasnaya Polyana. During this time I had a trip to a monastery with Sonya.⁴³ It was very good. I haven't rid myself of it, haven't overcome it; it has merely passed. Wrote about Hadji Murat very badly, in rough. Continued work on my exposition of religious belief. The Chertkovs have left. Sonya has been in Moscow since the 3rd. I waited for her impatiently today and was almost in distress. Lyova and his wife have come. She's a child. They're very nice. Now all three sons and their wives are here.⁴⁴ Had a letter from a Dutchman who has refused to serve. I wrote a foreword to the letter.⁴⁵ I also wrote a letter to Kalmykova with some very sharp opinions about the government.⁴⁶ The whole month and a half was compressed into it. Oh yes, I've also had my usual illness and my stomach is still not strong.

Yes, and during this time there was a letter from an Indian, Tod, and a delightful book of Hindu wisdom, *Joga's Philosophy*.⁴⁷

Thought during this time: [. . .]
(7) One of the most powerful means of hypnosis – of external influence on a man's spiritual condition – is dress. People know this well: that's the reason for monastic garb in monasteries and uniform in the army.
(8) Thought of two splendid subjects for stories: the suicide of the old Persiyaninov and the substitution of a child in a foundling hospital.⁴⁸ [. . .]

Today is 10 October, Yasnaya Polyana. Haven't written my diary for nearly a month, but it seems it was only yesterday. During this time I finished my exposition of religious belief, although in very bad shape. During this time some Japanese came with a letter from Konissi.⁴⁹ They, the Japanese, are incomparably closer to Christianity than our ecclesiastical Christians. I liked them very much. Lyova is weak. Relations with Sonya are all right, though not stable, but I struggle on with love. I want to write the whole exposition of religious belief from the beginning again. Yesterday there was a good letter from Pyotr Verigin.⁵⁰ [. . .]

Today is 20 October, Yasnaya Polyana (morning.) [. . .]
(1) In a work of art the main thing is the soul of the author. Therefore in the case of average works, those by women are better and more interesting. The woman will force her way through from time to time, will express the very secrets of her soul – that's what is needed – and you can see what it is she really loves, although she pretends she loves something else. When an author writes, we – the readers – put our ears to his breast and listen and say: breathe. If there are wheezing sounds they will be heard. And women don't know how to conceal them. But a man can learn literary devices, and you won't be able to see him because of his manner of writing; you only know that he's stupid. But what there is in his soul – you won't be able to see. (Not good, spiteful.) [. . .]
(4) Refinement and the power of art are almost always diametrically opposed.
(5) Is it true that works of art are produced by assiduous work? What we call works of art – yes. But is that real art?
(6) The Japanese sang – we couldn't refrain from laughing. If we had sung before

the Japanese, they would have laughed. Even more so if we had played Beethoven to them. Hindu and Greek temples can be understood by everyone. Greek statues can also be understood by everyone. And our best painting can also be understood. And so architecture, sculpture and painting, having attained their perfection, have also attained cosmopolitanism, universal accessibility. The art of speech has also attained this in some of its manifestations – in the teachings of Buddha and Christ, in the poetry of Sakyamuni, Jacob and Joseph. In dramatic art – Sophocles, Aristophanes – it has not been attained. It is being attained in some modern works. But music has lagged behind completely. The ideal of any art towards which it must aspire is universal accessibility, but the arts, and especially music today, are getting bogged down in refinement.

(7) The main thing I would like to say about art is that it doesn't exist in the sense of a great manifestation of the human spirit as it is now understood. There is amusement, consisting in the beauty of buildings, the sculpting of figures, the depicting of objects, dancing, singing, the playing of various instruments, poetry, fables and fairy stories, but all this is only amusement, and not an important matter to which one can consciously devote one's strength. This has always been understood, and is understood, by the working people who have not been corrupted. And any person who has not withdrawn from work and life cannot look at it otherwise. This ought to be said, it really ought to be. How much evil has come from this importance attributed by the parasites of society to their amusements! [...]

Today must be 23 October, Yasnaya Polyana. All these days I've been out of tune with my work. Wrote a letter yesterday to the commander of the Irkutsk disciplinary battalion about Olkhovik.[51] It's now evening and I'm sitting down to write because I feel the special importance and seriousness of the hours of life which are left to me. And I don't know what I must do, but I feel the expression of God's will has ripened within me and is ready to bear fruit. Read *Hadji Murat* – it's not right. I can't get down to *Resurrection*. The drama[52] occupies me. A splendid article by Carpenter on science.[53] We all walk close to the truth and reveal it from different sides.

26 October, Yasnaya Polyana Still just as unwell. And I can't write. My head aches. Seryozha came yesterday. I wrote letters to Sonya and Andryusha. But I think that during this time of doubt I arrived at two very important positions: (1) the one that I had previously thought about and noted down: that *art* is a fiction. It is the temptation to amuse oneself with puppets, pictures, songs, *play*, fairy stories and nothing more. But to place art as people do (and as they do with science) on the same level as the good is a terrible *sacrilège*. The proof that it isn't so is that one can say about truth that truth is good, [...] and about beauty that it is good; but one can't say about good that it is beautiful (it usually isn't beautiful) or true (it is always true).

There is only one good – good and bad – but truth and beauty are good attributes of certain objects.

The other very important thing is that reason is the only means of making manifest the release of love. I think this is an important thought, omitted in my exposition of religious belief.

Today is 1 November, Yasnaya Polyana I've been unwell all the time and can't work. Only wrote some letters, including one to the Caucasian disciplinary battalion.[54] Yesterday, while walking at night across the snow in a snowstorm, I strained my heart, and it aches. I think I shall die very soon. For that reason I'm writing these notes. I think I shall die without fear or resistance. Just now I was sitting alone and thinking how surprising it is that people live their own separate lives: I thought about Stasov; how is he getting on now, what is he thinking and feeling? About Kolechka[55] too. And I suddenly became aware in such a strange new way that all these people are living, but I am not living in them, and that they are shut off from me.

2 November, Yasnaya Polyana [. . .] Thought today about art. It's play. And when it's the play of normal, working people it's good; but when it's the play of depraved parasites, then it's bad; and now it's reached the stage of decadence.

Today is 5 November, Yasnaya Polyana Morning. Yesterday was a terrible day. Already the day before yesterday I had expressed to Lyova in a heated and unrestrained manner my view about his incorrect understanding of life and of what is good. Then I told him that I felt I was to blame. Yesterday he began a conversation and said some very bad things, with petty, personal animosity. I forgot God, didn't pray and felt hurt, and I confounded my true 'I' with my evil one – I forgot God in me, and went off downstairs. Sonya came in, as she did yesterday, and was very good. Then in the evening, when everyone had gone, she began to beg me to hand over to her the rights to my works. I said I couldn't. She was distressed and said a lot of hard things to me. I was even more distressed, but restrained myself and went off to bed. I hardly slept all night, and was depressed. I've just found the *prescriptions*[56] in my diary and read them through, and felt easier; I must separate off my true 'I' from the one that is offended and angry, must remember that all this is not just a hindrance, or a casual annoyance, but the very task destined for me to do, and above all I must know that if there is any lack of affection in me towards anyone, then as long as that lack of affection is in me I am to blame. And when you know you are to blame you feel relieved. [. . .]

Yesterday I wrote eighteen pages of my introduction on art.[57]

You mustn't say of a work of art: you don't understand it yet. If you don't understand it, it means that the work of art is not good, because its task is to make understandable what was not understandable before.

6 November Alive. For the third day I'm continuing to write about art. I think it's good. At least I'm writing readily and easily. Sonya left today. I feel both at ease and ill at ease with her. Lyova and his wife have left for Ilya's. I'm ashamed that I feel relieved. Received a good letter from Van der Veer, and wrote another letter to the commander of the battalion in the Caucasus. Chertkov sent me a copy of a similar letter from himself. Rode to Tula today, a wonderful day and night. I'm going for a walk now to meet the girls. [. . .]

16 November, Yasnaya Polyana Morning. Still working just as badly and am depressed because of it. The day after tomorrow I'm going to Moscow, God willing. Lyova and his wife have gone to Moscow; I'm ashamed to say I felt depressed in their company. During this time I had a strange letter from a Spaniard, Sanini, with an offer of 22,000 francs for good works. I replied that I wanted to use it for the Dukhobors.[58] Will anything happen? Wrote to Kuzminsky about Witte and Dragomirov,[59] and the day before yesterday I spent the whole morning writing diligently *about war again*.[60] Will anything come of it? [. . .]

17 November Hardly wrote anything yesterday. I'm alone with my daughters. How good to be with them. It spoils me. It's a warm bath for the feelings. A letter from Andryusha, a very good one. A fight in the papers over Repin's definition of art as amusement.[61] How appropriate it is to my work. The meaning of art still hasn't been fully clarified. It's clear to me, and I can write about it and prove it, but not briefly and simply. I'm not able to do that. Yesterday there was a letter from Ivan Mikhaylovich.[62] About the Dukhobors again.

Amusement is all right if the amusement is honest and not corrupt, and if people don't suffer because of it. I'm thinking about that now.

Aesthetics is the expression of ethics, i.e. in Russian: art expresses those feelings which the artist experiences. If the feelings are good and elevated, then the art will be good and elevated, and vice versa. If the artist is a moral person, his art will also be moral, and vice versa. (No good.) Thought last night:
(1) We rejoice at our technical successes – steam . . . phonographs. And we are so pleased with these successes that if we were told that these successes are only being achieved at the cost of the destruction of human lives, we would shrug our shoulders and say: we must try to prevent it: the eight-hour day, workers' insurance, etc., but because a few people perish, we mustn't renounce the successes we have achieved, i.e. *fiat* the mirror and phonograph, etc., *pereat* a few people. One has only to concede this principle and there is no limit to cruelty, and it's very easy to bring about all sorts of technical improvements.

I had an acquaintance in Kazan who used to ride to his Vyatka estate 130 *versts* away) in this manner: he would buy a pair of horses at the market for twenty roubles (horses were very cheap), harness them and drive them the 130 *versts* to the place. Sometimes they would reach the place and he would still have the horses and the cost of the journey, sometimes they would only cover part of the road and he would hire some more. But it still worked out cheaper for him than hiring post horses. Swift even proposed eating children.[63] And that would have been very beneficial. In New York, city railway companies run over several pedestrians every year, and they don't change the crossings to avoid the possibility of accidents because such a change would cost more than paying money to the families of those run over every year. The same thing happens with the technical improvements of our own age. They are brought about by means of human lives. But one must value every human life – not value it, but rather place it above any value, and make improvements in such a way that lives should not be lost or damaged, and put a stop to any improvement if it is injurious to human life.

22 November, Moscow   Fourth day in Moscow. Dissatisfied with myself. No work. Was confused over my article on art and made no progress. Received a letter yesterday. She wants to separate from Seryozha. Wrote her a long letter today. Wrote from the heart what I think, and I believe it's the truth. Took it myself today to Petrovsko-Razumovskoye.[64] Gorbunov, Boulanger, and Dunayev were here. Went to Rusanov's myself. A very good impression. Read Plato: the embryos of idealism.[65] Thought of two subjects, very good ones:[66]
(1) A wife's betrayal of her passionate, jealous husband; his sufferings, struggle and the pleasure of forgiveness, and
(2) A description of the oppresssion of the serfs, and then exactly the same kind of oppression by landed property, or rather by depriving people of it.

Goldenweiser[67] has just been playing. One piece a fantasia and fugue: studied, cold and pretentious artificiality; a second – Arensky's *Bigarrure*: sensual and artificial; and a third – a ballade by Chopin: sickly and nervous. Neither the first, nor the second, nor the third can be of any use to the people.

The devil attached to me is still with me and torments me.

Today is 2 December, Moscow   Five days have passed and very painful ones. Everything is still the same. Yesterday night I went for a walk; we had a talk. I understood my guilt. I hope she also understood me. My feelings: I discovered a terrible, purulent sore on myself. They promised me they would heal it and bandaged it up. The sore was so disgusting to me and it was so depressing to think it was there, that I tried to forget about it and persuade myself that it wasn't there. But some time has passed – the bandage has been taken off and although the sore is healing it's still there. And this was agonisingly painful to me and I began to reproach the doctor, unjustly. Such is my condition.

The main thing is the devil attached to me. Oh, this luxury, this wealth, this lack of concern for the material life is like ground that has been over-manured. Unless people grow good plants on it, and weed and clean all round them, it will become overgrown with terribly nasty things and will be horrible. But it's difficult – I'm old, and hardly able. [. . .]

12 December   I've suffered a lot during these days and, I think, I've made progress towards peace and goodness – towards God. I'm reading a lot about art. Things are becoming clearer. I'm not even trying to write. Masha has left. The Chertkovs have come. Today I wrote an afterword to the appeal.[68]

15 December, Moscow   It's now 2 o'clock in the morning. I've done nothing. Had stomach-ache. I feel at peace; I've no desire to write. Sonya has a strange need to feel concerned. She just came to ask me whether one should go and visit Pelageya Vasilyevna.[69] It's strange.

I've made a few notes: I won't copy them all out. One thing struck me very much: it's my clear awareness of the weight, of the constraint of my own person – of the fact that I am – I. It makes me glad because it means that I'm aware of and recognise at least in part the *non*-personal 'I' in me.

Today is 19 or 20 December 20 December, Moscow. Five days have passed and this feeling of constraint, of the weight of my body, and then the awareness of the existence of that which is not body, has increased terribly. I want to throw off this weight, to free myself from these chains and at the same time I can feel them. I'm sick of my body. All this time I've done no work and I feel a depressing melancholy. [. . .]

I've noted various trifles about art:

(1) People adduce as evidence that art is good the fact that it makes a great impression on you. But who are you? On the decadents, their own works make a strong impression. You say that they have been corrupted. But Beethoven, who makes no impression on the working man, only makes such an impression on you because you have been corrupted. Who is right? What music is of undoubted value? That which makes an impression on the decadents and on you and on the working man: simple, comprehensible folk music.

(2) What relief everyone would feel, shut up at a concert listening to Beethoven's last works, if a *trepak* or a *chardash* or something like that were to be played to them. [. . .]

(4) Nothing confuses concepts about art so much as the acceptance of authorities. Instead of determining according to a clear and precise concept of art whether the works of Sophocles, Homer, Dante, Shakespeare, Goethe, Beethoven, Bach, Raphael or Michelangelo conform to the concept of good art, and precisely which works do so, they define art itself and its laws on the basis of the existing works of those who are recognised as great artists. And yet there are many works by famous artists which are beneath criticism, and many false reputations, many who have acquired fame by chance: Dante, Shakespeare.

(5) I'm reading a history of music:[70] among sixteen chapters about artificial music there is one short chapter about folk music, and people know next to nothing about it, so that the history of music is not a history of how real music originated and spread and developed – the music of melodies – but the history of artificial music, i.e. of how real, melodious music was deformed.

(6) Artificial music, the music of gentlemen and parasites, feeling its own impotence and emptiness, and in order to replace real interest by artificial, has recourse at times to counterpoint and fugue, at times to opera, at times to illustration.

(7) Church music was good because it was accessible to the masses. Only that which is accessible to everyone is undeniably good. And so it's true to say that the more accessible the better.

(8) The different characters expressed by art only move us because in each one of us there are possibilities which exist in any conceivable character. (I've forgotten.)

(9) The history of music, like all histories, is written to a plan, namely to show how

it has gradually reached the position in which the subject whose history is being written now finds itself. And the present state of music, or the subject whose history is being written, is assumed to be the highest. But what if it is not only the lowest state, but a completely distorted one, a chance aberration, resulting in distortion?

(10) Belief in authorities causes the mistakes of the authorities to be accepted as models.

(11) People say that music strengthens the impression of the words of an aria or song. It's not true. The music outstrips the impression of the words to an unimaginable degree. A Bach aria. What words can compete with it when it is being performed? Words by themselves are a different matter. Whatever music you set the Sermon on the Mount to, the music will be left far behind when you have penetrated the meaning of the words. Faure's *Crucifixe*.[71] The music is pathetic alongside the words. It's a case of two quite different feelings – and they are incompatible. In a song they only harmonise because the words set the tone. That's not accurate. I'll say more about it elsewhere. [. . .]

(13) The Scylla and Charybdis of artists: either a thing is comprehensible, but shallow and vulgar, or it is pseudo-exalted, original and incomprehensible.

(14) Popular poetry has always reflected, and not only reflected, but predicted and paved the way for popular movements – the crusades, the Reformation. What can the poetry of our parasitical circle predict and pave the way for? love and debauchery; debauchery and love.

(15) Popular poetry, music, and art generally have dried up because all those with talent have been won over by bribes to become jesters to the rich and famous: chamber music, operas, odes . . .

(16) In all arts there is a struggle between the Christian and the pagan. The Christian begins to prevail and then comes the onset of the new wave of the fifteenth century – the Renaissance – and only now, at the end of the nineteenth century, is Christianity rising again, and paganism in the form of decadence, having reached the ultimate degree of absurdity, is being destroyed.

(17) Apart from the fact that the most talented representatives of the people have been won over to the camp of the parasites, the reasons for the destruction of popular poetry and music were first of all the enserfment of the people, and then – most importantly – printing.

(18) Chertkov said that we are surrounded by four walls of ignorance: in front, the wall of the future, behind, the wall of the past, on the right the wall of ignorance of what is happening somewhere where I'm not present, and the fourth, he says, is the wall of ignorance of what is going on in another person's soul. In my opinion that isn't so.

The first three walls are as he says. One shouldn't look over them. The less we look beyond them the better. But the fourth wall of ignorance of what is going on in the souls of other people – that wall we ought to break down with all our strength, and strive towards a union with the souls of other people. And the less we look beyond those other three walls, the closer we shall get to other people in that direction.

(19) After death in importance, and before death in time, there is nothing more important, more irrevocable, than marriage. And just as death is good only when it is unavoidable, while any intentional death is bad, so it is with marriage. Marriage is not an evil only when it is irresistible.

21 December, Moscow I.I.A. I'm still writing on the 20th   I'm still just as depressed. Help me, Father. Give me relief. Strengthen Thyself in me, subdue, eliminate, destroy the impure flesh, and all that I feel through the medium of it. Just now there was a conversation about art and the opinion that one can only engage in art for the sake of a person one loves.[72] And there was an unwillingness to say this to me. And I wasn't amused or sorry, only hurt. Father, help me. However, I feel better already. What consoles me particularly is the task, the test of humility, of humiliation, an entirely unexpected, exceptional humiliation. In chains or in prison one can be proud of one's humiliation, but here it is merely painful unless one accepts it as a trial sent by God. Yes, learn to endure it calmly and joyfully, and to love.

21 December, Moscow   I'm a bad learner. I'm still suffering, and feel weak and helpless. Only in rare moments do I rise to the consciousness of my entire life (not just this one), and my duties in it.

Thought (and felt). There are people lacking both in aesthetic and ethical (especially ethical) feelings, to whom it is impossible to make clear what is good, the more so when they do and love what is bad, and think that the bad is good. Sonya has just been; we had a talk. It only made me even more depressed.

22 December, Moscow   I.I.A. It's beginning to be very doubtful; my heart aches incessantly. I can hardly find rest anywhere. Only Posha cheered me up today. It's disgusting that I want to cry over myself, over what is left of my life which is being ruined to no purpose. But perhaps it must be so. Yes, it certainly must be so.

25 December, Moscow   9 o'clock at night. I feel better at heart. But I've no intellectual or literary work, and I long for it. I'm now experiencing that peculiar Christmas tenderness and emotion, the need for poetry. My hands are cold, I want to cry and love. Over dinner my sons' rudeness hurt me very much.

26 December, Moscow   I'm still not writing anything, but my thoughts seem to be reviving. My devil still won't leave me. Thought today about *The Notes of a Madman*.[73] [. . .]

1897

5 January, Moscow   Still nothing good to note about myself. There's no necessity to work, and the devil won't go away. I've been unwell for about six days.

Began to re-read *Resurrection*, and gave it up in disgust when I got as far as his decision to marry. It's all untrue, made-up and weak. It's difficult to put right something that is flawed. To put it right it will be necessary: (1) to describe her feelings and life and his alternately. And in her case positively and seriously, and in his case negatively and sardonically. I doubt if I'll finish it. It's all very flawed.

Yesterday I read Arkhangelsky's article 'Who should we serve?',[1] and it made me very glad.

Finished writing my notebook. Here are some extracts from it: [. . .]
(2) (For *Notes of a Madman*) or the drama. Despair over the folly and wretchedness of our life. Salvation from this despair lies in the recognition of God and of one's sonhood to Him. The recognition of sonhood is the recognition of brotherhood. The recognition of the brotherhood of man and the cruel, brutal, unbrotherly way of life which is justified by man inevitably leads to the recognition of oneself or the whole world as mad. [. . .]

Today is 12 January, Moscow   Early morning. I can't sleep for depression. And it's not gall, or egoism and sensuality which are to blame, but this agonising life. Yesterday I sat at table and felt that the governess and I are both equally superfluous, and both equally depressed. The talk about the acting of Duse and Hofmann, jokes, fine clothes, and sweetmeats – it all goes over us and through us. And it's the same all day and every day. There's nobody to rest on. Poor Tanya would have been willing at one time, but hers is a weak nature, with weak spiritual demands. Seryozha, Ilyusha . . . In other people's lives there is at least something serious and humane – say science, the service, being a teacher or doctor, young children, not to mention earning a living or serving people, but with them there is nothing except playing all sorts of games, and eating, and senile *flirtation*[2] or even worse. It's revolting. I'm writing so that people might know it, at least after my death. It's impossible to say it now. People who shout are worse than the deaf. She's ill,[3] it's true, but it's an illness which is taken for good health, and which people help her to bear, instead of trying to cure. What will come of it, how will it end? I pray incessantly, blame myself and pray. Help me, as Thou knowest how.

15 January, Moscow   Early morning. Hardly slept all night. Woke up from a dream about the same shameful thing.[4] My heart aches. Thought: it doesn't matter, I've got to die of something. If God won't let me die for the sake of His work, I'll have to die foolishly and weakly like this of my own accord and for my own self. One good thing is that it eases my passage from this life. Not only am I not sorry, I actually want to leave this nasty, humiliating life. I had the particularly painful and unpleasant thought that after sacrificing everything to do with God, a life of service to God, after the distribution of my property and the withdrawal from my family in order not to destroy love – instead of that love, I had to witness this humiliating madness. [. . .]

Thought last night how necessary it is to write the Notes.[5] That's the main thing now, and I must set about it before I die.

4 February, Nikolskoye, at the Olsufyevs'. This is the fourth day I've been here. Unspeakable depression. I'm writing badly about art. Prayed just now, and was horrified how low I've sunk. I think, wonder what to do, and doubt and hesitate, as thought I don't know, or have forgotten who I am and therefore what I have to do. I must remember that I'm not a master but a servant, and must do what I was sent to do. With what difficulty did I struggle to acquire, and did acquire that knowledge, how indisputable that knowledge is and how could I forget it nevertheless – not exactly forget it, but live without making use of it.

Sonya has read this diary in my absence, and is very distressed that people might *afterwards* conclude from it that she was a bad wife. I tried to console her – our whole life and my attitude to her of late will show what sort of wife she was. If she looks at this diary again, let her do what she likes with it, but I can't write with her or subsequent readers in mind, or write a reference for her, as it were. One thing I know is that last night I vividly imagined that she would die before me, and I became terribly afraid for myself. The day before yesterday I wrote to her that once again, and particularly by degrees (which always means particularly strongly) we had begun to grow closer together four or five years ago, and it would be good if this relationship were to grow stronger and stronger until the death of one of us – until my death – which I feel is very near. But enough of that. I'll copy out what I've been thinking during this time.

(1) Ultimately it is those people who are the victims of oppression, i.e. those people who obey the law of non-resistance, who always rule. So women seek rights, but it is they who rule, just because they are the ones subjected to force – were, and still are. Institutions are in the power of men, but public opinion is in the power of women. And public opinion is a million times stronger than any laws and armies. The proof of the fact that public opinion is in the hands of women is that not only is the organisation of houses and food determined by women – they spend the money and consequently control the labour of men – but the success of works of art and of books, even the appointment of rulers is determined by public opinion, and public opinion is determined by women. It was well said by somebody that men need to seek emancipation from women, and not the other way round. [. . .]

(3) Poets and versifiers twist their tongues in order to be able to express any thought at all in every possible variation of words, and to make up from any words at all the semblance of a thought. Only people who are not serious can indulge in such an exercise. And that's the way it is. [. . .]

(5) Twenty times have I repeated it, and twenty times the thought comes to me as though it were new, that release from all agitation, fear and suffering, both physical

and especially spiritual, lies in destroying in oneself the illusion of the union of one's spiritual and physical *I*. And this is always possible. When this illusion is destroyed, the spiritual *I* can suffer only from the fact that it is joined to the physical, but no longer from hunger, pain, sorrow, jealousy, shame, etc. In the first case, while it is joined, it does what the physical *I* wishes: gets angry, censures, abuses, strikes; in the second case, when it is separated from the physical, it only does the things that can free it from that painful bond; and only the manifestation of love can free it. [. . .]

(7) I noted down: 'the harm done by art, especially music', and was going to write that I'd forgotten what it was, but as I was writing I remembered. The harm done by art is chiefly that it takes up time and conceals from people their idleness. I know that it is harmful both for producers and consumers when it encourages idleness, but I cannot see any clear way of determining when it is permissible, useful and good. I would like to say that it is only when it is a respite from work, like sleep; but I don't know yet if that is so. [. . .]

(10) Art is – I had written food, but it's better to say sleep – which is necessary for sustaining the spiritual life. Sleep is good, it is necessary after work, but artificial sleep is harmful – it doesn't refresh or stimulate, but leaves one weak.

(11) I've been listening to contrapuntal singing *a capella*. It's the destruction of music, a means of perverting it. There are no thoughts or melodies, and any old meaningless sequence of sounds is taken, and from a combination of these insignificant sequences some boring semblance of music is put together. The best thing is when the last chord dies away. [. . .]

6 February, Nikolskoye Gorbunov came in the morning; in the evening a telegram to say that the Chertkovs are going on Thursday. I got ready to go with Sonya. We're just about to leave.[6] Health better.

7 February, Petersburg Went to the Chertkovs'. They were in a joyful mood. Then to Yaroshenko's.[7] The evening at home with Sonya. Things are well with us. I pray that I may not abandon, here or anywhere else, the awareness of my mission, which will be accomplished by doing good.

[16 February] Back again at the Olsufyevs' in Nikolskoye. 16 February. Returned on the morning of the day before yesterday and fell ill. Was better yesterday. Wrote well about art. Sonya left today after a conversation which distressed her. Women don't consider the demands of reason binding upon them and can't progress as a consequence of them. This sail is not unfurled for them. They row without a rudder.

17 February, Nikolskoye I feel unwell. Tried to write about art. Tanya came. A good, clear-sighted woman. I told her everything. Received some letters: an adaptation of *On Life* from an American.[8] Wrote two letters to Sonya, yesterday and today, and sent them off. Thought before going to Petersburg:
(1) For the appeal:[9] describe the condition of factory workers, servants, soldiers,

agricultural workers as compared with the rich, and show that it's all the result of fraud. The first fraud is that of land; the second fraud is that of taxes and customs; the third fraud is that of patriotism, defence: and finally, the fourth fraud, the worst of all, is the (religious) fraud of the meaning of life, of two sorts: (*a*) that of the church and (*b*) atheism.

(2) In the Middle Ages, in the eleventh century, poetry was common to all – to the people and the masters, *les courtois* [the well-born] and *les vilains* [those of humble origin]; then it split up, and *les vilains* began to imitate the poetry of the masters, and the masters that of the people. It must be united again. [. . .]

(5) People don't run after a poet or painter as they do after an actor, and particularly a musician. Music has a directly physical effect, sometimes acute, sometimes chronic.

(6) We quite wrongly ascribe intelligence and goodness to talent, as we do to beauty. This is great self-delusion.

Today is 20 February, Nikolskoye 7 o'clock in the evening. I still feel just as bad . . . Fell asleep in the morning, then went for a walk without even trying to work. Extraordinary weakness. I'm at peace at heart, only bored that I can't work. The house is full of people. Received a letter from Sonya today. All this has brought us closer. And I think I'm now quite free from it.[10] Yesterday I wrote a lot of letters. Thought as I walked:

(1) There is no greater cause of errors and confusion of ideas – the most unexpected and otherwise inexplicable – than the recognition of authorities – i.e. of the infallible truthfulness or beauty of people, books or works of art. Matthew Arnold was a thousand times right when he said that the business of criticism is to separate the good from the bad in everything that has been written and made, and principally the bad from the sphere of what is recognised to be excellent, and the good from what is recognised to be bad, or not recognised at all.[11] The most striking example of such an error and the terrible consequences of it which have held back the progress of Christian mankind for centuries is the authority of the Scriptures and the Gospels. [. . .]

24 February, Nikolskoye Got up today feeling jaded, and after breakfast fell asleep at once. Between 1 and 2 I walked to meet the sleigh riders. Drove back home and had dinner. I'm fighting successfully against heart-burn. Went for a walk in the evening. Read and am still reading Aristotle (Bénard) on aesthetics.[12] Very important. Thought during these days: [. . .]

(2) They tell me when I condemn religious propaganda . . . you preach too. No, I don't preach, mainly because I haven't anything to preach. I won't even preach God to an atheist (if I have done so I was wrong). I only draw conclusions from what people accept, pointing out the contradictions in what they accept, and which they don't notice.

(3) A guest here – a general – imposing, clean, correct, with thick eyebrows and an important appearance (and exceptionally good-natured, but lacking any moral impulse), suggested to me the striking thought as to how and by what means

people who are most indifferent to public life, to the common good – how it is precisely these people who involuntarily reach the position of being rulers over other people. I can see him being in charge of an institution on which millions of lives depend, and just because he likes cleanliness, elegance, choice food, dancing, hunting, billiards and every kind of amusement, and doesn't have any means himself, taking up a position in those regiments, institutions and societies which have all these things, and gradually, as a good and inoffensive person, making his way up and becoming a ruler of people – just like F – and their name is legion. [. . .]

1 March, Nikolskoye [. . .] Thought of two things:
(1) That death now seems to me just like a change of scene: retirement from a former post and appointment to a new one. I think that I've already retired from my former post, and am no longer any use.
(2) Thought about Adam Vasilyevich[13] as a type for a drama – good-natured, clean, spoiled, pleasure-loving, but good, and at the same time unable to accommodate radical moral demands. [. . .]

Good heavens, how many days I've missed. Today is 9 March, Moscow. I've spent two of the last four days writing about art, and wrote quite a lot today. Wanted very much to get on with *Hadji Murat*, and my thoughts about it were rather good – and moving. A letter from Posha: wrote to Chertkov and Koni about the terrible thing that happened to Vetrova.[14]

Today is 4 April, Moscow Haven't written my diary for almost a month (twenty days) and have lived badly during that time – because I did little work. I'm still writing about art – I've become confused in recent days. And I've written nothing for two days now. [. . .] I've prayed a lot recently that my life should be better. But I'm ashamed and depressed by the awareness of the anomalous nature of my life. Had some very good thoughts yesterday about *Hadji Murat* – that the main thing is to express in it the betrayal of trust. How good he would have been but for that betrayal. I also think more and more often about the appeal. I'm afraid that the theme of art has occupied me recently for personal, egotistical and bad reasons. *Je m'entends* [I understand what I'm saying]. [. . .]

Today is 3 May, Yasnaya Polyana Haven't written my diary for nearly a month. Not a good or fruitful month.
  Worked quite hard on the article about art. It's now in a state where it's possible to understand what I wanted to say, but it's still said badly and there are many *lacunes* and inaccuracies. Came here yesterday with Tanya. I feel physically and mentally and morally weak. The moral man is beginning to wake up and is dissatisfied. [. . .] A wonderful spring. I've just come back from Kozlovka and brought some clover and lilies of the valley.
  Thought a lot and made no notes. I've done no good. Capua.[15] The hairs of the Lilliputians have bound me so fast that I soon won't be able to move a single limb

unless I can break them. I'm sad, sad, and not because of any external dissatisfaction. I don't want anything from life, and don't regret the past at all,[16] but I loathe myself, I'm ashamed of myself, and am sorry for my soul. [. . .]

9 May, Yasnaya Polyana Night. 12 o'clock. I was about to go to bed, but came downstairs to make a note of my astonishing mental condition: a depression which is painful and not good. I don't know whether it's illness or mental weakness, but I suffer very much. I pray. The Molokans from Patrovka came today; I wrote a rough draft of a letter to the Tsar.[17] It should be good.

16 May Wrote the letter and sent it off on the 11th, I think. It must have been delivered by now. On the 13th Sofya Andreyevna was here. Received a letter from her yesterday. It's always the same thing. Didn't sleep all night. Never have my sufferings reached such intensity. Father, help me. Teach me. Enter into me. Grow in strength within me. I can't come to any decision. Should I stop thinking about it? That's impossible. I can't decide anything. I can't pity her, and from pity I can't oppose her. Help me, God.

17 May [18 May] I.I.A., which is very doubtful. My heart aches terribly. There are tears in my throat. Once I start, I shall cry my heart out.

I've got the day wrong. Today is 18 May. My heart still aches incessantly. I haven't slept for three nights, and feel I won't sleep today either. Can't do any work. I think I've come to a decision.[18] It will be difficult to carry out, but I can't and mustn't do otherwise. Yesterday the Molokans returned, having thrown my letter on to the dung heap.[19] I was annoyed. Boulanger came today. Copied out the letters and sent them off with him.[20] Good letters from Chertkov, but I can't see or feel anything. I'm not living. Lyova and his wife have just left.[21] [. . .]

Today is 16 July Have written nothing in my diary, not just for one, but for two and a half months. I've lived through many very hard things and many good ones.

I've been ill. Very severe pains at the beginning of July, I think. I've worked all the time on my article on art, and the further I got the better. I've finished it and am revising it from the beginning. Masha got married[22] and I was sorry for her, as one is sorry for a thoroughbred horse that is made to cart water. She doesn't cart water, but she's been broken and made useless. What will come of it I can't imagine. Something monstrously unnatural, like making pies out of children. Tanya has also saddled herself with a lot of suffering.[23] Misha is tormenting himself. There's the same trouble at Pirogovo too.[24] It's terrible! Instead of moderating and allaying passion, the source of our greatest calamities, we rouse it up by every means and then complain that we suffer. I've felt sorry for Sonya all the time recently. Good letters from Chertkov. Shidlovsky, a peasant from Kiev, has been. I feel lonely – feel that my life is not only not interesting to anyone, but that people are bored and ashamed that I go on occupying myself with such stupid things.

Thought during this time:

(1) There is a type of woman – there are men like that too, but there are more women – who are unable to see themselves, whose necks, as it were, can't turn round in order to look at themselves. It's not that they don't want to repent, it's that they can't see themselves. They live as they do, and not otherwise, because that way seems good to them. And so whatever they have done, they did because it was good. Such people are frightening. And such people may be clever or stupid, good or evil. When they are stupid and evil, it's terrible. [. . .]
(3) The second condition of art is novelty. For a child everything is new, and so it has many artistic impressions. But for us, what is new is a certain depth of feeling, the depth at which a person encounters his own individuality, separate from that of everyone else. That is so for indifferent art. But for the highest art, novelty lies only in religion, since religion is the most advanced world philosophy.
(4) For the drama. They bring a ragamuffin to the table and laugh at the inappropriateness of it and at his awkwardness. Indignation.[25]
(5) When you happen to think of something and forget what you thought about, but you remember and know the nature of your thoughts – sad, dismal, oppressive, gay, cheerful – and even remember their sequence: at first you felt sad, then were consoled, etc. – when you remember things that way, that's exactly what music expresses.
(6) A subject: a passionate young man in love with a mentally sick woman.[26]
(7) God gave us His spirit, love and reason in order to serve Him, but we use this spirit to serve ourselves, we use the axe to plane the handle. [. . .]

17 July [. . .] Rode on my bicycle to Yasenki. I like this exercise very much. But it makes me ashamed. [. . .]

Missed three days. Today is 21 July. I'm working quite well. I'm even satisfied with my work,[27] though I'm changing a lot. Today everything has come into focus and has gained a lot from it. I've been looking through it all again from the beginning. The life round me is very miserable. The children give me no joy. I don't know why: whether it's my stomach, or the heat or excessive physical exercise – but I feel very weak in the evenings. A good speech by Crookes about how a microscopic man would understand the world.[28] [. . .]

Today is 7 August, Yasnaya Polyana During this time a whole host of guests: Ginzburg[29] (pleasant), Kasatkin (less so), Goldenweiser (not unpleasant). Two German decadents. A naive and rather stupid Frenchman. Novikov the clerk was here (very strong), and Bulakhov, also a strong man morally and intellectually.[30] I'm living very badly and weakly. The Stakhoviches and the Maklakovs also came today.[31] There's very little goodness in them. I'm continuing to work on my article about art. And, stange to say, I like it. Yesterday and today I read it to Ginzburg, Sobolev,[32] Kasatkin and Goldenweiser. The impression it made on them is the same as it makes on me. A letter from Crosby enclosing a joyful letter from a Japanese.[33] Good letters from Chertkov. My correspondence has been very neglected. I'm quite alone and growing weaker. [. . .]

8 August A peasant was here who had his arm broken off by a tree and amputated. He ploughs with a sling attached.

9 August [. . .] Noted down in my book: (1) Servants make life false and corrupt: as soon as you have servants you increase your needs, complicate life and make it a burden: the joy of doing something yourself turns into vexation, but the main thing is that you renounce the main business of life, the fulfilment of the brotherhood of man. (2) The aesthetic and the ethical are two arms of one lever: to the extent to which one side becomes longer and heavier, the other side becomes shorter and lighter. As soon as a man loses his moral sense, he becomes particularly responsive to the aesthetic. [. . .] (4) It's a common phenomenon that old people love to travel, to go far and to change places. Isn't this a preview of, and a preparation for the last journey?

15 August, Yasnaya Polyana [. . .] Tanya has just come from seeing Sukhotin. She called me to her room. I felt very sorry for her. But what can I say to her? What will be will be. I only hope there is nothing sinful. A shocking report about the missionary congress in Kazan.[34] [. . .]
(5) Since I've become old, I've begun to mix people up: for example, the children: Seryozha with Andrey, Misha with Ilya, and I also mix up strangers who belong to one type, or are registered as such in my mind. And so I don't know Andrey and Seryozha, but I know a collective personality to which Andrey and Seryozha belong. (6) We are so accustomed to the thought that everything is for us, that *the earth is mine*, that when we come to die we are surprised that my earth, something belonging to me, will be left, but not me. The chief mistake here is thinking of the earth as something acquired, an appendage of me, whereas I am acquired by the earth and am an appendage of it. (7) How good it would be if we could live with the same concentration – could perform life's task and above all communion between people – with the same concentration as we play chess, read music, etc.

Today is 19 September Haven't written my diary for more than a month. Everything is the same. The work has been making progress all the time. And it could have made much more progress in the sense of form, but there's absolutely no time. There's so much work to do. A typist is typing out a fair copy on the Remington. I've reached the 19th chapter, inclusive. The important thing during this time was Boulanger's exile.[35] My work has only been interrupted by a letter to the Swedish newspapers about the Dukhobors apropos of the Nobel prizes.[36] Sonya is afraid. I'm very sorry, but I can't help doing it. It was also interrupted by ill health: a terrible boil on my cheek. I thought it was cancer, and am glad it wasn't very unpleasant to think so. I'm receiving a new appointment, one which in any case I can't escape.

St John[37] has been, a gentleman and a serious person, but I'm afraid it's more for worldly fame than for himself or for God. Work was also interrupted by the arrival of the Molokans from Samara – about the children who were taken away. I wanted to write abroad, and even wrote a very sharp and, I thought, strong letter, but changed my mind. It wouldn't have been right in the sight of God. I must try again. Wrote letters today to the Emperor, Olsufyev, Heath and L. I. Chertkova, and saw the Molokans off.[38] [. . .]

Today is 22 September, Yasnaya Polyana Wrote a letter to Sonya yesterday to say that I can't be guided in my writing by her opinions.[39] Wrote from the heart, and with a kind feeling. And she accepted it with the same feeling. Yesterday I finished the translation with Langlet.[40] Today I've been busy with *Art*, but couldn't get on with it at all, and then disliked what I had already written. Sonya came today. Thought during the night about the separation of lust from love, and about the fact that either is an extra-sensory notion. [. . .]

Today is 14 October, Yasnaya Polyana It's the third day since Sonya arrived. I'm alone with her. She's doing some copying. She helps very much. I'm still writing about art. Revised the 10th chapter today. And clarified what was unclear. I must copy up my notebook, I'm afraid I've forgotten a lot.
(1) Nothing does more to support a quiet, egotistical life than the occupation of art for art's sake. Despots and villains must certainly love art. I'd noted down something like that, but can't remember it now. [. . .]
(4) Details for *Hadji Murat*: (1) the shadow of an eagle runs across a mountain slope, (2) there are tracks of wild animals, horses and people in the sand by the river, (3) as they ride into the woods, the horses snort briskly, (4) a goat jumped out from behind a holly bush.
(5) When people are carried away by Shakespeare or Beethoven they are carried away by their own thoughts and dreams evoked by Shakespeare or Beethoven, just as people in love don't love the object of their love, but what it evokes in them. [. . .]
(7) [. . .] Generally speaking – I don't know why – I don't have that religious feeling I used to have previously when I wrote my diary just for myself. The fact that people have read it and may read it in future destroys this feeling. But the feeling was precious and helped me in life. Starting from today, the 14th, I'll begin to write again as I used to, – so that nobody should read it during my lifetime. If there should be any thoughts which deserve it, I can copy them out and send them to Chertkov. [. . .]
(14) You get angry with a woman because she doesn't understand something, or she understands, but doesn't do what reason tells her. She can't do this. Just as a magnet acts on iron and doesn't act on wood, so the conclusions of reason are not binding on her, are not motive forces. Feeling and the conclusions of reason are only binding on her when they are transmitted by an authority, i.e. the feeling of a desire not to lag behind others. And so she won't believe or follow an obvious demand of reason unless it is confirmed by an authority, but she will believe and follow the greatest folly as long as everyone does so. She can't do otherwise. And we get angry. There are many men like that as well – womanish. [. . .]
(18) Rode past the out-buildings. Remembered the nights I used to spend there, and the youth and beauty of Dunyasha[41] (I never had a liaison with her), her strong,

womanly body. Where is it? It's long been nothing but bones. What are those bones? What relation have they to Dunyasha? There was a time when those bones formed part of that separate being which was Dunyasha. But then that being shifted its centre, and what used to be Dunyasha became part of another being, enormous in size and inaccessible to me, which I call the earth. We don't know the life of the earth and so we consider it dead, just as an insect which lives for only an hour considers my body to be dead because it doesn't see its movement. [. . .]

The letter to Stockholm has been printed.[42]

Today is 16 October, Yasnaya Polyana Didn't write my diary yesterday. Health quite improved. Sonya still works a lot with me and helps me.[43] A letter from Olga Dieterichs,[44] and one from Chertkov. Obviously he – and therefore they too – have had a hard time. Yesterday evening and today I wanted to get on with *Hadji Murat*. Made a start. It seemed quite good, but I didn't continue because I wasn't in complete control. I mustn't spoil it by forcing it. The *Petersburg Gazette* hasn't printed my letter yet.[45]

Noted: (1) I've noted many considerations and rules which, if they were remembered, would ensure a good life. Yes, there are too many rules, and it's impossible always to remember them all. It's the same with counterfeit art. Too many rules, and it's impossible to remember them all. Art should come from within, and be guided by feeling. [. . .]

Today is 21 October, Yasnaya Polyana Received proofs of Carpenter's article from the *Northern Herald*, and began to write a foreword.[46] [. . .]

Today is 10 November, Yasnaya Polyana I've lived through a lot these two weeks. Still doing the same work. I think I've finished it. Wrote some letters today, and among others, one to Grot asking him to set up the type.[47] Sonya has been; she left for Moscow from Pirogovo, where we went together. It was good there. Since I returned I've had back-ache and a fever in the evenings. Alexander Petrovich[48] is here writing. Went to Yasenki today with Lyova, and he started a funny conversation about culture. He wouldn't be a bad fellow if it wasn't for this enormous denominator below a very small numerator.[49]

Wrote nine letters today. Only one left, to Khilkov. His business and his situation are terrible.[50] Mikhayla Novikov has been, and also a peasant from Kazan, a poet.

Thought: (1) The situation of people who are stupefied by false religion is the same as in blind man's buff: their eyes are bandaged, then they are taken by the arm and turned round. Then they are released. It's the same for everybody. They aren't released until this is done. (For the Appeal.) [. . .]

(3) Walked through the village, looking into the windows. There was poverty and ignorance everywhere, and I thought about the slavery of old. Formerly one could see the cause, one could see the chains which bound people, but now there aren't any chains – and in Europe there are only hairs, but just as many of them as the ones which bound Gulliver. In our country one can still see ropes, or anyway

twine, while over there there are only hairs, but they hold them so tightly that the giant people can't move. The only salvation is not to lie down, not to go to sleep. The deception is so powerful and so cunning that you often see the very people who are being sucked dry and destroyed passionately defending their bloodsuckers and attacking those who are against them. With us it's the Tsar.

12 November, Yasnaya Polyana Pyotr Osipov came today: 'where we live they've started to sell indulgences'. The Virgin of Vladimir was there, and the village elder was ordered to drive the people into church.[51] Lyova has found ore, and finds it very natural that people should live underground, in danger of their lives, while he gets the revenue.[52] The day before yesterday there was a telegram from Tanya to say that she had been held up. I look forward to her coming very much. The most important thing is that I've decided to write the Appeal: there's no time to postpone it. Today I revised the article on science. It's now evening. I've got two versions of the Appeal and want to work on it.

14 November, Yasnaya Polyana A disgruntled letter from Sonya. And Tanya writes that she is displeased that I'm not going. I only want one thing: to do as well as possible in the sight of God. I still don't know how. Slept badly last night – bad, evil thoughts. And apathy. No desire to work. Revised the foreword on science. Made the following notes:
(1) Read about the actions of the British in Africa.[53] It's all terrible. But it occurred to me that perhaps it was unavoidably necessary in order that enlightenment should get through to these peoples. At first I thought hard, and thought it was necessary. What nonsense! Why can't people living a Christian life not simply go and live with them, like Miklukho-Maklay;[54] why do they need to trade, make drunkards of them, kill them? [. . .]
(3) Thought as a *pendant* [counterpart] to Hadji Murat of writing about another Russian brigand – Grigory Nikolayev – in such a way that he should see the whole lawlessness of the life of the rich, should live as a caretaker of an orchard on a wealthy estate with a lawn tennis court.[55]

Today is the 17th, Yasnaya Polyana For the second day I've been thinking particularly clearly about the following:
(1) My life – my awareness of my own personality – is getting weaker and weaker, and will get weaker still and end in marasmus and the absolute cessation of the awareness of personality. At the same time, absolutely simultaneously and parallel with the destruction of my personality, the things that my life has done, the consequences of my thoughts and feelings, are beginning to live and are growing stronger and stronger: are living in other people, even in animals and in dead matter. And so I would like to say that this is what will live after me. [. . .]
(2) I also thought today quite unexpectedly about the charm – actually the charm – of awakening love, when, against the background of joyful, pleasant and sweet relationships, that little star sudddenly begins to shine. It's like a sudden waft of scent from a lime tree or the first shadow falling as the moon comes out. It's not yet

fully light, and there is no clear light and shade, but there is joy and fear of the new and the fascinating. It's good, but only when it's for the first and last time.
(3) I also thought about the illusion which everyone is subject to, and especially people whose activity is reflected in others – the illusion that having been accustomed to see the effect of your actions on other people, you test the correctness of your actions by their influence on other people.
(4) I also thought: for hypnotisation it's necessary to have belief in the importance of what is being suggested (the hypnotisation of all artistic delusions). And to have this belief, ignorance is necessary, and the cultivation of credulity. [. . .]

Today is the 20th, evening, Yasnaya Polyana Got on with the foreword to Carpenter. Thought a lot about *Hadji Murat* and prepared my material. Still can't find the right tone. Letters from Sonya, one of them unpleasant. But a good one today. I think about the journey to Moscow with horror. [. . .]
Yesterday an angry conversation with Lyova. I said a lot of unpleasant things to him, he remained silent for the most part, and towards the end I felt ashamed and sorry for him, and began to love him. There is much good in him. I forget how young he is. [. . .]

21 November Alive. Still thinking and collecting material for *Hadji Murat*. Today I thought a lot, read, started to write, but stopped at once. [. . .]
(1) Thought about death – about how strange it is that one doesn't want to die, although nothing holds one – and thought about prisoners who have become so much at home in their prisons that they don't want to, and are even afraid to leave them for freedom. In the same way we too are at home in the prison of this life and are afraid of freedom. [. . .]

22 November Dreamed very vividly that Tanya fell off a horse, broke her head, and was dying and that I was weeping over her.

24 November, Yasnaya Polyana Tanya arrived safely today. Masha is still poorly. But she wasn't distressed by my letter.[56] I love them both very much. All their weaknesses are understandable and touching. Tanya is going to Moscow tomorrow. I promised to go with Lyova, but I'm seized with fear when I think about it. Yesterday and today I prepared some chapters to send off to Maude and Grot.[57] No letters for a long time from Maude or Chertkov. A nice letter today from Galya.
Beautiful weather. I walked a long way along the Tula road. In the morning I worked hard on revising *Art*. Yesterday I got on with the preparations for *Hadji Murat*. I think it's clear . . .
Thought during this time:
(1) A strange fate: anxieties and passions begin in adolescence, and you think: you'll get married and it will all pass. And it did pass for me, and there was a long period – some eighteen years – of peace. Then came the striving to change my life, and a set-back. Struggle, suffering and finally, it seemed, a haven and a respite.

But it wasn't so. The real difficulties have begun and are continuing and will probably stay with me till death. [. . .]

25 November   Alive. Tanya has gone. She's very dear – and good. I was wrong to talk to her about my situation. Revised *Art*. Wrote quite a good letter to Maude. A good letter from Galya. Thought:
(1) It always seems to us that we are loved because we are good. But we don't suspect that we are loved because those who love us are good. You can see this if you listen to what that miserable, disgusting and vain person says whom you have taken pity on with a great effort: he says that he's so good that you couldn't have acted otherwise. And it's just the same when people love you.
(2) 'Lobsters love to be boiled alive.' That's not a joke. How often do you hear it, or have said it, or say it yourself. Man has the faculty of not seeing the sufferings he doesn't want to see. And he doesn't want to see the sufferings he has caused himself. How often have I heard it said about coachmen who are kept waiting, or about cooks, man-servants or peasants that 'they are very happy' at their work. Lobsters love to be boiled alive.

Today is 28 November, Yasnaya Polyana   Haven't written my diary for two days. Still busy working on *Art* and the foreword to Carpenter. A pained letter from Sonya. I was wrong to say what I did and Tanya was wrong to pass it on. Makovitsky came today, a nice, gentle, pure man. He told me many joyful things about our friends. I went to Yasenki: a good letter from Maude and a bad one from Grot. I've been in bad spirits these last days. Fancy being in Moscow in such a condition! [. . .]

Today is 2 December, Yasnaya Polyana   A sad, melancholy, depressed state of body and spirits, but I know that I'm alive and can feel this *I* of mine, if only a little, independently of this condition. A letter from Tanya today to say that Sonya was upset by my sending the foreword to the *Northern Herald*. I'm terribly afraid about this.[58] During these last days I had an absurd, irritable letter from Grot. So far nothing has been decided.[59] I've been busy all the time with corrections and additions to *Art*. The main thing during this time was that Dušan[60] was here; I've begun to love him more and more. He is forming, with his Slavonic *Intermediary*, a centre of a small, but I think godly enterprise. Still no news from Chertkov. Melancholy – gentle, tender melancholy – but still melancholy. Were it not for my awareness of life, my melancholy would probably be embittered. Thought: [. . .]
(2) Had a talk with Dušan. He said that since he had involuntarily become my representative in Hungary, how was he to act? I was glad of the opportunity to tell him and make clear to myself that to speak about Tolstoyanism, to seek my guidance and to ask my decision about problems was a serious and crude mistake. There is no Tolstoyanism or teaching of mine, and never has been; there is only one eternal, universal, world-wide teaching of the truth as expressed particularly clearly for me and for us all in the Gospels. [. . .]
  I think I've finished *Art*.

3 December My work on *Art* has cleared up a lot of things for me. If God bids me write works of fiction, they will be entirely different ones. And it will be both easier and more difficult to write them. We'll see.

Today is 6 December, Moscow
On the 4th I went to Dolgoye. The tumbledown house made a very moving impression on me. A swarm of memories.⁶¹ I've written almost nothing for two days – only prepared some chapters of *Art* and packed my things. Very depressing letters from Sonya. Arrived on the 5th. She wasn't there. She had gone to the Troitsa Monastery in a terrible state of excitement. It was all due to my article in the *Northern Herald*. I unwittingly made a mistake. Stupid letters from Grot. He's mentally ill. Went to see Trubetskoy. I've given in to them.⁶² Sonya came back in the evening, more composed. We had a talk, and felt better. Made no notes. Woke up feeling ill.

7 December Talked more and more yesterday, and I heard from Sonya something I'd never heard before: an admission of guilt. It was a great joy. I thank Thee, Father. Whatever should happen in future, this has already happened, and it is a great good. Went to Storozhenko's. Kasatkin came in the evening. I asked about examples.⁶³ In the morning I revised *Art*. Made no notes – too much noise. Health good.

11 December [. . .] Rostovtsev's stories about Chertkov, and Ivan Mikhaylovich's letter made a sad impression.⁶⁴ Then Tanya, Vera, Varya, Sonya – they're all suffering. Well, with them it's forgivable, but how can a Christian suffer? During this time Grot's condition has become clear. He's mentally ill, like all people who are not Christians. [. . .]

Today is the 13th Morning. Wrote a letter to the Chertkovs. I think I've revised the 10th chapter very well. Read St John's correspondence on the sexual question yesterday, and was very indignant and had an unpleasant talk with him at Rusanov's. Rusanov has the same sort of head as Hadji Murat. Wanted to get on with *Hadji Murat* this morning. Lost the plan. Made some notes. Want to make a note now of subjects which can be, and deserve to be worked up properly:
(1) *Sergey*.⁶⁵ (2) *Alexander I*.⁶⁶ (3) *Persiyaninov*.⁶⁷ (4) *The Story of Petrovich, the Husband who Died a Pilgrim*.⁶⁸ (5) The following are not so good – *the Legend of the Descent of Christ into Hell and the Rebuilding of Hell*.⁶⁹ (6) *The Forged Coupon*. (7) *Hadji Murat*. (8) *The Substitute Child*.⁷⁰ (9) Probably the drama of a Christian resurrection,⁷¹ and (10) *Resurrection* – the trial of a prostitute. (11) Excellent – a brigand who murders defenceless people.⁷² (12) The mother.⁷³ (13) The execution in Odessa.⁷⁴

It's depressing at home. But I want to be cheerful and will be. [. . .]

Diary, 1897. 21 December, Moscow I'm beginning a new exercise book, as though in a new state of mind. For five days or so now I've done nothing. I've been thinking about *Hadji Murat*, but without enthusiasm or confidence. *On Art* has been published. Chertkov is displeased.[75] So are people here. Received an anonymous letter yesterday with a threat of murder if I don't reform by 1898. I'm only given until 1898. I'm both apprehensive and pleased. Sonya is very weak, and I'm terribly sorry for her. She is undergoing a crisis too. I've been skating. It's a sign of my inactive state of mind that I've made no notes. Have just read Chekhov's story *On the Cart*. Excellent for its descriptiveness, but rhetorical as soon as he wants to give a meaning to the story. My head is wonderfully clear, thanks to my book on art.

Alive. Today is 29 December, Moscow. Morning. Thought about *Hadji Murat*. All day yesterday a drama-comedy, *The Corpse*, was taking shape in my head.[76] I'm still unwell. Went to the Behrs' yesterday. Received letters with threats of murder.[77] A pity there are people who hate me, but it doesn't interest me much and doesn't worry me at all. [. . .]

1898

Two days have passed. 1 January, 1898. I greet the New Year very sad, depressed and unwell. I can't work, and my stomach still aches.

Received a letter from Fedoseyev in Verkholensk about the Dukhobors,[1] a very touching one. Another letter from the editor of *The Adult* about free love.[2] If I had time, I would like to write about this subject. I probably shall write. The main thing is to show that it's all a question of guaranteeing for oneself the greatest possible pleasure without thinking about the consequences. Apart from that, they preach something which already exists and is very bad. And why should the absence of external *restraint*[3] make everything all right? I am, of course, against any regulation and in favour of complete freedom, but the ideal is chastity, and not pleasure.

I've been thinking about one thing only during this time, and, I think, an important one, namely:
(1) We all think that our duty, our vocation, is to do various things: bring up children, make a fortune, write a book, discover a scientific law, etc., but there is only one thing for all of us to do: to shape our own life, and to make of it something whole, rational and good. [. . .]

Today is the 4th already. I'm a little better. I feel like working. Yesterday – Stasov and Rimsky-Korsakov,[4] coffee, and stupid conversation about art. When will I follow the rule that much talk means much bother. [. . .]

Today is 13 January, Moscow   Haven't written my diary for more than a week. And I've hardly done anything. I'm still unwell. And dejected. Sometimes good and composed, sometimes anxious and not good. The day before yesterday I felt miserable. Then some peasants came: Balakhov with Stepan Petrovich and two from Tula. And I felt so relieved and cheerful. One mustn't give in to one's own circle. One can always enter the circle of God and His people. Haven't felt so dispirited for a long time. A letter from Posha. Wrote to Posha, Ivan Mikhaylovich, the Chertkovs, Maude and Boulanger. Still trying to find a satisfactory formula for *Hadji Murat*, and still can't, although I think I'm getting near. Yesterday we celebrated Tanya's nameday – it was depressing. A telegram today about my article *What is Art?*[5] I've made a note and, I think, an important one.
(1) Something of enormous importance, and which will have to be properly expounded: organisation, any organisation, which frees people from any sort of human, personal or moral obligations – that is the source of all the evil in the world. People are flogged to death, debauched, stupefied – and nobody is to blame. For the story about the rebuilding of hell – this is an important new method of approach. [. . .]

3 February   Still as unproductive mentally. [. . .] Read Lyapunov's *The Ploughman*⁶ and was very touched. Noted the following:
(2) Women use words not to express their thoughts, but to achieve their aims. And they look for the same purpose in other people's words. And for that reason they often understand people in such a contrary fashion. And that is very unpleasant. [. . .]
(5) An inorganic thing is merely a thing whose life we cannot understand. For a flea, my finger nail is inorganic. In just the same way, evil is good which we haven't understood.
(8) One of the most common delusions is to consider people good, evil, stupid or clever. Man is in a state of flux and contains within himself every potential: he was stupid and is now clever, he was evil and is now good, and vice versa. That is man's greatness. And for that reason one mustn't judge a man. What is he like? You judge him and he is already a different person. And one mustn't say: 'I don't love him.' You say it, and the situation is already different.
(9) People say about the Tsar that it's not he who is to blame, but his entourage. That's not true: he alone is the cause of everything. One can and must pity him, but one must know where the cause lies.
(13) Power resides in the working people. If they endure their oppression, it's only because they are hypnotised. This is the whole gist of the matter – one must destroy this hypnosis.

5 February   [. . .] When I was copying up my notes I forgot:
(7) Jean Grave,⁷ *L'individu et la societé*, says that revolution will only be fruitful when *l'individu* is forbearing, disinterested, kind, ready to help his neighbour, not vain, not condemning other people, and aware of his own merit – i.e. when he has all the merits of a Christian. But how is he to acquire these virtues if he knows that he is only a fortuitous chain of atoms? All these virtues are possible and natural, and in fact they cannot be absent from a Christian philosophy, namely that we are the sons of God, sent to do His will; but these virtues are incompatible with a materialistic philosophy. [. . .]

Today is 19 February, Moscow   Haven't written my diary for a long time. At first I was unwell. For about five days I've been better. During this time I've kept revising and adding to and spoiling the last chapters on *Art*. I decided to send off Carpenter and my foreword to the *Northern Herald*. I've been revising this foreword too. The general impression made by this article *On Science*, as well as that of chapter 20, is – remorse. I feel that it's true and that it's necessary, but it hurts me that I should offend and distress many good, deluded people. Obviously 999 people out of 1,000 won't understand on what account I condemn our science, and will be indignant. I ought to have done it with more kindness. And I'm to blame for this, but it's too late now. [. . .] Made the following notes:
(1) People are quite unable to agree about the non-reality of everything material. 'But the table exists and always will do, and if I go out of the room it will still be there, and it will be just the same table for everybody as it is for me' – they usually

say. Yes, but when you cross over two fingers and roll a ball with them, don't you undoubtedly feel two? Isn't it the case that every time I hold a ball like that, there will be two, and for everyone else who holds a ball like that there will be two, and yet there are not two balls. In the same way the table is a table only for the crossed fingers of my senses, but it might be half a table, or 1/1,000 part of a table, or indeed no part of a table at all, but something quite different. So that what is real is only my ever recurring impression, confirmed by the impressions of other people. (5) A priest, or any ecclesiastical person ought, in order to expiate his sins, to repent of his deception from the pulpit in front of all the people and say: 'forgive me for deceiving you . . .' What a powerful scene! And what a truthful one. [. . .]

19 March Haven't written my diary for more than three weeks. Today is 19 March, Moscow. Finished all my letters. During this time I've written some important letters: (1) to the American colony,[8] (2) to the *Petersburg Gazette* about the Dukhobors,[9] (3) to the English newspapers, also about the Dukhobors,[10] and (4) a foreword to the English edition of *What is Art?* – about the censor's mutilations.[11]

My inner life is just the same. As I foresaw; my new awareness of living for God, for the perfection of love, has become blunted and grown weak, and when it was needed the other day it proved to be, if not ineffectual, at least less effectual than I expected. The main event during this time was the permission for the Dukhobors to emigrate. *What is Art?* is now, I think, completely finished. Sonya left for Petersburg yesterday. She is just as unstable. I haven't done much work all this time. [. . .]

Today is 21 March, Moscow I'm continuing copying out my notes. [. . .]
(6) The socialists will never destroy poverty and injustice, and the inequality of talents. The most intelligent and the strongest will always make use of the most stupid and the weakest. Justice and the equality of goods can never be attained by anything less than Christianity, i.e. by renouncing the self and recognising the meaning of one's life to be in the service of others. [. . .]
(8) Intelligent socialists recognise that to achieve their goal the important thing is to raise the intellectual and physical level of the workers. This can only be done by religious education, but they don't recognise this, and so all their work is in vain. [. . .]
(10) For the *Appeal*. All are agreed that we don't live as we ought to and as we could. The remedy for some is religious fatalism, and, still worse, scientific, evolutionary fatalism; others comfort themselves with the fact that everything is gradually getting better and better of its own accord – the gradualists; a third group promises that everything will come right once things reach their very worst – the socialists: the government and the wealthy classes will have full control of everyone, i.e. the workers, and then power will somehow transfer itself all of a sudden not simply to the workers, but to infallible, disinterested, self-sacrificing, saintly workers who will then run everything without mistakes, and without wrongdoing; a fourth group says that things can only be put right by exterminating villains and evil

men. But there is no indication where evil people end and where harmless ones, if not good ones, begin. Either the evil people will not all be exterminated, or, as in a big revolution, the good will be caught up with the bad. Once you begin to judge people strictly, nobody will be innocent. So what is to be done? There is only one means: a religious change in people's thinking. And it is precisely such a change which is being prevented by all these imaginary remedies. [. . .]
(13) How good it would be to write a work of art in which one could clearly express the shifting nature of man; the fact that one and the same man is now a villain, now an angel, now a wise man, now an idiot, now a strong man, now the most impotent of creatures. [. . .]
(16) There is an English toy called a 'peepshow'[12] – first one thing and then another is shown underneath a glass. That's the way to show Hadji Murat: as a husband, a fanatic, etc. [. . .]
(20) Ambition in the service and the greed of misers are so attractive because they are very simple. With any other aim in life you have to think and reflect a lot, and you never see results clearly. But in this case it's so simple: one star becomes two, one million becomes two million, etc. . . . [. . .]
(22) Had a talk with Peshkova[13] about the woman question. There is no woman question. There is the question of freedom and equality for all human beings. But the woman question is an irritant. [. . .]

Today is 27 April, Grinyovka[14] My third day here. I'm all right. A little unwell. Sonya left this morning – sad and distraught. She's very depressed. And I'm very sorry for her and I still can't help her. All the time in Moscow recently I was finishing *Carthago delenda est*. I'm afraid I haven't finished with it, and it will come back to me again. But it's reasonably good. I've done no work here. The famine disaster isn't nearly as great as it was in 1891. There are so many lies to do with everything in the upper classes, everything is so tangled up in lies, that it's never possible to answer any question simply: for example, is there a famine? I'll try to distribute the money entrusted to me as well as possible.[15]

Yesterday we had a talk again about the same thing. Is exclusive love good? This is a resumé of it: the moral man, whether he is married or single, will look on exclusive love as evil and will fight against it; the less moral man will consider it a good thing and will encourage it. The completely immoral man doesn't even understand it and makes fun of it.

The Russian Gazette has been banned because of the Dukhobors and me[16] – it's a pity, and I'm annoyed.
(1) A proverb. Don't make a fortune for a good son; don't leave a fortune to a bad one. [. . .]

Today is 29, morning Grinyovka. I've been very weak. Felt better since yesterday. But haven't been able to write anything. Walked to Lopashino and compiled some lists.[17] Read Boccaccio.[18] The beginning of ruling-class immoral art. No letters. Seryozha has been. I'll continue: I thought:
(1) You look at and examine a person's life, especially a woman's life, you see from

what world view their actions stem, you see above all how inevitably all arguments opposed to this world view bounce off them, and you can't imagine how this world view could change, how it could begin to germinate – just like a date stone – but there are conditions under which change goes on and is accomplished from within. A man who is alive can always be born anew, a seed can always germinate. [. . .]
(4) One of the most urgent needs of man, as urgent as, if not more urgent than food, drink or sexual desire, and the existence of which we often forget, is the need to project oneself – to know that it was actually I who did this. Very many actions, otherwise incomprehensible, can be explained by this need. One ought to remember it both when educating people and when having dealings with them. The main thing is to try to ensure that it manifests itself as action, not boasting. [. . .]
(8) I began to think about soup-kitchens, the purchase of flour, and money, and I felt so unclean and sad at heart. The realm of money, i.e. any kind of use of money, is a sin. I accepted money, and undertook to use it only in order to have a pretext for getting away from Moscow. And I acted *badly*. [. . .]

Today is 11 May, Grinyovka Yesterday I wrote a little of *The Appeal*.[19] Then went to Mikhaylin Brod. Dreamed about Strakhov, who said to me that I should write out clearly for the plain man what God is. [. . .]

Today is 27 May, Grinyovka, morning During this time I've been getting on with *The Appeal*, and wrote an article on the condition of the people. [. . .]

Today, I think, is 12 June, Yasnaya Polyana [. . .] Sonya has arrived, sick herself, and terribly overcome with fear on my behalf.[20] It's about four days since I arrived at Yasnaya, and I'm making a good recovery. I've written a lot of letters. Received up to 4,000 roubles, which I can't use this year. Masha and her husband and Ilyusha are here. And the Westerlunds. Dora has had a baby.[21] Tanya is definitely going to get married. I'm sorry for her, but perhaps it's necessary for her soul. Today, quite unexpectedly, I started to finish *Sergey*.[22] No news from England. I've made a great many notes. [. . .]
(12) The sight of my children owning land and making the people work has such a strange and depressing effect on me. Like pangs of conscience. And this is not a reasoned judgement, but a feeling, and a very strong one. Was I wrong not to have given my land to the peasants? I don't know.
(13) Leskov has made use of my theme,[23] and badly at that. My wonderful idea was – three questions: what time is the most important? What person? And what act?

The time is now, this minute; the person is the one you are now dealing with; and the act is to save your own soul, i.e. to perform an act of love. [. . .]

14 June, Yasnaya Polyana Evening. Both days I've been getting on with *Father Sergey*. It's making out quite well. Wrote some letters. Today was the christening. Still can't be altogether kind to Lyova. It's difficult. But I don't despair.

Today is 22 June, Yasnaya Polyana On the 16th I took seriously ill. I've never felt so weak and near to death. I'm ashamed to take advantage of the care bestowed on me by those near to me. Could do nothing at all. Only read and made a few notes. I'm much better today. Ukhtomsky made a fuss of my article, but still refused to print it.[24] I telegraphed to Menshikov to ask him to try the *Herald of Europe* and *Russian Labour*. I'm afraid I'm getting on his nerves. The young folk have been sent packing. They've been forbidden to hand out the flour they bought.[25] Lyova talked about his story.[26] I told him hurtfully that what he had done was 'uncivilised' (his favourite expression), not to mention the fact that it was stupid and untalented. His very crude and uncivilised, but very good-natured *beaux parents* [parents-in-law] left today.

Received a letter from Chertkov, a good one. Dieterichs arrived. Dear Dunayev came. They talked about the big riot of the factory workers. I'll finish writing later.

Today is 28 June, Yasnaya Polyana Evening, I've only now recovered, and am experiencing the pleasure of *convalescence*. I feel nature particularly keenly and vividly, and my thoughts are very clear . . . I've written a little more of *The Appeal*. Today I've been getting on with *Father Sergey*. Both are quite good. Wrote quite a lot of letters. The ones I received yesterday were all unpleasant, from Monet,[27] and especially from Galya with the news that they have quarrelled.[28] Posha is going to Switzerland and Boulanger to Bulgaria. Tanya has gone to Masha's, Ilya arrived yesterday. Misha and Sasha came today. Misha is in very poor shape spiritually. Things were very difficult with Lyova, through my own fault of course. I understood and felt this particularly vividly on getting news of the quarrels in England. Only one task, one real task, has been given to us: to live lovingly with our brethren, with everyone – we must renounce the self. I've written to my friends about this and will endeavour to do it myself. [. . .] Noted:
(1) Paul Adam gives a cruel description of the peasant, and of the worker generally:[29] he is coarse, egotistical, a slave and a fanatic – all this may be true, but the one thing is that he can exist without us, but without him we should all be utterly lost. And therefore it's not for us to judge him. (Something wrong here.)
(2) It's particularly unpleasant for me when people who have lived little and thought little don't believe me, and argue about moral questions without understanding me. It's for the same reason that a veterinary surgeon would be annoyed if people not versed in his art were to argue with him. The only difference is that the art of the veterinary surgeon, the cook or the samovar maker, or whatever art or science you like, is recognised as an art or science in which only those people are competent who have studied that subject; but in matters of morality all people consider themselves competent because everyone needs to justify his own life, and life is only justified by theories of morality. And everyone makes them up for himself.
(3) I have often thought about being in love – good, ideal love, excluding all sensuality – and I could find no place or meaning for it. But it does have a very clear place and function: to lighten the struggle between sexual desire and chastity. Being in love should be for young people unable to remain completely chaste, it should precede marriage and rescue young people in the very critical years from

sixteen to twenty or more, from their painful struggle. That's the place for being in love. But when it erupts into the lives of people after marriage, it is out of place and disgusting. [. . .]

17 July, Yasnaya Polyana Morning. Nothing special happened these last eleven days. Decided to let my stories *Resurrection* and *Father Sergey* be published for the benefit of the Dukhobors.[30] Sonya has gone to Kiev. An inner struggle. I don't much believe in God. I don't rejoice at the examination, but am oppressed by it, knowing in advance that I won't pass. Didn't sleep all last night.[31] Got up early and prayed a lot. The Dieterichs and Gorbunovs came today. I enjoyed being with them. Took up *Resurrection* and at first it went well, but since I became worried I haven't been able to do anything for two days. [. . .] Made many notes. [. . .]
(4) For *Father Sergey*. On his own he is good – with people he falls. [. . .]

3 August, Pirogovo Everything is just the same again. My life is just as repulsive again. I've lived through a great deal. I haven't passed the examination. But I don't despair and want a re-examination. I did particularly badly at the examination because I had the intention of transferring to another institution.[32] I must abandon these thoughts and then I'll study better. During this time Sonya returned and dear Tanya Kuzminskaya has been. Worked on *Resurrection*; it's going very badly, although I think I've thought it out much better.

The third day at Pirogovo. Uncle Seryozha is not as well as before – he's out of sorts. Marya Nikolayevna. For two days no thoughts have come into my head. During this time there has been alarming news about the situation of the Dukhobors[33] and the fact that M. N. Rostovtseva has been imprisoned.[34] No letters from the Chertkovs for a long time. They are probably intercepted. I'll continue to copy out what I haven't copied: [. . .]
(2) There are two forms of human activity, and according to which of these two kinds of activity people primarily adhere to, there are two kinds of people too: one kind uses its reason to discover what is good and what is bad, and acts according to this knowledge; the other kind acts as it wishes and then uses its reason to prove that what it did was good and what it didn't do was bad. [. . .]
(4) Even if what Marx predicts were to happen, then the only thing that would happen would be that despotism would be transferred. Now the capitalists are in power, then the workers' bosses would be in power.
(5) The mistake of the Marxists (and not only of them, but of the whole materialistic school) is that they don't see that the life of mankind is advanced by the growth of consciousness, the advancement of religion, and a more and more clear and general understanding of life which provides a satisfactory answer to all problems, and not by economic causes.
(6) The main misjudgement, the main error of Marx's theory is the supposition that capital will pass out of the hands of private individuals into the hands of the government, and from the government, representing the people, into the hands of the workers. The government does not represent the people, but is these same private individuals who have power, somewhat different from capitalists, but partly

coinciding with them. And so the government will never hand over capital to the workers. It is a fiction, a deception, that the government represents the people. *If only there were such a system whereby the government actually did express the will of the people, such a government would have no need of force, nor would there be any need for a government in the sense of an authority.* [. . .]

(13) I pray to God that He might rescue me from the suffering which torments me. But this suffering is sent to me by God in order to rescue me from evil. The master whips his cattle in order to drive them out of a burning shed and save them, but the cattle pray not to be whipped.

(14) There are some common misunderstandings of my views, sometimes deliberate, sometimes not, which, I confess, irritate me: (1) I say that the God who created the world in six days and who sent His son, and also His son himself, are not God, but that God is the one existing, incomprehensible good, the beginning of everything; but people accuse me of denying God. (2) I say that one ought not to resist violence by violence; but people accuse me of saying that one ought not to fight against evil. (3) I say that one ought to strive towards chastity, and that the highest stage on this path is virginity, the second a pure marriage and the third an impure one – i.e. not just marriage – but still marriage; but people accuse me of denying marriage and preaching the cessation of the human race. (4) I say that art is an infectious activity, and the more infectious art is, the better it is. But whether this activity is good or bad doesn't depend only on how far it satisfies the demands of art, i.e. on its infectiousness, but also on how far it satisfies the demands of religious awareness, i.e. morality, conscience; but people accuse me of preaching tendentious art, etc.

(15) Woman – the legends say – is the tool of the devil. She is generally stupid, but the devil lends her his brains when she works for him. And lo and behold, she performs miracles of intelligence, far-sightedness and constancy in order to do something nasty, but when there is no need for anything nasty, she can't understand the simplest thing, can't think beyond the present moment and has no endurance or patience (except over bearing children and looking after them).

(16) All this concerns the woman who is not a Christian, not a chaste woman – like all the women of our Christian world. Oh, how I would like to show to women the full significance of a chaste woman. A chaste woman (the legend of Mary is not in vain) will save the world. [. . .]

(19) For *Resurrection*. It wasn't possible to think about and remember his sin and be satisfied with himself. And he had to be satisfied with himself in order to live, and so he didn't think, he forgot. [. . .]

Today is 24 August, Yasnaya Polyana During this time I've received no letters from Chertkov, and I'm very puzzled. I think the Dukhobors came during this time.[35] Letters from Khilkov and Ivan Mikhaylovich.[36] Answered them all. Suller came today.[37] I'm still working on *Resurrection*, and am satisfied, very satisfied even. I'm afraid of clashes. Sonya is unwell; but she is in good spirits. So am I. The house is full of people: Mashenka, Stakhovich, Vera Kuzminskaya, Vera Tolstaya. I'll copy out my notes. [. . .]

(7) Egoism, all egoistic life, is only justified until reason is awakened; as soon as it is awakened, egoism is only justified to the extent to which it is necessary to support oneself as an instrument to be of service to people. The purpose of reason is to serve people. The terrible thing is that it is used to serve oneself.

(8) Man gives in to the illusion of egoism, lives for himself and suffers. He has only to begin to live for others and his suffering is relieved and he obtains the greatest good in the world: the love of other people.

(9) Just as one can cure oneself of smoking and of bad habits, so one can and must cure oneself of egoism. If you want to increase *your own* pleasure, if you want to project *yourself*, to arouse the love of other people – stop. If there's nothing you can do for others or if you don't want to do anything, don't do anything, – only don't do anything for yourself.

(10) A Bavarian was telling me about their life. He boasts about the high degree of freedom, but at the same time they have compulsory and crudely Catholic religious teaching. That is the most dreadful despotism. Worse than ours.

2 November It's terrible to see how long I've gone without writing my diary – more than two months. And not only has there been nothing bad, but rather everything has been good. The jubilee[38] was not so repulsive and depressing as I expected. The sale of the story and the receipt of the 12,000 roubles which I gave to the Dukhobors was well organised.[39] I was displeased with Chertkov and saw that I was to blame. A Dukhobor came from Yakutsk. I liked him very much. Seryozha is very close to me in deed and feeling. I deliberately don't provoke him with words. Things are very well with Sonya. I love her more than before. Masha is to be pitied for her weakness, but she is just as close in spirit. Tanya has broken things off,[40] but is very unstable. Andryusha is going to marry Dieterichs[41] and is much closer to me. Misha and Lyova are strangers. But praise God and thanks be to Him that He has come to life and is on fire within me, and that it is natural for me either to love and rejoice, or to love and pity. What happiness!

Archer[42] came here yesterday, from Chertkov; I took a liking to him. There's very much to do, but I'm entirely engrossed in *Resurrection*; I'm saving water and only using it for *Resurrection*. I think it will be quite good. People praise it, but I don't believe them. I made some notes – all very important. I'll write them out later, but now I want to note that I was walking along the path this evening, and not only thought clearly but felt clearly too.

(1) Under my feet is the hard frozen earth, round about me are enormous trees, above my head is the cloudy sky, I feel my body, I feel a pain in my head, I'm busy thinking about *Resurrection*, but at the same time I know and feel with my whole being that the hard, frozen earth and the trees and the sky and my body and my thoughts are all only the product of my five senses, my imagination, a world built by me, because such is my separate compartment of the world as it is at present. And I know that once I die, all this will not disappear, but it will be altered, just as transformations take place in theatres: bushes and stones become palaces and towers, etc. Death is nothing else but such a transformation, depending on another separate compartment of the world, another personality; now I consider myself, my

body and its senses to be me, but then something quite different will be allotted to me. And then the whole world will become different. For the world is only as it is and not something else, because I consider myself to be what I am and not something different. And there can be an infinite number of divisions of the world. This is not altogether clear to others, but it is very clear to me.

14 November Again I haven't noticed how eleven days have gone by. I've been very absorbed in *Resurrection*, and am making good progress. I'm quite near the end. Seryozha and Suller have been, and both went to the Caucasus with my letter to Golitsyn.⁴³ Sonya arrived yesterday. Things are very well. It's a long time since I've felt so hale and hearty mentally and physically. [. . .]
(9) You watch people kissing an icon, crawling up to it, worshipping it and fearing it. If people can be deceived like this, there's no deception to which they won't succumb. [. . .]
(11) God manifests himself in us through consciousness. If there is no consciousness there is no God. Only consciousness provides the possibility of goodness, restraint, service and self-sacrifice.
Everything depends on what consciousness is directed towards.
Consciousness directed towards the animal 'I', kills and paralyses life; consciousness directed towards the spiritual 'I', stimulates, elevates and liberates life.
Consciousness directed towards the animal 'I' strengthens and inflames passion, produces fear, struggle and the horror of death; consciousness directed towards the spiritual 'I' *liberates love. This is very important, and if I'm still alive I will write about it.* [. . .]
(15) The moral progress of mankind only takes place because there are old people. Old people grow kinder and wiser and hand on their experience of life to succeeding generations. Were it not so, mankind would not have progressed. And what a simple means! [. . .]
(17) Technical progress is welcomed and encouraged by everyone, but moral and religious progress is held back by priests. Hence the main calamities of life. [. . .]

Today is 25 November, Yasnaya Polyana Sonya went away full of good feelings, and I promised to come on 1 December. Misha is worrying her and she is depressed. I want to join her as soon as possible. I also want to go to Pirogovo. We are alone: Tanya, Masha and Kolya. There's only Liza Obolenskaya. I'm working just as hard on *Resurrection*. Last night I thought about an article on why the people are corrupted. They have no faith. They christen children by force, and then consider any argument about faith apostasy and any deviation to be a criminal offence. Only the sectarians have faith. Perhaps I'll put this into the *Appeal*.⁴⁴ A pity. I thought it out well during the night. *Resurrection* is getting bigger. It will hardly fit into 100 chapters. Noted down the following, and I think it's very important. It ought to go into a statement of faith.
(1) We are very accustomed to arguments about how to organise the lives of other people – people in general. And such arguments don't seem strange to us. And yet such arguments could never arise between religious, and therefore free people:

such arguments are the consequences of despotism: the rule of one man or more over other men. This is how both the despots themselves and the people corrupted by them argue: they say, if I had the power I would do so with other people. This delusion is harmful, not only because it hurts and degrades people who are subjected to the violence of despots, but also because it weakens in all people their consciousness of the need to improve themselves. And this is the one and only effective means of influencing other people. [. . .]

A DIALOGUE[45]

Last night there was a conversation and a scene which had a far greater effect on me than her last journey.[46] In order to describe the conversation it must be said that I had returned the same day after 11 o'clock at night from a journey of eighteen *versts* to inspect Masha's estate. I don't say that this was hard work for me, it was a pleasure; but still I was rather tired, having done about forty *versts* on horseback, and not having slept during the day. And I'm seventy.

Under the influence of my conversation with you, my tiredness and a good, happy frame of mind I went to bed intending to say nothing about what had happened, and hoping that it would all blow over of its own accord, as you consoled me by saying. We went to bed. We said nothing for a while. Then she began to speak.

She: Will you go to Pirogovo and abuse me in front of Seryozha?
I: I haven't spoken to anybody, not even to our daugher Tanya.
She: But you spoke to my sister Tanya?
I: Yes.
She: What did she say?
I: The same as she said to you . . . she defended you to me, and probably spoke up on my behalf to you.
She: Yes, she was terribly hard on me. Too hard. I don't deserve it.
I: Please don't let's talk about it, it will sort itself out, settle down, and, God willing, disappear.
She: I can't help talking about it. It's too depressing for me to live in constant fear. If he[47] calls now, it will begin again. He didn't say anything, but he might call.

The news that he would come – as always 'might come' meant in fact that he certainly would come – was very depressing to me. I had just intended to stop thinking about it, when this depressing visit cropped up again. I remained silent, but couldn't get to sleep and couldn't refrain from saying:

I: I was just hoping for some peace, and now you seem to be preparing me again for an unpleasant prospect.
She: But what can I do? 'It's possible,' he said to Tanya. I didn't invite him. Perhaps he won't call.
I: Whether he calls or not isn't important, even your journey isn't important; what is important, as I said to you before, as I said to you two years ago, is your attitude towards your feeling. If you acknowledged your feeling to be bad you wouldn't even have thought about whether he would call, wouldn't even have spoken about him.

She: Well, what am I to do now?
I: Repent at heart of your feeling.
She: I can't repent, and I don't understand what it means.
I: It means discussing with yourself whether the feeling which you have for this man is good or bad.
She: I don't have any feeling, good or bad.
I: That's not true.
She: The feeling is so unimportant, insignificant.
I: All feelings, and therefore the most insignificant also, are always either good or bad in our eyes, and therefore you too must decide whether this was a good feeling or a bad one.
She: There's nothing to decide, this feeling is so unimportant that it can't be bad. And there's nothing bad about it at all.
I: No, the exclusive feeling of an old, married woman for another man is a bad feeling.
She: I have no feeling for a man, only for a person.
I: But this person is a man.
She: He isn't a man for me. It isn't a question of any exclusive feeling, it's a question of music being a comfort to me after my sorrow, but there isn't any special feeling for the person.
I: Why tell lies?
She: All right. There was once. I was wrong to have gone,[48] to have distressed you. But it's over now. I'll do anything not to distress you.
I: You can't do that because it's not a matter of what you do – of going, or receiving him or not – it's a matter of your attitude towards your feeling. You must decide yourself whether it's a good or a bad feeling.
She: But there isn't any feeling.
I: That's not true. And this is just what is bad for you that you want to hide this feeling, to suppress it. But until you decide whether this feeling is good or bad, and until you acknowledge that it is bad, you won't be able to help hurting me. If you acknowledge, as you do now, that this feeling is good, then you will never be able to stop wanting to satisfy this feeling, i.e. to see him, and since you want to do so, you won't be able to help ensuring that you do see him. If you avoid opportunities of seeing him, you will be melancholy and depressed. Therefore it's all a matter of deciding what sort of feeling it is, good or bad.
She: I did wrong to hurt you, and I repent of that.
I: This is just what is bad, that you repent of your actions, but not of the feeling which controls them.
She: I know that I haven't loved and don't love anyone more than you. I would like to know how you understand my feeling for you. How could I love you, if I loved someone else?
I: Your discord is due to the fact that you haven't made clear to yourself the meaning of your feelings. A drunkard or a gambler loves his wife very

much, but can't refrain from gambling and drink, and never will refrain until he decides in his own heart whether his love for gambling and drink is a good feeling. Only when that has been decided is deliverance possible.

She: Always the same old thing.
I: But I can't say anything else when it's as clear as day that it's all to do with this.
She: I've done nothing wrong.

So the conversation would keep coming back to the same point with different variations. She tried to show that this feeling was very unimportant, and therefore couldn't be condemned, and there was no reason to fight against it. I kept returning to the point that if a feeling is acknowledged in one's heart to be good, there is no deliverance from it, and no deliverance from those hundreds of thousands of trivial actions which stem from this feeling and sustain it.

She: Well, what will happen if I acknowledge the feeling to be bad?
I: The fact that you will fight against it, and will avoid everything that sustains it. You will get rid of everything connected with it.
She: But it's all just in order to deprive me of my only consolation – music. I'm in a terrible *cercle vicieux*. I'm depressed. I can only get rid of this depression by playing the piano. If I play, you say that it's all connected with my feeling; if I don't play I'm depressed, and you say that my feeling is the cause of it.
I: I only say one thing: you must decide whether the feeling is good or bad. Without that our torments will never end.
She: There isn't any feeling, there's nothing to decide.
I: As long as you say that, there's no way out. But if a person has no moral judge to tell him what is good and bad, that person is like a blind man who can't distinguish colours. You don't have this moral judge, and so let's not talk any more – it's two o'clock.

A long silence.

She: Well then, I ask myself absolutely sincerely: what sort of feeling do I have, and what would I wish for? I would wish for nothing more than that he should come once a month to stay a while and play, like any good acquaintance.
I: But by these very words you yourself confirm that you have an exclusive feeling for this person. Surely there isn't any other person whose monthly visit would be a joy for you. If a visit once a month would be pleasant, then once a week or every day would be more pleasant still. By saying this you unwittingly acknowledge your exclusive feeling. And without deciding the question whether this is good or bad, nothing can be changed.
She: Oh, always the same old thing. It's torture. Other people are unfaithful to their husbands, but they aren't tormented as much as I am. Why is it? Because I love music. You can reproach people for their actions, but not for their feelings. They aren't under our control. And there haven't been any actions.

I: No actions? What about the journey to Petersburg, and to this place and that, and all this music?
She: But what is special about my life?
I: What do you mean what is special? You live an exclusive life. You've become a sort of lady of the conservatoire.

These words for some reason angered her terribly.

She: You want to torment me and deprive me of everything. It's so cruel of you.

She reached a state of semi-hysteria. I was silent for quite a long time, and then remembered God. I prayed and thought to myself: 'She *cannot* renounce her feeling, she cannot use reason to influence her feelings. With her, as with all women, feeling is paramount, and any change of feeling takes place, perhaps, independently of reason . . . Perhaps Tanya is right that it will gradually disappear of its own accord in that special way women have which is incomprehensible to me. I must tell her this, I think, and say it with compassion for her and the desire to calm her down – that perhaps I'm mistaken in putting the question so much from my own point of view, that perhaps she will come to the same conclusion in her own way, and that I hope so. But at the moment her anger has reached its peak.'

She: You have tormented me, for two hours you have been using the same phrase over and over again: exclusive, exclusive feeling, good or bad, good or bad. It's terrible. Goodness knows what your cruelty will lead to.
I: But I prayed and wanted to help you.
She: It's all lies, pharisaism, deceit. You can deceive other people, but I can see right through you.
I: What's the matter with you? I just wanted to do good.
She: There's no good in you. You're evil, you're a beast. *I will love good and decent people, but not you. You're a beast.*

Whereupon there followed nonsensical, not to say terrible and cruel words: threats, suicide, curses on everyone, on me and our daughters. And some sort of threats to publish her stories if I published *Resurrection* with a description of the chambermaid.[49] And then sobs, laughter, whispering, nonsensical and, alas, hypocritical words: my head is splitting, look here, where the parting is, cut the vein in my neck, here it is – and all sorts of nonsense which could be dreadful. I held her in my arms. I knew that this always helps, and I kissed her on the forehead. She couldn't get her breath for a long time, then she began to yawn and sigh and dropped off to sleep, and is still sleeping.

I don't know how this madness can be resolved. I don't see any way out. She obviously values this feeling of hers as dearly as her life, and won't acknowledge it to be bad. And since she won't acknowledge it to be bad, she can't be rescued from it, and will go on taking actions provoked by this feeling, actions which it is painful and shameful for me and the children to see.

1899

2 January, Yasnaya Polyana The last time I wrote my diary was on 25 November, consequently a month and a week ago. I wrote it at Yasnaya Polyana, then went to Moscow, where I didn't write it at all. At the end of November I went to Pirogovo. I returned[1] on the first and haven't been quite well since then – the small of my back ached and still does, and recently I've had a sort of bilious fever. This is the second day I've felt better. All this time I've been working exclusively on *Resurrection*. There have been dealings to do with the Dukhobors and an infinite number of letters. Kolechka Gay is with me, it's refreshing to be with him. Things are not happy in the family: Masha has been ill (it ended yesterday, she had a miscarriage). Tanya is worried and lifeless. Misha is crazy. Andryusha is equivocal. I get on well with Sonya. I'm at peace, as old men are. That's all. There are quite a lot of notes to write out. I'll write them out on the pages I left blank. Recently my interest in *Resurrection* seems to have waned, and I rejoice to feel other, more important interests – the understanding of life and death. Much seems clear.

2 January My notes. [. . .]
(3) Our art is like dressing to food. If there is nothing but dressing it tastes nice, but you won't feel full and your stomach will be upset. [. . .]
(6) Complexity of knowledge is a sign of its falseness. What is true is simple. [. . .]
(10) I suppose it's more important to know what one shouldn't think about, than to know what one should.
(11) Women are weak, and not only don't want to know their weakness, but want to boast of their strength. What can be more disgusting?
(13) The sole concern of rulers is not, as they say, to establish religion firmly among the people but, on the contrary, to cut the people off from religion. And in Russia they have almost achieved this.
 This was written on 2 January.

Today is 21 February Haven't written my diary for more than six weeks. I'm still in Moscow. At first *Resurrection* went well, then I cooled off towards it completely. Wrote a letter to a sergeant-major,[2] and to the Swedish newspapers.[3] It's three days since I resumed work on *Resurrection*. I'm making progress. A students' strike. They keep trying to involve me. I advise them to behave passively, but I've no wish to write letters to them.[4] Tanya is weak in body and spirit. My back is better. An interesting and lively Frenchman, Sinet,[5] is staying with us. The first religious Frenchman. There's a great deal I need to write down. I've been in a very bad mood, but am all right now.

26 June, Yasnaya Polyana Haven't written my diary for four months; I won't say

I've spent the time badly. I've been working intensively on *Resurrection*, and still am. There's a lot in it that isn't bad, things for whose sake it is being written. The other day I was seriously ill. I'm well now. Sonya is going to our sons' today. She has been seriously ill, and is still weak. The critical time is not over yet. I'm often very tenderly sorry for her. I felt so today when she said goodbye. Relations are difficult over the printing and translations of *Resurrection*.⁶ But most of the time I'm at peace. Correspondence has been neglected. People keep sending money for the famine victims, but I can't do anything except send it on by post. Kolechka⁷ is with me, helping me with the work. Seryozha makes me glad every time he comes. Tanya worries me with her frivolity; she has withdrawn into egotistical love. I hope she will come back. I'm continuing to copy things out from my notebook. [. . .]
(17) It seems to us that real work is work on something external – making or collecting something: property, a house, cattle, fruit: but working on one's soul is nothing special, just fantasy; and yet any work except work on one's soul, acquiring the habit of doing good – any other work is child's play.
(18) People don't obey God, they worship Him. Better not to worship, but to obey. [. . .]
(21) It seems strange and immoral that a writer, an artist, when he sees people suffering, doesn't so much sympathise as observe, in order to reproduce these sufferings. But it isn't immoral. The suffering of one person is insignificant compared with the spiritual effect which a work of art – if it is a good one – will have.
(25) The military class is a survival which has no use – a caecum.
(27) The evil in the world has a very simple cause. Everyone seeks *midi à quatorze heures* [looks for difficulties where there are none] – both in the economic and the political sphere. I've just been reading the debate in the German parliament about how to keep the peasants from running off to the towns. But there is only one solution to all problems, and nobody acknowledges it or is interested in it. And this one solution is clear and indisputable: those in power have been corrupted because they have power, and have made up for themselves a religious doctrine to accord with their corruption. And this doctrine they vigorously implant in the people from childhood on.
There is only one salvation; the destruction of that false doctrine. [. . .]
(34) The press is falsehood *with a vengeance*.⁸ [. . .]

28 September, Yasnaya Polyana I've been working all the time on *Resurrection*. I'm now bogged down in the 3rd part. Haven't made any progress for a long time. Sonya is in Moscow. I have evolved for myself a state of peace and quiet which hasn't been disturbed yet: not to speak, and to know that this is necessary, and that I must live in these conditions. Ilya, Sonya and the children, Andryusha and his wife, and Masha and her husband are here. I keep thinking more and more often of the philosophical definition of matter – space and time. I'll make a note of it today if I have time.
Read an interesting book about Christ never having existed, that it was a myth.⁹ There is as much to be said *for* the likelihood that this is true, as there is *against*.

Cleared up all the letters yesterday with the help of Masha. Left many unanswered. Thought during this time:

I'm still ill. There's hardly a day without pain. I'm dissatisfied with myself morally too. I've let myself go very much: I'm not working physically and am preoccupied with myself, with my health. How difficult it is to endure illness with resignation, to go to one's death without resistance, but I must. [. . .]
(3) I picked a flower and threw it away. There are so many of them that I wasn't sorry. We don't value the inimitable beauty of living creatures and destroy them without pity – not only plants, but animals and human beings. There are so many of them. Culture – civilisation – is nothing else but the destruction of these beautiful things and their replacement. What by? The tavern, the theatre . . . [. . .]
(5) The most valuable thing on earth is good relations between people, but these relations are not formed as a result of conversation – on the contrary they are ruined by conversation. Talk as little as possible, especially with those people with whom you want to maintain good relations. [. . .]
(8) Brotherhood is natural and proper to people. Non-brotherhood, separation, is studiously cultivated. [. . .]
(14) People who assure others that reason cannot be a guide to life are people whose reason is so distorted that they can see clearly that it will lead them into a bog.
(15) The only instance when a person can and should be preoccupied with himself is when he feels unhappy. Unhappiness is the best condition for improving oneself, for rising to a higher level; unhappiness is an indication of one's imperfection. One should be glad of these instances. They are the preparation of oneself for work, they are spiritual food. [. . .]

Today is 2 October, Yasnaya Polyana Still unwell. I'm not suffering, but feel constantly threatened. I'm better morally – I think more about God within me, and about death. I think I've got over the difficult passage in *Resurrection*.[10] Andryusha has changed strikingly for the better. Perhaps he'll get worse, but the fact remains, and will leave its mark. Kolechka has left. Sonya has arrived – she's unwell. I'm continuing to copy things out from my notebook. [. . .]
(4) Conscience is the memory of society as assimilated by the individual person. [. . .]

Today is 13 October, Yasnaya Polyana I'm still not altogether well – that's as it should be. But it doesn't prevent me from living, thinking and progressing towards the appointed end. *Resurrection* is making slow progress; I've sent off four chapters, which I don't think will pass the censor, but at least, I think, I've settled on one thing, and I won't make any more changes. I never cease to think about my brother Seryozha,[11] but because of the weather and my ill health I can't bring myself to go. Tanya, I think, has finally decided to get married. Sonya has been to Moscow, and is going again today. Today is a sort of mental holiday for me, and not only today but all recent days. I've thought up some good scenes for *Resurrection*. I keep thinking more and more often and more and more clearly about that separate existence, which appears to us as matter in space and movement in time. I've also received from America some brochures by Westrup about money,[12] which impressed me by making clear to me everything that was unclear about financial questions and reducing everything, as was bound to be the case, to the coercion of governments.

If I have time I will write it down. There is another important, happy thought which, although an old one, came to me as a new one and makes me very happy, namely:

(1) The main cause of family unhappiness is the fact that people are brought up to think that marriage brings happiness. Sexual attraction is an enticement to marriage, and it takes the form of the promise or hope of happiness which is bolstered up by public opinion and literature; but marriage is not only not happiness, but always suffering, which is the price one pays for the satisfaction of sexual desire, suffering in the form of lack of freedom, slavery, satiety, disgust, all sorts of spiritual and physical defects in one's partner which have to be borne – malice, stupidity, falsehood, vanity, drunkenness, idleness, meanness, greed, debauchery – all defects which are particularly hard to bear when not in oneself but in somebody else, and from which one has to suffer as if they were one's own; and similarly physical defects: ugliness, dirtiness, nasty smells, sores, insanity, etc., which are even more difficult to endure in other people. All this, or at least something of it, will always be so, and everyone has to bear these hardships. But the things that ought to compensate – care, contentment, help – all this is taken as a matter of course, while all the defects are not taken as a matter of course, and the more people expect happiness from marriage, the more they suffer from them.

The main cause of these sufferings is the fact that what is expected doesn't happen, and what always happens isn't expected. And so the only escape from these sufferings is not to expect joys, but to expect what is bad and be prepared to endure it. If you expect everything that is described at the beginning of *The Thousand and One Nights*, if you expect drunkenness, nasty smells, disgusting diseases, then stubbornness, untruthfulness, even drunkenness can be, if not forgiven, at least not be a matter for suffering, and you can be glad that what might have happened didn't happen – the things described in *The Thousand and One Nights* – nor madness, cancer, etc. And then everything that is good will be appreciated.

Isn't this also the main means to happiness in general? Isn't this the reason why people are so often unhappy, especially the rich? Instead of acknowledging themselves to be in the position of a slave who has to work hard for himself and for others and to work hard in the way his master wishes, people imagine that all sorts of pleasures await them and that they only have to enjoy them. Given this, how can one fail to be unhappy? In that case all things – hard work, obstacles, illnesses, the necessary conditions of life – appear as unexpected, terrible calamities. The poor, therefore, are usually less unhappy: they know in advance that they are faced with hard work, struggle and obstacles and so they value everything that gives them joy. But the rich, who expect only joys, see a calamity in every obstacle, and don't notice and don't value the good things which they enjoy. Blessed are the poor for they shall be comforted; the hungry, for they shall be fed; and woe unto you, the rich . . .

27 October, Yasnaya Polyana We are on our own – Tanya (her time is near and I'm sorry for her), Olga, Andryusha, Julie and Andrey Dmitriyevich.[13] Things are all right, but I'm often ill: more days sick than well, and for that reason I'm not writing much. Sent off twelve chapters, very much unfinished. I'm working on the ending. I've had many thoughts and, I think, good ones. [. . .]
(2) War, lawcourts, executions, the oppresssion of the workers, prostitution and much else – all this is a necessary and inevitable consequence and condition of that pagan system of life in which we live, and to change one or many of these things is impossible. What is to be done? Change the very system of that life, the thing on which it rests. How? First of all by not taking part in the system, and in what maintains it: military service, the lawcourts, taxes, false teaching, etc., and secondly by doing that one thing which a person is always free to do: replacing in one's heart selfishness and everything that flows from it – malice, greed, violence, etc. – by love and everything that flows from it: reasonableness, humility, charity, etc. Just as it's impossible to turn the wheels of a machine by force, as they are all connected with cogs and other wheels, but it's easy to turn the steam on and off which sets them in motion, in the same way it's terribly difficult to change the external conditions of life, but it's easy to be good or bad. And it's this – being good or bad – that changes all the external conditions of life. [. . .]

20 November, Moscow There's a lot I haven't written down. I'm in Moscow. Tanya has gone off with Sukhotin for some reason.[14] It's shameful and offensive. For seventy years I've been lowering my opinion of women more and more, and I need to lower it still further. The woman question! Of course there's a woman question! Only it's not a question of women beginning to control our life, but of their ceasing to destroy it. [. . .]

Today is 18 December, Moscow Haven't written my diary for nearly a month. I've been seriously ill. It was very painful for twenty-four hours, then a respite and weakness. And death became something more than natural, almost desirable. And so it remains now that I'm getting better. It's a new, joyful step. Finished *Resurrection*. It's not good. Not revised. Too hurried. But I'm free of it, and it doesn't interest me any more.

Seryozha, Masha and her husband and Marya Alexandrovna[15] are here. I feel well. Haven't started to write anything yet. Philosophy interests me most of all, but I've no great wish to do anything. I'm resting. Wrote some letters. I'll try to copy out my notes.
(1) (A trifle.) About polyphonic music. A voice ought to say something, but in this case there are many voices, and each one says nothing. [. . .]
(4) Matter is everything that is accessible to our senses. Science makes us suppose that there is matter which is inaccessible to our senses. In this area there may be creatures made up of such matter and aware of it – this matter which is in-

accessible to our senses. I don't think that there are such creatures; I only think that our matter, and our feelings which are aware of it, are only one of *innumerable* possibilities of life. [. . .]

(6) Read about Engelhardt's book.[16] The evolution of the progress of cruelty. I think that there's a great deal of truth in it. Cruelty has increased primarily because a division of labour has taken place, which has contributed to the increase of people's material wealth. Everyone talks about the advantages of the divison of labour, without seeing that a necessary condition of the division of labour, apart from the *mechanisation* of man, is also the elimination of those conditions which give rise to moral association between human beings. If we do exactly the same thing as agricultural workers, it's understandable that a system of mutual aid will be established between us, but there can't be any association between the shepherd and the factory-weaver. (This seems wrong. I'll think about it.)

(11) People usually say: 'This is very profound, and therefore not fully comprehensible.' That isn't true. On the contrary. Everything that is deep is transparently clear. Like water, which is murky on the surface, but the deeper it is, the more transparent it is. [. . .]

Today is 20 December, Moscow Health not good. Mental condition good, I'm ready for death. A lot of people in the evenings – I'm tired. *Resurrection* didn't appear in No. 51,[17] and I was sorry. That's bad. I'm thinking over philosophical definitions of life. Thought today about *The Coupon* – good. Perhaps I'll write it. [. . .]

1900

1 January, Moscow I'm sitting in my room, *and everybody is here, celebrating the New Year.* All this time I've written nothing in my diary, I've been unwell. There's a lot to note down. [. . .]

(2) If it has once been instilled into a child that he must believe that God is man, that God is 1 and 3, in a word that $2 + 2 = 5$, the instrument of his knowledge is damaged for ever; faith in reason is undermined. And this is just what is done to all children. It's terrible. [. . .]

(4) I recalled to mind my adolescence, especially my early and late youth. No moral rules were instilled into me at all – none; yet round about me *grown-ups* were self-assuredly smoking, drinking and leading a dissolute life (especially the latter), beating people and demanding hard work from them. And I did a lot of bad things, without wishing to – simply from imitating grown-ups. [. . .]

(7) Seryozha and Usov were talking about various conceptions of the structure of the world: the continuity or discontinuity of matter. In my own conception of life and the world, matter is only the idea I have of it which stems from my being separate from the world. And movement is the idea I have of it which stems from my being in contact with the world, and so for me the question of the continuity or discontinuity of matter doesn't exist.

(8) I was riding along in a horse-drawn tramcar, looking at houses, signboards, shops, cabmen, and people driving or walking by, and suddenly it became so clear to me that all this world, including my life in it, is only one of an innumerable number of possibilities of other worlds and other lives, and for me only one of innumerable stages through which *it seems to me* I am passing in time. [. . .]

(1) We respect and worship people: courtiers – tsars, ecclesiastical people – bishops, etc., only because the higher the person we are subordinate to (for our own advantage), the more justified we are, not only in other people's eyes, but also in our own.

(11) Eve tempted Adam, and it's always like that. The female decides everything. [. . .]

8 January Evening. I've done nothing for several days. I've put aside the letter to the Dukhobors,[1] and only revised the article on the 36-hour day.[2] Got nearer the end today. Masha is here (I was just going to write about them and stopped, because they would read it).[3] I'm in good spirits, despite the fact that my health is undermined. I feel the pangs of death, i.e. of a new birth. I can't regard them in any other way, especially when ill, and the more ill I am, the more clearly and calmly I regard them.

Stasov has just said goodbye and left. A model *intellectual type.* How I would like to depict it. It's something quite new.

News today from Syzran. I'm sorry for Seryozha.⁴ There's not much to note down.

(1) I read newspapers, journals and books and still can't get used to ascribing any real value to what is written there, namely: the philosophy of Nietzsche, the dramas of Ibsen and Maeterlinck and the science of Lombroso and that doctor who makes eyes. Surely this represents complete poverty of thought, understanding and feeling.

(2) I'm reading about war in the Philippines and Transvaal, and am seized with horror and revulsion. Why? The wars of Frederick and Napoleon were honest wars and therefore not without a certain grandeur. This was so even with the Crimean War. But the wars of the Americans and the British in the midst of a world where even schoolchildren condemn war are terrible. [. . .]

16 January, Moscow [. . .] Lizanka has come from Syzran⁵ and Vorobyov from Nalchik.⁶ Nothing, it seems, could be worse. But that's not true: it could be worse. And so I mustn't feel regrets. Physical sufferings and sufferings of self-love – pride, vanity – almost always lead to spiritual progress. Always, especially the sufferings of pride. But we, stupid people, complain. Received letters from St John and Sinet – good ones.

Thought today that my situation – any situation – is undoubtedly useful to me. A magic wand has been given to me. Only I must learn how to use it.

Must note:

Gorky has been.⁷ We had a very good talk. And I liked him. A real man of the people.

What a wonderful flair women have for recognising celebrity. They discover it, not from impressions received, but from how and which way the crowd is running. [. . .]

Notes:

(1) One can't be too much on one's guard against the stimulation of one's vanity – love of praise. If an enemy wanted to destroy a man, it would be safer to praise him than to get him drunk. It fosters morbid sensitivity – which leads to idle relaxation when people praise you, and to bitterness and despondency when they blame you. About all it increases morbidity and vulnerability.

(2) Read Chekov's *Lady with the Dog*.⁸ It's all Nietzsche. Previously people who hadn't evolved for themselves a clear philosophy of life, which could distinguish good and evil, used to seek anxiously; now they think they are beyond good and evil, but remain on this side, i.e. they are almost animals. [. . .]

(7) The best attitude to sexual desire is (1) to suppress it altogether. Next best⁹ (2) to have relations with one woman only, chaste and of the same faith, and to raise children together and to help one another. (3) Next worse⁹ to go to a brothel when tormented by desire; (4) to have casual relations with various women without living with them; (5) to have an affair with a woman and then abandon her; (6) still worse, to have an affair with someone else's wife; (7) worst of all, to go on living with your own unfaithful and immoral wife.

I must tear this sheet out.

27 January, Moscow Haven't written my diary for nearly two weeks. Went to see *Uncle Vanya* and was shocked.[10] Wanted to write my drama *The Corpse*, and sketched out a draft.[11]

Was very depressed by the appearance of G.[12] Retribution still not complete. Serves him right. Wanted to copy things from my notebook – but I can't. I've been well, though not mentally vigorous. I've been worse the last couple of days.

13 March Haven't written my diary for more than two months. Masha left, then Andryusha and Olga left. My health improved significantly during this time.

Continued writing (1) a letter to the Dukhobors, which I finished and sent off, (2) an article on patriotism,[13] which I copied out many times and which is terribly weak, so that I decided yesterday either to abandon it or to begin it all from the beginning again, and I think I have something to say from the beginning. I must show that the present situation, especially the Hague conference, has shown that nothing can be expected from the highest powers, and that this terrible, pernicious situation can only be sorted out, if at all, by the efforts of private individuals.

On the 36-hour day will, I think, turn out all right. Above all, it will show that the now forthcoming emancipation will be just like the emancipation from serfdom, i.e. that one chain will only be released when there is another one to hold things secure. Slavery was abolished when serfdom was consolidated. Serfdom was abolished when land was taken away and taxes instituted; now people are being relieved of taxes when their means of production have been taken away. The workers will be given back – the intention is to give them back – their means of production, but only on condition that work is made compulsory for everyone. [. . .]

I'll copy out my notes: [. . .]

(5) Had a dream: one man was standing on a pillar and people were admiring him and praising him, a second man, to outdo him and go one better, was dancing on nails. A third man was simply good. [. . .]

(11) In a workhouse a priest was interpreting the first commandment of the Sermon on the Mount to the people and was explaining that one may and should get angry, as the authorities do, and that one may kill on the orders of the authorities. It was terrible.

One can forgive everything except the distortion of the highest truths which mankind has arrived at with such effort. [. . .]

(12) Lessing, I think, said that every husband says or thinks that there is only one bad and untruthful woman in the world and that is his wife.[14] That is because a wife is an open book to her husband, and cannot deceive him any more, as everyone else deceives him. [. . .]

(15) People want to equate man and woman. It's not a question of precedence, but of difference. Every female, from a queen bee to a woman, attracts many males, all of whom are ready to satisfy her. She chooses. That's her vocation. The male and the man are not in that position. That's the basic difference. [. . .]

19 March, Moscow I'm working little and unsuccessfully, although I'm well. But there is good work going on in my head. I've been reading psychology,[15] and with great advantage, although not for the purpose for which I'm reading it.

Today is 24 March, Moscow   Yesterday Tanya had a terrible operation.[16] I understood without any doubt that these clinics erected by merchants and factory owners who have ruined and continue to ruin tens of thousands of lives are a bad thing. The fact that they can cure one rich man, having ruined hundreds, if not thousands of poor men, is obviously a bad thing, a very bad thing. And the fact that thereby they are allegedly learning to lessen suffering and prolong life is also bad, because the means they use for this purpose (they say 'up to now', but I think essentially) are such that they can save and alleviate the sufferings of only a few chosen people; but mainly because their attention is directed not towards prevention and hygiene, but towards healing deformities which are continually and constantly occurring.

I'm getting on at times with *Patriotism*, and at times with *The Slavery of Money*.[17] I've improved the first one a lot, but I've done no writing for two days now. I'm reading psychology. I've read Wundt and Höffding. Very instructive. Their mistake and the source of it are obvious. In order to be exact, they want to keep to experiment alone. It is certainly exact, but on the other hand completely useless, and in place of the substance of the soul (which I deny) they put a still more mysterious parallelism. [...]

Thought during this time: [...]

(5) All our concern for the good of the people is like somebody trampling on young shoots, mutilating them and then trying to heal each little tree and blade of grass separately. This applies especially to education. Our blindness towards the question of education is astonishing. [...]

6 April, Moscow   It's evening now. Seryozha is playing, and I feel for some reason moved to tears, and drawn to poetry. But I can't write at such moments. I'm keeping fairly well; I'm still doing the same work which has stood in the way of my literary work, and I long for literary work. I crave for it very much.

Went to Obolensky's lecture and a strange thing happened: I spoke to his son.[18] And another strange thing happened: the same evening, as I was going to Olsufyev's to hand on a petition from the Molokans, an American missionary arrived with a petition to the Tsar about religious toleration in the Caucasus.[19] It was unpleasant for me to be beholden to Olsufyev, despite his good nature. [...]

I noted in my book: [...]

(10) There exists a naive, popular opinion that a husband, especially if he is older than his wife and his wife is very young, can educate and mould his wife. This is a gross delusion. Women have their own traditions, their own methods of handing them on, their own language as it were. And so a man can never influence a woman except through her desire to attract him. Women live quite independently of a man's spiritual life (of course there are exceptions, although very rare ones) and never yield to the influence of men, while they themselves, by their persistence and their cunning, have an indirect influence – not a direct one since men don't

understand women's language either – on the whole of life, and therefore on men as well. [. . .]

2 May, Moscow Haven't written my diary for nearly a month. I've been busy all the time with the two articles. And I would like to think I've finished them. There have been hard things, but good things too. More good things. Apart from work I've had few thoughts. Work has swallowed up everything. Tomorrow I'm going to Masha's:[20]

I noted in my book:
(1) You sometimes get angry with people for not understanding you, not following you or going along with you, although you are standing right next to them. That's just like walking through a labyrinth (such as there are in parks) and demanding that a man standing right next to you, only on the other side of the wall, should walk in the same direction as you. He has to walk a whole *verst* in order to catch you up, and to go first of all not in the same direction, but in the opposite one, in order to catch you up. But you know that he has to follow *you*, and not you *him*, only because you have already passed the place where he is standing.
(2) Every art represents a separate field of its own, like a square on a chess board. Every art has an art adjacent to it, just as a chess board square has adjacent squares. When the top surface of a field has been exploited, one has to go deeper in order to work in it, i.e. to produce something new. That's difficult. So people occupy adjacent squares, and produce something new out of this mixture. But this mixture – music with drama, printing, or lyric poetry and vice versa – is not art, but the perversion of art. [. . .]
(4) Our life as masters is so ugly that we can't even rejoice at the birth of our children. It's not servants of men who are born, but enemies of men, parasites. There's every likelihood that that's what they will be. [. . .]

Today is 5 May, Pirogovo Had a good journey. I'm fully fit. The country gave me new life. Saw Seryozha. It was sad, but truly good. Tanya has left. Masha, I think, has had another miscarriage.

Thought over *The New Slavery* from the beginning, and changed a lot today and improved it.

Made no notes. Thought:

People who don't know repentance are both fortunate and unfortunate. Having brought misfortune to others, they will die with the assurance of having done them a favour. It would be too hard for them to understand all their guilt. That would only crush them, not make them better.

I'm thinking about the peasant novel.[21]

I'm beginning a new notebook, 19 May, Yasnaya Polyana. Got back yesterday from Pirogovo, where I spent a wonderful fifteen days. Finished *Slavery* and wrote two acts.[22] I feel well here too. My health was on the point of breaking down. Now it's better. Read through a pile of letters. Nothing important. I've been writing the last chapter today.

It's late. Tomorrow I'll copy up my notes.

23 June, Yasnaya Polyana   Haven't written my diary for more than a month. I haven't spent these thirty-five days badly. I've had moods of depression, but religious feelings got the better of them. All this time I've been continuously and diligently writing *The Slavery of Our Times*. I've put in much that is new and clearer. I terribly want to write something literary, not dramatic, but epic – a continuation of *Resurrection*: Nekhlyudov's life as a peasant.[23] Nature moves and affects me: the meadows and woods – the corn, the ploughed fields, the meadowlands. I think – will this be my last summer? Well, never mind, that's all right. I'm grateful for everything – I've been infinitely blessed. How possible it is to be always thankful, and how joyful.

An American, Curtin,[24] Boulanger and St John have been here during this time. I've got to like St John. Health good. [. . .]

Today is 12 July, Yasnaya Polyana   Tanya is here. She's pitiable. I'm still writing *The Slavery of Our Times* every day. [. . .]
(2) Conscience is nothing else but the coincidence of one's own and the highest reason.
(3) Whoever sees the meaning of life in self-improvement cannot believe in death – in the fact that self-improvement should be suddenly interrupted. What is being improved only changes its form.
(4) When a person has many duties, he neglects the duties to himself, to his own soul; but they are the only important ones. Poor tsars, who imagine they have so many important duties. [. . .]
(33) I am seriously convinced that the world – countries and estates and houses – is governed by people who are quite mad. Those who are not mad refrain from taking part, or cannot do so.
(37) We destroy millions of flowers in order to erect palaces and theatres with electric light, but a single flower of a thistle is worth more than thousands of palaces. [. . .]

7 August, Yasnaya Polyana   Tanya is ill and is still in bed. I was seriously ill – terrible pains – and was a long time getting better. I'm better now. I feel the nearness of death and try to meet it calmly, and I think I shall meet it calmly; but while I'm well, as today, I can't readjust myself quickly to the process of transition.

Finished and sent off both *The Slavery of Our Times* and the article on Umberto's death.[25] I think I've done what I ought and what I could. [. . .]

Wrote a scene for *The Corpse* today. I'll now copy up my notes: [. . .]
(4) As an eye has an eyelid, so a fool has self-assurance to shield him from the possibility of his vanity being wounded. And the more they both protect themselves the less they see – they screw up their eyes.
(5) Our feelings for people paint them all in the same colour: if we love them they all seem white to us, if we don't they seem black. But there is black and white in everyone. Look for the black in the people you love, and especially the white in those you don't love. [. . .]

15 August All these days I've been fully fit, got on with *The Corpse* and finished it. And I'm getting further and further involved in it.

Sofya Andreyevna has gone to Moscow and to see friends. The consciousness of the need for love helps me. I notice it with Lyova. Tanya is better. [. . .]

Noted:

(1) Between old and young people, if both are normal, there is a strange misunderstanding. A person of twenty, addressing a five-year-old, knows this difference of understanding, and addresses the child accordingly. But a person of fifty doesn't address one of thirty-five like that, or even one of twenty. But the difference is the same. It's even the same between a person of eighty and one of sixty-five. For this reason it's necessary to respect old age and for old people to respect themselves and not put themselves on the same level as the young – and quarrel. What also contributes to this misunderstanding is the fact that all mankind is advancing, and a young man who has assimilated what is peculiar to his own time, thinks that he himself is in advance of an old man, and that he has nothing to learn from him.

(2) If you want to know yourself, notice what you remember and what you forget. [. . .]

(4) Marriage, of course, is good and necessary for the continuation of the race; but if it is necessary for the continuation of the race, then (a wonderful extract from Nietzsche) parents must feel they have the strength to bring up their children not as parasites, but as servants of men and God. And to do so they must have the strength to live not by other people's labours but by their own, giving more than they take from people. But we have the bourgeois rule that you can only marry when you are sitting firmly on people's necks, i.e. when you *have the means*. It should be just the opposite: only a person who can live and bring up a child *without means* should be able to marry. Only such parents can bring up children well. [. . .]

21 August, Yasnaya Polyana I've been writing the drama, and am altogether dissatisfied with it. There is no awareness that it is God's work, although it has been much revised: the characters have been altered.

Still the same examination and still the same practices. Things are a little better. The old temptation was aroused today.[26] Alexander Petrovich[27] has gone. Yesterday Boulanger and the editor came.[28] Read George Eliot and Ruskin, and appreciated them very much.[29]

The denunciation of unbelief and of the robber kingdom is taking clearer and clearer shape in my mind today. I *must* write about it.

Noted down in my book: [. . .]

(2) Why do people remember one thing, and not remember another? Why do I call Seryozha Andryusha, and Andryusha Seryozha? A character is inscribed in my memory. It's this thing that is inscribed in the memory without a name or designation, this thing that unites various faces, objects and feelings into one – it's this that is the subject of art. That's very important. I must clarify it. [. . .]

(6) A sign of the dissoluteness of our world is the fact that people are not ashamed of wealth, but are proud of it.

(7) It suddenly became clear to me how unjust it is when an old man says: 'I've

lived long enough, it's time to die'. An old man hasn't the right to say that. He is a fruit, a grain of corn. The stalk can be trampled down, but the corn must be eaten. This doesn't mean that an old man need fear death; on the contrary, he needs to live without fear of death. And only then is life easy and useful when you are not afraid of death.
(8) My position in the family is strange. They may love me, but I'm of no use to them, or rather I'm an *encombrant* [in the way]; if I am of use, then I'm of use to them, the same as to everyone. But it's less obvious to my family than to others what use I am to everyone. And so: a prophet is not without honour, save . . .

Today is the 26th Haven't written my diary all these days, although I've been well. Started to write on unbelief.[30] Changed a few things in the drama, and for the better, but nothing attracts me to work, although I like both things.
I'll try to copy up my notes:
(1) Mental work is bad in that until you are attracted to it, you feel yourself to be idle. And you don't feel like taking up physical work, both because it's hard and because it might seem unnatural. I thought that if you can't work either mentally or physically, you should devote all your strength and attention to being loving. It's work of the highest order and it's always possible, even in isolation – thinking about people with love.
(2) There are people who are gifted in the highest degree with moral and artistic feeling, and there are other people who are almost devoid of it. The first, as it were, grasp and know the integral immediately. But the second make complicated calculations which don't bring them to any final conclusions. It's just as if the first had done *all* their calculations *somewhere* before, and are now making use of the results. [. . .]

30 August, Yasnaya Polyana I'm seventy-two. I haven't been able to do any work all these days. I've had no desire to. I've had a few good thoughts – praise and thanks be to God – that's good. [. . .]
I once asked myself: do I believe, do I actually *believe* that the meaning of life is the fulfilment of the will of God, and that that will is to increase the amount of love (harmony) in myself and in the world, and that by increasing and uniting into one all that is loved, I am thereby paving the way for a future life for myself? And I was forced to answer that I don't believe it in such a definite form. But what do I believe in? I asked. And I answered sincerely that I believe that it is necessary to be good: to be humble, to forgive, to love. I believe in that with all my being. [. . .]

7 September, Yasnaya Polyana I've been unwell, but am better today. I'm struggling with myself all the time. Sometimes things are better. Never worse. And that's good. Sonya is at Masha's. Andryusha is leaving. It's terrible to see sixteen fully laden carts.[31] Salomon and Seryozha are here. No work is being done. Nothing is coming of the journal.[32] I've just tried to get on with the drama – it's no good.
Made the following notes: [. . .]

(3) Andryusha is travelling alone in his carriage, and it seems to him (and to almost everyone who looks at him) that if he travels and is dressed in such a magnificent way, he also has the virtues appropriate to such magnificence. I always used to think this myself when well dressed or in a good environment. How harmful luxury is for the spiritual life! The most harmful thing is – it increases the denominator without any foundation. [. . .]

(5) The source of all the disasters which people suffer from is the fact that they want to look ahead to the future: to work for it at first each one for himself, then for his family, then for the people. Man can only do what he ought, and must let life take the course which a higher will or fate wishes. Man walks, God leads.

But why is man given the ability to look ahead to the future? I can't answer that. I see that looking ahead and working with the future in mind is a source of evil, but also that such looking ahead is necessary for life: it's necessary, when sowing seeds, to look ahead to the fact that summer and autumn will come and they will grow, etc. I'll come back to this. [. . .]

(9) Learned explanations for the most part produce the impression that what was clear and comprehensible has become obscure and confused. [. . .]

(11) Thought for my big drama[33] about how to depict a good, decent creature completely lacking in the ability to understand the Christian philosophy of life.

(12) What is now called the Christian religion is the same sort of conventional propriety as the forms of address and signature on letters: 'Dear Sir' and 'Yours faithfully',[34] etc. [. . .]

(14) For my little drama:[35] Fedya says when he's dying: 'Perhaps I was wrong. But what is done is done. Put up with it.'

Today is 22 September, Yasnaya Polyana All this time I've been working badly. And working at something useless. Galya Chertkova wrote to ask if I couldn't give her the two unfinished appeals for her to print. I started to revise them and have been working at this all the time. In one of them I put in something good about Christian peoples having no religion.[36]

I've been in a very bad, unkind frame of mind the whole time. The thought that God is within me no longer helps.

I've been to Masha's and my brother Seryozha's. I felt very good at Andryusha's. I'm looking forward to something. But there's nothing to look forward to except work, good work in God's service, and death. Health poor. Latterly – depression, shivers and fever. At this minute, 11 o'clock in the evening, I'm well. Tanya has left. A nice letter from her today. Sonya is in Moscow.

Made the following notes:

(1) It seems to me that just as there is a critical sexual age and much is decided at that age, so there is a critical spiritual age – about fifty – when a person begins to think seriously about life and to try to solve the problem of its meaning. Usually what is decided at this time is irrevocable. It's a bad thing if it's wrong. [. . .]

Today is 5 October, Yasnaya Polyana Still busy with the same thing. I've sent off one article on work on the land.[37] I'm still working on the other. The cheerful

Boulanger has been. The journal hasn't been abandoned yet. We'll see what happens. Health good. I've been depressed, but was wrong to say that the awareness of God within me doesn't help. It does. I'm reading the Chinese classics.[38] Very important. Wrote ten letters. I've a few notes to write, but there's no time today.

9 October Health continues to be good. I had many visitors – all literary people except Dunayev and his daughter and I. I. Bochkaryov: Veselitskaya (very pleasant), Totomiants, a young Marxist, also pleasant; yesterday Posse and Gorky.[39] They were not so pleasant. State of mind middling. [. . .]

Still finishing *Must It Be So?* I think it will be finished today, and I'll send it off tomorrow.

I'm not reading much. Not much mental exertion at the moment.

During these days the important thing has been that – I don't remember on what occasion, after inwardly reproaching my sons I think – I began to recall all the nasty things I've done. I vividly recalled all, or at least most of them, and was horrified. How much better are the lives of other people and of my sons than my own life. I shouldn't be proud of the past, or even of the present, but should be humble, be ashamed, hide myself – ask forgiveness of people. I wrote '*of God*', and then crossed it out. I'm less to blame before God, than before people. He made me, He allowed me to be like this. My only consolation is that I've never been evil; there are two or three acts on my conscience which tormented me at the time, but I've never been cruel. But still I'm a disgusting, repulsive creature. And how good it is to know this and remember it. You at once become kinder towards people, and that's the main thing, the one thing necessary. [. . .]

(2) Writers and their works have an improper significance and importance ascribed to them, because the press which forms public opinion is in the hands of writers. Only this can explain these strangely serious deliberations by critics about the significance of the heroes of poems and novels . . . It also explains the exaggerated significance attached to art. They all belong to the same clique. [. . .]

(4) A terrible, insoluble problem: how can clever, educated people – Catholics, Orthodox – believe in the absurdities of the teachings of the Church? It can only be explained by hypnosis. In childhood, and later on in moments of depression, people have ideas suggested to them, and they become so firmly implanted that the people are unable to free themselves from them afterwards. When I was reading books about hypnosis last year, I could find no answer in them to the question: how is one to free oneself from hypnosis? I think there is only one way: breaking off relations with the hynotiser, a natural way of life and, above all, an advance into the realm of spiritual self-help.

I must think about this. It's terribly important.

People say: hynotisers should be liable to prosecution for suggesting actions which are illegal. But suggesting all the horrors of the Church's teaching in childhood at an age when people are susceptible to hypnosis, is not only not forbidden, but it is forbidden not to do so. This is terrible. [. . .]

16 October, Yasnaya Polyana Tomorrow, if nothing prevents me, I'm going to Tanya's. All this time I've been well, but today I began to have a stomach-ache. And apart from that I fell down some three days ago and damaged my bad arm. It's better now.

In spite of good health I've done nothing outstanding during these days. I've finished *Must It Be So?* and since sending it off, I haven't started anything else. I'm well, and mentally inactive. Only the day before yesterday, when out walking, I had a lot of good thoughts – only I didn't think them through. Nemirovich-Danchenko came about the drama.[40] But my enthusiasm for it has gone.

Thou Shalt Not Kill is in all the papers, even the Italian ones, with omissions. I'm expecting visitors.[41] [. . .]

Today is 27 October, Kochety I've been at Tanya's for ten days now,[42] and haven't written my diary or anything, although my health is good. Today is not 27, but 28. [. . .]

Thought:
(1) Life is continual creation, i.e. the formation of new, higher forms. When this formation comes to a stop in our view or even goes backwards, i.e. when existing forms are destroyed, this only means a new form is taking shape, invisible to us. We see what is outside us, but we don't see what is within us, we only feel it (if we haven't lost our consciousness, and don't take what is visible and external to be the whole of our life). A caterpillar sees itself shrivel up, but doesn't see the butterfly which flies out of it.
(2) Memory destroys time: it unites things that seem to have taken place separately.
(3) I've just been for a walk and thought: there is a religion, a philosophy, a science, a poetry, an art of the great majority of the people; a religion, although covered over with superstitions, a belief in God as the origin of things, in the indestructibility of life; an unconscious philosophy: of fatalism, of the material nature and the reasonableness of all that exists; a poetry of fairy tales, of true happenings in life, of legends; and an art of the beauty of animals, of the products of labour, of carved shutters and weather-vanes, of songs and dances. And there is a religion of true Christianity: philosophy from Socrates to Amiel; poetry: Tyutchev, Maupassant; art (I can't find any examples from painting) – Chopin in certain works, Haydn. And there is also a religion, a philosophy, a poetry, an art of the cultured masses: religion – the Evangelicals, the Salvation Army; philosophy – Hegel, Darwin, Spencer; poetry – Shakespeare, Dante, Ibsen; art – Raphael, the Decadents, Bach, Beethoven, Wagner. [. . .]
(10) Thought that if I'm to serve people by my writing, the one thing I'm entitled and obliged to do is to expose the lies of the rich, and reveal to the poor the delusion practised on them.

30 October In the morning I began writing an epistle to the Chinese.[43] Wrote the beginning of it – briefly and badly. [. . .]

7 November, Moscow I.I.A.

Was very depressed until I realised that there is only one thing I need to do: I don't need to prepare myself for a future life, but to prepare for a future life by living this life well. [. . .]
(2) Thought about three articles: (1) about the letter to the Chinese, (2) about the fact that everything is based on murder,⁴⁴ and (3) about the fact that we quasi-Christians have no religion.⁴⁵ Had a lot of good thoughts about this when walking today:
(1) About the might of a savage, tempered by patriarchal hospitality; (2) about the terrible might of our world, not tempered by anything; (3) about the fact that historical fate forced the acceptance of Christianity, and (4) above all about the fact that technology – gunpowder, weapons, telegraphs – provide a semblance of peace, and constantly conceal murder or the threat of it.

12 November, Moscow (Morning.) Health very good. I'm not writing anything; I'm studying Confucius and feel very well. I'm storing up spiritual strength. I want to write down how I now understand *The Great Teaching* and *The Teaching of the Mean*.⁴⁶ [. . .]
(2) Was amazed by the news that Princess Vyazemskaya,⁴⁷ apparently the quintessence of aristocracy – horses à la Daumon and French prattle – has nineteen inns to her name in the Tambov province, bringing in 2,000 roubles each. And people say there's nothing to write about, and they write about adulteries. [. . .]

14 November, Moscow Received bad news from Masha.⁴⁸ Wrote letters to Seryozha, Masha, Marya Alexandrovna. I'm studying Confucius, and everything else seems worthless. It's going quite well, I think. The main thing is that the teaching that one must pay particular attention to oneself when one is alone has a powerful and salutary influence on me. If only it would stay as fresh as it is now.

18 November, Moscow [. . .] Heard talk about Lyova's work and had a glance at his book and couldn't overcome my disgust and annoyance.⁴⁹ I must learn.

I'm writing my diary again in the morning, 19 November, Moscow. In the morning, because I can't do anything. I'm trying to get used to it and not grumble. The work inside me is going on, and so I must not only not grumble, but rejoice. Man is wonderfully organised. Either you can work here, or you can prepare for work there. But the best work here is when you prepare for work there.
Walked a lot with Mikhail Sergeyevich.⁵⁰ I'm beginning quite simply to love him. Went to Boulanger's. He's very ill. Talked with Filippov⁵¹ about Marxism. [. . .]

23 November, Moscow [. . .] Confucius' teaching about paying particular attention to oneself when one is alone continues to bear fruit.
Thought during this time:
(1) The song from the Caucasus,⁵² (2) I've forgotten it all, but there was something, (3) I only remember:

(1) We, the wealthy classes, ruin the workers, we keep them doing dirty, non-stop work while we enjoy leisure and luxury. We don't give them the opportunity, oppressed as they are by work, to produce the spiritual flowers and fruits of life: poetry, science, religion. We take it upon ourselves to give them all this, and we give them pseudo-poetry, 'Why did you hurry away to the fateful Caucasus', etc.; pseudo-science – jurisprudence, Darwinism, philosophy, the history of the tsars – and pseudo-religion – Church dogma. What a terrible sin. If only we hadn't sucked them dry, they would have developed a poetry and a science and a teaching about life.

I feel unwell now.

24 November, Moscow I.I.A. Alive and writing. Seem to feel a bit stronger. Received letters from Masha and Seryozha. Wept tears of joy. How blessed is misfortune.[53] [. . .]

26 November, Moscow Morning. For more than a month now, since my move to Tanya's on 18 October, I've written nothing; it seems to me at least that I *can't* work; I've no enthusiasm, no thoughts, no belief in the importance of my thoughts or in the possibility of expressing them coherently. I rejoice only that this doesn't prevent me from working in the moral sphere, and, I think, not entirely unsuccessfully: I feel no ill will. *Success in being good is good for the additional reason that one can't be proud or boast about it, or even be comforted by it. Such success is only success when one doesn't notice it oneself.*

I'm reading the Gospels in Dutch[54] and many passages strike me afresh. Thus, I was awfully struck by the Sermon on the Mount. [. . .]

28 November, Moscow Morning. Still the same apathy. Read Novikov's article[55] yesterday and was very impressed by it: I remembered what I'd forgotten: the life of the people – need, humiliation, and our guilt. Oh, if only God would bid me express all I feel about this. I must give up my drama *The Corpse*. And if I write anything, it must be the other drama, and the continuation of *Resurrection*. [. . .]

1 December, Moscow [. . .]
(1) What a terrible quality self-assurance, self-satisfaction, is. It freezes a man, as it were: he becomes covered with a crust of ice through which there can be neither growth, nor communication with others, and this crust of ice gets thicker and thicker. These thoughts were prompted by my relations with many people: they are all – it's a terrible thing to say – swine before whom one oughtn't to cast pearls. [. . .]

8 December During this time I received a letter from Canada about wives wanting to join their husbands in the Yakut province, and wrote a letter to the Tsar, but haven't sent it yet.[56] [. . .]

A nice letter from Masha. How I love her, and how joyful is an atmosphere of love, and how oppressive is the opposite. Thought during this time:

(1) Any philosophical or religious teaching is only a teaching about what one ought to do. And what if we measure the teaching of Nietzsche by this yardstick? [. . .]

Today is the 15th One thing that happened is that Davydov proved of my letter to the Tsar and undertook to send it.[57] I'm trying in my own consciousness to separate myself off from this affair, so that the *affair* should be the object of concern. [. . .]
(2) Walked past a bookshop and saw *The Kreutzer Sonata*. And I recalled: I wrote *The Kreutzer Sonata* and *The Power of Darkness* and even *Resurrection* without any thought of preaching to people, of being of use to them, and yet all of them, especially *The Kreutzer Sonata*, have been of great use. Will it be the same with *The Corpse* too? [. . .]
(4) Historical materialism is only an echo of physiological materialism, already demolished by the materialist scientists themselves (Claude Bernard, Du Bois-Reymond[58] and someone else). It has been proved that life cannot be reduced to mechanical processes. And if there is an x in life, there must be x to the x degree (xx) in the history of *the life of lives*. But since people devoid of religion become stupid and brutalised, they think that xx is far simpler and more comprehensible than God. The main thing is that on the basis of xx it's convenient to indulge in pseudo-scientific chatter.
(5) Thought about the fact that Schopenhauer's *Parerga und Paralipomena* is far more powerful than his systematic exposition.[59]

I don't need to (and I've no time to) – but above all I don't need to write out a system. My view of the world will become clear from what I write down here, and if any people need it, they will make use of it.
(6) Sasha just said something rude. I was offended, but then I tried hard to summon up love, and it all blew over. How wonderful it is the way love unties all knots.
(7) A thought that is very important and dear to me. People usually think that morality is nurtured on culture, like a flower. It's just the opposite. Culture only develops when there is no religion, and therefore no morality (Greece, Rome, Moscow). It's like a luxuriant tree, from which an ignorant gardener expects an abundant crop of fruit because it has a lot of splendid branches. But it has a lot of splendid branches only because it hasn't, and won't have any fruit. Or like a barren calf.

19 December, Moscow I've been unwell these last four days and very weak. I'm better today. Lyova came and started a conversation about his writing. I offended him by speaking the truth. It was bad. I should have done it more gently and kindly. [. . .]
(2) An artist, in order to produce an effect on other people, must be a seeker, his work must be a search. If he has found everything and knows everything and teaches or deliberately amuses, he produces no effect. Only if he is seeking does the spectator, the listener or the reader join with him in his search. [. . .]
(3) The two most terrible plagues of our time: Church Christianity, or rather the

dogmatic, supernatural Christianity instilled into *people* from childhood and maintained throughout their lives by hypnosis – and materialism, physiological, anthropological and, above all, historical, i.e. the conviction that everything proceeds automatically according to the laws of mechanics, physics, chemistry, biology and even psychology (in the sense of materialistic psychology), and therefore all efforts to be good or do good are vain and pointless. And this materialism lies in wait for people once they are freed from dogmatic Christianity. No sooner are they freed from the immoral lies of the Church than they fall into the even worse lies of materialism.

(4) Determinism is fatalism just the same, only stupid fatalism, because it is without God.

(5) They used to say *cherchez la femme*, but there is no point in searching now: clearly all disasters, or an enormous proportion of them, are due to the dissoluteness of women. There are some plants whose flowers are particularly harmful, but whose fruits are harmless and useful. Women are like that. They are harmless only when they are engrossed in motherhood. Aferwards they are terrible, and they are only harmless when controlled by the habit of modesty, virginity or the *vénérabilité* of old age. I vividly imagined a world in which all young women were occupied with motherhood, the very young with preparing for it and the old with assisting with it, and it became obvous to me how much grief and suffering *such a world* would be spared from knowing. (*All this is unclear* and not right.) [. . .]

Today is 20 December, Moscow [. . .] Read the Buddhist Suttas.[60] Very good. [. . .]

Today is 29 December, Moscow Lyova's child has died. I'm very sorry for them. Grief always has its spiritual reward and enormous profit. Grief calls – God has visited you and remembered you . . . Tanya gave birth to a stillborn baby, and is very good and sensible. Sonya is at Yasnaya. Ilya is here. He's astonishingly childish. [. . .]

Must note down the following:

(1) Read about some amazing machines which are a substitute for human toil and suffering. But it's just like inventing a complete apparatus, by means of which one can flog and kill without toil and effort. It's simpler not to flog and not to kill. It's the same with machines which make beer, wine, velvet, mirrors, etc. The whole complexity of our urban life lies in the fact that people think up and accustom themselves to harmful requirements, and then use all their mental energies to satisfy them or reduce the harm caused by satisfying them: all medicine, hygiene, artificial lighting, and all our harmful urban life. *Before speaking about the goodness of satisfying one's requirements, one ought to decide what requirements constitute goodness.* That's very important.

(2) Read Nietzsche's *Zarathustra*, and his sister's note about how he wrote it,[61] and am absolutely convinced that he was completely mad when he wrote it, and mad not in a metaphorical sense, but in the straightforward and most exact sense: incoherence, jumping from one idea to another, comparisons with no indication of

what is being compared, beginnings of ideas with no endings, leaping from one idea to another for contrast or consonance, and all against the background of the *pointe* of his madness, his *idée fixe*, that by denying all the higher principles of human life and thought he is proving his own superhuman genius. What will society be like if such a madman, and an evil madman, is acknowledged as a teacher? [...]
(5) It's amusing, the opinion people have that non-resistance to evil by force or paying back good for evil are very good rules for individuals, but can't be applied to the state. As though the state isn't a combination of people, but something separate from people. Oxygen has such and such properties. But they are only the properties of the atoms and molecules of oxygen. But oxygen in big compounds acquires quite different, opposite properties. This opinion alone that states have properties which are the opposite of human ones is the most obvious proof of the obsolete nature of the state as a form of government.
(6) People talk about the equality of men and women. There is complete equality in an immaterial sense, but not in a sexual one. In a sexual (animal) sense, the difference is enormous: the male is always ready for any female, because sexual intercourse doesn't disturb his activity: deer, wolves, hares, drones. There are always a lot of males running after one female. But the female isn't always ready. But when she is ready, she gives herself up entirely, and is fit for nothing else when she is producing offspring. There are many conclusions to be drawn from this. [...]

31 December, Moscow I'm still not writing, and am in a very low state of morale. I've just received a letter from a gentleman who is organising a library.[62] He seems to be reproaching me with mercenariness in selling my works: a tax on the poor, etc.... And I became terribly offended that he should suspect and reprove me without knowing my attitude towards this. Furthermore, I felt hatred towards him, and was at a loss how to act: whether to say nothing, or to tell him to approach my wife at the warehouse. And all this was bad. I wanted to rise above it and couldn't, until I suspected that it was all a question of my attitude towards him. I mustn't hate him, but love him: must explain his mistake to him, help him. Yes, only love unties all knots. Thought: [...]
(2) Thought today that the main unnatural feature of dramatic works is the fact that all the persons speak for an equally long time, and people listen to them. In real life this is not so: every person is able to speak and listen according to the nature of his character and his oratorical skill. I wanted to revise my drama accordingly. But evidently my writing career is over. If so, that's all right.

1901

1 January, Moscow   I'm writing in the morning because I'm doing nothing except reading. Read *Six Systems of Indian Philosophy*[1] and a report by the Finance Minister.[2] And I remain indifferent to them both. [...]

9 January, Moscow   I've written nothing all this time except some worthless letters. I've been ill recently, and am still not well now. Letters from Chertkov about the misuse of money and reproaches for intending to take part in the journal.[3] [...]

19 January, Moscow   All this time I've been ill and weak. On the good days granted me I wrote a long letter to Serebrennikov in Nizhny.[4] Mental state quite good, if only there was less empty talk.
  Noted during this time:
(1) People live by their own thoughts or other people's thoughts, their own feelings or other people's feelings (i.e. understand other people's feelings, are guided by them). The very best person is the one who lives primarily by his own thoughts and other people's feelings; the very worst sort of person is the one who lives by other people's thoughts and his own feelings. The whole difference between people stems from various combinations of these four bases and motives for doing things.
  There are people who have almost no thoughts, either their own or other people's, and no feelings of their own, and who live only by other people's feelings: they are self-sacrificing fools and saints. There are people who live only by their own feelings – they are animals. There are people who live only by their own thoughts – they are wise men and prophets; there are those who live only by other people's thoughts – they are learned fools. From various permutations of the strength of these properties stems the whole complex music of characters. [...]
(5) A man should raise himself to the level of a woman's chastity; a woman shouldn't lower herself to the level of a man's debauchery, as happens now. [...]
(9) We all – and this is not a simile, but is almost a description of reality – we all grow up and are reared in a robbers' den, and only when we are grown up and look about us do we understand where we are and what we are taking advantage of. And then we begin to have various attitudes to this situation: some join the robbers and rob, others think they are not to blame if they take advantage of robbery without approving of it and even trying to stop it, others again are indignant and want to destroy the den, but they are weak and few in number. So what must be done? [...]

6 February, Moscow   What a terribly long time since I've written my diary. All this time I haven't been altogether well, or rather, I'm getting older and closer to death. During this time I've written nothing except some unimportant letters. I've been a little less strict in my attention to myself, but I can't complain, I maintain my composure and good-will. Tanya is due to arrive today. Misha's wedding has taken place. I'm afraid she is even more irreligious than most women.[5] But perhaps it's quite the opposite. God grant it may be so.

I've made quite a lot of notes, and, it seemed, important ones.

(1) Above all one must try to destroy the delusion, continually upheld by the government, that everything it does, it does for the good order and wellbeing of its subjects. Everything it does, it does either for itself (robbing its victims), or in order to *leur donner le change* [put them on the wrong track] and assure them that it does it for their sake. [. . .]

(6) All things designed to flatter the five external senses such as a beautiful house, beautiful household equipment and above all beautiful clothes, especially women's, are the things which inflame lust. Or things like music, perfume, gourmet food, smooth surfaces pleasant to the touch. The brilliance, light and beauty of the sun, the trees, the grass and the sky, even the sight of the human body without artificial ornaments, the singing of birds, the scent of flowers, the taste of plain food and fruit or the feel of natural substances do not arouse lust. It is aroused by electric light, adornments, fine clothes, music, perfume, gourmet dishes and smooth surfaces.

Today is 8 February, Moscow I understood yesterday for the first time, and understand from the reserved, cold and wily *NN*, how and why he and all those who don't share a Christian view of life, hate and are bound to hate not me, but what I profess. But to divorce me from what I profess is too difficult. [. . .]

(9) [. . .] People usually say: 'Why impose your religious convictions either on adults or on children? Let everyone form his own.' What a strange confusion of ideas! To impose – i.e. to deprive a person of the possibility of seeing and knowing anything else, as churchmen do – is of course bad, but to hand on both to children and to adults all that human thought has evolved in the field of religion is not only not bad, but necessary. Why, if I teach a child or an adult that the sum of the squares on the sides adjacent is equal to the square of the hypotenuse, or that electricity has two poles and acts according to such and such laws am I not coercing; but if I teach that people have a spiritual essence which is immortal, and that one ought to behave towards others as one would wish them to behave towards oneself, I *am* coercing? Such a strange opinion only exists because it is usual to consider the only important and necessary fundamental science – the science of religion and morality – not a science, but something arbitrary and unimportant. [. . .]

(11) I had a good fresh think again about what time is. And I felt its reality with my whole being, or at least the reality of what it is based on. It is based on the movement of life, on the process of the expansion of frontiers, which is going on incessantly in man. Time itself may be a category of thought, but without the movement of life it would not exist. Time is the relationship of the movement of one's own life to the movement of other creatures. Does it not move slowly at the beginning of life and quickly at the end because the expansion of frontiers is taking

place with ever-increasing speed? The measure of the speed is the awareness of this expansion. In childhood I advance one *vershok* while the sun traverses its annual cycle and the moon its twelve cycles. Since the measure is within me I actually say that it is quick.

The speed of this expansion is analagous to the fall of an object – in inverse proportion to the square of the distance from death. [. . .]

11 February, Moscow I'm alive, but very weak, and above all, bad. I struggle, but can't conquer ill feelings towards people. I don't yield to them, but don't overcome them either. I'm reading Chicherin's book *Science and Religion*.[6] The point of view is correct, but the self-assurance, opaqueness of expression and preconceived ideas make it superficial and *sans portée* [without significance]. A mass of letters which I can't answer. The one good thing about my state of mind is that I look on sufferings and the approach of death not only without grumbling, but sometimes with pleasure. [. . .]

Read the speech at the agricultural congress.[7] Pompous, empty, stupid and self-satisfied. We all want to help the people; but we are beggars who are fed and clothed by them. What can beggars give to the rich? This must be understood once and for all, and then our attitude to the people will be corrected. Only stand aside, you beggars who latch on to the people, don't interfere with them, like the beggars in Italy, and they will do everything; not the stupid things you propose for them, but things which you have no conception of.

I thought further that I must put aside the appeal to the Chinese. It can be entitled simply: *A Godless Time* or *The New Fall of Rome*. And I can start simply by pointing to the lack of religion.

Almost a month has passed. Today is 19 March. I've written nothing all this time except an appeal to the Tsar and his aides,[8] and some alterations, all bad ones, to *Hadji Murat* which I took up again reluctantly.[9]

During this time there was my strange excommunication from the Church,[10] and the expressions of sympathy caused by it, and then the business of the students which assumed a public nature and made me write an appeal to the Tsar and his aides and a programme.[11] I tried to be guided only by the wish to serve, and not personal satisfaction. I haven't sent it yet. As soon as it's ready I'll send it. I've been ill all the time with pains in the legs and body and stomach. I'm better today.

Wrote the following in my notebook:
(1) How necessary it is to remember and not forget what was said by Coleridge [. . .] 'He who loves Christianity better than the Truth proceeds to love his Church or sect better than Christianity and ends in loving himself better than all.'[12]

This is the absolutely essential answer to those who are afraid to repudiate the divinity of Christ.
(2) Those who have the people and the good of the people in mind, including myself, are quite wrong to ascribe importance to student riots. They are really strife between oppressors, between fully fledged oppressors and those who still only want to be such. [. . .]

(6) Women have only two feelings: love for men and love for children, and those which derive from these feelings, such as love of fine clothes for the sake of men and of money for the sake of children. All the rest is cerebral, imitation of men, means of attracting men, pretence, fashion.
(7) No sooner does religious feeling diminish in society, than the power of women increases. In a completely religious world they are powerless; in a world without religion like ours all the power is in their hands.
(8) An atheist says: 'I don't know God, I don't need this concept.' To say this is the same as saying to a man sailing across the sea in a boat that he doesn't know the sea and doesn't need this concept. The infinity which surrounds you and on which you are moving, the laws of this infinity, your attitude towards it – this is what God is. To say that you can't see Him is to act like an ostrich. [. . .]
(12) The longer I live, the more horrified I am by the consequences of alcohol and nicotine. Not to mention the obvious and crude consequences of the increase of crime, illness and terrible loss of life, these narcotics stifle in people (it's particularly noticeable in our circle) the highest thoughts and feelings, the most important and necessary flower of reason. Because of this you see people who can serve, write books, produce works of art, but cannot understand the most important thing – the meaning of life – and even think that it's quite unnecessary to do so. What spiritual eunuchs. And their name is legion. I'm surrounded by them.

Today is 28 March, Moscow The day before yesterday the appeals were sent off to the Tsar and others. During this time I wrote a reply to my unknown correspondents,[13] and a bit of *Hadji Murat*. Only made one note – something that has become absolutely clear – that our whole Orthodox faith is a magic antidote to fear. And the root of it is – belief in the miraculous. A good letter from Vlasov.[14] Yesterday evening, as I sat on my own, I vividly imagined death: I looked in that direction, or rather, pictured to myself the whole change awaiting me more clearly than ever before, and felt a little apprehensive, but good.

31 March, Moscow Morning. I think I've finished *A Reply to the Synod*. Nothing from Petersburg. Wrote a short address to the Petersburg writers.[15] Continue to receive greetings and abuse. Health good. Wanted to finish *Hadji Murat*, but didn't feel like working. A letter from Chertkov. Replied to him. Nothing interesting.

Haven't written my diary for nine days. Today is 8 April, Moscow. I've been sick a few times. Finished the reply; wrote some letters today. I've done nothing else. Collected material for *The Notes*.[16] Still continue to receive addresses and greetings.
   Noted: [. . .]
(5) The only happy periods of my life have been those when I gave up my whole life to the service of people. They were: the schools, service as a mediator, famine relief, and religious aid.
   Yesterday I read about and saw pictures of the tortures in French disciplinary battalions[17] and sobbed with pity both for those who suffer, and more so for those who deceive and corrupt.

22 April, Moscow Haven't written my diary for a long time. I'm still ill. Pains in my arms and legs, and weakness. I must get used to living, i.e. to serving, even as a sick man – i.e. until death. The *Reply* is having a good effect, I think. But it's not my business. I've written nothing. But I must: (1) answer letters; (2) write to Posha about education;[18] (3) write to the soldiers;[19] (4) write about the lack of religion;[20] (5) finish *Hadji Murat*. All these things are as good as ready, but they must be done. And I'm not doing anything.

Made the folowing notes: [. . .]
(7) There are three branches of pedagogics because there are three kinds of thinking: (1) logical, (2) experimental and (3) artistic. Science, learning, is nothing else but assimilating what clever people before us have thought. Clever people always thought in these three ways: either they made logical deductions from a situation – generated thoughts: mathematics and the mathematical sciences; or they isolated an observed phenomenon from all others and made deductions about the causes and consequences of phenomena; or they described what they saw, knew and imagined. More briefly: (1) they thought, (2) they observed and (3) they expressed. And so there are three kinds of sciences: (1) mathematical, (2) experimental and (3) languages. [. . .]

7 May, Moscow We want to leave tomorrow. Health a bit better.
(1) The type of people who always want to be right is a terrible one. They are ready to condemn innocent people, saints, God himself, just in order to be right. [. . .]
(4) Dreamed about a type of old man whom Chekhov forestalled me in describing.[21] The old man was particularly good because he was almost a saint, but at the same time given to drink and bad language. I clearly understood for the first time the force which types acquire from boldly superimposed shadows. I'll do this with Hadji Murat and Marya Dmitriyevna.[22] [. . .]
(7) Thought about the requirements of the people and came to think that the main one is ownership of land; that if it could be decreed that there should be no private ownership of land, but that land should belong to those who cultivate it, this would be the most secure guarantee of freedom. More secure than *habeas corpus*. For even *habeas corpus* isn't a physical guarantee, but only a moral one – namely that a man feels himself entitled to defend his house. Equally so, and even more so, he should feel himself entitled to defend his own land – the land by which he feeds his family.

Dear Tanya is here. Received a letter from Chertkov about the freedom of the press and I'm afraid my reply was unfriendly.[23] Wrote a long letter about education.

10 May, Yasnaya Polyana It's two days since I arrived. Health better, but not completely. Haven't written either day. I've been walking and thinking. Solitude is pleasant. [. . .]

11 May, Yasnaya Polyana Evening. I'm copying up what is in my notebook:
(1) Must include in my foreword to *Büttnerbauer* that Orlov has something to say

and knows how to say it.²⁴ And what he has to say is that he loves the peasant, the person who feeds us. This is why people take notice of Gorky. We all know that tramps are human beings and brothers, but we know it in theory; but he has shown us them full-scale, with love for them, and has infected us with this love. Their talk is inaccurate and exaggerated, but we all forgive him for having broadened our love. [. . .]

(8) Women lie like children, without noticing it. To achieve their aim they need to lie, and they are so occupied with achieving their aim that they don't notice their lies.

(9) Moreover, they have no religion except the one instilled into them.

(10) In my search for the cause of evil in the world I've been delving deeper and deeper. At first I imagined the cause of evil to be evil people, then the rotten structure of society, then the violence which upholds this rotten structure, then the participation in violence of the people who suffer from it (the army), then the lack of religion in these people, and finally I became convinced that the root of it all is religious education. And therefore, in order to eliminate evil, there is no need to replace people, to change the structure, to eliminate violence, to dissuade people from participating in violence or even to refute false and expound true religion, but only to educate children in the true religion. [. . .]

Today, I think, is 13 May, Yasnaya Polyana. I'm writing in the morning. I haven't been able to work for two days. Sonya and I are alone. I feel well. I'm thinking about this and that, but can't find the forms and subdivisions of the subjects; apart from works of fiction there are: (1) on religion and the lack of it, (2) on education, (3) on the requirements of the people – land (*habeas corpus*), (4) on the notorious fact that power is only upheld by the army. [. . .]

Today is 8 June. Haven't written my diary for almost a month. Health a bit better. Relations with all the family are good.

I'm writing *To the Working People*.²⁵ Sasha is diligently copying it out. I've noted about sixteen points. I'll write out at least a few of them now:

(1) Physical work without overtaxing one's strength produces a good-natured desire to communicate with people. I was walking past the watchman. He was ploughing, his dogs jumped up at me, but he still boasted about them in a good-natured way. [. . .]

Today is 9 June, Yasnaya Polyana. I want to note:

(1) One of the most harmful things, especially in view of the goal which people want to achieve, is the teaching of art, i.e. the models which are considered best, the taste which prevails. Nothing holds back the development of art so much. Surely we know what monstrous tastes have been considered the highest, and what disgraceful things – models.

16 July, Yasnaya Polyana Haven't written my diary for more than a month. Was seriously ill from 27 June, and before that was unwell for a couple of weeks. My illness was one long spiritual holiday: heightened spirituality, and calmness at the approach of death, and expressions of love from all sides . . .

Finished *The Only Way*. Not particularly good, too weak.

I'm noting down things noted a long time ago. [. . .]

(3) In order to be heard by people one has to speak from Golgotha, to imprint the truth by suffering, or still better by death. [. . .]

(6) The Chinese say: 'Wisdom consists in knowing that you know what you know – and that you know that you don't know what you don't know'; I would add to that: 'There is still greater wisdom in knowing what needs to be known and what can be left unknown, what it is possible not to know, and what to know first and what to know later.' [. . .]

(9) Women are only known by their husbands. Only husbands see them behind the scenes. For that reason Lessing said what all husbands say: 'There is only one bad woman, and that is my wife'. But in front of other people they dissemble so cleverly that nobody sees them as they really are, especially when they are young.

(1) Women's main aptitude is for guessing what role pleases what person, and playing the role that pleases.

(11) Motherhood is their real life and their great concern, but they imagine that motherhood interferes with their life; i.e. they dissemble, to suit the taste of the men they have chosen. [. . .]

18 August, Yasnaya Polyana   Haven't written my diary for exactly a month. During this time I've written two sets of notes – they aren't bad.[26] I also want to write about religion and the lack of it, and a letter to Nicholas.[27] Then I can relax over something literary. Although a Christian drama is certainly service to God.

During this time it's been decided we should go to the Crimea.[28] I'm rather pleased about it. My health is much weaker: my heart is weaker. But I'm improving and, unfortunately, I've lost the *élan* I had during my illness. Masha is here and so is Mashenka.[29] I'm continuing my inner work without much success, but I don't despair. 'Unless we serve God in every voluntary act of our lives we don't serve Him at all,' says Ruskin.[30] That's what one must do and remember.

Noted during this time: [. . .]

(6) You often hear young people saying: 'I don't want to live by someone else's brains, I'll think things out for myself.' But why think out what has already been thought out? Take what is available, and go on from there. Therein lies mankind's strength. [. . .]

[10 October] It's terrible to say so: I haven't written my diary for almost two months. Today is 10 October, *Gaspra, on the south coast*.[31]

My health is still just as bad. Sometimes worse, sometimes better, but not much. My old state of health has gone for good. [. . .]

Arrived here on 8 September with Boulanger, Masha and Kolya.[32] Sasha is very dear. Seryozha is here now.[33] My inner work seems to be progressing a little.

Adam Vasilyevich has died. And a very good death.[34]

I've been working all this time on *Religion*.[35] I think it's progressing, but I've become mentally weaker, I can't work so long.

Noted during this time:
(1) It's difficult to live for God by oneself in the midst of people who don't even understand the idea, and live only for themselves. How glad one is in such a situation to have the help of people of the same belief. [. . .]
(10) One of the most common and serious mistakes people make in their judgements is that they consider to be good the things that they like. [. . .]
(13) Life is a serious business! Oh, if only one could always remember that, especially in moments of decision! [. . .]
(16) Entrepreneurs (capitalists) rob the people in that they are intermediaries between the workers and the suppliers of the instruments and means of labour, and merchants likewise rob the people in that they are intermediaries between consumers and vendors. Similarly state robbery is organised under the pretext of mediation between wrongdoers and the wrongly done by. But the most terrible deceit of all is the deceit of the intermediaries between God and men. [. . .]

11 October, Gaspra I.I.A.

Today is 24 October, Gaspra. The words I.I.A. acquire more and more significance. During this time I've been writing *On Religion*. Health still *chancelante* [shaky], going downhill. Still have to write about the revolutionary brochure received from Ivan Mikhaylovich,[36] and about *the right* to have a relationship with God, apropos of the speech by Stakhovich.[37] Yesterday I had a bad stomach. Today, especially now this evening, I'm in a very bad mood which I can't get over. Chetverikov and Sasha Dunayev are here,[38] both drunk. And the whole company [four or five words erased] are very alien to me. Sasha[39] is very dear. [. . .]

29 November, Gaspra Haven't written my diary again for nearly two months. I've been unwell all the time. And I'm seldom any better. The main thing is rheumatic pains and weakness. I think since the 14th I've begun to have arsenic injections. Today I feel more cheerful, and so I'm writing my diary. Tanya has had another stillborn child; she has taken it well.

I think I've finished *On Religion*. As always, I doubt the importance and goodness of this work, but with more justification now, I think, than on previous occasions.

Things are well at home. I don't see much of Masha. I'm glad that I find both Gorky and Chekhov pleasant, especially the former.[40] Good letters from a member of the court,[41] and it was pleasant to get to know Mikhaylov and the Stundists better.[42]

I've only made a few notes. This is what I noted:
(1) When a stream of water flows evenly, it seems as if it's standing still. And it seems just the same with one's own life and with life generally. But you notice that the stream isn't standing still, but is flowing, when it gets weaker, and especially when it becomes a trickle; and it's just the same with life.
(2) When I am dying, I would like to be asked whether I continue to understand life as I used to understand it, as a growing nearer to God, an expansion of love. If I'm unable to speak, I'll close my eyes if the answer if yes, and raise them upwards if it's no. [. . .]

(4) They say that women love courage and beauty, or the people who love these things. That's quite untrue. They give themselves to those who are sure they will do so. And having given themselves, they justify themselves by loving those they have given themselves to. [. . .]
(9) People differ again in that some think first and then speak and act, while others speak and act first, and then think.
(10) Another difference between people is that some are aware of others first and then themselves, while others are aware of themselves first – I was going to say, and then others – but for the most part such people are limited to an awareness of themselves alone. This is a terrible difference. [. . .]
(12) All people are corked up, and that is terrible. But they are corked up for one person and open for another. Every person has an opening through which he can apprehend the truth, but the truth is not transmitted to him from the side where the opening is. The only way is to pour out truth into the world *if you have it in you*, and it will find an opening. [. . .]

Today, I think, is 1 December. [. . .] Our folk have gone to Uchan-Su.[43] I'm alone at home with Tanya, and out of sorts. A wonderful chapter in Polenz's novel[44] spurred me on very much to write – but in vain. Once again I can see death, better, nearer and clearer.

26 December, Gaspra Things seemed to get better for me, then worse again. I went to Yalta for the night and was taken ill there with heart trouble. Spent a week at Masha's. I'm beginning to get well again. Dear Boulanger has been. He left today. I've finished *On Religion*. But I'll probably revise it again. I've been writing about religious tolerance for about ten days, and am bored with it. It's too unimportant. But I'm not very keen even on writing the letter to the Tsar.

Had one or two thoughts: [. . .]
(3) The most immediate task of our lives is so clearly apparent. It is to replace a life based on struggle and violence by one based on love and reasonable agreement. And the enormous material which needs to be spiritually worked up for this purpose still lies untouched within the working people of all races and beliefs.
(4) Every person is chained to his loneliness and condemned to death. 'You must live for some reason alone, with your desires unsatisfied, grow old and die.' It's terrible! The only salvation is to free oneself from one's I, to love someone else. Then you have two throws instead of one, more chances of winning. And as a person strives in that direction he can't help loving people. But people are mortal, and if there is more grief than joy in life, it's the same in other people's lives too. And so the situation is just as desperate. The only consolation is that company in distress makes trouble less. The only complete salvation would be love for an immortal being, for God. Is that possible? [. . .]

1902

Today is 22 January, Gaspra   Almost the whole time I've been ill, i.e. getting closer to death. And I've lived quite well. During this time I wrote a letter to the Tsar and sent it via Nikolay Mikhaylovich.¹ Both the letter and he himself are in Petersburg today. I don't know whether he'll hand it over. An excellent book by Mazzini, and Ruskin's thoughts.²

Grauberger³ came today and said quite rightly that for a Christian in our time there is only one decent abode – prison. [. . .]

23 January   Still weak. Bertenson came.⁴ Of course it's nothing serious. Some wonderful verses:

> The old man started to groan,
> The old man started to cough,
> It's time for the old man to get under the shroud,
> Under the shroud and into the grave.⁵

How wonderful is the language of the people. Picturesque and moving and serious.

Thought:
There is no more obvious proof of the false path which science finds itself on than its confidence that it will find *everything* out.

5 May   Haven't written my diary for three and a half months. I've been seriously ill and still haven't recovered yet. I want to write down what I thought and noted during this time:
5 February.⁶ [. . .]
(2) One person commits the most terrible crime and suffers agony, and is aware that it was bad and that he could have avoided doing it. Another person commits an apparently trivial immoral act and justifies himself and lives happily and peacefully. The first person's crime only produces material evil, which often turns into spiritual good for himself and others. But the second person's act produces incalculable disasters both for himself – by leaving the way clear for other bad acts – and for others – by his example of peace of mind and complacency in his evildoing. [. . .]

February (1) *De mortuis aut bene aut nihil* [Either speak well of the dead or say nothing] – what a false, pagan rule! Speak well or say nothing about the living. How much suffering this would save people from, and how easy it is. But about the dead, why not speak ill as well? In our world, on the contrary, there is an established rule: to speak only terribly exaggerated praises, and consequently only lies about the dead, with obituaries and jubilees. And this does terrible harm to people, blurring and rendering indistinguishable the concepts of good and evil.

(2) It's necessary to suffer a serious illness in order to be sure what life is: the weaker the body, the stronger becomes one's spiritual activity. [. . .]
21 February. [. . .]
(3) Peaceful deaths under the influence of the Church's rites are like death under the influence of morphine. [. . .]
8 March.
(1) Belinsky, with no religion, is on the bottom floor. The religious Gogol is on the top.[7] [. . .]
21 March. [. . .]
(3) There are three fashionable philosophers I can recall: Hegel, Darwin and now Nietzsche. The first tried to justify everything that exists; the second tried to put man on the same footing as an animal and to justify struggle, i.e. the evil in men; the third contends that what it is in human nature that resists evil is merely wrong upbringing, error. I don't know how much further one can go. [. . .]
(9) Life, whatever it is, is good, there is no higher good. If we say that life is evil, it is only in comparison with another, better or imaginary life. There may be evil in life, but life itself cannot be evil. Good can exist only in life. And so one can't say that the absence of life can be good.

Health can only exist in the body, and so one can't say that the absence of the body is health.
10 April, Gaspra [. . .]
(3) (*To the Working People*).[8] You have no right to demand an eight-hour day, etc. But you do have an inalienable right, even a duty towards your children, to demand land for your sustenance. [. . .]
(5) Is not all pleasure – recollection? All that is recollection gives joy.
(6) People say: 'End the existing regime and everything will perish.' It's like saying: 'The river will thaw and everything will perish. No, ships will go along it and real life will begin. [. . .]
(12) The poorer people are (tramps, etc.) and the more despised, the freer they are, and vice versa. And the richer and more important they are (the Tsar), the more they are slaves. [. . .]
(15) In the past irreligious people were enemies of society, now they are its leaders. [. . .]

Today is 22 May, Gaspra. The typhus is over.[9] But I'm still in bed. I'm waiting for a third illness and death. I'm in a very bad mood. There are a few notes to copy in but I'm putting them off. I'll pray now. And prayer, as always, helps.

23, 24 May, Gaspra Was very weak yesterday. Better today. Wrote a little of *To the Working People*. It's beginning to take shape. They wanted to move me out of doors, but there's a cold wind. I'm ashamed that I behaved badly towards Tanya for trying to dissuade me from going out. Transferred to the armchair. I seem to have no legs.

25, 26, 27 May, Gaspra For three days I've been out of doors, at first for four or five, and today for six hours. I'm gradually recovering. I felt the pangs of death, i.e. of a new life, and I've been given a respite. Received the sad news today of the arrest of Suller.[10] A Persian pedlar has been, a thoroughly educated man, said he was a Babid.[11]

It's now gone 6. I'm working bit by bit on the appeal to the people (not bad).

Today is 3 June   I'm continuing to spend the days out of doors, working. I've almost finished the appeal. It's not bad. I'm recovering, but I see it's not for long. [. . .]

1 July, Yasnaya Polyana   It's three days since we arrived from Gaspra. The journey was hard physically. I was getting over it, but yesterday I was feverish and weak again. I don't resent it. I'm preparing myself for, or rather, trying to live my last days and hours as well as possible. I've been revising *To the Working People* all the time. It's beginning to take shape and I think I've finished it. [. . .]

5 August   I never expected I wouldn't write my diary for so long. On 22 July I sent off *To the Working People*[12] and since then I've been getting on with *Hadji Murat*, sometimes enthusiastically, sometimes reluctantly and with shame. During this time there have been visitors – I can't remember who. For the fourth day I've written nothing. I was stuck over my ideas for *Hadji Murat*. Now I think I've got it clear. Health generally better, but my stomach is weak.
(1) An astonishing thing: I know myself how bad and stupid I am and yet people consider me a man of genius. So what must other people be like? [. . .]
(4) In music there is an element of noise, contrast, speed, which acts directly on the nerves and not on the feelings. The more there is of this element, the worse the music is. It's the same in other arts too: in poetry – declamation, in painting – brightness of colours. [. . .]

8 August, Yasnaya Polyana   A very hard day. My liver aches and I can't get over my bad mood.

I'm getting on with *Hadji Murat*, and am ashamed all the time. The priest's brochure hurt me.[13] What do they hate me for? I must write to them with love. Help me.

Mashenka and Liza are here; Glebova has been.[14] Letters from Seryozha.

20 September, Yasnaya Polyana   Haven't written my diary for six weeks. I've been getting on with *Hadji Murat* all the time. Health improving. I can be satisfied with my state of mind. I've no bad feelings towards anyone. I've thought a lot. There's a lot to be copied down.
(1) If people in authority have been able to bribe the Church to justify their position, why shouldn't they be able to bribe science? [. . .]
(7) Thought about the immorality of medicine. Everything about it is immoral. Immoral is the fear of illness and death induced by medical aid, immoral is the use of the exclusive aid of doctors, available only to the rich. It is immoral to enjoy

exclusive comforts and pleasures, but to enjoy the exclusive possibility of preserving life is the height of immorality. Immoral is the requirement of medicine to conceal from a patient the danger of his situation and the nearness of death. Immoral are the advice and requirements of doctors that a patient should look after himself – his bodily functions – and in general should live as little as possible spiritually, but only materially: should not think, should not excite himself, should not work.

(8) Socialists see in trusts and syndicates the realisation, or the progress towards the realisation of the socialist ideal, i.e. that people work collectively and not independently. But they only work collectively under pressure of force. What evidence is there that they will also work when they are free, and what evidence that trusts and syndicates will pass into the workers' hands? It is far more probable that trusts will produce slavery, in liberating themselves from which the slaves will destroy the trusts which they themselves did not set up.

(9) The hypnosis of tradition, i.e. willing people to repeat what their ancestors did, is the main barrier to progress – to the liberation of mankind.

(10) My recovery is like dragging a carriage out of a quagmire in which it is stuck, not in the direction in which one inevitably has to go, but in the opposite one. There is no avoiding going through the quagmire.

23 September, Yasnaya Polyana I've been revising *Hadji Murat* all the time. This morning I wrote a little of my article *To the Clergy*.[15] [...]

I've just been thinking this morning about an article on the lack of understanding between Christianity and irreligion, which ought to come before my article *To the Clergy*. 'The main cause of the evil or disasters of our time.' That's what the title should be.[16] Thought on this subject: [...]

(2) People say that Christianity is a teaching of weakness. [...] To reproach Christianity with weakness is like reproaching an army in battle with weakness when it doesn't advance on the enemy with its fists, but, under enemy fire and without replying to it, builds batteries and erects cannons on them which will surely destroy the enemy. [...]

26 September, Yasnaya Polyana Health good. Abandoned *Hadji Murat* and have no desire to continue *To the Clergy*, but somehow feel like writing something literary. Wrote a letter to Schmitt and sent money, and one to a young man faced with conscription.[17]

Had some good thoughts during this time. Some of them I've forgotten.

(1) I imagined very clearly to myself the inner life of each individual person. How can one describe what each individual 'I' is like? Yet I think one can. Then I thought that that is actually what constitutes the whole interest, the whole importance of art – poetry. [...]

(3) Ilya asked me: can women be clever? I couldn't answer, but then I understood: women can be very clever, generally speaking no more foolish if not more clever than men, but their mind is not in the right place, like a joist that is put, not under a roof, but on top of it. With a man, whatever his mind is like, it serves as a guide to

action; with women mind is a plaything, an adornment. A woman's life is guided by what you will: – vanity, motherhood, cupidity, love – only not the mind. [. . .]

27 September, Yasnaya Polyana Haven't written anything good, only today I seemed to get caught up in *The Appeal to the Clergy*. Lyova is staying with us, and I'm extremely glad about the good, simple relations between us. Wrote some unimportant letters. Some interesting visitors from Chernigov – one wants to refuse military service. I wrote to him. Health good. State of mind good too. I feel the approach of death calmly. [. . .]

6 October, Yasnaya Polyana Yesterday I began to revise and continue *The Forged Coupon*. I'm still writing *To the Clergy*. It's weaker than I expected. Gorky and Pyatnitsky have been.[18] Epictetus says: 'Strengthen in yourself contentment with your lot. With it you will overcome everything.'[19]

Today is 4 November, Yasnaya Polyana   Important things during this time: the conviction of Afanasy,[20] the arrest of Novikov,[21] the death of Mikhaylov's mother[22] and the arrival of Pyotr Verigin.[23] There's a lot to note down. I'll note down now what I've been thinking:
(1) I'm reading V. Hugo's *Postscriptum de ma vie*.[24] He writes about the *infini*, about the distances of the stars and the speed and direction of time, and sees something grand about it. This has never puzzled or frightened me, I have always seen it as a misunderstanding, and never acknowledged the reality of such passionate feelings for the magnitudes of space and time. [. . .]
(3) Consciousness stands still, the events of life move through it, but it seems to us that consciousness moves, like clouds racing past the moon. [. . .]
(5) People want freedom, and to attain it they enter into the slavery of institutions from which they never emerge and never will.
(6): (1) To be aware of the Christian truth – that's the first step; (2) the attempt to put it into practice now in life; (3) indignation and bitterness against the enemies of truth; (4) despair; (5) attempts at reconciliation; (6) everything in oneself, in the sight of God, with no thought for the consequences.
  Noted the same things down differently:
  (1) Delight at knowing the truth.
  (2) The desire and hope to put it into practice now.
  (3) Disillusion over the possibility of putting it into practice in the world; the hope of doing so in one's own life.
  (4) Disillusion over this, and despair.
  (5) Everything for one's soul, with no thought for the consequences.
  (This is the programme for the drama.)[25]
(7) The main difference between a revolutionary and a Christian is that the former does everything with the consequences in view, while the latter does everything for God, leaving Him to determine the consequences.
(8) Read Merezhkovsky on Euripides and understood his Christianity.[26] One person wants Christianity together with patriotism (Pobedonostsev, the

Slavophiles); another with war, another with wealth, another with lust for women, and everyone arranges his own Christianity for himself according to his own requirements.

Today is 30 November, Yasnaya Polyana [. . .] Finished the legend,[27] took up *Hadji Murat* again and ought to finish it tomorrow I.I.A. [. . .]

11 December
(1) We know that without physical efforts we won't achieve anything. But why do we think that in the spiritual realm it's possible to achieve something without effort? [. . .]

13 December
(1) Critics are wrong to think that the intelligentsia as a movement can guide the popular masses (Milyukov).[28] It would be still more wrong for a writer to think that he can consciously guide the masses by his works. [. . .]
(2) If in answer to the question: 'Can you play the violin?' you reply: 'I don't know, I haven't tried yet', we would understand at once that it was a joke. But when in answer to the question: 'Can you write books?' we reply: 'Perhaps I can, I haven't tried', we not only do not take this for a joke, but we continually see people acting on the basis of such reasoning. This only goes to prove that anyone can pass judgement on the ugliness of meaningless sounds made by an untrained violinist (absurd people will be found who will find even such music beautiful), but that refined sensibility and intellectual maturity are needed to distinguish between a collection of words and phrases and a true literary work of art.
(3) The whole first half of the nineteenth century is full of attempts to destroy despotic state regimes by revolutionary violence. All attempts ended in reaction, and the power of the ruling classes only increased. Obviously revolution cannot now overcome the power of the state. There is only one thing left: a change of outlook on life by the people, whereby they would cease to minister to the violent acts of governments. Only religion, and actually the Christian religion, can produce such a change. But this religion is so perverted that it might as well not exist. And what is worst of all is that its place is occupied. And so not just the main, but the sole means in our time of serving mankind is by destroying perverted Christianity and establishing the true Christian religion. That is the very thing that everyone considers most insignificant; and not only does nobody do it, but the smartest, quasi-intellectual people are busy doing just the opposite: making perverted Christianity even more confused and obscure.

1903–1910

The last years of Tolstoy's life were eventful ones for Russia. The disastrous war with Japan was followed by Bloody Sunday, the *Potyomkin* mutiny, the 1905 revolution and the setting up and speedy dissolution of the first Duma. Tolstoy's life continued to revolve physically round the Yasnaya Polyana–Moscow axis, but mentally he was even more involved than before with issues of world significance. He openly accused the government of complicity in the savage pogroms in Kishinyov in 1903 and wrote three stories for an anthology (published in Warsaw) in aid of the Jewish victims. In the same year he wrote *After the Ball*, a telling indictment of physical violence and brutality, and in 1904 completed his long essay *Shakespeare and the Drama* with its hostile criticism of *King Lear*. Among his numerous publicist articles of the 1900s which were widely read abroad are the pamphlet *Bethink Yourselves* on the subject of the Russo-Japanese War and the powerful onslaught on capital punishment *I Cannot Be Silent*. In a letter to the Russian Prime Minister he forcefully advocated the Henry George solution to the land problem and the abolition of private property, and his outspokenness on almost every issue of social, political and religious importance meant that he was the focus of attention of men and women throughout the world. Yasnaya Polyana became a place of pilgrimage, where Tolstoy held reluctant court. Letters poured in from many countries, from Gandhi and Bernard Shaw as well as from hundreds of obscure sympathisers and critics. Some people came to film him, others to record his voice, others again to take down all he said. It is hard to believe that Tolstoy, despite his vanity and egoism, welcomed this world-wide publicity which made the last few years of his life so wearisome and helped to aggravate the tensions of an already difficult family life. The death of his favourite daughter and disciple, Masha, in 1906 was a grievous blow to him. His wife's increasing neuroticism and hysterical outbursts (not without provocation), and the bitter wrangling over his will and the problems of copyright, brought matters to a head. At the age of eighty-two Tolstoy found his position so intolerable that he finally took the decision he had long been contemplating and left home for good. The story of his last days and his death on the railway station at Astapovo makes painful reading, and a tragic conclusion to his long, searching and restless life which his diaries and vast correspondence so brightly illuminate.

1903

6 January   I'm now experiencing the torments of hell. I'm recalling all the nastiness of my early life, and these memories won't leave me and are poisoning my life.[1] People usually regret that an individual doesn't retain his memories after death. How fortunate that he doesn't! What torture it would be if in this life I were to remember all the bad things that pain my conscience which I had done in a previous life. And if the good things are to be remembered, all the bad things must be remembered too. How fortunate that memory disappears with death and only consciousness remains – consciousness which represents a sort of total resultant of good and bad, a sort of complex equation reduced to its simplest expression: $x = a$ positive or negative, a big or a small number. Yes, it's very fortunate, the destruction of memory; one couldn't enjoy living with it. But now, with the destruction of memory, we enter life with a clean, blank sheet on which one can write afresh the good and the bad.

5 February, Yasnaya Polyana   Haven't written my diary for a month. I've been ill for two months and am ill now. My heart is weak. And that's good. It reminds me very vividly of the nearness of death. During this time I've been busy mostly with my own memoirs. I'm making progress bit by bit. But so far – it's not good. I've also begun to write an afterword [to the appeal] to the working people,[2] but I'm making no progress. I'm busy too with a philosophical exposition of the true life.[3] Am I mistaken? I feel very clearly that there is something new and useful here.

Today is 12 February, Yasnaya Polyana. My heart is still weak, but I'm gradually recovering my strength. The afterword is still no good. I've made a little progress with my memoirs. The philosophical exposition of life still lacks clarity.

I'm reading a wonderful theosophical journal;[4] it has much in common with my understanding of things. The letter about the Saxon princess has been published, and I'm very sorry.[5] [. . .]

20 February, Yasnaya Polyana   Health a bit better. For the second day I've been out for a drive. Can't work. I've no enthusiasm.

Yesterday I received Posse's article about my appeal *To the Working People.*[6] They are very upset. They are obviously hypnotised, believing in a theory which won't stand up to criticism.
(1) Supporters of socialism are people who have the urban population primarily in mind. They don't know either the beauty and poetry of rural life, or its sufferings.

If they did know, they wouldn't want, as they do now, to destroy this life and replace it by the comforts of urban life, but would only try to free it from its afflictions. [. . .]

1 March, Yasnaya Polyana Read Mechnikov's article, on the same theme again:[7] if you cut out the large intestine, people won't think any more about the meaning of life, and will be as stupid as Mechnikov himself. No, joking apart. His idea is that science will improve man's organism, free him from sufferings and then it will be possible to find the meaning, the purpose of life. Science will reveal it. But how shall we all live until then? After all, billions of people have lived already with their large intestines. And what if, according to this science of yours, the sun grows cold and the world comes to an end before the human organism is fully perfected? Why talk such nonsense? [. . .]

9 March, Yasnaya Polyana [. . .] An excellent philosophical article by a Pole.[8] [. . .]

11 March, Yasnaya Polyana I'm still writing my definition of life and am still dissatisfied. Got on with it the day before yesterday, and must recast it again. But before doing so, I want to note down some desultory thoughts I've had recently. [. . .]
(2) It hasn't been made altogether clear that often (perhaps even always) our satisfaction or dissatisfaction with life, our impressions of events, stem not from the events themselves, but from our state of mind. [. . .]
(4) Often people – liberal statesmen and all sorts of doctrinaire people in general – consider it good to fight against only one of the manifestations of falsehood and to tolerate the others and not fight against them. It's as though, in the course of a flood, you were only to halt one of the streams of water pouring over you, and to allow the others to drown you. [. . .]

14 March [. . .]
(4) Read *Opinions sociales* by Anatole France.[9] Like all orthodox socialists and devotees of science, and therefore repudiators of religion, he says that there is no need for mercy or love, only for *justice*. That is true, but in order to have real *justice*, it is necessary for our striving and our ideal to embody self-denial and love. In order to have an honourable marriage, it is necessary to strive towards complete chastity. In order to have true knowledge, it is necessary to strive towards a knowledge of the spiritual world. (Then there will be knowledge of the material world. Otherwise there will be ignorance.) In order to have a fair distribution of services, it is necessary to strive to give up everything, and not to take anything for oneself. (Otherwise there will be robbery of other people's labour.) In order to hit the target it is necessary to aim above and beyond it. In order to swing high on the 'giant's footsteps', it is necessary to run further away from the pole.[10]

Today is 20 March, Yasnaya Polyana Wrote letters yesterday and today. Wrote twenty-six of them. Health a bit better, but I mustn't forget the nearness of the crossing over. [. . .]

14 April, Yasnaya Polyana Haven't written my diary for a long time. I've been weak all this time. I've been unwell for three days now: a cold and a cough. And today, weak as I was, I read Thoreau and was mentally uplifted.[11] [. . .]

I'll write in here what I noted down before 2 April.
(1) People usually measure the progress of mankind by its technical and scientific successes, supposing that civilisation leads to good. That isn't true. Rousseau and all those who enthuse over the uncivilised, patriarchal state are just as right, or just as wrong, as those who enthuse over civilisation. The good of people who live and enjoy the highest, most refined civilisation and culture, and the good of primitive, uncivilised people is absolutely identical. Increasing the good of people by science – civilisation and culture – is just as impossible as making the water on a flat stretch of water higher in one place than in others. Increasing the good of people only comes from increasing love, which by its very nature makes all people equal; but scientific and technical successes are a matter of age, and civilised people are just as little superior to uncivilised people in their happiness as a grown-up man is superior in happiness to a juvenile. Good only comes from increasing love. [. . .]

I'm continuing to write on 29 April, Yasnaya Polyana. During this time I've been working continually on the afterword.[12] I think I'm coming to the end. It's quite respectable. Wrote a letter about the Kishinyov affair and a telegram.[13] My health has been good. Caught a chill – there's been a cold spell – but I'm better today. A book from Mechnikov.[14] I'd like to write about it. [. . .]
(4) Everything is alive. Everything is an organism. We don't recognise some things, either because they are too big like the earth or the sun, or too small like particles of minerals or crystals. [. . .]
(7) How terrible are angry workers who won't work! Which is worse: they or Nicholas Pavlovich? That's another question. [. . .]
(13) Somebody asked me: 'Does fate depend on man, or man on fate?' The more you live a spiritual life, the more you are independent of fate; and vice versa.
(14) In our age there exists a terrible superstition that we eagerly accept any invention which reduces labour, and consider it necessary to make use of it, without asking ourselves whether this invention which reduces labour increases our happiness or whether it doesn't destroy beauty. We are like a peasant woman overeating beef because there is plenty of it, although she isn't hungry and the food will probably be bad for her. Railways instead of walking, motorcars instead of a horse, hosiery machines instead of knitting needles.
(15) The methods of the natural sciences which base their conclusions on facts are the most unscientific methods. There are no facts. Only our perception of them. And so we only need the sort of method which talks about perception, about impressions. [. . .]

Today is 13 May, Yasnaya Polyana [. . .] Finished the afterword and sent it off.[15] Tanya and her husband are here, and Strakhov with his terrible story.[16] [. . .]

17 May I think, Yasnaya Polyana. [. . .] I've been revising *Hadji Murat*. Got as far as Nicholas Pavlovich,[17] and I think it's becoming clearer.
    One thing to note:
(1) A proof that memory is consciousness and vice versa, is the fact that the longer you live, the weaker your memory gets, and the stronger your consciousness.

26 May, Yasnaya Polyana [. . .]
(1) Life here is not an illusion and not the whole of life, but one of the manifestations, the eternal manifestations of eternal life.

29 May, Yasnaya Polyana Went to Pirogovo yesterday. Had a good trip and found everything well. I find N. N. very unpleasant.[18] I'm struggling with varying success. Wrote a small addition to the afterword today and sent it off. [. . .] Went for a walk in the evening and admired the beauty of nature. [. . .]

3 June, Yasnaya Polyana Stomach still out of order. I'm still struggling. Wrote well about Nicholas yesterday. Wrote some letters today and made the following notes:
(1) Any authority is aware that it only exists thanks to the ignorance of the people, and so it is instinctively and rightly afraid of education and hates it. There are, however, conditions under which authority has to make concessions willy-nilly to education; then it pretends that it is protecting it, takes it into its own hands and perverts it. But there are also conditions – so great is the power of the authority – under which this isn't necessary. Nicholas lived in such conditions – and he understood it and acted accordingly.
(2) Nicholas considered all people to be like those who surrounded him. But those who surrounded him were scoundrels; and so he considered all people to be scoundrels. [. . .]

Today is 4 June, Yasnaya Polyana Didn't sleep much. My stomach still hurts. Yesterday I gave Misha my diaries to copy for Posha. There's a lot in them of interest to me. Settled down to work today; wanted to continue my memoirs, but couldn't: *they don't grip me.* Yesterday I read *Nicholas I*.[19] Very much of interest. I must finish reading it before going on.

9 June, Yasnaya Polyana Health better. I'm making some progress with Nicholas Pavlovich. Thought up three new things.[20] It's time to die, and I'm still thinking up things. (1) A story about a ball and running the gauntlet. (2) The cry of the devil at the approach of Christ, and (3) Who am I? – a description of myself now with all my weaknesses and good sides. [. . .]

18 June, Yasnaya Polyana [. . .] I'm doing no work or hardly any. Decided to leave Nicholas Pavlovich almost as it is, and, if necessary, to write about him separately.[21] [. . .] Thought up three new things:
(1) The cry of the lost people of today: the materialists, the positivists, the Nietzscheans, is the cry (Mark I, 24): 'Let us alone; what have we to do with thee, thou Jesus of Nazareth? Art thou come to destroy us? I know thee who thou art, the Holy One of God.' (That would be very good.)[22]
(2) For the Jewish anthology:[23] a gay ball in Kazan, I'm in love with Koreysha, the beautiful daughter of a military commander – a Pole – I dance with her; her handsome old father takes her lovingly on his arm to the mazurka. And the next

morning, after a sleepless night in love, the sound of a drum, and a Tatar made to run the gauntlet, and the military commander giving orders to beat him till it hurts more. (That would be very good.)[24]
and (3) A description of myself in all truth, as I am now, with all my weaknesses and follies, alternating with what is good and important in my life. (That would also be good.)[25]

All this is more important than the stupid *Hadji Murat*.

19 June [...]
(2) Read *St Francis of Assisi*.[26] How good that he addresses the birds as brothers! And his conversation with frère Léon about what joy is! [...]

23 June, Yasnaya Polyana Health good. I'm eating berries and riding a lot on horseback. Mental inertia.

One thing to note:
(1) I'm a person with very bad qualities, very slow to understand good, and so I need to make geat efforts not to be a complete scoundrel. Yury Samarin once put it very well when he said he was an excellent mathematics teacher because he was very slow to understand mathematics. I'm absolutely the same with mathematics, but, most important, I'm just the same with what is good – very slow – and so I'm not at all a bad teacher – no, I'll be bold and say I'm a good teacher.

30 June, Yasnaya Polyana [...] A lot of guests. Kiester was here, a colonist who has to do military service. The Hunters were here yesterday.[27] [...]

4 July, Yasnaya Polyana Copied out my thoughts. Revised *Hadji Murat*. Health not bad. Only it's a bit weaker than before. I'm thinking up a lot of things to write: obviously unrealisable. I was reading today how soldiers used to be trained.[28] How good it would be to tell about it in a naive manner. [...]

21 July, Yasnaya Polyana Health still just as good; I'm still living the same vegetable life. Tried to write a fairy tale,[29] but it was no good. [...]
(3) I can't repeat often enough to myself (and to others) that there are three driving forces in human life: (*a*) the feeling flowing from a man's various communications with other creatures; (*b*) imitation, suggestion, hypnosis, and (*c*) the conclusions of reason. Of a million acts performed as a result of the first two forces, scarcely one is performed on the basis of the conclusions of reason. This proportion is the same for each man (i.e. of a million acts, he performs one according to reason) and for all sorts of men.

The Pope – the election and Serafim.[30] What an illustration of the power of suggestion.

25 July, Yasnaya Polyana Wrote three fairy tales.[31] Bad as yet, but they could be quite good. [...]

9 August, Yasnaya Polyana   I've been well all this time. Wrote *Daughter and Father* in one day.³² Not bad. Finished the fairy tales. [. . .]

20 August   Only finished the tales today – and not three, but two.³³ Dissatisfied with them. On the other hand, *But You Say* isn't bad.³⁴ Health still good. I'm going to Pirogovo today. [. . .]

27 August, Yasnaya Polyana   Night. I've been to Pirogovo. Seryozha is better than I expected. I was glad to see Masha. Added the third tale I left out to the other two. I'm well, and ride a lot on horseback; went to Taptykovo yesterday. I'm still thinking about Nicholas I. I must finish it, otherwise it will block the way for other works. [. . .]

3 September, Yasnaya Polyana   Alive, but unwell. On the 29th we went riding; my horse trod on my foot, then I had a bilious attack and feel quite unwell and my foot isn't getting better. The 28th was a depressing day. The congratulations are frankly depressing and unpleasant – they're insincere, the words 'of the Russian land', and all that sort of nonsense.³⁵ No flattering of my vanity, thank God. Probably there is nothing to flatter. It's high time.

I was thinking of something very important, but couldn't think it out properly. I'll come back to it later, but I'll write it down now as I understand it:
(1) I often mix people up: my daughters, some of my sons, my friends, and people I find unpleasant, so that my consciousness contains not individual persons, but collective mental beings. And so I'm mistaken, not when I call one by the wrong name but when I consider each to be an individual being. That's not clear. But *je m'entends* [I understand what I'm saying].
(2) About literature. We spoke about Chekhov: in a conversation about Chekhov with Lazarevsky,³⁶ it bcame clear to me that he, like Pushkin, has made an advance in form. And that's a great service. But, like Pushkin, he hasn't any content. Gorky – there's a misunderstanding. The Germans know Gorky, but they don't know Polenz.³⁷

Today is 22 September, Yasnaya Polyana   I've been writing for a few days (more than a week) a foreword to Shakespeare.³⁸ Health good. My foot is healing up. Not many thoughts: [. . .]

Today is 6 October, Yasnaya Polyana   My health has taken a turn for the worse, and there's still the same inertia and poverty of thoughts. Still writing the foreword to Crosby. [. . .]

Yasnaya Polyana, 14 November   Haven't written my diary for five weeks. All the time I've been busy with my Shakespeare, which has kept growing and growing; I think I've reached the end. I can't boast about my intellectual energy during this time, but my state of mind is good. About three days ago I had a bad bilious attack.

Thought completely calmly about death, only with a certain impatience in case I were to suffer for long. Of course that's wrong, sufferings themselves may be of use for life's eternal purpose. I partly understood that that may be so, but not with my whole being.

Went to Pirogovo. On the 9th, I think. Was very glad to be with my brother. He is disintegrating bodily, like me, and, like me, growing spiritually; only I'm particularly glad to see this in him, with his peculiar simplicity and truthfulness. When talking to me about his sorrow and illness, he said: 'God has cast His eye on me too, as the peasants say.'

I've noted in my book:

(1) When people's lives are immoral and their relationships are based not on love but on egoism, all technical improvements, the increase of man's power over nature – steam, electricity, telegraphs, all kinds of machines, powder, dynamite, roburite – create the impression of dangerous toys which have been put into the hands of children. [. . .]

(3) People usually think that progress consists in the increase of knowledge, in the improvement of life, but that isn't so. Progress consists only in the greater and greater clarification of the answers to the basic questions of life. The truth is always accessible to a man. It can't be otherwise, because a man's soul is a divine spark, the truth itself. It's only a matter of removing from this divine spark (the truth) everything that obscures it. Progress consists, not in the increase of truth, but in freeing it from its wrappings. The truth is obtained like gold, not by letting it grow bigger, but by washing off from it everything that isn't gold. [. . .]

(9) Read Gegidze's university essays.[39] The poor, sincere young man sees the folly of university science and of all culture, and the horror of the debauchery into which he is falling. In one place, when speaking about what to do, what aim to set oneself in life, and having decided in advance that such an aim cannot of course be self-improvement, he runs through all other aims, and none of them satisfy him. May God forgive the people who instilled, and instil, in our young generations the idea that external activity is necessary and praiseworthy, but that self-improvement, the only vocation for a man which satisfies all the demands both of his soul and of all external conditions – that such self-improvement is not only not necessary, but is amusing and even harmful. The poor young man rushes about in search of a worthy aim in life, and naturally the poor, misguided creature comes to rest on women's love, naively imagining that such love is man's chief and highest vocation. Not having any spiritual aim before him, he naturally thinks that the urge to continue the race, implanted in man's animal nature and expressing itself in a more or less poetic love, is man's highest vocation. I would like to write a few words apropos of this.

Today is 24 November, Yasnaya Polyana I'm still dawdling over the forewords to both Shakespeare and Garrison.[40] I've almost finished. Health good, but I'm intellectually sluggish. I've just thought of something very important, I think, namely: (1) We are aware of two lives in ourselves: the spiritual life, known to us through our inner consciousness, and the physical life, known to us through external observation.

Normally people (myself included) who recognise the spiritual life as the basis of life deny the reality, the necessity, the importance of studying the physical life, which evidently cannot lead to any conclusive results. In just the same way, those who only recognise the physical life completely deny the spiritual life and all deductions based on it – deny, as they say, metaphysics. But it is now absolutely clear to me that both are wrong, and both forms of knowledge – the materialistic and the metaphysical – have their own great importance, if only one doesn't wish to make inappropriate deductions from the one or the other. From materialistic knowledge based on the observation of external phenomena one can deduce scientific data, i.e. generalisations about phenomena, but one should not deduce any guiding principles for people's lives, as the materialists – Darwinists for example – have often tried to do. From metaphysical knowledge based on inner consciousness one can and should deduce the laws of human life – how should we live? why are we living? – the very thing that all religious teachings do; but one should not deduce, as many people have tried to do, the laws of phenomena and generalisations about them.

Each of these two kinds of knowledge has its own purpose and its own field of activity. [. . .]

I think it's 30 November, Yasnaya Polyana. I've finished the foreword – it's not bad. Wrote a few letters. Andryusha's misfortune.[41] Still haven't finished Shakespeare, although it's nearing the end. Health has been good all this time. [. . .]
(3) The day before yesterday I dreamed I was writing a story, comic in form but a moving story, about a peasant who has picked up a lot of incomprehensible words. And it was very good. Generally speaking my brain was working all night in a particularly lively way: I imagined three more popular types: one – a strong man, a Hercules, a slow mover, but subject to fits of madness, whereupon he becomes a wild animal. The second – a chatterbox, a braggart, a poet, tender and self-sacrificing for a few minutes at a time. The third – an egoist, but refined, attractive, gifted and a ladies' man.

I want to write at least a little of my memoirs each day.

2 December, Yasnaya Polyana Health so-so. Still toying with Shakespeare, and decided to stop writing it in the mornings, and to begin something new, either a drama, or something on religion, or else finish *The Coupon*. If I feel like working in the evenings I'll revise Shakespeare and write my memoirs. [. . .]

19 December, Yasnaya Polyana Andyrusha's behaviour distresses me. I'm trying to do what I can. Health very good: but my mental activity is still feeble. I'm trying to accept it as right and proper, and I'm partly achieving my aim. Finished working on Shakespeare and began something on the importance of religion.[42] But only wrote two beginnings, and both are bad. Wrote a bit of my memoirs, but unfortunately didn't continue. No enthusiasm for it. Thought about *The Forged Coupon*, but didn't write any of it.

Noted a few things down in my book: [. . .]

(2) I can put myself in the shoes of the most terrible villain and understand him, but not in those of a foolish man. Yet that is very necessary. [. . .]

(4) The artist, the poet and the mathematician, or the scholar generally. The poet can't do the scholar's job, because he can't see one thing only and stop seeing things in general. The scholar can't do the poet's job because he always sees one thing only, and can't see everything.

(5) There are machine people who work splendidly when they are set in motion, but can't set themselves in motion.

(6) A truly virtuous unmarried woman who devotes all the strength of the maternal self-sacrifice she has been endowed with to the service of God and man is the finest and happiest human creature (Auntie Tatyana Alexandrovna).

25 December, Yasnaya Polyana I've begun to write *The Forged Coupon*. I'm writing very carelessly, but it interests me in so far as a new form, very *sobre*, is taking shape. [. . .]

30 December, Yasnaya Polyana Went for a ride. 20° of frost. Health good, but haven't the strength to work, although I've thought about a lot of things. I'd like to write:

(1) A popular story for the people about an angel who killed a child;[43] (2) about a peasant who doesn't go to church;[44] and (3) about a dissenter in prison and a revolutionary;[45] (4) about my own confused weak, psychical condition; (5) Why didst Thou, Jesus, Son of God, come to torment us.[46] [. . .]

1904

2 January, Yasnaya Polyana Wrote a story *The Divine and the Human* in my old diary. Was unwell for two days. I'm better today. Some good thoughts [...]

3 January, Yasnaya Polyana Health not altogether good: biliousness – my liver. Went riding; a thaw. Seryozha and Aunt Tanya are here. Some very good thoughts. I'm making a little progress with *The Forged Coupon*. But it's certainly very disorganised. I'm also busy revising the *Thoughts*.[1] Thought:
(1) Am I afraid of death? No. But at the approach of death or the thought of it, I can't help experiencing the sort of trepidation that a traveller must experience as he approaches the place where his train drops down to the sea from an enormous height or who rises to an enormous height in a balloon. The traveller knows that nothing will happen to him, that it will only be the same as happens to millions of creatures, that he will only change his method of travel, but he can't help experiencing trepidation as he approaches the place. Such is my feeling too about death.
(2) I thought at first that it was possible to establish a good life for people while retaining those technical devices and those forms of life under which mankind now lives, but I'm now convinced that this is impossible, that a good life and the present technical refinements and forms of life are incompatible. Without slaves we would not only be without our theatres, confectioners' shops, carriages and objects of luxury in general, but probably all our railways and telegraphs too. And besides, people have become so accustomed over generations to an artificial life that none of our town dwellers are fit any longer for a true life, don't understand it and don't want it. I remember Yusha Obolensky saying when he arrived in the country during a snow-storm that life in the country, where you get so snowed in that you have to dig yourself out, is impossible. Nowadays there are people, and they are those who are considered the best educated, who are surprised not at how people could have arranged their lives in such a way that snow-storms or darkness or heat or cold or dust or distance no longer exist for them, as people in towns have done, but who are surprised at how people living in the midst of nature can struggle against it. [...]

6 January, Yasnaya Polyana Health a bit better. Wonderful weather. I've been compiling a new calendar. Today I'm getting on with *The Forged Coupon*. Must note:
(1) Two types of mind: one mind in the material field – observations, deductions, reasoning about what is observed, and another mind in the spiritual field: attitude to God, to people, to other creatures, moral demands... Usually, or even always, the more there is of one mind, the less of the other.

11 January, Yasnaya Polyana I've been unwell with liver trouble for four days or so. Haven't written my diary. Finished my addition to Garrison yesterday and worked on the calendar.[2] [. . .]

14 January, Yasnaya Polyana Woke up today feeling healthy, physically strong, and with an overwhelming awareness of my own nastiness and worthlessness, and of a life badly lived now and in the past. And up to now – midday – I'm still under the influence of this salutary mood. How good, how profitable even, to feel, as I do today, humiliated and vile! You don't require anything of anybody, nothing can offend you, you deserve everything that is bad. Only one thing is necessary, namely that this humiliation should not turn to dejection and despair, should not hinder the effort to free oneself at least a little from one's own stinking pit – should not hinder one from working and serving as best one can. Something occurred to me just now. I must also note down an earlier thought:
(1) What a useless occupation all our literature is which has to be censored! All that needs saying, all that can be useful to people in the field of internal and external policy, economic life and above all religious life, all that is reasonable is forbidden. It's the same with social activity. All that is left is children's games. 'Go on playing, children. The more you play, the less opportunity you will have of understanding what we are doing to you.' How undoubtedly clear this has become to me. [. . .]

16 January Wrote about religion yesterday.[3] Health not bad. I can't write anything today, didn't sleep well. Sonya has arrived. Boulanger was here yesterday. Kept trying to work on the calendar today, but couldn't do anything. Thought yesterday: [. . .]
(2) How right Amiel is that every feeling and thought has its own high point which one ought to try to hold on to – to commit that thought or feeling to writing. If you let go of it, it's gone for good.[4] A couple of days ago I thought so clearly and with such power about government robber bands, but now it's all cold and powerless.

18 January, Yasnaya Polyana [. . .] Added a little yesterday to Shakespeare, and looked through the *Coupon* and the *Stone*. Felt good at heart.

22 January, Yasnaya Polyana Health still good, but death is near. Work is going badly. Worked today on the *Coupon* and am hesitating whether to leave the devils in or get rid of them.[5] Cleared up all my letters yesterday and today. Thought:
(1) It's necessary to explain one's attitude to the government. And this attitude can be twofold: either the government is a necessary condition for maintaining order and one must submit to it and serve it; or one must recognise, as I recognise and as one is bound to recognise, that the government is a band of robbers, and then it is necessary, as well as trying to enlighten these robbers and persuade them to stop being robbers, to refrain as far as possible oneself from sharing with these robbers in the enjoyment of their spoils. Above all one must not do what the liberals are now doing: recognise that the government is necessary and fight it with its own weapons. That's a childish game. [. . .]

27 January, Yasnaya Polyana For three days I've had a cough and cold, and for three days I haven't written anything. And I'm weak enough to think that this is bad. Made a few notes in my book. And I've just been for a walk and thought:
(1) The war,⁶ and hundreds of arguments about why it has come about, what it means, what will result from it, etc. Everyone is arguing about it, from the Tsar to the lowest trooper. And apart from arguments about what results the war will have for the whole world, they will all have to face the argument about what must *my, my, my* attitude be to the war? But nobody is arguing in this way. They even think that there's no need to, that it's not important. Seize a man by the throat and start to strangle him and he will feel that the most important thing of all for him is the life of his *I*. And if the life of his *I* is the most important thing of all, then, apart from the fact that he is a journalist, a tsar, an officer, a soldier, he is also a man who has come into the world for a short time and has to leave it again at the will of Him who sent him. What then can be more important for him than what he has to do in this world, more important obviously than any arguments about whether the war is necessary and what it will lead to? And what he obviously has to do as regards the war is not to fight, and not to help others to fight if it is no longer possible to restrain them.

28 January, Yasnaya Polyana Still haven't recovered. My liver and a cold in the head. Revised a bit of the *Coupon* today. And had some good thoughts about the war that has begun. I'd like to write about the fact that when such a terrible thing as war takes place, everybody puts forward hundreds of opinions about all the various meanings and consequences of the war, but nobody argues about his own situation: what should he or I do in regard to the war?⁷ This is the best and clearest illustration of the fact that nothing can remedy the evil that exists except religion. [. . .] Noted:
(1) In order to have a serious attitude to life I not only need to understand and remember that I shall die, but also that I have not existed before. [. . .]
(4) The peoples of Europe are in debt to the tune of 133 milliards. Who is in debt to whom? The poor people, the workers are in debt to the rich people, the owners of shares. Perhaps one day it will be different, but up to now the interest on debts is paid by the toiling workers; while the people who receive the interest are the rich, the shareholders.
Liver still bad; I've no energy for working.

19 February, Yasnaya Polyana I'm still writing about war. It won't come right yet. Health not bad. But my heart has been weak for some time. I can't welcome death at all. I've no fear, but I'm full of life, and I just can't. I've been reading Kant, and was carried away, and am now carried away by Lichtenberg.⁸ He's very close to me. Thought I should write about the three stages of consciousness. Wrote about it today to Chertkov.⁹ Wrote some letters. How important the three stages of consciousness were in my head, and how feeble their expression turned out to be. But I'll come back to it again. [. . .]

23 February, Yasnaya Polyana I'm writing about war; health good. I want to write a continuation of *The Divine and the Human*; I like it very much. [...]

25 February, Yasnaya Polyana [...] Today I revised Nicholas Pavlovich in *Hadji Murat* and then gave it up. If there's time, I'll write about Nicholas separately.

7 March, Yasnaya Polyana Had a very good trip to Pirogovo with Sasha. Masha, judging from a letter, is worse. I can't help feeling sorry. I'm still revising my article on war. It's quite reasonable. Not good, but quite reasonable. [...]
(2) An excellent saying: *the living think about life*, i.e. while a person is alive he can't help giving himself up entirely to the interests of this world. For this reason death is so terrible when a person who is full of life thinks about it. But when death is near because of a wound, or illness or old age, a person ceases to think about life and death ceases to be terrible.
(3) Death is a window through which one observed the world, and which has been slammed shut, or lowered eyelids and sleep, or a walk from one window to another.
(4) The more foolish and immoral the things people do, the more solemn they are. I met a retired soldier out walking, and we got talking about the war. He agreed that to kill is forbidden by God. 'But what is one to do?' he said, as he thought of an example of the most extreme case of attack or insult which an enemy could inflict. 'What if he were to defile a sacred object or wanted to take it away from you?' 'What sort of thing?' 'A standard.' I have seen how standards are venerated. And the Pope, and the Metropolitans and the Tsar. And the courts. And the mass. The more absurd, the more solemn.
(5) I had a dream. I was talking to Grot and knew that he was dead, and yet I went on talking calmly without being surprised. And in the course of the conversation I wanted to recall some opinion about Spencer, or an opinion of Spencer's – the distinction wasn't made clear in the dream. And I knew this opinion, and had already expressed it before. So that the opinion existed both before and after. The fact that I was talking to Grot although he was dead, and the fact that the opinion about Spencer existed both before and after and belonged both to Spencer and to someone else – all this was no less true than what existed in reality, spaced out chronologically. When asleep you often dream things which, when you space them out chronologically, seem to be absurd, but what you find out about yourself when asleep is far more true than what you think about yourself when awake. You dream that you have the weaknesses which you consider you are free from when awake, and that you don't have the weaknesses which you are afraid of when awake, and you see what you crave for. I often see myself as a soldier, often see myself being unfaithful to my wife and am horrified by it, often see myself writing only for my own pleasure.

The dream I had today made me think about this. Dreams are really moments of awakening. In these moments we see life outside time, we see joined together in one point what has been broken up chronologically; we see the essence of our life – the extent of our growth.

10 March, Yasnaya Polyana [. . .] Wrote some epigraphs, and revised the ending.[10] [. . .]

Missed out a day; today is 12 March, Yasnaya Polyana. Health good. Still revising *On War* and am dissatisfied with it. Went for a walk. Yesterday Arensky was here, today Olga came to ask advice.[11] I'm sorry for her. And I don't know what to advise. Read about Nicholas I.

16 March, Yasnaya Polyana I.I.A. Very unwell. Heart weak. Irregular heart beats and pains. Went for a walk. Cold. Wrote *On War*. Almost finished it. Read *Maine de Biran*.[12] Very interesting to me.

I'm writing on the 19th. Didn't write my diary yesterday. Went for a walk. Ate too much. And felt unwell. Think I've finished *On War* – gave it to be copied. [. . .]
 Read *Maine de Biran* and Nicholas I. It became clear to me that the whole interest in Nicholas I will be in showing the baseness of those who left their comrades in the lurch for the sake of success: Rostovtsev, Shipov, Bludov.[13] *Cette canaille, ces malfaiteurs*.

29 March, Yasnaya Polyana Still revising *On War*. Today I revised *The Divine and the Human*. Health weak. This is as it should be – the boundary walls are crumbling.

[5 April] – Haven't written my diary for five days. Today is the 5th. I haven't been ill, but have been weak the whole time and have had no mental urge to work. Apart from that there have been visitors: Koni and others. I've done no work the whole time. Must note: [. . .]
(2) Thought today about Nicholas I, about his ignorance and self-assurance, and about what a terrible thing it is that people of inferior spiritual strength can influence and even control people of superior strength. But this is only as long as the spiritual strength which they control is in the process of ascendancy, and hasn't reached its highest point, at which it becomes more powerful than anything else.
 I'd like to write about the Decembrists.
(3) I'm still thinking about an explanation for hypnosis. And I can't find a clear definition.
(4) Today I was reading a philosophical book about Spinoza's ethics:[14] it summoned up many thoughts. The basis for ethics can only be the recognition of the divine nature of what we call ourselves. But how to *beibringen* [impart] this idea to backward people? By suggestion. I'd like to explain the role of suggestion in the life of society.
 Began writing *The Corner-Stone*, but couldn't continue.
 Alexandra Andreyevna has died.[15] How simple and good it is.
 I feel very well.

29 April, Yasnaya Polyana All this time I've been writing another addition to the article on war. Finished it today and am satisfied with it. [. . .] Thought of something very important today. [. . .]

(2) A man can only know something fully from the experience of his own life. I know myself fully, my whole self from the curtain of birth until the curtain of death. I know myself from the fact that I am I. This is the highest, or rather the deepest knowledge. The next kind of knowledge is knowledge acquired from feelings: I hear, I see, I feel. This knowledge is external: I know that something exists, but I don't know – in the way that I know myself – what the thing I see, hear or feel is like. I don't know what it feels or is aware of. The third kind of knowledge is less deep, it is knowledge acquired by reason; knowledge deduced from one's own feelings or transmitted by word from other people – reasoning, prediction, deduction, science.

The first kind. *I am sad, hurt, bored, joyful.* There is no doubt about this.

The second kind. *I smell the scent of a violet, I see light and shade, etc.* Here there may be mistakes.

The third kind. *I know that the earth is round and rotates, and that Japan and Madagascar exist, etc.* All that is doubtful.

Life, I think, consists in this, that both the second and the third kinds of knowledge change into the first, that a man experiences everything within himself. [. . .]

7 May, Yasnaya Polyana The day before yesterday I met a beggar in the street, in rags. I got talking to him: he was an ex-pupil of the Pedagogical Institute. A Nietzschean *sans le savoir* [without knowing it]. And what a convinced one. 'Service to God and one's neighbours, the suppression of one's passions is narrow-mindedness, the violation of the laws of nature. One must follow one's passions, they give us strength and greatness.' It's astonishing how Nietzsche's teaching, egoism, is a necessary consequence of the whole aggregate of quasi-scientific, artistic and, above all, quasi-philosophical and popularising activity. We are not surprised and we don't doubt that, if seeds fall on well-cultivated land and if moreover there is warmth and moisture and nothing tramples down the crops, certain plants will grow. Likewise it is possible to determine accurately what the spiritual consequences of certain intellectual, artistic and scientific influences will be.

(2) It seems to me more and more that there are things that can and must be said about the causes of the suppression of people's spiritual life and the means for remedying it. It's always the same old thing; the cause of it all is violence – violence which reason tries to justify, and the means for remedying it is: religion, i.e. the awareness of our relationship to God. I'd like to express this in literary form. Nicholas I and the Decembrists. I'm reading much that is good on this subject.[16] [. . .]

Recently sent off *On War*,[17] and am awaiting the effect, although I know that there won't be any and I shouldn't expect any.

8 May, Yasnaya Polyana Received a letter today from a sailor from Port Arthur.[18] *Is it God's will or not that the authorities should compel us to kill?*

This doubt exists, and I am writing about it, but I also know that an enormous number of people are in great darkness. But, as Kant says, as soon as the truth is clearly expressed, it is bound to prevail over everything. When? That is another question. We would like it to be soon, but for God 1,000 years is like a single hour. It seems to me that for wars to cease (and with wars, legalised violence), the following historical events are necessary: it is necessary (1) that England and America should be beaten in wars by countries which have introduced universal military conscription; (2) that as a result of this they should introduce universal military conscription themselves; and (3) that only then will everyone come to their senses.

11 May, Yasnaya Polyana   Health better. Mikhaylov and Nikolayev have come, and the Merezhkovskys are coming.[19] I've written nothing all these days. An Englishman with a letter from Chertkov.[20] Mental state *good*. [. . .]
(1) Ilya Vasilyevich the man-servant is in a bad temper as a result of the holiday and the carousing. And before I know where I am I am infected by the same bad, unfriendly mood. One of the most important rules in life is: *don't yawn when other people yawn*. Don't yield to any suggestion without testing it. Only yield to the sort of suggestion you acknowledge to be good – to that of Christ and Marcus Aurelius, but not Maupassant, etc. And don't forget either that you too are able to suggest. [. . .]

20 May, Yasnaya Polyana   The last few days I've been writing a foreword to Chertkov's article.[21] Added a few things to *On War*. [. . .]

30 May, Yasnaya Polyana   Unwell for the third day – my liver – but feel much better today. Added a bit to *The Divine and the Human*. It's not bad, I think. As for *The Corner-Stone*, i.e. *On Religion*, I've decided to throw away what I've written and begin again. [. . .]
(2) Yesterday I read *Time and Eternity* and *The Eternal Question*.[22] Both good books. About time and the philosophy of the spirit.

2 June, Yasnaya Polyana   Wrote some letters yesterday. I don't feel like starting on any work. Saw Briggs off. A clever fellow. Gegidze has been. No use. Health a bit better. The war and the call-up torment me. Thought: (1) A man, a grown-up man, without any religious philosophy and without faith, is a spiritual and moral cripple; he can only do what is natural to man, that is he can only live, thanks to artificial contrivances: amusements, art, lust, ambition, greed, curiosity, science. And such a man – like a cripple – is always in everyone's power, you can do what you like with him. And all our intelligentsia, all the European (and American) intelligentsia, is like that. This cripple-like intelligentsia doesn't believe in anything, can't do anything except trivialities, but knows that it has to live. And it can only live by other people's labours. But it can only force those people to feed it and maintain it who are also without any religion. And so all its efforts are directed either to perverting the faith which the people have, or depriving the people of it altogether. The clergy especially are occupied with the former; scholars – science, literature and art – with the latter. [. . .]

4 June, Yasnaya Polyana Haven't felt like writing for several days. Health not too good. The war, the call-up of reserves – I suffer continually. Tried to write my memoirs yesterday – it was no good. Thought: [. . .]
(2) War is the product of despotism. If there were no despotism, there could be no war; there might be fights, but not war. Despotism produces war, and war supports despotism.

Those who want to fight against war should fight only against despotism.

6 June Yasnaya Polyana Wrote a bit of *The Stone* yesterday. [. . .] Soldiers' wives are walking about unhappy and abandoned. I read the papers and it seems that all these battles, these consecrations of standards, are so firmly rooted that it's useless to rebel, and I sometimes think that I was wrong to have written my article which only caused hostility, but then you look at the people, at the soldiers' wives, and you regret that you wrote so little and so feebly. [. . .]

9 June, Yasnaya Polyana [. . .] I'm not writing anything. Visitors: Davydov, Bestuzhev, Kun, Michael Davitt today.[23] [. . .]

13 June, Yasnaya Polyana Still the same mental weakness, and I feel unwell. My liver. Yesterday I revised Posha's biography.[24] Made a few insertions. It's poor. Went for a ride. Behaved badly towards an officer. Didn't forget myself, but couldn't do otherwise. I'll go and see him now. I must write down two things: about God and His ministry. I'm afraid I'm in a bad mood today and will write badly. Thought of something else good, and have forgotten it. Saw Andryusha off.[25] It's astonishing why I love him. To say it's because he's sincere and truthful isn't true. He's often untruthful (indeed, it's obvious at once). But I feel at ease and well with him, and I love him. Why? [. . .]

18 June, Yasnaya Polyana Health not too good. I'm not writing anything. Thought about myself:
(1) Am I not deceiving myself when I praise poverty? I saw this with my letter to Molostvova.[26] I see it with Sasha. I'm sorry for them, I'm afraid for them with no carriage, no cleanliness, no riding-habit. There is only one explanation and justification: I don't like poverty, I can't like it, especially for other people, but I like still less, I hate, I can't help hating what brings wealth: ownership of land, banks, interest. The devil has so cunningly ensnared me that I can see all the privations of poverty clearly before my eyes, but I can't see the injustices which rescue people from it. All that is hidden, and it's all approved by the majority. If the question were put directly, however much it hurt me, I would resolve it in favour of poverty. I must put the question to myself directly and resolve it directly. [. . .]

20 June, Yasnaya Polyana [. . .] Some things I think of and forget, some things I remember, namely: [. . .]
(7) Man in the present, i.e. outside time, is always free, but when we look at his behaviour in time, it always seems to be the result of a preceding cause. Every act

of behaviour is preceded by some other act or state, and not only one act or state but a countless number of acts and states, and therefore every act can be related to some other act or state, or some aggregate of preceding acts or states, as a consequence of it or of them. And therefore man is free, but seems unfree. It's just the opposite of what the determinists say, when they say that man is unfree, but seems free. And Lichtenberg is absolutely right: *you say that man is unfree because we know for certain that every action has its own cause, but I say that the thesis that every action has its own cause is untrue because I know for certain that man is free.*

22 June, Pirogovo   I've been at Pirogovo since yesterday. My brother is in a very bad state, not so much physically as spiritually. True, his condition is very serious, a stroke, mouth distorted, slobbering and pains; but it's becoming more serious because he doesn't want to give in to it. In such a condition there are only two solutions: defiance, irritability and an increase of suffering, as with him, or, on the contrary: submission, gentleness and a decrease of suffering, even to the extent of eliminating it altogether. [. . .]

Yesterday the *Russian Gazette* expressed an opinion about my article published in England.[27] It pleased me very much, pleased my vanity, and that's bad.

24 June, Yasnaya Polyana   Letters from Chertkov and an Englishman apropos of my article *On War*.[28] I'm afraid that it caused annoyance because it wasn't thought out with God's help. It both gratified my vanity and made me aware of a bad deed. Everything can be said lovingly, with God's help, but I didn't manage to do so. I still remember everything, and live in a state of higher consciousness. Masha is here. And she is not only as near as ever, but even nearer to me, without the need for words. [. . .]

27 June   Yesterday my stomach and liver were upset. Sluggishness, lethargy and even a bad frame of mind. Caught myself grumbling at Ilya Vasilyevich. I was ashamed. But everything else is good. I'm not forgetting my station. [. . .]

28 June, Yasnaya Polyana [. . .]
(5) Called to mind military drill in the time of Nicholas Pavlovich (Rosen's *Notes*:[29] beat up three, make a soldier out of one); called to mind serfdom and the attitude I felt towards a human being, as though he were an object or an animal; a total lack of consciousness of brotherhood. That's the most important thing of all that I would like to write about Nicholas I and the Decembrists. [. . .]

2 July, Yasnaya Polyana   Wrote a lot of letters yesterday – Grishenko about free will and Toll about my article.[30] I seemed to wake up yesterday, but am sluggish again today. Thought a lot about the same things: movement, matter, time, space . . . [. . .]
(2) There was a time when anarchy was unthinkable. The people wanted to worship and obey, and the rulers were sure of their vocation and didn't think about consolidating their authority and did nothing about it. But now the people no

longer worship, and not only don't want to obey, but want freedom, while the rulers don't do what is considered necessary for their own and their people's glory, but are busy maintaining their own power. The peoples sense this, and no longer put up with power, but want freedom, complete freedom. One must first of all throw a certain amount off a heavily-laden wagon in order to be able to overturn it. The time has come not to throw things off gradually any more, but to overturn the wagon.
(3) Is a reasonable life thinkable in a state where the head of it blesses people with icons, kisses them and makes others kiss them?

17 July, Yasnaya Polyana   I'm still writing just as little. I'm thinking of a few things and working a bit on the foreword.³¹ I've been to Pirogovo. Seryozha won't rest, he's putting up resistance. And it's painful for him and for the others. On the way there I saw a new horse-collar bound together with bast, and thought again about the Robinson theme – a migrant rural community. And I wanted to write a second part of Nekhlyudov. His work, tiredness, nascent grand seigneurism, temptation by a woman, fall, mistakes, and all against a background of a Robinson community.³² [. . .]
(3) Socialism – apart from the immediate relief of the condition of the workers – advocates the establishment of external forms, the *future* economic organisation of human societies. And therefore *il a beau jeu* [it has a good hand]. Everything is conceived in the future, without substance and without realisation in the present, apart from the struggle to improve the life of the workers. The main mistake people make in their understanding of socialism is that they confuse two things by this concept: (a) the struggle against the exploitation of capital and (b) imaginary progress towards the realisation of a socialist society. The first is a useful and natural thing, the second – an impossible and fantastic concept.

18 July, Yasnaya Polyana   Was unwell yesterday and had no dinner. *I've overdone it*, as the German said. I'm all right today. I'm now sitting in my room and listening at a distance to the incessant talk, and I know that this talk has been going on since early morning and will go on until late evening, and went on yesterday as well, and the day before, and before that again, and is always going on and will do so as long as the people talking have no need to work. And the main thing is that everything has been said; there's nothing more to say. The only way to pad out the talk is to say malicious things about people who are not there, or to argue in a malicious way with people who are. Idleness is a terrible calamity. People are created in order to work, but they have created slaves for themselves, and emancipated themselves from hard work, and now they are suffering, and suffering not just from boredom and idle talk, but from atrophy of the muscles and the heart, from losing the habit of hard work, from maladroitness, cowardice, lack of courage, and illnesses.

But these are only the sufferings which idle people heap upon themselves; but how many of the best joys of life are they deprived of: hard work in the midst of nature, association with fellow workers, enjoyment of relaxation, food when it goes to replenish used up energy, association with animals, an awareness of the fruitfulness of one's work . . . My life has been ruined, has been corrupted by this terrible idleness. How I would like to warn others against similar ruin.

Oh, how I would like to write a second part of Nekhlyudov!

Must note down:

(1) Dreams can never be studied and examined enough. Nothing reveals the secrets of the mental life as much as they do. [. . .]

(3) We constantly forget that we are not standing still, but are moving, each person individually in his lifetime and all of us together with the centuries. This delusion is particularly strong in childhood. Children like everything to be as it always has been, and don't want to believe in the movement in which they are taking part. But with the years, this movement gets quicker, like a stone falling from a height, and old men can already see this quick and obvious movement. For a right life it is always necessary to remember that we are not standing still but are moving, and we must not cling to what we are moving away from.

22 July, Yasnaya Polyana There's a big new work asking to be written, a necessary, important and enormous work. I don't even want to say here what it is.[33] I wanted to begin it today but couldn't, I had no enthusiasm. Finished the foreword. Still the same lack of enthusiasm or ability to work. Health reasonably good.

24 July, Yasnaya Polyana Began it yesterday and gave it up. It was no good. But I'm still thinking. Last night I thought about the same thing, and thought well. Yesterday I travelled to the fire victims at . . . (I can't remember) . . . Gorodna. (My memory is getting very feeble.) Unpleasant; false philanthropy. Things are well at home. Well, without any effort from me. What was not good was listening to *The Divine and the Human*, and being agitated. Still I think I'll finish *The Stone* today. I feel I must. It's really the awareness of my duty to say what people don't know and where they are going astray. I'll try to do it as briefly and simply as possible.

29 July, Yasnaya Polyana [. . .] People often visit me, and three days ago I thought of noting down who they all were. They were: (1) A peasant from Gill's who had had an accident in a mine. I sent him to Goldenblat.[24] (2) Then a soldier's wife, about the return of her husband. I wrote her a petition. (3) Then some lads from the railway. I selected some booklets for them. (4) Then a lady from Tiflis about religious education. I told her what I thought. On Monday and Tuesday too there were just as many visitors. Note:

(1) Still on the same thing: how everything seems to me to be growing and expanding, but this is an illusion: there can be no infinite growth and expansion. For the infinite, there is no more or less. So what seems to me to be growing and expanding is movement in a circle – a snake biting its tail. [. . .]

2 August, Yasnaya Polyana Still can't write. Decided yesterday for a start to write about the importance of religion without, or almost without any corrections. And I thought it over carefully. All my sons came to see Andryusha off, and Olga also.

The war disturbs me, but less so now because all my efforts have gone into my work. I must note down things in general, and something for my article on religion, namely: (1) As I listened to music and asked myself the question why there is such and such a sequence of sounds, apparently determined in advance, in such and such a tempo, the thought occurred to me that it is because in the art of music or poetry the artist lifts a curtain on the future – shows what ought to be. And we agree with him, because we see after the artist what ought to be, or already is in the future. It's the same – and to a greater degree – with moral preaching and with prophecy. [. . .]

15 August, Pirogovo I've been here three days. I've been gradually getting worse, and yesterday was quite bad: fever, and above all severe heartburn. It was very depressing being with Seryozha. He is suffering cruelly both physically and morally, and won't resign himself to his fate. I couldn't do or say anything good or useful to him. On the first day I did some translating. Yesterday I did nothing, and today I unexpectedly hit upon a beginning for an article on religion and wrote one and a half chapters. My head suddenly became clear, and I realised that it had been my illness coming on. Hence my stupidity.

I must give it a title: *The One Cause of Everything*, or *The Light has become Darkness*, or *Without God*.

Note:

(1) People think up symbols of greatness: tsars, military leaders, poets. But it's all false. Anyone can see through them, can see that there's nothing there and the tsar is naked.

But what about wise men and prophets? Yes, they seem to us more useful than other people, but not only are they not great – they are not even one whit greater than other people. All their wisdom, saintliness and prophecy is nothing compared with absolute wisdom and saintliness. And they are no greater than others. There is no greatness for human beings, there is only the fulfilment, the greater or lesser fulfilment or non-fulfilment of one's duty. And that is good. It's better that way. Do not seek greatness; seek to do your duty. [. . .]

17 August, Pirogovo Much better today; I'm recovering. I'm thinking of going to Seryozha's. Sat out in the open air yesterday and went for a walk. Made some notes. Was just thinking that I definitely must abandon the idea of polishing up my writings. Rather I should write whatever has taken clear shape in my head according to various sub-divisions: (1) wisdom – religion – philosophy; (2) works of fiction: (*a*) *Resurrection*, (*b*) The Decembrists, Nicholas, (*c*) obvious corrections to the works of fiction I write; (3) Memoirs. I must without fail note down my memories as I recall them; those times, conditions and feelings which I vividly recall and which seem worthy of recording. This would be very good. I don't know if I'll succeed.

Note:

(1) The sort of blasphemy which exasperates me is not deliberate but spontaneous; not an icon in a cess-pit or a Gospel used instead of packing paper or any other

sort of paper (although I feel something unpleasant about that too), but people speaking in sport and jest, and amusing themselves with sophisms about morality, the good, love, reason and God, like Jerome Jerome whom I'm reading now,[35] and like many, many science writers and writers of journals and fiction, both intentionally and unwittingly.

(2) While out walking, I vividly recalled my state of mind when young, especially after military service. Even before that the yearning towards self-improvement was alive, just about alive in me. I couldn't define, and didn't know in whose name this was necessary, but I felt there was something. But after military service I was absolutely free of all spiritual bonds, i.e. the complete slave of the animal in me. There was only one thing in whose name I could still sacrifice the lusts and even the life of an animal (war, a duel for which I was always preparing myself), and only that one thing; otherwise everything was possible. And so it was till the age of fifty. How I would like to save people from this! [. . .]

19 August, Pirogovo Seem better today. Slept without pains or heartburn. Yesterday Sergey Vasilyevich[36] said that Seryozha was afraid he would die in the night. I'll go and see him at once.

I'm reading Taine.[37] I find him very opportune.

(1) He describes the disasters of the anarchy of 1780 to 1790. They are hardly greater than the disasters of the present Japanese war, under the most orthodox system of government. [. . .]

20 August, Pirogovo Much better today. Received some letters yesterday. Sonya isn't expecting me particularly. Still I want to go tomorrow, God willing. Pleasant news from Chertkov about the foreword, and from Lucy Mallory too.[38] I'm walking a lot. And I'm still reading Taine. It's very important for me.

When reading the history of the French Revolution, it becomes undoubtedly clear that the foundations of the Revolution (which Taine attacks so unjustly) are undoubtedly correct and ought to be proclaimed, and that, as he says, *imaginary man*, i.e. the ideal man, is far nearer to reality than the Frenchman of a given time and place, and that it is far more *practical* to be guided by this *imaginary man* for the purpose of organising our lives than to be guided by considerations of the qualities of such and such a Frenchman; the only mistake was in supposing that the principles proclaimed could become reality in the same way as the previous abuses: as a result of force. *L'assemblée construante*[39] would have been absolutely right had it declared the same principles, namely: that no one may own another man, or may own land, no one may collect taxes, no one may execute anybody or deprive him of freedom; had it declared that as from today no one, i.e. no government, would support these rights – that and nothing more. What would have happened as a result of this I don't know, and no one knows what would happen now if it were declared; but of one thing there can be no doubt, that what happened in the French Revolution could not happen.

Private people could never kill or slaughter or rob one thousandth part of the number of people killed and robbed by governments, i.e. by people who arrogate to themselves the right to kill and rob. Perhaps French society was not ready for such a revolution then; perhaps it is not ready even now; but there can be no doubt that this revolution is bound to take place, that mankind is preparing itself more and more for this revolution, and that the time will come when mankind is ready for it.

22 August, Yasnaya Polyana Came back from Pirogovo yesterday. Seryozha is dying. He didn't need me. [. . .]

26 August, Pirogovo Seryozha has died. Quietly, without the awareness, the express awareness, that he was dying. It was a secret. It's impossible to say whether it's better or worse that way. Effective religious feeling was denied to him (perhaps I'm still deceiving myself, but I think not). But all is well with him just the same. Something new and better has been revealed to him. And to me too. The degree of this illumination is valuable and important, but it doesn't matter at what stage in an infinite cycle it comes.

I've been working for two days on the calendar, things are becoming clearer. But it's still difficult.
(1) People talk about the disasters of anarchy, even accompanied by terrorism. But can they be compared with the disasters of, for example, the present Japanese war? [. . .]

1 September, Yasnaya Polyana I've had a stomach-ache for three days now. All this time I've been translating, and reading for the *Cycle of Reading*, and have written a foreword. Work is progressing, but there's a great deal of it. [. . .]

15 September, Yasnaya Polyana Haven't written my diary for two weeks. I've been busy all the time with extracts for the *Cycle of Reading*. I've collected enough material for a full year and probably for another whole year. I'm not reading the papers, but am reading Amiel, Carlyle, and Mazzini,[40] and feel very good at heart. Health not bad. State of mind – I'd like to boast about it, but I'm afraid to; still, I'll say that it's very gratifying. There are a lot of things to be noted: [. . .]
(2) A strange thing: I very often feel myself drawn more to immoral, even cruel, but single-minded people (Vera, Andryusha and many others) than to liberal people who serve other people and society. I've found an explanation for this. People are not to blame if they can't see the true meaning of life, if they are still blind – not like owls, but like puppies. The one good thing they can do is not to lie, not to be hypocritical, not to do what resembles real, humane, religious activity, but is not. But when they are hypocritical, or do things for other people's sake, not for God's, or seek to justify themselves, then they are repellent. [. . .]
(8) There's a wonderful fairy tale by Andersen about the peas which saw the whole world as green as long as their pod was green; then the world became yellow, and then (I'm going on a bit) there was a crack and the world came to an end. And the peas fell to the ground and began to grow.[41] [. . .]
(10) Carlyle says that atheism leads to 'valetism'.[42] The man who doesn't recognise the power of God invariably recognises the power of man.

22 September, Yasnaya Polyana Haven't written my diary for a week. Health good. Mentally drowsy. Started to write *Light in the Darkness*,[43] but hadn't the enthusiasm to continue. Did one or two things for the *Calendar*. Must copy out the biographies.[44] Read Kant.[45] His God and immortality, i.e. the future life, are remarkable for their lack of proof. However, he says himself that he won't remove from one side of the scales his wish to prove immortality. But the basic idea of a will outside time, of the thing in itself, is absolutely correct and known to all religions (e.g. the Brahmin), only there it's more simply and clearly expressed. There remains one service he has performed, but it is an enormous one: *the conditional nature of time*. That's a great thing. You feel how much you would have missed if, thanks to Kant, you had not understood this.

Sonya is in Moscow. The weather is wonderful.

Note:

(7) Religion is a philosophy comprehensible to everyone; philosophy is a religion to be proved, and therefore involved and systematised.

(8) Oh, how I would like to write a catechism of morality (without questions and answers) for everybody, especially children – a comprehensible and convincing one! Then I could say: 'Today your sins are forgiven'.

22 October, Yasnaya Polyana Haven't written my diary for an age. All this time I've been busy with the *Cycle of Reading*. I've worked a lot and done a lot. But the further I get, the more I see that it could have been better. I don't know where I'll stop. It's nice to realise that it's only enthusiasm for the work itself that I feel in this case. [. . .] Something particularly important happened today:

(1) A thought comes to me, as used to happen so often in the past, which seems strange, a paradox; then it comes again from a different direction, a second and a third time, and I begin to think about objects and thoughts connected with it, and suddenly I become convinced that not only is it not a paradox, a chance thought, but a most important and fundamental one which will open up a new, important side of life. This is what happened to me with the thought about man's vocation to improve himself. I used to react cautiously and timidly to this thought because to some people it seemed a truism and to others something unpleasant, foolishly comic, against which they would angrily rebel. But now I am convinced that this thought resolves all doubts, and that therein lies the clear meaning of life and the only one accessible to us.

Why it is necessary to the source of life, to God, or simply why it is necessary at all for us to improve ourselves, I do not and cannot know. I can only guess that it is necessary in order that the greatest good might come to pass both for individual people and for people collectively, since nothing promotes the good of the one and the other so much as the striving towards improvement. But if I do not know why, I do know without doubt that therein lies the law and the purpose of our lives.

I know this from three very convincing arguments: in the first place because all our life is a striving towards good, i.e. towards the bettering of our situation. Self-improvement is the most undeniable way of bettering our situation. And the striving towards self-improvement is not a prescription of reason, but an innate property of man. Every man is always striving towards it consciously or unconsciously. That's the first point. In the second place it is the one and only activity of all human activities which cannot be halted, and which can be pursued as freely as ever in times of distress, suffering, illness and death itself. That's the second point. The third proof of the fact that this is man's vocation is that for a man who consciously sets himself such activity as a goal, all that we call evil disappears, or rather is transformed into good. Persecutions, insults, need, physical suffering, one's own illnesses and those of people near to one, the death of one's friends and one's own death – all this is accepted by such a man as something which not only should be, but which is necessary to him for his self-improvement.

The parable of the talents says this very thing. Life is an enlarging of one's soul, and good is not a question of what sort of soul it is, but of the extent to which a man has enlarged, expanded and improved it. Why is this? Nobody knows or can know. But we all vaguely feel that it is so, if we don't actually know it, and we are capable of knowing it. [. . .]

(14) If we dislike people, it's not because they are evil; we consider them evil because we dislike them. [. . .]

(22) People ask 'why do children die, young people who have not lived much?' How do you know they have not lived much? It is your crude measurement in terms of time, but life is not measured by time. It's like saying: 'Why is this aphorism, this poem, this picture, this work of music so short; why was it broken off and not expanded to the length of the longest speeches and plays, or the biggest pictures?' Just as the measurement of length is not applicable to the importance (the greatness) of works of wisdom, neither is it (applicable) to life. How do you know what inner growth this soul has achieved in its short time span, and what influence it has had on others?

The spiritual life cannot be measured by physical measurements. [. . .]

Today is 24 November, Yasnaya Polyana Weakness and indecision about what to write. Began *The Stone* today. But it's poor. I must write three things. These are the most essential:
(1) *The Stone*, (2) on the form of the state, and (3) a profession of faith.[46] If I have the time and strength in the evenings, then my memoirs, in any order just as they come. I've begun to remember things very vividly. I don't know whether I'll succeed in expressing them vividly. [. . .]

1 December, Yasnaya Polyana I've finished the hard work on the *Cycle of Reading*. I've begun *Who am I?* Feel very good at heart. [. . .] Note:
(1) The existing social system is in its fundamentals so much at variance with the consciousness of society that it cannot be repaired, just as the walls of a house whose foundations are sinking cannot be repaired. It all has to be rebuilt from the very bottom. One cannot repair the existing system with its absurd wealth and over-indulgence for some and its poverty and deprivation for the masses, its right to own land and to levy state taxes, its seizure of territory by countries, its patriotism, militarism, and knowingly false religion, upheld by force. One cannot

repair all this by constitutions, universal suffrage, pensions for workers, the separation of Church and state and suchlike palliatives. [. . .]

7 December, Yasnaya Polyana I don't feel like work at all. I'm living cheerfully. I feel particularly strongly the temporary nature of this life of service, and that's good. Began the exposition of my faith, and am doing a few things for the *Cycle of Reading*.

11 December, Yasnaya Polyana Health worse. Pains in the stomach, and I don't feel like work. Stopped work on the exposition of my faith, and have been translating Pascal[47] for two days. He's very good. Read Spinoza and chose some extracts.[48] [. . .] Note:
(7) Medical science and practice is, together with drunkenness, militarism, luxury and the oppression of the workers, one of the greatest calamities of our time and has the same origin as all the other calamities, namely the absence of religion, i.e. the recognition of one's situation in the world. The basis of a reasonable (religious) understanding of life is *memento mori*, the memory of death – not so much the memory of it, as the understanding of the brevity and fleeting nature of life. But medical science is bound to look only at life, in search of ways to prolong it. [. . .]

13 December, Yasnaya Polyana I.I.A.

Alive, but have missed many days. Today is 22 December, Yasnaya Polyana. Began a little of *The One Thing Needful*, and began it not badly, but hadn't any enthusiasm for continuing. Also wrote several letters. I'm afraid I distressed Molostvova.[49] Worked on the *Cycle of Reading*; included Spinoza. There's much to note down, above all the joyful, steadfast, serene, almost always loving state in which I find myself. The question is: where does it come from? Why, given my vile life, do I have so much happiness? [. . .]

Today is 31 December, Yasnaya Polyana All this time I've been overcome by a sort of weakness. It's my heart, I think. I'm not the least bit unwilling to depart (to die). The only thing is the inertia of my life and thought: it's as though I had come to a stop in the middle of a fast race and felt embarrassed and even in pain. Tried to get on with *The One Thing Needful*, but only made a mess of it, and nothing came of it. Tried to continue my memoirs. Also badly.

During these last days my letter to Nicholas II has appeared.[50] Chertkov printed it following the consent I had given via Dušan. I found it unpleasant. If any measures had been taken against me, no matter what – the harder the better – I would have been pleased, but I think I behaved indelicately towards Nicholas II and Nikolay Mikhaylovich.[51] It was particularly unpleasant for me because I had been in a sad mood all this time (not unkind and not discontented, but sad) because of the state of my body. [. . .]
Note: [. . .]
(4) The surrender of Port Arthur caused me grief and pain.[52] It's patriotism. I was brought up in it, and am just as much a slave to it as I am to personal egoism,

family egoism, even aristocratic egoism. All these egoisms are alive in me, but there is in me also the awareness of the divine law, and that awareness keeps these egoisms in check so that I don't have to be their servant. And bit by bit these egoisms are becoming atrophied. [. . .]

1905

1 January, Yasnaya Polyana A mass of people, and they make me tired. But I'm glad that, like the appearance of the letter,[1] this disagreeable congregation of people is not causing me displeasure, but is a stimulus to inner work: to behave in the best way possible towards what is disagreeable. I've just been thinking about this:
(1) We conjecture about, we seek, we desire happiness, i.e. the conditions under which things should be good for us, but things can only be good for us as a result of our efforts to overcome what is not good for us. And so the result is the complete opposite of what we thought it would be: the very things that we call happiness: health, wealth, fame, beauty – all that is Capua,[2] it all weakens our energy, does away with the opportunity, or at least doesn't stimulate the need, to make an effort – the very thing that brings true good. And conversely: everything that is considered unhappiness stimulates these efforts. This is the foundation for the terrible delusion that the external forms of social life constitute the good, and need to be properly organised. I feel like expressing the paradox that the better the forms of social life are, the lower are people's minds and characters (America before the emancipation of the negroes). To seek what are called fortunate circumstances in life: wealth, fame, health, beauty, attractiveness – is just like warming oneself by the stove, rather than by healthy hard work in the fresh air.
(2) Organising the external forms of social life without inner self-improvement is just like trying to rebuild without lime, but in a new style, a dilapidated building of undressed stones. However you build it, it still won't be weather-proof and will collapse. [. . .]

20 January, Yasnaya Polyana Haven't written my diary for a long time. [. . .] Note: [. . .]
(2) Music is the stenography of the feelings. What I mean is: the quick or slow succession of sounds, their pitch, their volume – all this, in speech, embellishes words and their meaning, indicating those shades of feelings which are associated with our parts of speech. Music without speech takes these expressions of feelings and shades of feelings and combines them, and we get a play of feelings without the things that gave rise to them. For this reason music has such a particularly strong effect, and for this reason the combination of music with words is an adulteration of the music, a retrogression, a writing out in letters of stenographic signs. [. . .]

[29 January] I've missed more than a week. Today is 29 January, Yasnaya Polyana. I'm writing *The One Thing Needful*, and either because I have combined two different beginnings, or simply because I'm not in the mood, the writing is going badly. Posha has been here the whole time. I'm very fond of him. Sasha has gone to Petersburg. Sonya is in Moscow. Seryozha is here, and relations are difficult between us. I want to master myself, but I still can't. I'm glad that after one quarrel to begin with (not a very serious one), I didn't go any further. Today I received a second letter from Galya – not a good one.[3]

There are signs of irritability and a lack of serious inner religious work. One shouldn't, and therefore one mustn't quarrel or argue either. This morning there was a letter via Lederle from two sailors who have refused military service: they are in prison in Kronstadt. I want to write to them and their commander at once. Looked in the calendar for their commander's name and couldn't find it. Changed my mind about writing.

In the morning a nice person, Kipiani,[4] came from Nakashidze, and told wonderful stories about what is happening in the Caucasus: in Guriya, Imeretiya, Mengreliya, Kakhetiya. The people have resolved to be free of the government and to organise things for themselves. Dušan took notes. I must write about it. It's a great thing. I experience various states: shame, sadness, anger, tenderness; but today my state is one where nothing is important, nothing is interesting, nothing matters.

Still, I have a lot of things to note down:

(1) I was listening to some political discussions, arguments and censure, and went into another room where people were singing to a guitar and laughing. And I clearly felt the sacred quality of cheerfulness. Cheerfulness and joy – these are one of the means of fulfilling God's will.

(2) I felt recently how far I've fallen spiritually from that moral, spiritual height to which I was raised by being in association with the best and wisest people whose works I've been reading and whose thoughts I've been pondering over for my *Cycle of Reading*. There is no doubt that you can raise and lower yourself spiritually through the company of the people you associate with, whether present or absent. [. . .]

Today is 1 February, Yasnaya Polyana. I'm still writing my article *The One Thing Needful*. It either goes badly or not at all, and I continue to be in a state of 'it's not worth it'. The vanity and folly of political interests is more and more apparent. Relations with Seryozha have been unpleasant. I was unkind. And I'm suffering for it. Lyova has been seen by the Tsar, and I'm glad of it.[5] Strange to say, this has quite freed me from the desire to influence the Tsar. Astonishing news from Guriya of how they have overthrown the government and set themselves free, and at the same time have begun to lead a better life and have become freer. I must note down something very important; I don't know whether I'll have the strength. I've been writing a little of my memoirs for two days. [. . .]

[18 February] Haven't written my diary for an age, i.e. eighteen days. Today is 18 February, Yasnaya Polyana. I've been mentally weak all this time. It's my liver. I feel a bit fresher today. I'm still writing *The One Thing Needful*. And it's still bad. There's still no end to it. I don't like the *Cycle of Reading*. Strakhov has taken on the job. And I'm very glad.[6] [. . .]

24 February, Yasnaya Polyana   Began to write *Korney Vasilyev*.⁷ It's poor. I'm still weak. Busy with the *Cycle of Reading*. I'd like to start writing *about life*. [. . .]

Today is 28 February, Yasnaya Polyana   I've been writing *Alyosha*;⁸ it's quite bad. Gave it up. Revised Pascal and Lammenais.⁹ Finished writing *Korney*. It's reasonable. [. . .]
(2) Most people live as though they are walking backwards towards a precipice. They know there's a precipice behind, which they might fall over at any moment, but they don't look at it, and amuse themselves with what they can see.

6 March, Yasnaya Polyana   I'm feeling very happy. Revised Pascal and Lammenais. Looked through *The One Thing Needful*, and I don't think I'll revise it any more. Masha and Kolya are here. Wrote a few worthless letters. Must note down something that seems to me important:
(1) How ridiculous people are who try to explore greater and lesser infinity with their telescopes and microscopes. They are just like a man trying to find his friends in a house in which he has been told that nobody has ever lived or could live. Infinity is only an indication of the fact that where the object of a man's study approaches infinity, as with stars and microbes, there must be a mistake in the formulation of the question, and its study can lead nowhere.
(2) I've been thinking about what is taught in our schools, our grammar schools: the main subjects are: (1) ancient languages and grammar – no use at all; (2) Russian literature, confined to near contemporaries, i.e. Belinsky, Dobrolyubov and yours truly. All the great literature of the world is a closed book. (3) History, by which is understood the description of the nasty lives of various good-for-nothing kings, emperors, dictators and military commanders, i.e. distortion of the truth, and (4) to crown it all – nonsensical and stupid legends and dogmas which are impudently called scripture.
   This is in our secondary schools.¹⁰ In our secondary schools everything that is reasonable and necessary is repudiated. In our colleges, with the exception of specialisations like technology and medicine, they deliberately teach a materialistic, i.e. a narrow and limited doctrine which is intended to explain everything and exclude any reasonable understanding of life.
   It's terrible! [. . .]

9 March, Yasnaya Polyana   I've been writing *Who am I?* It's neither good nor bad. I'm feeling very well. I'm thinking more and more about living for God, and training myself to do it. It's not difficult. A matter of habit. I think it's possible for the young too.

Today is 18 March, Yasnaya Polyana. For five days or so I've been feeling sluggish, sleeping and fighting against gloom. That's good. It needs an inner effort. [. . .]
   Must note one thing:
(1) Turgenev wrote a good piece, *Hamlet and Don Quixote*, and brought in Horatio at the end. But I think that the two chief characters are – Don Quixote and Horatio,

Sancho Panza and the *Darling*.¹¹ The former are for the most part men; the latter for the most part women. My sons are all Don Quixotes, but without the self-sacrifice; my daughters are all Horatios, ready for self-sacrifice.

20 March, Yasnaya Polyana Still unwell. I've written nothing except letters for three days. Haven't been out today. I'm fighting against the desire for worldly fame. Had some reproachful letters,¹² and couldn't overcome an unpleasant feeling. [...]

22 March, Yasnaya Polyana I'm awake today. Worked very well at *The One Thing Needful*. And I think, or rather I'm sure that I've finished it. There's a lot of work I want to do. [...]

30 March, Yasnaya Polyana I've had heart pains these last few days, and haven't been able to work at all as a result, and I very much want to: Chelčický, and Ilyusha's story. And Filka, and *An Unfortunate Girl*.¹³ And my profession of faith. Had some good thoughts about death. I continue to live in the sight of God. Wrote a letter about the overturned cart.¹⁴ Revised the proofs of the *Cycle*. Note:
(1) Two things above all are necessary for me: to overcome my concern for people's opinions about me, and to overcome my unkind feeling towards them.

For the former I must take advantage of every occasion when people censure or misunderstand me, without feeling bitterness and without correcting them.

For the latter it is very important not to allow myself to think unkindly of people. A test today with Lyova,¹⁵ and a test today also with regard to the former thing: a letter about my writings.¹⁶ [...]
(3) How right the Slavophiles are when they say that the Russian people try to avoid power, that they run away from it. They are prepared to offer it to bad people rather than be soiled by it themselves. I think that if that is so, they are right. Anything is better than being compelled to use force. The situation of a person in the power of a tyrant is far more conducive to a moral life than the situation of a voter, or a sharer of power. [...]

3 April, Yasnaya Polyana I've had heart trouble. Death is becoming more and more simple, more and more natural. In spite of ill health, I've got a few things done, namely: a foreword to *The Net of Faith* (not bad), and excerpts from *The Net of Faith* (8) and a foreword to *The Teaching of the Twelve Apostles*.¹⁷ Not so good, but it will do. And the letter about the overturned cart. [...]

6 April, Yasnaya Polyana For two days (including today) I've written nothing. Made an attempt yesterday at *The Green Stick*.¹⁸ It was no good. It's still not right. I can't combine the whole truth as I understand it with simplicity of exposition. [...]

16 April, Yasnaya Polyana All this time I've had heart pains. I didn't notice anything before, but now I feel it: constriction, irregular heartbeats. It's both good, and it's serious. I haven't been able to work because of it. And I very much want to write an exposition of my belief and also something about Henry George, whom I read in Nikolayev's edition[19] and was delighted by once more.

There have been moments recently when I've had a clear understanding of life such as I've never had before. It's as if a complex equation had been reduced to the most simple expression and solution. [. . .]

Today is 21 April (evening), Yasnaya Polyana. My heart has been better during this time. I've begun to write *Defenders of the People*.[20] It's not bad. And Henry George.[21] Was at Pyotr Osipov's yesterday with Buturlin, and he reproached me bitterly for saying what I do while buying up land.[22] It hurt me and was good for me. I felt how useful and fortifying censure is, especially when undeserved, and how harmful and ennervating praise is, and especially when undeserved (and it always is undeserved). Note: [. . .]
(5) I think more and more often about memory, about recollection, and this faculty seems to me more and more important, more and more fundamental. I receive an impression. It doesn't exist in the present. It only exists in the memory, when I begin to recall it, consider it, and combine it with other impressions and thoughts. I receive an impression of joy or offence. There is neither joy nor offence in the present; the impression only begins to operate in the memory. Of the innumerable number of impressions which I have received, I have forgotten very many, but they have left traces in my spiritual being. My spiritual being is formed from them. [. . .]

Today is 4 May, Yasnaya Polyana [. . .] During this time I finished *A Great Sin*.[23] Wrote a story about prayer.[24] It seemed good, and I was moved while writing it, but now I hardly like it at all. [. . .]

19 May, Yasnaya Polyana Haven't written my diary for more than two weeks. Health still as bad: continual heartburn and pains in my stomach and liver. But I'm not living too badly. The thought of the need for the awareness of life in the sight of God has ceased to have a strong effect as something new, but it has laid down a path, I hope, and part of it (the thought) has entered into my conscious activity. I've been revising *A Great Sin* all this time, and still haven't finished it. Sonya is ill. She had a severe attack of pain today. Note:
(1) I noted: consciousness brings time, i.e. illusion, to a stop.

News was received yesterday of the destruction of the Russian navy.[25] This news struck me particularly forcibly for some reason. It became clear to me that it could not have been, and cannot be otherwise: although we are bad Christians, it's impossible to hide the incompatibility between the Christian faith and war. In recent times (meaning the last thirty years or so), this contradiction has come to be felt more and more. And therefore in a war with a non-Christian people for whom the highest ideal is the fatherland and the heroism of war, Christian peoples are bound to be defeated. If Christian peoples have so far defeated non-Christian peoples, this has only happened because of the superiority of the technological and military advances of the Christian peoples (China, India, the African peoples, the people of Khiva and the Central Asians); but given equal technology, Christian peoples must inevitably be defeated by non-Christians, as happened in the war between Russia and Japan. Japan in the space of a few decades not only drew level with European and American peoples, but surpassed them in technological advances. The success of the Japanese in the technology not only of war, but of all material advances as well, has shown clearly how cheap these technological advances which are called culture are. It doesn't cost anything to copy them and even to invent new ones. What is valuable, important and difficult is a good life, purity, brotherhood, love, the very things that Christianity teaches us and which we have despised. That is the lesson for us.

I don't say this in order to console myself because the Japanese have beaten us. The shame and the disgrace remain just the same. But they don't consist in the fact that we were beaten by the Japanese, but in the fact that we undertook to do something which we are unable to do well and which is bad in itself.

(3) Didn't finish writing on the 19th and I'm continuing this morning.

24 May, Yasnaya Polyana Chertkov is coming today. All this time I've been revising and adding to *A Great Sin*. I think I've finished. But the final destruction of the Russian navy has prompted a number of thoughts which must be expressed. [...]

(7) As one grows old one regrets the joys of youth: gaiety, friendship, love ... Yet there is no need to be deprived of them. Grow old and live these joys in the young, putting yourself in their place, loving them and guiding them. [...]

(9) How ignorant we are of the life of the working people! We don't know all the sacrifice of life they endure for the sake of their work. I thought about all this as I watched them digging out Semyon Vladimirov who had been buried in sand.[26] Self-sacrifice, the joy of self-sacrifice, is obvious in Aleksey Zhidkov and Gerasim. It's wonderful. It must be made clear to people. [...]

(15) I very much want to insert my confession and my revelation about the peasants into Ilyusha's story.[27] Otherwise it won't be done. [...]

6 June, Yasnaya Polyana Chertkov left the day before yesterday. My relations with him were very good, better than I expected. I had a depressing talk with S. (my son). A difficult examination. I won't pass. Shortened *A Great Sin*, and discarded a lot. I regret it. Dear Posha has come. Sonya's health is not good. I was going to write 'dubious', but was afraid she would read it. I'll leave it, because it really is dubious. A disciple of Malevanny[28] came today, a very good man, but I'm not looking forward to Dolgorukov[29] coming.

A lot of people were sitting down together yesterday: old and young, husbands and wives, young girls and children, and it became so clear to me that they were all openings – windows through which I see God. They all open up for me alike as the curtain which covers them is drawn aside. And once I understand this, how can I be angry with them; how can I expect identical understanding from them?

Began bathing four days ago. Bowels not functioning at all. That's good. I'm often directly aware of what is good. Note: [...]

(4) The older I become, the more vivid my recollections become. And surprisingly,

I only recall what is joyful and good, and enjoy my recollections no less than, and sometimes more than I enjoyed the reality. [. . .]
(6) The analogy between the Church and science is confirmed in everything: like each other they don't argue, don't explain, don't try to understand dissent, but make assertions, don't listen and get angry. [. . .]
(8) People compare me to Rousseau. I am greatly indebted to Rousseau and I love him, but there is a big difference. The difference is that Rousseau rejects every kind of civilisation, while I reject the pseudo-Christian kind. What people call civilisation is the growth of mankind. Growth is necessary, one cannot talk about it being good or bad. It exists – life consists of it. It's the same with the growth of a tree. But the branches, or the life forces that grow in the branches, are bad and harmful if they absorb all the strength of the growth. That's the case with our pseudo-civilisation.
(9) If people walk over and trample down a good meadow, I regret it but I'm not indignant, but when, on the pretext of the good of the people or of love for them, but really because of greed, popular esteem and other various purposes, people dig up a meadow and sow it with absinthe or ruin it, and it becomes overgrown with wormwood, I can't help being indignant. I know it's bad, but I can't help being indignant with the self-satisfied liberals who are doing this. [. . .]

12 June, Yasnaya Polyana I've been in a very bad mood. Tried to take advantage of it. Wrote a story, *Berries*, in two days.[30] It's not bad. Misha has just been and we had a good talk. It's very possible that life will stir in him. It's bound to stir in everyone. I suffer more and more from my prosperity and the poverty round about me. [. . .]

18 June, Yasnaya Polyana I've been feeling very unwell physically for over a week: my stomach and bowels. I've only written the introduction to *A Great Sin*[31] and a few insignificant letters. Must note down a few things that seem to me important.
(1) (For *The Tower of Siloam*.)[32] It's the destruction, not of the Russian army and navy or of the Russian state, but the destruction of all pseudo-Christian civilisation. I feel it, am aware of it, and understand it with the greatest clarity. How good it would be to be able to express it clearly and forcefully. [. . .]

29 June, Yasnaya Polyana I've had stomach trouble for over a week. I've done hardly anything. Lyova is here. I'm sorry for him with all my heart, but it's impossible to help him. Perhaps it's necessary that way. And he is happy in his blindness. Just today I've written a little of *The Pool of Siloam*.[33] The more I see Posha, the more I value him and love him. Sasha is becoming coarse. Either she has no ideals, or else very low ones. Sonya's state of health is uncertain. Most probably it's nothing bad. Relations with her are very good. Note: something very important. [. . .]
(2) (For *The Tower of Siloam*.) A change in the state system can only take place when a new central authority is established, or when people form themselves locally into the sort of associations in which government authority will not be

necessary. Outside these two situations there can be riots, but no change of system.
(3) Tocqueville says[34] that the great revolution took place actually in France and not anywhere else, actually because everywhere else the situation of the people was worse, was more depressed than it was in France. *En détruisant en partie les institutions du moyen âge on avait rendu cent fois plus odieux ce qui en restait* [In partially destroying the institutions of the Middle Ages, people have rendered what is left of them a hundred times more hateful][35] That is correct. And for the same reason the new revolution, the forthcoming revolution of the freeing of the land is bound to take place in Russia, since everywhere else the situation of the people with regard to the land is worse than it is in Russia. [. . .]
(6) I have known three attitudes to married life during my lifetime: (1) marriage is indestructible; whether it's happy or unhappy, put up with it as you do your own body, without violent outbursts, despair or love affairs; (2) harmony of souls, passion, poetic love, Werther, the sufferings of love; and (3) if you don't like your husband or your wife, separate and take a new one.
(7) It would be good to write about the attitude of uncorrupted children towards vegetarianism – how they know unhesitatingly that one shouldn't take life.
(8) The only revolution that is beneficial is the one which destroys the old only through having already established the new (the people of Guriya). One mustn't patch up the wounded place, or amputate it, but replace it with new cellular tissue. [. . .]
(10) Freedom is liberation from the illusion, from the deceit of the personality.
(11) As the French were called in 1790 to make a new world, so the Russians have been called to the same task in 1905.

31 July, Yasnaya Polyana   Haven't written my diary for twenty-eight days. I'd no idea it was so long. All this time I've been quite well physically, but weak spiritually; I haven't written much. I haven't made much progress with *The End of the World*.[36] But I think I've had quite a few thoughts, and perhaps interesting ones, during this time. I'll make a note of them now. During all this time I've suffered from great indolence, weakness and a bad mood which, thank God, has only shown itself *a little bit*. I'll copy out my notes.
(1) This is a note I made: a passive revolution has begun in Russia.
(2) In times of trouble such as now in Russia, the first thing that's necessary is to refrain from helping one side or the other; the second: to look for means of reconciliation.
(3) the intelligentsia has contributed a hundred times more evil than good to the life of the people [. . .]
(5) The revolution now can in no way repeat what happened a hundred years ago. The revolutions of '30 and '48 did not succeed because they had no ideals, and they were inspired by what was left over from the great revolution. Now the people who are making the Russian revolution have none: economic ideals are not ideals.
(6) The only revolution that is fruitful is the one which cannot be halted. [. . .]
(10) For the existence of a reasonable, moral society, it is necessary for women to be under the influence of men. But in our society it is the reverse: men are under the influence of women.

(11) It is far better for women to flirt with their shoulders and behinds, than with principles and convictions. [...]
(24) The Rusian revolution is bound to destroy the existing order, only not by force, but passively, by disobedience. [...]

Today is 10 August, Yasnaya Polyana I've been to Pirogovo. For two or three days I felt particularly weak, but after three days the work began to get going, and I've almost finished *The End of the World*. It was very good being alone and with Masha. Came back on the 7th, and things were good here. Yesterday I sinned; I was annoyed about my works – the printing of them.[37] Of course I'm entirely to blame. I don't know whether it's good or bad, but always after such a sin the bonds of love are loosened – it's like an aching wound. [...] Note:
(1) The difference between a man and a woman: a man always feels lust, but it's possible to suppress it. A woman – only from time to time – but it's irrepressible.
(2) What a patent absurdity – to try to put down force by force. A story: a substituted baby.[38]

27 August, Yasnaya Polyana I've been writing *The End of the World* all this time. It's quite reasonable, I think. I've almost finished it. Still 'almost'. *The One Thing Needful* and *A Great Sin* have come out,[39] and I think that *A Great Sin* has run up against an obstacle, but is pushing on and perhaps demolishing it. I've just read a criticism by an American.[40] Obviously it rubbed him up the wrong way, and it hurts. It's the same attitude in Russia: either silence, or irritation at being hurt. That's all right.

How clear to me has the history of my attitudes to Europe now become: (1) joy that I, an insignificant person, am known by such great people; (2) joy that they value me on a level with their own people; (3) that they value me more than their own; (4) that I am beginning to understand who the people are who value me; (5) that they hardly understand me; (6) that they don't understand me; (7) that they don't understand anything at all, that the people whose appreciation I valued are stupid and barbaric. Today I received a pathetic criticism of *A Great Sin*, and a *Questionnaire* from the editor of *Echo* about capital punishment, why it is necessary and justified.[41] And the editor's name is – Sauvage.

I wake up in the morning and ask myself: what is in store for me? and I reply: nothing, except death. There's nothing I desire. Everything is good. But what am I to do? How am I to live? I must fill up the rest of my life with the things that are necessary to Him who sent me. And how easy! How restful! How free! How joyful!
Note:
(1) Who is more free: The Mongol who is a slave of Ghenghis Khan or of the Chinese Emperor who can take his property, wife, children and life away from him, or the Belgian or American who allegedly governs himelf by means of elections? [...]
(7) In childhood people want everything, in youth and manhood – some one thing, in old age – nothing.
(8) Living is dying. To live well means to die well. Try to die well.

(9) The chief and greatest feat accomplished at the beginning of this century in the Far East is the feat of the Chinese, who have held their ground in the world despite all the injustices, cruelties and horrors perpetrated against them. They are Christians, and we, white peoples, are savage heathens. I ought to write about that. [. . .]

9 September, Yasnaya Polyana Bad news from Masha.[42] I'm very sorry for her, and I can't relieve the pain. All this time I've been writing *The End of the World*, and I've rarely been so satisfied with anything. I think it's good. It could and should have been much better, but it's all right as it is. Just before this I was very sad for some reason. I feel lonely and want love. Of course it's wrong. Things are very good as they are. I'm still just as often too clearly aware of the meaning of life, and this cruel, senseless life depresses me. A Jew came today, a correspondent of *Rus*. At the end of our talk, as a result of my disagreement with him, he said: 'So you even consider the murder of Plehve a bad thing?' I said to him 'I regret having talked to you', and walked out angrily, i.e. I behaved very badly. [. . .]

19 September, Yasnaya Polyana I've completely finished *The End of the World*, and have rarely been so satisfied with what I've written.[43] It will be less understood than anything else I've written, but nevertheless it will leave its mark in people's consciousness.

Masha has again lost a stillborn child. Tanya is still holding her own. I'm very sorry for them. All the time I've been relatively well, and working quite well in the mornings. I'd like to find a replacement for the story *The Tsar and the Hermit*[44] for the *Cycle of Reading*. I dislike it very much. It's all invented. [. . .] I'm reading Kant. It's very good.

21 September, Yasnaya Polyana A state of depression. I began to think it's because nobody loves me. I started counting up all those who don't love me. But then I thought, why should people love me? There's really no reason. It's only up to me to love; what they do is their affair. And people do love me much more than I deserve.

Then during the night I thought a lot about myself. I'm an exceptionally bad, vicious man.
(1) I have all the vices, and to a very high degree: envy, and greed, and meanness, and sensuality, and vanity, and ambition, and pride, and malice. No, not malice, but bitterness, deceitfulness and hypocrisy. Everything, everything, and to a far higher degree than the majority of people. My only salvation is that I know it, and have been fighting – fighting all my life – against it. For this reason they call me a psychologist. [. . .]

23 September, Yasnaya Polyana Finished *The End of the World*. Masha is out of danger. A nice, spiritual letter. Just now – this morning – there was a letter from an intellectual son of a peasant with a venomous reproach against me, under the guise of praise for *A Great Sin*, for not giving up my own land myself. I was terribly offended. But it turned out for my own good. I realised that I had forgotten that I am living in the sight of God, and not for the good opinion of this correspondent. And I felt relieved, very much so. Yes, one must never forget the absolute seriousness of life.

27 September, Yasnaya Polyana   I've been in rather a bad, depressed and gloomy mood. Thought during this time: it's good for a person to suffer a little not only physically, but spiritually too. If one were to live in contentment, harmony and love with everyone, how would one die then? I've quite finished *The End of the World* and am equipping myself for new work. I don't know what: *the teaching* or *the drama*?[45] [. . .]

6 October, Yasnaya Polyana   Continue to be well, but haven't done much work during this time. Finished *The End of the World* and read Alexander I and made notes.[46] A very weak and mixed up creature. I don't know whether I'll start to write about him.

Can't remember if there's anything to note. There is one thing: I'll write separately about the importance of old age, as a foreword to *The Green Stick* or to my teaching on how to live and how to bring up children.[47]

12 October, Yasnaya Polyana   Haven't written my diary for six days. I've been unwell for four days – my liver. I've written nothing. *Fyodor Kuzmich*[48] engages my attention more and more. I've been reading about Paul.[49] What a subject! Wonderful!!! I've also been reading Herzen's *From the Other Shore*[50] and was also thrilled. One should write about him – so that people of our time can understand him. Our intelligentsia have sunk so low that they are no longer able to understand him. His readers await him in the future. And, far above the heads of today's crowd, he is handing on his thoughts to those who will be able to understand them. [. . .]

23 October, Yasnaya Polyana   Haven't written my diary for a long time. All the time I've been revising and adding to *The End of the World*. I continue to be satisfied. I've finished it. I won't do any more to it. Chertkov sent the proofs of *The Divine and the Human*, and I disliked it very much, and would like to alter it, but doubt if I'll have the strength. A matter of enormous importance: one's attitude to death. I have a plan, but how shall I manage to carry it out?

The revolution is in full swing. People are being killed on both sides. A new and unexpected element, and one absent in previous European revolutions, has arisen – 'the black hundreds', 'the patriots': in actual fact men with a crude, false, and contradictory idea of the people and their demand not to use force. The contradiction, as always, is in the fact that people want to curb and put an end to force by force.

Generally speaking the frivolity of the people who are making this revolution is astonishing and disgusting: childishness without the innocence of children. I say to myself and to everyone that the main thing for each person to do now is to look to himself, take a strict attitude to every action of his and not take part in the struggle.

But this is only possible for a person who takes a religious attitude to his life. Only from a religious point of view is it possible to be free of involvement, free even of sympathy for one side or the other, and to further one's aim: the pacification of both sides.

I feel depressed amid the surrounding company.

3 November, Yasnaya Polyana Haven't written my diary for nearly two weeks. I've been unwell recently – biliousness: weakness and a bad frame of mind. I was to blame yesterday with Ilya. We quarrelled. It's depressing at times. Got on quite well with *The Divine and the Human*. Planned an appeal to the people.⁵¹ It's not good. A few notes:
(1) Went for a ride and thought about my life: about the emptiness and weakness of the greater part of it. Only in the mornings do I fulfil my vocation – writing. That's all that is needed of me. I am someone's tool.
(2) This present revolution completely lacks any ideal. And so it isn't a revolution, but a riot. [. . .]

22 November, Yasnaya Polyana During this time I've been correcting *The Divine and the Human* and am still dissatisfied with it. But it's better. Began *Alexander I*.⁵² Was distracted by *Three Untruths*.⁵³ It's no good. My health – a gradual ebbing away of life. That's very good. A great event – Tanya has had a baby.⁵⁴ Masha and her husband have arrived. I'd very much like to get on with *Alexander I*. Read about Paul and the Decembrists.⁵⁵ I can imagine it all very vividly. I go out riding every day. [. . .]

9 December, Yasnaya Polyana During this time I finished *The Divine and the Human*. Wrote: *Freedoms and Freedom* as a separate article, and included it today in *The End of the World* and sent it to Moscow and England. It's probably too late. Let is stay as it is.⁵⁶ Continued with *Alexander I* yesterday. Wanted to get on with my *Memoirs*, but hadn't the strength. Continual strikes and riots. And I feel more than ever the need for, and the tranquillity of a retreat into myself. The other day I prayed to God and understood my position in the world in relation to God, and it was very good. Yes, I forgot, the day before yesterday I got on with *The Green Stick*. Note: [. . .]
(2) When a new and reasonable, a more reasonable, form of social life emerges, people will be surprised at the fact that the compulsion to work used to be considered an evil, and idleness a good thing. Then – if there is any punishment then – to deprive people of work would be a punishment. [. . .]
(5) The transition from state violence to a free, reasonable life cannot happen suddenly. Just as the life of the state took thousands of years to take shape, so it will take thousands of years to disintegrate.

16 December I've written a bit of *Alexander I*. But it's bad. Tried to write my memoirs – worse still. I've written absolutely nothing for two days. My stomach is still upset, and I've been very drowsy mentally and even spiritually. Nothing interests me. I haven't yet got used to enduring such periods patiently. The horrors of brutalisation are continuing in Moscow. No news, the trains are not running. I sometimes think of writing an appeal to the intelligentsia and the people, on the lines of my appeal to the Tsar and his assistants.[57] But I've no strong desire, although I know clearly what to say. [. . .]

Oh yes, something else: a clear idea for a story – a comparison between a paralysed old woman, rejoicing at the fact that she can still get as far as the stove, and the bald Pototsky: '*Ah, que je m'embête* [Oh, how bored I am]!'[58]

18 December, Yasnaya Polyana   Feel a bit better, but my mental weakness continues. Wrote nothing yesterday. Today I began writing *Alexander I*, but poorly and reluctantly. I must make a note of a dream I had. Someone said to me: 'Are you a good man?' I said: 'To say that I am a good man would be an immodest thing to do, i.e. would mean that I am not a good man; to say that I am bad would be an affectation. The truth is that I am sometimes a good man and sometimes a bad one.' Life as a whole goes on just like an accordion – it contracts and expands and contracts again, from the bad to the good and back again to the bad. To be good only means wanting to be good more often than bad. And that is something I desire.

23 December, Yasnaya Polyana   Health better; I feel fresher mentally. Talked about the revolution and couldn't resist the temptation to write it all down in short form: 'The government, the revolutionaries, the people.' I've been writing it all these days, and I think it will do. [. . .] Note: [. . .]
(2) One of the chief motives for revolution is the feeling which makes children want to break their toys, the passion for destruction.
(3) Now, in the course of the revolution, three sorts of people have been revealed with their virtues and their failings. First the conservatives – people who want peace and quiet and a continuation of their pleasant life and don't want any changes. The failing of these people is egoism; their virtues – modesty and humility. Secondly, the revolutionaries – they want change and are arrogant enough to decide what change is needed, and they are not afraid of force in order to implement their changes, nor are they afraid of hardships and sufferings. The failing of these people is arrogance and cruelty; their virtues – energy and the readiness to suffer in order to achieve an aim which appears to them to be good. Thirdly, the liberals – they haven't the humility of the conservatives nor the readiness to make sacrifices of the revolutionaries, but they have the egoism and the desire for peace and quiet of the former and the self-assurance of the latter.

Thought that for my memoirs – should I ever write them in detail – I ought at least to write down the most characteristic scenes, events and inward states from each period of my life.

27 December, Yasnaya Polyana   All these days I've been revising *Government, Revolutionaries and the People*. I think I've finished, but don't know what to do with it. I feel, and am, quite well. Today – this morning – I saw off Dunayev and

Nikitin; there's a crowd of Sukhotins here, and I feel weak. Received a letter from Velikanov.[59] I must reply as well as possible, not only by letter, but by deed. It's difficult. All the better. Try and solve the difficult problems. Yesterday I revised the proofs of the *Cycle of Reading* for July. I didn't like it *at all*. Playing cards leaves me with an unpleasant feeling, but still it's incomparably better than talk. Note: [...]

(2) Dunayev is horrified at people's bestiality. I am not horrified. This seems surprising, but is due to the fact that the horror which he is now experiencing at the bestiality displayed (the reason for which is the absence of religion) I experienced twenty-five years ago when I saw myself as an animal endowed with reason, devoid of any understanding of the meaning of my life (religion), and saw that all the people round about me were the same. I was only horrified and surprised then at the fact that people were not killing or strangling one another. And I'm not just saying that I was horrified then. I really was horrified then, almost more than people are horrified now. What is happening now is just the same as what I was horrified by and what I expected. I am like a man standing on the tender of a train rushing down an incline who is horrified to see that it is impossible to stop the train. But the passengers are only horrified when the crash has happened. [...]

(6) I also have in mind a clear character sketch of Alexander I – if only I could manage to get even half way with it. The thing is that he wanted sincerely and with all his heart to be good and moral, and he also wanted with all his heart to reign at all costs. I must show the duality of desires – common to all people – which sometimes takes two completely opposite directions.

It is now the night of 31 December 1905 and the beginning of 1906 All this time I've been adding to *Government, Revolutionaries and the People*. Sometimes it seems necessary, sometimes weak. My health isn't bad. But my thoughts lack vitality. Only two things to note:

(1) When reading Stroganov on Romme,[60] I was struck by his heroism when combined with his weak and pathetic figure. It reminded me of Nikolenka. I think that this is very often the case. Strong men, sensual people like the Orlovs, are usually cowards, while these others are the opposite.

The second thing. (2) My duality: at times in the morning and at night I'm a truly wise and good man; at times I'm a weak, pathetic creature who doesn't know what to do with himself. The difference is that the former state is the real one, while in the second state I know that I'm enveloped in delusion. [...]

1906

4 January, Yasnaya Polyana All these days I've been revising and altering *Government, Revolutionaries and the People*, and I still haven't finished. *The People* is bad because I tried to work into it the unsuitable *Three Untruths*. I hope it will turn out all right. And that it will be useful. I'm reading *The Thoughts of Wise People* every day, and with great profit to my soul. These last two or three days, with no people here, I've been working on myself incessantly: I don't allow myself any bad thoughts or frivolous behaviour like gymnastics or fortune-telling. And that's good. If only I can keep it up until death! [. . .]

6 January, Yasnaya Polyana Still revising *Government, Revolutionaries and the People* and I think I've finished it or am near the end. I feel very gloomy. I try to overcome it but can't. I don't give expression to my badness in any way, but feel and think bad things. Note:
(1) In *The Thoughts of Wise People* today, the 6th, is Ruskin's idea that the sin of human beings is the sin of Judas, namely that people don't believe in their Christ and sell him. For the first time I understood: yes, the chief mistake – the source of all sufferings and disasters – is the fact that we don't believe in our divinity and sell it for the mess of pottage of physical joys.
(2) The Jewish faith is the most irreligious. A faith in which the denominator is infinity. A proud faith that they are God's only chosen people. [. . .]

18 January, Yasnaya Polyana Still unwell. I'm working a little on the *Cycle of Reading*.
Thought today about what I, an old man, should do. I haven't much strength, and it's getting noticeably weaker. Several times in my life I've considered myself close to death. And – how foolishly! – I would forget, or try to forget it – forget what? That I would die, and that in any case – whether in five, ten, twenty or thirty years – death is still very close. And now, because of my years, I naturally consider myself close to death, and there's no point in trying to forget it, and I can't forget it. But what should I, an old feeble person do? I asked myself. And it seemed that there was nothing to do, that I had no strength for anything. But today I realised so clearly the clear and joyful answer. What should I do? It's already been revealed – I must die. This is my task now, as it always has been. And I must perform this task as well as possible: die, and die well. The task is before you, a noble and inevitable task, and you are searching for one. This made me very glad. I'm beginning to get used to regarding death and dying not as the end of my task, but as the task itself.
Yesterday and today I've been reading *Siberia and Penal Servitude*, by Maximov. Some wonderful subjects: (1) the waiter in the inn, whipped as a punishment to hide a merchant's daughter's shame; (2) *The pilgrim*: a wonderful subject.[1]

22 January, Yasnaya Polyana Health good. Did some of the *Cycle of Reading*. Yesterday and the day before I wrote a story based on Maximov.² The beginning isn't bad. The ending is awful. Sonya arrived from Moscow. As was to be expected, nobody liked *Government, Revolutionaries and the People*, and it's inconceivable that it will be published. [. . .]

2 February, Yasnaya Polyana Health reasonably good on and off. I've been writing *What for?* One day it was reasonably good, but I still can't finish it. I'd very much like to write *Cycle of Reading* for children and the people, but haven't got the time. [. . .]

6 February, Yasnaya Polyana [. . .] Today I revised a bit of *What for?* It's reasonably good. The morning brought me much joy. Yet all joys are dangerous, worldly, and not for God: a nice letter from Sasha, *Cycle of Reading* and *On Life*.³ *Fais ce que dois, advienne que pourra* [Do what you must, come what may].

Yesterday or the day before I read an excellent brochure by D. Khomyakov.⁴ It's all very good. The trouble is that he considers Christianity and Orthodoxy to be synonymous and includes among the spiritual demands of life *everyday existence*. That is quite wrong and a patent sophism.

Today is 18 February, Yasnaya Polyana All this time, i.e. since the 10th, I've been in a (physically) depressed condition, but very well at heart. I still haven't lost the disposition to live only for God, to multiply what has been given to me (my talent). Very welcome letters from my daughters, and from Sheyerman⁵ and Toki-Tomi.⁶ Seryozha and Andryusha have been, thank God. There is much for me to note, and, I think, worth noting. I'm still revising *What for?* It's slow going, but becoming more tolerable. Note: [. . .]
(9) We don't remember a previous life because memory is an attribute of this life only. [. . .]
(13) In extreme old age other people, and frequently old people themselves, usually think that they are only living out their days. On the contrary, it is in extreme old age that the most valuable and necessary life both for oneself and for others is lived. The value of life is in inverse proportion to the square of the distance from death. It would be good if old people themselves, and those close to them, could understand this. [. . .]

2 March, Yasnaya Polyana Haven't written my diary for twelve days. I've felt both good and bad physically; more often bad. I'm just about surviving. I'm working on myself inwardly and, I think, well. The trouble is, and it's a good thing too, that just as when you fly in a balloon you don't feel either the wind or the movement because you move with the wind, so you don't feel your improvement because it is only what ought to happen, what is actually happening. You only feel the wind when you come to a stop, i.e. when you live badly. [. . .] During this time I've been revising *What For?* and have also sent off the proofs of the second volume of the *Cycle of Reading* to be set up. There is much to note down, I think, and it isn't bad. [. . .]
(4) We are so used to seeing people of our circle engaged in politics, i.e. concerning

themselves with how to improve the organisation of people's social life and putting all their efforts into this activity, that we are not surprised at this phenomenon. And yet it is very surprising.

People who are completely negligent about carrying out their economic, family and personal affairs, put all their energy into the future imaginary organisation of society and, in spite of the differences between all the parties, stubbornly defend their own position. There is only one explanation: a person needs activity, and the assurance that his activity is useful. He makes a mess of his personal, economic or family affairs, and not only lacks the assurance of behaving reasonably, but quite the contrary. And so he chooses an activity where the results are not visible, and he can comfort himself with the assurance that he is doing a useful and necessary thing. Confirmation of this is the fact that the more tormented a person's private life is, the more energetically he devotes himself to politics. [. . .]

(8) What I once wrote long ago to Khilkov almost as a joke, as a piece of fantasy, namely that our life is a dream about the sleep into which we were plunged in a former life, and that death will be an awakening to a new form of life – this idea no longer seems to me a piece of fantasy, but a great probabilty. Our dreams in this life are echoes of life as a whole, pointers to its laws. [. . .]

(14) Philosophical systems are badly constructed arches, smeared over with lime so that their flimsiness should not be visible. An arch made of unpolished stone, if it holds, will most likely last. But the arch which lasts the longest is the one built unconsciously, like natural caves. [. . .]

5 March, Yasnaya Polyana   I'm writing in the morning. These last days I've written nothing of substance, except letters, and they are worthless. Busy with the *Cycle of Reading* for children,[7] i.e. an exposition of scripture. It's going badly. I haven't taken it seriously enough.

9 March. In a bad state. I've only revised my note about government and power. The title should be: *From my Diary. On the Origin and Self-destruction of Power.*

No, that's not good.[8] [. . .] Note: [. . .]

(2) How clearly was the usual, corrupting effect of power seen in the revolutionaries when they began to seize power: self-importance, pride, vanity and above all lack of respect for man. [. . .]

10 March   Was in a dull, miserable state all day. By evening this state changed to one of emotion – the desire for affection – for love. I felt, as in childhood, like clinging to a loving, pitying creature, and weeping emotionally and being comforted. But who is the creature I could cling to like that? I ran through all the people I love – nobody would do. Who could I cling to? I wanted to become young again and cling to my mother as I imagine her to have been.

Yes, yes, my dear mother whom I never called by that name, since I couldn't talk. Yes, she is my highest conception of pure love – not a cold or divine, but a warm, earthly, maternal love. This is what attracts my better, weary soul. Mother dear, caress me.

All this is stupid, but it's all true.

11 March Haven't written my diary for about four days. Yesterday I was in a particularly depressed state. I feel everything unpleasant particularly keenly. That's what I tell myself; but in actual fact I seek out what is unpleasant, I am receptive to, and not impervious to what is unpleasant. I wasn't able to get rid of this feeling at all. I tried everything: prayer and the consciousness of my badness. And it was no good. Prayer, i.e. the vivid conception of my situation, doesn't reach down to the depths of my consciousness, and the recognition of my worthlessness and rottenness doesn't help. It's not that I want something particular, but I'm painfully dissatisfied with something, and I don't know what. I think it's life; I want to die.

By evening this state changed into a feeling of loneliness and the emotional desire for affection and love: I, an old man, wanted to become a child, to nestle up against a loving creature, to snuggle up, to complain, to be caressed and comforted. But who is this creature I could nestle up against and in whose arms I could weep and complain? Nobody now alive. So what is this feeling? It's the same old devil, egoism, who in this new crafty guise wants to deceive and take possession of me. This latest feeling explained to me my previous state of melancholy. It was only a weakening, a temporary disappearance of the spiritual life and egoism asserting its rights (egoism which, once aroused, can find no food for itself and turns to melancholy). There is only one remedy against this: to serve somebody in the simplest way, the first way that occurs, to work for somebody.

(1) Read Aschenbrenner's notes about Schlüsselburg.[9] How clearly they show that life is in oneself, and that the bounds of external freedom, however narrow some seem and however wide others, are almost, or indeed entirely, irrelevant.

19 March, Yasnaya Polyana Still in the same bad, depressed state. I'm struggling against it. I think I've overcome the feeling of unkindness and reproachfulness towards people, but my apathy is just as bad. I can't do any work at all. Went riding yesterday and argued with myself all the time. The weak, worthless, physical, egotistical man said: 'Everything is vile', while the spiritual man said: 'You're lying, everything is fine. What you call vile is the whetstone without which the most precious thing in you would be blunted and grow rusty.' And I told myself this so insistently and convincingly that in the end I convinced myself and returned home in a very good mood. [...]

(1) Thought about the fact that I'm not writing my diary for myself but for other people – primarily for those who will be alive when I am not here physically – and that there's nothing bad about that. It is, I'm inclined to think, what is required of me. Well, but what if these diaries are burnt? Well, what of it? Perhaps they are necessary for other people, but for me I'm sure they are not just necessary – they are me. They are a good thing *for me*. [...]

2 April, Yasnaya Polyana Easter. All the time recently (two weeks) I've felt poorly. I've hardly written anything. Weakness and physical depression. But it's a strange thing. In those rare moments of clarity of thought which came to me, my thoughts worked more clearly and profoundly than in periods of constant mental activity.

It's bound to occur to one that the revelation of life goes on all the time at a steady pace. If it seems to me that life is standing still within me, it isn't standing still but going on underground, and later on reveals itself all the more forcibly the longer it has been held in check. Whether this is true will be seen from what I've noted down and am now entering in my diary for these two weeks. Note:
(1) It has become absolutely clear recently that an agricultural way of life is not merely one of various ways of life, just as a book – the Bible – is not one of various books, but *is* life, life itself, the only human life which alone makes possible the manifestation of all the highest human qualities. The chief mistake in the organisation of human societies and one which eliminates the possibility of any reasonable organisation of life is that people want to organise society without agricultural life, or with the sort of organisation in which agricultural life is only one form, and the most insignificant form, of life. How right Bondarev is![10]
(2) A remarkable thing! One only has to tell people, to disclose to them somehow the good one feels or does or wants to do, and immediately that inner force and joy which the awareness of good has given one – disappears. It's just like steam released from a steam-engine. What you do for God, do only for God. Keep your secret with God and He will help you. As soon as you blurt it out to people, He turns away from you. 'You have told it to other people, let them help you.'
(3) I would like to write a story, *The Dream*, on the following theme: a person dreams about himself being judged after death and his deeds being weighed in the scales. He waits for people to bring out and put on the scales the work he has done for the people, his philanthropy, his scientific works, his family virtues, and they are brought out, and they all weigh nothing at all, or else they have the reverse effect: the scales rise. It was all done for worldly fame. Then suddenly they bring out something he had forgotten: how he suppressed his irritation during an argument, picked up a toy for a little girl . . . (I must think of something better) – everything that people didn't know of or didn't appreciate. One could also compare two holy fools (*yurodívye*): the one recognised as a holy fool, a professional holy fool, and the other a person whose involuntary folly (*yurodstvo*) nobody knows about. And how the first is not pleasing to God, but only the second.[11] [. . .]
(13) Peace is the highest material good of human society, just as the highest material good of the individual is health. That is what people have always supposed. And peace is only possible for agricultural workers. Only agricultural workers feed themselves by their own direct labour. Townspeople inevitably have to be fed by one another. The state originated among townspeople, and is possible and necessary for them. For agricultural workers it is superfluous and harmful. [. . .]
(16) I'd like to write a story about how a politician, after twenty or thirty years' work in one direction and after achieving his goal, suddenly discovered that he had a soul which needed to be served, and which he had neglected and which had shrivelled up, grown hard and unresponsive, and could neither give nor receive any joy. (He is ill or in prison.)[12]
(17) People write pompously in books that where there are rights, there are also obligations. What audacious nonsense – what lies. Man has only obligations. MAN HAS ONLY OBLIGATIONS.

(18) People talk and argue about Henry George's system. It isn't the system which is valuable (although not only do I not know a better one, but I can't imagine one), but what is valuable is the fact that the system establishes an attitude to land which is universal and the same for everybody. Let them find a better one if they can.

17 April, Yasnaya Polyana [. . .] I'm still busy with *Two Ways*. Progress is slow. But the importance of the subject is becoming clearer and clearer, and capturing my attention. I've been revising the *Cycle of Reading* for a few weeks. I've written a few letters. Received an article today from Tregubov about persecution for refusal to do military service, and must send it off and add something of my own.[13] There is much to note, and I think it's not unimportant.
(1) People in exalted places – tsars and heroes – shouldn't perform ordinary human functions, shouldn't disport themselves. Otherwise you get a terrible, disgusting contrast. Elizabeth going to the Troitsa Monastery.[14] Catherine . . .
(2) The Western peoples have given up agriculture, and all want to exercise power. They can't exercise power over themselves, and so they search for colonies and markets.
(3) A sensible, moral life is only possible when everyone is engaged in agriculture. Agriculture points to what is most necessary and what is less so. It is the guide to a reasonable life. One must be in contact with the earth.
(4) The emotion and enthusiasm which we experience from the contemplation of nature is a recollection of the time when we were animals, trees, flowers, the earth. More exactly: it is the awareness of our unity with everything, an awareness concealed from us by time.

Today is 25 April, Yasnaya Polyana I am better physically, and yet I haven't felt in such a weak condition spiritually for a long time, not throughout my illness. Read in the paper about Gorky's reception in America and caught myself feeling angry.[15] Read Velikanov's arguments and criticism of my writings and felt displeased.[16] Then a printed article which had been sent to me which says that I am as good as summoning the Cossacks to Yasnaya Polyana, and I was hurt.[17] Yet it's good that I feel that it's a weakness uncharacteristic of me. During this time I revised *What For?* – badly – and read through the proofs of the *Cycle of Reading* – also badly. Whether it's true that the thoughts I had during my illness where such as to compensate for my lack of work will be shown by what I have to write down:
(1) Epictetus says: you don't get angry with a blind man because he can't see . . .[18] Yes, but it's difficult not to get angry when the blind man is sure that he can see, and that you are blind, and when he is leading you towards a pit. There is no need to follow him, but still there is no reason to get angry. [. . .]
(12) The thought came to me clearly today that people's propensity for handing on power and the right to use violence to other people is not a good and Christian feature, and that therefore its fruits – violence and murder – are even worse sins than if one were personally involved in them. That is very important. [. . .]
(24) I dreamed that I was trying to drive my son away: my son – a combination of Ilya, Andrey and Seryozha. He wouldn't go. I was conscience-stricken because I

had used force, but also because I hadn't gone the whole way. Stakhovich was present, and I felt ashamed. Suddenly this collective son began to edge me off the chair I was sitting on with his backside. I put up with it for a long time, then jumped up and waved the chair at my son. He ran away. I felt even more conscience-stricken. I knew that he hadn't done it deliberately. My son had gone. Tanya turned up in the hall and told me I was in the wrong. And she added that she was beginning to be jealous of her husband again. The whole psychology was exceptionally accurate, but without time, or space, or personality. [. . .]

30 April, Yasnaya Polyana I'm trying to work as before, but my strength is deserting me. And a good thing. [. . .] Note: [. . .]
(2) The power of one person over another is ruinous in the first place to the person who exercises power. Wealth and money are just the same sort of power as direct power. They are likewise ruinous in the first place to those who possess it, and the more ruinous because their evil is concealed. [. . .]

It's already 22 May, today, Yasnaya Polyana. All this time I've been in a poorly and weak condition. I'm still writing and rewriting *Two Ways*. And it's still not quite clear. There have been many joyful things recently: an old man from Kolomna, a Jew who is renouncing military service and a young man, Ofitserov, in the grip of regeneration.[19] There have been some letters too. One today from the Mironovs in Samara. I'm afraid that Dobrolyubov's influence on them is not straightforward and not likely to last.[20] A letter from Morrison Davidson and one from Toki-Tomi.[21]

Recently I have had moments of silent despair at the lack of effect that the truth has on people. Especially at home. All my sons are here at present, and it's particularly depressing. What is depressing is the unnaturalness of conventional intimacy and the greatest spiritual remoteness. Sometimes, as today, I feel like running away and disappearing. That's all nonsense. I make a note of it to confess my weakness. It's all good and necessary and may bring me joy. I can't feel sorry for those blind people who think they can see, and strenuously deny what I can see. [. . .]

29 May, Yasnaya Polyana Very depressed about the shamefulness of my life. And I don't know what to do. Lord, help me. I'm still dawdling over *Two Ways*. I think quite well now and then about death, and often frankly desire it. That's good. There's a great deal to be noted. [. . .]
(9) We all live by robbery and alms and hard work. The only question is what percentage of each. I live entirely by alms and robbery. And it torments me. [. . .]

6 June, Yasnaya Polyana I feel well. I'm not sleeping much, and am weak; and that's good. *Two Ways* seems to be progressing. A correspondent has been, and I wrote down a few things about Henry George and told him about the Duma and the repressions.[22] The Denisenkos are here. Began reading the *Cycle of Reading* with Onya.[23] Some good, if not deep, thoughts and feelings. I'm on good and loving terms with all my sons; with Andrey it's terribly difficult. What a plague their general self-assurance is! What a lot they lose because of it. I'm still fighting against my concern for public opinion, and am trying to establish a direct relationship with God. On rare occasions – I can. [. . .]

3 July, Yasnaya Polyana Haven't written my diary for a long time. My stomach has been upset. I've worked spasmodically on *Two Ways*. My spiritual condition is one of great joy and freedom, and I live mostly in accordance with God's will. Note: [. . .]
(13) We often look on the ancients as children. But we are children compared with the ancients, compared with their deep, serious and uncontaminated understanding of life. [. . .]
(15) If the Russian people are uncivilised barbarians, then we have a future. But the Western peoples are civilised barbarians, and they have nothing more to look forward to. For us to imitate the Western peoples is just like a healthy, hardworking, uncorrupted lad envying a bald-headed rich young Parisian sitting in his hotel. *Ah, que je m'embête* [Oh, how bored I am].

Don't envy or imitate, but have pity. [. . .]
(21) The Indians have been conquered by the British, but they are freer than the British: they can live without the British, but the British can't live without them.
(22) What a terrible habit it is to give orders! There is nothing which does more to corrupt and destroy the relationship of one natural, good and reasonable man to another. Poor people and subordinates are ignorant of this evil; and their ignorance abundantly compensates for the disadvantage of their situation. Everyone must get out of the habit of giving orders. [. . .]

Today is 30 July, Yasnaya Polyana Haven't written my diary for a very long time. I think I've finished the article *Two Ways* and it seems not bad. I was even very pleased with it. Like Fet with *Two Lime Trees*.²⁴ Chertkov is here, and it's very pleasant for me. I decided to let *Government, Revolutionaries and the People* go with some alterations. There is a lot to be noted:
(1) Does God exist? I don't know. I know that there is a law governing my spiritual being. The source of, and the reason for that law I call God. [. . .]

24 August, Yasnaya Polyana Haven't written my diary for twenty-four days. I've spent the time well. And now, thank God, still better and better. During this time Chertkov arrived. I went with him to Masha's. I found Chertkov very pleasant, but I'm afraid that that was largely because he has a very high opinion of me. Menshikov has also been, and, thank God, was so pleasant for a completely different reason that I recall our relations with pleasure. I was going to write that Masha is very dear to me, but everyone reads my diaries. And it's better like that.

Worked a lot on *Two Ways* and I think I've quite finished it. I think it's necessary, and may be useful. But I can't know that. I know that it was necessary for me to write it. The consciousness of being a servant of God has not grown much weaker, although it has lost its novelty; but it has taken root and, thank God,

I live by it. Often when I'm out walking, or when I put out the candle as I lie in bed, I experience a new, joyful feeling of life, gratitude and quiet contentment. I crossed out 'quiet', because the feeling, although not unquiet, is very vital and strong. Note: [. . .]

(2) Read in Mendeleyev[25] that the vocation, the ideal of man is multiplying. It's awfully silly. This is stupidity (not the word itself, but the use of it) – the result of too much self-assurance. Animals eat one another and therefore have to multiply, and multiplying may be the ideal of rabbits. Eating others and multiplying are mutually restrictive. But with people who have been rescued from being eaten by other animals, multiplying can only be restricted by the consciousness of goodness, by the striving for self-improvement. Self-improvement includes chastity. That is the restriction. How terribly immoral and simply stupid is Mendeleyev's multiplying. After all, if people invent chemical food, multiplying will reach the stage where they will be standing shoulder to shoulder. The multiplying of animals and the eating of other animals is an equilibrium established in the realm of egotistical, physical life. In the realm of spiritual life that equilibrium is – love, domesticity, chastity. [. . .]

(7) Thought about what the government should do now, and it became absolutely clear that the main thing is to put an end to all repressions, to agree to all demands – not so that things should be better (they couldn't be worse, and very possibly could be better), but in order not to be party to evil, not to be obliged to restrain or punish. [. . .]

(14) I am counted among the anarchists, but I am not an anarchist, but a Christian. My anarchism is only the application of Christianity to human relationships. The same is true of anti-militarism, communism, vegetarianism. [. . .]

(21) Recently, as I look at people without any religion, I have begun to respect people who believe in God, although they conceive of Him in the most crude forms. Belief in the Iberian Mother of God is better than the complete absence of acknowledgement of a higher law. [. . .]

1 September, Yasnaya Polyana Haven't written my diary for six days. Sonya's illness is getting worse and worse.[26] Today I felt particularly sorry for her. But she is touchingly sensible, truthful and good. I don't want to write about anything else. Three of my sons: Seryozha, Andryusha and Misha, are here, and two daughters: Masha and Sasha. The house is full of doctors. It's depressing: instead of devotion to the will of God and a solemn, religious mood, I find pettiness, recalcitrance, egoism. I had some good thoughts and feelings. Thank God.

I don't live in time, nor does the whole world live in time, but the immovable world, previously inaccessible to me, is revealed to me in time. How much easier and more comprehensible it is like that. And given such a view, death is not the cessation of something, but a complete revelation . . .

2 September, Yasnaya Polyana They operated today. They say it's been successful. But it was very hard for her. This morning she was very well in herself. How death assuages one! I thought: isn't it obvious that death is being revealed both to me and to her; and when she dies, it will be completely revealed to her. 'Ah, so that's what it is!' But we who are left behind can't yet see what has been revealed to the person dying. It will be revealed to us afterwards, in its own time. During the operation I walked to the fir tree woods. And I was nervously exhausted. Then I wrote a bit about Henry George[27] – not well. Note: [. . .]

(9) The Western peoples are far ahead of us, but ahead of us on the wrong path. For them to get on the right path they need to go a long way back. But we only need to turn a little way off the wrong path which we have just started on, and along which the Western peoples are coming back to meet us. [. . .]

5 September, Yasnaya Polyana I'm terribly sad. I'm sorry for her. Her sufferings are great, and probably in vain. I don't know, I'm sad, I'm sad; but that's very good.

15 September, Sonya is well. Evidently she is recovering. She's suffered a great deal.

I've finished the article, also the one on the land, and have begun a letter to a Chinaman, all on the same thing.[28]

I'd like to write something quite different. Something more truthful. There's a lot to note down. But I won't today. [. . .]

24 September I've finished all the works I've started and written a foreword to Henry George. Recently my stomach hasn't been quite right, and my thoughts are few and sluggish. Began the *Cycle of Reading*, but it's going sluggishly and not well. I even thought today I couldn't go on with it. Wrote a venomous letter in reply to an enquiry about a visit by some Englishmen,[29] and am glad I didn't send it. This is just what is lacking when one is asleep: moral effort. For example I had a long dream today and lied about something, I don't remember what, and then remembered there was no need to lie, but I couldn't restrain myself. But when one is awake it's always possible to restrain oneself. And this is the crux of our whole life and the difference between waking and sleeping.

Must note: [. . .]

(12) How much more valuable and important than writing is the business of living – direct relationships with people. In that case you have a direct effect on people, you can see success or failure, you can see your mistakes and can correct them, but with writing you don't know anything, perhaps you had an effect, perhaps not; perhaps you were not understood, perhaps you said the wrong thing – you don't know at all. [. . .]

30 September, Yasnaya Polyana Looked through the proofs that have been brought. Tried to begin a story about a priest. A wonderful subject, but I began too boldly, in too much detail. I'm not ready yet, but would very much like to write it.[30] The philosophical, metaphysical-religious question nags at me, and requires a clearer expression. And I think that if I haven't found the solution today, I've got very close to it.

I'm reading Goethe[31] and can see all the pernicious influence of this insignificant, bourgeois-egotistical, gifted man on the generation which I encountered, – especially poor Turgenev with his veneration of *Faust* (a thoroughly bad work) and Shakespeare – likewise Goethe's doing – and especially with the particular importance ascribed to various statues of Laocoon and Apollo and various poems and dramas. How much I suffered when, because of my love for Turgenev, I wanted to love what he rated so highly. I tried to with all my strength and was quite unable to. What terrible harm is done by authorities, celebrated great people, and false ones moreover! [. . .]

2 October, Yasnaya Polyana I've just been through a difficult test with a blind man. He came here and began to reproach me for not having given my land up, and for not buying land back now, since he assured me I had the money. I walked away from him. I could have been friendlier. And I didn't quite pass the test. I continue to be tired, but can think well, and it seems my definition of life is becoming clearer. I'll try and expound it now in a letter to Chertkov. [. . .]

3, 4 October, Yasnaya Polyana Wrote some letters yesterday: one to Chertkov with an exposition of my understanding of life. I must insert it here.[32] And one about the revolution – to Yagn.[33] It's morning now. I want to write a bit of *Vasily of Mozhaysk*.

10 October, Yasnaya Polyana I haven't carried out my wish. I was struck by a conversation on the high road with a young peasant-revolutionary from Lomintsevo, and by reading in the papers next morning about twenty-two people executed, and I began to write about it.[34] The result was very bad, but for three days I've been writing about it bit by bit, and it's still bad. I'd like to answer the question: What is to be done?
 There's a lot to be noted: [. . .]
(6) Went for a walk. A wonderful autumn morning, still and warm, the winter crops, the smell of leaves. And in place of this wonderful nature with its fields, woods, water, birds and animals, people are creating another, artificial nature for themselves in the towns, with factory chimneys, palaces, locomotives, phonographs . . . It's terrible, and one can't do anything to improve it . . .
(7) A very important thing. The people of our time boast about their science. The fact that they are so proud of it shows better than anything that it is false. True science can be recognised by this fact – or rather an undoubted sign of true science is – the awareness of the insignificance of what you know compared with what is being revealed. But of the fact that our science is false there can be no doubt. Not because what it investigates is wrong, but because it is unnecessary: some of it relatively so in comparison with what is important and has not been investigated, but much of it totally unnecessary. And I am firmly convinced that people will come to understand this and begin to develop the one true and necessary science which is now neglected – THE SCIENCE OF HOW TO LIVE.
 It would be good to devote the rest of my life to pointing this out to people. [. . .]

11 October, Yasnaya Polyana I'm writing about the revolution. But it's going badly. [. . .]

(4) I ought to compile the *Cycle of Reading* in such a way that for every day there is one religious, metaphysical thought, defining the position of man in the world, and a second one – a useful rule helping one to live a good life. [. . .]

14 October, Yasnaya Polyana   [. . .] Dear Ivan Ivanovich[35] was here yesterday. I re-read with pleasure my articles that are now in print. And also the one on education and teaching. Found Chertkov's letter and his opinion about me unpleasant. It's unhealthy and I really feel hurt – it's harmful. [. . .]

20 October, Yasnaya Polyana   [. . .] Health worse and worse. All this time I've been busy with the concluding chapter.[36] And it was so bad that I gave it up. Read Chamberlain on the Jews.[37] Not good, although it evokes many thoughts. I'd very much like to write something literary, and also something religious and metaphysical. [. . .]

23 October, Yasnaya Polyana   Last time I wrote that I continue to enjoy the awareness of life, but today I have to write the very opposite: I've grown weaker spiritually, mainly because I desire and seek the love of people – both near and far. Went to Yasenki today and brought back some letters, all unpleasant. The fact that I could find them unpleasant shows how low I've sunk. Two argumentative ladies, vague, muddle-headed and tiresome (I could and should have treated them more affectionately, as I decided after a little thought), and then a feuilleton in a Kharkov paper by that young student who lived here in the summer.[38] [. . .] He condemns me for something I'm not guilty of. But if he knew all the nastiness that used to exist and still does exist in my soul, he could justly condemn me many times more severely. And if I feel cross because he condemns me for something I'm not guilty of and judges me falsely, then I can only be sorry for him, as I would be sorry if he had made a mistake and told lies about another person. Oh, how good it would be never to lose that direct relationship with God which rules out all interest in people's opinions. And this is possible. One can be strong or weak, one can be idle, but one mustn't give way to the temptation of wanting people to love you. This is a terrible temptation which began with me in early childhood and still has a hold on me, or rather, continually tries to subject me to its power. At present I'm free, thanks to the feuilleton. But will it be for long?

All this time I've been busy with the *Afterword*,[39] and it still seems bad at times, and reasonably good at times, and I can't decide which. And in this case too, it's only necessary to rid myself of any consideration about other people's opinions and feelings, and the decision will be simple. [. . .]

I'd very much like to write about the priest, but I thought again about the impression it would make.[40] [. . .]

24 October, Yasnaya Polyana   Received a pile of letters, including a roundly abusive one from Velikanov and two eulogistic ones which could go to my head. Just like a glass of wine. I won't drink it. I'm in a good mood. I think I've finished the *Afterword*. Rode up above Salomasovo and back home through the Zaseka wood. Very good. [. . .]

Today is 26 October, Yasnaya Polyana I've finished all my things. The *Afterword* is poor, but I've sent it off. I've written all my letters, even the autographs. Yesterday Sasha upset me, and I'm still depressed because I can't bring myself to talk to her. It's evening now, and I'm in a very bad mood. I want to arouse in myself the vital awareness of my spiritual principles, and I can't. Recalled my past, and thought about the terrible blindness of youth. I censure Andryusha and Sasha. But what was I like at twenty-seven? The Caucasus, the Turkish War, Sevastopol. And what was I like at twenty-two? Gambling, Chulkovo,[41] hunting. Yes, life consists of shaping and improving oneself, and it goes on as long as it can in that form. But there is a limit. The limit is absolute self-sacrifice, but that is impossible for the human animal. And so it is necessary to die, i.e. to change into a different form. Isn't that so?

I'd very much like to write down everything that a person thinks – everything – if only for a period of six hours. This would be awfully novel and instructive.[42] [. . .]

Today is 9 November, Yasnaya Polyana I've been unwell for several days – my stomach – and have suffered great physical weakness. My state of mind is reasonably good. Wrote a letter to Sabatier – it's not good, but I decided to send it in the sight of God.[43] Thank God, I'm not going backwards. Note:
(1) Only a person who considers himself free can submit to other people. A person who does what he wants considers himself free; but a person who does what he wants is a slave of everything. The only person who *is* free is the one who considers himself a slave of God, and only does what God wants and what nobody and nothing can prevent. (Good.) [. . .]
(4) Thoughts only move our life forward when they are arrived at with one's own mind, or answer a question which has arisen in one's own soul; but other people's thoughts, apprehended only by the mind and memory, have no influence on life and can coexist with actions which are contrary to them.
(5) Brotherhood, equality, freedom make no sense when they are understood as the requirements of an external form of life. This was the reason for the addition: *ou la mort*. All three conditions are the consequences of human attributes: brotherhood is love. Only if we love one another will there be brotherhood between people. Equality is humility. Only if we don't have a high opinion of ourselves, but consider ourselves lower than everyone else, shall we all be equal. Freedom is the carrying out of the law of God, common to everyone. Only by carrying out the law of God shall we all be free for certain. (Good.) [. . .]
(10) A person stubbornly holds on to his ideas mainly because he has arrived at those ideas himself, perhaps very recently, after condemning his previous ones. And suddenly it is suggested that he should condemn these new ideas of his, and embrace still newer ideas which he has not yet arrived at himself. And here we have yet another of those very ludicrous and harmful superstitions, namely that it is shameful to alter one's convictions. It is shameful not to alter them, because the meaning of life lies in the greater and greater understanding of oneself and the world, and so it is shameful not to change them. [. . .]
(17) It's astonishing that people don't see that both the deep inner cause and the

consequences of the revolution now taking place in Russia cannot be the same as the causes and consequences of the revolution that happened more than a hundred years ago. [. . .]

17 November, Yasnaya Polyana A whole week. I wrote *What I Dreamed About*[44] (reasonably well) and corrected proofs of *What Is To Be Done?* which had been sent to me and worked a bit more seriously with Dorik.[45] Things are well with me. The awareness that the meaning of life is in fulfilling God's law has not weakened, but rather is growing stronger. Oh, I'm afraid of boasting. Chertkov is ill and I was very frightened of losing him. Can that be caring about myself? A touching letter from Sutkovoy.[46] I tried to start writing *Father Vasily* today, but found it boring and worthless. I'm still thinking more and more about the meaning of the dilemma to be resolved by the revolution.[47] I'd very much like to write about it. Note:
(1) That dreams are memories is obvious from the fact that you don't know what came before and what after. You string together all your memories into a succession of events the moment you wake up. Hence it seems that a long dream ends and merges with a real sound, the sound which woke you up. [. . .]
(7) One can understand the beliefs of Buddhism that you will always return to life (after death) until you reach absolute self-renunciation. Nirvana is not destruction, but that new, unknown, incomprehensible life in which self-renunciation is no longer necessary. Buddhism is only wrong in not recognising the meaning and purpose of *this* life which leads to self-renunciation. We cannot see it but it is there, and so this life is just as real as any other. [. . .]

21 November, Yasnaya Polyana [. . .] Yesterday I wrote *To The Young* for *The Spring*.[48] It's reasonably good. I haven't revised it yet. An interesting article today about the revolution in a Japanese journal, and one yesterday in an Indian journal about yellow and white civilisations.[49]

23 November, Yasnaya Polyana I'm in a very good state of mind and full of love for everyone. I've been reading St John's epistle.[50] It's wonderful. Only now can I fully understand it. Today there was a great temptation which I just couldn't resist entirely. Abakumov ran after me pleading and complaining that he had been sentenced to prison because of the oak trees. It hurt me very much. He can't understand that I, a husband, can't do as I want, and sees me as a scoundrel and as a pharisee, hiding behind my wife. I hadn't the strength to put up with it in a loving spirit, and told Abakumov that I couldn't go on living here. And that wasn't good. Generally speaking people are abusing me more and more on every side. That's good. It drives me towards God. If only I could stand firm where I am now. Generally speaking I feel at this very moment one of the biggest changes that have ever taken place in me. I feel it in my calmness and joyfulness and good feelings (I daren't say love) towards people. I dislike almost all my earlier writings of recent years, except the Gospels and a few others, for their lack of goodness. I don't want them to be published.
   Masha greatly alarms me. I love her very, very much. Yes, I would like to draw a dividing line under all my past life and begin a new, very short, but purer epilogue.

27 November, Yasnaya Polyana Just now, one o'clock in the morning, Masha died.[51] A strange thing. I didn't feel horror or fear or the awareness of anything exceptional taking place, nor even pity or grief. I seemed to consider it necessary to arouse in myself a special feeling of emotion, of grief, and I did so, but at the bottom of my heart I was more composed than I would have been in the case of another person's bad or improper behaviour – not to mention my own. Yes, this event belongs to the realm of the body and is irrelevant. I watched her all the time she was dying: wonderfully calmly. For me she was a creature experiencing revelation before my own revelation. I watched her revelation, and it made me glad. Now this revelation in the realm accessible to me (life) has ended, i.e. the revelation has ceased to be visible to me; but what was revealed exists. 'Where?', 'When?' – these are questions relating to the process of revelation here, and cannot be related to the true life outside space and time. Note:
(5) In serious moments when, as now, the body of a loved one lies still unburied, one sees clearly the immorality and wrongfulness and depressing nature of the life of the rich. The best remedy against grief is work. But they have no essential work, only amusement. But amusement is unseemly, and all that remains for them is automatically false, sentimental chatter. I've just received some falsely sympathetic letters and telegrams, and met the simple-minded Kynya who knew Masha. I said: 'Have you heard about our grief?'

'Yes, I've heard' – and then said immediately: 'Give me a copeck.'

How much better and easier that is.

29 November, Yasnaya Polyana They've just taken her away to be buried. Thank God, I'm still in good spirits, as before. Things are easier with my sons now. [...]

28 December, Yasnaya Polyana [...] During this time I've been doing some writing: a revised *Cycle of Reading* and a children's scripture.[52] It's very difficult, but if God wills I can do it. There is much that needs to be noted, and it's good, but I can't do it now – it's late in the evening.

I go on living and often recall Masha's last minutes (I don't like calling her Masha, that simple name is so unsuitable to the creature who has left me). She *sits* here, surrounded by pillows, and I hold her thin, dear hand and feel life departing, feel her departing. These quarter hours are among the most important, significant times of my life.

29 December, Yasnaya Polyana I feel weak physically, but good mentally. *What Is To Be Done?* has come out. It's unpleasant and feeble, but undoubtedly true. I didn't want to write any more articles, but an article on the meaning of the revolution, a letter from an officer and a notice today about *What Is To Be Done?* requires me to.[53] The main thing is, I must write that all their historical-economic theories are only a justification for their nasty life, only tramping up and down in a blind alley from which there is no exit. Note:

(3) I'd made a note 'Spartanism or effeminacy . . .'. I can't remember what I meant, probably that our society has lost the awareness of the sin of effeminacy. All, or the greater part of the inventions we are proud of, from railways to telephones, are aimed at increasing effeminacy. [. . .]

(10) Just as all the convictions of every kind of politician, socialist and revolutionary with regard to a better organisation of society are futile, so too are my own futile. Do what you can for yourself in the field in which you are competent, and leave the consequences to that force on which they depend.

(11) I have often been surprised at the confusion of ideas of such clever people as Vladimir Solovyov (I would say Bulgakov too, if I regarded him as clever), and now I realise clearly why. It's all due (as with all modern science) to regarding the state as something which exists independently of people's will, something pre-ordained, mystical, immutable.

(12) I am distressed by the fact that I shan't see in my life-time the consequences of my activity, and at the same time I am distressed that I shan't find in life an opportunity for the sort of activity in which I could be completely sure that I wouldn't be guided by the desire for worldly fame. I have exactly what I need, but I still complain.

(13) In the literature of today, everything that is produced is available to us with equal power to attract. The further back one goes, the less is available: the greater part has been whittled away by time; even more, if one goes back still further. The literature that is available has the shape of a cone standing on its point. Near the point are the wisdom of the Brahmins and the Chinese, Buddhism, Stoicism, Socrates, Christianity; further away, as it gets wider, come Plutarch, Seneca, Cicero, Marcus Aurelius, the mediaeval thinkers, then Pascal, Spinoza, Kant, the Encyclopaedists, then the writers of the nineteenth century, and finally our contemporaries. It's obvious that even among our contemporaries there are those who will survive, but it's difficult to find who they are, first because there are so many that it's impossible to go through them all, and secondly because only the very worst things are exposed to view, since the masses are always stupid and lacking in taste. [. . .]

(16) I've been noting down some simple rules for the children's scripture: (1) Don't condemn. (2) Don't overeat. (3) Don't kindle the passions. (4) Don't stupefy yourself. (5) Don't quarrel. (6) Don't pass on bad things about other people. (7) Don't be lazy. (8) Don't lie. (9) Don't quarrel. (10) Don't take anything away by force. (11) Don't torture animals. (12) Don't demand work from other people. (13) Be good to everyone. (14) Respect old people.[54] [. . .]

(21) You, the politician, say that love for the people guides your activity. You labour for their future good. But surely there is an enormous field before you, apart from political action, in which you can demonstrate your love, and not in the future but in the present, and without any admixture of that evil which is inevitable in your activity. [. . .]

(28) How difficult it is to distinguish whether you serve people for their good (to satisfy an inner striving to love), or for the gratitude and praise you will get from them. There is only one way of telling: would you do the same thing if you knew that

nobody would know? With every action which is not the result of an animal impulse, ask yourself: who for? [. . .]

(30) It is characteristic of man to strive to have more. This can be a striving to have more roubles, pictures or horses, more titles, muscles or knowledge, but it is only necessary to have more of one thing: more goodness. [. . .]

1907

14 January, Yasnaya Polyana I've been unwell all these last two weeks and still haven't recovered yet. All this time I've been reading: Plutarch, Montaigne and Waliszewski, yesterday a book about St Paul and today I finished the *Memorabilia*.¹ It's very interesting to compare the high state of moral understanding with the simplicity of life and the low level of technical development. Now this side has advanced so far and the moral side has fallen so far behind that it is hopeless to establish a correct relationship. I made a few notes during this time, but couldn't do any work at all. With the big new *Cycle of Reading* and also the one for children which I've started I seem to have taken upon myself work which is too much for me. There's a lot to note down, and it's quite good, I think.
(1) I was thinking today that it's impossible to live peacefully with a high opinion of oneself, and that the first condition for a peaceful and good life is what St Francis said about himself in case he should not be allowed in.² And today I've been busy all morning reducing my own denominator. And I think it hasn't been useless: I vividly recalled in myself all the things I now condemn in my sons: passion for gambling, hunting, vanity, dissipation, meanness . . . The main thing is to understand that I am a man well below average as far as concerns morality, weakness, intelligence, and especially knowledge, a man whose mental faculties are becoming feeble, and not to forget this; and then how easy life will be. Value the estimation of God, not men. Acknowledge the justice of people's low estimation of me. [. . .]

2 February, Yasnaya Polyana Haven't written my diary for more than a fortnight. I've been unwell – and I'm not fully recovered yet. I had a letter yesterday from my son Lev, a very painful one.³ I only read the beginning and threw it away. I was going to write a reply of silver words, but calmed down and preferred golden ones. Went for a ride and only then regained my composure. [. . .]
 During this time I wrote a great many letters: to Bolton Hall, Crosby's relatives, the Daniels, and Baba Bharati (which I haven't sent yet) and many short Russian letters.⁴ [. . .]

Today is 13 February, Yasnaya Polyana I don't think I've noted that I wrote a long letter to Baba Bharati. I'm afraid he covets fame. During this time I tried to write some lessons for children, but always unsuccessfully.⁵ Yesterday I read them two lessons, and was very dissatisfied with both. Wrote a letter to Reichel.⁶ Dušan Petrovich translated it. I don't know whether I'll send it. I don't despair of the scripture for children and I'm glad that with this work I don't have any purpose outside the work itself. I only want to use the time left to me in this world in the very best way I can. There's a lot to note down: [. . .]
(5) Revolutionaries are guided above all by envy and ambition and love of power.

And the worst thing of all is that these nasty feelings are concealed by a would-be love of freedom: they make themselve slaves of power, the most terrible form of captivity, out of love of freedom! [. . .]

14 February, Yasnaya Polyana   It's probably unnecessary to write Yasnaya Polyana. There's not much likelihood of my going away anywhere before I die. [. . .]

17 February, Yasnaya Polyana   Health worse. I'm well on my way to the passage over. I'm busy with La Bruyère.[7] Yesterday I read about Shakespeare – *Le Nazaréen, le grand corrupteur de l'humanité*.[8] Tanya just said about Ivan[9] that he hates the masters, and envies them. And it hurt me so sorely and made me so sad. How can one live under the burden of such hatred?!

22 February [. . .]
(2) Children need dogmatism, it doesn't hurt them.

17 March, Yasnaya Polyana   Haven't written my diary for a very long time, but I've made many notes in my notebooks. During this time I've only been working on the lessons for children. The further I get, the greater and greater are the difficulties I see, and at the same time the greater the hope of success. All that I've done so far is hardly any use. Yesterday I divided the children into two classes. Today I thought about what to do with the lower class. [. . .]
   There's a great deal to note down.
(1) Something strange and quite new to me is the reason why sons don't love their fathers (in non-Christian families, of course): it's envy on the sons' part and rivalry between sons and fathers. [. . .]
(5) I feel the blessings of old age and illnesses which release me from caring about other people's opinions. The fact that I am more abused than praised is a help in this respect.
(6) Only in the realm of consciousness is man free. But consciousness is only possible in the actual present moment. [. . .]
(8) Philanthropy is like a man draining off lush meadows by means of drainage ditches and then irrigating those meadows in the places where they seem particularly dry. You take away from the people everything they need, thereby depriving them of the possibility of feeding themselves by their own labour, and then you try to support the weak ones by sharing out among them a part of what has been taken away from them. [. . .]
(14) It would be good to forget one's self, but it's impossible, and so one must try at least to strike a balance: to do unto others as you would have them do unto you.
(15) If you notice in an argument that a person is defending his outward situation, cut short the conversation as soon as possible. [. . .]
(19) I remembered so vividly the nice young boy Nikolasha and the fact that it seemed to me that I was he, that I was smiling his smile and my eyes were sparkling like his eyes. That's how it is when you love someone. Surely this is clear evidence that one spirit is alive in all of us and that love does away with divisions. [. . .]

(22) Only old men and children, free from sexual desire, live a true life. The rest are only a stud for the continuation of the animal species. That's why debauchery is so disgusting in old men and children. Yet people think that all poetry is to be found in the sexual life alone. All true poetry is always outside it. [. . .]

5 April, Yasnaya Polyana Haven't written my diary for more than a fortnight. I've lived reasonably well all this time. I've had a heavy cold, and now feel very weak. The lessons for children and the preparation for them have been entirely absorbing me. I notice my physical and mental powers growing weaker, but in inverse proportion to my moral ones. There's a lot I would like to write. But there's a lot I've already left unfinished for good, or not even begun. Note – though I doubt if I'll manage to today:
(1) A story about two enemies trapped down a mine.[10] [. . .]
(5) I must write the life of a man who has experienced all the three temptations of Christ in the wilderness.[11] [. . .]
(10) The whole difference between a man and an animal is that a man knows he will die, but an animal doesn't. It's an enormous difference. [. . .]

9 April, Yasnaya Polyana As soon as I got up yesterday, I experienced a strange, joyful – more than joyful – a blessed feeling of calmness and assurance – of old age. *Je m'entends* [I understand what I'm saying]. A feeling of assurance that my life is lived in the spirit, not in the body; and so of freedom, of satisfaction . . . And at the same time I felt very poorly all day physically. Today there was an unpleasant business with the wife of Volodkin, who was buried in the sand pit.[12] I didn't pass the test. I feel better towards Lev. I enjoy being with Tanya. Things are getting on gradually with the boys, but I'm dissatisfied and far from assured. [. . .]

16 April, Yasnaya Polyana Five days have passed and I'm in quite a different mood today. I can't overcome my dissatisfaction with those close to me. I feel melancholy and want to cry. Everything seems depressing. Just now after dinner and a lesson with the children – only two came – I sat alone and thought that only now was I fully and completely entrusting myself to the will of God. Come what may. There was no point in wanting to perform any task – writing a scripture for children or whatever it may be; I had to surrender myself entirely to Him, retaining only my love for Him, privately and publicly . . . and suddenly Sonya came in and we started talking about the wood, about people stealing, and about the children selling things at half price, and I couldn't suppress my anger. As if it wasn't all the same to me. Lord, help me. Help me. I'm sorry for myself and feel disgusted with myself.

22 April, Yasnaya Polyana I thought I wrote my diary the other day, but eleven days have passed. I've been in a very good, joyful and peaceful mood all this time. I only want to give thanks and rejoice. I've been busy with the Gospels, the *Cycle of Reading* for children and my lessons. A strange thing happened in bed last night. It was as if someone was blowing on me. I felt a fresh breath of air and my spirits revived together with the awareness of the nearness of death. I can't say I was afraid, but I can't say I was calm either.

A work of fiction, *Three Centuries*, is taking clearer and clearer shape in my mind. It would be good to work on it.[13] [. . .]

Today is 30 April, Yasnaya Polyana   I've been living very well all this time. I've been busy with the same things. I'd like to write a work of fiction, but I'm hardly capable of it now. However, the main thing is not to wish for anything for oneself. The *Cycle of Reading* for children is a sufficient service. I feel very poorly and weak today. Note. [. . .]
(2) The true life is lived above all by children, who enter life and are not yet aware of time. They never want anything to be changed. The longer they live, the more they become subject to the illusion of time. As old age approaches, this illusion grows weaker and weaker – time seems to go quicker – and finally old people enter more and more into a life without time. And so it is children and old people who live the true life most of all. But people who live the life of the flesh are preparing material for the true life rather than living it themselves.
(3) People condemn egoism. But egoism is the basic law of life. The point is what one regards as one's *ego*: one's consciousness or one's body – or rather, one's spiritual or physical consciousness. [. . .]
(11) Noted down six themes for stories for children:[14]
   (1) A cruel landowner whom an old woman took pity on;
   (2) A never despairing, cheerful fellow in adversity;
   (3) Agafya Mikhaylovna's pity for dogs, cats, mice and cockroaches;
   (4) Enemies trapped down a mine;
   (5) A truce during war;
   (6) Three temptations. [. . .]
(23) *It isn't the sun which moves, but the earth which rotates in its direction; likewise it isn't time which runs on, but the world that has been concealed by time, which reveals itself.* N.B.
(24) How mysterious everything is for old people, and how clear to children! [. . .]
(27) Personal egoism is a small evil, family egoism a bigger one, party egoism a bigger one still, and state egoism the most terrible of all. [. . .]

Today is 22 May, Yasnaya Polyana   Haven't written anything in my diary for nearly a month. During this month, I've continued lessons with the children and preparations for them. Apart from that, almost all I've done is to jot down my thoughts about Paul as the falsifier of Christianity.[15] Among the visitors was Dobrolyubov. Yesterday – Loizner, a 'free Christian'. He's very busy combating the influence.[16] Dear Nikolayev and his boys.[17] The depressing business of Andrey.[18] The murder of the good Vyacheslav.[19] Yesterday evening I had a very nasty quarrel with Kolya;[20] today, thank goodness, I asked his forgiveness. Wrote yesterday about Skoworoda.[21] Something else to do: to compile biographies of Epictetus, Socrates, Pascal and Rousseau, as well as those of Buddha and Confucius. This is an old man's dispersal of effort. [. . .]

28 May, Yasnaya Polyana I've been unwell, and so have asked Sasha to write my diary for a few days. [. . .]
(1) Today, 13 May, I woke up and experienced a strange new state of mind: I seem to have forgotten everything. I can't remember whether Yuliya Ivanovna is here or not, I can't remember what the date is or what I'm writing. But at the same time I have a particularly vivid impression, not so much of the images, but of the feelings of my dreams today.
(2) We must make use of the freedom of the revolution in order to rid ourselves of the superstition of the necessity of power. 'But the people are not ready.' It's a *cercle vicieux*. The people won't be ready as long as the power that corrupts them exists.
(3) Just as a tutor always considers his pupil unprepared, so too do probationary tutors. The anarchists see the evil of power, but believe in it – believe in it as a means. [. . .]
(5) What comes first, and what next? First people must be freed from slavery, and then their work made easier by means of machines. And not as now, when the invention of machines only makes slavery worse. [. . .]

7 June, Yasnaya Polyana Haven't written my diary for a long time. My previous illness is over, but a new one seems to be starting. I'm very, very sad today. I'm ashamed to admit it, but I can't summon up any joy. I'm calm and serious at heart, but not joyful. I'm sad mainly because of the darkness in which people so stubbornly go on living. Because of the bitterness of the people, and our senseless luxury. Gorbunova told me about the terrible corruption of children. A letter yesterday from Andrey made me feel good. I felt the joy of solitude with God. Today I looked over my *Cycle of Reading* for children. The children didn't come. There was a letter from Sutkovoy, and I wrote one to him about the Dobrolyubovtsy sect.[22] I'm sad, sad. Lord, help me, burn up the old carnal man in me. Yes, the only consolation, the only salvation is to live in eternity, not time. [. . .]

I thought how harmful it is to write *articles*, to compose articles and not to express one's thoughts and feelings just as they come.

9 June, Yasnaya Polyana I've woken up today. I feel good at heart. I remembered that Nikolayev, in his book, was expressing my thoughts about man being a detached, spiritual creature, conscious of his own detachment in space and time, and I felt displeased.[23] And then again, just as with Andrey's letter, when I measured this question against the business of my life, against my relationship to God, the feeling not merely passed, but changed from a depressing and unpleasant one to one that was joyful and sublime. [. . .]

10 June, Yasnaya Polyana Physically weak. I'm well at heart. Loving relationships are becoming a habit. Oh, if only this habit could be acquired in childhood! Is it possible? I think so. A few things to note:
(1) I suffer more and more, almost physically, from inequality – of wealth and of the extravagances of our life in the midst of poverty; and I can't reduce this inequality. Therein lies the secret tragedy of my life. [. . .]

16 June, Yasnaya Polyana   The Chertkovs are coming. That makes me very glad. I'm not writing much or thinking much. I was in a very bad mood a couple of days ago. I held myself in check more or less. I think I've caught a cold again. There are a few things to write down from my notebook. I'll write something down now immediately: [. . .]
(3) Self-assured and therefore worthless people always impress modest and therefore worthy, intelligent and moral people precisely because a modest person, judging by himself, simply cannot imagine that a bad person could respect himself so much and speak with such self-assurance about something he knows nothing about. [. . .]

27 June, Yasnaya Polyana.   The Chertkovs have been, and spent three days with us. It was very enjoyable. Nesterov[24] is here – a pleasant man. Sergeyenko has been. Yesterday there were eight hundred children here.[25] My state of mind is good. [. . .]
(5) There exists something not transient and not variable; in brief, something not spatial and not temporal, not partial, but whole. I know that it exists, I am conscious of myself within it, but I see myself limited by my body in space and by my movement in time. I can imagine that my human ancestors have existed for the last thousand centuries, and before them their animal ancestors, and the ancestors of the animals – all that has been and will continue to be in infinite time. I can also imagine that I and my body occupy one definite place amid infinite space and am conscious that not only has all this been and will continue to be, but that all this, both in infinite space and infinite time, is actually me.

Herein lies the at first seemingly strange, but essentially very simple understanding of one's own life: I am a manifestation of everything in space and time. All that exists – all that is me – only limited by space and time. What we call love is only a manifestation of that consciousness. This manifestation is naturally more alive with regard to creatures who are nearer to one in space and time. [. . .]
(10) All passions are only an exaggeration of natural – and legitimate – inclinations: (1) vanity – the desire to know what people want of us; (2) meanness – the thrifty use of other people's labours; (3) lust – the fulfilment of the law of the continuation of the race; (4) pride – the consciousness of one's divinity; (5) malice, hatred of people – hatred of evil. [. . .]

1 July, Yasnaya Polyana   I'm getting weaker and weaker. Can't do any work. Did a few things for the *Cycle of Reading*. Haven't worked with the children for two days. I've many plans, but no strength. Feel very good at heart. [. . .]

20 July, Yasnaya Polyana   Haven't written my diary for a hundred years, i.e. more than a month. During this time there have been many outward events: the children, the murder of Zvegintseva's servants,[26] above all the Chertkovs. Joyful relations with the Chertkovs, and a mass of visitors. The children's lessons have 'come to nothing'. The arrival of Tanya and her husband, the arrival of Andryusha: he's well. [. . .]

During this time my health has been reasonably good, too good, 'to judge by our sins'. I've given up the *Cycle of Reading* and wrote a brochure, *Kill No Man*, apropos of the imprisonment of Felten.[27] Read it to Chertkov and the others yesterday, although I hadn't finished it. Now I feel like writing a letter to Stolypin[28] and a story, *Hands Up*,[29] which came into my head while Goldenweiser was playing. People have been paying a lot of attention to me recently for some reason, and this does me a lot of harm. I look for my name in the paper. This darkens and obscures life very, very much. I must fight against it. Note: [. . .]

(2) If the proposition that the three angles of a triangle equal two right angles were opposed to people's interests, they would find ways of proving the opposite (Hobbes). [. . .]

(5) Old age is good because it does away with concern for the future. For an old man there is no future, and so all concern, all efforts, are transferred to the present, i.e. to the true life. [. . .]

(12) Before I knew where I was I fell into temptation, and began to ascribe special importance to myself – the founder of a philosophical-religious school – began to ascribe importance to this and wished it were so, as though it were of some importance *for* my life. All this is of importance not *for* my life but *against* it; it stifles it and distorts it. [. . .]

(15) What a bad habit it is when you meet a person to start off with a joke. God is in that person, and you mustn't joke with God. When you meet a person, always talk to him in all seriousness. [. . .]

6 August, Yasnaya Polyana Haven't written my diary for a hundred years. Today I handed over *Kill No Man* to Chertkov, and I hope I've finished it and it's not bad. I've just started on the children's *Cycle of Reading* for Ivan Ivanovich.[30] I've a lot to write down both about life and from my notebooks, but at the moment I'll only write down what I thought today, namely:

(1) I thought that the peasants were far better morally during serfdom than they are now. Why was that? I think because oppression, want and suffering assist the process of moral improvement, while freedom, sufficiency and outward blessings are harmful to it. Harmful because they are heavy and demanding. A person can settle down better and more easily in a little house than in an enormous palace. However strange and odd this seems, I believe it's true. And the conclusion from this for me is that a person's wellbeing is only spiritual, and this wellbeing is undermined more than anything else by concern for physical, material wellbeing. The further conclusion from this is that there is nothing more harmful for a person than to concern himself with his own physical wellbeing. But what should we do if we don't concern ourselves with our own spiritual wellbeing? We should concern ourselves with the wellbeing of others with the assurance that others will concern themselves with us. Self-denial is thus the most fundamental law of human life.

Today is 8 August, Yasnaya Polyana I feel a considerable weakening of everything, especially memory, but at heart I feel very, very good. I've finished the article, and apart from letters and my diary I'll now work on the children's *Cycle of Reading*. Being with Chertkov makes me very happy. I had some very good thoughts today. [. . .]

(4) A pilgrim said to me: 'Life has become impossible. The landowners have completely crushed the people. They've nowhere to go. And the priests. The way they live! They fleece widows and orphans of their last copeck. And those who stand up for truth and for the people are imprisoned. How many good people have been hanged?

He went on his way – and there are thousands like him – to earn his daily bread, and that is the most effective form of propaganda.

(5) In the past we had the Saint Francises, now we have the Darwins.

(6) The young generation nowadays not only doesn't believe in any religion, but believes, actually believes, that all religion is rubbish, nonsense. [. . .]

(9) Intelligence only springs from humility. Stupidity – only from conceit. However great his intellectual faculties, a humble person is always dissatisfied – always seeking; a self-assured person thinks he knows everything, and doesn't try to delve deep. [. . .]

(15) Kant is considered an abstract philosopher, but he is a great religious teacher. [. . .]

(18) There is almost no freedom of choice over physical conditions: you burn yourself and you recoil, you haven't slept for two days and you fall asleep. There is more freedom of choice over actions: shall I go or not? Shall I do this job or another one? There is more freedom of choice still over thoughts – almost complete freedom. [. . .]

22 August, Yasnaya Polyana I can't say that I've been in a weak state of mind, rather the opposite, but my nerves have been very weak, and I've been tearful. Tanya is arriving shortly. Yesterday I said goodbye to Malevanny, and he and his companions – both Dudchenko and Grauberger – made, I won't say a bad, but an unnecessary impression on me. I thought hard today about the sequence of the *Cycle of Reading*. Perhaps I'll change it again, but it's all right as it is. I'm freeing myself more and more from worrying about people's opinion of me. What freedom, what joy, what strength this gives! God help me to free myself entirely.

I've just read in the papers about murders and robberies with threats of murder. Murders and cruelty get worse and worse. What's to be done? How can we stop it? People are locked up, sent to penal servitude, executed. But the crimes get no fewer – on the contrary. But what are we to do? One thing and one thing only: each of us must devote all his powers to living a godly life, and we must implore them, the murderers and robbers, to live a godly life too. I, with my hands raised at their command, will implore them to stop living badly. 'They won't listen, they'll go on doing the same thing.' Well, what *am* I to do then? There's nothing more that *I* can do. Yes, something good needs to be said about this. Note: [. . .]

(3) I've been reading Kropotkin on communism.[31] It's well written and the intentions are good, but it's remarkable for its inner contradiction: violence must be used to put a stop to violence by some people over others. The point is, how are you to stop people being egoists and perpetrators of violence? According to their programme, you need to use fresh violence to achieve this purpose. [. . .]

7 September, Yasnaya Polyana I've looked through my notebook from 22 August. I've only been working on the *Cycle of Reading*. I've got little to show for it, but it was good for the soul. It has fortified me particularly in my fight against people's opinions. I had some very important thoughts about this today. I'll write them down later. Received a depressing letter from Novikov and replied to him.[32] Being with Chertkov still makes me just as happy. I'm afraid I've been suborned by his liking for me. Had a look yesterday at *The Collected Thoughts*.[33] It would be good if they were to be as useful to people as they seem to me in my moments of conceit. During this time my state of mind has been good rather than bad. I felt just now how constrained I am in writing this diary by the knowledge that it will be read by Sasha and Chertkov. I'll try to forget about them.

For the last two or three days I've been in a depressed state of mind which I haven't been able to overcome until today, because some cabbage thieves fired shots during the night, and Sonya complained and the authorities appeared and arrested four peasants and their womenfolk and their fathers turned to me. They can't accept the fact that I'm not the master – especially since I live here – and so ascribe everything to me. It's depressing, very depressing, but it's good because it makes it impossible for people to have a good opinion about me, and drives me into the realm where people's opinion counts for nothing. For the last two days I couldn't overcome this bad feeling.

News of Boulanger.[34] I hope and believe that he's escaped. The governor and *tout le tremblement* [the whole caboodle] have just been. It's disgusting and pathetic.[35] It was good for me in the sense that it strengthened my genuine sympathy for these people. [. . .]

(4) I'd like to say this to people:

Dear brothers, why do you torment yourself and other people, why do you try to change and improve people's lives, change and improve people themselves? Neither you nor anybody else can do that. By trying to change and improve people's lives you only torment yourselves and other people, damage your own and other people's lives. No person in the world has been called on to reform other people, and nobody can do so. Everybody is called on to reform and improve himself only, and everybody should and can do so. [. . .]

(7) I heard some children talking behind the acacias: they were smoking and swearing. I called a young boy over and began to admonish him; he began lying and blaming the others. The state of mind of these children is worse than any physical afflictions. [. . .]

15 September Both days I've been writing 'talks with young people'.[36] It turned out to be neither one thing nor the other. A depressing conversation with Sonya. I'm truly sorry for her. Note: [. . .]

(2) To love a bad person seems impossible. And it is indeed impossible. But one can and must love not the person, but the crushed and stifled God in him, and love that God and try to set Him free. That is not only possible, but a source of joy. [. . .]

(7) Women of our circle, well-to-do people, have an enormous advantage over men of this circle, which country women and working women in general don't have: it is

that in bearing and bringing up children, they are doing a real job which is undoubtedly necessary and laid down by a higher law. But our men for the most part live their lives in military headquarters, university departments, law courts, administration and trade, not only not doing a real job, but doing nasty, stupid and harmless jobs. On the other hand, women with no children, if they are not saints, and don't devote themselves to deeds of love, but take to being idle like the men, are even nastier, more stupid and more complacent in their nastiness than the most corrupt men of the idle classes. [. . .]

26 September, Yasnaya Polyana I'm a bit constrained in my writing by the fact that Repin is painting my portrait[37] – it's unnecessary and tiresome, but I don't want to distress him. Things are well with me. For a long time now I've felt an awareness of my great blessings. There were four days or so of depression and struggle as a result of my sickly condition. Thank God, I've nothing particular to repent of.

I've been compiling a new *Cycle of Reading* all this time and have finished it very roughly. A great many visitors. I'm fashionable just now. And that's depressing. Posha has been. I love him very much. I miss Chertkov. Repin, the founder of the commune,[38] has been – passionate and therefore dangerous. I've had some good thoughts. I'd like to write abut women and about the crazy way the world is organised. And there are some interesting letters to answer. Note:
(1) Why is it that people who can't read and write are more sensible than scholars? Because in their consciousness the natural and sensible order of importance of objects and questions has not been disturbed. It is pseudo-science that causes this disturbance.
(2) The demands of the family cannot justify actions contrary to morality any more than a contract one has entered into can justify dishonest settlements of accounts with suppliers. [. . .]

10 October, Yasnaya Polyana Haven't written my diary for a long time; one day during this time I was in a melancholy state because of the watchmen who are alarming the peasants.[39] Aunt Tanya and Mikhail Sergeyevich and the two Tanyas are here.[40] The unexpected and unpleasant abuse caused by my letter saying that I own no property was unpleasant.[41] I felt offended, and, surprisingly enough, this was just the very thing I needed: freedom from the desire for worldly fame. I feel a big step forward in that direction. More and more often I experience a sort of special delight, a *joie de vivre*. Yes, one has only to free oneself, as I am now doing, from temptations: anger, lechery, wealth, to some extent lasciviousness and most of all, the desire for worldly fame, and suddenly an inner light blazes forth. It makes me particularly happy. During this time I've been working on the children's *Cycle of Reading*, fitting it into the same subdivisions as the main one. It's work which requires a great deal of effort, but it's going reasonably well. Note:
(1) Life is not a joke, but a great and solemn business. One's life should always be as serious and solemn as one's death. [. . .]
(9) Man doesn't know what is good and what is bad, but he writes a research paper on a fallen aerolite or the origin of the word 'cowl'.

12 October, Yasnaya Polyana My health is good, but in my soul is paradise – or almost paradise. It's becoming more and more second nature to live lovingly, without thinking about myself for the sake of myself (my body), or about myself in the opinion of other people. And it makes me wonderfully happy. It must be because of my age which has freed me from passion – whether in anger, lust or the desire for worldly fame; but I think it's possible for everybody. I'm receiving many letters, and very good ones. A letter from Ikonnikov made me burst out crying like an old woman when I heard it.[42] And that's good. Very good. I must write down one thing which isn't in my notebook:

(1) People say, and so do I, that printing has not furthered people's wellbeing. More than that. Nothing which increases the possibility of people exerting influence on one another – railways, telegraphs, telephones, steamers, cannons, all military devices, explosive materials and everything called 'culture' – has done anything to further people's wellbeing in our time; on the contrary. And it could not have been otherwise among people, the majority of whom live an irreligious, immoral life. If the majority are immoral, then the means of exerting influence will obviously only further the spread of immorality.

The means culture has of exerting influence can only be beneficial when the majority, if only a small one, live a religious and moral life. What is desirable is that the relationship between morality and culture should be such that culture should only develop at the same time as, and a little behind moral progress. But when culture outstrips morality, as is the case at present, the result is a great disaster. It may be, as I think, that it is a temporary disaster, that although there are bound to be temporary sufferings as a result of the elevation of culture over morality, the backwardness of morality will cause sufferings as a result of which culture will be held back and the progress of morality speeded up, and a correct relationship will be re-established.

I'm still occupied, and very assiduously, with the children's *Cycle of Reading*, and although it's slow, I'm making progress. I thought today that I would do three *Cycles of Reading*. One – in sections – for children; the second – a similar one for adults. The third would be without sections, the old one revised.[43]

20 October, Yasnaya Polyana I've got stuck in my work. And I've done nothing for two days. I very much dislike the enumeration of my sins and temptations.[44] Today I seem to be disentangling myself a little. During this time I've been unwell – my stomach – and I still haven't recovered. I've had visits from Zabolotnyuk, who's refusing to do military service, and today Novichkov.[45] I'm receiving threatening telegrams and terribly abusive letters. To my shame, I must admit that they distress me. The universal condemnation and animosity caused by my letter are still quite incomprehensible to me. I said what is true and asked them not to trouble themselves unnecessarily, and to leave me in peace. And suddenly... It's astonishing and incomprehensible. The only explanation is that they like to think that everything I said and say about Christianity is lies and hypocrisy, so that they can take no notice of it. Sutkovoy has been – he's going to Samara. [...]

26 October, Yasnaya Polyana For a long time – three weeks or so if not more – I've been in very low spirits. I've no longer felt any *joie de vivre*, or the joyful and necessary and (for me) important thoughts and feelings that used to come crowding in before. During this time I've done nothing particularly bad. I'm still working on the *Cycle of Reading*. Decided today to change many things in it. It's about six days since I started lessons again with the children. They aren't going particularly well. Worse than I expected. Gusev has been arrested.[46] Visits from: Novichkov, Liza, today Olsufyev, Varya and Natasha.[47] Today for the first day I've woken up spiritually, and have climbed back up to my old rung, perhaps even a little higher. [. . .]

Must note also: [. . .]

(7) (Very important.) Non-resistance to evil by force is not an injunction, but a manifest, consciously understood law of life for every individual human being and for all mankind – even for every living creature.

This law is constantly being obeyed. Wolves die, rabbits multiply. This law, like any law, is an ideal towards which every living creature unconsciously strives of its own accord, and towards which every individual human being *must* strive.

This law only seems wrong when it is conceived of as a demand which must be fulfilled in full, and not (as it ought to be understood) as a continual, incessant, conscious and unconscious striving towards the fulfilment of the law.

(8) It's strange that I have to remain silent in front of the people who live round about me, and only talk to those far away in time and place who will listen to me.

8 November, Yasnaya Polyana I thought I'd written my diary recently, but it's been almost two weeks. About three days ago I was in Krapivna seeing Gusev.[48] A very painful but significant impression. I'd like to write about it, and also a drama about Bulygin's son.[49] Their life made a very joyful impression on me. [. . .] Note: [. . .]

(4) If the brain is occupied with scientific knowledge, there can be no room in it for religious and moral knowledge. This explains the irreligious nature of our upper classes. Physical labour leaves the brain free, but it isn't so with mental labour.

(5) The tragedy of our situation is that there is no other choice except crude, pagan ecclesiasticism or true Christianity. But in true Christianity man is alone; not merely alone, but the majority are hostile to him. And so people choose neither the one nor the other, and are left without a faith of any sort of all. [. . .]

(7) I know that these simple and clear truths about life which I'm writing now are sure to be defined by scholarly readers of the future as mysticism or some other such name, which will enable the readers, without trying to understand them, to continue to remain in complacent, self-satisfied ignorance. [. . .]

(10) The most tragi-comical thing about our Christianity is that it is introduced and propagated among the poor and the weak by the strong and the rich – the very people whose existence is repudiated by Christianity. [. . .]

22 November, Yasnaya Polyana I feel very well, full of tenderness and joy, and – a surprising thing – I've forgotten everything: forgotten who Gusev is and why he's in prison. Got up in the morning and had tender thoughts and feelings about Andryusha and wrote him a letter. Looked for the sketch plan of my article and couldn't find it.[50] It seemed so good and important, but now I can't remember anything. I'm still thinking about the drama. It would be a good thing.

All this time I've been strenuously occupied with the *Cycle of Reading*. I've finished it in rough, but the work is endless. If I compile, i.e. rewrite five or six sayings a day, there will be work for more than a year, more than four hundred days. But I'm almost certain that I won't live that long. The nearer death is, the stronger I feel the obligation to say what I know, what God says through me. And I feel that this is necessary, all the more because there is nothing personal about it, no desire for worldly fame. Note: [...]
(8) Yes, idleness is the mother of all vices, especially intellectual ones: false arguments – politics, science, theology.
(9) If a rich man has a conscience, he will be ashamed of his wealth and will want to get rid of it: but to get rid of it is almost as difficult as it is for a poor man to get rich. The main difficulty is the family. One can overcome habits – but the family... [...]
(15) The Russian government knows and can't help knowing that in our country everything is supported by religion, and it bases itself on religion, but the religion on which it bases itself was unsteady even before; now it is ceasing to give any support at all. [...]

29 November, Yasnaya Polyana Haven't written my diary for only a week, but it seems a terribly long time. Life is so full. There is quite a lot I need to note down, but I won't today. I'll only note down the most important thing, namely that I now feel the benefit of the mental activity to which I've devoted myself. Although I'm in a very bad physical condition and state of mind, I feel well. Not only well – happy. How astonishing it is: *de gaieté de coeur* [out of sheer wantonness] people ruin their lives by allowing themelves to become irritable. It all depends 'on you', as Syutayev used to say. Look with love at the world and its people, and they will look at you in the same way. I'm still busy with the *Cycle of Reading* and I think I'm making progress. Seryozha, Masha, Andryusha – I get on well with them all. Must write down from my notebook:
(1) At first it seems strange why a person who has done an evil deed should become more evil. You would think he ought to be content: he has done what he wanted. But the reason is that his consciousness, his conscience reproaches him and he needs to justify himself, if not before others at least before himself, and to justify himself he does a new evil deed *with a vengeance*.[51] [...]

[16 December] Haven't written my diary for a terribly long time. Today is 16 December, Yasnaya Polyana. On 29 November I fell off my horse and hurt my arm. It's getting better now. During this time much has happened, I've had more and more good letters. I don't get carried away and I don't desire publicity as I used to before, but I'm simply glad that I could and can be at least of some service to people. How strange that with goodness comes humility – modesty. I don't need now, as I did before, to pretend to be humble. As soon as my inner self gets to

work, I see at once that there is not only nothing to be proud of, but nothing to be glad about. I'm only glad that I feel undeservedly well, and more and more so the nearer I approach death.

I'm still busy with the *Cycle of Reading*. The main thing is the order of the sections. I think the distribution of material is nearly finished, but the editing of the thoughts themselves is still an enormous job. Only three sections have been copied out. Andrey has been with his new . . .[52] It was very difficult, although I tried my best and did nothing wrong. I get on well with Seryozha, and with everybody, even the watchmen. 'Rejoice if people revile you.' There's a great deal to note down, I think. They still haven't released Gusev, although as long ago as the 22nd they promised to do so both in Tula and Petersburg. . . .

30 December, Yasnaya Polyana   Haven't written my diary for two weeks. The only thing of importance is that Gusev has been released.[53] Seryozha and his wife are here. I still continue to receive heartening letters. A very good letter today from Molochnikov to Stolypin.[54] Wrote about it to Olsufyev. I'm still occupied with the *Cycle of Reading* and, thank God, everything is getting clearer and clearer. I'm going through the sections a second time. There are thirty-one of them. And, I think unintentionally, there have turned out to be four sins, four temptations and four deceptions. Yesterday I had a very heated – and therefore bad – argument with Seryozha about science. How astonishing is the belief in science and its complete analogy with the Church. [. . .]

1908

Today is New Year's Day, 1 January, 1908, Yasnaya Polyana. I'm finishing copying up my notebook. I'm still just as busy with the *Cycle of Reading*, and I'm making progress, I think. Andrey and Seryozha and their wives are here. I'm fighting against my feelings towards . . .¹ [. . .]
(11) The fact that life only consists in moral endeavour is evident from the fact that in dreams you are incapable of moral endeavour, and you do the most terrible deeds.
(12) The life of people who lack moral endeavour is not life, but a dream.
(13) My arm was broken, and I watched it get better. But now it is all right again, and I feel there is something lacking. There is nothing for me to watch. And our whole life is watching things grow like this: muscles, riches, fame. True life is moral growth, and the joy of life is watching this growth. But what a childish, senseless idea heaven is, where people are perfect and therefore don't grow and so don't live. [. . .]

13 January, Yasnaya Polyana Haven't written my diary for twelve days. I've finished the *Cycle of Reading in rough* and have written out the sections. I'm keeping quite well, only I lost my way in the Zaseka wood the day before yesterday and got very tired, and my heart aches today. Slept badly. Wrote some letters – cleared everything up. I'm expecting Chertkov the day after tomorrow. I'm copying up my notebook. I've been thinking about a drama for two days.² I doubt if I'll have enough interest to write it. Note: [. . .]
(4) Almost all technical improvements satisfy either egotistical aspirations towards personal enjoyment, or family, class, civic or national pride (war). [. . .]
(8) From a newspaper: 'They tell me: "be chaste", but I say: "as long as it doesn't harm my health".' What a terrible thing. Firstly, losing one's chastity is far more of a threat to one's health than retaining it, and secondly, most important, health and the moral law are two incommensurate conditions of life. To violate the moral law for the sake of health is the same as pulling down the house you live in in order to use it for fuel. [. . .]
(10) Don't borrow other people's answers to questions until the questions have arisen in your own mind. [. . .]

20 January, Yasnaya Polyana Chertkov is here, and a mass of people, all welcome. However, I'm in the state of mind, thank God, when everyone is welcome to me. The Abrikosovs, Gusev, Plyusnin. Yesterday Posha came. Sofya Andreyevna is in Moscow. Andrey was here yesterday. A pitiable man, pitiable for his imperturbable self-assurance. I write it and don't regret it. Perhaps if he reads it after my death, it will pierce the armour of his self-satisfaction at least a little bit. I've begun writing

an article. On decadence, unbelief and non-resistance.³ It's not too bad, but it's weak. I feel generally weak myself. Death must be near. And I approach it as I approach my destination when travelling. The comparison isn't exact, because the journey gets better the nearer one gets to the destination. I've finished the sections.⁴ Note. [. . .]
(8) If, as scholars think, man might remain in ignorance of the meaning of life and his guide through life without the study of complex and difficult sciences which requires leisure time, this would be a far more scandalous injustice than the fact that one man has millions, and another has no shoes. [. . .]

31 January, Yasnaya Polyana Began to revise my old *Cycle of Reading*. And it proved to be more work than I expected, and not bad work at that. I've almost finished eight months – I still have to re-arrange and make additions – but the main work is done. Sasha is a long time in Moscow. I try not to fear for her. Things are very well with everyone. Yesterday Mikhail Stakhovich was here. I had a good talk with him. But I can't talk about intimate matters without tears. Today I've been revising my exposition of the Gospels for children at the wish of dear Marya Alexandrovna.⁵ I've written two long letters during this time: one to Stolypin, and the other was probably to a Pole – Zadago.⁶ Both, I think, are not bad, at least I wrote them from the heart. [. . .]
Note: [. . .]
(5) How good it would be and how necessary for life not to forget that a person's rank is so much higher than any possible human rank, and that one must behave in exactly the same way to a tsaritsa as to a prostitute, etc.[. . .]
(7) I have come to know the blessing and the teaching of life only at the end of my own life, and so I can't make use of the knowledge. And therefore it's necessary and it's my duty to hand on what I know to other people. For the first time I have felt this duty keenly. [. . .]
(18) I've been reading Shaw.⁷ His triviality amazes me. Not only does he not have a single thought of his own rising above the triviality of the urban masses, but he doesn't understand a single great thought of the thinkers of the past. The only special thing about him is that he can express the most banal trivialities in a very elegantly distorted, new manner, as though he were saying something new and original. His main characteristic is his terrifying self-assurance, only equalled by his complete philosophical ignorance. [. . .]

9 February, Yasnaya Polyana During this time I've been busy revising my *New Cycle of Reading*. I've finished correcting the old one, although there is still some work to be done on it. Butkevich has been with a young teacher, and I have had some good letters. My state of mind gets better and better. The spiritual life, the work of the spirit within, is replacing the physical life more and more, and I feel better and better at heart. What seems like a paradox – that old age, the approach of death and death itself are a good thing and a blessing – is the undoubted truth. I am experiencing it. A letter from Gr. Petrov,⁸ asking if he can come. I'll try to see in him only a brother, a son of God. Health not bad. [. . .]

(4) I asked myself: why am I writing this?[9] Is there not a personal desire here for something for myself? And I can confidently answer no, that if I am writing it, it's only because I can't be silent and would consider it a bad thing to be silent, just as I would consider it bad not to try to stop children falling down a precipice or under a train.

(5) (Also for the appeal.) It would be possible to remain indifferent to what I say if I were saying something I had invented, something that might happen or might not, but the destruction I am speaking about is bound to happen, is inevitable. It would have been possible to think hard about whether to do or not to do what I say if this meant doing something dangerous, difficult, shameful, degrading or incompatible with human nature; but on the contary, what I'm appealing for is safe and easy and noble, and compatible both with the awareness of one's dignity and with human nature. [. . .]

10 March, Yasnaya Polyana Haven't written my diary for exactly a month. I've been busy at the desk with my article. It's not progressing, but I don't want to give it up. But my inner work is progressing, thank God, without pause, and it's getting better and better. I want to write down what is going on in me and how it is going on; something I haven't told anyone and which no one knows. There have been many letters and visitors. None particularly important. People have organised a jubilee clebration,[10] and this is doubly irksome for me: both because it's stupid and the flattery is unpleasant, and because from force of habit I slip into a state of finding in it not pleasure, but interest. And that is offensive to me. Chertkov has been. I got on particularly well with him. About a week ago I felt ill. I had a fainting fit. And it made me feel very good. But the people round about me made a *fuss*[11] over it. Yesterday I read a wonderful article by an Indian in Nazhivin's translation.[12] My thoughts, unclearly expressed.

This is how I live: I get up, my head is clear, good thoughts occur to me as I sit on the pot and I note them down. I get dressed and I empty the contents of the pot with an effort but with pleasure. I go for a walk. On my walk I wait for the post from force of habit, although I don't need it. I often guess to myself how many steps it will take to get to such and such a place, and I count them, dividing each one into four, six and eight breaths: one and *a* and *a* and *a*; and two and *a* and *a* and *a* . . . Sometimes, from force of habit, I'm disposed to guess that if there are as many steps as I suppose, all will be well. But now I ask myself: what is 'well'? and I know that everything is very well as it is, and there's no need to try and guess. Then when I meet someone I try to remember – though for the most part I forget that I wanted to remember – that he and I are one. It's particularly difficult to remember during a conversation. Then my dog Belka barks and prevents me from thinking, and I get angry and reproach myself for getting angry. I reproach myself for getting angry with a stick I stumble over. Yes, I forgot to say that as I wash and dress I remember the poverty of the village and feel bad about the luxury of my clothes, but cleanliness is a habit. When I get back from my walk I start on the letters. Begging letters irritate me. I remember that they are all my brothers and sisters, but always too late. Praise is irksome. I am only glad when there are expressions of unity. I read the newspaper *Rus*. I'm horrified at the executions, and to my shame, my eyes look out for T. and L.N., but when I find them it's rather unpleasant. I drink coffee. Always too much – I can't restrain myself – and settle down to my letters.

21 March I'll continue this description some time, but now it's 21 March, Yasnaya Polyana. All this time – not all the time but for about five days – I've been unwell, but have continued to feel very well at heart. The most recent day, yesterday, I was very weak. Today I slept until 9 o'clock, and in spite of ill health got on very well with my article. Everything that was unclear became clear, and I thought it over on my walk, and it all seems clear and I'll finish writing it. I've recently been working on a new edition of the *Cycle of Reading* (Gusev is helping so well and lovingly) and also on dear Marya Alexandrovna's favourite Gospels for children as we call it. And both the one work and the other were very pleasant, especially the work on the Gospels. I've begun working with the children in the mornings, but often miss lessons. During this time there has been unwelcome concern about the jubilee; not mine – mine has only been about how to stop it. I've just received an abusive letter apropros of it. I want to carry out the wish of the writer – send a letter to a newspaper and use the opportunity to express my views clearly and definitely.[13] That's all. Sasha is copying things out of my notebook. I'll copy some things out too.

(1) With knowledge it's not the amount of knowledge that is important or even its accuracy (because there never is and never will be completely accurate knowledge), but the sensible coordination of it: so that it should illuminate the world from all sides. It's the same thing with buildings. A building can be magnificent or mean, a winter palace or a cabin, but both buildings only make sense when they protect you on all sides from bad weather and enable you to live in them both in winter and summer; but the most magnificent three walls without a fourth, or four walls without a roof or without windows and a stove are much worse than a mean hut in which you can take shelter and not suffocate or be frozen. And it's the same with scientific knowledge, the present-day knowledge of scholars compared with the knowledge of an illiterate peasant farmer. This truth should be the basis of upbringing and education. Knowledge ought to be increased uniformly.

23 March If it were known that death makes our situation worse, life would be terrible in view of inevitable death. But if there was no beginning, there will be no end either. [. . .]

The law of life is beautifully illustrated by fingers in a glove: separate them in the belief that you will make each finger warmer and they will all be cold, and the better they are separated the colder they will be; do away with the divisions, join all the fingers together, and they will all be all right. [. . .]

27 March[14] [. . .]
(2) How good that I understood today – *vaut mieux tard que jamais* [better late than never] that people – Seroyozha and Sonya, and their name is legion – disagree with me not because they can refute, or think they can refute my arguments (as I used to

think), but because none of the arguments interests them, and they don't know and can't know anything concerning problems of religion. [. . .]

4 April   A woman does a great thing: she gives birth to children, but she doesn't give birth to thoughts; a man does this. A woman always follows only what has been introduced by a man and what has already been disseminated, and she disseminates it further. Likewise a man only educates children, but doesn't give birth to them.

12 April, Yasnaya Polyana   Health – my stomach is very weak. I can't sleep, and I'm in a bad mood, which I fight against more or less successfully. I want to make some notes now.
(1) If men knew all women as well as husbands know their wives they would never argue with them and would never value their opinion. [. . .]

19 April, Yasnaya Polyana   Health better. The article is progressing, but it's weak. There's a lot to note down. Just now I'll note the following, which is very good:
(1) A sure sign of the fact that all my activity is futile is that not only am I not persecuted, but that people praise me. That's good for humility.
 I feel the great burden of foolish outward charity combined with the absurd luxury of my own life.
 Semyonov has been.[15] He's not yet ready for himself. There's much good to be had from associating with people. I don't want to name names [. . .]

28 April, Yasnaya Polyana   They are trying hard to cure me. Shchurovsky[16] has been. Very painstaking, but like all of them he wants to know and to believe he knows, but he doesn't know anything. For several days, indeed almost all the time I've felt bad . . . Yesterday, I think, I finished the article.
 This morning as I lay in bed, I experienced a feeling of doubt about everything which I haven't experienced for a long time. Ultimately there is one thing left, though: goodness, love – the good which no one can take away. Yesterday I received a point by point letter of reproach from a young Marxist, and to my shame it depressed me.[17] I'm still a long way from living only for the soul (God), and worldly fame still disturbs me. Yes, as Pascal said yesterday,[18] there is only one true good, the one which no one can give or take away. If only one could acquire it and live for it.

6 May, Yasnaya Polyana   I'm still busy with the article. I've devoted about four days to my recollections about the soldier[19] for Posha. They're not too bad, but they're provocative. No letters today, but a conversation about the rights to my works after my death. I found it difficult to put up with. There is much in my notebooks for me to copy out, but at present I want to note:
(1) The fact that just now, while out walking, I clearly and fully understood for the first time the beneficial nature of condemnations, reproaches, and public disgrace. I understood how this drives one in on oneself – if, of course, there is somewhere in oneself one can go to. It really is a good and desirable thing.

(2) To die means to go back to where you came from. What is there there? It must be something good, judging by the wonderful creatures, the children, who come from there.

9 May   Consciousness and knowledge. Consciousness is the study of one's own inner being, knowledge is the study of everything external. The one is always at the expense of the other. The more of one, the less of the other.

12 May, Yasnaya Polyana   Something new and unusual happened to me today, I don't know whether it was good or bad; it must be good because everything that was, is and will be, is only good: what happened was that I woke up with a slight headache, and, for some strange reason, having forgotten everything: what time it was, what I was writing, where I had to go to. But a surprising thing! At the same time I felt particularly receptive to good: I saw a boy sleeping on the ground – and felt sorry for him; women were working – I felt particularly ashamed. Vagrants – I wasn't angry, but sorry. So it was all for the better, not for the worse at all.

Read passages from my work *The Law of Violence and the Law of Love* and was pleased, and I finished it. Yesterday I was particularly painfully depressed at the news of the twenty peasants who had been hanged.[20] I began to dictate into the phonograph, but couldn't go on. [. . .]

A nightingale sang beneath my window and moved me to tears of joy. I've only just remembered that on my walk before tea today I forgot to pray. I've forgotten everything. It's amazing! I'm just reading my letter to Anatoly Fyodorovich[21] and can't remember who he is.

14 May, Yasnaya Polyana   [. . .] Yesterday, the 13th, I wrote an appeal, a denunciation – I don't know what it was – about the executions,[22] and another about Molochnikov.[23] I think it's what's needed. Muravyov has been and told me many painful things.[24] Yesterday my sons Andrey and Mikhail were here, pitiable and very remote. Sasha has come. I went for a walk and had some good thoughts. [. . .]

15 May   For *Thou Shalt Not Kill.*[25] And all this is done for our sake, for the sake of peaceful citizens. Whether we want it or not, we are made a party to these horrors.

And all this is done among people and by people who say that they worship and accept as God the one who said: 'It is said unto you . . . All are brethren . . . Love all, forgive all, not seven times, but seventy times seven'; the one who said about punishment, 'Let him who is without sin cast the first stone'. This is a dreadful thing, and this most terrible, forbidden deed is done by the most respected people and with the complicity of the teachers of this faith. It is done in a country where the people consider it a duty to help the unfortunate.

I can see Europeans reading this with a smile of contempt. It's very different with us, the English and other peoples will say. It's all so organised with us that it's simply a pleasure. It's all done by a machine. You don't see anything, only the flag.

20 May, Yasnaya Polyana   My state of joyful animation has passed, but I can't say that things are bad with me. What is good is that not only do I feel no resistance to death, but I even want it. Stakhovich is here. Sonya is in Moscow and Petersburg, I'm very glad to be with Sasha. I've been revising my article on the executions. I think it's not bad, and I think it's necessary.

Two disciples of Dobrolyubov from Samara have been – not an altogether good impression. They lack the quality of simplicity which is valuable to me. Their good life is artificial, and I feel it smells of glue and varnish. Consciousness is necessary and essential, but I think that it's only necessary in order to test oneself, not to falsify oneself. I can't say it clearly, but I know what I mean.

Thought today (1) that my life is good because I carry the whole burden of a rich life which I hate: the sight of people working for me, requests for help, condemnation, envy, hatred – and I don't enjoy its advantages, even that of liking what is done for me, helping those who ask, etc. [. . .]

21 May, Yasnaya Polyana Haven't felt as unwell as I did yesterday for a long time. Weakness and gloominess. But, thank God, nothing bad. 120 children from a railway school came. They were very nice. Got on a bit with *Capital Punishment*, and read *Figner* with revulsion.[26]

This morning an old beggar of eighty-two was here. He called back after eighteen years, a gentle, peaceful man, and then two students came. One was a literary person, the other a revolutionary. The revolutionary bluntly asked the question: if I could have been the executioner at the hanging of twenty people and by hanging one could have saved nineteen, ought I to have hung that one? Obviously this question was important to him, and my opinion about it disturbed him. Then he brought up other similar examples. When I said to him that one must do what one thinks right and not do evil, he said: 'And won't the result be that this person who does no evil will, despite the sufferings round about him, walk with his head high in the air saying: "Look what a good person I am."' I said to him that every one of us has too many sins of all kinds to feel ourselves free of sin for not committing the sin of compromise. Yes, this service to the people, this doing good to others, is a dreadful evil; I must write about this particularly. All the evil of government, all the evil of the revolutionaries, all the evil of education, all economic evil stems from it.

29 May, Yasnaya Polyana What I wrote about my ill-health on 21 May still holds good. I've never felt myself so weak. But every cloud has a silver lining: at such times, when I feel my nearness to death, I rejoice at this nearness. There have been so many visitors and letters that it's impossible to find time to note everything down. I'm beginning to feel the spread of my fame which, as always, arouses both good feelings and correspondingly bad ones too.

Yesterday the very tedious K. was here.[27] On the other hand, it's about three days since the very agreeable Stamo and her son arrived.[28] I'm very glad about the arrival of Chertkov, he's in Petersburg. Sasha has been to Tanya's and came back today. I fear for her. The Stakhoviches have also been. Sonya has been to Petersburg and come back. During this time I finished my article *On the Executions* and wrote a letter to a peasant about the land, and while writing it became convinced that as long as state oppression exists there are no means of improving anyone's position. Had a good talk about this yesterday with Nikolayev and Stamo. I've forgotten to note the arrival during this time of the nice Nikolayevs and the visit of my daughter-in-law Sonya and Unkovskaya.[29] More photographers – Prokudin-Gorsky and Kulakov – and an American and his wife,[30] and another nice couple... There's a lot to note down. Before copying up my notebook I'll note down what I've just been thinking:

(1) We want to make people's lives happy and just, but as long as we have known people's lives, and have known that they have always aspired towards this goal, we have known that they have never attained it. Beyond the stage of good attained, another subsequent stage is always immediately revealed, one just as urgently necessary as the one only just attained had seemed to be; and so it has continued up to the present time, from cannibalism to the nationalisation of land. And so it is natural not merely to suppose, but to be certain that it will always be so.

And so it will, and so it should be. The situation of a man advancing towards the good which keeps moving away from him can be compared with what people do with stubborn horses, so I'm told. They fasten on the shafts in front of them a piece of bread with salt on so that the horse can smell it but can't reach it. And it stretches forward and moves in its desire to reach the bread, but its very movement moves the bread further away and so *ad infinitum*. And it's the same with people: the good can never be reached, because in attaining one good a new one immediately presents itself. And good is infinite perfection, like God.

What is the conclusion from this?

Only that a man can and must know that the good in his life is not in attaining the goal in front of him, but in progress towards the highest goal which he can never reach. [...]

3 June, Yasnaya Polyana Received a letter the day before yesterday reproaching me for my wealth and hypocrisy and oppression of the peasants, and to my shame I was hurt. I've been sad and ashamed all day today. I've just been out riding, and it seemed such a desirable and joyous thing to go away and be a beggar, thanking and loving everyone. Yes, I'm weak. I can't live by my spiritual 'I' all the time. And when I can't live that way, everything irritates me. The one good thing is that I'm dissatisfied with myself and ashamed, only I mustn't pride myself on it.

Finished *I Can't be Silent* and sent it to Chertkov. Almost finished the other one, the big one, too.[31] Had a seizure. It's good that nearness to death doesn't make me sad, but rather is something to be desired, if not enjoyed. I can think well and vigorously. I'd like to write a new *Cycle of Reading* and also something artistic – about the revolution.[32]

10 June I've been weak for several days, but slept well today and wrote about Molochnikov and the sentence.[33] I think it's not bad. Began a letter to an Indian, but got stuck.[34] Chertkov revised it splendidly. I think it's finished. Gave the big article to be copied. The two Seryozhas and Countess Zubova are here.[35] Some good letters and some good people: Kartushin. Note:

(1) I walked round the garden this morning and, as always, thought about my mother, my 'mamma', whom I don't remember at all, but who remains for me a sacred ideal. I never heard anything bad about her. And as I walked along the avenue of birches and approached the avenue of walnut trees I saw the imprint in the mud of a woman's foot, and thought about her, about her body. And to imagine her body was beyond my powers. Anything physical would defile her. How good my feelings were towards her! How I would have liked to have the same feelings towards everyone: women and men. And it's possible. It would be good when having dealings with people to think like that about them, to feel that way towards them. It's possible. *I'll try.*

13 June I've hardly written anything for two days. There's a mass of people here. I can't speak about my mother without tears. Molostvov has been copying extracts out of her diaries.[36] [. . .]

17 June, Yasnaya Polyana During this time I've written an article about Molochnikov's sentence and have been busy again with the big article. I worked on it yesterday, and today I've written very well – so it seems to me – about non-resistance, and have done a general revision.

I'm reading about Herzen. The author is a narrow socialist.[37]

There was a clash at table. I'm very sorry. I can't summon up good feelings, and that's depressing. Went to Marya Alexandrovna's[38] yesterday, and corrected proofs with dear Nikolayev. I've just found Sonya in a rage over the wood that was cut down. Why, why does she torment herself? I'm sorry for her, but it's impossible to help her.

I'm more and more deeply ashamed of my position and of all the folly of the world. Is it only an illusion of my thoughts and feelings that it can't continue? No, it can't.

19 June Couldn't sleep half the night because of a headache. The pain is quickly getting worse. Will it lead to the end? Well, that's all right. I try when I'm weak, as today, to think just as well, calmly and even joyfully about death as I do when I'm strong and cheerful. Yesterday Bulygin told me a strange and moving story to do with his son.[39] I've finished Herzen. I've just suddenly had such a stabbing pain in my head that it made me wince. What I've written about violence is bad.

21, 22 June, Yasnaya Polyana Chertkov is here.[40] I'm very glad. My health is waning away. Thank God, there's not the slightest resistance. Only I'd like to finish what I've planned to do, sinner that I am. And then I remember how trivial and worthless it all is compared with the change that is in the offing. I've just caught myself, not so much thinking as being conscious of the fact that this diary is read, and that while writing it I have readers in mind. I'll forget it, I'll set myself free. [. . .]

24 June, Yasnaya Polyana A very severe headache tormented me during the night and I found it hard, very hard to endure – I groaned and woke up Yuliya Ivanovna and Dušan. The main thing is, I haven't been able to find happiness in a life of suffering. I said to myself: it's a chance to learn to endure, and it brings me nearer to liberation, and there is happiness in everything. Still I couldn't overcome the burden of suffering.

I didn't think that suffering is the friction which moves me on towards the blessed goal of liberation. And that's the main thing. It hurts now, though not as it did during the night. I'll try not to weaken. It's possible. I've begun to write something for Orlov's album;[41] perhaps it will be good.

26 June   I didn't write my diary yesterday. I passed a very good night and *regretted* that I wasn't in pain, that there was no chance to correct yesterday's weakness. I haven't written anything. I tried Orlov, but without success. An American was here, a correspondent.[42] Had a good talk with him. A conversation with Kuzminsky – impenetrable darkness. But I said my say.

Had a bad night. Was in pain. Behaved well and didn't grumble. But the pain was only slight. [. . .]

I've just thought:

It's bad that a stone is hard if you want to break it up, but if you need a stone to sharpen something on, the harder and stronger the better. It's the same with what we call sorrows. [. . .]

Wrote quite well about Orlov. Felt today for the first time the possibility, as Vivekananda says, of everything becoming 'you' instead of 'me' – felt the possibility of self-renunciation not in the name of anything in particular, but in the name of common sense. It's difficult to give up the habit of tobacco, difficult for a drinker to give up alcohol, but it's more difficult and at the same time more necessary to lose the habit of that terrible intoxication with oneself, with one's 'I'. But I'm beginning – now, just before death – to feel the possibility of such renunciation. It's no great merit.

30 June, Yasnaya Polyana   The day before yesterday a blind man came and abused me. Yesterday I went to see him at Nikolayev's and told him I loved him (1) because he was seeking God's truth, (2) because he – as a man who hated and gave offence – ought to be loved and (3) because he might perhaps need me, and as I said goodbye I shook his hand. Before he left he wanted to see me. I was glad. He said: 'I didn't mean to shake your hand, I can't shake hands with a scoundrel, a villain, a pharisee, a hypocrite . . .' Sofya Andreyevna told him to go, but I managed to say, and say sincerely, that I loved him. Oh, if it were only so with everyone! [. . .]

2 July, Yasnaya Polyana   A depressing conversation yesterday. I'm still bad. The one good thing is that I know and feel it. I still can't understand and feel the salutary nature of physical sufferings, but I know that it exists. On the other hand I know and even feel the salutary nature of insults, reproaches and slanders. Revised Morozov today,[43] and a bit of the article. I'm handing it over entirely to Chertkov.

How glad I am that I haven't the slightest desire for success or praise. Health good. But in a gloomy mood. I must pull myself together.

4 July, Yasnaya Polyana I seem to have finished the article yesterday. It's high time. My mental state is better, although my physical one is worse. Read Vivekananda's excellent article about God.⁴⁴ I must translate it. I've been thinking of the same thing myself. [. . .]

9 July, Yasnaya Polyana I've experienced some very painful feelings. Thank God I've experienced them. There's been a countless number of people here, and it would all have been enjoyable had it not all been poisoned by my awareness of the folly, the sin, and the vileness of our luxurious life with servants, and the poverty and excessive strain of hard work all around us. I suffer painfully and incessantly from this, and I'm on my own. I can't help wishing for death, although I want to make use of what is left as well as I can. Enough of that for now.

I think it's 11 July, Yasnaya Polyana. More and more letters of sympathy about the article *I Cannot be Silent*.⁴⁵ It's very pleasant. I feel very well today. Tanya came. She's not as close to me as I thought. Still a mass of people here. Today Buturlin, Berkenheim and Mikhail Sergeyevich.⁴⁶ [. . .]

20 July, Yasnaya Polyana Noted on 11 July: 'Letters of sympathy about the article.' Now there are letters of abuse, and quite a lot. And I'm sad. [. . .]

Today is 5 August, Yasnaya Polyana I'm still in bed. My leg is better. I feel good, even very good at heart. Worked on a new *Cycle of Reading* and reached the 26th. There's still plenty of work. I was moved by Chertkov's and other friends' work on the collection. Sometimes I think it's worth it, sometimes I doubt it. But I'm pleased – pleased by this integration of my spiritual 'I'. Abusive letters about *I Cannot be Silent* are increasing in number. I'm reading Dickens' *Our Mutual Friend*;⁴⁷ it's very poor. Vivekananda doesn't satisfy me much either. 'Terribly clever.' Two concerts by Sibor and Goldenweiser.⁴⁸

I've thought a lot recently while people were playing and have tried to define every piece of music by a certain feeling or mood, and to transfer it to the realm of literary art, and it turned out that there always was one: sometimes tenderness, sometimes joyfulness, sometimes passion, sometimes alarm, sometimes tender love, sometimes spiritual love, sometimes solemnity, sometimes sorrow, and many other moods, but one thing there never was – there was never anything bad: malice, censure, ridicule, etc. Could one write works of fiction like that?

11 August, Yasnaya Polyana I'm depressed and in pain. I've had a constant fever these last few days, I feel ill and find it hard to put up with. I must be dying. Yes, it's difficult to live in the absurd conditions of luxury in which I have had to live my life, and still more difficult to die in these conditions of fuss and bother, medicine, and apparent relief and cure, while there can be neither the one nor the other, and they are unnecessary, and there can only be a worsening of one's state of mind. My attitude to death is not fear at all, but intense curiosity. More about that later, however, if I have time.

I would like to say a few things, trivial though they are, about what I would like done after my death. First, I would be glad if my heirs would make all my writings public property; if not, then certainly all my writings for the people, for example the *Primers*, and the *Readers*. Secondly, although this is the most trivial thing of all, I do not wish any rites to be performed during the burial of my body. A wooden coffin; and anyone who wishes can carry it or convey it to the Zakaz wood opposite the gully, to the place where the green stick is.[49] At least there is a reason for choosing this place rather than another.

That's all. From force of habit, which, nevertheless, I haven't got rid of, I think I could still do one or two more things – strangely enough I'm thinking first of all of a work of fiction. Of course it's nonsense, I simply wouldn't have the strength to do it well. [. . .]

17 August, Yasnaya Polyana   (For a work of fiction.)
(1) The child of a wealthy, atheistic, liberal-scientific bourgeois family devotes himself to religion. Fifteen years later he is a revolutionary and an anarchist.
(2) The gentle, sincere son of a priest does well at school and theological college, and is married and ordained. The daughter of a neighbour in his parish gives his mother, a vain intellectual woman, a book to read. He reads Tolstoy and questions begin to arise.
(3) A young boy, the sixth son of a blind beggar, arouses the sympathy of the wife of a leading liberal atheist. He is taken from home and sent to school, shows brilliant ability and gets a science degree. He goes abroad, meets some of his comrades, is shocked, thinks everything out again, renounces science and sees the one truth and salvation in belief in God.
(4) One of his comrades had started up in business and made a million, and now lives on the labours of his workers, while playing the liberal.
(5) The son of an aristocratic family introduces clients to a procuress; then philanthropy; then the renunciation of everything.
(6) One son of a ruined half-aristocrat, a vain man, makes a career through marriage; another son, a reserved man, makes a career as a hangman. The second used to pander to the first, now he gives himself airs.
(7) A similiar sort of aristocratic writer, the son of a bourgeois, lives by journalism, feels the vileness of it and can't go on.[50]

21 August   Haven't written my diary since the 12th. Health just the same, my leg is better, my general state worse, i.e. I'm nearer to death. Last night I experienced for no apparent reason a particularly strong – not merely pleasant but, to put it mildly, joyful and serious feeling – of the complete disappearance not of the fear of death simply, but of being at odds with death. I'm very glad of this because this feeling, I know, is not fortuitous or transitory, but it can go on existing in the depths of the soul without being experienced all the time, and that is very good.

This feeling is like what a man might experience if he discovered unexpectedly that when he thought he was somewhere a long way away from home he was right beside it, and what he had thought of as something strange and alien was really his own home.

I'm still working with Nikolay Nikolayevich[51] on the *Cycle of Reading*. I can't say I'm very satisfied, but I'm not dissatisfied either. I feel the nearness of the 28th by the increased number of letters.[52] I'll be glad when it's over, although I'm also glad that I'm completely indifferent to this or that attitude people have towards me, although I'm also less and less indifferent to my attitude towards them.

I've written a letter to M. and am unrepentant.[53]

26 August, Yasnaya Polyana   I am better, but still in bed. I've been working on the *Cycle*, and the further I get the more and more faults I see and correct. I've reached the 8th. People are making a fuss about the jubilee, and I'm glad that I feel quite calm. An unkind letter and an undeservedly unkind letter disturbs me far more than all that is being done for the sake of the jubilee. I feel well at heart and think I'm making progress. I'm enjoying work on the *Cycle*. It helps to clear up a lot of things. And what joy my friends are – and what friends! I'm tired, I don't want to write anything more.

14 September   I'm recovering bit by bit. The jubilee brought much pleasure for the baser soul, but made it hard for the higher soul. But I can't complain much about myself. I'm continuing to pull through bit by bit. I took my notebook out today actually in order to note that this morning and last night I *felt* for the first time, actually *felt* that the centre of gravity of my life had already shifted from the carnal to the spiritual life: felt my complete indifference to everything physical and an unflagging interest in my own spiritual growth, i.e. my spiritual life. [. . .]

28 September, Yasnaya Polyana   My leg is better, but the general state of my body – my stomach – is bad. I feel well at heart. Work is progressing. Only now is it real work, only now at eighty, is life beginning. And this is not a joke if one understands that life is not measured by time. I'm still working on the *Cycle*. It's not altogether good. But perhaps it's useful. Something literary and important keeps wanting to intrude. Many letters, and good ones. How good that one won't see the consequences! This is life: preparing for good consequences – at least wishing they might be good – which one won't see. [. . .]

26 October, Yasnaya Polyana   Haven't written my diary for almost a month. I'm still busy with the *Cycle of Reading*. I want to call it *The Teaching of Life*. I still feel very well at heart, nearer and nearer to death which I welcome, like everything to come in the future, as a blessing. I've begun something literary.[54] But it's hardly likely I'll finish writing it, or even go on with it. I've also begun a letter to a Serbian woman.[55] I keep wanting to express more clearly and concisely the mistaken way of life of the Christian peoples. Received a book yesterday from a Chinaman.[56] It makes me think. I'm thinking a lot. I want to note down some trifles.

(1) I receive letters from young people which try to smash my whole conception of life to smithereens. Previously I used to get angry with their frivolous self-assurance and narrow-mindedness, then I wanted to demonstrate to them all their stupidity, but now the letters hardly interest me at all – i.e. they interest me as long as I'm looking to see if they contain any justified reproach, but then I lay them aside. After all, I've only to think how in my own family no arguments, no intimacy, not even love can make people stop asserting that $2 + 2 = 5$; so why should I want to make remote strangers change their minds? Like the socialist yesterday or the embittered Christian-peasant.[57] Yes, it was a great thing Francis of Assisi said: when perfect joy should reign.[58] Yes, many of my followers only take from Christianity the side of it which rejects evil. True Christianity is not angry at people's un-Christian acts, but only tries not to act in an un-Christian way itself – not to be angry.
(2) What astonishing madness: to kill people for their own good!
(3) How splendid that I've forgotten all the past and freed myself from thoughts of the future. Yes, I'm beginning in this life to depart from it, from its main condition: time. [. . .]

28 October, Yasnaya Polyana [. . .]
(2) What an incomparable and wonderful joy it is – and I'm experiencing it – to *love* everyone and everything, to feel this love in oneself or, more accurately, to feel oneself through this love. [. . .]

Yes, a great joy. And whoever has experienced it will not compare it with any other, will not desire any other, and will spare nothing and do all he can to obtain it. And in order to obtain it, only one small thing – but a difficult thing in our corrupt world – is necessary; one thing: to wean oneself away from the habit of hatred, contempt, disrespect and indifference towards anyone. And this is possible. I've done so little in this respect, but I already seem to have received in advance an undeserved reward. [. . .]

31 October, Yasnaya Polyana Yesterday I looked through and revised the Serbian letter. I think it will turn out tolerably well. I've revised some more today. A letter from an Indian.[59] I must make much the same reply. Worked a little bit on the *Cycle of Reading*. [. . .]
I've missed a day. Today is 2 November, Yasnaya Polyana. Worked yesterday on the Serbian article. I'm reaching the end. Not bad and not good – middling.

Felt depressed at heart yesterday, or rather depressed *physically*, because I didn't give in to it. Now it's morning and I want to make the following notes:
(1) I walk about, sit on a bench and look at the bushes and trees, and I think that two big, apparently bright orange shawls are hanging on a tree; but it's really two leaves on a nearby bush. I attribute them to the trees in the distance, and they become two big shawls, and they are *bright* orange because I attribute that colour to the distant object. And I think: the whole world as we know it is only the product of our external senses: sight and touch . . . and our ideas. And how can we believe in the reality, the one and only reality of the world as we imagine it to ourselves? What

is it like for fleas? What is it like for Sirius, for a creature unknown to me and endowed with senses unknown to me? And space and time – it's all constructed by me. What I call infinitely small creatures are no smaller than me. And what I call a moment is no less than what I call eternity. One thing, only one thing, exists, namely that which has consciousness, and not that which it is conscious of, and how.
(2) On the feeling of moderation in art: lack of moderation exposes to view the producer of art, and for that reason destroys the illusion that I am not perceiving it, but creating it.

10 November, Yasnaya Polyana My health isn't bad. Except for heart-burn. I've felt dejected since this morning. I'm ashamed. Still ashamed. I like it. [. . .]

15 November, Yasnaya Polyana Played cards yesterday until 12 o'clock. I'm ashamed, and disgusted, and I thought: people will say: 'A fine teacher he is, he plays *vint* for three hours on end.' Then I thought in earnest: that's just what is needed. Therein lies real humility, which is necessary for the good life. But it will be said a general should behave like a general, an envoy like an envoy and a teacher like a teacher. That's not true. A man should behave as a man. And what is natural to man first and foremost is humility, the wish to be humble. This doesn't mean that it's necessary to play cards if you can do something else that people need, but it does mean that it's unnecessary to be afraid of people's opinions and, on the contrary, to be well able to put up with them *sans sourciller* [without turning a hair]. [. . .]
(4) Yesterday I got into a rage with my horse. How loathsome!

28 November, Yasnaya Polyana I never thought I hadn't written my diary for so long. It's only three days since I woke up a bit, and before that I was asleep and had no proper mental life. I'm still writing the letter to the Indian. It's all repetition. Physical health poor, but I feel good at heart and when I'm asleep, and when I'm awake I always feel tenderness and joy.

Yesterday Misha and his wife and the young Vyazemsky came.[60] I invited them in and read the *Cycle of Reading* to them and talked to them. And I'm glad I did. This couple, Misha and his wife, are becoming more and more dear to me. I've just added something to the Indian letter. I don't know what I'll write when I've finished it. Probably nothing literary. I had the inclination, but it's passed.

29 November, Yasnaya Polyana Physically I'm – I was going to say not good, but that's not true – I feel weak, but that's *good*. Got on yesterday with the *Letter to an Indian* and read Sunderland all evening in order to answer the letter.[61] Dreamed during the night that I was partly writing and composing, and partly experiencing the drama of Christ. Myself – and Christ and a soldier. I remember him putting on his sword. Very vividly. Sonya has gone to Moscow. [. . .] From my notebook: [. . .]
(8) The most necessary science is the science of religion. A comparison of all religions would show what religious truths are common to all, and what are fortuitous excrescences. [. . .]

3 December, Yasnaya Polyana State of mind very good. Slept a lot. Began by seeing in myself all my vileness, the prevalence of my desire for worldly fame over the real demands of life. I saw this too (it's something I've long sensed) in the feeling of depression I got from the letter of a woman who reproached me for my letter, and from the degree of interest with which I looked for the word 'Tolstoy' when I read the newspapers. How far I still am from being even moderately decent, how bad I am. I write this now and wonder: am I not writing it for the sake of those who will read this diary? I suppose so, partly. Yes, I must work on myself – do now at eighty what I used to do with particular energy when I was fourteen or fifteen; strive to improve myself; only with this difference that then my ideals of perfection were different: muscles, and generally speaking what was needed for worldly success. Oh, if only I could train myself to put all my energy into serving God, to drawing near to Him. But drawing near to Him is impossible without serving other people. [. . .] Note. [. . .]

(2) I've lost my memory. And surprisingly enough – I haven't once regretted it. I can regret the fact that I'm losing my hair, and do regret it, but not my memory; the loss is so obviously the consequences of something acquired which is not compatible with memory. Just as the residue is thrown away when the butter has been taken, so it is with memory. It is only material from which an understanding of the meaning of life can be formed. [. . .]

4 December, Yasnaya Polyana I was very busy yesterday: wrote my diary, wrote about Ertel[62] and revised the foreword to the new *Cycle of Reading*. A painful conversation with Sonya. During the conversation I was sorry for her, and afterwards I felt moved. Noted down something very important:

(1) When thinking about your impending actions, and if possible when performing these actions, ask yourself whether you are doing what you are doing for yourself or for God, for your own conscience or for other people, for their approval. Ask yourself: would you do what you are doing if you not only knew that no one would know about it, but also that the deed which your conscience judged to be good would be a pretext for other people to condemn you.

One must train oneself to do this. It's the only important thing in life, both for a boy of fourteen, and for me, an old man of eighty.

Sometimes I can't help seeing the philanthropic nature of my good actions, and can't help being moved and being glad. But remember that the important consequences won't be seen by you, but still exist. [. . .]

Today is 6 December, Yasnaya Polyana [. . .] I'm still plodding away at the *Letter to an Indian*. I think it's rubbish and all repetition. I must finish it and tear myself away. I'd like to do something literary, but I'm not making a start because there isn't anything which I'm itching to write, which I can't stop myself from writing, in the way that one should get married only when one can't stop oneself from marrying.

I want to prepare something real and close to my heart for the phonograph.[63] [. . .]

(2) How particularly fortunate I am. If many people hate me *without even knowing me*, how many people love me more than I deserve. People who ought to hate me because of their quasi-religious views which I demolish, love me for those trifling things like *War and Peace*, etc., which seem to them very important.

The Serbian letter has come out in the *Voice of Moscow*, and I'm very pleased.

Today is 14 December, Yasnaya Polyana Haven't written my diary for six whole days. Finished the *Letter to an Indian*; it's weak and repetitive. Wrote a few letters. Sonya is in Moscow. I've been weak physically the last four or five days. I haven't been too bad mentally, but today the hanging and torture of people roused me to indignation and a bad, evil feeling towards the hangmen. I'm thinking about something literary, and it seems to be germinating. [. . .]

18 December, Yasnaya Polyana Haven't written my diary for three days. Sonya is back. Repin and Nordman have come.[64] I still feel just as weak. I'm turning over in my head something literary. I think I could do it. Wrote a very embittered foreword and a worthless beginning.[65] I'm mentally weak. Yesterday evening I received an unfriendly letter saying I was making a fortune out of my works, and was so weak that I took it to heart and answered it (I threw the letter away).

Today I've been turning over my diary entries, but can't write anything. I've just seen Repin off. Sonya is unwell. I'll write out what's in my notebook. [. . .]
(3) It's a big mistake to think that all inventions which increase people's power over nature in agriculture, and in the extraction and chemical combination of substances, and which increase the possibility of people's greater influence over one another, such as ways and means of communication, the press, the telegraph, telephone, phonograph, etc., are good. Both power over nature and an increase in the possibility of people's influence over one another are only good when people's activity is guided by love and the desire for other people's good, but are an evil when guided by egoism and the desire for good for oneself alone. Metals dug out of the ground can be used for the comforts of life or for cannons; the consequence of increasing the fertility of the land can be to provide people with guaranteed food and it can also be the cause of the increased spread and consumption of opium and vodka; communications and the means of communicating ideas can spread abroad good and evil influences. And so in an immoral society like our ostensibly Christian one, all inventions which increase man's power over nature and all means of communications are not only not good, but are an undoubted and obvious evil. [. . .]

27 December, Yasnaya Polyana I've missed two days. There have been many visitors and good letters. I've been working all the time on an article about Stolypin's article,[66] and I think in vain. A work of fiction is clear in my head, but I've no desire to write it. [. . .].

When I was out walking yesterday a young man met me with tears in his eyes, but he spoke so incoherently and incomprehensibly about what he needed that I walked away from him with unkind feelings and even unkind words. And thank

God, I immediately began to suffer, and tried to find him. Fortunately he hadn't gone away and I had a splendid talk with him.

Some Petersburg students came with an address.[67] It's difficult. But I must remember the one thing that lasts for ever: love here and now.

28 December, Yasnaya Polyana   Gave my article to Chertkov; tried to write *The Lost Ones*,[68] but nothing came of it. Yet there is something I have to say. I feel well at heart. I'm still learning gradually not to think unkind thoughts. That's the whole thing. One can get used to it. May God 'who is within thee' help me.[69] The students have been. It was depressing. I forgot I had to behave in a God-fearing way. Still I'm making progress. The trouble is *l'esprit de l'escalier* [being wise after the event]. But I'm making progress, I'm making progress.

Today is 29 December, Yasnaya Polyana   I feel very well. For the first time I've been writing enthusiastically, although badly. I don't know what to call it. Perhaps: *No One Is To Blame*. I can imagine it, I see the possibilities and it gives me pleasure. [. . .]

30 December, Yasnaya Polyana   Nikolay Nikolayevich[70] has arrived. I received a touching letter from Petrova in prison. Replied to her.[71] Visits today from a peasant suppliant about the partition, then a student with an astonishing question about a woman student's demand that he should marry her. Then Andrey with money matters, then a madman, then a letter from a student demanding that life should be evil. Felt very good at heart yesterday, full of joy and love; I'm worse today but, thank God, still full of joy and gratitude. Began to write *No One Is To Blame*, but couldn't get on with it. They're getting ready for a masked ball.[72] I'm sorry. [. . .]

Secret diary for 1908[1]

2 July, Yasnaya Polyana I'm starting a diary for myself – a secret one.

My position would be agonising were it not for the awareness that all this is good for the soul if one assumes that the soul has a life.

If I had heard about myself from an outsider – heard about a man living in luxury, surrounded by guards, taking everything he can from the peasants, putting them in prison, and professing and preaching Christianity, and giving away five-copeck pieces, and hiding behind his dear wife for all his vile deeds – I would have no doubts about calling him a scoundrel! And yet this is just what I need to free myself from the desire for worldly fame and to live for the soul.

I've been revising Vasily Morozov's story.[2]

My soul is sorely depressed. I know it's good for my soul, but it is depressing.

At times I ask myself: what should I do – go away from everyone? Where to? To God, to die. In a sinful way I wish for death.

After writing this there was an incomprehensibly boorish and cruel scene over the fact that Chertkov had been taking photographs.[3] Doubts occur to me whether I'm doing right in remaining silent, and even whether it wouldn't be better for me to go away and hide like Boulanger.[4] I don't do so primarily because it would be for my own sake, in order to escape from this life which is poisoned on every side. And I believe that actually enduring this life is what is necessary for me.

Help, Lord, help, help!!!!

Death is the only place one can really go away to.

3 July I'm still struggling just as agonisingly, but struggling badly. Life here at Yasnaya Polyana is completely poisoned. Wherever I go – there's shame and suffering. Either it's the Grumant peasants in prison, or the guards, or the old man V. Suvorov saying: 'It's sinful, Count, oh, it's sinful, the Countess has insulted me.' Or it's this stupidity and disgracefully selfish and unjust road.[5] It's difficult. I don't know whether it's because I'm in a bad mood, or whether I'm in a bad mood because of all these horrible things. Oh, help, help me, God within me.

4 July I'm a bit better, but still depressed. Had a good talk with Sasha. How strange heredity is: men inherit their fathers' intelligence and their mothers' character and vice versa.

6 July Agonising and painful is the ordeal to be suffered, or the retribution to be paid for lust. The retribution is terribly painful. Chertkov has just told me of a conversation he had with her. 'He lives, and enjoys every luxury and says . . . "it's all pharisaism, etc." I'm the one who is sacrificing herself.'

Help me, Lord. Again I want to go away. And I can't make up my mind. But I haven't given up the idea either. The main thing is: shall I be doing it for my own sake if I go away? The fact that I'm not doing it for my own sake if I stay – that I do know. I must think with God. And I will do so.

7 July It was agonising yesterday. I counted up my money and thought about how to go away. I can't see her without unkind feelings. It's better today.

How clearly one can see in her all the horrors of love of body, love of self, carried to the extent of the loss of all spiritual sense of obligation. It's terrible both for others and for herself. I must have pity. I'll try and write it down as well as I can – I can't say it.

So much for her. But I'm forgetting myself. I'm bad, very bad. I couldn't help thinking about myself yesterday, my repulsive self.

Yes, I – my body – is like a repulsive latrine – take off or raise the lid of spirituality a little, and there's a loathsome stench.

Today I'll try to live for my soul.

But she's right about asparagus.[6] I must learn to live.

9 July I'm thinking of writing her a letter. I've no unkind feelings, thank God. Only one thing is more and more agonising to me: the injustice of this insane luxury amid the unwarranted poverty and need amid which I live. Everything is becoming worse and worse, more and more depressing. I can't forget it and I can't fail to see it.

They're all writing my biography – and it's the same with all biographies – there won't be anything about my attitude to the seventh commandment. There won't be any of that terrible filth of masturbation and worse, from thirteen or fourteen to fifteen or sixteen (I don't remember when my debauchery in brothels began). And it will be the same up to the time of my liaison with the peasant woman Aksinya – she's still alive. Then my marriage in which again, although I have never once been unfaithful to my wife, I experienced a loathsome, criminal desire for her. Nothing of this appears or will appear in the biographies. And this is very important – very important as the vice of which I at least am most conscious, and which more than any others is forcing me to come to my senses.

14 July It's still very depressing to bear with and endure Sonya's unhappy character. Egoism that excludes everything that is not herself and which goes to comic lengths, vanity, self-satisfaction, cockiness, condemnation of everybody, irritability. I had to write it down. I'm sorry for her. No one says anything to her, and she thinks she is the height of perfection.

18 July My unkind feelings have passed. I've been distracted by other thoughts. Two runaway sailors were here yesterday. I gave them some money and regretted it. I'm having some good thoughts. Sasha is back from the wedding[7] – a dear, good woman. I love her too exclusively, it's not good. My leg hurts. And I don't care at all.

1909

3 January, Yasnaya Polyana I've been unwell for two days, but my state of mind is calm and resolute. I think more and more often about the story,[1] but it's now morning, and I'm sitting at the table pen in hand and feeling that I shall think of something. And how necessary, how necessary it is to write, and, thank God, it's not for my own sake that I consider it necessary. During this time I've been revising the end of Stolypin.[2] I think it's quite good.

Yes, my health isn't good, but my state of mind seems to be more composed with the start of the new year. [. . .] (My diary, my attitude to the fact that people read it is doing me harm. Please don't read it.) [. . .]

6 January, Yasnaya Polyana Yesterday it seemed that I could write something literary.[3] But it wasn't so. I'd no enthusiasm. Today I can't at all. And there's no need to. [. . .]

The day before yesterday a real intellectual came, the literary man Gerschenson,[4] supposedly with questions about my metaphysical principles, but really with the secret (but obvious) idea of demonstrating to me the complete groundlessness of my belief in love. [. . .]

Yesterday I read Chertkov's correspondence with Ertel.[5] Once again the same self-assured, frivolous, intellectual chatter on Ertel's part, and a clear, firm understanding on Chertkov's.

The only thing that I derived from these two impressions is an awareness of the vanity of arguments. Oh, if one could answer only when asked a question, and otherwise keep silent all the time. If it were not a contradiction to write about the need for silence I should write now: 'I can be silent.' 'I must be silent.' If only I could live in the sight of·God – through love alone. But I've just written about Gerschenson without love – it's vile. Help, help . . . I can't name anyone.

8 January, Yasnaya Polyana Health tolerable. I've done no work for two days. Wrote a few letters yesterday and tried to go on with *Pavlusha*. It was no good. Today – it's 12 o'clock now – I've done nothing all morning. Wonderful weather. Went a walk in the morning and met a Bulgarian officer – I was nervous and excited. It was depressing. A letter from Lev Ryzhy;[6] I wrote a reply but won't send it. Chertkov insists on my special importance. I can't, I simply can't believe it, and I don't want to. Thank God. Two things to note: [. . .]
(2) I thought during the night how good it would be to define clearly those infamous occupations which not only a Christian, but simply any decent man – anyone who isn't a scoundrel or doesn't want to feel a scoundrel – cannot undertake. I know that a tradesman, a manufacturer, a landowner, a banker, a capitalist, a harmless functionary such as a teacher, a professor of painting, a

librarian, etc. lives off the proceeds of theft and robbery, but one must make a distinction between the thief or robber himself and those who live off the proceeds of theft. And it is these thieves and robbers who ought to be separated off from the rest, and the sinfulness, cruelty and shamefulness of their activity clearly demonstrated.

And the name of such people is legion. (1) Monarchs; ministers: (a) of internal affairs, with their police violence, executions, and suppressions; (b) of finance – taxes; (c) of justice – the courts; (d) of the armed forces; (e) of religious faiths (deceit of the people); and all civil servants, the whole army and the whole clergy. There are millions of them. If only one could explain to them what they are doing. [...]

10 January, Yasnaya Polyana Yesterday I almost wrote with enthusiasm, but badly. It's not worth making the effort. I've no enthusiasm at all today, and yesterday's writing seems weak, or simply bad. The day before yesterday I had a conversation with Andrey, a very edifying one for me. It began with the fact that the brothers, all of them, are short of money.
I: How is that?
He: Well everything has got more expensive, and we live in a particular milieu.
I: You should live better, more abstemiously.
He: May I object?
I: Go on.
He: You say that people should live as follows: not eat meat, refuse military service. But what is one to think about the millions who live like everybody else?
I: Don't think about them at all, think about yourself.

And it became clear to me that there is no other guiding principle for him in life except what *everybody else* does. It became clear that that is all that matters, that with minute exceptions everybody lives like that, and can't help living like that, because they have no other guiding principle. And therefore to reproach them and advise them differently is useless and harmful to oneself, since it causes ill feelings. For thousands of years mankind has progressed by the century, and you want to see this progress by the year. It progresses because people of advanced views change the environment little by little, pointing the way to an eternally remote state of perfection, pointing the way there (Christ, Buddha, yes, and Kant and Emerson and others), and little by little the environment changes. And these people do like everybody else again, only in a different way than before.

Intellectuals are people who do the same as 'everybody else' – as other intellectuals.

I've done nothing today and have no wish to. I'm writing this in the evening, at 6 o'clock. I woke up, and two things became especially and absolutely clear to me: (1) that I am a very worthless man. I say this absolutely sincerely, and (2) that it would be good for me to die, and that I would like to do so.

I'm very bad-tempered today. Perhaps I go on living in order to become just a little less vile. Very likely that is the reason. And I will try. Help me, Lord.

11 January, Yasnaya Polyana [...] A mass of executions and murders.⁷ No, they are not animals. To call them animals is to slander animals, they are much worse.

I feel the need to do something. An irresistible need, but I don't yet know what. This is the time when I say from the heart: help me, Lord! I don't want anything at all for myself. I'm prepared for sufferings and humiliations, if only I could know in my own mind that I'm doing what I should. What an easy, and what a terribly difficult word – what I *should*. I think there's nothing more I need to, or want to write. [...]

12 January, Yasnaya Polyana I feel very well today. But I did nothing before 12 o'clock except play patience. Yesterday's music excited me very much.⁸ I've been to the Chertkovs'. Very pleasant – not pleasant, but much more than that – was the equality of their relations with everybody. Of course even with them it isn't complete, but there isn't the agonising presence of 'servants', serving up sweet things to eat which they mustn't touch themselves. Life in these conditions gets more and more depressing. [...]

I've just been thinking a lot about work. Literary work such as: 'It was a fine evening, there was a smell of...'; is impossible for me. But work is necessary, because it's an obligation. A speaking-trumpet has been put into my hands, and I'm obliged to handle it, to make use of it. Something is asking to be done, I don't know whether it will be successful. What is asking to be done is for me to write without any form – not in the form of an article or a discourse or anything literary – but to express and pour out as best I can what I feel strongly. And I feel painfully strongly the horror and depravity of our situation. I want to write what I would like to do and how I imagine to myself what I would do. Help me, God. I can't help praying. I'm sorry that I don't pray enough. Yesterday I treated Sonya badly, today a petitioner. Yes, help, help me.

14 January, Yasnaya Polyana Began writing yesterday: I don't know what I'll call it.⁹ I've an ardent desire to write, but what I've written is weak. But it's possible. Landowska¹⁰ is coming, I don't know whether that's good. I want to collect some thoughts for children for Ivan Ivanovich.¹¹ [...]

15 January, Yasnaya Polyana Landowska came yesterday. A poor impression. I'm very tired. Had a good walk. Wrote nothing. I feel somehow ashamed, ashamed, constantly ashamed. Slept badly. A letter from the Regiment of God.¹² [...]

16 January, Yasnaya Polyana I'm somehow ashamed about my relations with Landowska, and the music. Generally my state of mind is one of dissatisfaction with myself, but not of depression; on the contrary. *Fais ce que dois*... and it's all right. An important letter from the Regiment of God. Today there was a visitor whom I treated badly, but I recovered myself. I can't write, but I'd like to and I'm thinking. Perhaps it will come. I want to say something very, very much, and the need is choking me. [...]

17 January, Yasnaya Polyana [. . .] Read a report about the Almanac,[13] and recognised all my worthlessness: how people's opinions interest me exclusively. Praise and thanks be to God – I came to my senses. Incidentally the present *Cycle of Reading* is precisely about that. [. . .]

The second thing planned by me[14] could be a work of terrifying power. That doesn't mean that I anticipate its influence, its visible influence, on people, but the terrifying power of the revelation of His law. [. . .]

18 January, Yasnaya Polyana I've missed a day. I was physically very weak all day yesterday, and wrote nothing either yesterday or today. Today I've only written a small addition to the article on Stolypin, an addition about the Tsar, with the secret aim of arousing persecution against me.[15] The aim is not altogether good, but the unloving attitude towards him is altogether bad. I'll have to improve it. I've corrected the article a little and made it better. Thank God – I think I've overcome my desire for worldly fame.

Last night I was very unwell, but experienced a very pleasant feeling of waiting for death without wanting it, but without the slightest resistance either, rather regarding it like any natural and reasonable act or event. I think that in any case it – death – must come soon, i.e. in weeks or at most months. Played patience all morning today, but didn't start any work since I felt too weak. But the themes are very good ones and I don't want to spoil them. A new theme occurred to me. It is the attitude to the newspaper, to what is written in the newspaper, of a free man, i.e. a truly religious man.[16] I must show the full extent of the perversion, slavery and weakness of people – their lack of human dignity. Some very good thoughts. I don't know how I'll manage to write them down. Perhaps tomorrow. It's now evening. I'm waiting for Chertkov, and won't start anything.

22 January, Yasnaya Polyana [. . .] Yesterday the bishop[17] came; I talked to him frankly, but too cautiously, and didn't express all the sinfulness of his cause. And I should have done so. Everything was spoiled for me by Sonya's story about his conversation with her.[18] He would obviously have liked to convert me, or if not convert me, then destroy or diminish my influence – pernicious in their view – on belief in the Church. What was particularly unpleasant was that he asked to be informed when I was dying. I'm afraid they'll think up something to assure people that I 'repented' just before my death. And therefore I state, or I think, repeat, *that to return to the Church, to take communion before dying, is just as impossible for me as to utter obscene words or look at obscene pictures before dying, and that therefore anything that people might say about my repentance and taking communion on my deathbed is lies.* I say this because if there are people for whom, in accordance with their religious understanding, taking communion is a religious act, i.e. a manifestation of a striving towards God, then for me any such outward act as communion would be a renunciation of my soul, of the good, of the teaching of Christ, of God.

I repeat on this occasion also that I ask to be buried without any so-called divine service, and for my body to be interred in the ground so that it should not stink. [. . .]

24 January, Yasnaya Polyana   [. . .] I've just been reading *Fellowship*.[19] It contains many good things. The Behai[20] are very interesting. When I was out walking today I thought about two things: *The Wisdom of Children*,[21] and about education – about the fact that just as I was persuaded when young to direct all my energy to the bravado of hunting and war, so children can be persuaded to direct all their energy to the struggle against themselves, to the increase of love. [. . .]

I've just flung a book on to the shelf; it had slipped off and fallen on to the floor, and I was angry and swore at the book. My anger with a person who doesn't do what I want must be just as obvious and just as shameful.

4 February, Yasnaya Polyana   Yesterday I was very ill physically. Did nothing. Struggled against unkind feelings. Read Artsybashev.[22] He's talented, but has the usual ill-bred off-hand literary manner, particularly in descriptions of nature. Great and small talents from Pushkin to Gogol have worked this way: 'Ah, that's not right, how can I make it better?' People today say: 'Oh, it's not worth bothering, it'll do as it is.'

Artsybashev not only has talent, he has ideas too: unfortunately all these people, Artsybashev included, while knowing all the incorrect and frivolous thoughts that have been expressed about the problems of life, are astonishingly ignorant about everything that has been done by the great thinkers of the past. With an awareness of their own great boldness and wisdom, they often allow themselves – in their own fashion and very feebly – to express doubts about what is being professed by everybody in their circle, and they don't know that not only their doubts, but everything that follows from their doubts, have long since been thought about and clarified, so that there is no longer an America waiting to be discovered in these problems. But still, with Artsybashev there are thoughts at work – and original ones – which isn't so with Gorky or Andreyev. There is mere talent without content in Kuprin; in Artsybashev there is both talent and content. But still they are both incomparably higher than Andreyev and Gorky, especially Artsybashev. His story *Blood* is splendid. *Gololobov* is good too. *Kupriyan* suffers from careless descriptions of things the author doesn't know about. But enough of this.[23] [. . .]
(1) From having experienced how unpleasant it is to put up with it, I've realised – it's funny to say so, at the age of eighty – that you shouldn't talk to other people about what interests you, but try and detect what interests them and, if there is anything, talk about that. [. . .]
(3) I also wanted to note that I'm compelled to believe whether I like it or not that people have accorded me a somewhat inappropriate reputation as an important, a 'great' writer and man. And this position of mine has its obligations. I feel that I've been given a speaking-trumpet which might have been in the hands of others more worthy to make use of it, but *volens nolens* [willy-nilly] it is in my hands, and I'll be to blame if I don't make good use of it. But recently, I think, I've been making use of it for empty chatter and the repetition of old things. I'll try harder.
(4) I still hear complaints and receive letters – there are probably some in the press as well – reproaching me for not having given my land away to the peasants. I can't help admitting it would have been better not to have been afraid of the reproaches

of my family and to have given my land away to the peasants (which ones? – still I could have organised it somehow) but for good or bad I didn't do so, though certainly not because I valued this property. For twenty years and more I've hated it and I don't need it and can't need it, thanks to my writings, and if not my writings, then my friends. The only advantage of not having given my land away is that I've been censured and abused, and still am censured and abused.

But now I ask my heirs to give away the land after my death to the peasants, and to make my writings freely available for general use, not only those that I have made available myself, but *all of them, all of them*. If they decide not to fulfil both my requests after my death, let them at least fulfil one; but it will be better – for them as well – if they fulfil both.

13 February   Read Croft Hiller.[24] The toleration of violence in order to re-establish the law of God is false and artificial. Only love – but love is only love without violence. The main thing though – and here I was mistaken – is that love is doing its work even now in Russia with its executions, gallows, etc.

14 February, Yasnaya Polyana   [. . .]
(3) Capital punishment in our time is good in that it shows clearly that our rulers are evil, misguided men, and that therefore to obey them is just as harmful and shameful as to obey the chief of a robber gang.

15 February, Yasnaya Polyana   Yesterday evening I spoke harshly to Zosya[25] – censured her and was angry. Health good; had a talk with Vanya.[26] I can't do so without tears. Thought of something apparently new this morning – thought with such joy that:
(1) To censure people behind their backs is mean – and to their faces unpleasant, dangerous and likely to cause anger. And therefore there is only one possible, sensible, and therefore good attitude to take towards people who behave badly – such as Stolypin did in my view with his speech[27] – compassion – and the attempt to explain to them their errors and delusions.
(2) A beggar has just been, a peasant, a former soldier, who spoke in unnecessary, foreign words, but the sense of his speech was always the same: hatred of the rulers and the rich, envy and self-justification in everything. A terrible creature. Who created him? The revolutionaries or the government? Both. [. . .]

18 February, Yasnaya Polyana   [. . .] I don't know and never have known a single *woman* spiritually higher than Marya Alexandrovna.[28] She is so high that she is now beyond price. [. . .]

19 February, Yasnaya Polyana   Slept well. Revised *Incomprehensible*; started *The Wisdom of Children*.[29] Looked through *The Devil*. Painful and unpleasant. Had some good thoughts while out riding. [. . .]

20 February, Yasnaya Polyana   A painful physical condition, just the same as yesterday. It's probably the liver, and I can't do any work at all. Tried taking up *Pavel*[30] and re-read it. It could be not bad, but I've no enthusiasm for it. I've no enthusiasm either for *The Wisdom of Children*. A letter from Petrov – not quite it.[31] I must reply. Misha is here with his wife and sister-in-law. They're very pleasant. Nothing to note. I doubt if I'll be able to write anything literary. Revised *An Issue of a Newspaper* – not good. Yesterday and the day before I had good talks with Chertkov. But I was terribly weak by the evening.

25 February, Yasnaya Polyana The day before yesterday, i.e. the 23rd, I can't remember at all. I don't think I wrote anything except letters about non-resistance and the school. Very cold. On the 23rd I went for a walk, I think. Zosya rode behind me. On the 24th I got on well with *Pavel*. It may turn out all right. There is very much that is good and useful which can be said. Had a visit from a man who has been stupefied and corrupted by the revolution. He hates and condemns everyone, but thinks everything is permissible for him. Read V. Hugo. The prose is splendid, but I can't stand the poetry.[32]

Answered some old letters this morning – wrote no fewer than fifteen, very cheerfully and enthusiastically. [. . .]

1 March, Yasnaya Polyana Didn't write my diary yesterday, but was well. In the morning I read and wrote something for *The Wisdom of Children*. Probably walked too much and my leg is sore. Some pictures of India at the Chertkovs' in the evening.[33] Very good. [. . .]

Today is 2 March, Yasnaya Polyana Sat yesterday without moving because of my leg, and am doing just the same today as well. Did absolutely nothing yesterday except read. They brought the Indian pictures round. I revised the English translation of *Letter to an Indian*.[34] Yesterday there was a man from Tula of remarkably strong religious faith – as always, an ex-revolutionary – Mikhail Perepelkin. Read Grabovsky's *Geistige Liebe*.[35] Much that is very good and profound. I must look at it carefully. [. . .]

5 March I'd never have thought I hadn't written my diary for four days. During these four days the pain in my leg has confined me to my armchair, and made me dependent on the help of others. I can't boast about my spiritual condition, especially in the evenings. But I'm not weakening. I know that I'm bad. I'm dissatisfied that I feel no state of joy or love. Spent all day yesterday just writing two sections of *The Wisdom of Children* and reading Gogol.[36] Made some notes in my book about Gogol. Sasha will write them in here:
(1) Gogol – an enormous talent, a wonderful heart and a weak, i.e. unadventurous, timid mind.

The best product of his talent is *The Carriage*, the best product of his heart – some of his letters.

The chief misfortune of his whole activity is his submissiveness to the established, pseudo-religious teaching of the Church and the state, just as it is. It would have been a good thing if he had simply accepted all that exists, but as it was he tried to justify it, and not by himself, but with the help of Slavophile-sophists, and he was a sophist himself, a very bad sophist of his own childish beliefs. His desire to attach religious significance to his own literary work adversely affected and confused the character of his thinking still more. The letter about *The Government Inspector*, the second part of *Dead Souls*, etc.

When he surrenders himself wholly to his talent, the result is works which are splendid and truly artistic; when he surrenders himself wholly to the moral and the religious, the result is something good and useful; but as soon as he wants to introduce religious significance into his works of art the result is dreadful, disgusting nonsense. That's the case in the second part of *Dead Souls* and elsewhere.

One must add to this that it's all because he ascribes to art a significance which is inappropriate to it. [. . .]

6 March, Yasnaya Polyana I feel very – I was going to say bad, but no, not bad – good – but weak: I have a sinking feeling at heart and I can't think logically at all. And my leg is worse. I didn't know what to do. And I asked myself: what ought I to do in the sight of God, my master? And at once it became clear, at least what I ought not to do, what is not worth doing.
(1) I read in the paper both about the executions, and about the evil deeds which led to the executions, and I realised so clearly the corruption being practised by the Church – in hiding Christianity from view, in perverting people's consciences – and by the state – in legalising, in not simply justifying but in extolling pride, ambition, self-interest, the humiliation of other people, and, in particular, all forms of violence, murder in war, and executions. One would think that this was so indubitably obvious, but nobody sees it, nobody wants to see it. And they – both the Church and the state – although they see the evil growing greater and greater, continue to perpetrate it. What is going on is rather like what people would do who only knew how to plough and only had the implements for ploughing and could only exist by their work, by their ploughing – if such people were to plough fields in which corn shoots had already sprung up.

If the works of the Church and the state might have been necessary at one time, they are patently harmful in our time, and yet they continue to be practised.

7 March Sad news yesterday. Chertkov is being expelled.[37] He came here sick, weak and agitated. However painful it is for me to lose him, I was sorry only for him – the ruin of all his non-personal plans. But that is his ordeal and no doubt a blessing, a true blessing. Yesterday I felt very, very weak. Wrote *nothing*, which is rare for me. Sonya has written a letter and is indignant.[38] Oh, if only she could rise above herself . . . I tried to write a comedy yesterday[39] – it's no good, and I don't feel like it.

Thought a lot about Gogol and Belinsky. A very interesting comparison. How right Gogol is in his ugliness, and how utterly wrong Belinsky is in his resplendence, with his contemptuous reference to *some* God or other.[40] Gogol searches for God in the beliefs of the Church, in the place where He is misinter-

preted, but still he searches for God, but Belinsky, thanks to his belief in science which is just as absurd as, if not more absurd than the beliefs of the Church (it's worth recalling Hegel and his *alles, was ist, ist vernünftlich* [all that is is rational]), and undoubtedly even more harmful, doesn't need any God. What a theme for a necessary article! Note:
(1) How good it would be to write about how our life, the life of the wealthy classes, is non-stop theft and robbery which, for those born and brought up in this atmosphere of robbery is at least partially mitigated but which, for those who compound the robbery by accepting posts from capitalists or from the government, is baseness. But in everyone's case it is hypocrisy.[41] [. . .]

9 March Yesterday I didn't write anything in here, and indeed I didn't write at all. I only dictated a letter to a priest which wasn't bad.[42] The Tsar has granted Chertkov a respite at his mother's request. He is weak physically, and partly spiritually as well – he is sorry for his family and his work. But he knows himself. And that's the main thing. I've copied out from my diary everything that's necessary. Sasha copied it out.

Mikhail Novikov came yesterday evening. He has written about *A New Religion*.[43] Very much of it is good, but it's long and monotonous. I feel well at heart. Health better. Thought today with great remorse about the letter I wrote for Andrey to Timiryazev.[44] The conventions of our life require us to express our estimation of people: a compassionate loathing for the P. Stolypins, the Gerschelmans[45] and ministers of all sorts, a respect for the peasant, and a compassionate respect for the down-and-out worker. Both yesterday and today thoughts ran through my mind with great clarity and force, but I can't concentrate. I tried the little comedy, I tried *The Wisdom of Children*. Neither was any good. I'll wait. I've babbled long enough as it is. No notes to copy out.

10 March, Yasnaya Polyana
(1) All misfortunes are the result of tradition, the inertia of the olden days. A blouse comes apart at all the seams, we've grown out of it so much, but we daren't take if off and replace it by one that fits, and we walk about almost naked out of love for the olden days. [. . . .]

16 March However ashamed I am to admit it, yesterday, *15 March*, I waited for something very probable – death. It didn't come, but my health is still poor, still feverish. Only today am I a bit better. I'm not writing anything. There's a great deal I would like to write: *The Police Constable* and *Pavel* and *The Elder* and *The Wisdom of Children*.[46] Note: [. . .]
(3) Fighting against sexual lust would be a hundred times easier were it not for the poeticising both of sexual relations themselves and the feelings which lead to them, and also of marriage as something particularly beautiful and something which brings happiness (while in fact marriage, if it doesn't always ruin one's whole life, does so 9,999 times out of 10,000); if only it could be instilled into people in childhood and also when fully mature that the sexual act (one only has to imagine a

being one loves indulging in this act) is a disgusting, animal act which only acquires human meaning when both parties are aware that its consequences will lead to the difficult and complicated responsibilities of bringing up children and educating them as well as possible.
(4) A peasant thinks with his own mind about what he needs to think about, while an intellectual thinks with somebody else's mind about what he doesn't need to think about at all. But a peasant only thinks like that while he is at home, in his own environment; as soon as he associates with the intelligentsia, he thinks with the mind of somebody quite different and speaks with somebody else's words. [. . .]

Today is 20 March Haven't written my diary for several days; I felt very poorly physically and depressed mentally, but not angry, thank God. Wrote some trifling letters and read. Dear Posha, Ivan Ivanovich[47] and Nikolayev came. Today I feel better than I've felt for a long time. Chertkov is depressed and I'm sorry both for him and for myself. I feel more and more keenly the need to write for the *grand monde*[48] and for it alone. Ivan Ivanovich with his little booklets has revived the desire very much. All this morning I've been reading the legend of Krishna.[49] And the very thing that I rejected with our circle in mind is excellent for the people: a legend similar to the Christian one, but among a different, foreign people. We decided on: (1) A sketch of India, its history and present position, (2) The legend of Krishna and (3) The sayings of Krishna. Then perhaps: (4) The sayings of the moderns – Ramakrishna and Vivekananda. Then (5) A survey of China and the three religions, (6) Buddhism, (7) Confucianism, (8) Taoism, (9) The sayings of Mohammed, (10) Babism. Sasha and the five Sukhotins are coming back tomorrow – I'm glad. There were two visitors yesterday: a Kalmyk intellectual, a literary man, going back to the land, and a woman-revolutionary – she asked for a thousand roubles for the release of her fifteen-year-old brother, sentenced to twelve years' penal servitude.

21 March, Yasnaya Polyana First of all it must be understood that there can be no heroic feats, no heroism, nothing 'great'. There is only doing one's duty and not doing it. It's just as if a stable-man cleaning out the stables or a ploughman or a reaper were to talk about what a heroic feat he had performed, what heroism he had shown, what a great deed he had done yesterday in cleaning out the stables or ploughing up a field or mowing a meadow.

22 March [. . .] A correspondent from the *Russian Word* came. I finished writing about Gogol and gave it to him.[50] Perhaps it has distracted me from work. I couldn't write anything. Only letters. Chertkov has been. Felt very good at heart this morning, and later when I was reading and answering letters, in fact all the time except when I was talking to the correspondent, and that's a pity. [. . .]

24 March Yesterday I wrote a long appeal.[51] Not bad, I think. [. . .]

26 March Didn't write my diary yesterday. Health still good. And my state of mind. Read Kant: *Religion within the Bounds of Reason Alone.*[52] It's very close to me. I've been reading the same today. [. . .]

Yesterday I wrote a rather bad dialogue for *The Wisdom of Children*. Today I've been getting on with *The Revolution of Consciousness* – not bad. Things went particularly well with Sonya in the morning – how glad I was. Behaved badly towards L.[53] in my thoughts. I must overcome it, I must. 'So help me, Lord.'

27 March, Yasnaya Polyana Alive. Got up very early. Chertkov took our pictures in the morning. This didn't stop me from writing. Revised *The Revolution*. I still don't know what to call it. Chose some splendid epigraphs.[54] [. . .]

29 and 30 March After dinner the day before yesterday I looked through the account compiled by Strakhov.[55] It seemed very good. But I looked at it yesterday morning, and it seemed very bad. Got on quite well yesterday with *The Old and the New*. [. . .]

The fact that people read and copy out my diaries spoils my method of writing the diary. I'd like to say things better and more clearly, but I've no need to. And I won't. I'll go on writing as before, without thinking about other people, just as things occur to me.

1 April Chertkov left yesterday. I wanted to go and see him off, but was very weak and didn't write anything; I began and gave up. I was in a very bad mood, and I can't boast at all even now. I'm tormented by this senseless life (worse than senseless, compared with the poverty-stricken life in the village), in the midst of which I'm doomed to live out my days, I don't know how. I've obviously made progress in this awareness of injustice, if in nothing else. And the luxury shames and torments me, and poisons everything, and my sons depress me by their aloofness, and the exceptional self-assurance they share with the whole family – and it's the same with my daughters too. [. . .]

Thought further about how the grammar school harms and corrupts children (Volodenka Milyutin – there is no God),[56] how impossible it is to teach history, mathematics and scripture side by side. A school of unbelief. One should be teaching moral instruction.

Read *Korney Vasilyev* yesterday and was moved.

3 April Some good letters yesterday: one from Krasnov. I replied to him and the others. Did a little writing. None of it good. The title – *The New Life*. Weak. Sonya left for Moscow. I'd like to write something on inheritance for *The Wisdom of Children*. And two booklets for Ivan Ivanovich,[57] and *Pavel*.

8 April Snow fell during the night. I never thought I hadn't written my diary for so long. During this time I was unwell, on the 5th I think, and ate nothing for a day and a half. And it was very good. Some good letters again. *Ils m'en diront tant* [They'll tell me so many things] that I shall really believe I'm a very important person. No, they won't fool me. [. . .]

It was nice yesterday or the day before, when I had just thought how happy I was, to tell Sonya who had come to say goodbye to me that I was happy, and that she was the reason for it. [. . .]

How good, necessary and profitable it is, when conscious of all the wishes that arise in me to ask myself: whose wish is this: Tolstoy's or *mine*? Tolstoy wants to condemn, to think badly of NN, but *I* don't want to. And as long as I remember this, remember that Tolstoy is not *I*, then the question is resolved once and for all. Tolstoy is afraid of illness, condemnation and hundreds and thousands of trifling things which affect him one way or another. But one has only to ask oneself: and what do *I* want? And that's the end of it, and Tolstoy says nothing. Whether or not you, Tolstoy, want this or that is your affair. But to carry out what you want, to recognise the rightfulness and lawfulness of your wishes – that is *my* affair. And you know that you are bound to listen to me and cannot help it, and that in listening to *me* lies your happiness.

I don't know how this will seem to others, but this clear division of myself into Tolstoy and *I* makes me feel wonderfully glad, and is a fruitful influence for good.

Wrote nothing today. Only re-read Confucius.[58]

11 April Haven't written my diary for two days. Health not good. I don't feel so good at heart as before. Tolstoy is getting the upper hand over *me*. And he's wrong. I, I, only I exist, and he, Tolstoy, is a dream and a nasty stupid one. Cold weather and snow. Some good letters yesterday. I was so glad! Answered a few of them. I still can't answer Bulgakov as I would like. I'll try to write today.[59] Things are well with my daughters. Revised Krishna together with Nikolayev.[60] I wanted to work on the Chinese, on Confucius, today, and still do. [. . .]

[17 April] Didn't write my diary yesterday; today is 17 April. I was very weak and irritable yesterday. Kept going somehow. Petitioners, both in person and in writing, have been irritating me. I must think carefully about this. Dear Nikolayev has been, always kind, always serious. An excellent letter yesterday from a conscientious objector. And I talked to Misha about military service – it's hopeless. Rode round to Galya's;[61] she burst into tears. A good, wise woman. I did no work. Only one short chapter for the article. I think the whole article is useless. Sasha distresses me with her irritability. [. . .] Received a letter about Petrazhitsky and 'the law'. I'd like to write about it.[62] But generally speaking, however shameful to admit it, I'd like to die.

20 April I've just been out on to the balcony and was besieged by petitioners, and I couldn't sustain my good feelings towards everyone. Some astonishing words yesterday from Sergey: 'I feel and know,' he said, 'that I now have such powers of reasoning that I can discuss and resolve everything correctly . . . It would be good if I could apply these powers of reasoning to my own life,' he added, with astonishing naiveté. The whole family – but especially the men – have a self-assurance that knows no limits. But I think it is greater in him than in all the others. Hence his incorrigible narrow-mindedness. I write this on purpose, so that he should read it after my death. But I can't say it. Yesterday I came across my letter to an Indian in the *Russian Gazette*. I read it and relived the thoughts it contained with emotion; and immediately afterwards I read the memoirs of the actor Lensky.[63] I couldn't help bursting out laughing. The contrast was so sharp. Went for a ride. A Frenchman came[64] – a pleasant man. Chertkov's letter is intelligent and good, but it would have been better not to have written it.[65] Wrote yesterday morning about *Landmarks* and a letter from a peasant.[66] Feel unwell; my head aches. Wanted to write yesterday. Began something about work for *The Wisdom of Children*.[67]

23 April Haven't written my diary for two days. Yesterday was the 22nd. Nikolayev came in the evening; I read Krishna. Drove to dear Galya's with Mikhail Sergeyevich and Tanya. In the morning I read my article on education to Mikhail Sergeyevich and revised it.[68] The day before yesterday Strakhov was here; he talked about Orlov[69] and played with the girls. In the morning I revised my article *On Landmarks*. There's no need for *On Landmarks*, I think. It's not good.

I was very touched by what is written in the *Cycle of Reading* about the fact that one should only behave towards other people with love. I still haven't forgotten this, I think about it when associating with people, and it's very good. I feel the division of my person less strongly. But I do feel it sometimes. I'm still getting gratifying letters. Very unwell today. Did nothing all morning. Read *Landmarks*. The language is astonishing. I must beware of that myself. Un-Russian, made up words denoting implied new shades of thought, unclear, artificial, conventional and unnecessary. These words can only be necessary when one is talking about what is unnecessary. These words are only used and have meaning when the reader has a great desire to indulge in speculation, and ought always to be accompanied by the addition: 'Surely you understand this, surely we both understand it.'

It's a strange thing, Strakhov's stories aroused in me the desire to do some literary work; but a real desire – not as before with a definite purpose, but without any purpose – or rather with an invisible purpose beyond my reach: to look into the human soul. And I want to very much. I'm too weak.

Today is 26 April The day before yesterday I began writing something literary,[70] and wrote a lot, but it wasn't good and I didn't copy it out. But I didn't despair, and I want to improve it and know how to. Yesterday I revised *The Law*.[71] I thought I'd finished, but revised it much better today. I also revised the article on education. It's much better now. Yesterday I read Lozinsky.[72] The negation is very good, though strained, but the conclusion is very poor. There's only one thing I can and must note:
(1) Gorky writes about individualism.[73] This is the word in intellectual jargon for the life of the personality. And these people think they have discovered something new when they conclude that 'individualism' is not good, but socialism, the commune, the people *et tout le tremblement* are good. It never occurs to them that in the opposition between personality, the 'I' divorced from the whole, and the

awareness of this whole (God) together with the 'I' – that in this opposition lies the whole essence and secret of life which people were aware of thousands of years ago, but with this difference only that these people oppose personality to some collection of people, while in reality it is opposed to the whole, i.e. God, and to all mankind, every living thing, everything.

Dušan has discovered gangrene in my heels.[74] That's good, very good. Had a letter from Chertkov, and wrote a short letter to him. I'm just going to Galya's.

30 April Didn't sleep much, but am well. Yesterday I thought I'd completely finished the article on education. This morning I revised it again on Gusev's advice. [. . .] Yesterday Sonya spoke to me in distress about how she could see in my diaries my dissatisfaction with her. I'm sorry about this, and she is right that *in the long run*[75] I've been happy with her. Not to mention the fact that all is well now. And it's good that I'm sorry that I caused her distress. She asked me to write that the deletions in my diaries were made by me. I'm very glad to do so.[76] [. . .]

1 May Pasternak and his wife came yesterday and also Mogilevsky.[77] Mogilevsky played magnificently. I wept continually. Polished up the article[78] in the morning; it's not bad, I think. Went to Galya's. All is just as well with her. When I woke up I learned that Andrey and his wife had met Olga. Both women were nice and kind and friendly to one another, but Andrey was terrible. He's as pleased as Punch with himself. Nothing can pierce his self-satisfaction. It's astonishing that two good women can't share between them . . . I know that it's bad to write and think this, but I can't help it. Perhaps he'll read it one day and smell his own stench.

Wonderful weather; I didn't sleep much. Yes, I forgot that Molochnikov came yesterday. I was very glad to see him. Didn't note down the most important thing that happened yesterday: namely that dear Tanya left. I saw her off with emotion, and think about her with emotion and joyful love.

3 May Worked a lot on my article. I've made good progress. I think it's not bad. Wrote a conversation for *The Wisdom of Children*.[79] I'm depressed, i.e. I behave badly towards both Ss,[80] who don't love one another precisely because they are very like one another. The harder they are, the softer must I be. Molochnikov and Strakhov came; I was glad to see them both, but came in tired from work and was wrong not to have spoken to them. Went for a pleasant ride. Marya Alexandrovna, Olga[81] and her children. Read and talked in the evening. Was depressed again. Spoke to Sasha on the balcony. I'm afraid she's impervious . . . still [. . .]

5 May Worked badly yesterday. Did nothing really. Prepared some Confucius and Lao-Tzu for Ivan Ivanovich. It's not very clear. Had a good drive with Dušan to Marya Alexandrovna's. Slept. A very pleasant Serb came.[82] Was out of sorts all day. Struggled with myself. I still don't know how to be – not to seem to be, but to be – loving towards everyone. Some good letters. A melancholy condition – dissatisfaction – obviously an internal one because I experience the same condition in dreams – in dreams things never seem to turn out well for me. The reading of

Lao-Tzu was very important for me. I actually even had a nasty feeling, in direct contrast to Lao-Tzu: pride, the wish to be Lao-Tzu. And he says it so well: the highest spiritual condition is always combined with the most complete humility.

I've just been out on to the terrace. There were nine petitioners there, beggars, the most unfortunate of people, and Kurnosenkova. And I just couldn't sustain a feeling of kindness towards them all. You would think it was time I learned, but so far from learning, I'm still only making slow progress. [. . .]

7 May I've been revising the article and I'll put it aside. It's not good at all. *Landmarks* is also poor. An officer from the Semyonov regiment came – he claims to have acted against men of his own regiment.[83] God grant that it's true. I had a good talk with him. Went to see Galya and Olya. As always, it was nice. And she, Galya, is enduring her lot well.

Uspensky was here; letters in the evening and Vostorgov's unkind brochure.[84] [. . .]

Nothing particularly bad has happened. I'm busy with the article and *Landmarks*. *Dans le doute abstiens toi* [when in doubt, don't]. I'm giving up *Landmarks*.[85] Had a good ride with Dušan. I don't think I've infringed the sacrament of love, or only very little. Just a little with Sonya, apropos of the reading of Kuprin's *Pit*.[86] There's progress. And that's good. I feel weak. I'd like to write about what true Christianity consists of, and why the Church's belief distorts it, and destroys its whole meaning for our life. I'd also like to write *There are no Guilty People in the World*. It's cold. Sasha has gone to Mtsensk. I've accumulated a lot of tiresome work; I must free myself of it and do what is most needed in the sight of God. There isn't much time left. [. . .]

9 May Woke up very early. I feel well at heart. Yesterday I revised the article (it's not good, especially the ending). Saw off dear Ivan Ivanovich and Marya Alexandrovna. A Baptist peasant came, a petitioner. I restrained myself. Had a long ride with Dušan. In the evening I read the article and Kuprin. It's very poor, crude and unnecessarily dirty. [. . .]

10, 11 May Wrote nothing in my diary yesterday. I don't remember the day before. Now I remember: I wrote about love.[87] I've done nothing particularly good or bad. Went to Galya's. A curt refusal for Chertkov.[88] I felt anger – malice towards Stolypin – but, thank God, I restrained myself, and it turned into genuine compassion. In the evening a splendid conversation with Nikolayeva. Tregubov came.

Yesterday I got up very early. Wrote some trifle for Tregubov. But thought of something very, very important.

In the first place, that I must write a letter, which Sasha will deliver, asking her to think about her soul, and about the true life;[89] secondly, I mustn't give up my diary and mustn't write anything for publication during my lifetime. I make an exception now for what I write about love. That is necessary. I may be wrong, but I think it's of the utmost importance. [. . .] Note:

(5) He writes to his wife:[90] 'Forgive me. I have forgiven you, but I can't help saying, if only from beyond the grave, what I couldn't bring myself to say when alive so as not to anger you, and therefore to lose the chance, to lose it for ever even, of helping you – namely to say that you live a bad life, a life that is bad for yourself, tormenting yourself and other people, and depriving yourself of the greatest good – love. Yet you are capable – very much so – of all that is the very best. I have seen these seeds in you many times. Help yourself, my dear. Just begin – and you will see how your own self, your best and true 'I', will help you.' [. . .]

13 May   Yesterday I revised *On the State*[91] and *On Love*. [. . .]

I wrote quite a lot on love. It's not bad, it's making progress. Sonya was dreadful at breakfast. It turned out she had read *The Devil*,[92] and the old rancour began to ferment in her, and it was very painful for me. I went into the garden. I began to write a letter to her to be given to her after my death, but I didn't finish it; and gave it up, mainly because I asked myself: 'why?' and was aware that it wasn't done in the sight of God for love. Then at 4 o'clock she spoke her mind, and, thank God, I calmed her down and began to cry myself, and we both felt better.

14 May   Yesterday evening passed as usual. Pleasant news about Felten and his trial.[93] Today I got up early, went into the garden and wrote a letter to Molochnikov. Overheard a conversation between Kopylov and a passer-by – filthy words and lies – and what astonishing, terrible unbelief. I felt depressed. I'm still depressed from yesterday. I'm better than before, but there isn't that joyful calm which I felt at first. I also received some depressing letters – Kopyl, and a peasant making accusations.[94] And there were petitioners. I want to die, I want to die. [. . .]

15 May   No, it's not good. Not good at all. I've sunk very low morally. I felt bad all day yesterday and all evening. Einroth[95] came and Nikolayev also. I began to complain to them about my life. Apart from that there were two malicious letters – one from Kopyl, the other from a peasant-revolutionary, and also some verses about the land; I was quite overcome by it all. [. . .]

I've just been out: first there was Afanasy's daughter with a request for money, then Anisya Kopylova stopped me in the garden about the wood and about her son, then the other Kopylova whose husband is in prison.[96] And I began to think again about how people would judge me. 'He is supposed to have given everything away to his family, but he lives for his own pleasure and doesn't help anybody' – and I felt hurt and began to think how I might go away, as if I didn't know that we must live in the sight of God in ourselves and in Him, and not only not worry about people's opinions, but rejoice at humiliation. Oh, I am bad, bad. The only good thing is that I know it – although not always – I've only just remembered it now. Well then, I'm bad, but I'll try to be less bad. Just now I couldn't restrain myself from angrily sending Kopylova away when she caught me as I was beginning to write my diary. Einroth is a very original and serious person, modest, simple and profound. Tanechka[97] is ill – they are running round to all the doctors and squandering money, while people are dying of poverty in the village. No, I mustn't go away, there's no need, but I still want to die, although I know that it's bad, very bad. Yesterday I revised the article *Revolution*⁹⁸ – it's not bad. [. . .]

16 May Yesterday evening the post came. The letters were unimportant, but the papers published my letters to the priest and to Tregubov.⁹⁹ And these letters were to me like wine to a drinker, and immediately caused me concern for people's opinions. No doubt because I no longer feel physical desires, I feel vanity particularly painfully, and can't rid myself of it. Yesterday, knowing that these letters would make me talk about them, I thought I mustn't do so, especially in front of my son Seryozha. And so I abstained from vanity for the sake of my concern for people's opinions, for the sake of vanity. I've never suffered so much before from heartburn as yesterday evening and all this morning. Slept well and got up late. There were about ten petitioners; I refused them all without getting annoyed, but it could have been better. Then I went into the garden to correct the proofs of the *New Cycle of Reading*. I didn't like it at all. [. . .]

Today is 19 May What I ended up by saying the day before yesterday that I'm getting used to the awareness of my dependence on God alone and consequently my independence of people's opinions actually turned out to be wrong yesterday evening and today. I read a foolish article about myself apropos of Ertel¹⁰⁰ – and felt annoyed and couldn't regain my composure and steadfastness in God. Spent the day well yesterday. Revised the letter about religious education¹⁰¹ and *The Inevitable Revolution* quite well. Had a very painful conversation with Sonya about the price for the land she is giving up. I said nothing, but it was painful to listen, and all because the connection with Him has been lost. Dear Nikolayev came twice. What a wonderful worker he is in the Henry George sense, and what a good person in general. Went for a ride, spoke to Grushetsky by telephone and read Goethe and the newspapers.¹⁰² [. . .]

20 May Yesterday revised *On Education, The Revolution* and the letter to an American. The letter is still not what it could have been. Went to Telyatinki. The evening as usual. Read some letters. Was a great nuisance to the people closest to me. An article about me by Roosevelt.¹⁰³ The article is silly, but I was pleased. It aroused my vanity, but it was better yesterday. [. . .]

21 May [. . .] Yesterday morning there was a correspondent from the *Russian Word*. I talked to him and dictated something to him about *Landmarks*. Nothing particularly bad, but it would have been better not to have done it. I'd very much like to make public the letter from the peasant¹⁰⁴ – and rightly so. Lina and the children came.¹⁰⁵ Dušan has returned, the danger has passed 'for the time being'.¹⁰⁶ In the evening I upset Lina, I think, by talking about the religious education of children – that was bad. A wonderful spring. It's now gone 10 o'clock. I feel well at heart, but I've no desire to write. And that's fine. Yesterday there was a very interesting man who had come on foot from Simbirsk. He said many good things, but the best thing was that in his opinion: *The main thing the people need now is spiritual food.*

22 May Yesterday I dabbled about with the letter to an American and *On Love*. I'm behaving quite well, but in my relations with people I don't always remember the reverence for God in man. Every time – *l'esprit de l'escalier* [wise after the event]. A lively, talkative Moscow worker has been, but one who talks and doesn't listen. Drove to Telyatinki. Went to the Nikolayevs'. Went to Galya's. Felt very good at both places. Lina, Masha and the children are at home. In the evening Seryozha upset me with his talk about the law. Some good letters. Got up early today. Walked round the garden. Sat down for a rest and saw a peasant woman coming towards me. I did well to remember that it was God coming in her. It turned out to be Shurayeva, poor woman; her granddaughter had died, and she was asking for money. I tried to enter into her soul, in the depth of which is the same God who is in me and everyone, and I felt so good. Help me God. May it always be so.

(1) The fêting of me is a bad sign. The fêting of Mechnikov[107] made me think of this. We are both, obviously, very empty people if we have pleased the masses so much. What comforts me a little is the fact that I am abused – not by envious people, but abused in earnest both by the revolutionaries and by the clergy, the churchmen. [. . .]

(6) A man is funny when he boasts about his face and his gracefulness, and a woman about her strength and intelligence. [. . .]

24 May Wrote a bit again about love and about education. Not much. Went to the Chertkovs'. Behaved badly towards the person investigating Chertkov's case; I didn't give him my hand and then I didn't manage to say what I should have done. Mikhail Sergeyevich came – pleasant as always. In the evening the merchant Letyshev was here again. He talked a long time about his theory which offers a mystical explanation of the sacraments. Then Kalachov and dear Nikolayev came. My brain is very tired.

I didn't get up early today. Sonya came back. Constant worries and unkind feelings. A beautiful album from Polenov.[108] [. . .]

25 May Yesterday I seemed to have finished both *On Love* and the letter to an American. Sonya came back. She is very pitiful. Rode hard to Tula. Had a good trip. Mikhail Sergeyevich is here; I gave him *The Inevitable Revolution* to read. He made some just observations. Goldenweiser. Today I was late getting up, and as I walked round the garden I thought about the speed, and above all the monotony of time: day and night, again and again, and the years and the decades fly by. [. . .]

26 May [. . .] A painful conversation with Sonya about the estate. I'm sorry I didn't speak about the sin of owning land. At dinner too she was confused, poor woman. She's an interesting creature when you love her; when you don't love her she's too simple. It's the same with everybody. [. . .]

27 May A very touching meeting yesterday evening with a student who had come from the Caucasus to see me. Gusev said that he thought he was a petitioner. He gave me an envelope and asked me to read it. I refused at first, then began to read the end of it. About monism and Haeckel. I began to speak to him unkindly. He was terribly agitated. Then I learned that he was a consumptive, a hopeless case. He was about to leave and said that the reading of *On Life* had been a great event for him. I was astonished and asked him to stay. I read his note right through. He turned out to be a person quite close to me. And I had offended him and caused him anguish. I was hurt and ashamed. I asked him to forgive me. He stayed the night in the village. This morning he came back and we had a moving talk. A very touching case. I grew fond of him. [. . .]

28 May Lev came. It's depressing to be with him. Thank God I didn't betray the demands of love, but I can't help avoiding him, and remaining silent when listening to him. I only broke my silence twice: when he was talking about his dissatisfaction with life I said what I thought about the need to live a spiritual life, and the other time I expressed my disgust when he voiced sympathy and justification for the murders of Stolypin. [. . .]

29 May [. . .] Note: [. . .]
(4) I'd very much like to show in *There are no Guilty People* how everyone lives for himself alone and is deaf to everything else.
Dear Ivan Ivanovich was angry with Chertkov.[109] Some quite pleasant letters. Wrote a letter about women and an answer to some accusations.[110] An astonishing story about Kashinskaya.[111] An argument about vegetarianism between Nikolayeva and . . . (I've forgotten). I interrupted and probably angered NN. And it hurt me.

30 May Didn't sleep much; got up early. Mechnikov came, and some correspondents.[112] Mechnikov is pleasant and apparently broad-minded. I haven't had a chance to talk to him yet. [. . .]

31 May Continuation of 30 May. Mechnikov turned out to be a very superficial person – *areligious*. I deliberately chose a time to talk to him alone about science and religion. On science – nothing, except a belief in the very status of science, the justification of which I was asking him for. On religion – silence; evidently a denial of what is considered religion, and both a failure and an unwillingness to understand what religion is. The old aestheticism of Hegel, Goethe and Turgenev. And very talkative. I let him talk, and was very glad I didn't interrupt him. As always, the talk made me depressed by the evening. Goldenweiser played splendidly.
Got up late; didn't sleep well last night. Had a terrible dream . . . A type of scholar-revolutionary is emerging.[113] I wanted to get on with it, but began to revise *The One Commandment*, and worked all morning at it. A reporter came; it was unpleasant and false. Vera from Pirogovo came. It's painful to recall her situation.[114] I did *not* behave badly. No unkind feelings towards anyone. But the folly and self-torment of people depresses me. I'm going to have dinner.

1 June After dinner there were three visitors: a worker from the *Union of the*

Russian People who had drunk too much tried to persuade me to return to the Church, a good-natured man but completely mad; then a woman with two huge envelopes demanding that I should read what was in them ... 'a cry from the heart'. Vanity, mania to be a writer, and greed. I was angry – I should have been calmer. Then a reporter from *Early Morning*.[115] How glad I am that my relations with Lev are no longer strained. I just couldn't manage to ask Vera about her child. How could it happen?

1 June Woke before 5 and noted down many good and important things for *There are no Guilty People in the World*, and for *The One Commandment*, and also more about God. Also the outlines of a conversation with some girl-students.[116] I understood very clearly and vividly, strange to say for the first time, that either there is no God, or that there is nothing except God. Began writing *The One Commandment* very well, but soon, towards midday, my concentration relaxed and I abandoned it. The editor of a vegetarian journal came.[117] Went riding for a bit. [...]

2 June Yesterday evening I read my letters. Few of interest. Slept a lot today and am fresher than I've felt for a long, long time. A telegram from Henry George's son,[118] then someone from the *Russian Word* with the proofs of the Mechnikov article.[119] Corrected the proofs and wrote about Henry George and sent it to the *Russian Word*. They probably won't print it.[120] Then I looked right through *The Inevitable Revolution*. It's all good as far as chapter 8. I must work a bit on the ending. Wrote till 3, had no lunch and didn't go riding, but walked round the garden. Rain. It's now 5 o'clock. I'm going to lie down. Note:
(1) Cruelty is not natural to man and can only be explained by narrowness of aim, by the concentration of life's efforts on that aim. The narrower the aim, the greater the likelihood of cruelty. Love has as its aim the good of others, and so by excluding any other aim is incompatible with cruelty.

5 June Troyanovsky played very nicely yesterday. Chertkov and the Goldenweisers came. Health still bad. Did nothing today: revised *The One Commandment* and the article on George a little bit. George's son came with a photographer. A pleasant person. [...]

6 and 7 June Yesterday I wrote some quite serious letters, especially one about Haeckel and suicide.[121] And a little on *The One Commandment*, I think. Troyanovsky played again in the evening. I got up in rather better spirits today. Worked very hard on *The One Commandment* with a great effort. Sent a telegram to Tanya to say that Sofya Andreyevna and I are travelling tomorrow. [...]

8 June Kochety. Got up early and set off. A good journey. A talk with a marshal from Mtsensk[122] – Orthodox, conservative, impermeable. Dear Tanya and Misha and, least not last,[123] little Tanechka. I felt particularly keenly the insane immorality of the luxury of the rulers and the rich, and the poverty and down-trodden state of the poor. I suffer almost physically from the awareness of being party to this madness and evil. I've been accommodated here in insane luxury together with the three others who brought me here: my doctor, secretary and servant. And unfortunately, all the *Cycle of Reading* for 9 June is on this theme. [. . .]

11 June The revises of *On Love* are poor. I must do more work on them. Wrote a prayer for Sonechka in bed in the morning. Everything is bad. I couldn't work at all. Read forty-one letters with unkind feelings. Went riding and was very tired. But the main thing is the tormenting feeling of the poverty – not the poverty, but the humiliation – the oppressed state of the people. The cruelty and madness of the revolutionaries is pardonable. Then at dinner Sverbeyeva,[124] French talk and tennis; and side by side hungry, ill-clad slaves, oppressed by work. I can't stand it, I want to escape.

Read Bakunin on Mazzini.[125] [. . .]

14 June Haven't written my diary for three days. [. . .] Yesterday, the 13th, I did no work all morning. Only late on did I work a bit on *The Commandment of Love*. The young people – tennis – unkind feelings and unjust accusations. A very interesting book on Persia.[126] Theoretically the land cannot be an object of private ownership. The shah is an oppressor and is regarded as a bad man. Soldiers are recruited voluntarily. But in practice their land is taken away from them; the shah rules and is worshipped, the soldiers are enlisted and the government authorities are bought off. [. . .]

19 June Yesterday, I think, I worked a bit on *The One Commandment*. Walked a lot. Slept. Many people for dinner. Was depressed by the emptiness of the conversation. In the evening, thanks to Lyubov Dmitriyevna, I managed to have a serious talk with the girls. The boys are afraid.[127] [. . .]
(1) A man robs a whole village, piles up what he has robbed in a heap and guards it. A man in rags comes along and takes away a shirt. The robber catches him and punishes him according to the law which he drew up himself. Surely it's just the same with all rich people surrounded by the poor, and especially with landed proprietors: they continually rob thousands of people of millions of roubles. People take food from their land for a cow or a horse, and it isn't the robber that is tried and punished, but the person who takes what he needs from the land which is his according to the most incontestable deeds.

Before drawing up laws forbidding the theft of a horse collar, or wood, or hay, one should draw up laws forbidding the robbery of people's most legitimate property – land.

20 June [. . .] Yes, yesterday I read Engels on Marx[128] . . . Today I woke up from a dream about a clear, simple refutation of materialism comprehensible to all. When I was awake it wasn't so clear as when I was asleep, but something remained – namely that materialists must grant the absurdity of a creator in order to explain how matter took shape in such a way that out of it were formed individual creatures, first of all 'I', and with such properties as feelings and reason.

But for the non-materialist it is clear that everything that I call the material world is the product of my own spiritual 'I'. The chief mystery for him is my own and other creatures' separate identity. [...]

22 June As far as I remember, I did nothing yesterday except revise *The One Commandment* and a few letters, one of which, an appeal, I scrapped. Then I rode in the woods with the three Tanyas. Set off from there on foot and came across some reapers – the whole village. Talked with them about many things, about the land, military service and the fact that they are enslaving themselves; about how difficult it is to be rid of poverty, but even more difficult of wealth; that one should live for one's soul, and all will be well. Had dinner and read. Felt in comparatively good spirits. [...]

23 June [...] It's time to understand that if you want to serve people you must work for the *grand monde* – the working people – and have them before you when you write. Our folk, the great majority of them, are without hope. But these others are thirsty. [...]

26 June Quite unexpectedly missed a day. The day before yesterday I revised *The One Commandment* again. Read the *New Cycle of Reading*. It's not bad. Went a short walk. Zosya arrived. Went to meet her and met Vasily Panyushkin.[129] Had a long walk and talk with him. A fine young man. In such people, and only such people, is there hope for the future. And even if nothing comes of them, it's good for them and for me and for everyone that they exist. Yesterday the 25th. The same again. *The Execution of Yevdokim* is crying out more and more to be written.[130]

29 June [...] Zosya has gone. Her partiality towards me is funny. It's like running after a person for his money, when the person knows he doesn't have any.

3 July Missed two days. 30 June. Went to Chertkov's, a joyful meeting with him. In the evening I went back again.

1 July In the morning I wrote quite a good reply to a peasant about education. I haven't finished it yet.[131] Went to the fair. It was good, but I expected more. In the evening to Chertkov's. It was good, but I expected more. In the evening to Chertkov's. It was very good again. He made some just remarks about *The One Commandment*. [...]

5 July, Yasnaya Polyana Set off on the 3rd, as resolved. Visited dear Abrikosov. Tanya accompanied me as far as Mtsensk. Travelled third class, and it was very pleasant – a policeman and some settlers. The very people who are treated like cattle, but who alone make life and history (if anyone is interested). All well at home. Sasha is just as good as ever. [...] Note: [...]
(2) I can't help being amazed at why God chose such a repulsive creature as me to speak to people through.

Today is 11 July [...] Decided to go to Stockholm.[132] I'm well at heart.

12 July Slept very little. In the morning I behaved badly towards a silly young boy who asked for my autograph. Twice I began to talk seriously to him, and both times he interrupted me, asking for a souvenir. Yesterday evening I was depressed by Sofya Andreyevna's talk about publication and prosecution.[133] If only she knew and understood how she alone is poisoning the last hours, days, months of my life! But I can't say so, and I don't expect any words to have any effect on her.

In the morning before coffee I got on with *On Science* and revised it, but was quite exhausted. Tiredness of the brain. Made a few notes for the congress in bed in the morning. [...]

14 July [...] Note: [...]
(2) For Stockholm: begin by reading old letters and then recent ones by conscientious objectors. Then say that it's all said very well there, but it's just like all of us having keys to open the door of the apartment we wish to enter, and then asking people hidden from us behind an impenetrable door to open it, not using our own keys for the purpose and teaching others to do likewise. The main thing is to say that the root of everything is the military. If we take soldiers and teach them murder, we repudiate everything we can say in favour of peace. One has to tell the whole truth: how can one talk about peace in the capitals of kings, emperors and commanders-in-chief of armies whom we respect just as much as the French respect M. de Paris?[134] As soon as we stop lying we shall be expelled from there at once.

We express the greatest respect for the commanders of the military, that is for those deluded people who are needed not so much for foreign enemies, as for keeping in submission those whom we oppress. [...]

19 July [...] Today I got on with *On Science*, then some peasants from Kolpna came, then some nice young workers from Thiel's courses.[135] We had a good talk. I went riding. Sonya is still just as sick. I had a talk with her, painful at first, then good and moving. [...]

20 July Last night I received a telegram from Popova,[136] the mother of a man on trial, to say she was coming. When I woke up this morning I began to think what I could do for him, and wrote a letter to Stolypin, not a bad one, I think. The feeling was good. But now it's gone 12 and she still isn't here. [...] For two days I've been reading Mechnikov's book,[137] and was horrified by its superficiality and downright stupidity. I meant to write something unkind. Decided today that if I do write, I'll write something loving. Note: [...]
(3) The first thought at the news of the flight across the Channel – how can aeroplanes be used for war, for murder?[138] [...]

I've just been re-reading for Stockholm both my letter to the Swedes,[139] and *The Kingdom of God*. Everything seems to have been said. I don't know what more to say. I'm thinking of a few things that can and ought to be said. We'll see.

When reading these old writings of mine, I'm convinced that my present writings are worse, are weaker. And thank God, I'm not distressed by this. On the contrary, I'll refrain from writing. There is other, more important and necessary work ahead of me. Help me, my God.

21 July In the evening Sofya Andreyevna was weak and irritable. I couldn't get to sleep till 2 or later. I woke up feeling weak. Somebody had woken me up. Sofya Andreyevna hadn't slept all night. I went to see her. It was something quite mad. Dušan had poisoned her, etc. A letter from Stakhovich[140] which I ought to have told her about because she thought I was hiding something from her made her condition still worse. I'm tired and I can't do any more and I feel quite ill. I feel the impossibility, the absolute impossibility of a reasonable and loving relationship. At present I only want to withdraw and take no part in anything. I can't do anything else, and I've already thought seriously of running away as it is. Well then, show your Christianity. *C'est le moment ou jamais* [It's now or never]. But I terribly want to go away. My presence here is hardly of use to anybody. A sorry victim, and harmful to everyone. Help me, my God, teach me. The only thing I want is to do not my will, but Thine. I write this and ask myself – is it true? Am I not putting on an act for myself? Help, help, help. [. . .]

22 July Yesterday I didn't eat or sleep at all, as usual. Was very depressed. I'm still depressed, but feel good at heart. Yes, love them that do us evil, you say. Well, try it. I do try, but badly. I'm thinking more and more about going away and disposing of my property. [. . .]

23 July Decided to give up the land. Talked yesterday to Ivan Vasilevich.[141] How difficult to be rid of this nasty, sinful property. Help, help, help.

Wrote yesterday morning. Did nothing sensible during the day. Finished dictating some trifling letters, and dictated a statement to the peace congress (very bad). Went to Telyatinki. Dear Tanya came. Dear, but still remote – not as much so as my sons – but dear, seeking to be closer to me, not fighting against the truth. Read a wonderful story about executions.[142] Slept very little, and was again restless at heart. [. . .] Note: [. . .]

(4) While thinking people of our time are concerned about how to be rid of private property generally, and especially its most criminal variety, landed property – people in our country are concerned about consolidating the feeling for private property. It's as if in the middle of the last century people in our country had been concerned about strengthening and consolidating the feeling for serf ownership and serfdom.

24 July Yesterday, as foreseen, I did no work. A few unimportant letters. Ginzburg and Posse came. Posse is an example of 'the intelligentsia'. I think he's a good man, very probably so. Went for a drive with Onechka. After dinner I talked with dear Tanya – a very good talk. She pointed out my old sin – correctly. In the evening the children came, and they all enjoyed themselves and danced. Sonya is a little better, but she is very pitiful. This is where I could help, and not turn away, thinking about myself. [. . .]

25 July Read a little of *The Cycles*. Then began to write for the peace congress. It's better, but still weak. Came across a little volume of my letters in French.¹⁴³ Very well translated and the content is good. I've obviously grown worse mentally. I mustn't write stupid things.

26 July Yesterday my brother-in-law Al. Behrs and his family came. I couldn't suppress a feeling of disgust, though I didn't show it. I've grown worse in my relations with people. Went riding for a bit. Wrote a few worthless letters. [. . .] I feel well at heart. Sofya Andreyevna has already said that I promised her not to go to Sweden. Her health is better. Wrote a bit about war, and a letter in French to Styka.¹⁴⁴ [. . .]

Yes, this is a good definition of love: *Être un homme n'est rien; être homme est quelque chose; être l'homme voilà ce que m'attire* [To be a man is nothing; to be man is something; to be *the* man – that is what attracts me] – Amiel.¹⁴⁵

My son Sergey and Buturlin came to dinner, and Maklakova also came in the morning. After dinner I began to talk about the trip to Sweden, and there was a terrible hysterical outburst of anger. She wanted to poison herself with morphine. I snatched it out of her hands and threw it downstairs. I struggled. But when I went to bed and thought about it calmly, I decided to give up the trip. I went and told her so. She is pitiful, and I'm truly sorry for her. But how edifying. [. . .]

27 July Didn't sleep much, but got up without any pain. Went for a walk, prayed and was moved to tears from inner joy and gratitude. And now there are echoes of this wonderful feeling. I came back. Wrote a letter to Mechnikov¹⁴⁶ and one in French to Styka. Revised the Swedish one a little.¹⁴⁷ [. . .]

28 July Written down during the night of 28/29. There are creatures in the world who all live off the produce of the land, but in order to make it as difficult as possible for them to feed themselves, they have divided their land up in such a way that only those who don't work on it can use it, while those who do work can't use it and suffer and die, generation after generation, from the impossibility of feeding themselves off the land. Furthermore these creatures elect one or several families out of many and renounce their own will and reason for the sake of slavish obedience to everything that these elected people want to do with them. These elected people are the most evil and stupid of all. But the creatures who elected them and obey them extol them in every possible way. These creatures speak in various languages incomprehensible to one another. But instead of trying to eliminate this cause of misunderstanding and dissension, they divide themselves up further, irrespective of language differences, into various combinations called states, and as a result of these combinations kill thousands and thousands of people like themselves and ruin one another. In order to ruin and kill one another more conveniently these creatures put on special, identical, and for the most part motley coloured clothes, think up ways of killing one another and teach the many who give obedience to one man alone the best methods of murder.

Moreover these creatures, in order to explain their life and its meaning and purpose, assure themselves and one another that there exists a creature like themselves, only endowed with those qualities which they would like to have, and therefore capable of doing all sorts of stupid and nasty things, and they think up various and quite unnecessary ways of gratifying this imaginary creature, and devote an enormous part of their labours to this gratification, although they need these labours for the most part to feed themselves. In order that this fabrication should never cease to deceive their children, parents assiduously teach their children all sorts of fabrications about this creature called God, about how he created the world, how he became man, and then gave people his body to eat and then flew off to heaven, which they know doesn't exist, and suchlike things. And not only do they require their children to repeat all this, but they require it of other people too, and kill, and have killed, hundreds of thousands of creatures like themselves for disagreeing with it.

But not content with continually doing all these nasty and stupid things and suffering from them, and knowing that they are suffering precisely because of these nasty and stupid things, they not only continue to do them, but elect from among themselves people who are obliged to think up arguments from which it would emerge that it is unavoidably necessary to do all these stupid and nasty things, that it is impossible not to do them. All these arguments, very involved and incomprehensible to anybody, most of all to those who think them up, they call science. And all these justifications for nasty and stupid things, and various completely unnecessary sophistries are considered a very important matter, and all children are taught these sophistries, and all parents and the young people themselves consider it a great honour to study this science.

These creatures multiply by means of such a filthy, repulsive and monstrous act that they are ashamed of it themselves, and not only do not perform it in front of others, but always do so in secret. Moreover the consequences of this act – the birth of similar new creatures – are not only painful for that species of creature from whose womb these new creatures come, helpless at the beginning of their lives, but are in the highest degree troublesome for those who beget them, and who find them a burden. Apart from that, the incessant multiplication of these creatures threatens famine disasters for everyone, since their reproduction goes on at too fast a rate for people to be able to produce food for everyone. These creatures know all this and talk about it, yet in spite of this, they not only perform this repulsive act on all occasions when they can to the detriment of their interests, health and general considerations, but actually extol it in every possible manner. Some eulogise it in incoherent and involved words called poetry; others not only eulogise, but bless this loathsome act in the name of that fictitious creature they call God.

I won't speak of the millions of stupid and nasty things which are done by these creatures: how they poison themselves and consider it a pleasure; how they congregate in enormous numbers in the places which have been most infected by themselves, in the midst of enormous unoccupied expanses of land, and build houses of thirty stories on one site; or how they are not concerned about better ways of transport for everyone, but are concerned only that a few people should be able to travel and fly as fast as possible; or how they arrange words so that their endings should be the same, and having put them together, then admire this arrangement of words and call it poetry; or how they arrange other words without endings, but just as stupid and incomprehensible ones, and call them laws and as a result of these words torment in every conceivable manner, imprison and kill each other in accordance with these laws. One could go on and on.

What is most surprising of all, moreover, is that these creatures not only do not see reason, or use their reason in order to understand what is stupid and bad, but on the contrary use it in order to justify all their stupidities and nastinesses. And so far from wishing themselves to see the stupidities and nastinesses which torment them, they do not allow anyone among them to point out why they should not do what they are doing, and why they can and ought to do something quite different and not torment themselves so. It is only necessary for a person who uses his reason to appear among them and all the rest of the people become angry and indignant and horrified, and abuse such a creature in all manner of ways and beat him, and either hang him on a gallows or on a cross, or burn him or shoot him. And the strangest thing of all is that when they hang or murder this one reasonable creature among all the unreasonable ones, and he is no longer in their way, they gradually begin to forget what this reasonable creature said and begin to think up for him what he allegedly said but never did say, and when everything that was said by this reasonable creature has been well and truly forgotten or distorted, these same creatures who previously hated and tortured this one reasonable creature, the one among many, begin to extol the tortured and murdered one, and sometimes even recognise him – thinking thereby to do this creature the greatest honour – as the equal of that imaginary evil and foolish God whom they revere.

These creatures are astonishing. These creatures are called human beings. [. . .]

29 July Didn't write my diary yesterday. The day before yesterday there were a lot of people here in the evening: Sergey, Rayevsky, Goldenweiser. Had an unpleasant argument with Sergey. Of course I was entirely to blame. I said some unpleasant things to him. Yesterday I hardly slept at all. During the night I painted in my diary an imaginary picture of human beings and their life. Did nothing at all. Sofya Andreyevna's painfully excited state has begun again. I'm both depressed and sorry for her; and, thank God, I managed to calm her down. Mashenka[148] came, it was very pleasant. Did nothing today. Began the Swedish speech, but it was no good. [. . .]

30 July Went a ride yesterday to Kolpna and to the Chertkovs'. Was in a bad mood – was even angry with the horse. In the evening Goldenweiser came. A talk with Sofya Andreyevna. Things seem to be better. I must note something about music.

In the modern music of our masters an embellishment has come into use which consists of interrupting the rhythmical expression of the melody, making antimelodic and antirhythmical digressions quite foreign to the melody and then, in order to *rehausser* [enhance] the charm of the melody, going back from these digressions to the melody. As time goes by people have begun to imagine the point of the music to be in these digressions.

Today I slept very well; the correspondent Spiro came. I gave him some information and finished the article for the congress.[149] Gusev gave a wonderfully good account of *On Science*.[150] Read extracts from my diary to Buturlin. A conversation with Sofya Andreyevna, impossible as always. It's now 2 o'clock, I'll go for a ride.

1 August Went to Kolpna the day before yesterday. I'm wrong. I don't think I went anywhere. In the evening Buturlin and Goldenweiser came. Yesterday I translated the congress article[151] and went for a ride with Sasha. In the evening I read aloud my speech to the congress – it's not good. Revised it today. It's better. I'm very depressed. Probably, even certainly, I'm to blame. I'm better today. I still haven't changed my mind about the plan.[152] [...]

2 August Yesterday I walked through the rain *d'une humeur de chien* [in a vile temper]. Did nothing bad, but I'm sick at heart and have no feelings of love. Spent the evening with everyone. Woke up today at 5 and had some good thoughts. I thought about true belief in God, belief which has no need of miracles and is not interested in nature and its study. Then I thought about the congress and made some notes before getting dressed. Then went for a walk and wrote two letters to the peasants. Read my letters. Sofya Andreyevna came in and announced that she would go,[153] but all this will surely end with the death of one or the other of us, and there will be innumerable difficulties. And so I certainly won't go in such conditions. [...] Note: [...]
(3) The company of women is useful in that you can see that you mustn't be like them. [...]

5 August Two days have passed without any entries. Yesterday evening the bandits came for Gusev and took him away.[154] His leave-taking was very good: the attitude of all of us towards him, as well as his attitude towards us. It was very good. I wrote a statement about it today. A pile of letters. Many begging ones. Some wonderful letters from Alexander.[155] It will soon be one o'clock. Yesterday, the 4th, I revised the congress article and, I think, it's almost all right. Went for a ride with Onechka. Read *The One Commandment* to everyone. Onechka understands. The day before yesterday, the 3rd, Vera came. Went for a ride a long way into the Zaseka wood with Onechka, and lost my way. In the morning – the congress article as well. That's all. [...]

Sofya Andreyevna is getting ready to go to Stockholm, and as soon as she speaks about it, she falls into despair. She takes no notice of my suggestions not to go. The only salvation is: live in the present and remain silent.

8 August Two days have passed again. 6 August was an important day. I went for a walk as usual, then settled down to work at *On War*, and Sofya Andreyevna came in and announced that the congress had been postponed.¹⁵⁶ Alexander Stakhovich told me the same thing. I talked to him, and his self-assured, free and easy, good-natured narrowness irritated me. Behaved badly; listened only to myself. But the important thing was not on the 6th, but on the evening of the 5th. The police came for Gusev and took him off to prison and then to Cherdyn. It all passed off very well. He behaved well, as is his nature, and everyone expressed the love and respect for him which he deserved. [. . .]

10 August Missed yesterday, and it was interesting. Did nothing special in the morning. Went for a walk, but not far; I was too weak. Before dinner they brought Gusev back.¹⁵⁷ And I couldn't refrain from laughing as they let in Sasha, Dušan and Marya Alexandrovna one by one to see him. He is very excited, but well. [. . .]

11 August In the morning I received a telegram to say that the article about Gusev *will* be published. Then a telegram from *Matin* also about Gusev. Read Kant,¹⁵⁸ and keep thinking about movement and matter, space and time. [. . .]

12 August Got up very early, quite well. Yesterday my article came out, almost in full.¹⁵⁹ In the morning I had some good thoughts both at home and on my walk. Read a little Kant. Received some letters, mostly unpleasant: from the socialist Antonov and from Velikanov.¹⁶⁰ On the other hand there were good ones which moved me very much. Drafted replies. Thank God I didn't send the letter about giving up my property – how weak one is at times!¹⁶¹ [. . .]

13 August Yesterday I read my article through. Alexander Stakhovich and Struve came. Not very interesting and heavy-going, especially Struve. Read *On Science* to them, in vain, and talked in vain. [. . .]

15 August Yesterday evening I was bored. Today, having advised Mashenka to go to mass, I got up at 6 and went to see the priest.¹⁶² A wonderful morning. How much we lose by sleeping late in the morning. Read *Modern Philosophy*.¹⁶³ How artificial and unnecessary. Received some letters, one from Velikanov again, and felt depressed again. Why? A letter from Gusev. He was depressed. Went for a ride with Zosya. Sad. Nothing particularly nasty. [. . .]

16 August Was very bored again all evening. I'm so remote from what all those around me live by. Two workers came, well-to-do, intelligent, socialists. Terrible conceit and narrow-mindedness. No individuality – one isn't a person, one is a party member. After talking to them, I came to a conclusion that has long been suggesting itself and has only now become clear. There are two sorts of people. With some people their thoughts are bound up with their lives. Whether they like it or not they have to do what their thoughts demand, and they cannot go on calmly doing what is contrary to their thoughts: their thoughts rule their lives. With other people the transmission belt has been removed from the fly-wheel, and their thoughts (for the most part other people's) are independent of their lives. The driving forces of these people's lives are animal lusts and worldly fame. To try to prove to these people something that is contrary to their lust and desire for worldly fame is as useless as putting a belt on a small cogwheel only. The wheel turns, and they are glad, and they even boast that their wheel turns faster than the driving wheel.

Today I slept better. But woke up feeling weak, and full of tender emotion.

> And I'm somehow glad at heart
> And still I want to weep,
> How gladly would I rush
> Into the arms of eternity. [. . .]¹⁶⁴

Thought about worldly fame. In this need for people's good opinion about you – for their love – there is something irresistible and legitimate. And it occurred to me now that just as the desire for the praise and love of people in one's lifetime is false and culpable, so is the desire for the continuation of one's life in the souls of other people after one's death good, just and legitimate. In this desire there is nothing to indulge the personality, nothing exclusive; there is only the desire for participation in a common, universal, spiritual life, participation in the work of God, an unselfish, impersonal desire. I think that is right.

20 August Did nothing yesterday except for some short replies to letters.

Went to Ovsyannikovo. Boulanger hasn't arrived yet. A conversation with Tenishev about the single tax.[165] Felt peaceful and tender-hearted. Spent the evening pleasantly with Mikhail Sergeyevich. Still weak.

Today I woke up still weak and mentally jaded. Went to meet the horses and thought on the way about one thing only, and a very important one in practice, namely the fact that I must bore everyone by my incessant writings all the time on one and the same thing (at least it must seem so to the public at large), just as Croft Hiller bores me,[166] and that I ought to keep quiet and get on living; but if I do write, should I want to very much, it should only be something literary for which I often have the urge. And, of course, not for success, but in order to say to a wider audience what I have to say, and to say it not by forcing my work on to people, but by offering it as a challenge. Help me, God. [. . .]

21 August Yesterday I answered some unimportant letters. Went to Telyatinki with Mikhail Sergeyevich and Sasha. A lady with a plan for education. During dinner the Botkins came – it was boring. Talked to Goldenweiser and Nikolayev about the single tax. Today I woke up early; very, very weak. Began reading Pauthier on China.[167] Good, kind letters which I don't deserve. I don't feel like writing anything. [. . .]

24 August [. . .] Read the Gospels; very good. Good feelings too about Gogol. I especially liked the way he is prepared to embrace mankind, but not man.[168] Gusarov[169] came with Dimochka. Had a good talk with Gusarov. [...] Saw Gusarov's wife – how good that she is very ugly. [...]

Dinner as usual. In the evening I read Confucius[170] and had a good long talk with Ivan Ivanovich about editions of book about religions and cheap editions of *For Every Day*.

25 August Got up feeling quite cheerful, went out – and things went wrong from the start. A peasant from Novosil asked for help, and I was in a hurry to go on and spoke unkindly to him. And immediately I felt ashamed. And I was so glad when he overtook me and I spoke to him as a brother and asked his forgiveness. I sat down on the roadside to make a note of something and saw a man and a young girl coming. This time I made no mistake and welcomed him and had a good talk with him. He had seen me on the road and wanted to meet me. He had read a few things, but set store by the Church and said that ceremony was necessary. Then I met a young man, a teacher. Also had quite a good talk. He had come to get advice.

At home I began to compile the first booklet: *for the soul*.[171] There should be twelve books. (1) For the soul. (2) The whole law consists of love. (3) God is in you. (4) Fear sin. (5) Fear temptation. (6) Fear false faith. (7) Only one law for all. (8) True science. (9) True freedom. (10) Life consists of coming closer to God. (11) There is no death. (12) All is good. These are the titles, or something similar. Some not very important letters. An argument with Mashenka about whether there are saints who overcame all human temptations. I was slow to respond, but argued. And that was bad. It was bad too that I read Menshikov's article and had an unpleasant feeling.[172] Note: [...]
(2) Something very important. Although this is very immodest, I can't help writing down that I earnestly beg my friends who collect my notes and letters and note down my words not to attach any importance to what I have deliberately not committed to print. I read Confucius, Lao-Tzu, Buddha (I could say the same about the Gospels too) and see, side by side with profound thoughts linked together into one coherent teaching, the most strange sayings, either uttered fortuitously or else misquoted. And it is precisely these strange and sometimes contradictory thoughts and sayings that are useful to those who are exposed by the teaching. One cannot insist on this often enough. Every man is weak at times and expresses things that are patently stupid, but people write them down and then make much of them, as though they were a most important authority. [...]

26 August [...] I've been busy putting together the other completed parts of *For Every Day*. I'm beginning to think more and more of a literary work about three generations.[173] It could be very good. I'm depressed by what always depresses me. Went for a drive with Dušan. The Tsar is to pass by. They aren't letting people through any more.[174] I'd also like to express my thoughts in a letter to a Polish woman about the crude and blatant nature of violence and deceit.[175] Note:
(1) I thought about how I used to shoot birds and animals, despatch birds with a quill in their heads and hares with a knife in their hearts without the slightest

compassion, and do things which I can't think about now without horror. It's surely the same with people who now judge, imprison, sentence and execute. It's wrong to think that these people know that what they are doing is bad, but yet still do it. Somehow or other they become ignorant of the fact that what they are doing is bad. That was the case with me and the hares. [. . .]

27 August Got up very early. Apart from the *Cycle of Reading*, I read *The Christian Teaching* and thought about a revision of it. [. . .] Noted during the night:

I feel that the attitude of people – the majority – towards me is no longer an attitude towards a man but towards a celebrity, above all a representative of a party or a tendency: either complete devotion and confidence, or, on the contrary, repudiation and hatred. [. . .]

28 August Yesterday evening nothing special happened. I woke up early. Went for a walk. I don't think I made any notes. In the morning Maklakov, Zinger and Semyonov came.[176] I invited Maklakov in and spoke to him about raising the question in the Duma. He said he knew nothing about Henry George, and that the question would not only not get through, but would not even provoke discussion. He is very clever in a practical sense, but completely deaf to all questions really necessary to people – like very, very many people. Finished revising *The Christian Teaching*. I think it's a little better now. Dima,[177] Goldenweiser, Marya Alexandrovna and Ivan Ivanovich came. Dinner, and I felt terribly, terribly sorely depressed. Letters from Berlin apropos of Sofya Andreyevna's letter and articles in the *Petersburg Gazette* which said that Tolstoy was a fraud and a hypocrite contributed to my depression.[178] To my shame I wasn't glad that they abused me, but was hurt. And all evening I was sorely depressed. Should I go away? I ask the question more and more often. Only with Zinger did I have a good and useful conversation about mathematics and higher geometry, and with the naive Mitechka about criminal law. Went to bed very despondent, sad and weak.

31 August Yesterday I was unkind to Seryozha (my son) inwardly, and even in the words I spoke. It's really a *cercle vicieux*; once you're in a bad mood you cease to love people, and the more you allow yourself to stop loving, the worse and worse your mood becomes. [. . .]

Yesterday I dictated to Sasha a letter to Stolypin – I probably won't finish it or send it.[179] This morning a sacristan came, and as soon as I discovered he was a petitioner I refused him and then felt ashamed. Then came a highly interesting man – a thirty-year-old eunuch, a strong man. He asked my opinion about castration, and I couldn't give him convincing proof that it was wrong. Then he spoke to Sasha and was surprised at the luxury of the life which he found me living. [. . .]

Today is 2 September Yesterday morning I went for a walk. Talked a bit to Behrs. The destruction, the *devastation*, of everything spiritual and the replacement of everything necessary by an indiscriminate hodge-podge is nowhere so apparent as in the case of very unintelligent people. I wrote a letter to the Polish woman. Quite good, I think. The man from Kiev and Muller came again,[180] and it hurt me to listen to the Kiev man's story of how he had met a peasant woman whose horse had been impounded and who was asked to pay a rouble, and how she abused me and all of us, calling us devils and fiends. 'They just sit and stuff themselves, the devils . . .' He also spoke of the fact that the peasants are convinced that I own everything and am a crafty customer, hiding behind my wife. It hurt me very much, to my shame. I even tried to justify myself. Then I went for a ride with Sasha and made inquiries about it on the way. Yes, it's an ordeal, I must endure it. And it's for my good. However, it was only today that I felt and understood that it's for my good, and then not entirely.

Dinner. Goldenweiser played very well. Ivan Ivanovich. Yes, yesterday I dictated to Sasha a letter to Dundukova. Met some revolutionaries on my walk returning from exile. Had a cordial talk with them.

Didn't sleep much today, but feel fresh. No sooner had I gone out than I met a woman who had had two cows impounded, and they still hadn't been released after two days. I was very depressed. But I'm better today. I acknowledge it to be an ordeal sent for my good, to liberate me from vanity.

During the night and in the morning I was overcome by a state of coldness never experienced, I think, before, a state of doubt about everything, above all about God, about the correctness of my understanding of the meaning of life. I didn't believe in myself, yet couldn't summon up the consciousness by which I lived and still live. Only this morning did I come to my senses and return to life. It's all a punishment for the unkind, unloving feelings to which I sank in the preceding days. And serve me right. However strange it is to say so: knowledge of God only comes through love. Love is the only organ for coming to know Him. [. . .]

Today is 3 September [. . .] The cinephotographers came, despite my refusal.[181] I let them photograph, but without my cooperation. [. . .]

4 September, Moscow We arrived safely yesterday.[182] I've waited a long time. It would have been good on the journey if it hadn't been for the curiosity and flattery – irritating and corrupting – of the passengers. Arrived safely. Spiro: I spoke too harshly to him about Sytin.[183] The dear Chertkovs, then Ivan Ivanovich. I was glad that relations were good between them, as they ought to be. Towards evening I felt very weak. Slept well. Went for a walk round town. Very strong impressions made by children. Oh, how good a literary description would be, not for myself, but as a service. [. . .] I walked along the streets and was horrified at the debauchery – no, not the debauchery, but the obvious lack of any moral, religious, restraining principle. Yet many, many people cross themselves as they walk past churches. Note: [. . .]

(1) However arrogant and self-assured it is, I can't help thinking and noting down for myself that I need to remember in my intercourse with people that with the vast majority of them I stand on such a high point in my outlook on the world that I have to come down often and very far for any intercourse to be possible between us. [. . .]

5 September, Kryokshino We went to Zimmermann's. The music was very good.[184]

Then I walked along Kuznetsky Bridge, then on the train there were demonstrations of sympathy – food for vanity – temptation. But I didn't yield too much. We arrived at Kryokshino. A great joy to see everyone. Everyone was cheerful and kind, to say nothing of their attitude towards me. I felt very unwell towards evening.

6 September   Alive. Woke up early. Went for a walk. Wrote quite well to the Polish lady. Noted one or two things in my book, and forgot one or two good things. Peasants from Kryokshino came and brought the 'Mignon' from Zimmermann's. Dined with everyone and listened to music. I'll go for a ride. [. . .]

8 September   Yesterday night I lost a lot of blood. At first I felt bad, but slept well and am quite cheerful. Went for a walk. Sonya is coming at 2 o'clock, which I'm very glad about. Revised my letter to the Polish lady for the last time, I think. [. . .]

Did little work. Listened to music. Many people came: three young peasants, one an evangelical, as persistent as ever. I had a pleasant chat with them. Then another young peasant, very serious. In the evening I read about peasant administration to Kalachov, and *To a Polish Lady* and a story by Chekhov to our folk.[185] [. . .]

9 September   Slept little. Went out early. Felt very good at heart. Everything moved me. A meeting with a Kaluga peasant. Made a note of it separately.[186] It was only touching for me, I think. Then I met a carter, and another one on foot; there was anger and hatred on both their faces because I'm a master. How depressing! How I would like to escape from it all. But obviously it will be like this till I die. At home I made a note of the meeting, then looked over *To a Polish Lady* and finished it, and then Lao-Tzu – also finished it.[187] Inserted something in my paper.[188] And now I'm finishing writing my diary. [. . .]

11 September   I'm well. Wrote down a conversation with the peasants.[189] [. . .]

12 September   [. . .] Intensive inner work continuing. Went riding with the Chertkovs. In the evening some peasants from Vyazyomy came. The eldest one was very clever. He spoke well about the terrible discontent among the uneducated people. The Tsar and the peasants – everything else will be wiped off the face of the earth. [. . .]

13 September   Still well. Got up late. Thought about what to say to the teachers.[190] But couldn't think about that or anything else. And wrote nothing all morning. Went out, and there were many people there: Dimochka, old Solomakhin and his son, then some ladies and a man wanted to kiss my hand. Then Chertkov's cinematograph and Tapsell,[191] then a whole mass of people: Sonya Ilyushina, musicians, Goldenweiser and his wife, Sibor, Mogilevsky, Tishchenko and many, many more I didn't know. Sonya hurt her leg and is in great pain. At home a treat for the peasants, about two hundred people. Chertkov *suffit à tout* [makes up for everything] . . . (that's for him). Then more folk. Had dinner. Letters of little interest. Didn't manage to sleep before dinner. They played trios by Arensky, Beethoven, and Haydn magnificently. [. . .]

14 September [. . .] Wrote a lot for the teachers and revised the conversation between a passer-by and a peasant. The Solomakhins and their wives and Lineva and her husband arrived;[192] had lunch and am going for a walk. It's gone 2.

Children and their teachers came from Khamovniki. Sonya is better. Slept a lot. After supper some songs by Lineva. Then two peasants from Vyazyomy. Then the teachers, a good, serious talk with them till late at night. Yes, and Klechkovsky[193] was here too. And in spite of his kindness, an unkind conversation with him on my part.

15 September [. . .] Note: [. . .]
(2) Everyone knows and everyone has remarked on those strange dreams which end with the sleeper being woken up by some external influence: either a knock or a noise or a touch or a fall; and furthermore this noise that actually happens, or the jolt or whatever, assumes in one's dreams the character of a final impression after the many others which, as it were, prepared the way for it. I remember, for example, the following dream: I arrived at my brother's house and met him on the steps with his rifle and dog. He invited me to go hunting with him; I said I didn't have a gun. He said that instead of a gun I could take, for some reason, a clarinet. I wasn't surprised, and went hunting with him through the familiar places, but we came by way of these familiar places to the sea (I wasn't surprised at that either). Boats were sailing on the sea, but they were really swans. My brother said 'Shoot'. I did as he wished, put the clarinet to my mouth, but couldn't blow at all. Then he said: 'Well, I will', and he fired. And the shot was so loud that I woke up in bed and saw that what had been the shot was really the noise of the screen opposite the window which had been blown down by the wind and fallen over. We all know such dreams, and are surprised how the thing that had just happened and woken us up could have been prepared for in our dream by everything we had dreamed about beforehand, and which had led up to this momentary event that had just happened.

This illusion of time has, in my opinion, a very important significance, namely this, that time does not exist, and that we imagine everything to take place in time because this is the nature of our mind. Exactly the same illusion is present in what we call real life, only with this difference that we wake up from life in death. Only then shall we know and be convinced that what was real in life was what was asleep and woke up in death.

What happened to you and what you thought you did in this life were just the same as happens to the man who is asleep and has dreams. The result of this is that just as when a man is asleep time does not exist for him, i.e. it's all the same to the sleeper whether he sleeps for one hour or a hundred, so for the man who lives in this world time does not exist. He is always living in the present.

It's very difficult to express all this, but there is something here and it's very important.

17 September Got up feeling cheerful. Met the photographer and cinematographer.¹⁹⁴ What was also unpleasant, was that this makes me aware of myself, not as a creature of God's, but as loathsome Lev Nikolayevich. Made one or two notes on the way. Talked to Chertkov about the children's intention of appropriating the works that were made public property. I simply can't believe it. [. . .]

At home the unpleasant news that Sonya was upset by the suggestion of travelling to Moscow separately. Went to see her. I'm very sorry for her; poor woman, she is ill and weak. I didn't entirely calm her down, but then she spoke so nicely and kindly, took pity and said 'forgive me'. I rejoiced and was deeply moved. [. . .]

18 September Didn't sleep much. Went for a walk. I didn't want to say goodbye to the musicians, felt conscience-stricken, came back, spoke stupidly and awkwardly and felt ashamed and went out. Almost lost my way again. Chertkov came again. At home I've just added something to the first conversation and want to revise the second.¹⁹⁵

The fuss and bother of departure. I want to go home. However nice it is for me here, I want peace and quiet. [. . .]

20 September, Yasnaya Polyana Had a good journey. Had a walk round. The cinematographer and photographers pursued me. In Moscow I was recognised and greeted – it was both pleasant and unpleasant, because it aroused bad feelings of conceit. Dinner, a quiet evening. Dunayev, Semyonov, Maklakov. Went to the cinematograph.¹⁹⁶ Very bad.

Woke up today at 10 o'clock feeling very weak. A lot of letters. Two very abusive ones. Wrote a letter to the newspapers about the abusive letters.¹⁹⁷ Twice went for walks. Weak. I'm thinking all the time – and well – about a letter to the Tsar and a meeting with him; I think I will write. [. . .]

24 September Didn't sleep much. Had a walk. Wrote a letter to an Indian, and received a pleasant letter from an Indian in the Transvaal.¹⁹⁸ The letter to the Indian is very weak.¹⁹⁹ Maude came.²⁰⁰ This interest that people show in me is tiresome. Cinematographers. Andryusha's arguments yesterday about how profitable the ownership of estates has become astonished me by their naive insensitivity: corn and rye are twice as expensive, labour is 20 per cent cheaper. Wonderful. [. . .]

25 and 26 September I'll go back. It's now 8 o'clock in the evening of the 26th. Had a pleasant, peaceful walk among the fir trees. Before that I had a chat with dear P. I. Biryukov who has just come, and before that I wrote quite a lot: *Anarchism*.²⁰¹ I don't know whether anything will come of it and whether I'll publish it. For the first time today for many days I wrote enthusiastically. Before that I read letters. Waking up at first was unpleasant because of the news Berkenheim told me that a fugitive had come from Gusev. Berkenheim himself attended to him, and when I went to look for him he had gone. In the morning I walked round the garden. On the 25th, in the evening, I had a good talk with Maude. He's sorry about his break with Chertkov, and probably feels he's not entirely justified, but it's good that Chertkov doesn't accuse him of anything.[202] Went for a long ride – to Goryushino. Did nothing all morning. Wrote a letter to the Indian.[203] Started writing *A Conversation* but gave it up.[204] Maude is translating the letters to the Indians. That's all. [. . .]

27 and 28 September [. . .] Note: [. . .]
(1) I'm thinking about a letter to the Tsar about the land, something of the very first importance I think, and at the same time the thought is running through my mind about what to say to Sofya Andreyevna about Ilya Vasilyevich's wish to have an increase in salary. The one thing is the good of the Russian people, to be discussed with the Tsar; the other: an increase in salary for a man-servant. But the second is more important than the first because the second requires my participation and decision, while the first is entirely my own affair. [. . .]

29 and 30 September I didn't go downstairs on the 29th; did some writing and wrote a great deal more of *Anarchism*. I think it's not bad. [. . .]

30th Woke up early. Eight beggars. I felt they were human beings, but couldn't deal with them humanely. Taras; had a good talk with him. Then settled down to work, to *A Conversation*, and wrote a lot, and, I think, quite well. Boulanger came, and I talked to him about Confucius.[205] [. . .]

5, 6, 7 and today, 8 October Yesterday, the 7th. I felt very bad. In the morning I walked to the forester's, and talked to Goldenblat about the Telyatinki peasants.[206] At home I did nothing. Read Andreyev and Chelyshev who are both coming.[207] [. . .]

9 October Yesterday Chelyshev came. A combination of intelligence, vanity and play-acting, and a peasant's common sense, independence and subordination. I can't describe him, but he's very interesting. Talked a lot. His idea about exerting influence on Europe by controlling exports and at the same time handing over to the peasants those commercial advantages which are now in the hands of the merchants is a very intelligent one. It's a crude, antireligious, patriotic idea, but it could be linked up with the single tax. I gave him a letter for Nikolayev. [. . .]

10 October [. . .] In the evening Ilya came. He has the same lack of higher interests as all my sons. But never mind.
  Dušan is ill. I went to see him. He was as gentle and calm as ever. I did nothing except some unimportant letters. Went to meet Sasha. Broke some stones and had a good talk with a father and son from Yasenki. In the evening I read Andreyev. I got the same very definite impression. The early stories are good, the latest ones beneath criticism.[208] Nothing to note, I think. A tiresome petitioner came. I treated

him badly at first, but managed all right later. Generally speaking I can't train myself to remember God when I'm in people's company. I remember afterwards. I'll learn.

14 October I've missed two days and haven't noticed it at all: I've been so weak these last days. I seem to be a bit more lively today, but did nothing in the morning except altering my reply to Struve,[209] and doing a few letters. Reading Andreyev made me think more vividly about literary work. I'd like to, but there's no irresistible need. The day before yesterday, the 10th, I think, I revised *A Conversation* for the last time, wrote a few letters and went for a walk. It's turned cold. Nobody came. Read Andreyev and don't remember anything worth noting. A boy came; he didn't ask for anything at first and I pressed a rouble on him, and he came back the next day to ask for fourteen roubles. I don't remember any great deviations. I'm beginning to get used to being on my guard in my associations with people. Yesterday, the 13th. Got up still feeling weak, wrote a venomous note in reply to Struve's article, and also some letters. Went for a walk. Very weak. Finished Andreyev. His denominator is disproportionately big compared with his numerator. Note: [. . .]
(2) A work of art is only real when the person perceiving it cannot imagine anything different from what he actually sees or hears or understands; when he experiences a feeling similar to recollection – that this thing has already happened, and happened many times, that he has known it for a long time but has been unable to say it, and now somebody has expressed this very thing for him. And above all, when he feels that what he hears or sees or understands cannot be otherwise, but must be just as he perceives it. [. . .]
(3) There are bipartite arts: music, drama, partly painting, in which the thought – the purpose of art – and its execution are separated: in music, composition and performance; similarly in drama – the writing of a play and its performance; partly too in painting, and in plastic art generally, the intention and the performance; and entirely so with illustration. And it is in these bipartite arts that false art is most commonly encountered: false, empty thought and wonderful execution by musicians or actors or painters. It's especially so in drama and music. There are dramatists (Andreyev is one of them) and composers who, without bothering about the content, significance, novelty or truthfulness of their drama or musical composition, think only about its performance, and adapt their works to the appropriateness and the impact of that performance. [. . .]

Went for a very pleasant ride. After dinner I read the *Vedic Magazine*.[210] I ought to write a letter of thanks to the Indian for his wonderful exposition of Maya. [. . .] Late in the evening I played duets with Sofya Andreyevna. My hands won't work properly.

[. . .]*16 October* Semyonov came, and he persuaded me that I couldn't refuse the phonograph recording that I had promised.[211] It was very unpleasant for me. I had to agree. Received an abusive letter apropos of the conversation with Chelyshev that *one must* hang and go on hanging. I wrote a letter to the papers, but then thought about it and didn't send it.²¹² Enjoyed being with Semyonov. He's intelligent and has an original, peasant-style, i.e. good education. Then a Polish woman came, a doctor from Paris.²¹³ At first I found her scientific attitude and her *Hygiène morale* funny, but later I saw in her an intelligent woman. She and Semyonov enumerated the outstanding writers, and their name is legion, but what about the second – and third-rate? What a nasty and futile occupation. [...]

In the evening six people came with the gramophone and phonograph. It was very depressing. I couldn't refuse and I had to prepare something as best I could. [...]

19 October [...] Went for a long ride with Ivan. In the evening Andrey and his family came. I can put up with them more easily. Read *Russian Thought*: *The White Horse*, *The Birch Tree* and some poems. Without exaggeration: a madhouse; yet I value the opinion of these readers and writers.²¹⁴ Shame on you, Lev Nikolayevich.

20 October Slept a lot; weak. Had some good thoughts; I'll make a few notes. But during the day I did nothing except the *Cycle of Reading* and some letters. But even that is good if it's done in His sight. No, I did revise the conversation with the teachers a bit more. Ivan Ivanovich came and brought the books that have come out and some plans for new ones. It's pleasant to work with him. Dreamed very vividly of Gusev and wrote to him. Then a quite drab and bloated peasant from the Voronezh province came specially to see me. He smokes and drinks too, and condemns everybody, and denounces the clergy, but he's original and I liked him very much. He took some books and a photograph and went away. Yes, the only hope is in them, if one can allow oneself hopes and thoughts about the future. I can't [...]

Yes, I forgot to note: an unpleasant conversation with Sofya Andreyevna apropos of the Circassian and the attempted robbery at Taptykovo.²¹⁵ I could have been more gentle. But never mind. [...] Sofya Andreyevna is just leaving.

21 October Sofya Andreyevna came back yesterday, frightened by a car abandoned on the road.²¹⁶ I didn't sleep much, but had some good thoughts on my walk. Friedman came,²¹⁷ I don't need him. Began writing *Notes of a Priest*. It could be very good. Perhaps I'll finish it.²¹⁸ I'd like to do so, and also *Notes of a Manservant*.²¹⁹ [...]

I've just been talking to Sasha. She was telling me about the greediness of the children and their counting on my writings which will come to them after my death, and consequently counting on my death too. How I pity them. I gave up all my property to them in my life-time so that they should not be tempted to wish for my death, and still my death is what they wish for. Yes, yes, yes. How unfortunate are people, i.e. creatures endowed with reason and the gift of speech, when they use both the one and the other in order to live like animals. That's bad, I'm passing judgement on them. If they live like that it means they can't do otherwise. But I am passing judgement. Yes, I would like some literary work. One can express everything and unburden oneself without condemning anyone. [...]

22 October Woke up early. Dušan came with the news that there was a violinist and his wife here. I went downstairs. Probably a Jew; he wanted to play. I left it to my daughters to decide. They refused.[220] [. . .]

Wrote nothing. Revised the conversation[221] a little. Went for a ride with Dušan. Before dinner Sasha came in to announce that they had all returned – the musicians and Friedman. What could I do? They didn't seem very sympathetic. A Catholic priest and a Frenchman came to dinner. The Frenchman flattered me grossly. The priest, obviously, doesn't believe, but wants to convince himself. A sophist of his own traditions. And he doesn't need my opinion, but he needs to express his own opinion to me. Then the musicians began to play. Magnificent. He's of gipsy origin. I was particularly moved by a *Nocturne* of Chopin's.[222] And they turned out to be very nice people.

23 October Slept well. I still want to write. Went for a walk. Weak. A pain in the small of my back. Came back, didn't feel like it at first, but then wrote down my dream about Henry George.[223] Not entirely good, but not entirely bad either. [. . .] Note:
(1) One of the main reasons for the narrowness of the people of our intellectual world is their pursuit of the contemporary, their effort to find out about, or at least to have some idea of what has been written recently. 'We mustn't miss anything.' Yet mountains of books are written in every field. And they are all accessible, because of ease of communication. Whatever subject one talks about people say: 'But have you read Chelpanov, Kun, Breding? If you haven't, you can't talk about it!' And you must hurry up and read them. And there are mountains of them. And this haste, this stuffing one's head with the contemporary, trivial and confused as it is, excludes any possibility of serious, true, necessary knowledge. How obvious the mistake is, you would think. We have the results of the thoughts of the greatest thinkers who have stood out from milliards and milliards of people in the course of thousands of years, and these results of the thinking of these great people have been sifted through the sieve of time. All that is mediocre has been discarded, and only the original, the profound, the necessary is left; what is left are the religious faiths, Zoroaster, Buddha, Lao-Tzu, Confucius, Mencius, Christ, Mohammed, Socrates, Marcus Aurelius, Epictetus and the moderns: Rousseau, Pascal, Kant, Schopenhauer and many others. And the people who try to keep up with the contemporary don't know any of this, but go on trying to keep up with it and stuff their heads with chaff and rubbish, which will all be sifted out and none of it will remain. [. . .]

24 October [. . .] Read Gorky.[224] Neither one thing nor the other. [. . .]

25 October Yesterday evening I read Gorky's *Philistines*. It's worthless. Got up today feeling just as weak. Went for a walk; I can only walk with difficulty. Read *For Every Day*, the little *Intermediary* booklets, and my letters. Didn't start on anything – I'm so weak. But I'm well at heart. Zinger came, and I had a good talk with him about physics generally, then read about physics in Brockhaus[225] and found confirmation of my thoughts about the triviality of 'science' and physics with its hypotheses about ether, atoms and molecules. [. . .]

All physics (as all the other natural sciences too) has only one basis – the study of the laws of getting to know objects by means of the external senses. The basic sense is the sense of touch, subdivided into its varieties: sight, hearing, smell and taste. The first two have been investigated. The others are not worth mentioning.

That which ought to be the basis of all knowledge, if not the only object of knowledge – the teaching of morality – has become for some people an object not devoid of interest, and for the majority of 'educated people' an unnecessary fantasy of backward, uneducated people.

26 October Didn't get to sleep until 3, and felt miserable, but didn't succumb entirely. Woke up late. Sofya Andreyevna has returned. I'm glad to see her, but she's very agitated. Yesterday I found a letter from Leonid Semyonov. Today I had a more brisk walk. Wrote letters to Leonid, Koni, Tolstoy and Nazhivin. Strakhov came. Did nothing in the morning. A good letter from Chertkov. He tells me more clearly what I thought myself. The conversation with Strakhov was painful on account of Chertkov's demands, because it's necessary to have dealings with the government. I think I'll decide everything in the most simple and natural way – Sasha. I want to include the earlier ones too, up to 82.[226] [. . .]

Evening. Another conversation with Strakhov. I agreed. But I regret that I didn't say that all this is very painful to me, and the best thing would be – doing nothing.

1 November I certainly didn't think that I'd missed two days. Yesterday Leonid[227] returned. He moves me very much by his serious religiosity. I feel that he prays almost every minute. Didn't write anything. Zosya Stakhovich came. Answered a few letters and read Ramakrishna.[228] Weak. In the evening I almost said goodbye to Leonid. The day before yesterday was almost the same, or else I've forgotten. Mikhail Sergeyevich is alien to me. Yes, Seryozha came to dinner – he too, unfortunately, is alien. Today Goldenweiser and Strakhov came and brought the papers from Chertkov. I altered them all.[229] [. . .]

I forgot; the day before yesterday I had a very interesting trip to the district court. [. . .]

2 November Slept well, but I'm still weak. I think I'm played out as a writer of literary works. I can't concentrate on one thing. But there's a lot I want to do. Yesterday I did nothing except letters. Had quite a frivolous chat at table. A pleasant evening with Bulygin, Strakhov and Goldenweiser. Today I wrote some letters as well and read *The Horrors of Christian Civilisation*.[230] Not as good as I expected – too narrow. But splendid as far as the form. [. . .]

4 November Missed yesterday. Did no work yesterday; read and marked passages in the Lama's book. Very powerful. Tried to write a foreword – it was no good.[231] [. . .]

On the evening of the 2nd something very important happened. I spoke about the fact that, if I went to Kryokshino, Chertkov had promised to arrange my passage through Moscow so that no one would see me. Sofya Andreyevna suddenly lost control of herself. It was very painful. Thank God – I refrained from evil. I kissed her as I said goodbye, and very much wanted to do something particularly pleasant for her. I understand life's greatest joy – paying back evil with good – but I only understand it, and I couldn't do anything that evening or the next day. I could only restrain myself when speaking, but in my heart there was *rancune*. [. . .] Note: [. . .]

(3) People often ask me in letters, is it good, or is it necessary to get married? I think this answer will clearly express what I think and feel about this question:

It is always better to refrain if you can – destroy the sex in yourself if you can, i.e. be a human being, not a man or a woman. That's the first thing. But if a man cannot and is unable to see in women his sisters, or a woman to see in men her brothers – if sexual feelings violate the main thing in life, a brotherly, spiritual and loving attitude towards all people without distinction – then marry and bind yourself inseparably for life to one person, trying, of course, to find in that one person you bind yourself to the greatest possible agreement with your own understanding of life, and if you enter into that sort of sexual relationship, you must know that you are thereby taking upon yourself the obligation to raise and bring up children – the natural consequence and justification of marriage.

5 November Yesterday I went for a ride with Zosya. In the evening I read some books on the Hindu faith. One excellent book on the meaning of life[232] [. . .]

Wrote my impressions of the recruits who were setting off – weak.[233] [. . .]

7 November Yesterday morning I received a wonderful letter from Polilov about Henry George and replied to him,[234] and something else that was pleasant too – Tolstoy's pedagogics in Bulgarian.[235] Revised *The Recruits*. It turned out quite well. [. . .] After dinner I read Gorky – weak. He lacks the main thing – a sense of proportion; his denominator is too big.

9, 10 November In the evening I read Gorky.[236] A knowledge of the lowest strata of the people, and wonderful language, i.e. the idiom of the people. But a completely arbitrary and quite unjustified psychology – i.e. the attribution of feelings and thoughts to his characters – which gets more and more heroic, and then an exclusively immoral milieu. And on top of that a slavish respect for science.

Yesterday, the 9th. I walked round the garden, then wrote a great deal, relatively speaking, of *A Dream*, and some letters too. *A Dream* could be quite good. Relations with the family are pleasant, peaceful and loving. I still can't overcome my interest in other people's opinion of me. Went to Telyatinki with Dušan. Talked to Alexey about the murder of a man.[237] Less interesting than I expected. Sleep, dinner, reading Gorky. [. . .]

Had a good journey. It was pleasant at Marya Alexandrovna's. At home in the evening I finished reading Gorky. All imaginary, unnatural and tremendously heroic feelings, and falseness. But a great talent. And yet, like Andreyev, he has nothing to say. They ought to write poetry, or – as Andreyev has also chosen to do – dramas. With poetry the permissible obscurity would save them, with drama the setting and the actors. It was the same with Chekhov, but there's a comic strain in him.

In the evening things were unpleasant, and I was wrong not to have spoken out about *A Captive in the Caucasus* and *Polikushka*, about making them public property.[238]

11 November Slept well till 5, then couldn't sleep, and only dropped off towards morning. Had a splendid walk. But did not work. I'm thinking about an article about unemployed people, suggesting organising aid for them.[239] It would be good. [. . .]

12 November [. . .] A wonderful story by Sonya about rescuing a girl on the Khodynka;[240] [. . .]

Today is 17 November Was very weak and lay in bed till 12. Got up, read the letters, a theosophy journal, the paper, and, as usual, *For Every Day* in the three editions. In the morning I wrote down something for *The Wisdom of Children*, not entirely good. And began writing about the government. I didn't finish, but I intend to complete it.[241] [. . .]

18 November [. . .] A peasant from Telyatinki came. His son had been conscripted as a soldier and was to be tried for saying that icons were wooden boards. I'd very much like to write about it, but I'm trying to do too much. [. . .] Yes, I received an abusive letter with an article of Menshikov's: *an old buffoon*.[242] And to my shame, it distressed me. But I'm all right now, I've got over it.

19 November Alive. Slept little, but am agreeably excited. But did absolutely no work again. First I received twenty-eight letters, secondly dear Gusarov came to say goodbye, and thirdly I'd written something more down during the night about consciousness and was correcting it. Received a second and third letter censuring me for the article on science, and all from the same type of people: people who 'believe' in science like a religion, who have made it their ideal to master this science, who have achieved a certain degree of mastery over it and suddenly . . . an unbeliever ventures to deny this one and only sacred object. Apart from that, they are all party people. Then it would also appear that the article plays into the hands of *The Union of the Russian People*, that it's contrary to the programme, etc.[243] [. . .]

20 November The musicians came.[244] I was sorry I invited them. It's all very artificial. Even the elegantly artificial return to the past. They are all Frenchmen, very nice, flattering people, and Goldenweiser. The music excites me very much physically. Worried absurdly about my French. [. . .]

Today is 21 November Dreamed about yesterday's musicians. I'm still not sleeping much and am tearful. In the morning a girl came from Moscow with some questions.

The poor girl is seeking, but youth and lust tell in the form of falling in love; then Lopatin, a nice man who went to prison because of me, came just to thank me.²⁴⁵ [...]

23 November Missed out yesterday. Got up in good spirits. A passer-by, a nice man, admitted with his first words that drink was the culprit. There are very many like him, probably the majority. In the morning I was busy with letters, then got down to the foreword to *For Every Day*, and it turned out to be a great deal of work. [...]

Yesterday I read the indictment against Gorbunov.²⁴⁶ It's a terrible, astounding thing. *C'est le cas ou jamais de dire* [Now if ever is the time to speak]. I cannot be silent. It's just as uncontrollable as coughing during a concert. [...]

Read about Gorky after dinner. And it's strange, I have an unfriendly feeling towards him, which I struggle against. I try to justify myself by the fact that, like Nietzsche, he is a harmful writer: a great talent and a lack of any religious convictions – i.e. convictions which comprehend the meaning of life – and at the same time a self-assurance bolstered up by our 'educated' world, which sees in him its exponent, and which is infecting this world more and more. For example his saying: 'If you believe in God, God exists; if you don't believe in God, He doesn't exist.' A vile saying, but all the same it made me think hard.²⁴⁷ Does the God in Himself about whom I speak and write exist? It's true, one can say of that God: 'If you believe in Him, He exists.' And I always thought so. And for that reason in Christ's words 'love *God* and your neighbour', love of God has always seemed to me superfluous, incompatible with love of one's neighbour; incompatible because love of one's neighbour is so clear, clearer than anything can be, while love of God on the contrary is very unclear. You can accept that He exists, this God in Himself, that's true, but can you love Him? This is where I encounter what I have often experienced – the slavish acceptance of the words of the Gospel.

God is love – that is so. We know Him only because we love Him; but that God in Himself exists is a rationalisation, and often a superfluous and even harmful one. If I am asked: 'Does God in Himself exist?' I am bound to say and I will say 'yes, probably, but I don't understand anything about Him, this God in Himself'. But it isn't so with the God of love. Him I know for certain. He is everything for me, the explanation and the purpose of my life. [...]

25 November [...]Read some Dostoyevsky and *L'immolé*.²⁴⁸ The folly of life generally, and Russian life in particular is becoming more and more clear to me, and I think I'll soon be ready to express my thoughts about it. [...]

Walked round the garden and the pond. Daniel and A. Sergeyenko came.²⁴⁹ Slept heavily. Had dinner and spoke English with difficulty. Daniel is a clever, cold person. [...]

28 November [...] It was difficult with Daniel because of my lack of knowledge, or rather my half knowledge of the language. [...] Read *L'immolé* in the evening. It's interesting, the seriousness attached to Catholicism. [...]

29 November Got up in very good spirits. Before getting dressed I began working on the foreword to *For Every Day*. Went out – there was a woman there; I wanted to refuse her from a bad habit of mine. It turned out, on the contrary, a joyful occasion.[250] I'll try to describe it elsewhere. [. . .]

30 November I'm only writing my diary so as not to neglect it. There's nothing to write, and I've no wish to. Got up feeling tired. Petitioners came about their goods being sold to pay taxes.[251] Worked a little bit on the foreword. Went to Novaya Kolpna. There the clerk told me how the taxes are collected. Andrey came. I couldn't bring myself to speak lovingly to him. I wasn't kind at home either, although I didn't do anything bad. Had dinner without Andrey. Read *L'immolé*. The description of the miracle performed by the Lourdes Mother of God is astonishing. Read about Rousseau in the lexicon.[252] A professor 'examined and condemned him'. The folly of people horrifies me more and more. [. . .]

1 December In the morning I walked to Kurnosenkova's and dropped in at Shintyakov's.[253] The condition of the bare-bellied children at Kurnosenkova's is dreadful. I very much want to write *Three Days in the Country*. Worked on the foreword. A letter about the property transferred to my wife distressed me very much, to my shame. [. . .]

3 December Missed out yesterday. Walked to the village to see the headman. The petitioners are cheating me. Everything is just as wretched. Worked well on the foreword. I think I've finished it. Walked to the skating rink. Admired Sasha (when you copy this, remember that I want to admire in you the same sort of spiritual energy). [. . .] Note four things:
(1) To be an artist of the word, one has to have the faculty of rising to the heights and falling to the depths spiritually. Then all the intermediate stages are known, and one can live in the imagination, live the life of people who stand on the various rungs.
(2) I don't like it, and even consider it bad poetically speaking to treat religious, philosophical and ethical questions in a literary or dramatic manner, as in Goethe's *Faust*, etc. One should either say nothing about these questions, or only speak with the greatest caution and attention, without rhetorical phrases, and – God have mercy upon us – without rhyme. [. . .]

I don't want to be a Christian, as I wouldn't advise, and wouldn't want people to be Brahmins, Buddhists, Confucianists, Taoists, Mohammedans, etc. We must all find, each in his own faith, what is common to all, renounce what is exclusive to one's own and hold on to what is common. [. . .]

6 December [. . .] In the evening Dušan brought round *Anarchism* with his observations. The last one is very true that the ending is weak, and I took it into consideration and revised it, but still came to the conclusion not to publish it.[254] It's a bad article – there's no need for it.

9 December [. . .] Yesterday evening I read Posse.²⁵⁵ Got up not too late this morning, health better. Beautiful weather. Worthless letters. Revised the addition to *On Science*, began to revise *Conversation at Dinner*,²⁵⁶ but didn't finish it. [. . .]

12 December [. . .] Revised *A Dream*. There's still some work to do on it. But this form could be successful. [. . .]

13 December [. . .] Something interesting happened today, something very helpful in freeing me from my concern for worldly fame: I was sent an article from the *Russian Standard* which speaks about me being a preacher of 'materialism' (*sic*), who denies everything spiritual,²⁵⁷ and in James' book it is said that I'm a melancholic, close to mental illness.²⁵⁸ It's very helpful; I can feel the good influence already. [. . .]

14 December Woke up with a cold, and it got worse and worse until it became an extraordinary fit of shivering, then a temperature of 42°, and I forgot everything. During the night I dreamed about Andrey, some doctor or other and Boulanger. Was bad all night, but recovered and feel as well at heart as I could wish. I don't need to make an effort to love everyone. True, it's easy when one is surrounded only by those who love you. [. . .]

Was ill the whole evening. Sofya Andreyevna arrived. It's very unpleasant. I simply can't put up with it patiently. And I still feel no less weakly what I felt three days ago that I am a worker, and only need His approval, which I always know of in my heart, and know when I don't deserve it. Read James' book. A wrong attitude to the subject – a scientific one. Oh, all this science!

16 December A very bad night again. Insomnia and heartburn. Got up; had an interesting conversation with Nikitin about medicine. [. . .]

Had a little dinner with all of them. Read a Japanese book.²⁵⁹ It's remarkable, the patently naive corruption of the people for their own ends by means of the monopoly of the influence of education. It's the same with us, only not so openly. [. . .]

17 December [. . .] Looked through and wrote the ending to *Pauperism and the People*.²⁶⁰ Not bad. Read Menshikov's article about the *Cycle of Reading*.²⁶¹ It's just like the article in the *Russian Standard* about my materialism: he has a command of language, even the talent of a writer, and that's partly the reason why these people don't think about things at all, aren't afraid of falsehood, aren't even interested in the question whether what they write is true or false. And that's very reassuring. [. . .]

18 December Ivan Ivanovich is being tried today.²⁶² The craziness of our life is becoming more and more incomprehensible, and my powerlessness to express my understanding of it more evident. Got up late. Went for a walk. A teacher's wife came, a pathetic woman. I wasn't deceived by her. At home I did nothing except letters. Read Smetana.[263] It's good. A peasant from Saratov came, an old man. He'd sold his horse to come and have a heart-to-heart talk. [...]

19 December Got up in quite good spirits. Again, to my great joy, I felt a strong and reassuring awareness of my being a worker. [...]

Went for a walk and a ride with the visitor from Saratov. All is still well. He wants to go over to 'my' faith, and I try to explain to him that there isn't such a thing as 'my' faith. He told me a terrible story about murder and execution.

Slept. After dinner I read an empty 'scientific' book by Guyau.[264] A pity about the money, two and a half roubles, and my wasted evening. Read *Conversation with a Passer-by* to the Saratov peasant as he was about to leave. It's good. Had a walk in the morning and thought that it's time to give up writing for deaf 'educated people'. I must write for the *grand monde* – the people. And I jotted down about ten articles: (1) on drunkenness, (2) on swearing, (3) on family dissensions, (4) on sharing out property, (5) on cupidity, (6) on truthfulness, (7) on fisticuffs and beatings, (8) on women and respect for them, (9) on compassion for animals, (10) on a clean life in the towns, (11) on forgiveness.[265] [...]

20 December Went for a walk. Met a wretched Cossack; he said he had been exiled for distributing my books. I gave him some books. [...]

21 December Got up late, a snow-storm, walked a bit. Thank God, I'm loathsome and worthless to the last degree. *A Dream* is vile.

I've discarded everything and left just the dream. [...]

23 December Many petitioners. Bulgakov came; he's compiled an account of my outlook on the world.[266] I revised both articles again and answered letters. An unpleasant letter from some workers.[267] I couldn't be indifferent to it. Said goodbye to Marya Alexandrovna. Went to Demenka. Terrible poverty. Slept. After dinner I read Bulgakov's work. It's poor on the whole – not his work, but mine.

25 December, evening. Yesterday evening I read Epictetus.[268] Played cards. Got up late today. Didn't get to sleep last night until 3. Letters: one reproachful one about handing over my property to my wife. Wrote a reply. I don't think it was bad. Revised *A Dream* again. It's a bit better. Drowsiness and weakness. A strange feeling. I'm experiencing something special, new and complex, which I'd like to express. And preferably as something literary and figurative. Read *A Sentimental Journey*. It reminded me of my youth and the demands of art.[269] [...]

29 December Slept well, woke up almost in good health. Went for a walk. Some good letters. Wrote *Poverty*.[270] It's weak. But I must get it off my hands. Dimochka came and I went for a ride with him. He told me about Lev and his father.[271] How I need to, and how I want to try to understand people and the motives for their conduct, and not condemn them. It's now 6 o'clock. I'm going for dinner.

In the evening Landowska played. I was bored. Her flattery is particularly unpleasant. I must tell her.

30 December Got up early. Noted down in bed something which seemed to me important. Went for a walk. Some interesting letters; wrote a good reply to Semyonov and to Gusev's friend.²⁷² Then revised *A Dream*. Walked around outside the house. A thaw. They're getting the Christmas tree ready. I feel very good at heart. [. . .]

1910

Missed two days. Today is the 2nd [January], 1910. Yesterday everything was as usual. Revised *A Dream* again. The Landowskis left.[1] I went for a ride. Called on Marya Alexandrovna and Boulanger. I never cease to be ashamed of my life. I'm at least making a little progress though in the sense of refraining from unkind feelings.

Dimochka[2] came to say goodbye. A long business letter from Chertkov. I didn't have time to answer it. In the evening a talk about the land with Seryozha. They all have their own theories. Played chess and cards with dear Adamych.[3]

The day before yesterday, the 31st, in the morning, I revised something, I think. Went to the district offices. The people are indignant.[4] The Landowskis are a bit tiresome, but I liked him. Olsufyev arrived in the evening. Seeing the New Year in with insane luxury was very painful, both in itself and because I took part.

3 January I'm well. Good, interesting letters. Revised *The Poverty of the People* and *A Dream*.[5] Letters. Went riding with Olsufyev. He is Orthodox from a sense of propriety, and therefore defends it heatedly. Yes, if religion doesn't take the first place, it takes the last. It's only a static religion that people champion heatedly, i.e. a religion taken on trust. [. . .]

4 January [. . .] Very sad. Those around me are very alien. I thought about my relations with the people of our world, irreligious people. They're like my relations with animals. I can love them and pity them, but can't enter into spiritual intercourse with them. [. . .]

5 January Woke up early. Walked round the garden. It becomes more and more depressing to see slaves working for our family. [. . .]

I'm going to dinner. In the evening I read *A Dream* to the whole company. Many objections. But I think it's good. *Vint*, and I'm still sad and ashamed.

6 January Many letters, not many interesting ones. The cinematographer came.[6] [. . .] Yesterday a Jew came, demanding a concise exposition of the meaning of life. Everything I said to him was wrong, it was all subjective, it ought to be objective, based on 'evolution'. It's astonishing, the stupidity and obtuseness of those who have tasted learning. [. . .]

8 January I've recovered, but am very weak. A peasant from the Volynsky Province wants to be a book pedlar. Yes, I would like to go into the wilderness. A good letter from Gusev, and one to Sasha from Chertkov. How they both . . . well – all's well that ends well.[7] Chertkov's letter is so heartfelt and serious. And Sasha can understand and feel what he says about the main thing, which is independent of me personally. God grant it. I only answered one or two letters. Began to write about taxes,[8] but gave it up: I didn't feel like it. [...]

In the evening I read an interesting almanac, *Coenobium*[9] – interesting because one feels the dissatisfaction of all more or less advanced people with their spiritual condition. *Vint* in the evening. Did no writing yesterday.

9 January In the morning I got up very early and added something more to my letter to Schmitt on science.[10] Then letters, then finished writing about taxes, quite well. In the evening I read.

10 January [...] Something very important to note.
(1) I thought how necessary it is to preach to people an equal love for ALL, for negroes, savages and one's enemies, because if you don't preach that, there won't be and can't be any deliverance from evil, there will only be what comes most naturally: one's fatherland, one's people, its defence, armies, and war. And if there are armies and war there will be no limits to evil.

An ideal is essential for life. But an ideal is only an ideal when it is PERFECTION. The direction can only be indicated when it is indicated mathematically by a *straight line* which doesn't exist in reality.

13 January The usual letters. Re-read all *Three Days*. And I'll finish it, I think. Went riding with Philip.[11] I'm going to dinner. Must write down one or two things. The woman whose husband killed her seducer.[12]
(1) It's not anarchism, the teaching by which I live. It's the fulfilment of the external law which doesn't permit violence or participation in it. But will the consequences be either anarchism, or, on the contrary, slavery under the yoke of the Japanese or the Germans? That I don't know and don't wish to know. [...]

I'm going to dinner. After dinner I went to see Sasha; she's ill. If Sasha wasn't going to read this, I would write something that would please her. Borrowed Gorky from her and read it. Very poor. But the worst thing about it is that the false evaluation of him is unpleasant to me.[13] I should see only the good in him. [...]

16 January Woke up in good spirits and decided to go to the court in Tula.[14] Read my letters and answered a few. Then set off. First came the trial of some peasants: lawyers, judges, soldiers, witnesses. All very new to me. Then came the trial of a political prisoner. The charge was that he had read and, at cost to himself, disseminated ideas for a more just and sane organisation of life than the one which now exists. Felt very sorry for him. People gathered to look at me, but not many, thank goodness. The oath upset me. I could hardly refrain from saying it was a mockery of Christ. My heart sank, and because of that I remained silent. On the way back I had a good talk with Dušan about Masaryk.[15] In the evening I rested, and couldn't help feeling glad about the publication in Odessa of the *Cycle of Reading*.[16] [...]

19 January Woke up in better spirits. Thought on my walk that it would be good to start a school again: to pass on what I know about faith and to test myself. [. . .]

21 January [. . .]
(4) We speak about life after death. But if the soul lives after death, it must have lived before life also. One-sided eternity is an absurdity.

23 January [. . .] Took up *For Every Day* and worked a bit on it. But the more I work at it, the more repulsive the whole thing is to me. I must recognise that it's all stupidity and unnecessary, and get rid of it as quickly as possible. [. . .]

26 January [. . .] Worked on *For Every Day*. Went riding. During dinner Sergeyenko came with a gramophone.[17] It was unpleasant for me. [. . .]

30 Janury [. . .] In the evening Dolgorukov came and brought the library.[18] [. . .]

31 January In the morning Posha came. He's still as serious, simple and good as ever. A correspondent and a photographer came. I began some new work on the booklets for *For Every Day*, and did the first one: *On Faith*.[19] Then I had to go to the library. Everything very contrived, unnecessary and false. Dolgorukov's speech, the peasants, the photographs. [. . .]

Today is 8 February I don't remember the day before yesterday. I know that I wrote the sixth booklet.[20] Yesterday Shmelkov came from the Caucasus.[21] A religious man. Bulygin came.[22] A touching letter from Felten.[23] I'm unwell, but wrote the seventh booklet; it will be good, I think. Today I wrote the eighth.[24] My alleged article is very stupid.[25] An explanation with Sasha, a touching one. I've just come back from Marya Alexandrovna's and am going to lie down before dinner.

Missed two days again. Today is 11 February. [. . .] Boulanger came the day before yesterday. I must write a foreword for him for his Buddha.[26] And there are many more things I need to do. But above all, the suffering caused by people's sins – including my own – which divide and torment people is crying out more and more to be revealed. I thought about this more clearly than ever today in the form of *Notes of a Man-servant*. How good it could be![27] Re-reading Dostoyevsky – it's not suitable.[28]

They are all ill at home: Dorik, little Tanechka and Sasha.[29] A greeting from D'Estournelles, my mutilated article, and some abusive letters.[30] Sofya Andreyevna is going to Moscow. [. . .]

Sofya Andreyevna has left. I spoke to her yesterday about my wish, and the unpleasantness caused by the fact that the *Readers* are being sold at a high price; she began to say she would have nothing left, and refused outright. [. . .]

15 February Got up rather late. Wrote a letter to Khiryakov.[31] A worker came, wanting to settle on the land. He wants to influence people. Yesterday I had a good talk with Bulgakov about his expected call-up. [. . .]

16 February [. . .] Boulanger came. He was dissatisfied with my article.³² It's a bit difficult when one has no practical interests to have dealings with people guided primarily by these interests. [. . .]

17 February Alive. Received a touching letter from a Kiev student urging me to leave home and live in poverty.³³ Health better. Spent all morning revising the letter about Buddha and answering letters. [. . .]

21 February [. . .] Finished all the booklets.³⁴ Went riding. Sasha is still ill. I thought about deliverance. Evening spent with the Molostvovs.

23 February [. . .] In the evening we read an article about *Barricade*.³⁵ Wrote letters to Lehr and one about Masaryk.³⁶ [. . .]

25 February Slept very badly. An astonishing condition – just like a young man in a dream. Got up early. Went for a walk. Had a good talk with a drunkard who admitted deceiving the women – cleansing them of the evil eye and drinking up all the money. The whole day I was *d'une humeur de chien* [in a vile temper]. Wrote a whole story, *Khodynka*; it's very poor.³⁷ Wrote an answer to Melnikov in bed.³⁸ Didn't go out in the afternoon. In the evening I read philosophy and on Dušan's advice wrote a letter to the Czechs.³⁹ It's now 12 o'clock, I'm going to bed.

27 February Got up in better spirits. Went for a walk. Two Cossacks came:⁴⁰ one wants to found the kingdom of heaven on earth: a mixture of the religious and the secular. Both worldly fame and the urge to organise. But they are touching. They came specially. I worked on the booklets: *God*, and *Sins, Temptations and Superstitions* – they're not good. Interesting letters from Chertkov and others. [. . .]

28 February Got up in fairly good spirits. Walked a lot. Wrote letters. Saw off the Cossacks and the sailor, and also an alcoholic Ukrainian and his wife. Sasha got up. I'll go for a ride in the sleigh as soon as I've had lunch.

Went riding with Lena. A pleasant evening with Sasha. Read *Super-Tramp*. Poor English jokes – and in Shaw's foreword as well.⁴¹

2 March [. . .] Shestov came.⁴² Not very interesting – a 'man of letters', not a philosopher at all. [. . .]

5 March Better today. Wrote letters and the tenth booklet.⁴³ Rode to Telyatinki with Andrey Tarasov and had an enjoyable talk with him and with Seryozha Popov.⁴⁴ In the evening I read an interesting novel, *Ecce Sacerdos*.⁴⁵ [. . .]

6 March Got up in better spirits than yesterday. Went for a long walk, then a letter. Only one, the confession of an ex-revolutionary, and it made me very happy and moved me.⁴⁶ You see the glad fruits now and again, and very glad they are. [. . .] Stakhovich came. His politics and luxurious living and quasi-aristocracy are very alien to me. [. . .]

7–8 March Yesterday I wrote two letters, I think. Went riding with Dušan. Read Alexandra Andreyevna's notes[47] and experienced a very strong feeling: firstly, emotion caused by happy memories, and secondly sadness and the clear awareness of the fact that she, poor woman, couldn't help believing in redemption and *tout le tremblement* [all the rest of it], because if she didn't believe, she would have had to condemn her whole life and change it if she wanted to be a Christian and have communion with God. People who are not religious can live without faith, and therefore have no need of an absurd one, but she needed a faith, but a rational faith would have shown her up. So she believed in an absurd one, and how she believed! Thirdly I also felt the awareness of how the external affirmation of one's own faith and the condemnation of others – how precarious and unconvincing this is. She insists on her own faith, with such assurance, and condemns others so resolutely. Fourthly, I also felt that I had often been wrong and not careful enough when touching upon other people's faith (if only in science). [. . .]

In the evening I read my letters to Alexandra Andreyevna again with emotion. One about the fact that life is work, struggle and mistakes is such that I wouldn't say anything different at all now.[48] Ivan Ivanovich and I have decided about publishing.[49]

10 March Got up early again. Met Tanya and her husband. Letters: one terrible one from a young man prepared to kill an old man in order to pass his matriculation exam. Worked a bit on the sixteenth book. A letter from Chertkov. Wrote a reply to the Japanese,[50] and a letter about *The Horrors of Christian Civilisation*,[51] and a reply about the 15,000 roubles.[52] Went riding with Dušan. I'm going to bed. Dinner, chess, gossip, cards, the gramophone, and I felt sorely ashamed and disgusted. I won't do it any more. I'll read.

11 March [. . .] Note [. . .]
(2) The revolution has made our Russian people suddenly see the injustice of their position. It's the fairy story about the Emperor's new clothes. The child who told the truth that the Emperor was naked was the revolution. The people have become aware of the injustice in various ways (most of them, unfortunately, with anger); but the whole people now understand it. And this awareness cannot now be destroyed. But what is our government doing? By trying to crush the ineradicable awareness of the injustice they have been suffering, it is increasing this injustice and provoking a more and more angry attitude towards this injustice. [. . .]

12 March [. . .] The book about Brahminism is splendid and has stimulated many thoughts.[53] [. . .]

[17 March] I've missed three days; today is the fourth, 4 o'clock on 17 March. I've been unwell all these three days. Worked badly on the letter to the Japanese, the foreword to *For Every Day*, and on 14 March – the sixteenth booklet.[54] [. . .] I think the foreword is better. But generally all this work on *For Every Day* is becoming a burden to me. There's a certain pedantry and dogmatism about it. Generally speaking it's loathsome. Two strong impressions of an identical character were the reading of Alexandra Andreyevna's letters and the thoughts of Leskov.[55] There is much to note, I think. [. . .]

(5) Life for the peasant is first of all labour, which enables not only himself, but also his family and other people to continue living. Life for the intellectual is the acquisition of that knowledge and those arts which are considered important in his circles, and by means of that knowledge the exploitation of the labours of the peasant. How then can the peasant's understanding of life and its problems not be sensible, and the intellectual's understanding of life not be mad? [. . .]

19 March [. . .] Read my letter to the Indian and very much approved of it.[56] But the one to the Japanese is terrible. But it's good that that isn't important to me. [. . .]

23 March Health good. Letters. Work with the booklets is very boring. Wrote a letter about suicide. I don't like it either. I'd like to write a play for Telyatinki.[57] [. . .]

24 March [. . .] Still not very satisfied with my work. I'm dissatisfied with its systematic nature. I'll try to overcome this. Some interesting letters; answered them. Worked a bit on the foreword. I want to write a play for Dimochka. But there's no need. If I don't, it doesn't matter. A moving letter from Molochnikov with terrible details about the prison. I still haven't managed to write down what I've been thinking.

25 March Went for a long walk. Met Dunayev. Sad. My thoughts agitate me. Either I don't have the strength, or I can't find the form to express them. A powerful article by Korolenko about the death penalty.[58] Went riding. Spent a tiresome evening at cards. I must stop. I'm going to bed.

26 March [. . .] Walked for more than an hour. Felt good. Revised the foreword. I'm going to lunch. A moving letter from a priest about Christ. In the evening I read Korolenko's article. It's magnificent. I couldn't help sobbing. Wrote Korolenko a letter.

[30 March] Missed two days. Yesterday was the 29th. In the morning on my walk I met Strakhov and then Masaryk. I like them both, especially Masaryk. On the 28th the Stakhoviches came. Rather tedious. He is very alien to me. Yesterday I had two good talks with Masaryk. Rode to Ovsyannikovo. Sketched out a comedy: perhaps it will turn out all right. Masaryk is a professor and still believes in a personal God and personal immortality. [. . .]

31 March [. . .] Felt today for the first time and with complete clarity my success in freeing myself from worldly fame. They were all trifling matters – not being embarrassed at being censured for drinking wine, playing cards and living in luxury – but all of a sudden, I felt an unexpected freedom. I think I'm not mistaken.

Slept well today. Spilled my pot and broke it, and was very tired cleaning and wiping it up, and got out of breath. It's near, and it's good that it's near. [. . .]

Went for a walk in the morning. A peasant revolutionary from Panino came to see me, and also his father who is just like him. Both had been in prison, both know me. But they need me only to the extent that they see something revolutionary in me. I gave him some books. Behaved badly in explaining my situation to him. Still, I think, it wasn't for the sake of worldly fame. He asked for money. That was depressing. Then I began to write the play. It was no good. A journalist from Finland came.[59] I received him and had a long and ardent talk with him, and it was good. Then Belinky brought a letter from Molochnikov. I blubbered as I asked a favour of Ryadzevskaya as she was leaving.[60] [. . .]

1 April Yesterday Dimochka came and related a story by Semyonov to me, and it was very good. I borrowed Semyonov's book and read it all evening.[61] Very good. [. . .]

3 April, [. . .] This morning I meant to write about my funeral and what should be read at it. I'm sorry I didn't write anything down. I feel death approaching nearer and nearer. There's no doubt that my life, and probably that of all people, becomes more spiritual with the years. The same happens to the life of mankind as a whole. In this lies the essence and meaning of all and every life, and so the meaning of my life lies only in this spiritualisation of it. If you are aware of this and act accordingly, you know you are doing the task assigned to you: you become more spiritual yourself, and by your life contribute at least to some extent to the general spiritualisation – to becoming better. [. . .]

7 April [. . .] An insanely lovely spring. Each time I can't believe myself. Can this beauty really come again out of nothing? Seryozha came in the evening. I've come to understand him. And I'm glad. Dimochka came with Bulgakov and the Sergeyenko boy. Wrote an answer to Gradovsky.[62] [. . .]

10 April I continue to be in a very bad mood. I can't even think of any original work to do. Corrected my thoughts *On Life*. Met Nikolayev. Received the proofs from Ivan Ivanovich.[63] Sasha is leaving.[64] She is sad. I had a good talk with her. We both blubbered. I only copied in: [. . .]

(3) What a great wrong I did in giving the property to the children. I did harm to them all, even my daughters. I see this clearly now.

12 April [. . .] Had no dinner. Felt a tormenting anguish from the awareness of the vileness of my life among people who are working so that they can just barely save themselves from a cold, hungry death, save themselves and their family. Yesterday there were fifteen people gorging pancakes, and five or six people with families were running about, barely managing to cook and hand round the fodder.

It was agonisingly shameful and terrible. Yesterday I rode past some stone-breakers, and it was as though I'd been forced to run the gauntlet. Yes, need and envy and anger against the rich are painful and agonising, but I don't know whether the shame of my own life isn't more agonising.

Today is 13 April Woke up at 5 and kept thinking how to escape, what to do. And I don't know. I thought of writing. Yet it's disgusting to write while continuing to live this sort of life. Should I speak to her? Go away? Change things gradually? [. . .] I think the latter is all I can and will do. But still it's depressing. [. . .]

14 April Yesterday was very depressing. [. . .] Did nothing except write a worthless letter. Went for a ride. It's depressing, and I don't know what to do. Sasha has left. I love her and I miss her, not for my work but for her soul. The Goldenweisers came to see her off. He played. My weakness made me jaundiced.

During the night I felt bad physically, and this had some effect on me spiritually. Got up later. Bodyanskaya came about her husband, sentenced in the Novorossiisk Republic case. Wrote to Olsufyev.[65] Behaved well with some beggars and a petitioner. Rode to Ovsyannikovo. I've been reading through my books. I oughtn't to write any more. I think in this respect I've done all I could. But I want to, I terribly want to. [. . .]

15 April I.I.A. Alive – just about. Got up in better spirits. A fuss again. Petitioners. Treated them all well, remembering to show gratitude for the joy of communion with them, except for a drunken woman whom I treated badly and refused. Letters. One to Shaw,[66] and one about a peace society.[67] Bad. Proofs. And I still haven't written anything. Solomakhin is very nice, and in the evening a railwayman came from Samara. I'm feeling a bit shiverish now. Wrote to Sasha.

16 April [. . .] Revised my thoughts *On Life* and am very dissatisfied. Some not very interesting letters. To my shame, I found Menshikov's judgement about me disagreeable.[68] [. . .]

17 April [. . .] A good letter from Chertkov and a journal of a Chinese leading progressive party. It interests me very much.[69] [. . .]

19 April [. . .] A visitor yesterday: a spy who had served in the police and had fired on revolutionaries came expecting sympathy from me. The sort of man, moreover, who obviously wanted to ingratiate himself with me by abusing priests. It's very depressing for me that I can't, i.e. that I don't know how to deal with everyone in a humane, i.e. in a godly manner, lovingly and reasonably. Only just today, two youths have been trying to teach me and catch me out: one demanded that I 'fight' with bombs; the other asked why I had handed over the copyright to my works before 1880. And again, I didn't know how to deal with them gently and without irony. [. . .]

This morning two Japanese came:[70] primitive people in an ecstasy of enthusiasm over European civilisation. On the other hand I had a book and a letter from an Indian[71] expressing understanding of all the shortcomings of European civilisation, even its utter worthlessness. [...]

20 April I.I.A. Still alive. Got up rather late. Walked through the young fir trees; the ants interested me. Made a few notes. The colonel came again, with apparently unkind feelings towards me.[72] Corrected the proofs of two booklets. *Sins, Temptations and Superstitions* and *Vanity*. Not bad. Went riding with Bulgakov. Few interesting letters. In the evening I read Gandhi on civilisation. Very good. Note:
(1) Progress is slow up the rungs of the generations. In order to progress a single step, it is necessary for a whole generation to die out. At the present time it is necessary for landlords to die out, and rich people in general who aren't ashamed of their wealth, and revolutionaries who are only driven on by the vainglory of revolution as a profession, and not by suffering at the discrepancy between life and consciousness. How important is the education of children – the future generations.
(2) The Japanese accept Christianity as one of the appurtenances of civilisation. Will they also be able, like our Europeans, to make Christianity so innocuous that it will not destroy what they take from civilisation? [...]

21 April Got up late in a very bad mood. A peasant came about the land. I behaved badly towards him. Then a lady came with her daughters. I talked to her as best I could. Read a book about Gandhi.[73] A very important one. I must write to him. Then Misha came, then Andreyev.[74] Not very interesting, but a pleasant, kindly manner. Not very serious. Bad news about Sasha.[75] I want to write to her at once. In the evening I read about suicides.[76] A very strong impression. [...]

22 April Alive. Went for a walk by myself, refused to go with Andreyev and a man who had come from Archangel. Had a talk later with Andreyev. He doesn't have a serious attitude to life, but touches superficially on these questions all the same. Letters. Revised two months of *For Every Day*. I liked it very much. Went for a walk. The Goldenweisers came. I'm still struggling. Wrote a letter to Sasha. I'm going to bed before dinner. A letter from Sasha which moved me very much. The music excited me greatly. He played wonderfully.

1 May Alive. Note:
(1) One of the main causes of suicides in the European world is the false teaching of the Christian Church about heaven and hell. People don't believe in heaven and hell, but all the same the idea that life should be either heaven or hell is so firmly fixed in their heads that it doesn't permit of a rational understanding of life as it is – namely neither heaven nor hell, but struggle, unceasing struggle, unceasing because life consists only of struggle; only not a Darwinian struggle of creatures and individuals against other creatures and individuals, but a struggle of spiritual forces against their bodily restrictions. Life is the struggle of the soul against the body. If life is understood in this way, suicide is impossible, unnecessary and

senseless. The good is only to be found in life. I seek the good; how then can I leave this life in order to attain the good? I seek mushrooms. Mushrooms are only to be found in the forest. How then can I leave the forest in order to find mushrooms? [. . .]

It's now evening. Sonya has arrived. I packed and went for a walk to watch the motor cars.[77] [. . .]

2 May, Kochety [. . .] Got ready to go, and left at 7.[78] It was depressing. The curiosity of people. Dear Tanya and Mikhail Sergeyevich. I lost my way in the park in the evening. Unwell.

3 May Got up feeling listless. Did no work. Walked round the park reading Masaryk.[79] Weak. Revised the foreword. Thought about suicide and re-read what I'd begun. It's good. It would be good to finish writing it. Wrote to Masaryk, Sasha and Sonya. I'm going to bed. 12 o'clock.

4 May Before dinner I walked round the wood and rejoiced in life, in its 'invisible forces'.[80] Had some dreams which were amazing for their psychological truthfulness. I thought I'd write about suicide, but when I sat at the desk I felt feeble-minded and disinclined. Again I feel acutely the burden of the luxury and idleness of a landowner's life. Everyone works except me. [. . .]

5 May Sleepiness again and feeble-mindedness. Wrote nothing and didn't try to. Read the old Frenchmen: La Boétie, Montaigne, La Rochefoucauld.[81] [. . .]

6 May [. . .] Note:
Habit – mechanical, unconscious actions – is the basis of true life, of moral striving for improvement. [. . .]

9 May [. . .] Sonya and Andrey have arrived. I wasn't good to Andrey, I was too abrupt. With Sonya I partly expressed for the first time what depressed me. And then, in order to soften what I'd said, I kissed her silently – she understands that language completely.

11 May Sleepiness and weakness again. I can barely move and don't feel like writing anything, but on my walk I noted down something which seemed to me important, and, thank God, I'm not angry and it's easy not to do wrong. Chertkov copied out and looked over the foreword for me. I don't feel like working on it. If God wills, I'll finish it and will write both *Insanity* and *There are no Guilty People in the World*. [. . .]

12 May Alive. In the morning I went for a walk and had some good thoughts. Then weakness, and I did nothing. Only read *On Religion*.[82] Learned something new about Chinese religion. And it stimulated my thoughts. Went riding with Bulgakov. It's depressing at home for several reasons. A note from Sasha. Talks with a shopkeeper and a village policeman. Note:

(1) How easy it is both for individuals and for peoples to acquire what is called civilisation, real civilisation! Go through the university, clean your nails, make use of the services of a tailor and a hairdresser, travel abroad, and the result is a very civilised man. And for peoples: more railways, academies, factories, dreadnoughts, fortresses, newspapers, books, parties, parliaments – and the result is a very civilised people. That's why people clutch at civilisation and not enlightenment – both individuals and peoples. The first is easy, it requires no effort and evokes approval; but the second, on the contrary, requires concentrated effort, and not only does it not evoke approval, but it's always despised and hated by the majority because it exposes the lie of civilisation. [...]

(3) The danger of conquest is destroying the religious obduracy of the East. An obvious advantage of militarism.

13 May Note:
(1) It's only necessary to say that most people wait for work as though it were charity for it to be clear how terrible our life is in its immorality, stupidity, danger and misery.
(2) With medicine it's the same as with all sciences: it's gone a long way without being tested: a few have knowledge of unnecessary refinements, while the people have no idea about health and hygiene. [...]

14 May Had a pain in my side. Got up in good spirits. Walked a lot. Made no notes. At home I read Veresayev and Semyonov.[83] [...]

15 May [...] Chertkov and Tanya are demanding that I give them the comedy,[84] but I just can't – it's so bad.

18 May [...] I'm still reading Réville[85] and there is much of interest in it. Among the Hottentots the chief judge who sentences a person to death must be the first to lay hands on the condemned man. They express it well that one should live like the moon: *vivre en mourant et mourir en vivant* [to live dying and to die living]. Réville is a very naive writer – he considers it the height of unenlightenment when people live without recognising either the state or property. Reading this book has suggested many thoughts to me. [...]

(4) Memory? How often people take memory for intelligence. And they don't see that memory excludes intelligence, is incompatible with intelligence – intelligence which solves problems in an original manner. The one is a substitute for the other.

19 May My last day in Kochety. It was very pleasant except for the seignorial way of life, well organised and alleviated by a just and kind attitude to people, but still a terrible, crying contrast which never ceases to torment me.

Revised the play and nothing else. Health good. Some photographs taken. [...]

20 May [...] Note: [...]
(2) The peasants consider it necessary to lie, and prefer lies to the truth, other

things being equal. This is because they have been taught to do so, since people always lie when talking to them or about them. [. . .]
(6) What a highly moral way of life it is that goes on in all peasant families: namely that the adult gives up all his earnings to support the old and the young.

Today is 22 May, Yasnaya Polyana Woke up early. Wrote up what Bulgakov had copied down.[86] Walked round the Zaseka wood, got lost and came out at the lieutenant's. Was very tired. Revised the play. It's a bit better, but still poor. A mass of petitioners. I don't think I behaved very badly in applying my rule of not worrying about their opinion, but about my own state of mind. Ivan Ivanovich came for dinner with some proofs, and then a remarkable objector from the Tula district who had suffered for eight and a half years. I asked Bulgakov to write down his story. Gave him ten roubles; his name was Fokin.

An unpleasant talk with Sonya.[87] I behaved badly. She did everything I asked. [. . .]

Today is the 24th Got up early and it's now 7 o'clock. Note:
(1) People come to see a person who has acquired a reputation for the importance and clarity of expression of his thoughts; they come and they don't let him say a word, but talk and either tell him something which has been said much more clearly by him, or something whose absurdity has long ago been proved by him. [. . .]

25 May I'm well. Walked a little. My mind is working feebly. Carefully revised and looked over the *booklets*, and they're not bad. Took them round to Ivan Ivanovich. Wrote one letter. Received a letter from Gusev and a book *Christenthum und Monistische Religion*.[88] It all amounts to the same thing. I don't want to think. Feel very weak, thank God. A letter from Sasha. Seryozha came. Nothing to note, a sign of feeble-mindedness. Yes, a young teacher came in the morning, threatening to commit suicide. I behaved badly towards him.

Today is 27 May [. . .] Yesterday evening I read a good article by Wipper about Rome.[89] I'd like to write about the soldier who killed a man.[90] Early in the morning – no, last night – I woke up and wrote down a very strong and new feeling:
(1) For the first time I felt vividly the arbitrariness of this whole world. Why do I, such a clear, simple, rational and good person, live in this confused, complicated, insane, evil world? Why?
(2) (On the courts.) If only these wretched, stupid, coarse, self-satisfied evil-doers could understand what they are doing when they sit in their uniforms at tables covered with green cloth repeating and gravely analysing senseless words printed in vile books which are a disgrace to mankind; if only they could understand that what they call laws are a crude mockery of those eternal laws which are engraved on the hearts of all people. Some people who, without any ill will, shot at birds in a place called a church have been sent to hard labour for sacrilege, but these other people continually commit and live by sacrilege against the most sacred thing in

the world: human life. The Tsar teaches his innocent son to kill. All this is done by Christians. A soldier who doesn't want to serve because he doesn't need to has deserted. Oh, how I need to and want to write about this.

27 May Sasha arrived. We both wept for joy. She is too cheerful. I'm afraid. I'm in a bad mood. *But I worked as best I could.* I'm going to lunch. Went for a ride with Bulgakov. Slept. A letter from Chertkov about Orlenev.[91] I'll have to try to finish the play. [. . .]

29 May [. . .] A talk with Sonya. She was agitated. I was afraid, but, thank God, it turned out all right. Trubetskoy came.[92] He's very nice. I also worked quite well. Finished all the booklets and gave them to Ivan Ivanovich. [. . .]

Today is 1 June Yesterday I wasn't in a good mood. I don't think anything bad happened, although there were a lot of petitioners. Not many letters. And to my shame I found this unpleasant. Revision of the play and the foreword again as usual. [. . .]

I've been reading Chernyshevsky.[93] His easy way of crudely condemning people who don't think as he does is very instructive. I have a very pleasant, kindly feeling towards Sonya – a good, spiritual, loving one. I feel well at heart despite my inactivity.

4 June Got up early. Dealt with the petitioners very well, and went for a walk. Then letters. One serious one, as an answer to the writing epidemic.[94] Began working on the comedy and gave up in disgust. Revised the foreword[95] reasonably well. Went out tired after work; there were a dozen women and I behaved badly, not towards them but towards dear, unselfish Dušan. I rebuked him. It was all disgusting.

Set off with Dušan. Had a good ride. Came back and found the Circassian who had brought in Prokofy.[96] Felt terribly depressed and really thought of leaving.

5 June And now today, on the morning of the 5th, I still don't consider it impossible.

Dear, dear Tanechka came. I sobbed as I talked to her.[97] This was vile of me. It's always me, me, my pleasure, and not my work. [. . .] Note:
(1) You tell a man to work and he says 'I don't want to'. And if you say everyone ought to work he says 'Let all those rich men who don't do anything set me an example. If they'll work I will, but if they won't I won't.'
(2) For *The Wisdom of Children*: how he ate a cake up by mistake, and how she taught him to repent.[98] [. . .]

I was very poorly all day. Did no work and felt sorry for myself all day and wanted others to feel sorry for me, wanted to cry, and blamed everybody else, like a spoiled child. But still I kept myself in check. The only thing was that I said at dinner that I wanted to die. And I do want to very much, and I can't help wishing it. In the evening Goldenweiser played well, but it left me cold. I went for a ride and sat for Trubetskoy.

Today is 6 June Once again the same state of sadness and self-pity. I walked to the Zakaz wood. Met a boy who asked me whether he could walk through, otherwise the Circassian would beat him. I became so depressed! Had some very good thoughts, but they were all disconnected and confused. Worked a bit on the foreword. Couldn't work on the comedy. A good letter from Chertkov. After lunch some workers from the Prechistenka workers' school came. Had a very good talk with them. Then Dima came with some people from Telyatinki. Dancing and another very good talk with the peasants. Goldenweiser came in the evening. I'm on better terms with Seryozha. [. . .]

7 June Slept badly, very little. Revised the foreword. Then spoke to Sofya Andreyevna about the Circassian, and there was the usual emotion and irritation. I'm very depressed. I keep wanting to cry. [. . .]

8, 9, 10 June [. . .] A girl came on crutches, with some vague requests to make of me as usual. I found the doctors disagreeable, especially Nikitin with his belief in his own superstition and his desire to convince others of it. Wrote a very bad letter to the newspapers about the impossibility of helping people with money. But I won't send it. There's no need. Orlenev was here. He is awful. Nothing but vanity, and of the basest physical variety. He's simply awful. Chertkov rightly compares him with Sytin. It's very possible that there's a spark in them both, very probable even, but I'm not able to see it.

On the 10th I was a bit better; I was able to work again on the foreword and read a lot about Babism with bad feelings towards myself. [. . .]

12 June [. . .] Had a difficult time with the two girls – they were to be pitied, but I couldn't give them any help and they took up my time.[99]

I've decided to go to the Chertkovs'. [. . .]

14 June I'm beginning a new notebook at the Chertkovs'. Walked through the fields. Worked on the foreword. Looked over my old diary. For seven months now I've been constantly busy with this and this only. Can it really all be a waste of time? Letters. Not many interesting ones. Walked to Lyubuchany[100] to see the madmen. One very interesting one: 'I didn't steal,' [he said], 'I took.' I said: '[We'll meet] in the next world.' He said: 'There's only one world.' This madman is far superior to many people who are considered sane. Slept. Dinner. Worked a bit more in the evening. Then a Czech came with questions about pedagogy.[101] We had a good talk. Only it was inhibiting having it written down. I'm going to bed.

15 June Went for a walk, then felt weak and did hardly anything all day: revised December,[102] scribbled a bit of the foreword and read *Notes of a Man-servant*. I'm more and more aware of the futility of writing, of all writing and especially my own. But I can't help speaking out. [. . .]

16 June Got up rather late; still the same weakness. Went for a walk; the people are affectionate. [. . .] At three o'clock I set off on foot to Meshcherskoye to see the madmen. Chertkov drove me the rest of the way. Walked round all the wards. I haven't analysed my impressions yet and so I'm not writing anything. And the impressions are less strong than I expected.[103] Worked a little on the proofs of the booklet *Sins, Temptations and Superstitions*. I very much want to be rid of this work. Sasha is better. Uninteresting letters. Read Kuprin.[104] He's very talented. *Measles* is inconsistent, but the imagery is vivid, true to life and simple . . .

18 June Slept little, but worked a bit better despite that. Revised three booklets. Dictated a bad letter to Belgrade[105] and looked over the foreword again, I hope for the last time. Rode to Meshcherskoye and Ivino with Chertkov. Women patients. A nice peasant writer. And the women are kind-hearted. One especially was no different from anybody else. Then an invitation from Troitskoye to a cinematograph show.[106] Slept, dinner, chess in the evening. Wrote to Sonya. Nothing to note. One good letter.

20 June Got up in good spirits. Revised *To the Slavs* and the foreword. And wrote something for *The Wisdom of Children*.[107] I want to try to win over Sonya consciously by means of goodness and love. From a distance it seems possible. I'll try to do so when she's close by as well. [. . .]

21 June [. . .] Dictated an account of my meeting with Alexander and how he immediately promised not to drink.[108] Then worked a lot on the proofs. Corrected three booklets – not bad. Strakhov came, and also a *skopets*.[109] Talked a lot with the *skopets*, or rather listened. Berkenheim also came. I didn't go for a walk. Read aloud *On Suicide*. Yes, and revised that too. Had a short nap. Orlenev read Nikitin. He's alien to me. We went to Troitskoye. The height of luxury there, a cinematograph. Sasha had a headache. And I was bored and depressed. The cinematograph is a nasty, deceitful thing.

23 June Alive. It's now 7 in the morning. Yesterday I had only just gone to bed and hadn't gone to sleep when a telegram arrived:[110] 'Beg you come 23rd.' I'll go, and I'm glad of the chance to do my duty. God help me.

Yasnaya Polyana. Found things worse than expected: hysterics and irritability. It's impossible to describe. I didn't behave very badly, but not very well either, not gently enough.

24 June, Yasnaya Polyana A lot to note down.
Got up, not having slept much. Went for a walk. During the night Sonya came in. She still can't sleep. She came to me in the morning. She's still agitated, but is calming down.
(1) Went out for a walk after an agonising talk with Sonya. There are flowers out in front of the house, and healthy, barefoot girls tidying up. They came back later with hay and berries – cheerful, calm and healthy. It would be good to write two scenes.[111]

Re-read the letters. Wrote a reply about drinking.¹¹² Nothing special in the evening. Peace and quiet.

25 June Got up early. Wrote about insanity and did some letters. And suddenly Sonya was in the same irritable, hysterical condition again. I was very depressed. Drove with her to Ovsyannikovo. She calmed down. I was silent, but couldn't be kind and affectionate, I wasn't able to. [. . .]

26 June [. . .] Sonya was excited again, and there were the same sufferings again for both of us. [. . .]

27 June Yesterday she spoke about moving somewhere. I didn't sleep all night. I'm very tired. [. . .]
Read *Psychiatry*.¹¹³ How obtuse, and often just stupid. In order to explain consciousness it talks about the subjective and the objective, as though the word subjective is anything else but a bad name for consciousness. [. . .]

28 June Didn't sleep much. Sonya has been in a wonderful mood since morning. She asked me not to go.¹¹⁴ But then she had a letter from Chertkov. A good letter from Chertkov. But she is still excited and angry with him. I talked to him and set off for Yasenki instead of Kozlovka. I gave a gasp and ran back home.¹¹⁵ We had a good journey. There were no horses, the telegram hadn't been sent off. We wasted about three hours. We got to Seryozha's. An unpleasant story by a newspaper woman. Had some pleasant talks with the workers. There was a mass of people at Seryozha's and I was bored and depressed. Walked to the sexton's and talked with the village women. How can we live amidst this terrible, acute need? [. . .]

30 June, Yasnaya Polyana Arrived at Yasnaya on the 29th. Nothing special on the way. Parted on pleasant terms with Tanya. In general my whole impression was very good. Sofya Andreyevna is better. I'm not quite well myself, although I can't complain of being in a bad frame of mind. Weakness and a headache. In the morning I received a French copy of *The Law of Violence and the Law of Love*,¹¹⁶ and a few good letters. Read it with great interest, and I must admit I approved of it. It's useful to re-read things so as not to repeat myself in what I write. I hope there won't be any repetitions in *On Insanity* and I can see it's worth writing, but I don't know if I shall be fated to. I'm talking about my strength. [. . .]
Apart from *The Law of Violence and the Law of Love* I received a brochure by a Frenchman, Polak, *La politique de l'avenir prochain*.¹¹⁷ It's interesting to read because he's obviously a scholar abreast of the latest philosophical thought, and shows astonishing lack of clarity and wrongness of understanding. It's enough to quote him that the three main activities of human life are: the satisfaction of the feeling for beauty – art; the satisfaction of the demands of reason – science; and finally, and in passing – morality. The more I read it, the more I felt the need to finish *On Insanity*. [. . .]

7 July Alive, but a bad day. Bad because I'm still out of sorts, and am not working. Didn't even correct the proofs. Went for a ride to Chertkov's. When I got home I found Sofya Andreyevna in an irritable mood and couldn't calm her down at all. Read in the evening. Goldenweiser came over late on, also Chertkov. Sonya had it out with him, and still didn't calm down. But late in the evening I had a very good talk with her. Hardly slept all night.

10 July Woke up at 5. Got up, but felt weak and lay down again. Walked to the village at 9. Went to Kopylov's. Gave him some money. It was very simple and not bad. Walked past Nikolayev's. He came out and we talked again about justice. I said to him that the concept of justice is an artificial one and unnecessary for a Christian. This line can't be drawn in reality. It's fantastic and completely unnecessary for a Christian.

At home I wrote a long letter to a worker in reply to his objections about *The Only Way*. Went for a ride with Chertkov. He spoke about non-resistance – in a strange way. I lay down. Woke up to find Davydov, Kolechka and Salomon there. Read an empty, pompous article, *Retour de l'enfant prodigue*,[118] and a charming story by Mille.[119] Then Sutkovoy and Kartushin came to say goodbye.[120] I like them very much. [...]

11 July Alive, just about. A terrible night. Until 4 o'clock. And Lev Lvovich was worst of all. He scolded me as if I were a little boy, and ordered me to go into the garden after Sofya Andreyevna.[121] In the morning Sergey arrived. I did no work – except for the booklet *Idleness*. Went walking and riding. I can't look calmly at Lev. I'm still ill. Sonya, poor woman, has calmed down. A cruel and depressing illness. [...]

14 July A very depressing night. Began writing her a letter in the morning and finished it.[122] Went to her room. She demanded the very things that I promised and granted. I don't know whether I did right, whether I wasn't too weak and submissive. But I couldn't do otherwise. They've gone to fetch the diaries. She's still in the same irritable condition, not eating or drinking. Worked on the booklets, did three. Then rode to Rudakov. I can't be kind and affectionate to Lev, and he doesn't understand or feel anything. Sasha brought the diaries. She went twice. And Sonya has calmed down and thanked me. I think it's all right. A touching letter from Batya.[123] [...]

15 July Alive, but depressed. Commotion again in the morning: I might run away, I must give her the key to the diaries. I said I wouldn't go back on what I'd said. It was very, very depressing. Before that I finished the proofs of the booklets. There's only a part of one left. Went for a ride with Dušan. In the evening an American,[124] and Chertkov, and Goldenweiser, and Nikolayev. Sonya is calm, but one feels it's all hanging by a thread. [...]

17 July [...] Read some letters and Pascal. A talk yesterday with Lev, and today he explained to me that I'm to blame. I must remain silent and try not to have unkind feelings. [. . .]

18 July Alive, but ill. Still the same weakness. I'm doing no work except writing worthless letters and reading Pascal. Sofya Andreyevna is agitated again. 'I've been unfaithful to her and that's why I'm hiding the diaries.' And then she's sorry that she's tormenting me. An uncontrollable hatred of Chertkov. I feel an unbridgeable distance between Lev and myself. And I'll tell him *son fait* [what I think of him], as lovingly as I can. A tiresome writer gentleman came. Rode to Tikhvinskoye. Very tired. Goldenweiser and Chertkov came in the evening, and Sofya Andreyevna was almost beside herself. I'm going to bed.

19 July Slept reasonably well, but am very weak; pulse irregular. Wrote a venomous article for the Peace Congress,[125] and some letters. Sofya Andreyevna was better this morning, but worse towards evening with the arrival of the doctors. [. . .]

20 July [. . .] Note: [. . .]
(4) I can't in my heart forgive Vera[126] for her fall. And I clearly understand at once all the cruelty and injustice of this. I only need to remember my own male sexual past. Yes, nothing shows so obviously that public opinion is formed not by women, but by men. Yet a woman should be less liable to condemnation than a man because she bears all the great weight of the consequences of her sin – childbirth, shame; while the man bears none. 'If you're not caught, you're not a thief.' As a fallen woman or an unmarried mother, V is shamed in the eyes of the whole world, or straightway becomes a member of the class of despised creatures, whores. But a man is pure and good and in the right, as long as he doesn't catch a disease. It would be good to make this clear.

21 July [. . .]
(3) (1) The scholarly type, (2) the ambitious type, (3) the self-interested type, (4) the conservative believer, (5) the debauchee type, (6) the robber, within accepted limits, (7) outside accepted limits, (8) the truthful, but mistaken man, (9) the writer ambitious for fame, (10) the socialist revolutionary, (11) the gay, dashing type, (12) the complete Christian, (13) the struggling one, (14) . . . There's no end to these types which I can feel.[127]

21 July I'm still just as weak, and still have the same unkind feeling towards Lev. Made notes about the characters. Must have a try. Did no work. Had a good ride with Bulgakov. Dinner. Read the *Herald of Europe*. Goldenweiser, Chertkov. Sofya Andreyevna had another fit. It's depressing. But I don't complain and don't pity myself. I'm going to bed. A nice letter from Tanya about St Francis.

22 July Slept very little. Did no work. Fell asleep before lunch. Went for a ride with Goldenweiser. Wrote it in the woods.[128] That's good. Irritability and agitation again at home. Even worse at dinner. I took it upon myself to invite her for a walk, and calmed her down. Chertkov came. It was strained, painful and depressing. Bear up, Cossack. I'm reading La Bruyère.

24 July The same again as regards health and my relations with Sofya Andreyevna. My health is a bit better. But Sofya Andreyevna's is worse. Yesterday evening she wouldn't leave me and Chertkov alone, so as not to give us the chance to talk just by ourselves. It's the same again today. But I got up and asked him whether he agreed with what I had written to him. She heard me and asked what I was talking about. I said I didn't wish to answer. And she went out, agitated and irritable. I can't do anything. It's unbearably depressing for me. I'm doing nothing: writing worthless letters, and reading all sorts of trash. I'm going to bed, unwell and restless.

25 July Sonya didn't sleep all night. She decided to go away and went to Tula where she met Andrey and came back quite well, but terribly exhausted. I'm still unwell, but a bit better. Did no work, and didn't try. Talked with Lev. It's no good. [. . .]

27 July The same again. But only, I think, the calm before the storm. Andrey came to ask if there was a document. I said I didn't wish to answer. Very depressing. I can't believe that they only want money. [. . .]
(1) The history of punishment is its continuous abolition. Ihering.[129] [. . .]

28 July Still the same ill health – my liver, and lack of mental activity. It's quiet at home. Zosya came. Went for a ride with Dušan. Seryozha was here. Thank God, everything has been exaggerated. Yes, I no longer have a diary, a frank, simple diary. I must start one.[130]

2 August Still just as depressed at heart, and still the same lassitude. Walked a lot in the morning. Not many letters. Feebly corrected some proofs. A splendid letter from Tanya. She is suffering for me, poor girl. Rode over to get some seed-rye. Sofya Andreyevna drove over to check on me. [. . .]

3 August I.I.A. Alive, and melancholy. But worked better on the proofs. A wonderful passage in Pascal.[131] Couldn't help being moved to tears as I read it and was aware of my complete accord with this man who died hundreds of years ago. What more miracles do you want when you experience one like this?

Rode to Kolpna with Goldenweiser. In the evening there was a painful scene; I was extremely agitated. Did nothing, but felt such a rush of blood to the heart that I was not only frightened, but in pain.

5 August Note: [. . .]
(4) 1 August. The words of a dying man are particularly important. But surely we are always dying and it's particularly obvious in old age. So let an old man remember that his words might be particularly important. [. . .]

(6) How terrible, or rather how amazing is the impudence or folly of those missionaries who, in order to civilise and educate 'savages', teach them their own church's faith. [. . .]

6 August [. . .] Korolenko has come.[132] A very pleasant and intelligent man who talks well. But still it's painful to talk and talk.

7 August A state of despondency. Tried to write. On insanity. Couldn't do anything. Invited Korolenko to go for a walk with me in the morning and we had a good talk. He's intelligent, but dominated by the superstition of science. [. . .] For Sasha to copy:
(1) I've seldom met a person more endowed with all the vices than I am: lasciviousness, self-interest, malice, vanity, and above all self-love. I thank God that I know this, and have seen and continue to see all this loathsomeness in myself and still struggle against it. This is what explains the success of my writings. [. . .]

8 August I'd just got up when Sofya Andreyevna ran outside, not having slept all night, agitated and really ill. I went for a walk, then looked for her. Couldn't write anything. Went riding with Bulgakov. The young people from Telyatinki came. But five people who had promised to come[133] didn't come. It all seems like a trick. Thank God, I'm only sorry for them. [. . .]

9 August [. . .] At home there was the awful Ferre, awful because of his impervious, naive bourgeois nature. Then a Hungarian. I behaved badly towards them both.[134] Sasha had another clash with Sonya. [. . .]

13 August Health a bit better. It poured with rain; I walked along the terrace. A man came up to me, wet through and with no coat on. I didn't give him anything to eat or treat him at all in a brotherly fashion. I shook his hand. A stupid demonstration. Some quite interesting letters, but still no desire to work. Well, never mind. I feel well at heart – good. A former lady of good family was here, now a medical attendant. All the usual service to other people and sexual love.[135] Note:
 How good it would be to expose such love well and truly. To show the hypocrisy of such love.

15 August, Kochety[136] Woke up feeling unwell. Sofya Andreyevna is going with us. We had to get up at 6 o'clock. A depressing journey. Some insignificant letters. It's very pleasant at Tanya's. I'm just going to bed in a depressed state, physically and mentally. Read a book by Fyodor Strakhov: *The Search for Truth*.[137] Very, very good.
(1) What a strange thing: I love myself, but nobody loves me.
(2) Instead of learning to live a loving life, people learn to fly. They fly very badly, but they stop learning to live a life of love in order to learn to fly after a fashion. It's just as if birds stopped flying and learned to run or make bicycles and ride on them.

18 August Everything is just the same, the same mental weakness. Did nothing. Sonya was distressed by the news that Chertkov has been given permission to live at Telyatinki. Uninteresting letters. I feel quite good at heart, although sad. And that's bad. Seryozha and Dmitry Olsufyev came. Went to a performance at the school. Very good. Went riding.

19 August [. . .] Talked with Sofya Andreyevna and was wrong to agree not to be photographed. I mustn't make concessions. [. . .]

23 August Had a brisk walk and thought. Made up a fairy tale for children. And another one on the theme: *The Same for Everyone*, and the characters for it.[138] Sketched out the fairy tale. Walked in the park. Finished the booklets. *Vint* in the evening. I'm going to bed. Sofya Andreyevna is calm.

24 August Continue to feel well. In the morning I read *Le Bab* [?].[139] It's very interesting and new to me. Then letters. I ought to have written down the children's fairy tale. Tanechka told it well. For some reason I've no desire to write. But I ought to. Walked on my own to Alexandrovka. In the evening I finished reading *Le Bab*. I'm going to bed. Sofya Andreyevna is well. If only she didn't worry herself, didn't get suspicious. Note: [. . .]
(7) It's bad when the rich are not ashamed and the poor are not without envy.
(8) *The Same for Everyone* – the title for the character sketches.
(9) Formerly the government, with the help of the Church alone, used to deceive the people in order to exercise power over them; now the same government is gradually preparing science as well for this task, and science is getting down to the task very willingly and assiduously. [. . .]

26 August I'm well at heart. The children's fairy tale isn't a success. Received letters and proofs. Read the *Vedic Magazine*. The account of the Vedas and *Areia Samai*[140] is very good. [. . .]

27 August I.I.A. Alive. But still doing no work. Busy all day with Chepurin, a worker who has been to England, America and Japan. I read his book in manuscript,[141] very badly written, and talked with him.

29 August An empty day again. Walks, letters. I'm thinking, and thinking well, but can't concentrate. Sofya Andreyevna was very agitated, went into the garden and didn't come back. She came in after 12. And she wanted to have it out again. I was very depressed, but I restrained myself and she calmed down. She has decided to leave today. Thank goodness, Sasha has decided to go with her. She said goodbye very movingly and asked everyone's forgiveness. I feel a very great and loving pity for her. Some good letters. I'm going to bed. Wrote her a note.

30 August It's sad without her. I'm afraid for her. There's no tranquillity. Walked along the roads. Was just about to start work. Mavor came.[142] A professor. Very lively, but a professor, and a supporter of the state, and an irreligious man. The classic type of the good scholar. [. . .]

Today is 1 September [. . .] We went to the Matveyevs'.[143] Felt a very strong impression of the contrast between strong, sensible, hard-working people, worthy of respect, who are completely in the power of idle, debauched people on the lowest level of development – almost animals. I'm tired of them. They are all on the verge of insanity. [. . .]

The Mamontovs came. The insanity of the rich is more and more glaring. But I played cards with them until 11 o'clock and was ashamed. I want to stop playing all games. I'm tired and going to bed.

3 September Went for a walk in the morning, but didn't get as far as Obraztsovka. Came back and began writing with such enthusiasm as I haven't felt for a long time. Rode to Trekhanetovo to see a peasant. His horse had died. A strong impression. The old man was older than me. They were threshing at his place. Mamontova. Sasha came back. It's as painfully depressing as ever at home. Bear up, Lev Nikolayevich. I'm trying. I didn't want to play cards in the evening, but sat in for others.

5 September [. . .] Sofya Andreyevna came back. Very agitated, but not hostile. [. . .]

6 September, Kochety Woke up sick, probably gangrene from old age. The pleasant thing was that it not only didn't cause any unpleasantness, but rather a pleasant feeling of the nearness of death. Apart from that – weakness and lack of appetite. Pleasant news from the Transvaal about a colony of non-resisters.[144] I've eaten nothing, it's now evening and the cinematographer[145] has come. I'll try to go and watch. Talked with Sofya Andreyevna, all is well. [. . .]

7, 8 September [. . .] Only wrote letters, one to an Indian,[146] and one about non-resistance to a Russian. Sofya Andreyevna is becoming more and more irritable. It's depressing. But I'm bearing up. I can't yet go as far as doing what ought to be done calmly. I'm afraid of the letter we're expecting from Cherktov. [. . .] Sofya Andreyevna kept wanting Drankov to photograph both of us together. I don't think I'll work. I'm restless. Haven't written anything. Walked round the park and made a few notes. Received a letter from Chertkov, and Sofya Andreyevna received a letter from him. Just before that we had a painful talk about my departure.[147] I stood up for my freedom. I'll go when *I* want to. I'm very sad, of course, because I'm not well. I'm going to bed.

10 September Got up early. Didn't sleep much, but am fresher than yesterday. Sofya Andreyevna is still just as irritable. I was very depressed. Went riding for a bit with Dušan. A good letter from a peasant about faith. Answered it. And a very good one from an Italian in Rome about my philosophy.[148] Sofya Andreyevna has eaten nothing for the second day. They're about to have dinner. I'll go and ask her to come to dinner. Terrible scenes all evening.

12 September Sofya Andreyevna left in tears. She tried to summon me in for a talk; I evaded it. She took no one with her. I'm very, very tired. Read in the evening. I'm worried about her.

14 September [. . .]
(1) I must remember that in my relations with Sofya Andreyevna the point is not my own pleasure or displeasure, but the fulfilment of the task of love in the difficult conditions in which she places me.
(2) We are always urging time on. This means that time is the mould of our perception, and we want to free ourselves from this mould which constrains us.

15 September, Kochety [. . .]
(6) Motherhood for a woman *is not the highest calling*. [. . .]
(8) To think and say either that the world is the product of evolution, or that it was created by God in six days is equally silly. Still, the former is the sillier of the two. There is only one sensible thing to say about this: 'I don't know, and can't know, and there's no need to know.' [. . .]
(10) I can't get used to regarding her words as delirium. That's the cause of all my trouble.
   I can't talk with her because neither logic, nor truth, nor the words she herself has spoken, nor her conscience are binding on her – it's terrible.
(11) Not to mention her love for me, of which not a trace remains, she doesn't need my love for her either, she only needs one thing: for people to *think that I love her*. And it's this that's so dreadful. [. . .]

Missed two days: 16 and 17 September. Yesterday morning I revised the letter to Grot a little.[149] And then nothing special except a letter from Yasnaya, a very depressing one.
   Sixty letters, for the most part worthless. Busy again revising the letter to Grot. It's turning out better. Went riding with Dušan. A letter from Chertkov. His translation of my letter to Gandhi. A letter from Mrs Mayo.[150] A copy of the letter to Sofya Andreyevna. All very good. A few things to note down. Tomorrow.

20 September Wrote nothing 'tomorrow' (the 18th), nor the 19th. On the 18th I revised the letter to Grot and wrote a few letters. Unwell – my stomach. Walked for a bit. In the evening I read an interesting book: *Seekers After God*.[151]
   On the 19th I was still unwell; didn't touch the letter to Grot but thought seriously about it. Went for a walk in the morning. An interesting story by Kudrin on serving his 'punishment' for refusing military service.[152] Kupchinsky's book would be very good if it weren't for its exaggeration.[153] Read *Seekers Afer God*. A telegram from Yasnaya asking about my health and time of arrival. [. . .]

22 September [. . .] Yasnaya Polyana. Had a very good journey. Called on the dear Abrikosovs. Was sorry I didn't call in at Gorbov's school.[154] He came out with the children. At home I found Sofya Andreyevna in an angry mood: reproaches and tears. I remained silent.

23 September This morning Sofya Andreyevna went out somewhere; later she was in tears. It was very depressing. A pile of letters. Some interesting ones. Sasha was angry and unjust. Had dinner, read Max Müller's *Indian Philosophy*.[155] What an empty book. Lost my little notebook.[156] [. . .]

24 September Walked to Nikolayev's and the Kaluga men who were making felt boots. At home – books: a German one by Schmitt on science, the letter to an Indian, and the one on law. Schmitt is a scientific windbag. Maude is also preaching at me.[157] Went riding with Bulgakov. Dear Marya Alexandrovna. Sofya Andreyevna was unpleasant. It had passed off by evening. She is sick, and I'm sorry for her with all my heart.

Yes, I spent a while looking through *There are no Guilty People in the World*. I can go on with it. Note: [. . .]
(2) There's a difference between knowledge and science. Knowledge is everything, science is a part. It's just like the difference between religion and the Church.

25 September Got up, wrote a letter. Went for a walk. On my walk I wrote another letter to Malinovsky on the death penalty.[158] [. . .] Some unpleasant taking of photographs. [. . .]

26 September Slept badly; bad dreams. Got up and hung the photographs in their right place again.[159] Went for a walk. Began writing to the young Czechs;[160] continued working on the booklets *For the Soul*.[161] I'm a bit more satisfied. A student, Chebotaryov, came. He's faced with military service. He doesn't know how to act. A sincere person, I liked him. Went riding with Dušan. When I got back I found Sofya Andreyevna in an agitated state. She had burned the photograph of Chertkov. I began to say something, but stopped – it's impossible to understand her. In the evening Khiryakov and Nikolayev came. I was very tired. Sofya Andreyevna tried to speak again. I remained silent. I only said before dinner that she had rearranged my photographs in my room and then burned the photograph of my friend and that I seemed to be to blame for everything. The sequel to the day was the return of Sasha and Varvara Mikhaylovna,[162] summoned by Marya Alexandrovna. Sofya Andreyevna gave them a stormy reception, so Sasha decided to leave.

27 September In the morning I saw Sasha off '– she has gone to Telyatinki for good.[163] Went for a walk and wrote an addition to the letter to Grot. At home – the booklets and letters. Nothing more. Went for a ride in the Tula direction. Health good. I'm bearing up. Made a few notes. Khiryakov came. Sent the booklets to Gorbunov and Anishina's letter to the newspapers.[164]

28 September I.I.A. Alive. But, weak and unwell. Sasha came over. I did absolutely nothing and didn't make a start on anything except letters, and only a few of them. Rode to Marya Alexandrovna's. Nikolayev was there. On my way back, as I left the village, I met Chertkov and Rostovtsev. We talked for a bit and parted. He was obviously very glad. And so was I. In the evening I read. One book by a writer from the people, a rival of Gorky's,[165] and an interesting book, *Antoine le Guérisseur.*[166] A truly religious philosophy, only badly expressed. [. . .]

29 September Got up early. Frost and sunshine. I'm still weak. Went for a walk. I've just returned. Sasha came running in. Sofya Andreyevna couldn't sleep and also got up early before 8. She's very nervous. I must be more careful. On my walk just now I twice caught myself feeling dissatisfied because I had renounced my freedom of will and also because the new edition will be sold for hundreds of thousands of roubles,[167] but both times I put myself to rights with the thought that one needs only to be pure in the sight of God. And one is immediately aware of the joy of life. [. . .]

29 September, Yasnaya Polyana
(1) What terrible mental poison modern literature is, especially for young folk from the people. First of all they stuff their minds with the obscure, self-assured, empty chatter of writers who are writing for the modern reader. The chief peculiarity and harmfulness of such chatter is that it all consists of allusions to, and quotations from the most various of writers, the most modern as well as the most ancient. Phrases are quoted from Plato, Hegel and Darwin, about whom the writers themselves haven't the least conception, and alongside them are phrases from people like Gorky, Andreyev, Artsybashev and others, about whom it isn't worthwhile having any conception. Secondly, this chatter is harmful because, by filling their heads in this way it leaves no room or leisure for them to get to know the old writers who have stood the test of time not only for decades, but for hundreds and thousands of years.

Sasha has come. Sofya Andreyevna said she is ready to make peace with Varya.[168] Then I was moved by the fact that she thanked me for my affection towards her. It's frightening, but I would like to think that even she can be overcome by kindness. [. . .]

30 September I feel very poorly and weak. Did nothing except letters, and those badly. Went riding with Dušan – it was pleasant. In the evening I read my biography,[169] and it was interesting. It's very exaggerated. Sasha came. Sofya Andreyevna is calm. Note. [. . .]
(2) Sofya Andreyevna says she doesn't understand love for one's enemies, and that it's an affectation. She and many others don't understand it, mainly because they think that the partiality they feel towards people is love.

1 October Still the same listlessness. Received from Chertkov Lentovskaya's letters and an article of his,[170] and something else too. I read them. His work on the soul is interesting and good. Few letters, and those uninteresting. Wrote a bit about socialism for the Czechs. Sofya Andreyevna spoke about wanting to see Chertkov. I said that there was nothing to say, that she should simply stop being foolish and behave normally. Went riding with Bulgakov. The evening with Goldenweiser. Also read Maupassant. *The Family* is marvellous. [. . .]

2 October Got up feeling ill. Went for a walk. An unpleasant north wind. Made no notes, but thought very well and clearly during the night about how good it would be to depict in literary form all the vulgarity of the life of the wealthy and bureaucratic classes and of the peasant workers, and to put in the midst of both groups at least one person who is spiritually alive. It could be a man and a woman. Oh, how good it could be. And how it attracts me. What a great work it could be. And I'm actually thinking about it now without any thought of the consequences which are bound to follow with any real work, including any real literary work. Oh, how good it could be. Reading a story by Maupassant yesterday made me wish to depict the vulgarity of life as I know it, and during the night it occurred to me to place in the midst of this vulgarity a person who is spiritually alive. Oh, how good! Perhaps something will come of it.[171] [. . .]

3 October Yesterday I didn't finish writing about the evening. Had a good talk with Seryozha and Biryukov about Sonya's illness. Then Goldenweiser played beautifully, and I had a good talk with him. [. . .] Note: [. . .]
(2) Music, as indeed any art, but especially music, arouses the desire that everyone, or as many people as possible, might participate in the pleasure being experienced. Nothing demonstrates the true significance of art more emphatically than this: you are transported into other people, you want to feel through them. [. . .]

5 October I've been seriously ill for two days since the 3rd. Fainting spells and weakness. It began the day before yesterday, 3 October, after my nap before dinner. A good consequence of it was Sofya Andreyevna's reconciliation with Sasha and Varvara Mikhaylovna. But Chertkov is still as far away from me. I'm particularly sorry for him and Galya, for whom this is very painful. [. . .]

6 October Got up in better spirits, but very weak, and went for a walk. Made a few notes. Sasha will copy them out. To be noted now:
(1) On my walk I felt particularly clearly and vividly the life of calves, sheep, moles, trees: each tree has somehow put down roots and is getting on with its job – has put out a sucker during the summer: a seed becomes a fir tree, an acorn – an oak tree, and they grow and will do so for centuries, and new trees will grow from them, and it's the same with sheep, moles and people. And this has been going on for an infinite number of years, and will go on for the same infinite time, and is going on in Africa and India and Australia and in every corner of the globe. And there are thousands and millions of such globes. And when you understand this clearly, how ridiculous it is to talk about the greatness of any work of man or even

of man himself. Man is higher than all the other creatures we know, that's true, but just as there are below man an infinite number of lower creatures whom we know in part, so above man there must be an infinite number of higher creatures whom we do not know because we cannot know. And when man is in such a situation, to talk about any greatness in him is ridiculous. The only thing we can wish of ourselves as men is not to do foolish things. Yes, only that. [. . .]

(3) The most common reproach levelled against people who express their convictions is that they don't live in accordance with them, and that therefore their convictions are insincere. But if you think about it seriously, you will realise that it's just the opposite. Can an intelligent man who expresses convictions with which his way of life is not in accord help seeing this discrepancy? But if, nevertheless, he expresses convictions which do not accord with his way of life, this only shows that he is so sincere that he cannot help expressing what exposes his weakness, and that he is not doing what the majority of people do – tailoring his convictions to suit his weakness.

7 October [. . .] Sonya had a hysterical fit again; it was depressing.

8 October Got up early and went to meet the horses which had come to take dear Tanechka away. Said goodbye to her. Sasha and Varvara Mikhaylovna also saw her off and I came back home. Revised *On Socialism*. A shallow article. Then read Nikolayev.[172] At first I liked it very much, but then less so, particularly the synopsis of the first part. There are shortcomings, inaccuracies, far-fetched interpretations. Sonya came; I told her everything I wanted to but couldn't keep calm. I was very agitated. [. . .]

9 October Health better. Went for a walk and had some good thoughts in the morning, namely:
(1) The body? Why the body? Why space, time, causality? But surely the question 'why?' is a question about causality. And the mystery – why a body? – remains a mystery.
(2) I must ask: not why I live, but what I should do. [. . .]
  Spent the evening quietly and calmly; read about socialism and prisons in *Russian Wealth*. I'm going to bed.

10 October [. . .]
(3) When revolutionaries attain power, they inevitably must act as all people in power do, i.e. commit violence, i.e. do the things without which power does not and cannot exist.

11 October The days fly by without work. Got up late. Went for a walk. At home Sofya Andreyevna was agitated again by my imaginary secret meetings with Chertkov. I'm very sorry for her, she is ill. [. . .] Note: [. . .]
(2) One must be like a lamp, closed to outside influences – the wind, insects – and at the same time clean, transparent and burning warmly. [. . .]

12 October   Got up late. A depressing conversation with Sofya Andreyevna. I was silent most of the time. I've been busy revising *On Socialism*. Rode with Bulgakov to meet Sasha. After dinner I read Dostoyevsky.[173] The descriptions are good, although certain little jokes, long-winded and not very funny, get in the way. But the conversations are impossible, completely unnatural. In the evening there were painful speeches again from Sofya Andreyevna. I remained silent. I'm going to bed.

13 October   Still mentally lacking in vigour, but spiritually alive. Revised *On Socialism* again. It's all very insignificant. But I've started it. I'll be more restrained and economical in my work. There isn't much time left to me, and I'm wasting it on trifles. Perhaps I'll still write something useful.

Sofya Andreyevna is very agitated and is suffering. One would think it's so simple, what lies ahead of her: to live out the years of old age in harmony and love with her husband, not interfering in his work or his life. But no, she wants – God knows what she wants – she wants to torment herself. Of course it's an illness, and it's impossible not to pity her.

14 October   Everything is just the same. But I'm very weak physically today. There was a letter from Sofya Andreyevna on the table with accusations and an invitation to renounce something.[174] When she came in, I asked her to leave me in peace. She went away. I had a tight feeling in my chest and a pulse of over 90. Revised *On Socialism* again. A futile occupation. Before going out I went to see Sofya Andreyevna and told her that I advised her to leave me in peace and not to interfere with my work. It's depressing. [. . .]

16 October   Not quite well; listless. Went for a walk; couldn't think of anything. Letters; revised *On Socialism*, but soon felt weak and gave it up. Said at lunch that I would go to the Chertkovs'. A stormy scene commenced; she ran out of the house and ran to Telyatinki. I set off on horseback and sent Dušan to say that I wouldn't go to the Chertkovs', but he couldn't find her. I came back, she still wasn't there. Finally they found her after 6 o'clock. She came back and sat motionless in her outdoor clothes, and wouldn't eat anything. And this evening she tried to explain herself, not very well. Late at night she asked forgiveness very movingly, admitted she was tormenting me and promised not to go on tormenting me. Will anything come of it?

17 October   Got up at 8; walked round the Chepyzh wood. Very weak. Thought well about death and wrote about it to Chertkov. Sofya Andreyevna came in and behaved just as gently and kindly towards me. But she is very agitated and talks a lot. Did nothing except letters. I can't work or write, but thank God I can work on myself. I'm still making progress. Read Sri Sankara.[175] It's not right. Read Sasha's diary. Good, simple and truthful. [. . .]

18 October   Still weak. And the weather is bad. Thank God, without wishing it I feel a *readiness for death*, which is good. Didn't walk much. A depressing impression made by two petitioners – I don't know how to deal with them. I haven't done anything rude, but I feel guilty and it's depressing. And serve me right. Walked round the garden. Few thoughts. Slept, and got up feeling very weak. Read Dostoyevsky and was astonished at his slipshod manner, artificiality and fabrication, and read Nikolayev's *Concept of God*. The first three chapters of the first part are very, very good. [. . .]

19 October During the night Sofya Andreyevna came in: 'There's another conspiracy against me.' – 'What do you mean, what conspiracy?' – 'Your diary has been given to Chertkov. It's not here.' – 'Sasha has it.' It was very depressing; I couldn't get to sleep for a long time because I couldn't suppress an unkind feeling. Had a pain in my liver. Molostvova came. I walked through the fir trees, hardly able to move. [. . .]

Did nothing again, except letters. Health bad. The change is near. It would be good to live out the rest of my life a bit better. Sofya Andreyevna said she was sorry about yesterday. I made one or two remarks, especially about the fact that if there is hatred even for one person, there can be no true love. Talked with Molostvova, or rather listened to her. Skimmed through the first volume of *The Karamazovs*, and finished it. There's much that is good in it, but it's so disorganised. *The Grand Inquisitor* and Zosima's farewell. [. . .]

20 October I.I.A. Alive, and even a bit better. But still I didn't do any serious work. Revised *On Socialism*. A depressing impression made by the petitioners. Went a long ride with Dušan. Mikhail Novikov came. Talked a lot with him. A serious and intelligent peasant. Perevoznikov and Titov's son, a revolutionary, also came. In the morning I said goodbye to Molostvova. All quiet.

21 October [. . .] Tried to continue with *On Socialism* and decided to give it up. It's badly begun, and anyway there's no need for it. There will only be repetitions. Then came the Yasnaya 'recruits'. I talked to them. We're too far apart: we don't understand each other. [. . .]

22 October I'm still doing no work. Dunayev[176] is kind, impulsive and, in a natural sort of way, affected. A good letter from Chertkov. Didn't go riding, but went for a walk. Talked to some lavatory cleaners. Made no notes. In the letter to Dosev[177] there is much truth, but not the whole truth. It has its weaknesses too. I've no wish even to write my diary. Nikolayev's book is excellent.

23 October For me the letter to Dosev is above all a programme which I'm still so far from fulfilling. My talks with Novikov are enough to show that.[178] [. . .]

Dear Bulgakov has arrived. He had been reading a paper,[179] and vanity is already gnawing at him. A good letter from a priest; I answered it. Made a little progress with the article *On Socialism* which I've taken up again. Went for a ride. Spent all evening reading the cheap booklets and sorting them out. Wrote a note to Galya in the morning. A letter from Gusev about Dostoyevsky – just exactly what I feel.

24 October Today I received two letters: one, apropos of Merezhkovsky's article, denouncing me,[180] and the other from a German abroad, also denouncing me. I was hurt. [. . .]

Gastev and Mme Almedingen arrived.[181] Read letters and answered them, and did nothing else. In the morning I *made a real fool of myself*. Began doing some gymnastics, unsuited to my years, and brought down a cupboard on top of me. What a fool. I feel weak. But I've come to my senses, thank goodness. Worked a bit on *Socialism*. Gastev talked very well about Syutayev and a Cossack. The people must have a guide in the religious sphere and a leader in the secular one.
(1) I imagined very vividly a story about a priest trying to convert an unattached religious person, and how the converter is himself converted. A good subject.[182] [. . .]

25 October Got up very early, but did nothing all the same. Walked to the school and to Prokofy's, and had a talk with his son, an army conscript. A good lad; he promised not to drink. Then a bit of *On Socialism*. Rode to the school with Almedingen and then a long ride with Dušan. In the evening I read Montaigne. Seryozha came. I found him pleasant. Sofya Andreyevna still as troubled as ever.

26 October Had a dream. Grushenka, a romance it seemed with Nikolay Nikolayevich Strakhov. A wonderful subject.[183] Wrote a letter to Chertkov. Made notes for *On Socialism*. Wrote to Chukovsky about the death penalty.[184] Rode to Marya Alexandrovna's with Dušan. Andrey came. I'm very depressed in this madhouse. I'm going to bed.

27 October Got up very early. Had bad dreams all night. Had a good walk. At home – letters. Worked a bit on the letter for N.[185] and *On Socialism*, but had no mental energy. Went riding with Dušan. Dinner. Read about Syutayev.[186] A marvellous letter from a Ukrainian to Chertkov. Revised the article for Chukovsky. Nothing to note. That seems bad, but actually it's good. The burden of our relations is getting worse.

28 October, Optina Monastery Went to bed at 11.30. Slept till after two. Woke up, and again, as on previous nights, I heard the opening of doors and footsteps. On previous nights I hadn't looked at my door, but this time I did look and saw through the crack a bright light in the study and heard rustling. It was Sofya Andreyevna looking for something and probably reading. The day before she was asking and insisting that I shouldn't lock my doors. Both her doors were open, so that she could hear my slightest movement. Day and night all my movements and words have to be known to her and to be under her control. There were footsteps again, the door opened carefully and she walked through the room. I don't know why, but this aroused indignation and uncontrollable revulsion in me. I wanted to go back to sleep, but couldn't; I tossed about for an hour or so, lit a candle and sat up. Sofya Andreyevna opened the door and came in, asking about 'my health' and expressing surprise at the light which she had seen in my room. My indignation and revulsion grew. I gasped for breath, counted my pulse: 97. I couldn't go on lying there, and suddenly I took the final decision to leave. I wrote her a letter and began to pack the most necessary things, just so that I could leave. I woke Dušan, then Sasha, and they helped me pack. I trembled at the thought that she would hear and come out – that there would be a scene, hysterics – and I wouldn't be able to leave later without a scene.

Everything was packed somehow or other before 6; I walked to the stables to tell them to harness the horses; Dušan, Sasha and Varya finished off the packing. The night was pitch black, I lost my way to the outhouse, found myself in a thicket, pricked myself, bumped into some trees, fell over, lost my cap, couldn't find it, made my way out again with an effort, went back home, took another cap and with the aid of a lantern made my way to the stables and ordered the horses to be harnessed. Sasha, Dušan and Varya arrived. I trembled as I waited to be pursued. But then we were on our way. We waited an hour at Shchokino, and every minute I expected her to appear. But then we were in the carriage, the train started, and my fear passed, and pity for her rose up within me, but not doubt about having done what I had to do. Perhaps I'm mistaken in justifying myself, but I think it was not myself, not Lev Nikolayevich, that I was saving, but something that is sometimes, and if only to a very small extent, within me. We reached Optina. I'm well, although I haven't slept and have hardly eaten anything. The journey from Gorbachovo in a third-class carriage, packed with working people, was very edifying and good, although I was too weak to take it in properly. It's now 8 o'clock, and we are in Optina.

29 October, Optina Monastery – Shamardino[187] Slept uneasily; in the morning Alyosha Sergeyenko came. I didn't understand why, and welcomed him cheerfully. But the news he brought was terrible. When Sofya Andreyevna read my letter she screamed and ran into the pond. Sasha and Vanya[188] ran after her and dragged her out. Andrey has come home. They guessed where I was and Sofya Andreyevna asked Andrey to find me at all costs. And now, the evening of the 29th, I'm awaiting Andrey's arrival. A letter from Sasha. She advises me not to despair. She has written for a psychiatrist, and is waiting for Seryozha and Tanya to arrive. I was very depressed all day, and physically weak besides. Went for a walk, and yesterday I finished a note to *Speech* about the death penalty. Travelled to Shamardino. Mashenka made a very comforting and joyful impression on me, despite her story about 'the evil one', and so did dear Lizanka.[189] They both understand my situation and sympathise with it. On the journey I kept thinking as I was travelling about a way out of my situation and hers, and couldn't think of any, but there surely will be one, whether we want it or not, and it won't be the one we foresee. Yes, I should only think about not sinning. And what will be will be. That's not my business. I found a copy of the *Cycle of Reading* at Mashenka's, and just as I was reading the 28th, I was struck directly by the answer to my situation: this ordeal is necessary for me, it's beneficial for me. I'm going to bed now. Help me, Lord. A good letter from Chertkov.

30 October I.I.A. Alive, but not entirely. I'm very weak and sleepy, and that's a bad sign.
Read something from Novosyolov's philosophical library.[190] Very interesting – on socialism. My article *On Socialism* has been lost.[191] A pity. No, not a pity. Sasha has come. I was very glad. But also depressed. Letters from my sons. The letter from Sergey is good, business-like, short and kind.[192] Went to rent a hut in Shamardino in the morning. Very tired. Wrote a letter to Sofya Andreyevna.[193]

31 October, Astapovo They are all there at Shamardino.[194] Sasha and I were afraid they would catch us up, and we set off.[195] Sasha caught us up at Kozelsk; we got on the train and set off. We had a good journey, but between 4 and 5 I began to shiver, then my temperature was 40° and we stopped at Astapovo. The kind stationmaster has given us two fine rooms.

3 November, Astapovo Had a bad night. Lay for two days in a fever. Chertkov came on the 2nd. They say that Sofya Andreyevna has too. Seryozha came during the night, I was very moved. Today, the 3rd, Nikitin and Tanya came, then Goldenweiser and Ivan Ivanovich. So much for my plan. *Fais ce que dois, adv . . .* [Do what you must, come . . .]
And it's all for the good, for the others and above all for me.[196]

Diary for Myself Alone

1910, 29 July, Yasnaya Polyana I'm beginning a new diary, a real diary for myself alone. Today there is one thing I must note: namely that if the suspicions of some of my friends are right, an attempt has now begun to gain her ends by means of affection. For several days now she has been kissing my hand, something that never happened before, and there are no scenes and no despair. May God and good people forgive me if I am mistaken. And I can easily be mistaken over kindness and love. I can love her completely sincerely, which I can't say about Lev. Andrey is simply one of those people about whom it's difficult to think that they have a divine soul (but he has, remember). I'll try not to get angry and to stand my ground, chiefly by keeping silent.
One shouldn't deprive millions of people of what is perhaps necessary for their souls.[1] I repeat 'perhaps'. But even if there is the slightest possibility that what I've written may be necessary for people's souls, then one shouldn't deprive them of this spiritual food so that Andrey can drink and indulge in debauchery and Lev can daub away[2] and . . . But never mind about them. Get on with your own things and don't condemn others . . . It's morning.
The day was just like the previous ones: I felt unwell, but there was less unkindness in my heart. I'm waiting to see what happens, and that's bad.

Sofya Andreyevna is quite calm.

30 July Chertkov has involved me in a struggle, and this struggle is both very depressing and very repugnant to me.³ I'll try to wage it *with love* (it's terrible to say how far away I am from it).

In my present situation, what I probably need above all is *to do nothing and to say nothing*. Today I have clearly understood that I need only to avoid making my situation worse, and to remember clearly that I need *nothing, nothing at all*.

31 July Spent an idle evening. The Lodyzhenskys⁴ came, and I talked too much. Sofya Andreyevna couldn't sleep again, but she isn't angry. I'm waiting.

1 August Slept well, but am still bored, sad, listless and painfully aware of the lack of love round about me and, alas, within me. Help me, Lord! Sasha is coughing again. Sofya Andreyevna has been telling Posha all the usual things. It's all alive in her: jealousy of Chertkov and fear for the property. It's very depressing. I can't stand Lev Lvovich. And he wants to settle here. What an ordeal! Letters in the morning. Wrote badly; corrected one proof. I'm going to bed in a depressed state of mind. I'm ill.

2 August I.I.A. I've realised my mistake very, very clearly. I should have summoned all my heirs and announced my intentions, and not kept it secret. I've written this to Chertkov.⁵ He was very upset. I rode to Kolpna. Sofya Andreyevna drove over to check up and keep a watch on me; she rummages about in my papers. She's just been questioning me about who brings the letters from Chertkov: 'You're carrying on a secret love correspondence.' I said I didn't want to talk and left, but I was gentle. Unhappy woman, I can't help pitying her. Wrote a letter to Galya.

3 August I go to bed with anguish in my heart, and wake up with the same anguish. I just can't overcome it. Went for a walk in the rain. Worked at home. Went riding with Goldenweiser. Felt depressed in his company for some reason. A letter from Chertkov. He's very upset. I said 'yes', and I've decided to wait and not undertake anything.⁶ It's very good that I feel how worthless I am. In the evening an insane note from Sofya Andreyevna⁷ and a demand that I read it. I glanced at it and gave it back. She came in and began to talk. I locked myself in, then ran away and sent Dušan to her. How will this end? The only thing is not to sin oneself. I'm going to bed. I.I.A.

4 August Nothing depressing happened today, but I feel depressed. Finished the proofs, but wrote nothing. Lost my temper with some schoolboys, and was wrong to do so; then welcomed a student and his wife and gave them a book. A great deal of fuss and bother. Went riding with Dušan to the Lodyzhenskys'. Posha is leaving and Korolenko is coming.

5 August My thoughts were a bit clearer. My renouncing Chertkov's company is shameful, embarrassing, comic and sad.⁸ Yesterday morning she was very pitiable, and without any malice, I'm always so glad of this – it's so easy for me to pity and love her when she is suffering, and not making other people suffer.

6 August Today, as I lay in bed, I had a thought which, it seemed to me, was very important. I thought I would write it down later. And I forgot it, forgot it and couldn't remember it. I've just met Sofya Andreyevna, just here as I was writing this. She was walking quickly, looking terribly agitated. I became very sorry for her. I told them at home to watch her secretly and see where she went. But Sasha said that she was not walking about aimlessly, but was keeping a watch on me. I became less sorry for her. There is unkindness here, and I'm not yet able to remain indifferent to it – in the sense of loving what is unkind. I think about going away and leaving a letter, and I'm afraid to, although I think it would be better for her. I've just read my letters, taken up *Insanity* and put it down again. I've no desire to write and no strength. It's now after 12. This constant hiding and my fear for her are depressing.

7 August A talk with Korolenko. An intelligent and good man, but completely dominated by the superstition of science. The work I have to do is very clear to me, and it will be a pity not to write it, but I don't seem to have the strength. Everything is confused, and I don't have any tenacity or steadfastness of purpose in one direction. Sofya Andreyevna is calmer, but there is the same unkindness towards everyone, the same irritability. Read about 'paranoia' in Korsakov.⁹ It's as though it were copied from her. Sasha had had the book, and passages were underlined, probably by her. Korolenko said to me: 'What a fine person Alexandra Lvovna is.' There were tears of emotion in my throat, and I couldn't speak. When I recovered I said: 'I haven't the right to say so, she loves me too much.' Korolenko said: 'Well, but I have the right.'

It's still just as difficult for me with Lev, but, thank God, I have no unkind feelings.

8 August Got up early. Many, many thoughts, but all scattered. Well, never mind. I pray and pray: help me! And I cannot, I cannot help wishing and waiting for death with joy. My separation from Chertkov is more and more shameful. I'm obviously to blame.¹⁰ [. . .]

The same thing again with Sofya Andreyevna. She wants Chertkov to come. Again she couldn't sleep until 7 in the morning. [. . .]

My memory has gone, quite gone, and the astonishing thing is, I've not only not lost anything, but have actually gained a tremendous amount – in clarity and strength of *consciousness*. I even think that the one is always at the expense of the other.

9 August I'm taking a more and more serious attitude to life. Agitation once again. Talks with Ferre and Sasha.¹¹ Sasha is harsh. Lyova is a great and difficult ordeal.

10 August Everything is just as depressing, and I'm unwell. It's good to feel one is to blame, and I have this feeling. [. . .]

11 August Health worse and worse. Sofya Andreyevna is calm, but just as alien. Letters. Answered two. It's depressing with everyone. I can't help wishing for death. A long letter from Chertkov describing everything that has happened so far. It was very sad and depressing to read and to recall. He is absolutely right and I feel myself to blame towards him. Posha was wrong. I'll write to them both. All that I'm writing here.

12 August Decided yesterday to tell Tanya everything.[12] Since this morning I've felt a depressing, unkind feeling towards her, towards Sofya Andreyevna. And I must forgive and pity her, but I can't as yet.

Told Tanya. She is glad and agrees. Chertkov was very pleased with my letter according to Sasha. I didn't go out all day. In the evening Gay talked well about Switzerland. Sofya Andreyevna is very agitated, and always in this condition – she is obviously ill – I feel very sorry for her. I'm going to bed.

13 August Everything just the same, and her condition is just as depressing and dangerous. A good letter from Chertkov – telling me not to go and say goodbye if it might prevent my departure.[13] Tanechka is nice and sweet.

14 August Still worse and worse. She didn't sleep last night. In the morning she jumped out of bed. 'Who are you talking to?' Then she spoke about something terrible: sexual excitation. A dreadful thing to say [3 words crossed out].

It's terrible, but thank God, she's to be pitied and I can pity her. I'll put up with it. God help me. She has tormented everyone, and herself most of all. She's going with us. Apparently she's turning Varya[14] out of the house. Sasha is distressed. I'm going to bed.

15 August On the journey to Kochety I thought that if these disturbances and demands began again I'd go away with Sasha. And I said so. That's what I thought on the journey. Now I don't think so. We arrived peacefully, but in the evening I took my notebook from Sasha and she saw me. 'What's that?' 'My diary. Sasha is copying from it.'

16 August This morning she hadn't slept again. She brought me a note saying that Sasha was copying out my accusations against her from my diary to give to Chertkov. Before dinner I tried to console her by telling her the truth that Sasha was only copying out isolated thoughts, and not my impressions of life. She wants to be consoled, and is much to be pitied. [. . .]

17 August A good day today. Sonya is quite well. It was good, too, in that I felt anguish. And my anguish was expressed in prayer and consciousness.

18 August Sofya Andreyevna, having learned that Chertkov has been given permission to live at Telyatinki, was reduced to a state of morbidity. 'I'll kill him.' I begged her not to talk, and remained silent. And this seemed to have a good effect.

Something is going to happen. Help me, God, to be with Thee and to do Thy will. And what happens will not be my affair. Often, no not often but sometimes, I am in this state of mind, and how good it is then!

19 August Sofya Andreyevna has been begging me since morning to promise what I promised before and not to have photographs taken. I agreed, and was wrong to do so. A good letter from Chertkov. He is right in what he says about the methods which have the best effect on sick people.[15] At dinner I spoke inopportunely about Arago *tout court* [quite simply].[16] And I was ashamed. And ashamed that I was ashamed.

20 August Had a good talk with the watchman. It was bad that I told him about my situation. Went riding, and the sight of this seignorial domain so torments me that I'm thinking of running away and hiding.

Today I thought as I recalled my marriage that there was something fateful about it. I was never even in love. But I couldn't help getting married.

21 August Got up late. Feel fresher. Sofya Andreyevna is just the same. She told Tanya that she hadn't slept all night because she had seen a photograph of Chertkov. The situation is threatening. I want to speak, I want to speak, i.e. to write.

22 August A letter from Rossolimo,[17] a remarkably stupid one about Sofya Andreyevna's condition, and a very good letter from B.[18]

I'm behaving quite well.

23 and 24 August I'm reviving a little. Sofya Andreyevna, poor woman, suffers incessantly, and I feel the impossibility of helping her. I feel the sinfulness of my own exclusive attachment to my daughters.

25 August Varvara Mikhaylovna writes about the gossip at Zvegintseva's.[19] This irritates Sasha. It's all the same to me, thank God, but it impairs my feelings towards *her*. It shouldn't do. Oh, if only I could be gentle, but firm.

26 August Sofya Andreyevna spoke heatedly with Tanya last night. She is completely hopeless, her thinking is so inconsistent. I'm glad that I kept silent in response to her provocations and complaints. Thank God, I haven't the least bad feeling.

27 August She is terribly pitiable and difficult. This evening she began to talk about the photographs, from her own morbid point of view obviously. I tried to keep out of it all. And I went away.

28 August Things are more and more difficult with Sofya Andreyevna. It isn't love, but a demand for love which is near to hatred and is turning into hatred.

Yes, egoism is madness. She used to be saved by the children – an animal love, but nevertheless an unselfish one. But when that was over, all that was left was terrible egoism. And egoism is the most abnormal condition – madness.

I've just spoken with Sasha and Mikhail Sergeyevich, and both Dušan and Sasha refuse to recognise that it is an illness. And they are wrong.

29 and 30 August Yesterday morning was terrible, for no reason at all. She went into the garden and lay there. Then she calmed down. We had a good talk. As she left she touchingly begged forgiveness. Today, the 30th, I'm unwell. Mavor. Sasha telegraphed that it's all right.[20] What will happen?

31 August, 1 September I wrote Sonya a letter which flowed from the heart.

Today – 2 Sepember – I received a very bad letter from her. The same suspicions, the same malice, the same demand for love, which would be comic if it wasn't so terrible and agonising for me. Today in the *Cycle of Reading* – Schopenhauer: 'As the attempt to force people to love evokes hatred, so . . .'

3, 4 September Sasha arrived. She brought bad news. Everything is just the same. Sofya Andreyevna writes to say she will come. She is burning photographs and holding a prayer service in the house.[21] When I'm alone I'm ready to be firm with her and think I can be, but when I'm with her I weaken. I'll try to remember that she is ill.

Today, the 4th, I felt melancholy: I wanted to die and still do.

5, 6, 7, 8 September Sofya Andreyevna arrived. She was very talkative, but at first there was nothing depressing about it, but yesterday it began again, the hints, the searching for excuses to condemn. Very depressing. This morning she ran in to tell me some vile thing about Zosya. I'm bearing up, and will bear up as much as I can, and pity and love her. God help me.

8, 9, 10 September Yesterday, the 9th, she was in hysterics all day; she ate nothing and wept. She was very pitiable. But she won't accept any attempts at persuasion or arguments. I said one or two things, and, thank God, without any ill feeling, and she took them in the usual way, without understanding them. I was unwell myself yesterday – gloomy and despondent. She received a letter from Chertkov and answered it. A letter from Goldenweiser with extracts from V.M.'s diary which horrified me.[22]

Today, the 10th; still the same. She is eating nothing. I went in. Immediately there were reproaches, and about Sasha too, saying she ought to go to the Crimea. I thought in the morning that I couldn't endure it, and would have to leave her. There is no life with her. Only torture. As I said to her: 'My misfortune is that I can't be indifferent.'

11 September Towards evening she began making scenes – running into the garden, tears, screams. It even got to the stage that when I went out after her into the garden she screamed: 'He's a beast, a murderer. I can't bear to see him', and ran off to hire a cart and go away at once. And so it was the whole evening. But when I lost control of myself and told her *son fait* [what I thought of her], she suddenly became well again, and she is still well today, the 11th. It's impossible to talk to her because, first of all, neither logic nor truth are binding on her; nor is the truthful communication of the words which are said to her, or the ones she says herself. I'm very close to running away. My health is not good.

12 September Sofya Andreyevna has left after terrible scenes. I'm gradually becoming calmer.

16–17 September But the letters from Yasnaya are terrible. What is depressing is that among her crazy ideas is one to make me out as feeble-minded, and therefore to render my will, if it exists, invalid. Apart from that there are all the usual stories about me and avowals of hatred of me. I've received a letter from Chertkov confirming everyone's advice to remain firm and supporting my decision. I don't know whether I can hold out.

It's now the night of the 17th.

I want to return to Yasnaya on the 22nd.

22 September, morning I'm going to Yasnaya and I'm terrified at the thought of what awaits me. Only *fais ce que dois* . . . But the main thing is to remain silent and remember that she has a soul – that God is in her.

2

24 September, Yasnaya Polyana I've lost the little diary.[23] I'm writing in this one. The day began calmly. But at lunch they began to talk about *The Wisdom of Children*, and the fact that Chertkov, the collector,[24] had amassed a lot of things. What would he do with the manuscripts after my death? I begged her rather heatedly to leave me in peace. Things seemed all right. But after dinner she began to reproach me and say that I shouted at her and that I ought to pity her. I remained silent. She went to her room and it's now after 10 o'clock and she hasn't come out, and I'm depressed. A letter from Chertkov with reproaches and accusations. They are tearing me to pieces. I sometimes think I should go away from them all. It turns out she had been asleep, and she came out looking calm. I went to bed after 12.

25 September Woke up early, wrote a letter to Chertkov.[25] I hope he will take it the way I ask. I'm now getting dressed. Yes, all my business is with God, and I must be alone. A request again to stand for a photograph in the pose of a loving husband and wife. I agreed, and was ashamed all the time.[26] Sasha was terribly angry. It was painful for me. In the evening I called her and said: 'I don't need your stenography, but I need your love.' And we kissed each other, and both had a good cry.

26 September Scenes again because I had hung up the pictures where they were before. I began to say that it was impossible to go on living like this. And she understood. Dušan said that she fired a child's pistol in order to frighten me. I wasn't frightened and didn't go to her room. And really, it's better. But it's very, very difficult. Help me, Lord.

27 September How comic is the contradiction in which I live whereby, without false modesty, I am conceiving and giving expression to very important and significant ideas, and at the same time am involved in a woman's caprices and devoting a great part of my time to the struggle against them.

In the matter of moral self-improvement I feel myself a complete child, a pupil, and a bad pupil, not very diligent.

Yesterday there was a terrible scene with Sasha when she came back. She screamed at Marya Alexandrovna. Sasha left today for Telyatinki. And she [Sofya Andreyevna] is very calm as if nothing had happened. She showed me the toy pistol, and fired it, and lied. Today she drove after me on my walk, probably spying on me. I'm sorry for her, but it's difficult. Help me, Lord.

28 September It's very depressing. These expressions of love, this talkativeness and constant interference. It's possible, I know it's possible to love all the same. But I can't, I'm unwell.

29 September Sasha wants to go on living for a while away from home. I fear for her. Sofya Andreyevna is better. Sometimes false shame for my weakness comes over me and sometimes, as today, I rejoice in this weakness.

Today for the first time I saw the possibility of winning her over by kindness – by love. Oh, if only I could . . .

30 September Today everything is just the same. She talks a lot for the sake of talking and doesn't listen. There were some depressing moments today because of my weakness: I saw unpleasant and depressing things where they don't exist and can't exist for a true life.

1 October It's terribly depressing, my unkind feeling for her, which I can't overcome when this talking begins – talking without end and without meaning or purpose. Chertkov's article on the soul and God is, I fear, too clever by half.[27] It gladdens me that all truly original religious people have one and the same thing in common. Antoine le Guérisseur too.[28]

2 October In the morning her first words were about her own health, then reproaches and endless talking, and interruptions to the conversation. And I'm not well. I can't overcome bad and unkind feelings. Today I felt keenly the need for literary work and I can see the impossibility of devoting myself to it because of her, my obsessive feelings about her and my inner struggle. Of course this struggle, and the possibility of victory in this struggle are more important than all possible works of art.

3

5 October 1910 Handed over the brochures and am beginning something new today. And it seems necessary to begin something new: on the 3rd, after my nap before dinner, I lost consciousness. They undressed me, put me to bed and gave me an enema, and I said something but don't remember anything. I woke up and came round at about 11. Headache and weakness. All day yesterday I lay in a fever, with a headache; ate nothing and felt the same weakness. It was the same at night too. It's now 7 o'clock in the morning, and my head still aches, and my liver and my legs, and I'm weak, but better. The main thing about my illness is that it reconciled Sasha and Sofya Andreyevna. Sasha especially was good. Varya has come. We shall see. I'm struggling against my unkind feelings towards her, and can't forget these three months of torture for all those near to me and for myself. But I'll overcome it. Didn't sleep during the night, and while I can't say I thought, ideas wandered through my head.

7 October Yesterday was 6 October. I was weak and gloomy. Everything was depressing and unpleasant. A letter from Chertkov. He thinks it's no use. She is making an effort and has asked him to come here.[29] Today Tanya went to the Chertkovs'. Galya is very irritated. Chertkov decided to come at 8, and it's now ten minutes to. Sofya Andreyevna asked me not to kiss him. How disgusting. She had a hysterical fit.

Today is the 8th. I told her all I considered necessary. She objected and I grew irritated. And that was bad. But perhaps something will survive all the same. It's true that it's all a question of my not behaving badly myself; but I'm also sincerely sorry for her – not always, but most of the time. I'm going to bed, having spent the day better.

9 October She is calm, but contrives to talk about herself. I read about hysteria.[30] Everyone is to blame except her. I didn't go to the Chertkovs' and I won't go. Tranquillity is the most valuable thing of all. I feel in a stern and serious mood.

10 October It's quiet, but everything is unnatural and frightening. There's no tranquillity.

11 October This morning she was saying that I'd had a secret meeting with Chertkov yesterday. She hadn't slept all night. But thank goodness, she is struggling with herself. I behaved well and remained silent. Whatever happens she interprets as confirmation of her mania – never mind . . .

12 October More talking this morning and a scene. It seems someone told her about some will of mine bequeathing my diaries to Chertkov. I remained silent. An empty day; I couldn't work well. In the evening the same talk again. Hints and interrogations.

13 October It turns out that she found my little diary and took it away. She knows about some will leaving something to someone – obviously to do with my works. What torture she suffers over their money value – and she's afraid I'll interfere with her edition. Indeed she's afraid of everything, poor thing.

14 October A letter reproaching me for some paper about royalties,[31] as if the money question was all that was important; still that's better – it's clearer; but when she speaks in exaggerated tones about her love for me, and kneels down and kisses my hands, I find it very depressing. I still can't definitely declare that I'll go to the Chertkovs'.

15 October There was a clash with Sasha and general commotion, but it was tolerable.

16 October Today it was decided.
 I wanted to go to Tanya's, but I'm hesitating. A hysterical fit, a nasty one.
 The fact of the matter is that she proposed that I should go to the Chertkovs' and begged me to do so, but today, when I said I would go, she began to rave. It's very, very difficult. Help me, God. I said I would make no promises, and I'm not making any, but I'll do all I can not to anger her. I'll hardly be able to make my departure tomorrow. But I must. Yes, it's an ordeal, and my task is not to do anything unkind. Help me, God.

17 October Weak. Sofya Andreyevna is better and seems to be repentant, but there's a hysterical exaggeration about that too. She kisses my hands. She's very agitated and talks incessantly. I feel well morally. I remember who I am. Read Sri Sankara. The basic metaphysical idea about the essence of life is good, but the teaching as a whole is a muddle, worse than mine.

18 October Still the same depressing relations – fear and alienation. Nothing happened today. She began to talk about faith this evening. She simply doesn't understand what faith is.

19 October A very depressing conversation during the night. I took it badly. Sasha talked of a sale for a million.[32] We'll see what happens. Perhaps it's for the best. If only I could appear before the highest judge and earn his approval.

20 October There is nothing bad to write down. That's bad. I'll only write one thing: Sasha is a joy to me, and she is too sweet and dear to me.

21 October I'm bearing my ordeal with great difficulty. I keep remembering Novikov's words: 'When I used the whip she was much better', and Ivan's 'It's our custom to use the reins', and am displeased with myself. During the night I thought about going away. Sasha talked a lot with her, but I have difficulty in restraining my unkind feelings.

22 October There's nothing hostile on her part, but this pretence on both sides depresses me. A letter to me from Chertkov, with a letter to Dosev and the statement.³³ Everything is very good, but I'm not pleased about the violation of the secrecy of my diary. Dunayev talked well. It's terrible what he told me of what she said to him and to Marya Nikolayevna.

23 October The pretence on both sides is just as depressing as ever; I try to be natural, but it doesn't succeed. I can't stop thinking about Novikov. When I went for a ride, Sofya Andreyevna set off after me on foot, to see whether I had gone to Chertkov's. I'm ashamed to admit my stupidity even in my diary. Yesterday I began doing gymnastics – the old fool wants to get younger – and pulled a cupboard over on myself and hurt myself for nothing. There's an eighty-two-year-old fool for you.

24 October Sasha cried because she had quarrelled with Tanya. I did too. It's very depressing; the same tension and unnaturalness.

25 October Still the same feeling of depression. Suspicions, spying, and the sinful desire on my part that she should give me an excuse to go away. That's how bad I am. I think of going away, and then I think of her situation, and I feel sorry and I can't do it. She asked me for a letter of mine to Galya Chertkova.

26 October I'm still more and more oppressed by this life. Marya Alexandrovna tells me not to go away, and my conscience won't let me either. I must put up with her, put up with her without changing my outward situation, but working on my inner one. Help me, Lord.

[27 October] 25 October Dreamed all night about my painful struggle with her. I would wake up, drop off to sleep, and it would start again. Sasha told me about what was said to Varvara Mikhaylovna. I'm both sorry for her, and unbearably disgusted.

26 October Nothing special happened. Only my feeling of shame increased, and the need to take some step.

28 October, Optina Monastery During the night of the 27–28 came the impetus which made me take this step. And here I am at Optina on the evening of the 28th. Sent Sasha a letter and a telegram.³⁴

29 October Sergeyenko arrived. Everything is the same; worse even. If only I don't sin. And don't bear malice. I don't at present.

Notes

1895

1 Tolstoy and his daughter Tatyana were guests of the Olsufyevs from 1 to 18 January.
2 See 1894, Note 62. Sonya objected to Tolstoy being brought down to the level of the 'Tolstoyans' by being photographed with them.
3 *Master and Man*.
4 D. A. Olsufyev, one of the Olsufyev sons.
5 M. A. Olsufyev, another son, to whom Tatyana was attracted.
6 A. P. Sergeyenko, a writer and frequent visitor at the Tolstoys'. His books included *How Count Tolstoy Lives and Works* and *Tolstoy and his Contemporaries*. He also published three volumes of Tolstoy's letters.
7 In a speech of 17 January 1895 Nicholas II referred to discussions about the possible participation of the *zemstva* in government affairs as 'senseless dreams', and made it clear that he intended to uphold the principle of autocracy no less firmly than his father. On the initiative of D. I. Shakhovskoy, a meeting was organised of members of the liberal intelligentsia at which Tolstoy was present, but he refused to write a statement of protest against the Tsar's speech for publication abroad.
8 The cause of the storm, which presumably led to the page being torn out, was Tolstoy's opposition to his wife's publishing his new story *Master and Man* in her edition of his works in view of his renunciation of copyright, and his offer of the story free of charge to the *Northern Herald*.
9 Tolstoy eventually agreed to let his wife publish *Master and Man*, but also to allow the *Northern Herald* and *The Intermediary* to publish it simultaneously without charge.
10 His *Three Fables* were published at the invitation of the president of the Society of Lovers of Russian Literature in an anthology issued by the Society in 1895.
11 I. I. Gorbunov-Posadov.
12 Goltsev brought a petition from 114 public figures in Petersburg and Moscow asking the Tsar to grant freedom of the press, but Tolstoy refused to sign it because of his views on non-participation in government affairs.
13 Tolstoy had read a newspaper account of the disorderly behaviour of the students who were celebrating the 75th anniversary of the founding of Petersburg University.
14 A. A. Škarvan, a Slovak doctor, who sympathised with Tolstoy's views, refused to serve as a military doctor on conscientious grounds, and was later imprisoned and deprived of his medical diploma. M. V. Alyokhin, a landscape painter and one of three brothers who were all 'Tolstoyans', wished to pay allegiance to the new Tsar, but not to swear an oath. It is not known why Biryukov was fined.
15 Goryushin was a university student with social democratic sympathies; Pavel Petrovich Kandidov was employed at the time as a coach to Tolstoy's young sons and also acted as his wife's secretary in connection with her edition of Tolstoy's works.
16 Tolstoy's son Lev was a patient at the time in Ogranovich's sanatorium near Zvenigorod.
17 Tolstoy's youngest son Ivan died of scarlet fever shortly before his seventh birthday.
18 Probably A. N. Dunayev.
19 Eugen Heinrich Schmitt was an Austrian writer who shared many of Tolstoy's ethical beliefs and hoped to systematise them. He translated some of Tolstoy's articles into German and wrote a book about him (*Letters*, II, 515). Tolstoy wrote to him to propose founding an international *Intermediary* which would publish, perhaps in Switzerland, a series of cheap books and pamphlets in four European languages (see letter to Khilkov in *Letters*, II, 515). Nothing came of the project.

20 Of the stories listed, *Who is Right?* (a story about the famine), *Notes of a Mother*, and the projected novel about the settlers and the Bashkirs were abandoned. *The Devil in Hell* eventually appeared as the legend *The Destruction of Hell and its Rebuilding*. *The Coupon (The Forged Coupon)* was finished in 1904. The story about Alexander I was finished in 1905 and entitled *The Posthumous Notes of the Elder Fyodor Kuzmich*. The drama referred to is *The Light Shineth in Darkness*.
21 Vladimir Solovyov's *The Principle of Punishment from the Moral Point of View* in the *Herald of Europe*, 1895, No. 3.
22 N. T. Izyumchenko, the son of a peasant, was sentenced to two years in a disciplinary battalion as a conscientious objector, and Tolstoy and his wife visited him in a transit prison in Moscow. Khoklov was a patient in a psychiatric hospital.
23 Leskov, who had died in February 1895, left clear instructions in his will about how he was to be buried, and Tolstoy followed his example in wishing to avoid all ceremonies and speeches.
24 The subject of Tolstoy's will was later to become a major source of hostility between his wife and Chertkov.
25 Not really a foreword, but a note about Bondarev (1889, Note 174) for inclusion in *The Critical-Biographical Dictionary of Russian Writers and Scholars* being compiled by the literary historian S. A. Vengerov.
26 Tolstoy's annotated copy of A. G. Ritchie's *The Ruskin Birthday Book* (London, 1883) is in the Yasnaya Polyana library.
27 He did so in his article *Senseless Dreams*.
28 Nothing came of the idea.
29 *Herald of Europe*, 1895, No. 4, with Kovalevsky's essay on Benjamin Constant's youth, Pypin's article on Lomonosov and his contemporaries, Solovyov's article on Tyutchev's poetry and a story by the Polish writer Eliza Orzeszkowa. There is nothing by Bourget in the journal.
30 The Moscow circuit court, to collect material for *Resurrection*.
31 T. A. Kuzminskaya.
32 Y. I. Popov.
33 M. L. Tolstaya.
34 Tolsoy's eldest son was to marry Marya (Manya) Rachinskaya, the daughter of Professor K. A. Rachinsky, director of the Petrovsky Agricultural Academy, in July 1895.
35 Tolstoy went to the Maly Theatre to see an Ostrovsky play with his daughter Alexandra (Sasha) and a young friend of hers.
36 S. N. Tolstoy.
37 I. M. Tregubov, a 'Tolstoyan' and author of numerous pamphlets and articles on the Russian sects, later arrested and exiled for his views. He worked for *The Intermediary* for a time, and corresponded frequently with Tolstoy over the years.
38 Tolstoy and his daughter Marya were guests of the Olsufyevs from 19 to 31 May.
39 Tolstoy had received a copy of a German newspaper which referred to a booklet, *Graf Leo Tolstoi, von Anna Seuron* (Berlin, 1895). Anna Seuron, a Frenchwoman who had spent five years with the Tolstoys as a governess, had published her memoirs of that period which were considered to be so libellous that it was suggested that Tolstoy should issue a refutation.
40 A reference to *Resurrection*, and to the daughter of Tolstoy's old friend L. D. Urusov, on whom Tolstoy modelled Missy Korchagina in the novel.
41 A. M. Olsufyeva.
42 Major-General V. I. Poltoratsky had served with Tolstoy in the Caucasus, and his memoirs were later used by Tolstoy as a source of information on that area when he was writing *Hadji Murat*.
43 Sonya.
44 *Traité des hérétiques* by Sébastian Castellion, the Protestant theologian and professor of Greek at Basle.

45 Of his article *The Function of Criticism at the Present Time* in the *Northern Herald*, 1895, No. 6.
46 In the same issue of the *Northern Herald* Tolstoy read an article on the character of Ibsen's dramas, apropos of *Little Eyolf*.
47 *Mathematics as a Science and its School Surrogates*, by V. P. Sheremetyevsky.
48 By George Davis Herron, an American pastor, member of an American community called 'Christian Commonwealth' and founder of the Institute of Christian Sociology in the state of Iowa.
49 His reply to Arthur James Balfour's *The Foundations of Belief*, 1895, in the form of an article entitled 'Mr Balfour's Dialectic' in the *Fortnightly Review*, June 1895.
50 The one in English was to an Australian writer, S. A. Rosa, and reaffirmed his belief in Henry George's solution to the land problem.
51 A defence of cycling as a healthy form of exercise, against an attack on it by a neuropathologist!
52 Strakhov had just been operated on to remove a cancer. He died a few months later.
53 For the court scenes in *Resurrection*, which Tolstoy had in mind when he wrote earlier in the same entry 'things are progressing'.
54 By the English philosopher and sociologist Benjamin Kidd, author of *Individualism and After, Principles of Western Civilisation* and *The Science of Power*.
55 C. Strempf, the editor of the Stuttgart journal *Wahrheit*, had sent Tolstoy three issues containing articles by him about Tolstoy's religious teaching.
56 Letters, II, 522. A letter to *The Times* on the persecution of the Dukhobors which Tolstoy revised several times before eventually sending it off (see entry for 22 September).
57 Tolstoy is believed to have read about Weismann and his disbelief in the inheritability of acquired characteristics in Kareyev's book *Historico-philosophical and Sociological Studies*, Petersburg, 1895.
58 Chekhov had paid his first visit to Yasnaya Polyana the previous month and read the manuscript of *Resurrection* there, after hearing Tolstoy read it.
59 Biryukov had gone to the Caucasus to get more information about the persecution of the Dukhobors.
60 A letter from Professor M. E. Zdziechowski of Cracow University, who asked for Tolstoy's opinion about his article, *The Religious and Political Ideals of Polish Society*, which had been published under a pseudonym in the *Northern Herald*. Tolstoy's reply was published by Zdziechowski.
61 Paul Boyer, at the time a lecturer in Russian in Paris and a contributor to *Le Temps*. His later publications included *Chez Tolstoï: Entretiens à Iasnaia Poliana*.
62 M. O. Menshikov, a journalist who had at first been attracted by Tolstoy's ideas, but later turned against him and attacked him in the press (*Letters*, II, 520).
63 Biryukov's article on the persecution of Christians in Russia in 1895 and Tolstoy's own letter (see Note 56) – both of which were published in *The Times* on 23 October 1895.
64 A reference to *Resurrection*.
65 A. M. Bodyansky, a Russian landowner who emigrated to Canada in 1899 to live with the Dukhobors, but returned to Russia in 1905 and wrote a book about them. He was later arrested and imprisoned for distributing Tolstoy's banned works (*Letters*, II, 675).
66 It is not known who the visitor was.
67 Joseph Edwards, socialist editor of the British publication *The Labour Annual*.
68 M. A. Schmidt.
69 Policarpo Petrocchi, *La religione nelle scuole* (Milan, 1895).
70 The original name of Nekhlyudov's fiancée in *Resurrection* (eventually Missy Korchagina).
71 In which she asked him to delete all harsh references to her in his diaries.

72 Sonya had been to see Tolstoy's play which had been banned since 1887, and also the first performance of Taneyev's musical trilogy *Oresteia*.
73 The letters to his sons Andryusha and Misha are both translated in *Letters*, II, 524–6 and 527–32.
74 At Sonya's request, Tolstoy deleted 45 passages which were sharply critical of her.
75 With a description of Maslova, not Nekhlyudov.
76 I. I. Bochkaryov. He had been arrested and exiled in the 1860s for suspected revolutionary activities, but later became a member of the Tver *zemstvo* and frequently visited Tolstoy when living in Ovsyannikovo in 1895.
77 K. F. Walz, in charge of scene painting and shifting at the Maly Theatre in Moscow, had visited Yasnaya Polyana on 4 November with his producer to discuss details of the production of *The Power of Darkness*. It was first produced on 29 November 1895, and Tolstoy attended the dress rehearsal the previous day.
78 M. V. Syaskova, a teacher in the Tolstoy household and later a collaborator on *The Intermediary*.
79 M. A. Schmidt, who was ill at Ovsyannikovo.
80 In a Russian translation by F. V. Chernigovets.
81 *Shame*, published with some omissions in the *Stock Exchange Gazette* in 1895. Corporal punishment was not abolished until 1904.
82 L. A. Sulerzhitsky, an artist and art school contemporary of Tatyana Tolstaya's, who later became a producer at the Moscow Arts Theatre. He had been confined to a mental hospital in Moscow for refusing to do military service.
83 N. A. Filosofov, father of Sofya Nikolayevna Tolstaya, the wife of Tolstoy's son Ilya.
84 *Christian Teaching*.
85 *The Light Shineth in Darkness*.
86 John Manson had written to ask Tolstoy to express his views on the conflict between Britain and America over the frontiers of Venezuela. Tolstoy replied with an article which was published in the *Daily Chronicle* on 17 March 1896 under the title *Patriotism or Peace? Letter on Venezuela*.
87 The German novelist F. Spielhagen had written an 'open letter' to *Neues Wiener Tageblatt* severely criticising Tolstoy's foreword to Popov's biography of Drozhzhin on the grounds that it allegedly encouraged the young to resort to civil disobedience.

1896

1 *Patriotism or Peace?* See 1895, Note 86.
2 *The Light Shineth in Darkness*.
3 A peasant who refused to take the oath of allegiance to the new Tsar, and was fined and harassed in various ways.
4 See 1895, Note 82.
5 Dušan Makovitsky, a Hungarian Slovak doctor educated at Prague University, and a dedicated 'Tolstoyan'. He was Tolstoy's personal doctor, lived at Yasnaya Polyana from 1904 to 1910 and kept a detailed record of his conversations, published in full in *Literaturnoye nasledstvo*, No. 90, 4 volumes, Moscow, 1979. He accompanied Tolstoy on his last journey to Astapovo in 1910. The article referred to on the Nazarene sect in Hungary and its conscientious objection to military service was later published in Russian in England in 1898.
6 See 1895, Note 86. Manson had quarrelled with Kenworthy over the publication rights of *Patriotism or Peace?*
7 Davydov had been presented to the Tsar after his recent appointment as president of the Tula circuit court, and had been closely questioned by him about Tolstoy's life.
8 Ertel had written an article, *Is Russian Society in Decline?* in reply to Tolstoy's article *Shame* (1895, Note 81), advocating the role of public opinion in helping to

bring about the abolition of capital punishment; Spielhagen's letter – see 1895, Note 87.
9   Tolstoy corresponded frequently with M. A. Sopotsko who had worked with him during the famine years but later turned against him and bitterly denounced him (*Letters*, II, 526); M. E. Zdziechowski had initiated a correspondence the previous year (1895, Note 60).
10 A letter by Vera S. Grinevich to Tolstoy's daughter Marya, later published by Grinevich in a book of hers about the family. Tolstoy did not accept the challenge to write about the religious education of children.
11 George du Maurier's novel about the life of artists in Paris, which Tolstoy read in Russian translation.
12 *La suite du Menteur*, Corneille's sequel to his comedy *Le Menteur*.
13 These tentative ideas mark an early stage in the writing of *What is Art?*
14 M. P. Novikov, an army clerk who wrote several stories about peasant life which Tolstoy admired. He later wrote about his relations with Tolstoy, which lasted until Tolstoy's death and which profoundly affected his life (*Letters*, II, 679). His brother wished to obtain Tolstoy's banned work *What I Believe*, and was given a letter by Tatyana Tolstaya to take to M. M. Kholevinskaya, a Tula doctor, who gave him a copy. Kholevinskaya had previously been arrested for distributing Tolstoy's banned works, and in February 1896 her house was searched by the police and Tatyana's letter discovered. She was arrested again and imprisoned, and wrote a letter to Tatyana which greatly upset Tolstoy and to which he replied at length (*Letters*, II, 535).
15 *Christian Teaching*, as it was eventually called.
16 At the Bolshoy Theatre in Moscow. The next day he wrote to his brother criticising it severely.
17 *Denken und Wirklichkeit: Versuch einer Erneuerung der Kritischen Philosophie*, by the German-Russian neo-Kantian philosopher Afrikan Alexandrovich Spir (Leipzig, 1873).
18 Sonya took the young children to Moscow for the coronation of Nicholas II. Tatyana went to Sweden for the wedding of her brother Lev to Dora Westerlund.
19 'Koni's story' (*Resurrection*), or *The Light Shineth in Darkness*.
20 N. N. Ivanov, a minor author of short stories and poems who worked for *The Intermediary* and wrote some reminiscences of Tolstoy. Tolstoy had had some harsh things to say about his comedy *Sin*, which Ivanov had sent to him nearly ten years before, and relations were strained (*Letters*, II, 413).
21 In fact three articles with the same title, published in *Books of the Week*, 1896, 4–6, on the subject of non-resistance to evil by force. Tolstoy read the first two. Menshikov later renounced his pacifist views and turned against Tolstoy (see 1895, Note 62).
22 In Kareyev's book *The Historical World-outlook of Granovsky*, Moscow, 1896. Professor T. N. Granovsky was a distinguished historian and leader of the Moscow circle of pro-Western intelligentsia in the reign of Nicholas I.
23 *What is Art?*
24 A reference to Katyusha Maslova in *Resurrection*.
25 An allusion to the pomp and ceremony, autocratic and Orthodox, at the coronation of Nicholas II on 14 May.
26 *Christian Teaching.*
27 See 1889, Note 81.
28 The tragedy of Khodynka field, when crowds of people were trampled to death during the celebrations that followed the coronation of Nicholas II. Tolstoy wrote a story on the subject in 1910, based to some extent on a story by V. F. Krasnov entitled *Khodynka: The story of one not trampled to death* (*Letters*, II, 548).
29 An officer from Tiflis who came to Yasnaya Polyana to meet Tolstoy. Tolstoy gave him a copy of his book *The Kingdom of God is Within You*.

30 *My Refusal to Do Military Service: Notes of an army officer.* The notes were later published in England in 1898.
31 Tolstoy was probably reading an article in the *Northern Herald* entitled *The Poetry of Decadence*, which reproduced three poems in prose by Mallarmé. He returned to the subject in *What is Art?* (Chapter 10).
32 The second part of *Christian Teaching.*
33 Chertkov's wife, Anna Konstantinovna.
34 The police-spy told Tolstoy that he had been dismissed for admitting that he had been ordered to spy on Tolstoy while passing himself off as an artist and nihilist.
35 Nothing is known of any writing by Biryukov about the Khodynka tragedy.
36 K. I. Zlinchenko first met Tolstoy in 1895 and corresponded with him, as well as writing articles and reminiscences about him. He later became a member of the Social Democrats.
37 Of *Christian Teaching.*
38 *How to Read the Gospels, and What Their Essential Nature is* (London, 1898).
39 The first mention of the story *Hadji Murat*, one of the original titles of which was *The Burdock.*
40 Another reference to Tolstoy's jealousy of Taneyev.
41 Pride or indignation (see Note 40).
42 Tolstoy's tutor. See *Boyhood*, Chapters 14–16.
43 Tolstoy, still suffering from his jealousy of Taneyev, went with his wife to Shamordino Convent to see his sister. Their trip lasted six days, from 10 to 15 August.
44 Sergey and Marya Konstantinovna (née Rachinskaya); Ilya and Sofya Nikolayevna (née Filosofova); and Lev and Dora Fyodorovna (née Westerlund).
45 A letter from a Dutch journalist enclosing a copy of a letter by a Dutch socialist, J. Van der Veer, to a senior military commander explaining his refusal to do military service in Holland. Tolstoy's foreword, *The Approach of the End*, is really an afterword to Van der Veer's letter.
46 Translated in full in *Letters*, II, 539–47. It was a reply to a letter from three members of the former Petersburg Literacy Committee (including A. M. Kalmykova) which had recently been suppressed by the government together with the corresponding committee in Moscow. Kalmykova and her colleagues asked Tolstoy to express his attitude to the government's educational policies.
47 A letter from A. K. Datt (not Tod), who had sent Tolstoy a book by Swami Vivekananda entitled *Yoga's Philosophy: Lectures on Raja Yoga, or conquering the internal nature* (New York, 1896).
48 No stories were written on either subject.
49 Two journalists from Japan, with a letter of introduction from Masurato Konissi, a Japanese friend of Tolstoy's who was studying in Kiev.
50 From P. V. Verigin, leader of the Caucasian Dukhobors, who was living in exile in Siberia. Tolstoy approved of the doubts expressed by Verigin about the value of material progress and its harmful effects on morality.
51 A request for leniency toward Olkhovik and another peasant who were serving a sentence in Siberia for refusal to do military service. There was no reply.
52 *The Light Shineth in Darkness.*
53 *Modern Science* by Edward Carpenter, included in his *Civilisation: Its cause and cure and other essays* (London, 1889). Tolstoy later got his son Sergey to translate the essay into Russian, and wrote a foreword to it himself.
54 Another request to another commander of a disciplinary battalion, this time to show leniency towards Caucasian Dukhobors sentenced for refusing to do military service. Again there was no reply.
55 Nikolay Gay junior.
56 'Prescriptions' referred to in a diary entry of 20 October (not translated here) for helping to relieve sufferings caused by various passions.

57 *On What People Call Art.*
58 No money was ever sent by Sanini, a Spaniard from Barcelona.
59 Kuzminsky had told Tolstoy that the Finance Minister, S. Yu. Witte, wished to visit him to discuss the possible setting up of official temperance societies (a government monopoly on spirits had been instituted the previous year). Tolstoy told Kuzminsky that he did not want to discuss these matters with Witte, and also asked Kuzminsky to try to persuade General Dragomirov not to publish any more articles like his recent one in *New Times* which argued that wars were inevitable because they answered a basic law of nature.
60 His unfinished article *Carthago delenda est.*
61 Repin, in a letter to *New Times* in connection with the silver jubilee of his career as an artist, had compared an artist's work with that of other professional people and said 'We are lucky people – our work is amusement'. The letter caused an outcry, and Repin subsequently modified his view.
62 I. M. Tregubov.
63 *A Modest Proposal for Preventing the Children of Poor People from being a Burden to their Parents or the Country* (1729) – by using them as food for the rich.
64 Sergey's wife (née Rachinskaya) had written to Tolstoy to tell him that she wanted to separate from her husband. Tolstoy's reply (which has not survived) was delivered personally by him to her father.
65 A Russian translation of *Phaedon.*
66 Tolstoy did not write about the first subject, but *The Slavery of Our Times, The Root of Evil* and other articles developed the second theme.
67 A. B. Goldenweiser, a distinguished pianist and composer, later for many years a professor at the Moscow Conservatoire, and for a time its Principal. His memoirs of Tolstoy whom he knew well were published after the revolution and have been translated into English in abridged form as *Talks with Tolstoy.*
68 *Help!* – an appeal against the persecution of the Dukhobors.
69 P. V. Chizhova, Taneyev's aunt.
70 *Handbuch der Musik-Geschichte von den ersten Anfängen bis zum Tode Beethovens in gemeinfasslicher Darstellung* (Leipzig, 1878) by A. V. Dommer.
71 Jean-Baptiste Faure, the French operatic baritone and composer. He published many songs, including the very popular *Les Rameaux. Crucifixe* was a favourite duet of Tolstoy's.
72 An opinion expressed by Tolstoy's wife.
73 A story begun in the 1880s and left unfinished.

1897

1 An article by a former veterinary medical assistant explaining his reasons for coming to accept Tolstoy's religious and moral views.
2 In English in the diary.
3 Sonya.
4 His jealousy of Sonya's apparent infatuation with Taneyev.
5 An article on the army which was eventually written in 1901 and called *Notes for Soldiers.*
6 The Chertkovs had been exiled for publishing an appeal in support of the Dukhobors, and Tolstoy and his wife went to Petersburg to see them off on their way to England.
7 N. A. Yaroshenko, an artist friend of Chertkov's and one of the founders of the 'Itinerants'. He painted Tolstoy's portrait in 1895.
8 Ernest Crosby had sent Tolstoy the manuscript of a shortened version of Tolstoy's *On Life*, done by an American lawyer friend, Bolton Hall, who also edited the book *What Tolstoy Taught* (New York, 1911).
9 An 'appeal' directed against the existing political and economic structure of society,

	which eventually took the form of two articles, *Must it be so?* and *What is the Way Out?*
10	His jealousy of Taneyev.
11	A reference to Arnold's *The Function of Criticism at the Present Time*, later published in Russian by *The Intermediary*.
12	*L'Esthétique d'Aristotle* (Paris, 1889) by C-M. Bénard, quoted in *What is Art?*
13	A. V. Olsufyev. Nothing came of the idea.
14	A political prisoner in the Peter and Paul Fortress, and an acquaintance of Tolstoy's (she had been a teacher in the Yasnaya Polyana area) who committed suicide in prison by pouring oil from a reading lamp over herself and setting fire to it.
15	Tolstoy often used this word to denote idle frivolity (a reference to the alleged behaviour of Hannibal's troops in Capua after their victory over the Romans).
16	A slightly inaccurate quotation of a couplet from a poem by Lermontov.
17	Two peasant members of the Molokan sect in the Samara province came to ask Tolstoy to intercede on their behalf. A missionary congress in the area had ruled that their children should be taken away from them to be educated in church schools. Tolstoy wrote to the Tsar, but received no reply.
18	To leave home – a step not finally taken until 1910.
19	The Molokans took Tolstoy's letter to the Tsar, and other letters of intercession which he wrote for them at the same time, to Petersburg, but all the letters were destroyed on the advice of a servant in the household of one of the Grand Dukes where the Molokans had called in the hope of obtaining an interview.
20	This time the copies of the letters reached their destination, but no action was taken.
21	The two pages of the diary with the entries from 3 May ('Worked quite hard . . .') to 18 May ('Lyova and his wife have just left') had been torn out, but they were not destroyed and eventually fell into the hands of Boulanger and survived in his archive.
22	To her nephew N. L. Obolensky, the grandson of Tolstoy's sister.
23	She had fallen in love with M. S. Sukhotin, a married man, who was later to be her husband.
24	Tolstoy's niece Varvara (his brother Sergey's daughter) was living with a Pirogovo peasant as his common-law wife.
25	There is no such scene in *The Light Shineth in Darkness*.
26	Nothing came of this idea.
27	*What is Art?*
28	Tolstoy had read a report in *New Times* (*On the Relativity of Human Knowledge*) of a speech by the eminent English physicist Sir William Crookes. In *The Fruits of Enlightenment* Tolstoy mentioned Crookes' name when making fun of the attempt to prove the reality of spiritualistic phenomena.
29	A distinguished sculptor, who did a full-length model of Tolstoy on this visit.
30	M. P. Novikov (1896, Note 14) and P. A. Bulakhov, an Old Believer.
31	The two sisters of M. A. Stakhovich (1884, Note 40) and N. A. Maklakov and his wife, a grand-niece of Tolstoy's. Maklakov was Minister of Internal Affairs from 1912 to 1915.
32	M. N. Sobolev was a tutor of Tolstoy's son Mikhail.
33	The Japanese, who was living in America, had been inspired by reading Tolstoy's *A Short Exposition of the Gospels* to return to Japan to found a community where he could practise his new-found beliefs.
34	The missionary congress in Kazan (see Note 17) was proposing to apply for legislation to be introduced to force the children of dissenting parents to attend church schools.
35	Like Chertkov, Boulanger was compelled to go into exile abroad for helping Tolstoy's campaign on behalf of the Dukhobors.
36	Having learned that it was intended to offer the first Nobel prize for literature to him, Tolstoy wrote to the Swedish press suggesting that the money be given to the Russian Dukhobors.

37 Arthur St John, a British army officer in Burma, who was sufficiently influenced by Tolstoy's ideas to abandon his career, and who played a big part in the Dukhobor emigration (*Letters*, II, 579).
38 More letters on behalf of the Molokans (Note 17), no more successful than the previous ones. Heath, an Englishman, was a former tutor of Nicholas II. Chertkova – the mother of Vladimir Chertkov.
39 She was strongly opposed to Tolstoy's sending his letter to the Swedish press because of its unrestrained abuse of the Russian government. Relations between them were particularly strained at the time – see Tolstoy's letter to her (not sent) of 19 May 1897 (*Letters*, II, 558).
40 The translation into Swedish of Tolstoy's letter to the Swedish press, done by a Swede who was at Yasnaya Polyana at the time.
41 There were apparently three Dunyashas in the Tolstoy household. It is thought that Tolstoy was referring here to Yevdokiya Nikolayevna Orekhova, a housemaid he had once been fond of.
42 Tolstoy's letter about the Nobel prize was printed in the *Stockholms Dagblad* in October.
43 Despite their strained relations, Sonya was helping her husband by copying out *What is Art?*
44 The younger sister of Chertkov's wife, who married Andrey Tolstoy in 1899. She was living in England with the Chertkovs at the time and wrote about the serious crisis that her brother-in-law was passing through.
45 His letter about the Kazan missionary congress (Note 34). It had in fact been printed the previous day.
46 See 1896, Note 53.
47 Of *What is Art?*, which was to be printed in Grot's journal *Problems of Philosophy and Psychology*.
48 The copyist A. P. Ivanov.
49 See 1894, Note 8.
50 A reference to the break-up of Khilkov's marriage.
51 P. O. Zyabrev, a former pupil at Tolstoy's school, told him about a procession of monks carrying an icon of the Vladimir Virgin through the local parish and offering to sell indulgences.
52 Tolstoy's son had discovered that a coal seam ran underneath his land and was planning to exploit it, but the plan came to nothing.
53 Newspaper reports about British exploitation of the Indian population of South Africa.
54 The famous Russian explorer, geographer and anthropologist.
55 He later did so in *The Forged Coupon*.
56 Masha, who was staying with her husband in the Crimea, had written to ask whether her father felt any estrangement between them as a result of her marriage. He confessed that he did, but added that he did not wish to and would not do so in future.
57 To Maude in England and Grot in Russia, since *What is Art?* was to be published simultaneously in both countries.
58 Because of Sonya's objections, Tolstoy withdrew his foreword to Carpenter's article, but she later changed her mind and it was printed the following year.
59 Grot had had second thoughts about the simultaneous appearance of the full text of *What is Art?* in both countries, and wished to spread the Russian version over several issues of his journal.
60 Dušan Makovitsky, who had set up in Hungary a counterpart to *The Intermediary* for publishing the works of Tolstoy and other authors.
61 The main part of the Yasnaya Polyana house where Tolstoy had been born and which he had sold to pay his gambling debts had been re-erected at Dolgoye, some twelve

1895–1902

62   S. N. Trubetskoy, coeditor with Grot of the journal which was publishing *What is Art?* Tolstoy was eventually obliged to accept their conditions, and the work appeared in several successive issues.
63   Examples of what the artist Kasatkin considered to be true art.
64   N. D. Rostovtsev, a close friend of Chertkov's, had recently visited him in England and brought back gloomy reports. I. M. Tregubov had written to him on the subject of 'spiritual marriage'.
65   *Father Sergey*, finished in 1898.
66   *The Posthumous Notes of the Elder Fyodor Kuzmich*, finished in 1905.
67   Nothing is known about this.
68   The basis of the story *Korney Vasilyev*.
69   A revised version of *The Devil in Hell*. It was published in England in 1903.
70   Nothing came of this.
71   *The Light Shineth in Darkness*.
72   This subject was used in a draft version of a chapter of *Resurrection* and in *The Forged Coupon*. Tolstoy also wrote a children's story *Fedotka* on the same theme.
73   A story of this title was begun in 1891 in the form of a woman's diary but was never finished.
74   The execution in Odessa in 1879 of three men accused of an attempt on the life of Alexander II provided Tolstoy with material for his story *The Divine and the Human*.
75   Because the first five chapters of *What is Art?* were published in Russia sooner than in England.
76   The first mention of *A Living Corpse*.
77   One anonymous letter from a secret society calling itself *The Second Crusaders* threatened Tolstoy with death as 'an enemy of our Tsar and country'.

1898

1   N. Y. Fedoseyev organised one of the first Marxist circles in Russia. Exiled for revolutionary activities, he became acquainted with some of the Dukhobors in Siberia and twice wrote to Tolstoy about the conditions they were compelled to endure.
2   George Bedborough, editor of an English pedagogical journal, had written to ask Tolstoy some questions about free love, but Tolstoy did not reply. See Bedborough, *Love and Happiness; Letters to Tolstoy written in 1897 and now first published* (Letchworth, 1917).
3   In English in the diary.
4   The two men were in Moscow for the first performance in the Bolshoy Theatre of Rimsky-Korsakov's opera *Sadko*, and called on Tolstoy the following evening.
5   From Chertkov in England, where *What is Art?* had begun to be printed.
6   A poem by a Tula peasant which had been published in *Russian Thought* on Tolstoy's recommendation.
7   Editor of *Les Temps Nouveaux*, who wrote extensively on anarchism, the individual and society, patriotism and war.
8   To George Howard Gibson, a member of an American community called 'Christian Commonwealth'. Tolstoy's letter is translated in full in *Letters*, II, 515–17.
9   About collecting funds for resettling the Dukhobors. The letter was not published.
10 *Letters*, II, 567–70. Tolstoy's letter appeared in the *Daily Chronicle* on 29 April 1898.
11 In his foreword to the English translation Tolstoy mentioned the cuts made by the Russian censors in the version published in *Problems of Philosophy and Psychology*.
12 In English in the diary.
13 A. N. Toliverova-Peshkova, editor of a children's magazine and the monthly journal *The Woman's Cause*.

14 His son Ilya's estate, where Tolstoy had gone to help with the famine relief – the consequence of another harvest failure, though not so serious as the one in 1891–2.
15 The money received as a result of a letter he wrote to the *Russian Gazette* on behalf of the famine victims.
16 The Minister of Internal Affairs suspended publication of the *Russian Gazette* for two months for having collected money for the Dukhobors and handed it over to Tolstoy.
17 A village in the famine area where Tolstoy made notes about the condition and needs of the famine victims.
18 Selected stories in Russian translation.
19 See 1897, Note 9.
20 Fear of government reaction to Tolstoy's work for the famine victims, especially the publication abroad of his *Famine or No Famine?*
21 Lev Tolstoy's wife's first son, who died two years later.
22 *Father Sergey*, which had been left unfinished for seven years.
23 Leskov's *The Hour of God's Will*, drawing with Tolstoy's consent on the subject of his own sketch *The Wise Virgin*, a subject which Tolstoy later worked up in his story *Three Questions*, 1903.
24 *Famine or No Famine?*, which Ukhtomsky, the editor of the *St Petersburg Gazette*, refused to publish, and which only came out in Russia in a heavily censored version the following month.
25 Six young schoolchildren who had bought flour with the hundred roubles they had collected were prevented by the authorities from distributing it to victims of the famine.
26 *The Chopin Prelude*, a story taking sharp issue with the views on sex expressed in *The Kreutzer Sonata*.
27 The editor of an Italian journal, *Vita Internazionale*, to whom Tolstoy sent a copy of *Carthago delenda est* in response to a request for his views on war.
28 A quarrel between Chertkov, Biryukov and Boulanger over the Russian-language journal *Conscience* (subsequently called *Free Word*) which they intended to publish in England.
29 Tolstoy was reading the French novelist Paul Adam's story *Le Cuivre*.
30 Despite his statement in 1891 renouncing his copyright on works written since 1881. The new decision only applied in fact to *Resurrection*, which was published simultaneously in English, French and German, as well as Russian (in A. F. Marx's *The Cornfield* in Russia and Chertkov's *Free Word* in England.
31 Once again because of jealousy of Taneyev. On her way back from Kiev Sonya intended to call on some friends with whom Taneyev happened to be staying at the time.
32 In other words, to die.
33 A. K. Chertkova had written to say that Khilkov, who had gone to Cyprus to look for places for the Dukhobors to settle, had found conditions there unsuitable and advised them not to go.
34 On her return from England Rostovtseva (the Marya Nikolayevna referred to in the same entry) was found by Customs officials to be carrying some proofs of a work of Tolstoy's which was banned in Russia. She was arrested and imprisoned, but soon released.
35 Two representatives of the Dukhobors in the Kars district in the North Caucasus.
36 I. M. Tregubov.
37 L. A. Sulerzhitsky came for further discussions about the resettlement of the Dukhobors abroad.
38 Tolstoy's seventieth birthday.
39 Tolstoy had received an advance of 12,000 roubles from A. F. Marx, who agreed to pay 1,000 roubles a printer's sheet for the right to publish *Resurrection*.
40 A temporary rift with her future husband, M. S. Sukhotin.

41 He married Chertkov's sister-in-law in January 1899.
42 Herbert Archer, an English member of the Purleigh colony in Essex.
43 A letter asking Prince G. S. Golitsyn, civilian governor of the Caucasus, not to place any obstacles in the way of Sulerzhitsky and his son Sergey, who were to accompany the Dukhobors from the Caucasus to their new home in Canada.
44 See 1897, Note 9.
45 Tolstoy had intended to send the following record of a conversation with his wife during the night of 28 July about her relations with Taneyev to his sister-in-law, Tatyana Kuzminskaya, and it was therefore written in the form of a letter to her. He changed his mind and did not send it, and it was found among his papers.
46 See Note 31.
47 Taneyev.
48 To her friends on her way back from Kiev (see Note 31).
49 Part I. Chapter 17.

1899

1 To Moscow, where he stayed until 19 December before returning to Yasnaya Polyana. On 10 January the family moved back to Moscow again and stayed there until May.
2 To M. P. Shalaginin, on the incompatibility of war and Christianity.
3 To a group of Swedish pacifists who had asked him to express his views about the Hague Peace Conference. Tolstoy's reply was published in England in the form of a short article, 'Apropos of the Peace Congress' (*The Free Word News-sheet*, 1899, No. 6).
4 He did in fact write an article, 'The Student Movement of 1899', on the subject of the serious student disturbances which had broken out in February at Petersburg University and spread to other parts of the country.
5 An artist who had been sent to a disciplinary battalion in Algeria for refusing to do military service, and had escaped from there.
6 The English publishers had not been able to keep abreast of their Russian counterparts, and Tolstoy had held back the next instalment to Marx's journal by a week to enable the English translation to appear simultaneously.
7 N. N. Gay junior.
8 In English in the diary.
9 I. G. Verus, *Vergleichende Übersicht der vier Evangelien* (Leipzig, 1897).
10 The third and last part which was extensively revised and expanded to twenty-eight chapters instead of six.
11 He was distressed by the unfortunate marriages of his daughters Varvara and Vera.
12 Alfred B. Westrup, *Plenty of Money* (New York, 1899), dealing with the role of banking and finance in American government policy.
13 Tatyana Tolstaya (soon to be married); Andrey Tolstoy and his wife Olga; Yuliya Igumnova (Julie), an artist friend of Tatyana's who later did secretarial work for Tolstoy; and A. D. Arkhangelsky, a tutor of Tolstoy's son Mikhail, who came to Yasnaya Polyana to help Tolstoy with the copying out of *Resurrection* after having been expelled from Moscow University.
14 She had married Mikhail Sukhotin on 14 November, and immediately gone abroad with him.
15 M. A. Schmidt.
16 M. A. Engelhardt, *Progress as the Evolution of Cruelty* (Petersburg, 1899).
17 It came out in the next issue of *The Cornfield*, No. 52, 25 December 1899.

1900

1 A letter to the Dukhobors, now settled in Canada, many of whom had allegedly succumbed to the temptation to own private property. The letter was begun in December 1899 but not finished until February 1900. Tolstoy refers to sending it off in the entry for 13 March below.
2 *The Slavery of Our Times.*
3 She and her husband were copying out extracts to send to Chertkov for his collection of Tolstoy's thoughts.
4 See 1899, Note 11.
5 Y. V. Obolenskaya (Lizanka), Tolstoy's sister's daughter, had been to visit her cousin Varvara Tolstaya (Tolstoy's brother's daughter), whose unsuccessful marriage to a peasant had so upset her father.
6 Y. N. Vorobyov, an ex-ship's captain now farming in Nalchik in the North Caucasus, had come to ask Tolstoy's advice whether to give up agriculture for literature.
7 This was Gorky's first meeting with Tolstoy. Tolstoy allegedly called him 'a real Russian peasant'. Gorky reportedly referred to the occasion as being like a visit to Finland – 'neither home nor abroad, and cold as well' (*Letters*, II, 585).
8 Tolstoy took exception to Chekhov's treatment of the theme of adultery in the story.
9 'Next best' and 'next worse' are both in English in the diary.
10 At the Moscow Arts Theatre, where he had some disapproving things to say to Nemirovich-Danchenko, especially about the character of Dr Astrov.
11 *A Living Corpse*, which he returned to after an interval of three years but never completely finished. It was published for the first time the year after Tolstoy's death.
12 Gasha Trubetskaya, a former housemaid with whom Tolstoy had once had a liaison. She was employed by Tolstoy's sister, who was staying with him in Moscow at the time, and her reappearance there caused great distress to Tolstoy's wife. 'Serves him right': for 'him' read 'me'.
13 *Patriotism and the Government.* It first appeared in England later in 1900.
14 See 1893, Note 28.
15 Russian translations of Wilhelm Wundt's *Grundriss der Psychologie* (Leipzig, 1896) and the Danish professor Harald Höffding's *Studies in Psychology Based on Experience* – it is his views on the parallelism of body and soul that Tolstoy is referring to in the entry for 24 March below.
16 A trepanation of the skull.
17 *Patriotism and the Government* and *The Slavery of Our Times*.
18 The person sitting next to Tolstoy at a meeting of the Moscow Psychological Society, and to whom he spoke, turned out to be the son of the lecturer L. Y. Obolensky.
19 The coincidence was that both Tolstoy and the (unknown) American missionary were trying to petition the Tsar on behalf of dissident sects in the Caucasus (Tolstoy's friend A. V. Olsufyev was an aide-de-camp of Nicholas II and therefore able to get direct access to him).
20 To his daughter's estate at Pirogovo (where his brother's estate also was).
21 Perhaps an amalgamation of his earlier projected novel about peasant settlers in Siberia (see 1884, Note 97) and a continuation of *Resurrection* with Nekhlyudov in a new role.
22 Of *A Living Corpse*.
23 See Note 21. Nothing came of the idea.
24 Jeremy Curtin, an American scholar of Russian language and literature who had served in the Embassy in Petersburg and later became well known for his translations from Russian and Polish literature. He had come to Russia specially to see Tolstoy and the artist Vereshchagin.
25 Both *The Slavery of Our Times* and *Thou Shalt Not Kill*, written on the occasion of the murder of King Umberto of Italy by an anarchist, were sent to Chertkov for publication in England.

26 To leave home.
27 A. P. Ivanov.
28 Boulanger wanted to publish an illustrated weekly journal, *Morning*, with Tolstoy's participation and under the editorship of M. V. Dovnar-Zapolsky who came to Yasnaya Polyana with Boulanger. Permission was refused by the government.
29 Tolstoy's library contains Leipzig editions of *Adam Bede*, *Felix Holt* and *Romola* with marginal notes by Tolstoy, and also *The Mill on the Floss* and *Middlemarch*. It is not certain exactly what he was reading at the time, either by Eliot or Ruskin.
30 There is no article specifically on this theme.
31 Tolstoy's son Andrey was moving to his estate at Taptykovo, ten miles from Yasnaya Polyana, with what to Tolstoy was an unnecessarily large collection of goods and chattels.
32 See Note 28.
33 *The Light Shineth in Darkness*.
34 In English in the diary.
35 *A Living Corpse*.
36 In *Must it be so?*
37 *What is the Way Out?*, sent to Chertkov in England.
38 James Legge's *The Chinese Classics* (London, 1875–6).
39 A. N. Dunayev, see 1889, Note 13; Bochkaryov, see 1895, Note 76. L. I. Veselitskaya, a woman novelist who had visited Tolstoy on several occasions but whose memoirs of him, *Shades of the Past*, are not entirely reliable. V. F. Totomiants, a sociologist and theoretician of the cooperative movement (*Letters*, II, 696). V. A. Posse, editor of the Marxist journal *Life*, who wanted to publish Tolstoy's play *A Living Corpse*, but was refused permission as it was still unfinished.
40 Like Posse, he wanted to obtain the text of *A Living Corpse* (in his case to produce at the Moscow Arts Theatre), but permission was again refused for the same reason.
41 In other words, the police.
42 He stayed with Tatyana at Kochety from 17 October to 2 November.
43 On the subject of intervention in China by various foreign countries. The 'epistle' became a letter (see entry for 7 November), but it was never finished.
44 Nothing came of this idea.
45 The subject is dealt with in *What is Religion and What is its Essential Nature?*, 1902.
46 He wrote down his thoughts on the teachings of Confucius in some detail in an untranslated part of his diary entry for 12 November.
47 The wife of Prince K. A. Vyazemsky, who had become a monk on Mount Athos.
48 About Tolstoy's niece Vera Tolstaya who, unknown to her father, had secretly married, had a child and separated from her husband.
49 It is doubtful whether Tolstoy took his son's writings very seriously. Most of the copies of them in his library have not even been cut.
50 M. S. Sukhotin.
51 M. M. Filippov, editor of the weekly journal *Scientific Review* to which Lenin and Plekhanov contributed.
52 'Why did you hurry away to the fatal Caucasus?' – the popular song referred to later in the same entry.
53 Relations at Pirogovo between Tolstoy's brother (Seryozha) and his 'prodigal daughter' Vera had greatly improved.
54 Tolstoy had begun to study Dutch in the winter of 1897, probably as a result of his friendship with Van der Veer, and could apparently read it fairly fluently.
55 The manuscript of a brochure by M. P. Novikov, later published by the *Free Word* in London as *The Voice of a Peasant*, describing conditions in the Russian countryside.
56 Eleven wives of Dukhobors, having emigrated to Canada, wished to return to Russia to join their husbands in exile in Siberia. Tolstoy's letter to the Tsar had its effect and their wish was granted.

57 Thanks to the good offices of Tolstoy's friend Davydov, president of the Moscow circuit court, his letter reached its destination.
58 Claude Bernard, the founder of experimental physiology; Du Bois-Reymond, a German physiologist whom Tolstoy had heard lecture in Berlin in 1860.
59 There are three editions of this collection of essays and aphorisms in Tolstoy's library.
60 Tolstoy read the Buddhist Suttas, part of the Vedas, in a Russian translation of Professor T. W. Rhys-Davids' English translation from the Pali.
61 Tolstoy read *Also sprach Zarathustra* in the original; also the article by E. Förster-Nietzsche on the genesis of the work, published in *Die Zukunft* in 1900.
62 The letter has not survived, but was presumably one of many requests for free copies of Tolstoy's works for provincial libraries.

1901

1 By Max Müller in Russian translation.
2 *Autocracy and the Zemstvo*, a confidential report to the Tsar by the Finance Minister S. Y. Witte, arguing for a closer rapprochement between the two institutions.
3 The journal *Morning* (see 1900, Note 28) which, in any case, was banned by the government. Tolstoy justified his wish to take part on the grounds that it would enable him to write works of fiction which he would not otherwise write.
4 In fact via the book-dealer Serebrennikov to a peasant, V. K. Zavolokin, who had suffered for his religious and pacifist beliefs. There was a brief correspondence between the two men, and Tolstoy's letters to Zavolokin were published in England as a brochure entitled *On Reason, Faith and Prayer. Three Letters, Free word* (Christchurch, 1901).
5 Tolstoy's son Mikhail married A. V. Glebova, a maid of honour, and the Grand Duke Sergey Alexandrovich came to Moscow from Petersburg for the wedding. Tolstoy did not attend the ceremony.
6 The second, revised edition of Chicherin's book, originally published in 1879, which the author sent to Tolstoy.
7 By the political economist and philosopher S. N. Bulgakov, at the time a Marxist, who spoke in favour of adapting Russian agriculture to the needs of the West European market, especially trade with Germany, which would stimulate agricultural developments at home.
8 On the minimum reforms needed, in Tolstoy's view, to calm the social unrest at the time. The appeal was first published in England in 1901.
9 Tolstoy worked intermittently at the novel between 1896 and 1904, but it was not published until after his death.
10 By decree of the Holy Synod in February 1901, on the initiative of the Chief Procurator, K. P. Pobedonostsev (*Letters*, II, 347).
11 The appeal to the Tsar was prompted by social unrest stemming from the decision of the authorities to impose compulsory military service on some 200 students of Kiev and Petersburg Universities who had taken part in demonstrations; the 'programme' referred to was an unfinished article entitled 'What the Majority of the Russian Working People Want Most of All'.
12 A slightly garbled version of a saying of Coleridge's, which Tolstoy also used as an epigraph to his reply to the Holy Synod's decree of excommunication.
13 To the authors of the Holy Synod's decree of excommunication and the various people who had written to him about it.
14 A. V. Vlasov, who had been persecuted for his anarchical views and his refusal to pay taxes or swear an oath of allegiance to the Tsar, had first corresponded with Tolstoy in 1899. His letters were used by Tolstoy when creating the character of the old man on the ferry in *Resurrection*, Part III, Chapters 21 and 27.

15 A group of Petersburg writers including Maxim Gorky had protested against a police attack on a demonstration in front of the Kazan Cathedral on 4 March in support of university students who had been maltreated, as a result of which the Petersburg Union of Writers had been closed (Letters, II, 591).
16 *Notes for Soldiers* which Tolstoy was planning to write as a counter to the officially sponsored booklet by General Dragomirov.
17 In a book by G. Dubois-Desaulle, *Camisards, Peaux de Lapins et Cocos, corps disciplinaires de l'armée française* (Paris, 1901).
18 A reply to Biryukov's request for Tolstoy's views on the education of children (*Letters*, II, 592–7).
19 See Note 16.
20 See 1900, Note 45.
21 The old peasant in Chekhov's story *In the Ravine*.
22 Major Petrov's mistress in *Hadji Murat*.
23 Chertkov wanted Tolstoy to expand his 'programme' (Note 11) to include a point about freedom of speech and of the press, which Tolstoy was unwilling to do (*Letters*, II, 597–8).
24 In his foreword to the Russian translation of Wilhelm von Polenz's novel *Der Büttnerbauer*, Tolstoy had intended to mention the work of the painter N. V. Orlov who shared Tolstoy's views and painted many pictures of peasant life. He did not do so, but wrote a separate foreword to an album of Orlov's pictures of Russian peasants in 1908. For Polenz see *Letters*, II, 614.
25 An article on the labour problem, eventually called *The Only Way*, and first published in England in 1901.
26 *Notes for Soldiers* and *Notes for Officers*.
27 About the situation of the working people of Russia – eventually written and despatched in 1902 (*Letters*, II, 608–13). The Tsar did not reply.
28 For Tolstoy to convalesce after a serious illness. Countess Panina put her house and estate at Gaspra, near Yalta, at the disposal of the Tolstoy family and they lived there from September 1901 until June 1902. The house had previously belonged to Prince Golitsyn, Alexander I's Minister of Education and was built by an English architect, William Hunt, in so-called English Gothic style.
29 Tolstoy's daughter and sister respectively.
30 Tolstoy is quoting from *Selected Thoughts of John Ruskin*, translated from the English by L. P. Nikiforov.
31 For a description of Countess Panina's house at Gaspra see Tolstoy's letter to his brother in *Letters*, II, 605.
32 Kolya – Nikolay Obolensky, the husband of Tolstoy's daughter Masha.
33 Sasha – Tolstoy's daughter Alexandra; Seryozha – his son Sergey who joined them later.
34 Count A. V. Olsufyev. He apparently repeated: 'I never thought that dying was so easy.'
35 The article 'What is Religion and What is its Essential Nature?' was completed in 1902.
36 I. M. Tregubov, who was living in exile abroad, had sent Tolstoy some revolutionary pamphlets published in Geneva by Prince D. A. Khilkov and had asked for his opinion about them.
37 M. A. Stakhovich, although an Orthodox believer, had spoken out in favour of freedom of conscience in religious matters at a missionary congress in Oryol. Tolstoy responded with his article 'On Religious Toleration', first published in England in 1902.
38 D. I. Chetverikov, a factory owner and accomplished musician; A. A. Dunayev, the elder son of Tolstoy's old friend A. N. Dunayev, and in business as a tea merchant.
39 Not Sasha Dunayev, but Sasha (Alexandra) Tolstaya.

40 Gorky, who had been arrested earlier in the year, had been released on medical grounds and given permission to reside temporarily in the Crimea for health reasons. Chekhov had his own house in Yalta, and both writers often visited Tolstoy at Gaspra. Tolstoy wrote to Chertkov that Chekhov was a complete atheist but a kind person, while Gorky had far more depth but was overpraised.

41 S. P. Polyakov, a member of Kovno circuit court who had written an article on 'Count Tolstoy's Teaching on Life' (1900), had written to say that he intended to give up the law as a result of his sympathy for Tolstoy's views.

42 Probably M. A. Mikhaylov, a vine-grower, Tolstoyan sympathiser and brother of the artist K. A. Mikhaylov, who considered Tolstoy to be his 'spiritual father'. Tolstoy also got to know several members of the evangelical Stundist sect living in nearby Yalta and Feodosiya.

43 A famous waterfall near Gaspra.

44 Tolstoy was reading *Der Grabenhäger* at the time which he considered to be inferior to *Der Büttnerbauer*, despite one particular chapter which, he told Chertkov, made him wish to resume writing fiction himself.

1902

1 See 1901, Note 27. The Grand Duke Nikolay Mikhaylovich, grandson of Nicholas I and a distinguished historian, made Tolstoy's acquaintance in the Crimea and visited him on several occasions. The extant correspondence between the two men amounts to more than thirty letters. The Grand Duke was murdered by the Bolsheviks in 1918 (*Letters*, II, 615).

2 Tolstoy was reading Nikiforov's Russian translations of Mazzini's *The Duties of Man* and *Selected Thoughts of John Ruskin*.

3 A peasant sympathiser and unswerving exponent of Tolstoy's ideas, he was later imprisoned during the First World War for openly protesting against the war.

4 A well-known Petersburg doctor who had been called in to see Tolstoy at Sofya Andreyevna's request.

5 The words of a Russian folk song which Tolstoy had been reading and which, according to Dr Bertenson, he applied to himself and wept.

6 During Tolstoy's illness he occasionally dictated his thoughts to his family and later transferred them to his diary.

7 A comparison apparently suggested by the commemoration of the fiftieth anniversary of Gogol's death, with its reminders of Belinsky's famous letter to Gogol.

8 An article prompted by the spread of industrial unrest in Russia, and the workers' demands for reforms. The article was finished in September and published in England later in 1902.

9 After recovering from angina pectoris, which had almost led to his death, Tolstoy was smitten with typhoid fever, but he was spared a 'third illness' and was soon well enough to return to Yasnaya Polyana.

10 Sulerzhitsky had been arrested on a charge of being party to the illegal importing of the social-democratic journal *The Spark* into Russia. He was eventually acquitted.

11 Tolstoy was interested in the doctrines and practices of the Persian sect of Babids (or Babists), especially their preaching of equality and love of one's neighbour.

12 To Chertkov in England.

13 Possibly the article by a Moscow priest I. I. Solovyov on the Holy Synod's decree excommunicating Tolstoy, which is in the Yasnaya Polyana library.

14 Mashenka and Liza – Tolstoy's sister and daughter; Glebova – née Princess Trubetskaya, the mother of A. V. Glebova who married Tolstoy's son Mikhail.

15 An anti-clerical treatise, finished in December and first published in England in 1903.

16 The article was never written.
17 Eugen Schmitt, in serious financial straits as a result of illness, had asked Tolstoy for help, and Tolstoy sent him 300 roubles from the money received for *Resurrection* with the request to return it later. The other letter was to a young Moscow sympathiser who had written for advice about whether to serve in the army and do propaganda there for Tolstoy's ideas, or to refuse to serve and miss that opportunity.
18 K. P. Pyatnitsky had founded the influential journal *Knowledge* in 1898, and his friend Gorky collaborated with him in the enterprise.
19 A slightly abbreviated quotation of a saying by Epictetus, which Tolstoy had taken from an illustrated Russian desk calendar.
20 A. N. Ageyev, a local peasant convicted for speaking disrespectfully about icons.
21 M. P. Novikov was arrested for handing in to a Tula committee a note about the needs of the local peasantry, but was soon released, thanks to Tolstoy's efforts.
22 Mother of the artist K. A. Mikhaylov (1901, Note 42).
23 The Dukhobor leader, recently released from exile, called in to see Tolstoy *en route* for Canada.
24 Tolstoy was greatly impressed by this work which he read in a French edition of Hugo's posthumous writings, and later translated some parts of it for inclusion in his *Cycle of Reading*.
25 For *The Light Shineth in Darkness*, in which it was intended that Saryntsev should follow the same steps.
26 A speech by Merezhkovsky delivered before the performance of Euripides' *Hippolytus* at the Alexandrinsky Theatre in Petersburg, in which he spoke against Tolstoy's views on sex in *The Kreutzer Sonata* and argued that Christianity provided a synthesis of spiritual and carnal love.
27 *The Destruction of Hell and its Rebuilding*, not in fact finished until January 1903.
28 Tolstoy was referring to *The History of the Russian Intelligentsia* by the historian P. N. Milyukov, a founder of the Constitutional Democratic Party and later Foreign Minister in the Provisional Government.

1903

1. Biryukov had asked Tolstoy to recall what he remembered of his early years for the biography he was writing of him, and Tolstoy began to do so in his *Memoirs*.
2. It later became a separate article, *To the Politicians*, first published in England in 1903.
3. There are a few tentative entries on the subject in February's diary, which are not translated here.
4. A German journal, *Theosophischer Wegweiser zur Erlangung der göttlichen Selbsterkenntnis*, published in Leipzig. Tolstoy marked a number of aphorisms in his copy and translated a story from it, the theme of which he later used in his own story *Esarhaddon, King of Assyria*.
5. Tolstoy had been asked by an English correspondent, Michael Morrison, to express his opinion about the unorthodox behaviour of Louise, Crown Princess of Saxony, who had abandoned her children and had gone off to Switzerland, where she lived for a time with their tutor. Tolstoy replied, condemning her action in strong terms, but soon regretted it and sent a second letter to Morrison contradicting the first, which he asked him not to publish. Morrison, however, had already done so, and the letter received wide and sometimes adverse publicity.
6. V. A. Posse, the editor of the Marxist journal *Life*, had written a pamphlet, *Count L. N. Tolstoy and the Working People* (Geneva, 1903) sharply attacking Tolstoy's views as expressed in *To the Working People* and criticising his approach to land reform.
7. It is not known which article Tolstoy read, but he was familiar with the content of the lectures on human nature delivered the previous year by the Russian-born zoologist and director of the Pasteur Institute in Paris, I. I. Mechnikov, and the latter's view on the superfluousness of the large intestine.
8. *What am I?*, a Russian translation of the book *Czem jestem?* by Henryk Nusbaum, a specialist on nervous diseases and author of numerous medical and psychological works. Nusbaum's collection of philosophical essays appealed to Tolstoy for its advocacy of views on universal love which were similar to Tolstoy's own.
9. Tolstoy read France's *Opinions socialistes* (not *sociales*), Paris, 1902, and found his anti-religious and pro-socialist views distasteful.
10. 'Giant's footsteps' is the name of a swing on which a person holds on to the end of a rope attached by a swivel to the top of a fixed pole and runs round the pole in circles, getting further away from it each time until his feet leave the ground.
11. Tolstoy was a great admirer of the American self-styled 'mystic transcendentalist and natural philosopher', Thoreau. One of the works he read was *The Intermediary*'s publication entitled *Henry Thoreau: The philosophy of the natural life* (1903).
12. The article *To the Politicians*.
13. A letter to E. Linetsky and several prominent Jews about the anti-Jewish pogroms in Kishinyov in April 1903, and a telegram to the mayor of Kishinyov signed by Tolstoy and a group of Moscow intellectuals protesting against the actions of the authorities.
14. *Études sur la nature humaine*, with an inscription from the author. There is a reference in it to Tolstoy's attitude to death. He mentioned the book in a letter to his brother as being 'very interesting for its learned stupidity', but never wrote about it.
15. *To the Politicians* was sent to Chertkov in England and later published in the *Free Word*.
16. F. A. Strakhov's marriage had been declared invalid on the grounds of too close a degree of affinity between husband and wife, although they had been married for thirteen years.
17. Chapter 15, with its harsh assessment of the character of Nicholas I.
18. It is not known who is referred to by the initials.
19. N. K. Schilder's *The Emperor Nicholas I, his life and reign* (Petersburg, 1903).

20 See Notes 22–5.
21 Nothing came of this intention.
22 Another idea which led to nothing.
23 Tolstoy agreed to contribute to an anthology in aid of the victims of the Kishinyov pogroms – though not the story outlined in this paragraph (*Letters*, II, 631).
24 The basis of his story *After the Ball*. The girl's surname clearly suggests that of V. A. Koreysh, a student friend at Kazan University, and confirms the autobiographical nature of the story.
25 Nothing came of this idea either.
26 P. Sabatier's *Vie de S. François d'Assise*, which Tolstoy read in Russian translation.
27 Robert Hunter, an American socialist and friend of Ernest Crosby and the author of several books, including *Poverty* and *Socialists at Work*, visited Tolstoy with his wife and Sidney Cockerell, William Morris' former secretary, and spent a day at Yasnaya Polyana. Both men wrote about Tolstoy, Hunter in his book *Why We Fail as Christians* (New York, 1919), Cockerell in an article, *Count L. Tolstoy; Russian Novelist and Social Reformer. Notes on a Visit to Leo Tolstoy at Yasnaya Polyana on July 12, 1903*, published in Viola Meynell's *Friends of a Lifetime* (London, 1940).
28 Probably in Schilder's biography of Nicholas I.
29 *Esarhaddon, King of Assyria*, see Note 31.
30 A reference to the election of the new Pope Pius X, and to the recent canonisation by the Orthodox Church of Serafim, Elder of the Sarov monastery in the province of Tambov who had died in 1833, and the veneration of his relics.
31 *Esarhaddon, King of Assyria*, *Three Questions* and *Work, Death and Sickness*, all of which were published in Yiddish translation in the anthology compiled in aid of the Kishinyov victims (Note 23).
32 One of the original titles of *After the Ball*.
33 The third tale was finished a week later than the other two.
34 Another early title of *After the Ball*.
35 Some of the messages of congratulations on Tolstoy's seventy-fifth birthday included the words 'great writer of the Russian land', first used by Turgenev in a letter to Tolstoy shortly before his death in 1883.
36 V. A. Lazarevsky, a minor author and great admirer of Chekhov, wrote to Chekhov to tell him that Tolstoy had called him the Pushkin of prose.
37 Tolstoy believed that Gorky was overestimated as a writer, and regretted that the German novelist, essayist and dramatist Wilhelm von Polenz was less well known.
38 The article which was eventually called *On Shakespeare and the Drama* was originally begun as a foreword to Ernest Crosby's *Shakespeare and the Working Class*.
39 B. Gegidze, a student at Petersburg University and the author of several stories, attracted considerable attention by his book *At the University: Sketches of student life*, Petersburg (1903) which ran through six editions. It spoke of the emptiness of university life and the dissatisfaction of young people with the lack of worthwhile aims and ideals.
40 A foreword to the short biography of W. L. Garrison by V. Chertkov and F. Holah, published by the Free Age Press in English, and later in Russian.
41 Tolstoy's son Andrey's relations with a married woman, Anna Leonidovna Tolmachova, led to his separation from his wife and children in November 1903 (and his eventual divorce in 1907 when he wished to remarry).
42 What he began to write (at first called *The Stone* or *The Corner-Stone*) was eventually absorbed in his article *The One Thing Needful* (1905).
43 Tolstoy wrote a story, *Prayer*, on this theme in 1905.
44 A legend Tolstoy had taken down from a story-teller and which he worked up in 1907 for his *Cycle of Reading*.
45 A story which grew out of a rough draft in his diary after the entry for 30 December, and which was eventually called *The Divine and the Human*.

46 No stories were written on the last two subjects.

1904

1   An anthology in calendar form entitled *The Thoughts of Wise People for Every Day*, published in 1903 by *The Intermediary* and revised in 1904 with a new *Cycle of Reading* in mind.
2   See 1903, Note 40, and 1904, Note 1.
3   See 1903, Note 42.
4   A thought expressed (rather differently) in Amiel's diary for 30 December 1850, which Tolstoy read in the edition published in Russian by *The Intermediary* in 1894.
5   The devils representing man's evil actions were omitted from the final version of *The Forged Coupon*.
6   The Russo-Japanese War which began on 27 January 1904.
7   These thoughts were expressed in the article *Bethink Yourselves*! which Tolstoy began writing almost at once and which was widely read abroad.
8   Tolstoy was reading the German philosopher Georg Lichtenberg's *Vermischte Schriften*, in a four-volume edition of 1800–2. Many of his thoughts were included in Tolstoy's *Cycle of Reading*.
9   For the text see *Letters*, II, 637–8.
10 Of *Bethink Yourselves*!, in which each chapter was prefaced by an epigraph from the works of various well-known writers and thinkers.
11 The composer A. S. Arensky, and Tolstoy's daughter-in-law Olga, who had just been deserted by her husband (1903, Note 40).
12 Tolstoy was reading Ernest Naville's book on the French philosopher, *Maine de Biran, sa vie et ses pensées* (Paris, 1874).
13 Another of Tolstoy's unrealised intentions was to write about Nicholas I and the Decembrist rising of 1825, and to include the three statesmen mentioned who were all involved to some extent in the events of that month and later rose to positions of great influence. (Count Bludov was portrayed in Chapter 15 of *Hadji Murat*.)
14 R. Wahle's *Kurze Erklärung der Ethik von Spinoza . . .* (Leipzig, 1899).
15 A. A. Tolstaya.
16 Not only Schilder's biography, but various personal reminiscences in manuscript and article form.
17 The article *Bethink Yourselves*! which Tolstoy sent to Chertkov for publication in England.
18 The text of the letter is included in the last chapter of *Bethink Yourselves*!
19 K. A. Mikhaylov, art teacher and 'spiritual son' of Tolstoy (1901, Note 42); S. D. Nikolayev, a disciple of Henry George, who translated all George's main works into Russian. Dmitri Merezhkovsky and his wife Zinaida Gippius spent 11 and 12 May at Yasnaya Polyana, and both left accounts of their visit.
20 William Briggs, an Englishman who had originally intended to be a Unitarian minister but changed his mind because of religious doubts, was working at the time with Chertkov as a market gardener, and brought Tolstoy a letter with questions about who would be entitled to publish Tolstoy's works after his death.
21 Chertkov's article *On Revolution: Violent Revolution or Christian Emancipation?* had appeared in his journal in 1903, and he had asked Tolstoy to write a foreword to a separate edition of it which he was planning to publish.
22 Charles Allen Clarke, a Lancashire journalist, author and editor, was a prolific writer and had previously sent Tolstoy a copy of his book *The Effects of the Factory System*, which Tolstoy had had translated into Russian – see *Letters*, II, 640. In 1904 he sent Tolstoy a signed copy of *The Eternal Question. Shall a Man Live Again?* (Bolton, 1902) and also *Time and Eternity*.

23 N. V. Davydov was at the time president of the Moscow Circuit Court; V. N. Bestuzhev-Ryumin and A. V. Kun were, successively, in charge of the Tula armaments factory. Michael Davitt, the Irish nationalist, was a friend of Henry George and came to Russia to study the land question.
24 The manuscript of the first volume of Biryukov's biography of Tolstoy.
25 To Tambov, where he had been posted as orderly to General Sobolev.
26 A long letter to Y. V. Molostvova, the daughter of a rich landowner who was very close to Tolstoy in her views, in which Tolstoy replied to her own letter complaining about the unsatisfactory nature of her life with his advice on how rich people with a conscience ought to act.
27 *Bethink Yourselves!* was published in *The Times*, and got an enthusiastic reception, especially from the *Daily News*.
28 Chertkov wrote about some changes he had made to '*Bethink Yourselves!*'; an Englishman, P. W. Dougall, complained that Tolstoy was insulting the memory of Admiral Makarov and the officers who perished with him by speaking about their 'supposed patriotism'.
29 Baron A. Y. Rosen's *Into Exile: Notes of a Decembrist, 1825–1900* (Moscow, 1900).
30 Y. D. Grishenko, daughter of a Bessarabian landowner and a student in Moscow; S. D. Toll, daughter of Count D. A. Tolstoy, Alexander II's Minister of Education. She had written to Tolstoy accusing him of betraying his country by writing *Bethink Yourselves!*; he replied that he stood by the sense of the article, if not the tone.
31 To Chertkov's article (see Note 21).
32 This was never done.
33 Probably an unfinished article, *A New Life*, which was later incorporated into *The One Thing Needful*.
34 A Tula barrister to whom Tolstoy sometimes referred people in need of legal aid.
35 It is not known what work he was reading.
36 The son-in-law of Tolstoy's brother Seryozha.
37 Hippolyte Taine's *Les Origines de la France contemporaine* (1875–93).
38 Lucy A. Mallory, editor of the American journal *World's Advance Thought*, had written very favourably about *Bethink Yourselves!*
39 A mistake for *constituante*.
40 Extracts from Amiel's Diary (see Note 4); *The Riddle of the Sphinx* (Moscow, 1900) which was a translation of extracts from Carlyle's *Past and Present*; and Mazzini's *The Duties of Man*.
41 Hans Andersen's fairy tale *Five out of one Shell*.
42 *Past and Present*, Book 3, Chapter 3 (Gospel of Mammon).
43 Yet another title for the article referred to in the diaries as *The Corner-stone* and *A New Life*.
44 Biographies of saints and martyrs for the Sunday entries in his 'calendar' – an idea which was later dropped in favour of stories and articles, as with other days of the week.
45 The manuscript of a Russian translation of *Selected Thoughts of Kant*, to be published by *The Intermediary*.
46 The first two items were incorporated into *The One Thing Needful*; the third took the form of an article, *Who Am I?*, subsequently entitled *The Green Stick*.
47 Extracts from Pascal's *Pensées* for inclusion in the *Cycle of Reading*.
48 From a French translation of his works.
49 See Note 26.
50 The full text is translated in *Letters*, II, 608–13.
51 The Grand Duke Nikolay Mikhaylovich had personally delivered Tolstoy's letter (see Note 50) to the Tsar. Tolstoy was concerned because what had been intended as a private communication from one man to another had been published abroad by Chertkov.

52 Port Arthur with its garrison of 15,000 men surrendered to the Japanese on 20 December 1904 after six months' siege.

1905

1 To Nicholas II (see 1904, Note 50).
2 See 1897, Note 15.
3 A. K. Chertkova twice wrote to Tolstoy expressing her regret at his reply in an American newspaper, the *North-American*, to questions about *zemstvo* activities in which he spoke against 'political agitation' as a method of obtaining social improvement.
4 M. K. Kipiani, a Georgian who had been exiled to Siberia for revolutionary activities, told Tolstoy about widespread anti-government opposition in Georgia, which largely took the form at first of passive resistance.
5 Tolstoy's son had hoped to persuade the Tsar to convene the old *Zemsky Sobor*, the 'Assembly of the Land' in Muscovite Russia.
6 Of reading the proofs of the *Cycle of Reading*.
7 A tale Tolstoy had heard from a story-teller in 1897 and was reworking for publication in the *Cycle of Reading* about a peasant who left his wife to become a pilgrim.
8 *Alyosha Gorshok (Alyosha the Jug)*, a story Tolstoy wrote in a few days in 1905 but which was not published until after his death. Alyosha's nickname was the result of his being beaten for breaking a jug of milk.
9 Short biographies compiled by members of his family at his request for publication in the *Cycle of Reading*.
10 I have used 'secondary schools' and 'colleges' to translate *nizshiye* and *vysshye shkoly*.
11 In a much-quoted speech of 1860 Turgenev had attempted to classify the characters of Hamlet and Don Quixote as representing the two fundamental and opposite tendencies of human nature: the former – analysis, egoism and unbelief; the latter – belief in something eternal and unshakeable, belief in the truth. He referred also to Shakespeare's Horatio in *Hamlet* as a disciple in the best sense of the word, honest, loyal, self-sacrificing, warm-hearted, but with a rather limited mind. Tolstoy put Horatio on a par with Don Quixote, and added the character of the heroine of Chekhov's story *The Darling*.
12 See Note 3.
13 Tolstoy wrote an essay on the fifteenth-century Czech writer Chelčický, author of *The Net of Faith*; he intended to write a story on the theme of his son Ilya's story, *One Scoundrel Less*, but did not do so; the other two projects also came to nothing.
14 A reference to a letter from a semi-literate peasant to Tolstoy asking him how long the down-trodden peasantry would have to go on 'dragging an overturned cart'. Tolstoy's reply was published in article form in England under the title *How Are the Working People to Free Themselves?* – subsequently reworked and entitled *The True Freedom*.
15 A journalist visiting Yasnaya Polyana had just told Tolstoy that his son Lyova intended to publish a newspaper directed against his father's teachings (in fact he did not do so).
16 A complaint that Tolstoy's works were too expensive for poor people to buy.
17 Twenty years previously Tolstoy had translated *The Teaching of the Twelve Apostles* (published in 1883) and written a foreword to it. He wrote a new foreword in 1905 for publication in the *Cycle of Reading*.
18 See 1904, Note 46.
19 *Selected Speeches and Articles of Henry George*, compiled by S. D. Nikolayev and published by *The Intermediary*.

20 The original title of *A Great Sin*.
21 What began as an article about Henry George became part of *A Great Sin*.
22 This reproach of Tolstoy's foster-brother, the peasant Pyotr Osipovich Zyabrev, was really directed not at Tolstoy, but at his daughter Alexandra's purchase of the estate of Telyatinki from a neighbouring landowner.
23 It was not finished until June.
24 Tolstoy's story *Prayer* first appeared in the *Cycle of Reading*.
25 On 14 May 1905 two Russian naval squadrons were routed by the Japanese fleet off the island of Tsushima.
26 G. V. Fokanov, a Yasnaya Polyana peasant, was accidentally buried alive in a pit he was digging. Gerasim, mentioned in the next sentence, was his nephew.
27 His 'revelation' about the spirit of self-sacrifice on the part of the peasantry who tried to save Fokanov's life, which Tolstoy wished to include in his story referred to in Note 13.
28 K. A. Malevanny, an uneducated wheelwright who had been confined to a mental home and then to a psychiatric hospital for preaching non-resistance to evil, civil disobedience and opposition to military service.
29 Prince P. D. Dolgorukov, a member of the central committee of the Constitutional Democratic Party (Cadets).
30 It was written for, and first published in, the *Cycle of Reading*.
31 This introduction was omitted from the final version.
32 The original title of *The End of the World*, an article devoted to Tolstoy's belief that the coming social revolution would lead to a new social order based not on coercion but on love. The title is a reference to Matthew, 24:3.
33 Either an error on Tolstoy's part, or an alternative title (the pool of Siloam is mentioned in John 9:7 and 11, the Tower of Siloam in Luke 13:4).
34 In his *L'ancien régime et la révolution*.
35 Tocqueville actually wrote *une partie des institutions . . .* and *ce qu'on en laissait*.
36 It was first published in England in 1905; an edition published in Russia in 1906 was confiscated.
37 More precisely, the fact that his wife objected to his articles appearing without payment in the *Free Word* and *The Intermediary*.
38 A story which Tolstoy intended to write about a woman who gave up her own child and nursed another woman's. He had referred to it in diary entries in 1896 and 1897, and returned to it in 1905, but never wrote it.
39 The former in the August number of the *Free Word*; the latter in the July number of *Russian Thought*.
40 According to Makovitsky, Tolstoy was sent a copy of an American newspaper with a translation of *A Great Sin*, and also a review of the article in the *Spectator* of 5 August 1905.
41 From the editor of the Paris newspaper *Echo de Paris*, to which Tolstoy did not reply.
42 A difficult pregnancy resulting in a stillborn child.
43 In fact it was not finished until the end of the year.
44 Another name for the story *Three Questions* which had first appeared in *The Intermediary* in 1903 and was included in the *Cycle of Reading*, but was later removed.
45 An article on how to live and how to bring up children (see 6 October), which was never written, or the drama *The Light Shineth in Darkness*.
46 N. K. Schilder's book *The Emperor Alexander I, His Life and Reign* (Petersburg, 1904–5).
47 See Note 45.
48 *The Posthumous Notes of Fyodor Kuzmich*. The biographer of Alexander I, N. K. Schilder, was inclined to believe the legend that the Elder Fyodor Kuzmich was in fact the Emperor Alexander who had not died in 1825 but had withdrawn from the world.

49 N. K. Schilder's biography *The Emperor Paul I* (Petersburg, 1901) and the diary of Paul's tutor, S. A. Poroshin.
50 Tolstoy re-read Herzen's book after V. V. Stasov had mentioned it in a letter to him the previous month.
51 *An Appeal to the Russian People. To the Government, the Revolutionaries and the People* [*narod*]. The article was finished in 1906.
52 See Note 48.
53 An unfinished article on the three basic injustices of the private ownership of land, taxation and military service.
54 A daughter, also called Tatyana (Tatyana Sukhotina-Albertini).
55 The first volume of *Social Movements in Russia in the First Half of the Nineteenth Century* (Petersburg, 1905) with articles and materials on some of the Decembrists.
56 It was included in the second edition of *The End of the World* (Chapter 12), published by the *Free Word*.
57 Incorporated into the article referred to in Note 51.
58 The reference is obscure.
59 P. V. Velikanov, a teacher then living in Novgorod, who, unlike Tolstoy whose views he shared in many respects, believed in the need for political action.
60 Tolstoy was reading the Grand Duke Nikolay Mikhaylovich's book on Count Stroganov, with its description of the heroic death of Stroganov's tutor, Charles-Gilbert Romme, during the French Revolution.

1906

1 Nothing came of these particular subjects.
2 *What for?*, a story relating to the time of the Polish uprising of 1830.
3 The first volume of the *Cycle of Reading* had been published in Moscow on 30 January 1906; *On Life*, which Tolstoy had written in 1887–8, was not published in full in Russia until 1906.
4 *Autocracy* by D. A. Khomyakov, the son of the famous Slavophile poet, historian and theologian. Tolstoy agreed with him that the Russian people set greater store by the spiritual life than material wellbeing, but not with his views on Orthodoxy and autocracy as the mainstays of their life.
5 A landowner who sent Tolstoy a copy of his 'Open Letter to Landowners' announcing that he had given up nearly all his land to the peasants without payment, keeping only one peasant-size allotment for himself, and inviting his fellow landowners to do the same. Tolstoy had the letter published in a newspaper with a foreword by himself.
6 Kenjiro Tokutomi, a Japanese writer and editor of a periodical, who had written an essay on the life and work of Tolstoy and now wrote to him about the growing number of Tolstoyan sympathisers in Japan and their influence in the country.
7 It became part of the *New Cycle of Reading*, eventually entitled *For Every Day*.
8 This note, at first called *Two Ways*, grew into the article *On the Meaning of the Russian Revolution*.
9 *The Schlüsselburg Prison over Twenty Years. Reminiscences*, by a former member of the revolutionary party *The People's Will*, who was imprisoned there from 1883 to 1904. Published in *The Past*, 1906, No. 1.
10 A reference to his book *Hard Work and Slothfulness* and his belief in the moral superiority of work on the land.
11 Nothing came of this idea. See 1884, Note 21.
12 No such story was written.
13 Tolstoy wrote a short afterword to Tregubov's article calling on the Duma to pass a law enabling conscientious objectors to undertake other forms of service to the

community, and both the article and Tolstoy's supporting remarks were published in *The Word*, 3 May 1906.
14 A reference to the Empress Elizabeth's vow to make a pilgrimage to the Troitsa Monastery (present-day Zagorsk) whenever she was in Moscow, which she dutifully did on foot, escorted by her lovers. Tolstoy's source was Waliszewski's book *La dernière des Romanov*.
15 Gorky travelled to America with M. F. Andreyeva, and when it transpired that they were not married, some American newspapers and public figures gave him a hostile reception.
16 See 1905, Note 59.
17 An article in the *Stock Exchange Gazette* which accused the owner of Yasnaya Polyana of calling in the Cossacks to stop the illegal felling of trees on the estate – a charge which Tolstoy vehemently denied on his wife's behalf.
18 Tolstoy had come across this saying in slightly different form in Chertkov's book *Epictetus, a Roman Sage*, and included it in his *Cycle of Reading*.
19 F. D. Bykov, a carpenter who, according to Makovitsky, revered Tolstoy as a second Christ, and knelt before him, much to his embarrassment; Y. O. Dymshits, a Jewish pacifist and founder of a vegetarian society, whose Tolstoyan views did not all survive the October revolution; A. A. Ofitserov, a follower of Dobrolyubov (see Note 20), later imprisoned for distributing pacifist and anti-clerical literature.
20 A. M. Dobrolyubov, one of the first Russian symbolist poets. His religious fervour and the priority he gave to rural over urban life and to work on the land influenced a number of people in the Samara province, some of whom also became conscientious objectors.
21 J. M. Davidson, a prolific English writer on economic problems and author of *The Annals of Toil*, the second part of which was dedicated to Tolstoy personally (*Letters*, II, 588). In May 1906 he sent Tolstoy his latest book, *The Son of Man*, which Tolstoy thought highly of. Toki-Tomi – a misspelling of Tokutomi (see Note 6).
22 Y. D. Belyayev, correspondent of *New Times*. Tolstoy told him that the Duma made a 'comical, disturbing and revolting impression' on him for reasons which he enlarged on and which were summarised in Belyayev's article.
23 O. I. Denisenko, daughter of the lawyer I. V. Denisenko who married Tolstoy's niece.
24 A poem which Fet dedicated to Turgenev and which he particularly admired.
25 *Towards an Understanding of Russia* (Petersburg, 1906) by the distinguished chemist and writer on economic affairs, D. I. Mendeleyev, who regarded the growth of population and technological progress as important factors in strengthening the country's power.
26 She was suffering from serious abdominal pains which necessitated an operation.
27 A foreword to the Russian translation of Henry George's *Social Problems* published by *The Intermediary*.
28 *Two Ways* (*On the Meaning of the Russian Revolution*); an article entitled *The Only Possible Solution of the Land Problem*; and a letter to a Chinese writer, Ku Hung-Ming, who had sent Tolstoy his book on the moral causes of the Russo-Japanese War.
29 A request for Tolstoy to take part in a reception for an English parliamentary delegation which was due to visit Russia, and which he declined in rather strong language. The visit did not take place.
30 *Vasily of Mozhaysk*, later entitled *Father Vasily*, which was begun but never finished.
31 *Dichtung und Wahrheit*. Tolstoy was re-reading Goethe's memoirs since he was thinking of writing his own.
32 Tolstoy intended to insert in his diary the letter he wrote to Chertkov on 3 October defining his understanding of life.
33 A. A. Yagn, from Balanda in the Saratov province, had asked Tolstoy whether his views about the futility of political action had changed as a result of recent revolutionary events. In his reply Tolstoy said that they had not, and reaffirmed his belief in moral improvement.
34 An article which subsequently appeared under the title *What Is To Be Done?* (not to be

confused with *What Then Must We Do?*). The executions referred to had taken place the previous day in various parts of the Russian empire, the majority of them for robbery with violence.

35 Gorbunov-Posadov, editor of *The Intermediary*, which had recently published *inter alia* an article about Tolstoy's views on teaching and education.
36 Of the article *On the Meaning of the Russian Revolution*. The concluding chapter later appeared as a separate article, *What Is To Be Done?* (see Note 34).
37 Houston Stewart Chamberlain – a Russian translation of *Die Juden, ihre Herkunft und die Ursache ihres Einflusses in Europa*, which Tolstoy found superficial.
38 A scurrilous article entitled *At Yasnaya Polyana. Impressions of a Tourist* by a young student which claimed that the local peasants regarded Tolstoy as a typical serf-owner and a wolf in sheep's clothing.
39 To the article *On the Meaning of the Russian Revolution*.
40 See Note 30.
41 A gipsy settlement near Tula.
42 Nothing came of the idea.
43 In reply to a letter from the French Catholic writer Paul Sabatier, who had written about the apparent religious revival in the Catholic world, Tolstoy wrote a long letter explaining his views on the spiritual life of the West in general.
44 This story, based on an incident in the life of Tolstoy's brother Sergey, was first published posthumously.
45 M. S. Sukhotin's young son who was staying at the house and to whom Tolstoy read stories from the *Cycle of Reading*.
46 N. G. Sutkovoy, at the time a 'Tolstoyan', was a graduate of Petersburg University who had worked on the land in different parts of Russia and with Chertkov in England. A religious seeker, he had written to Tolstoy about moral self-improvement and universal love and extracts from his letter were included at Tolstoy's suggestion in Nazhivin's book *From the Life of L. Tolstoy*, 1911.
47 The dilemma of choosing between a form of society based on the laws of religion or on the power of the state.
48 A short address to the young (later published as *Have Faith in Yourselves*) which Tolstoy wrote at the request of the editor of the children's magazine *The Spring* which was celebrating its twenty-fifth anniversary.
49 The Japanese article has not been identified; the Indian article was entitled *The White Peril*, by the Indian philosopher Baba Bharati, published in the journal *The Light of India* in Los Angeles.
50 The first epistle of St John the Divine.
51 She died at the age of thirty-five of pneumonia.
52 See Note 7.
53 An article in the *Russian Gazette* took issue with *On the Meaning of the Russian Revolution* on the grounds that it postulated too great a change in human nature; the letter from an officer expressed doubts about Tolstoy's anti-militarism; and the notice about *What Is To Be Done?*, also in the *Russian Gazette*, accused Tolstoy of repeating his old views to no effect.
54 Tolstoy left a gap of three lines at this point in the diary.

1907

1 Plutarch's *Oeuvres morales* (a five-volume French translation); Montaigne's *Essais*; Waliszewski's *L'héritage de Pierre le Grand*; Renan's *Saint Paul*; and Xenophon's *Memorabilia*, which Tolstoy read in a Russian translation with parallel Greek and Russian texts.
2 A reference to an incident which Tolstoy read in Sabatier's life of St Francis in which

St Francis, in answer to the question 'what is perfect joy?' replied that if we were refused admission to a house when cold and wet and hungry, and were humble enough to accept that the janitor was right to refuse us, that would be perfect joy.
3   The letter has not survived.
4   Bolton Hall, president of the American Single Tax League, who shared many of Tolstoy's views and wrote about him in his book *Even as You and I*, 1900; Ernest Crosby, an American social reformer and Tolstoyan (*Letters*, II, 511), who had died recently and to whose sister and close friends Tolstoy wrote letters of sympathy; C. W. Daniel, editor of the London journal *The Crank* (*Letters*, II, 663) and his wife, to whom Tolstoy wrote about their journal and their articles about him; Tolstoy's letter to Baba Bharati (see 1906, Note 49) concerned Bharati's book *Sri Krishna* and Brahminism.
5   Some scripture lessons for Yasnaya Polyana children, out of which grew the *Children's Cycle of Reading*.
6   To the German author Eugen Reichel, apropos of his attitude to Shakespeare and to Reichel's book on the subject. See *Letters*, II, 664 for the full text of Tolstoy's letter, which was not sent until 2/15 March.
7   Tolstoy was translating and editing passages from La Bruyère's *Caractères de Theophraste traduits du grec avec les Caractères ou les Moeurs de ce siècle* ((1688). With G. A. Rusanov he translated from the French selected thoughts of La Bruyère, La Rochefoucauld, Vauvenargues and Montesquieu and wrote a foreword for *The Intermediary* edition of 1908.
8   A slightly inaccurate quotation from a French writer, Louis Thomas, who had responded unfavourably, together with other French writers, to Tolstoy's article *On Shakespeare and the Drama*, in the Paris journal *Les Lettres*.
9   A man-servant employed at Yasnaya Polyana.
10 Nothing came of this idea.
11 No such story was written.
12 See 1905, Note 26. Presumably his wife asked Tolstoy for money.
13 Nothing came of this idea.
14 The stories were never written.
15 In an unfinished article comparing St Paul's teaching unfavourably with the teaching of Christ.
16 A teacher who was trying to combat the excessive veneration of Malevanny by some of his followers in that part of the Kiev province where he, Loizner, taught.
17 S. D. Nikolayev and his family had settled in the village of Yasnaya Polyana for the summer to be near Tolstoy.
18 Tolstoy's son had divorced his first wife in order to marry the wife of the Governor of Tula, M. V. Artsimovich, with whom he had had a liaison. See *Letters*, II, 666–9.
19 Tolstoy's brother-in-law, a railway engineer, who had been shot dead in Petersburg by unknown assassins.
20 His late daughter Masha's husband, apparently over rent for land.
21 An article on the eighteenth-century Ukrainian philosopher and poet for the *Children's Cycle of Reading*.
22 See 1906, Note 46. In reply to Sutkovoy's description of the beliefs and practices of the Dobrolyubov sect in the Samara province, Tolstoy qualified his basic agreement with reservations about the danger of their becoming a clique of righteous men and about their hostile attitude to books.
23 P. P. Nikolayev's book *The Concept of God as the Absolute Basis of Consciousness* (Geneva, 1907).
24 The artist M. V. Nesterov spent a week at Yasnaya Polyana painting a portrait of Tolstoy and doing a number of sketches.
25 Schoolchildren from Tula and their teachers who had been invited for a day's outing.
26 Two servants of a wealthy landowner who lived near Yasnaya Polyana.

27 N. Y. Felten, editor of the publishing house *Renewal*, was arrested for publishing Tolstoy's article *Thou Shalt Not Kill*. He was soon released on bail.
28 P. A. Stolypin, Minister of Internal Affairs and President of the Council of Ministers (*Letters*, II, 689). Tolstoy wrote to advocate a Henry George-type solution to the problem of land, the unfair distribution of which was causing so much discontent among the peasantry.
29 The story was begun the following year but never finished.
30 I. I. Gorbunov-Posadov.
31 Probably *Communism and Anarchy* (Petersburg, 1906).
32 Novikov had written about his own impoverished condition, spoken out against wealthy landowners, and wondered whether one could continue to maintain, like the early Christians, that man lives 'not by bread alone' in view of the prevailing poverty of the peasantry.
33 A compilation of Tolstoy's thoughts by the Chertkovs which has not been published.
34 P. A. Boulanger, working at the time as an accountant on the railways, had squandered a large sum of government money at cards and had disappeared after leaving a note to say that he intended to kill himself. In fact he fled to the Caucasus, but settled near Tolstoy again in 1909 after a period abroad.
35 The governor of Tula and his colleagues visited Yasnaya Polyana in connection with a complaint by Tolstoy's wife that the peasants had been stealing cabbages.
36 Talks intended for the peasant youth who met from time to time at the Chertkovs' house at Telyatinki.
37 I. Y. Repin spent more than a week at Yasnaya Polyana painting a large portrait of Tolstoy and his wife seated at a table. Tolstoy had some very unflattering things to say about it in a letter to his sister-in-law, calling it 'incredibly funny'.
38 V. A. Repin, an ex-artillery officer who had founded a Tolstoyan colony near Tashkent in 1907. It was short-lived, and Repin had a mental breakdown.
39 At Tolstoy's wife's request two watchmen had been installed by the governor of Tula to protect the estate.
40 Tanya Kuzminskaya, Mikhail and Tanya Sukhotin, and their daughter Tanya.
41 Tolstoy's open letter to the press (*Letters*, II, 670), prompted by the numerous requests he received for aid, led to a series of abusive letters and adverse newspaper comment.
42 A letter from a young railway worker in prison describing the humiliating treatment he had received as a conscientious objector. Gusev read the letter aloud to relatives and guests of Tolstoy.
43 Eventually Tolstoy combined the *Children's Cycle of Reading* and the *New Cycle of Reading* for adults into a single anthology, *For Every Day*.
44 This catalogue of sins was part of the original plan of the *New Cycle of Reading*, which was subsequently modified.
45 The former a carpenter and ex-revolutionary who had come into contact with Tolstoy's writings in 1906–7 and had given up making iconostases for churches as a result; the latter a railway worker who had corresponded with Tolstoy intermittently since 1903.
46 N. N. Gusev, who had worked for *The Intermediary* publishing house since 1905, became Tolstoy's secretary in 1907 and stayed with him in that capacity for the next two years. He was arrested in October 1907 and briefly imprisoned, and arrested again in 1909 and sent into exile for distributing Tolstoy's banned works. His extensive writings included *Two Years with Tolstoy*, and from 1925 to 1930 he was director of the Tolstoy Museum in Moscow.
47 Liza Obolenskaya – Tolstoy's niece; D. A. Olsufyev – the son of Tolstoy's old friends and a member of the Council of State; Varya – V. V. Nagornova, another niece of Tolstoy's; Natasha – N. L. Abrikosova, the daughter of Liza Obolenskaya.
48 Visiting him in prison.

49 Sergey Bulygin, who gave up his studies to work on the land under the influence of Tolstoy's ideas, refused to do military service in 1910 and was exiled to Siberia during the First World War for his pacifist activities. Tolstoy's plan to write a drama with him as the hero came to nothing.
50 Probably the article he intended to write in connection with Gusev's arrest.
51 In English in the diary.
52 Tolstoy's son married his mistress Y. V. Artsimovich in November 1907 – a marriage of which Tolstoy strongly disapproved.
53 After nearly two months' confinement Tolstoy had campaigned vigorously for his release.
54 A letter from a fitter and Tolstoyan sympathiser to the Russian Prime Minister urging him to come to Tolstoy for advice on how best to satisfy the needs of the people.

1908

1 See 1907, Note 52.
2 See 1907, Note 49.
3 *There's an End to Everything*, later entitled *The Law of Violence and the Law of Love*.
4 The foreword to the *New Cycle of Reading*, in which the contents of the book are set out in sections.
5 M. A. Schmidt.
6 A second letter to Stolypin on the same lines as the first (1907, Note 28); and a letter to a Pole (Zimako, not Zadago) on the land question, militarism and the 'social question' which Zimako, unlike Tolstoy, considered to be an economic problem.
7 It is not known what Tolstoy was reading by Bernard Shaw (or Schaw as he calls him in the diary).
8 Grigory Petrov, a priest of liberal views, a popular writer, and briefly a member of the Second Duma. His religious views were too unorthodox for him to remain a priest, and Tolstoy did not even consider him to be a Christian when he stayed at Yasnaya Polyana for three days at his own request.
9 *The Law of Violence and the Law of Love*, two chapters of which were written in the form of an appeal.
10 For Tolstoy's eightieth birthday.
11 In English in the diary.
12 *God and Man* by Swami Vivekananda, a disciple of Ramakrishna.
13 This letter prompted Tolstoy to write to the press asking for the preparations to celebrate his eightieth birthday to be stopped – which they were.
14 The following entries for March and April which come after the entries for May in the diary have been restored to their proper place.
15 L. D. Semyonov, a graduate of Petersburg University and a young poet whose brief revolutionary activities led to a term of imprisonment, during which he read the Gospels and became deeply religious. A story by him on the death penalty made a great impression on Tolstoy. Subsequently his extreme views and his objection to military service led to further confinement in hospitals and mental homes.
16 A doctor who had treated Tolstoy in the Crimea, and later attended him on his death bed at Astapovo.
17 A letter from a peasant who had recently visited him, and reproached him for living in conditions of luxury which contradicted his principles.
18 In the previous day's entry in *Thoughts of Wise People*, to the effect that true good consists in the service of others.
19 His recollections about the Shabunin case (see 1889, Note 76) which he was writing for Biryukov's biography of him.
20 In the Kherson province, for a violent assault on the estate of a local landowner.

21 A. F. Koni, who supplied Tolstoy with the germ of the story of *Resurrection*.
22 *I Cannot be Silent*.
23 An article written in connection with the arrest and imprisonment of V. A. Molochnikov for distributing banned works of Tolstoy's.
24 N. K. Muravyov, a Moscow lawyer who later helped to draw up Tolstoy's will, had told him disturbing details about political trials in which he had been involved as counsel for the defence.
25 Later entitled *I Cannot Be Silent*.
26 Tolstoy read an account of the indictment and trial of Vera Figner, a member of the revolutionary *People's Will*, in a book entitled *Russian Women on the Scaffold*. He had no sympathy for her terrorist activities.
27 D. F. Kobeko, a member of the Council of State and director of the Imperial Public Library, who had come to discuss with Tolstoy's wife the possible acquisition by the Library of some Decembrists' letters belonging to a nun in the convent where Tolstoy's sister lived.
28 E. R. Stamo, a landowner from Bessarabia who shared Tolstoy's views and who had previously visited him at Yasnaya Polyana. She later wrote a pamphlet on Tolstoy and the Jews, which included an account of conversations she and her son had had with him.
29 Sonya Nikolayevna Tolstaya, the first wife of Ilya Tolstoy, and A. V. Unkovskaya, a violinist and pupil of Leopold Auer.
30 S. M. Prokudin-Gorsky, a professor of Chemistry and P. Y. Kulakov, founder of a stereographic firm, who were both interested in colour photography and had come to take some coloured pictures of Tolstoy to be published for his eightieth birthday. The American visitor was Jerome Hall Raymond, a professor of sociology in Chicago, with whom Tolstoy discussed the situation of the negroes in America, the American political parties and the forthcoming presidential elections.
31 *The Law of Violence and the Law of Love*.
32 Two short stories involving revolutionaries were begun at the end of the year but never finished.
33 The article *Apropos of the Imprisonment of V. A. Molochnikov*, published in abridged form in the newspaper *The Word* in July 1908.
34 A letter to the Indian writer Tarakuatta Das, editor of the *Free Hindustan*, published in North America, who had asked his opinion about the treatment of Indians by the British. Tolstoy's letter, begun in June and resumed much later in the year, grew into the article translated into English by Aylmer Maude as *Letter to a Hindu*.
35 Tolstoy's son, grandson and the mother of his daughter-in-law, Sergey's wife.
36 N. G. Molostvov was writing a biography of Tolstoy which was published jointly with P. A. Sergeyenko. The first part of it, which came out in 1910, was not favourably received by Tolstoy. The extracts from his mother's diaries which Molostvov copied out were included in the book.
37 Tolstoy was reading *A. I. Herzen* (Petersburg, 1908) by Ch. Vetrinsky.
38 M. A. Schmidt.
39 That his son was reading the Gospels and wished to be like St Francis of Assisi.
40 Chertkov and his family had returned from England, and came to Yasnaya Polyana on 20 June before settling in the neighbourhood.
41 A foreword to the artist N. V. Orlov's album of pictures *Russian Peasants*.
42 Herman Bernstein, a correspondent of the *New York Times*.
43 A story by his former pupil, the Yasnaya Polyana peasant V. S. Morozov, called *Just Because of One Word*, for which he also wrote a foreword.
44 It is not known which article he read.
45 The article was published on 3 July in both the Russian and the foreign press (although the Russian version was cut by the censor) and Tolstoy received more than sixty letters of appreciation.

46 A. S. Buturlin, a landowner from Simbirsk and an old friend of Tolstoy's who had at one time been imprisoned in connection with the Nechayev affair; G. M. Berkenheim, a Moscow doctor, formerly resident at Yasnaya Polyana as a house doctor; Mikhail Sergeyevich – Tolstoy's son-in-law, Sukhotin.
47 The title is in English in the diary, and presumably Tolstoy read the novel in English.
48 The recitals given by Goldenweiser and the distinguished solo violinist B. O. Sibor included – surprisingly enough in view of Tolstoy's strictures in *What is Art?* – two sonatas and a romance by Beethoven. One of the sonatas was the Kreutzer!
49 The green stick which, according to Tolstoy's brother Nikolenka, was buried there, and was a symbol of universal happiness and brotherhood.
50 Nothing came of any of these ideas.
51 N. N. Gusev.
52 28 August, Tolstoy's eightieth birthday.
53 A letter to the journalist M. A. Menshikov (*Letters*, II, 520) in reply to an article by Menshikov in *New Times* criticising Tolstoy for his opposition to government institutions and private property, and accusing him of inconsistent behaviour and of not giving his land to the peasantry.
54 It is not known what work is referred to.
55 To Anda Petrovič who had asked Tolstoy for his opinion about the recent incorporation of Bosnia and Herzegovina into the Austrian Empire. Tolstoy's reply grew from a letter into an article *On the annexation by Austria of Bosnia and Herzegovina* which was published in Russia with some cuts in December 1908.
56 Two books in English from a Chinese professor at Peking University, Ku Hung-ming. The book Tolstoy referred to was probably *The Universal Order or Conduct of Life: A Confucian Catechism*.
57 Tolstoy received a letter from a certain M. A. Antonov, a peasant living in Petersburg, who accused him of being unfair to the socialists. Tolstoy did not reply.
58 See 1907, Note 2.
59 A second letter from Tarakuatta Das which has not survived.
60 Tolstoy's son Misha had invited the young Prince D. L. Vyazemsky, a gentleman of the bedchamber and a rising politician, to meet his father.
61 J. T. Sunderland's book *The Bible, its Origin, Growth and Character* (New York, 1893) published in translation by *The Intermediary* in 1890 under the editorship of Chertkov. Tolstoy sent a copy of it in reply to a request for his opinion about certain passages in the Gospels concerning miracles.
62 A foreword to Ertel's novel *The Gardenins*, which his widow had asked Tolstoy to write.
63 Two men had been sent to Yasnaya Polyana by Edison to make a record of Tolstoy's voice. He recorded some thoughts in Russian, English and French.
64 N. B. Nordman, a writer and close friend of the painter Repin, contributed a number of articles on vegetarianism and the protection of animals to the *Vegetarian Review*. Her book *Intimate Pages* recalls her visits to Yasnaya Polyana in 1907 and 1908.
65 A reference to a new story, *Murderers* (never completed), about revolutionaries.
66 *The Death Penalty and Christianity*, an article Tolstoy wrote in response to one by Stolypin which attempted to justify capital punishment by a reference to some verses in Mark's Gospel. Tolstoy's article was finished in January 1909 and published with cuts in some Russian newspapers the following month.
67 They brought belated eightieth birthday greetings and a fulsome address.
68 An alternative title of the story *Murderers* (see Note 65).
69 A reference to the works of the sectarian peasant V. K. Syutayev.
70 N. N. Gusev.
71 K. A. Romanik-Petrova had written to Tolstoy describing prison life in the Butyrskaya prison in Moscow where she was serving a sentence for provoking unrest among the peasantry. Tolstoy in reply advised her to try to cultivate loving feelings towards both her fellow prisoners and her gaolers.

72 At the Chertkovs' house at Telyatinki.

SECRET DIARY FOR 1908

1 This diary 'for himself alone' was kept by Tolstoy for the short period from 2–18 July 1908. In August 1908 he gave it to Chertkov, asking him to copy out what he thought necessary and then destroy the manuscript. Chertkov copied out the whole manuscript before destroying it.
2 See 1908, Note 43.
3 Sofya Andreyevna was angry because Chertkov was frequently visiting Yasnaya Polyana with an English photographer, who took numerous pictures of Tolstoy.
4 See 1907, Note 34.
5 The road to Yasnaya Polyana was being remade in such a way that the interests of the peasants living in the village had been ignored.
6 A reference to Sofya Andreyevna's taunt that while preaching simplicity Tolstoy ate asparagus.
7 The wedding of her niece (Ilya's daughter) who married N. A. Holmberg.

1909

1 The story *The Monk Iliodor* (*Ieromonakh Iliodor*; ieromonakh – a monk with the office of a priest) which he began to write later that month.
2 See 1908, Note 66.
3 Tolstoy wrote a new beginning to his story *Who are the Murderers?* in dramatic form entitled *Pavlusha* (later incorporated into the text of the story).
4 M. O. Gerschenson, the historian and philosopher and active member of the *Landmarks* group, who had first met Tolstoy in 1904 and wrote his reminiscences of him.
5 In the proofs of the book *Letters of A. I. Ertel* (Moscow, 1909). The correspondence concerned the choice of contemporary works of literature suitable for publication by *The Intermediary*.
6 L. V. Tonilov (Lev Ryzhy), a member of various Tolstoyan colonies who was living with Chertkov at Telyatinki in 1908, wrote to Tolstoy to say that Chertkov idolised him (Tolstoy) and in turn wished to be idolised by those in his employ.
7 Press reports of a spate of executions of armed robbers and revolutionaries prompted Tolstoy to write about the subject in *The Death Penalty and Christianity*.
8 Goldenweiser's recital of Chopin at Yasnaya Polyana the previous evening moved Tolstoy to exclaim, 'It's good to be alive!'
9 Probably *The Monk Iliodor* which Tolstoy never finished.
10 The Polish pianist Wanda Landowska came to play at Yasnaya Polyana on three occasions, 1907, January 1909 and December 1909. As well as admiring her playing of Chopin, Bach, Handel and Mozart, Tolstoy claimed to have had some of his views on art confirmed. The 'poor impression' referred to below was apparently due to Landowska's overenthusiastic attitude to Tolstoy as a great writer, which he found embarrassing.
11 For the children's magazine *The Lighthouse*, edited by I. I. Gorbunov-Posadov.
12 From the leader of a Muslim sect who wished to come to Yasnaya Polyana to meet Tolstoy and was duly invited.
13 A notice about the publication of the *International Tolstoy Almanac* (Moscow, 1909) compiled by P. A. Sergeyenko.
14 *The Monk Iliodor*.
15 A reference to Nicholas II's reprieve of thirty-two men condemned to death for occupying the Yekaterinoslav railway in 1905. Tolstoy's insertion reproached the Tsar for only showing mercy to 'one per cent of those killed by his wish or with his consent'.

16 He soon began work on *An Issue of a Newspaper*.
17 The Bishop of Tula, who hoped to persuade Tolstoy to return to the Orthodox fold.
18 The Bishop had told Sofya Andreyevna that Tolstoy could not be given a church burial, but asked her to let him know if her husband became dangerously ill.
19 A religious journal edited in Los Angeles by Benjamin Fay Mills.
20 Behais or Babists, members of the Muslim sect founded in Persia in 1844.
21 A series of dialogues between children and adults on religious and moral issues, which Tolstoy began work on the following month.
22 The first volume of stories by M. P. Artsybashev, published by *Life* in 1908. In Tolstoy's copy there are marks awarded by him on a five-point scale. See *Letters*, II, 685 for further comments on Artsybashev's stories.
23 Tolstoy had been highly critical of Artsybashev's sensational novel *Sanin* which he read in 1908, and more favourably disposed towards Kuprin in 1910 when he called him a true artist who raised problems of life which were more profound than those in Artsybashev and Andreyev.
24 H. Croft Hiller had sent Tolstoy his book *Meta-Christianity. Spiritism established, Religion re-established, Science dis-established* (London, 1903). He subsequently sent various Appendices to it which Tolsoy refers to unflatteringly in a diary entry for 20 August.
25 Sofya A. Stakhovich.
26 I. O. Shurayev, a man-servant at Yasnaya Polyana.
27 A speech in the Duma calling for harsh reprisals against revolutionaries.
28 M. A. Schmidt.
29 *Incomprehensible* was one of the original titles of *An Issue of a Newspaper*.
30 *Who Are the Murderers? Pavel Kudryash*. Also *Pavlusha* (see Note 3).
31 The husband of Romanik-Petrova (see 1908, Note 71).
32 Nevertheless Tolstoy had included a prose translation of the poem *Les pauvres gens* in the first volume of the *Cycle of Reading*, and did a new translation of it for his projected *Children's Cycle of Reading*.
33 A. A. Korsini, a geography teacher in Moscow, gave a talk about India illustrated with slides, which she repeated the following day at the Tolstoys'.
34 Chertkov's translation of Tolstoy's letter to Tarakuatta Das (see 1908, Note 34).
35 *Die geistige Liebe*, Leipzig, 1902 by a doctor of medicine, Norbert Grabowsky.
36 Tolstoy was re-reading Gogol's works and Belinsky's letter to Gogol in connection with a request by V. A. Posse to write an article to commemorate the 100th anniversary of Gogol's birth on 19 March 1909.
37 The police authorities had issued an order expelling Chertkov from the Tula province on the grounds that his presence there was liable to disturb the peace.
38 A letter to the press protesting about Chertkov's expulsion.
39 Two versions have survived of the beginning of a comedy with no title. It was never continued.
40 A reference to a phrase in Belinsky's letter to Gogol.
41 Nothing came of the idea.
42 To a priest who exhorted Tolstoy to return to the Church.
43 Tolstoy tried unsuccessfully to have the article *A New Religion* by his peasant friend M. P. Novikov published.
44 A letter to the Minister of Trade and Industry, V. I. Timiryazev, thanking him for the help given to Tolstoy's son Andrey in obtaining a post in the Ministry.
45 A reactionary governor-general of Moscow who had been active in suppressing the revolutionary movement.
46 *The Police Constable* – the original title of the article *On the State*; *Pavel* – see Note 30; *The Elder* – the story *The Monk Iliodor*.
47 P. I. Biryukov and I. I. Gorbunov-Posadov.
48 Tolstoy's name for the working people.

49 Tolstoy was re-reading Baba Bharati's *Sri Krishna. The Lord of Love*, New York, 1904, in order to contribute to Gorbunov-Posadov's series of booklets on the religions of the East.
50 S. P. Spiro interviewed Tolstoy in connection with the centenary of Gogol's birth. His account of Tolstoy's views, together with an expanded form of the note Tolstoy had begun earlier that month, was published in the *Russian Word* on 24 March 1909.
51 An appeal which began with the words: 'Stop and think, for God's sake'. It was given various titles including *The Revolution of Consciousness* and *The Old and the New* in the course of writing, but was ultimately called *The Inevitable Revolution*.
52 A Russian translation of Kant's *Die Religion innerhalb der Grenzen der blossen Vernunft*.
53 His son Lev.
54 From the *Cycle of Reading* for the article which eventually became *The Inevitable Revolution*.
55 An account of Tolstoy's philosophy, which has not survived.
56 An incident from Tolstoy's childhood, recalled in *A Confession*, when the young Milyutin announced the discovery, made at school, that there was no God.
57 On the teachings of Confucius and Lao-Tzu.
58 The chapters on Confucius in Pauthier's *Les livres sacrés de l'Orient* (Paris, 1852).
59 While still a student at Moscow University before becoming Tolstoy's secretary, V. F. Bulgakov had asked Tolstoy to clarify some aspects of his views on education. Tolstoy's reply, begun in April but not finished until May, grew into the long article *On Education*.
60 Tolstoy edited Nikolayev's account of the legend of Krishna as recounted in Bharati's book and wrote a foreword to it, but the booklet which was intended for *The Intermediary* press was never published.
61 A. K. Chertkova's.
62 A letter from a Petersburg student asking for Tolstoy's opinion about Professor L. I. Petrazhitsky's book *The Theory of Law*. Tolstoy replied to it in his *Letter to a Student about Law*.
63 A. P. Lensky, an actor of the Maly Theatre in Moscow, who wrote about his early days on the stage.
64 André Mazon, at the time a teacher of French in Kharkov and later a distinguished Slavonic scholar.
65 A letter to Stolypin from Chertkov, recently expelled from the Tula province, asking for the police order to be reviewed. Tolstoy disapproved of appealing to the authorities for any form of assistance.
66 Gerschenson had sent Tolstoy a copy of the influential anthology of articles on the Russian intelligentsia, *Landmarks*, which had been published early in 1909. The anthology, whose authors were mainly Orthodox believers with Marxist backgrounds, examined the roots of the Russian revolutionary movement and its prospects for the future. Tolstoy wrote a critical article about it – he particularly disliked its foreign philosophical terminology – and included a quotation from a letter he had received from a peasant, I. V. Kolesnikov.
67 A dialogue entitled *On Remuneration for Work*.
68 See Note 59.
69 V. F. Orlov, a teacher in Moscow and a friend of both men (*Letters*, II, 354).
70 The story *There are no Guilty People in the World*.
71 See Note 62.
72 *Results of and Prospects for the Labour Movement in the West and in Russia* (Petersburg, 1909).
73 *The Destruction of the Personality* in the collection *Essays on the Philosophy of Collectivism* (Petersburg, 1909).
74 A mistaken diagnosis.
75 In English in the diary.

76 The deletions made by Tolstoy at his wife's request in the diaries for 1888–95 of passages particularly critical of her.
77 The artist Leonid Pasternak, his wife who was a concert pianist, and A. Y. Mogilevsky, a distinguished Moscow violinist. They played Bach, Beethoven and Mozart and Tolstoy was deeply moved.
78 *The Inevitable Revolution.*
79 A dialogue entitled *On Property*.
80 Sofya Andreyevna and their daughter Sasha.
81 Olga Konstantinovna Tolstaya, the divorced wife of Andrey.
82 A grammar school teacher in Belgrade, I. G. Maximovič, who left an account of his visit.
83 A certain Nazimov, who claimed to have saved eleven men from the firing squad during an armed rising in December 1905 which the Semyonov Regiment suppressed.
84 An abusive and libellous pamphlet by the archpriest I. I. Vostorgov entitled *Signs of the Times: Father Johann of Kronstadt and Count Lev Tolstoy*.
85 For various personal reasons Tolstoy did not wish to publish his article *On 'Landmarks'* and it did not appear in full until after his death.
86 Tolstoy spoke elsewhere about the 'cynical coarseness' of Kuprin's story which dealt with the life of prostitutes, part of which was read aloud in the family.
87 The article *On Love*, begun in May and finished in July, was eventually called *The One Commandment*.
88 A refusal by the authorities to reconsider the order expelling him from the Tula province.
89 Tolstoy began a letter, to be delivered to his wife after his death, but never finished it.
90 In his notebook this entry is prefaced by the words 'Letter to Sonya'.
91 See Note 46.
92 The story reminded her of Tolstoy's liaison with Aksinya Bazykina before he was married.
93 N. Y. Felten (see 1907, Note 27) had just been sentenced to six months' imprisonment for having published various articles by Tolstoy, but the sentence was deferred pending a fresh charge of publishing *What is the Way Out?*
94 Accusations of not really renouncing his property.
95 N. O. Einhorn (not Einroth), a retired army captain well read in Eastern philosophy.
96 Afanasy's daughter – the daughter of Afanasy Ageyev, a peasant friend of Tolstoy's; Anisya Kopilova – a widow whose son had been threatened by the police; Y. F. Kopylova – another Yasnaya Polyana peasant, whose husband was in prison for theft.
97 Tanechka Sukhotina, Tolstoy's granddaughter.
98 *The Inevitable Revolution.*
99 To the priest I. I. Solovyov about his attitude towards the official Church, and to I. M. Tregubov about freedom of conscience, both published in the *Voice of Moscow*.
100 By P. B. Struve, mainly devoted to *The Letters of A. I. Ertel*, but incidentally criticising Tolstoy's dogmatic morality.
101 To a Russian emigré, John Sevitt, who had written to him from Redlands, U.S.A., on the subject.
102 V. P. Grushetsky, a Tula doctor, whom Tolstoy spoke to about his granddaughter's illness; Goethe – Tolstoy was reading the *Goethe-Kalender auf das Jahr 1909*, sent to him from Leipzig.
103 Tolstoy read in the *Russian Word* the gist of an article by the American President Theodore Roosevelt entitled *Tolstoy* which had been published in the American journal *Outlook*, 1909, No. 2. The article was highly appreciative of Tolstoy's fiction, but critical of his social, political and religious views.
104 I. V. Kolesnikov – see Note 66.
105 Alexandra Vladimirovna Tolstaya, the wife of Tolstoy's son Mikhail.

106 The danger of gangrene (see diary entry for 26 April).
107 I. I. Mechnikov, the Russian director of the Pasteur Institute in Paris who had been awarded a Nobel prize in 1908, was visiting Russia and receiving a warm welcome.
108 The painter V. D. Polenov had sent Tolstoy an album of prints from his series of pictures on the life of Christ.
109 Now that Chertkov had returned to Russia from England, Gorbunov-Posadov could no longer count on receiving Tolstoy's new works for publication by *The Intermediary*, since Chertkov had assumed responsibility himself.
110 To Y. Dobrotina with his views on the question of women's rights, and to A. S. Cherkasov in answer to the latter's reproaches for his having handed over his property to his family.
111 By an edict of the Holy Synod the wife of Grand Duke Mikhail Yaroslavich, Princess Anna Kashinskaya, who died in 1338, had been canonised.
112 Mechnikov and his wife, together with reporters and photographers, came to see Tolstoy, and later wrote an account of his visit.
113 A reference to the story *There are no Guilty People in the World*.
114 Tolstoy's niece (his brother Sergey's daughter) had had an illegitimate child as a result of a liaison which was soon broken off.
115 To talk to Tolstoy about Mechnikov's visit for a newspaper article.
116 For an expected visit from some girl students from Petersburg, which never took place.
117 I. I. Perper, a teacher and editor of the *Vegetarian Review (Letters*, II, 685).
118 Henry George's son who had recently arrived in Russia asked Tolstoy if he could visit him at Yasnaya Polyana. Tolstoy readily agreed and the visit took place on 5 June. George later wrote about it in an article in the *New York World*, 14 November 1909, entitled *My Farewell to Count Tolstoy*.
119 S. P. Spiro's article *Tolstoy on I. I. Mechnikov*.
120 Tolstoy's article on the land problem, *Apropos of the Visit of Henry George's Son*, was not accepted by the *Russian Word*, but was published by the *Russian Gazette* on 9 June.
121 The publicist Yefim Kalvarsky had written to Tolstoy saying that he had consumption, could not afford treatment and wondered whether he should commit suicide to save his family from worry and expense. Kalvarsky had quoted Haeckel, who put *rational* considerations above all others in saying that the incurably ill should take morphine. Tolstoy argued that no amount of reasoning could enable one to foresee the future, and said that he sympathised more with Kalvarsky's *spiritual*, than physical illness.
122 On 8 June Tolstoy and his wife went to stay with their daughter Tatyana at Kochety, her husband's estate in the Tula province. He travelled in the same coach as the marshal of the nobility for the Mtsensk district to whom he talked about Henry George and the land problem without success.
123 *Sic* – in roman script in the diary.
124 A. V. Sverbeyeva, the wife of the then counsellor at the Russian Embassy in Vienna; they owned an estate near Kochety.
125 Bakunin's *Message to My Italian Friends*, addressed to a workers' congress convened by Mazzini on 1 November 1871.
126 *Mohammed Ali Shah. The Popular Movement in the Land of the Lion and the Sun* (Alexandropol, 1909).
127 L. D. Sverbeyeva, a niece of Tolstoy's son-in-law M. S. Sukhotin, arranged for Tolstoy to talk to the wife of Sukhotin's son by his first marriage and to her sister about the meaning of life and women's vocation in the world. 'The boys' – i.e. the three sons of Sukhotin by his first marriage – apparently fought shy of talking to Tolstoy.
128 Tolstoy read the article on Engels in the Brockhaus and Efron encyclopaedia which contained some pronouncements by Engels about Marx.
129 A young peasant from the village of Kochety.

130 The title of a new version of the story *There are no Guilty People in the World*.
131 A reply to a question about the importance of modern science which grew into the article *On Science*.
132 Tolstoy had been invited to take part in the 18th International Peace Congress in Stockholm in August.
133 Sofya Andreyevna wanted to prosecute the Petersburg publisher who had brought out *Three Deaths* and extracts from *Childhood* without her permission. Tolstoy said that if she did so, he would take away her authority to publish his works.
134 M. de Paris – a way of referring to the executioner.
135 Workers' courses at Thiel's tannery in Moscow, administered by Tolstoy's son Sergey.
136 A woman from Voronezh named Popova had asked Tolstoy to try to save her son who was about to be tried for revolutionary activity. Tolstoy wrote the draft of a letter to Stolypin, but Popova did not come and the letter was not sent.
137 *Essais optimistes* (Paris, 1907).
138 Shortly after Blériot's first flight across the Channel, Tolstoy read a newspaper report of a conversation between the French Minister of War and a journalist about the military importance of aviation.
139 The letter he wrote to a group of Swedish intellectuals in 1899 about the Hague Peace Conference of the great powers to discuss disarmament. He believed that only individual refusal to do military service would be effective, but that that was incompatible with a conference of governments.
140 M. A. Stakhovich had told Tolstoy that Prince Vasilchikov had been deeply offended by some remarks which Tolstoy had made in a letter to Molochnikov about the treatment of peasants on the Vasilchikov estates and which Molochnikov had quoted in a letter of his own to the prince. Tolstoy's reply to Stakhovich explaining that the remarks had been of a general nature and not directed specifically against Vasilchikov was seen by Sofya Andreyevna, who reacted angrily against Molochnikov.
141 To I. V. Denisenko about a will Tolstoy had asked him to draw up renouncing all his property and handing over the land that used to belong to him to the peasants.
142 The manuscript of a story *At the Gallows* sent to Tolstoy by its author P. P. Kazmichev, a barrister in Novocherkassk, and subsequently published with cuts in Korolenko's *Russian Wealth*.
143 *Léon Tolstoi, 'Appels aux dirigeants'* (Paris, 1902).
144 A letter of thanks to the Polish artist Jan Styka, then living in Paris, for sending Tolstoy a reproduction of his picture *Tolstoy at Work in the Garden*.
145 A quotation from Amiel's *Fragments d'un journal intime*.
146 A letter of thanks for the books which Mechnikov had sent him.
147 The paper to be given at the Stockholm congress.
148 Tolstoy's sister.
149 Tolstoy outlined the main points of his paper to the correspondent of the *Russian Word* and they were published there on 2 August.
150 To the correspondent S. P. Spiro, for inclusion in his article in the *Russian Word*.
151 Into French.
152 To leave Yasnaya Polyana for good.
153 To the Stockholm congress with Tolstoy, contrary to her previous intentions.
154 Gusev was arrested and exiled to the Cherdyn district for allegedly conducting revolutionary propaganda and circulating banned works of literature. Tolstoy wrote *A Statement about the arrest of Gusev*, which was published in the *Russian Gazette* on 11 August with the omission of a few words.
155 From A. N. Solovyov, sentenced to four years' imprisonment as a conscientious objector.
156 The congress had been postponed for a year because of a general strike in Sweden. Tolstoy believed that his decision to speak may have had something to do with the postponement.

157 To see Tolstoy, Makovitsky and other close friends before going into exile.
158 Tolstoy was re-reading *Die Religion innerhalb der Grenzen der blossen Vernunft*.
159 See Note 154.
160 Antonov asked for a reply to his first letter sent several months previously; Velikanov's abusive letter accusing Tolstoy of sheltering behind the backs of his friends was returned to the sender.
161 A reply to a midwife complaining that Tolstoy's practices often differed from his precepts.
162 To find out about the time of mass and to arrange for a chair in church for his sister.
163 H. Höffding's *History of Modern Philosophy* (Petersburg, 1900).
164 A free adaptation of a stanza of a poem by Lermontov.
165 Tolstoy asked V. V. Tenishev, a member of the 3rd Duma, to raise the question in the Duma of the abolition of private property and its replacement by Henry George's single tax, but Tenishev refused to do so.
166 See Note 24.
167 Tolstoy mistakenly called him Photer. The book which Tolstoy was reading in French was Jean-Pierre Guillaume Pauthier's *Chine, ou description historique, géographique et littéraire de ce vaste empire* (Paris, 1837).
168 A reference to Easter Sunday, in *Selected Passages from Correspondence with Friends*.
169 I. S. Gusarov, a Moscow peasant who had lived in an agricultural community. In August 1909 he set off with his wife and family to walk from Moscow to Bessarabia to settle on the land close to a friend of Tolstoy's.
170 In the first volume of James Legge's *The Chinese Classics*.
171 Part of a planned series of cheap booklets on the major religions of the world.
172 The journalist M. O. Menshikov's article in *New Times* calling Tolstoy a fashionable oracle and attempting to justify police persecution of his followers.
173 Nothing came of this idea, called elsewhere *Three Ages*.
174 Tolstoy and Makovitsky wanted to ride through the station at Kozlovka on their way to Ovsyannikovo, but were prevented from doing so at the time because the Tsar's train was due to pass through on its way to the Crimea.
175 To Stefania Laudyn, author of a book on the Polish question, who had asked Tolstoy to speak out in defence of the oppressed Polish people. Tolstoy's reply took the form of an article, *A Reply to a Polish Woman*.
176 V. A. Maklakov, a member of the 2nd and 3rd Dumas, whom Tolstoy hoped to persuade to raise the question of Henry George's single tax in the Duma; A. V. Zinger, a professor of physics at Moscow University; S. T. Semyonov, a peasant author.
177 D. A. Kuzminsky, the son of the Kuzminskys and a law student (also referred to as Mitechka below).
178 Certain people in Berlin, having heard that Tolstoy was planning to deliver his paper intended for the Stockholm Peace Congress in the German capital, tried to make use of two letters by Sofya Andreyevna refusing permission for selected works of Tolstoy's to be published free for distribution to schoolchildren, in order to discredit him. An article in the German language edition of the *St Petersburg Gazette* which carried the story was reproduced in a number of German papers and prompted charges of hypocrisy.
179 A harshly worded letter which was not sent accusing Stolypin of criminal behaviour and advising him to end the use of violence and especially the death penalty.
180 A hairdresser from Kiev and a deaf mute from a wealthy German family.
181 Sofya Andreyevna gave permission for Pathé cinephotographers to visit Yasnaya Polyana. Tolstoy was uncooperative, but pictures were taken while he was on his way to the station *en route* for Moscow.
182 The Tolstoys were on their way to visit the Chertkovs on their estate of Kryokshino outside Moscow.

183 About the publisher I. D. Sytin for his dilatoriness in publishing the *New Cycle of Reading (For Every Day)*.
184 At Zimmermann's music shop Tolstoy listened to a new recording machine called the 'Mignon' which was later taken round to Kryokshino (among other things he greatly enjoyed hearing Paderewski playing a Chopin *étude*).
185 Tolstoy read his article *The Inevitable Revolution* to Kalachov, and his letter to Stefania Laudyn (Note 173) and Chekhov's story *The Runaway* to his family and the Chertkovs.
186 In his essay *A Conversation with a Passer-by*.
187 Tolstoy corrected the proofs of *Sayings of the Chinese Sage Lao-Tzu, Selected by L. N. Tolstoy* and his foreword to it, *On the Essence of Lao-Tzu's Teaching*. The book was published by *The Intermediary* in 1910.
188 The paper originally intended for Stockholm, and which was to be read at a different meeting in Berlin.
189 A conversation between a passer-by and some peasants about their oppressed condition and the means of escaping from it eventually became a dialogue involving one peasant only – *A Passer-by and a Peasant*, which Tolstoy finished in October but which was not published in his life-time.
190 A visit was expected from a big group of teachers from the Zvenigorod district, and Tolstoy wanted to jot down some thoughts about education.
191 Thomas Tapsell, an English photographer, who was living with the Chertkovs and took numerous pictures of Tolstoy.
192 M. F. Solomakhin, a well-to-do peasant, and his son Semyon, a sectarian and disciple of Tolstoy's who printed and distributed some of his banned works; Y. E. Lineva, a former opera singer and collector of folk songs.
193 A teacher of music in Moscow secondary schools.
194 Thomas Edison had sent two Englishmen from London to Kryokshino with the latest cinematographic equipment to take pictures of Tolstoy.
195 See Notes 186 and 189.
196 To a cinema on the Arbat, where he saw a mixed programme of scenery, melodrama and comedy, which he found 'terribly stupid'.
197 Tolstoy wrote an open letter to the press explaining his thoughts about God and about life in response to a series of abusive letters he had received, but the letter was never sent.
198 Tolstoy replied to a letter from an Indian publicist Narain Bishen who had written to complain about the poverty-stricken condition of the people of India, and also received a letter from Gandhi (at the time in London) asking him to support the struggle of the Indian people in South Africa. For Tolstoy's letters to Gandhi see *Letters*, II, 691 and 706.
199 Gandhi had asked Tolstoy to verify his authorship of the *Letter to an Indian* and to confirm that the English translation was accurate since one of his friends wished to publish it in India. Despite Tolstoy's reservations about its weakness, it was translated into Hindi and published with a foreword by Gandhi.
200 To collect more material for the second volume of his biography of Tolstoy.
201 The original title of the article *It is Time to Understand*.
202 Maude and Chertkov had quarrelled over the publication of Tolstoy's works abroad.
203 To Gandhi (*Letters*, II, 691).
204 *A Passer-by and a Peasant*.
205 Boulanger's booklet on Confucius was edited and amended by Tolstoy.
206 Tolstoy discussed with the Tula lawyer Goldenblat the case of some peasants from Telyatinki who had approached him to ask for protection against police interference.
207 Andreyev first made contact with Tolstoy in 1901 when he sent him a volume of his collected stories (*Letters*, II, 608). The two authors corresponded from time to time, but only three letters from each have survived. Andreyev eventually visited Yasnaya

Polyana in April 1910. M. D. Chelyshev, a member of the 3rd Duma and an 'Octobrist', was an active campaigner against the evils of drink. Tolstoy was reading his booklet *The Main Cause of Our Unhappiness*. He hoped to persuade Chelyshev to raise in the Duma the question of the abolition of private property.

208   Of Andreyev's later works Tolstoy had serious reservations about *The Seven Who Were Hanged* which Andreyev wished to dedicate to him (*Letters*, II, 680).
209   P. B. Struve had written an article attacking the basic positions of Tolstoy's article *The Inevitable Revolution*, recently published in abbreviated form, and accusing Tolstoy of inconsistency while at the same time ascribing to him ideas which he did not hold. Tolstoy wrote a 'venomous' reply which he subsequently modified to some extent.
210   A journal published in India by Professor Rama Deva.
211   Tolstoy was regretting his promise to record his voice for the Society of Workers of the Periodical Press and Literature, but was persuaded to keep it.
212   A newspaper report referring to Tolstoy's advocacy of the abolition of the death penalty in his conversation with Chelyshev provoked more than one anonymous letter of abuse, but Tolstoy decided not to publish the reply he had written.
213   A woman doctor practising in the Vosges had come to ask Tolstoy for his advice about her medical research.
214   *Russian Thought*, No. 1, 1909 published Ropshin's (B. Savinkov's) novella *The Pale Horse* (not *The White Horse* as Tolstoy writes), Sologub's story *The White Birch Tree* (not *The Birch Tree*), and poems by Blok, Bryusov, Bely, Gippius, Merezhkovsky, Solovyov and Sologub.
215   Tolstoy was greatly upset by the fact that his wife had hired a Circassian to patrol the estate as a protection against theft. He tried to justify the armed attack by some peasants on Taptykovo, Andrey Tolstoy's estate, on the grounds of their poverty and the difficulty of alleviating it by legal means.
216   On her way back to the station to catch a train to Moscow, Sofya Andreyevna came across an abandoned car which she imagined in the dark was a carriage which had been attacked and robbed by highwaymen.
217   N. F. Friedman, a lawyer and a member of the 3rd Duma.
218   This story of a priest who began to lose his faith but was compelled by his family to continue in his office was never completed.
219   Tolstoy read *Notes of a Man-servant* by A. P. Novikov who had served Prince G. P. Volkonsky for twenty-six years, and wished to write a story of his own in similar form on social divisions, but never did so.
220   The violinist M. G. Erdenko and his pianist wife, both of whom went on to have distinguished musical careers, had come to Yasnaya Polyana to demonstrate their method of playing Russian music. Their offer was not accepted, but being unable to get railway tickets back to Moscow they returned to Yasnaya Polyana and were then admitted.
221   *A Passer-by and a Peasant*.
222   The recital eventually given by the Erdenkos, including some Jewish folk melodies and several pieces by Wieniawski, as well as Chopin's Nocturne, greatly moved Tolstoy who, according to M. G. Erdenko, danced across the room to the music of a mazurka.
223   Tolstoy had noted in his diary the previous day that he had had a wonderful dream about himself speaking impassionedly about Henry George. He wrote it down and included it as the final part of his trilogy *Three Days in the Country*.
224   The play *Philistines*.
225   The article on physics in the Brockhaus and Efron encyclopaedia.
226   Strakhov had brought a letter from Chertkov saying that Tolstoy's will signed at Kryokshino on 18 September 1909 whereby his family would retain the copyright only of Tolstoy's works published before 1881 was legally invalid. Tolstoy then

decided to renounce the copyright on all his works and to appoint his daughter Alexandra (Sasha) as executor. He later changed his mind again.
227 Leonid Semyonov.
228 *The Sayings of Sri Ramakrishna Paramahamsa* (Madras, 1905). Tolstoy marked some hundred sayings for translation and publication by *The Intermediary*, but nothing came of the idea.
229 The text of a new will, which Tolstoy amended and signed. This will also proved to be inadequate, since no second person was named in the event of Alexandra's death.
230 Bruno Freidank's *Die Greuel der 'Christlichen' Civilisation. Briefe eines Buddhistischen Lama aus Tibet* (Berlin, 1907). (The 'Buddhist Lama' was in reality the author.)
231 On Tolstoy's instructions the book was translated into Russian, and he wrote to I. I. Perper, the editor of the *Vegetarian Review*, recommending it for publication. It was duly published there in 1910.
232 Swami Abhedananda's *Vedanta-Philosophie* (Leipzig, 1907) the German text of which is in the Yasnaya Polyana library with Tolstoy's markings on it.
233 On 22 October Tolstoy had recorded in his diary the impressions made on him as he witnessed the leave-taking of a party of young Yasnaya Polyana recruits. His essay on the subject, *The Recruits*, was eventually entitled *Songs in the Village*.
234 P. Polilov was a pseudonym used by Tolstoy's daughter Tatyana who had written a popular account of Henry George's teaching and wanted to get her father's impartial opinion about it. Tolstoy was taken in and wrote an enthusiastic reply. Tatyana came to Yasnaya Polyana a few days later and revealed 'Polilov's' identity.
235 P. M. Noykov's *Pedagiyata na L. N. Tolstoya* (Sofia, 1903) which Tolstoy found very sound and comprehensive.
236 Presumably some of Gorky's early stories about down-and-outs. 'The lowest strata of the people' is a free translation of *naroda chernosotennogo* – a reference to the 'Black Hundred' anti-revolutionary groups active in Russia in 1905–7.
237 Alexey Leonov, a local peasant, who had killed a man while on military service.
238 Sofya Andreyevna was contemplating legal action against publishers who had issued cheap editions of the stories mentioned which, since they were written before 1881, were not public property – a fact which Tolstoy now regretted.
239 An essay entitled *Vagrants* which formed the first part of his trilogy *Three Days in the Country*.
240 This story by his wife may have prompted Tolstoy to write his own story about the disaster on the Khodynka field during the coronation celebrations of 1896.
241 What he wrote was eventually included in *Anarchism (It is Time to Understand)*.
242 Words from an article by Menshikov accusing the government of not dealing firmly with public unrest and criticising Tolstoy's opposition to the death penalty.
243 Tolstoy's article *On Science* was felt by some people to be playing into the hands of bodies such as *The Union of the Russian People*, a right-wing, nationalistic, anti-Semitic party founded in 1905.
244 Members of a Paris society for performers on ancient instruments, including Henri and Mariel Casadesus, whom Goldenweiser had brought to Yasnaya Polyana together with S. Kusevitsky (Sergei Koussevitzky).
245 N. P. Lopatin, a journalist who edited the liberal Moscow newspaper *Life*, had been fined and then imprisoned for printing a piece containing Tolstoy's views on capital punishment.
246 Gorbunov-Posadov had been accused of publishing without the censor's permission a book by Herbert Spencer, *The Right to the Use of the Earth*, which reprinted two chapters of Henry George's *The Perplexed Philosopher*.
247 A remark by Luka in Act 2 of Gorky's play *The Lower Depths*.
248 Tolstoy was reading the correspondence of Dostoyevsky and Aksakov which concerned the former's *Diary of a Writer*, and also Émile Baumann's novel *L'immolé*.
249 C. W. Daniel, the English editor of *The Open Road* and A. P. Sergeyenko, at the time Chertkov's secretary.

250 Tolstoy changed his mind and wrote a letter on behalf of the woman who had appealed to him for financial assistance.
251 The story told to Tolstoy by the Yasnaya Polyana peasants whose goods had been auctioned when they failed to pay their taxes was used by him in his short essay *Taxes* which eventually became part of *Three Days in the Country*.
252 In the Brockhaus and Efron encyclopaedia.
253 Kurnosenkova – the widow of a Yasnaya Polyana peasant; Shintyakov – a former yardman of the Tolstoys.
254 It was published posthumously under the title *It is Time to Understand*.
255 The first issue of Posse's new journal *Life for All*, which contained among other things an article on Andreyev.
256 One of the original titles of *A Dream*.
257 *The Tragicomedy of our Russian Life, Russian Standard*, 25 November 1909.
258 In William James' *Varieties of Religious Experience* which Tolstoy was re-reading in Russian translation.
259 A Japanese textbook and reader written by a Russian priest in Tokyo.
260 One of the original titles of *Vagrants*.
261 In his article in *New Times* of 13 December, Menshikov made fun of some of the sayings of wise people which Tolstoy had included in his *New Cycle of Reading*.
262 Gorbunov-Posadov. See Note 246.
263 Tolstoy read in German the Czech writer A. Smetana's *Die Geschichte eines Exkommunizierten*.
264 A Russian translation of Jean-Marie Guyau's *L'Irréligion de l'avenir*.
265 None of the articles was written, although a start was made on the first one on drunkenness.
266 Bulgakov brought with him the manuscript of his book *Christian Ethics: Systematic essays on L. N. Tolstoy's outlook on the world*. It was eventually published in 1917.
267 On the subject of Tolstoy's article *On Science* (entitled *On False Science* in the *Russian Gazette*).
268 Sayings of Epictetus in the anthology *For Every Day*.
269 Tolstoy had translated most of Sterne's novel in 1851 and 1852.
270 The original title of the essay *The Living and the Dying*.
271 Chertkov's son spoke about the relations between his father and L. V. Tonilov when the latter was living at Telyatinki in 1908.
272 Gusev's friend – P. V. Zlobin, living at the time in exile for having been a member of the Socialist Revolutionary Party.

1910

1 See 1909, Note 10.
2 Chertkov's son Vladimir.
3 D. A. Olsufyev.
4 About the severity of the tax-collecting measures. See 1909, Note 251.
5 See 1909, Notes 270 and 223 respectively.
6 A. I. Drankov, owner of a cinematographic office in Moscow, came to show the films he had recently taken and to take new ones.
7 Tolstoy's daughter Alexandra had quarrelled with Chertkov about who should publish Tolstoy's anthology *For Every Day*. Chertkov wanted Sytin to publish it, but Alexandra objected. Sytin began the publication of it, but it was continued in instalments in the newspaper *New Russia*.
8 See 1909, Note 223.
9 *Coenobium – Rivista Internazionale dei liberi studi*, Lugano, 1910, No. 2.
10 The article *More on Science*, written in reply to objections made to Tolstoy's earlier article *On Science* by the German publicist Eugen Schmitt.

11 The groom F. P. Borisov, who later accompanied Tolstoy to the station when he left home for good.
12 Presumably one of Tolstoy's numerous visitors in search of help and advice.
13 Tolstoy read the second volume of Gorky's stories published by *Knowledge* in 1902. He spoke to Makovitsky about the falseness, in his opinion, of the language, descriptions and similes in some of the stories.
14 Tolstoy heard two cases, one involving a mail robbery, the other membership of the Socialist Revolutionary Party and possession of banned literature. The sentences were comparatively light (the first was an acquittal), which some people attributed to Tolstoy's presence.
15 Thomas Masaryk, professor of philosophy at Prague University and later President of the Czech Republic, who corresponded with Tolstoy and visited him a second time on 30 March 1910.
16 The second volume, which had fallen foul of the Moscow censors, was published in full by a newspaper editor in Odessa in 1910.
17 Sergeyenko also brought recordings of Tolstoy reading extracts from the *Cycle of Reading*.
18 P. D. Dolgorukov, a major political figure in the Constitutional Democratic Party and President of the Moscow Society of Literacy, came to Yasnaya Polyana to open a local branch of the Society in honour of Tolstoy's eightieth birthday. He brought with him a catalogue of books and asked Tolstoy to choose some titles. (Dolgorukov emigrated after the revolution, but returned to Russia illegally and was shot.)
19 This new series of booklets, later entitled *The Way of Life*, differed from the *Cycle of Reading* and *For Every Day* by being organised thematically and not by the calendar.
20 *Sins, Temptations and Superstitions*.
21 An engine driver who came to ask Tolstoy's advice whether to give up his job on the railway and take up farming. Tolstoy apparently said that work on the railways was one of the more acceptable occupations for a Christian and advised him not to give it up.
22 M. F. Bulygin, a close friend of Tolstoy's and a former guards officer who owned a small farm near Yasnaya Polyana.
23 See 1907, Note 17 and 1909, Note 93.
24 The seventh and eighth booklets in *The Way of Life* series were entitled *Over-indulgence* and *Sexual Lust*.
25 Not an article by Tolstoy, but an extract from his diary for 1899 published by Chertkov in London in 1899 and translated into Russian via French. It appeared in *New Times* on 6 February.
26 Boulanger's article on the life and teaching of the Buddha with a foreword by Tolstoy was published by *The Intermediary* in 1910.
27 See 1909, Note 219.
28 Not suitable for inclusion in his series *The Way of Life*.
29 Sukhotin's son by his first marriage, his daughter by Tatyana, and Alexandra Tolstaya respectively.
30 Baron D'Estournelles de Constant, a former French ambassador in London with pacifist leanings and head of a French parliamentary delegation visiting Petersburg and Moscow, sent a telegram of greetings to Tolstoy while in Moscow; the 'mutilated article' refers to the diary extract published in *New Times* (see Note 25).
31 A. M. Khiryakov, who wrote extensively about Tolstoy and edited a posthumous collection of his works, corresponded with him from prison where he had been sentenced for editing a liberal newspaper in Petersburg.
32 With Tolstoy's foreword to Boulanger's article on the Buddha.
33 For Tolstoy's reply to the student see *Letters*, II, 697.
34 Or rather, the plan for the thirty booklets which were to comprise *The Way of Life*.
35 Tolstoy had received some cuttings from the French newspapers about a production of Paul Bourget's new play *La Barricade*.

36 To Elias Lehr, an Austrian writer on religious and moral questions, and to the executive committee of the Czech Progressive Party on the occasion of Masaryk's forthcoming sixtieth birthday.
37 Tolstoy's story about the disaster on the Khodynka field in 1896 was left unrevised and was not published in his life-time.
38 To a schoolboy who had written about a vice which was tormenting him.
39 See Note 36. Tolstoy wrote two letters, one about Masaryk's birthday and the other about the fifteenth-century Czech moralist P.Chelčický.
40 Two Kuban Cossacks who intended to become conscientious objectors.
41 Tolstoy read W. H. Davies' *Autobiography of a Super-tramp*, with a foreword by Bernard Shaw.
42 Lev Shestov's book *The Good in the Teaching of Count Tolstoy and F. Nietzsche. Philosophy and Preaching* had been published in 1907.
43 *Cupidity.*
44 Andrey Tarasov – a peasant from Tambov, ex-NCO, railway guard and revolutionary who was fired by Tolstoy's ideas of self-improvement; S. M. Popov – a young man of middle-class origin who abandoned his studies to work on a Tolstoyan colony and became a fanatical 'Tolstoyan'.
45 J. Raitz's novel *Ecce Sacerdos: Ein Zeitroman* (Dresden, 1909) which Tolstoy read in German.
46 A letter from a Bulgarian soldier sentenced to four years' imprisonment for refusing to do military service. The soldier referred in his letter to the influence which Tolstoy's ideas had had on him.
47 M. A. Stakhovich brought with him the manuscript of a book containing A. A. Tolstaya's correspondence with Tolstoy and her reminiscences.
48 *Letters*, I, 108–10.
49 Gorbunov-Posadov had decided to begin publishing the booklets which comprised *The Way of Life*.
50 To the Japanese Christian pastor who had written to Tolstoy to ask about his attitude to military service and to taxation.
51 A letter to I. I. Perper, editor of the *Vegetarian Review*, asking him to publish Bruno Freidank's book *The Horrors of Christian Civilisation*, which had been translated by A. A. Goldenweiser (see 1909, Note 230). See *Letters*, II, 698.
52 Tolstoy had been asked by a teacher how to dispose in his will of 15,000 roubles; he suggested that the money should be used to publish a popular encyclopaedic dictionary.
53 *The Light of Truth*, Lahore, 1906, an English book on Brahminism sent to Tolstoy by Rama Deva, editor of the *Vedic Magazine*.
54 *Vanity.*
55 A collection of aphorisms, including many by Tolstoy, which Leskov had compiled in a notebook. It was sent to Tolstoy by Sergeyenko.
56 See 1908, Note 34. Tolstoy re-read his letter on hearing that it had been widely circulated in India.
57 At the request of a group of young people at Telyatinki, Tolstoy began to write a comedy – at first called *One Good Turn Deserves Another* – for them to take part in. It was not finished but the draft was used for a performance at Telyatinki after his death. It is referred to again below on 30 March.
58 *An Everyday Occurrence, Russian Wealth*, 1910, No. 3. Tolstoy wrote an enthusiastic letter about it to Korolenko the following day (*Letters*, II, 699).
59 A correspondent of a Swedish-language newspaper published in Helsingfors, who wrote an article on the basis of his visit entitled *Lev Tolstoy on the Finnish Crisis* (*Hufvudstadsbladet*, 20 April).
60 Namely to ask her brother, M. A. Stakhovich, to do all he could to help Molochnikov (1908, Note 23) who had recently been imprisoned for a second time for allegedly 'seducing' two soldiers into becoming conscientious objectors.

61 V. V. Chertkov told Tolstoy the gist of the peasant writer S. T. Semyonov's story *Gavrila Skvortsov*, which prompted Tolstoy to re-read some more of Semyonov's *Peasant Stories* for which he had written a foreword in 1894.
62 To G. K. Gradovsky, chairman of the organising committee of the second all-Russian congress of writers, who had asked Tolstoy to send a message of greetings, which he did with some reservations, concerning government involvement in the congress.
63 The proofs of the first sections of *The Way of Life*.
64 Alexandra Tolstaya, who was suspected of having tuberculosis, was leaving for the Crimea for treatment.
65 To ask him to make efforts on behalf of Bodyansky, who had been sentenced to six years' hard labour for revolutionary activity.
66 Bernard Shaw had sent Tolstoy his play *The Shewing-Up of Blanco Posnet* and a letter indicating its connection with *The Power of Darkness*. For Tolstoy's reply see *Letters*, II, 700.
67 John Eastham, an English pacifist, had sent Tolstoy an invitation to speak at a meeting in London in May and a prospectus of the First Universal Races Congress which he was helping to organise. Tolstoy refused, mainly on the grounds that as long as separate peoples and states existed there would always be wars.
68 In an article in *New Times* written apropos of *Lev Tolstoy on the Finnish Crisis* (Note 59). Menshikov had accused Tolstoy of hating what exists in the name of the imaginary, and of hating Russia in particular.
69 Tolstoy read with approval an article on Chinese civilisation in an English-language bimonthly periodical, the *World's Chinese Students' Journal*, sent to him from Shanghai. 'If I were young,' he said, 'I would go to China.'
70 A headmaster who had been educated in America and an official who had been sent to Russia for further study.
71 A letter from Gandhi together with a copy of his book *Indian Home Rule*.
72 A retired colonel who came to reproach Tolstoy for his apostasy and for his hostility towards the state.
73 *M. K. Gandhi: An Indian patriot in South Africa* by Joseph Doke, Baptist Minister, Johannesburg. The book was published in Ilford in 1909.
74 Andreyev spent two days at Yasnaya Polyana where the two writers discussed among other things the works of Gorky, Sologub and K. Chukovsky. Andreyev wrote about the visit in an article entitled *Six Months Before Death* in the *Sun of Russia*, November 1911, No. 53.
75 The doctors believed that both her lungs were affected by tuberculosis.
76 An article in the *Modern World*, 1910, No. 3, entitled *Modern Suicides* by Dr D. N. Zhbankov, which Tolstoy discussed with Andreyev and corresponded about with Masaryk.
77 The motor car race from Moscow to Oryol which passed near Yasnaya Polyana.
78 Tolstoy travelled with Makovitsky and Bulgakov to Tatyana's estate at Kochety and stayed there until 20 May.
79 T. G. Masaryk's *Der Selbstmord als soziale Massenerscheinung der modernen Civilisation*, Vienna, 1881. Tolstoy considered it immature and too scholarly.
80 A quotation from a poem by Fet.
81 Tolstoy was reading *Essais de Montaigne, suivis de sa correspondance et 'De la Servitude voluntaire' d'Estienne de la Boétie* (Paris, 1854) and La Rochefoucauld's *Maximes*.
82 A Russian translation of the German Protestant theologian Otto Pfleiderer's book *Die Religion, ihr Wesen und ihre Geschichte*.
83 The Doctor, author and literary critic V. V. Veresayev's book *A Doctor's Notes*, and S. T. Semyonov's *Peasant Stories*.
84 See Note 57.
85 Albert Réville – Protestant theologian and professor of the history of religions at the

Collège de France. Tolstoy was reading his book *Les Religions des peuples non civilisés* (Paris, 1883) and taking notes from it.
86 Some thoughts which Tolstoy had expressed to Bulgakov while out walking.
87 About some Yasnaya Polyana peasants who had been arrested by the Circassian employed by Sofya Andreyevna to patrol the estate (1909, Note 215).
88 Professor H. Weinel's book *Das freie Christentum in der Welt* (Tübingen, 1909) summarised the papers given at an international congress of free churches in Boston in 1907, including one on *Monistische Religion*.
89 A public lecture given by the classical historian and professor at Moscow University R. Y. Wipper entitled *The Twilight of Mankind* which Tolstoy read in *Russian Wealth*, 1910, No. 5.
90 A reference to a story told to Tolstoy by his son Sergey about a soldier who killed a revolutionary in 1905 and suffered great remorse as a result. Tolstoy intended to use the story himself but never did.
91 P. N. Orlenev, a distinguished actor who had performed with acclaim in England and America, wished to start a travelling theatre for the people and to discuss the project with Tolstoy. He went to Yasnaya Polyana on 8 June but Tolstoy was not impressed (see entry under that date).
92 P. P. Trubetskoy, the Russian sculptor living abroad, came with his wife to stay for a few days at Yasnaya Polyana and did a sculpture, a portrait in oils and two pencil sketches of Tolstoy. When Sofya Andreyevna asked him whether he had read *War and Peace* he amused Tolstoy by confessing that he never read anything.
93 An article about Chernyshevsky in Siberia based on unpublished letters and the family archive which Tolstoy read in *Russian Wealth*, Nos. 4 and 5.
94 A reply by Tolstoy to the letter of a peasant blacksmith who wished to take up writing. Tolstoy made it very clear which occupation he thought preferable.
95 In this and other entries hereabouts the foreword mentioned is the one to *The Way of Life*.
96 P. V. Vlasov, a former pupil at Tolstoy's school.
97 Presumably Tolstoy talked to his daughter about his wish to leave home.
98 Tolstoy wrote a dialogue, *Repentance*, on this theme for the anthology, and later began to expand it into a story which was never completed.
99 Two girls (including the one on crutches mentioned earlier) had come a long way to ask Tolstoy's advice on how to live a fruitful, Christian life and also to get his opinion about their writings which they had brought with them. They had settled temporarily in the village to be near Tolstoy, and he visited them there on 12 June.
100 A branch of the Meshcherskoye psychiatric hospital.
101 Karel Velemínský, who translated into Czech and edited Tolstoy's educational writings.
102 The December section of *For Every Day*.
103 Tolstoy recorded his impressions in an article, *On Insanity*.
104 Tolstoy had a high opinion of many of A. I. Kuprin's stories and often spoke of his talent and vivid imagery, but was not enthusiastic about *Emerald* and was disgusted by *The Pit*.
105 To Sofia, not Belgrade, declining an invitation to take part in a conference designed to promote the unity of the Slavonic peoples on a cultural and economic basis. See also 20 June.
106 An invitation from some doctors from the psychiatric hospital at Troitskoye, which Tolstoy had visited on 17 June, to attend a cinema show for the patients.
107 See Notes 98.
108 A story dictated to his daughter Alexandra and published in the *Russian Gazette* on 14 July 1910, based on a meeting Tolstoy had with a peasant, A. P. Surin, which apparently had a great effect on the course of his life.
109 A member of a sect of *castrati* who had spent many years in exile in Siberia for his

	beliefs. Tolstoy, it seems, suggested that the tongue would be a better part of the body to cut off!
110	From Sofya Andreyevna, asking Tolstoy to return urgently.
111	Tolstoy's intention of contrasting life inside and outside the house.
112	To a man who had sought Tolstoy's advice on how to cure himself of drink.
113	*A Course in Psychiatry* (Moscow, 1901) by Professor S. S. Korsakov which had been sent to Tolstoy by doctors of a Moscow psychiatric hospital. Tolstoy was reading the book in connection with the article he was writing on insanity.
114	Sofya Andreyevna was going to Sergey's estate for his birthday and wanted Tolstoy to go with her. When she realised that he felt too tired to make the journey she changed her mind but Tolstoy did eventually go.
115	Engrossed in his conversation with Chertkov, Tolstoy took the wrong turning before suddenly realising his mistake and catching the others up, thanks to a lift in Chertkov's carriage.
116	A French translation of Tolstoy's article by Halpérine-(Galperin-)Kaminsky.
117	The book, published in Warsaw, was by Dr J. Polak, president of the Polish Society of the Friends of Peace.
118	André Gide's story, which Salomon brought from France at the author's request.
119	Pierre Mille's story *La Biche écrasée*, which the author sent to Tolstoy with a covering letter.
120	Two Tolstoyan sympathisers who were spending the summer of 1910 in the village of Yasnaya Polyana working with the peasants.
121	The terrible quarrel was largely the result of Sofya Andreyevna's determination to recover her husband's diaries from Chertkov. According to an eye-witness she ran into the garden shouting that she would kill Chertkov. Tolstoy woke up his son Lev and told him to go and look for her. In his memoirs *The Truth about My Father*, Lev Tolstoy claimed that she kept repeating 'I won't go back. He drove me out like a dog' and that he returned to the house and made his father accompany him in order to calm her down.
122	Tolstoy agreed not to give his diary to Chertkov for copying, to take back the old diaries which Chertkov still had and not to see Chertkov in future. For the full text of his letter see *Letters*, II, 700–2.
123	V. G. Chertkov.
124	Matthew Gering, a friend of the American politician and Secretary of State William Bryan, who had visited Tolstoy in 1903 and corresponded with him, asked to visit Yasnaya Polyana with a personal message from Bryan. Tolstoy agreed and Gering spent two days with him.
125	Tolstoy received an invitation to the Stockholm Peace Congress which was due to open in August, having been postponed from the previous year. He wrote a short addition to the paper he had prepared in 1909 but did not send it, confining himself to a brief letter instead.
126	Tolstoy's niece. See 1900, Note 48.
127	Tolstoy made a list in his diary and notebooks of some forty types or characters he would like to depict in future works.
128	His will, witnessed by Goldenweiser, Sergeyenko and Radynsky, bequeathed his entire literary heritage to his daughter Alexandra or, in the event of her death, to Tatyana. Further changes were made later, clarifying points of detail to do with the disposition of his writings after his death.
129	Rudolf von Ihering, a German legal theorist, whose book *Die Schuld im Römischen Civilrecht* is the source of the quotation.
130	From 29 July Tolstoy began to keep his *Diary for Myself Alone* parallel with his ordinary diary.
131	About the renunciation of the will and hatred of the self, which Tolstoy included in *Self-Denial* in his series *The Way of Life*.

132 V. G. Korolenko, editor of the influential journal *Russian Wealth* and vehement opponent of capital punishment, spent two days with Tolstoy. He returned to Yasnaya Polyana for Tolstoy's funeral.
133 To talk to Tolstoy about their intention to refuse to do military service.
134 A neighbour of Tolstoy's (a former vice-governor of Smolensk), and a Hungarian newspaper correspondent who had not heard of Henry George respectively.
135 A wealthy lady who had radically altered her life as a result of acquaintance with Tolstoy's writings came to question him about her service to the community and about being in love.
136 Tolstoy and his wife and daughter Alexandra left for his daughter Tatyana's estate at Kochety where Tolstoy stayed until 22 September.
137 A manuscript collection of articles which was published by *The Intermediary* in 1911 with an introductory letter by Tolstoy.
138 The only one of an intended cycle of 'character' stories to be written. See Note 127.
139 An unidentified book on Babism.
140 A religious society which aimed to combat English influence in India.
141 The manuscript is not known.
142 James Mavor, professor of political economy at Toronto University, who had helped the Dukhobors to resettle in Canada and had visited Tolstoy previously in 1889.
143 The Matveyevs and the Mamontovs were wealthy landowners in the neighbourhood of Kochety.
144 A letter from Gandhi and a friend who had set up a farm near Johannesburg for Indian residents who were resorting to civil disobedience.
145 A. I. Drankov (see Note 6). He spent three days taking pictures and showing ones he had taken previously.
146 A reply to Gandhi's letter (*Letters*, II, 706–8).
147 Sofya Andreyevna wanted Tolstoy to go back with her to Yasnaya Polyana, but he refused.
148 Giulio Vitali, author of several works on Tolstoy, had written to Makovitsky outlining what he considered to be the main points of Tolstoy's philosophy of life for a book which he intended to dedicate to him. Tolstoy confirmed their correctness, and the book was published in Rome in 1911: *Leone Tolstoi: Con ritratto, bibliografia e lettera autografa*.
149 To K. Y. Grot, with Tolstoy's reminiscences of his brother N. Y. Grot, for inclusion in the anthology *N. Y. Grot in Essays, Reminiscences and Letters* which was published in 1911.
150 Mrs I. F. Mayo, an English writer who edited the English translations of Tolstoy's works for the *Free Age Press* and was a contributor to the journal *The Open Road*.
151 By A. S. Pankratov, sent by the author to Tolstoy in March 1910.
152 A verbal account of the prison experiences of A. I. Kudrin, the son of a peasant friend of Tolstoy's from the Samara province, which was given to Bulgakov at Yasnaya Polyana in Tolstoy's absence and taken down in writing by him for forwarding to Tolstoy.
153 P. F. Kupchinsky's book *The Curse of War* was sent to Tolstoy by its author for his comments before its publication in 1911.
154 N. M. Gorbov, a neighbour of the Sukhotins, translator of Thomas Carlyle, owner of a valuable private library and a pioneer in the field of primary and secondary education.
155 A Russian translation by N. Kolayev of Max Müller's *The Six Systems of Indian Philosophy* (London, 1899).
156 Sofya Andreyevna had found Tolstoy's *Diary for Myself Alone* with his entries for the period 29 July to 22 September in the top of his boot. She did not return it, but made her own notes in it.
157 Tolstoy received German translations by Škarvan of his three articles: *On Science*,

Letter to an Indian and *On Law* with comments on them by Eugen Schmitt (the German translation of *On Science* was edited by Schmitt) and also the second volume of Aylmer Maude's biography.

158 A professor at Tomsk University, who had sent Tolstoy his book *Blood, Vengeance and the Death Penalty*.

159 In Tolstoy's absence his wife had moved the photographs of Chertkov and Alexandra Tolstaya which were hanging in his study.

160 The editors of a Czech newspaper, *Mladé Proudy*, had written to Tolstoy about the persecution of young socialists in their country and their wish to publish a 'Reader' containing socialist articles. Tolstoy, whose opinion and cooperation had been sought, replied with a letter which grew into an article, *On Socialism*, which he continued to work on until he left home for good.

161 Probably the proofs of the third chapter (*The Soul*) of *The Way of Life*.

162 V. M. Feokritova, a friend of Alexandra's, who worked at Yasnaya Polyana as Sofya Andreyevna's copyist and also helped Alexandra to copy out her father's writings. She accompanied Tolstoy and his daughter on Tolstoy's last journey, and was present at his death at Astapovo.

163 Because of the very strained relations with her mother, Alexandra moved temporarily to her house at Telyatinki, from which, however, she frequently came back to Yasnaya Polyana.

164 A. F. Anishina – a teacher who corresponded with Tolstoy about how his books *For Every Day* and *The Thoughts of Wise People* could be used in school.

165 M. Sivachov, a metal-worker, had sent Tolstoy an inscribed copy of his book *For the Reader to Judge! Notes of a Literary Makar*. Tolstoy thought him a poor writer, but acknowledged that the book made one think.

166 *Culte Antoiniste: Révélation d'Antoine le Guérisseur* – a biography of a Belgian worker and vegetarian who left the Catholic Church, became interested in spiritualism, and acquired a reputation as a healer.

167 Sofya Andreyevna's new (12th) edition of Tolstoy's works which came out in 22 volumes in 1911.

168 V. M. Feokritova.

169 The second volume of Aylmer Maude's biography.

170 M. A. Lentovskaya – a former medical attendant and wife of a naval doctor, who wrote a number of letters to Chertkov critical of some of the excesses of 'Tolstoyanism' as practised in particular by Tregubov. Chertkov had a very high opinion of her as a deeply religious woman and fellow thinker, and warmly recommended the letters to Tolstoy. He also sent Tolstoy the manuscript of his article *On Free Thinking*, which was never finished.

171 Nothing came of the idea.

172 *The Concept of God as the Perfect Foundation of Life*, published in two parts in Geneva by the Don Cossack philosopher, P. P. Nikolayev, who left Russia to live in Nice in 1905.

173 The first volume of *The Brothers Karamazov*. He had some critical things to say to Bulgakov about its unnaturalness and lack of artistry, while singling out for praise individual scenes such as those involving Father Zosima and the Grand Inquisitor. One particular reproach was that 'all the characters speak the same language'.

174 Sofya Andreyevna was alarmed that her husband, with the collaboration of Chertkov, had drawn up a will renouncing all copyright to his works, and that rich publishers would get richer while she and his children would starve.

175 A ninth-century Indian philosopher.

176 Dunayev (see 1889, Note 13) had arrived at Yasnaya Polyana the previous evening, having recently returned from Germany.

177 A reference to a letter Chertkov had written (and which had been forwarded to Tolstoy by Chertkov's wife) to the Bulgarian 'Tolstoyan' X. F. Dosev, trying to clarify

178 the relationship between Tolstoy and his wife and to correct Dosev's wrong impression that Tolstoy was a slave to Sofya Andreyevna.
178 On Novikov's recent visit to Yasnaya Polyana, Tolstoy had spoken to him about his intention of leaving home in the near future. On 24 October Tolstoy wrote to him to ask if he could find him a hut in his village, some sixty *versts* from Yasnaya Polyana, if he did leave home (*Letters*, II, 710).
179 At Moscow University on the subject of universities and science.
180 A Petersburg student, A. Barkhudarov, used Merezhkovsky's book on Tolstoy and Dostoyevsky as supporting evidence for his reproach that Tolstoy said one thing and did another.
181 P. N. Gastev (see 1891, Note 73), who had assisted Tolstoy during the famine year of 1891, had recently been working on a farm near Pyatigorsk; Natalya Almedingen was a journalist and editor of children's magazines in Petersburg, and also worked for *The Intermediary* publishing house.
182 The story was never begun.
183 Tolstoy evidently had in mind a story (never written) involving his old friend, the critic and philosopher Strakhov, and Grushenka from *The Brothers Karamazov*.
184 Korney Chukovsky had asked Tolstoy and other writers to write a few lines directed against capital punishment, suitable for publication in the newspaper *Speech*. Tolstoy's reply, which he was still working on during his last day at Yasnaya Polyana, was never properly completed, but came out after his death under the title *An Effective Remedy* – a title invented by the editor of *Speech*.
185 His 'farewell' letter to Sofya Andreyevna, telling her of his final departure. For the text and Tolstoy's movements after leaving home see *Letters*, II, 710–11.
186 P. N. Gastev's reminiscences about the peasant Syutayev whom he had met in a commune in 1890, which Tolstoy read in manuscript.
187 The convent where Tolstoy's sister had lived since 1889.
188 I. O. Shurayev, a man-servant.
189 Tolstoy's sister's daughter, Y. V. Obolenskaya, who was staying with her mother.
190 A booklet by V. Kozhevnikov entitled *The Relationship of Socialism to Religion in General and Christianity in Particular*, published in Novosyolov's Religious and Philosophical Library series.
191 It had been left behind at Yasnaya Polyana.
192 Saying in effect that his father was right to do what he had done.
193 His last letter to his wife, translated in *Letters*, II, 713–14, in which he ruled out a return home or a meeting with her.
194 Tolstoy wrote Sharapovo by mistake.
195 Tolstoy and Makovitsky.
196 Tolstoy's last written words, preceded by a shortened version of the favourite saying of his: *Fais ce que dois, advienne que pourra*.

DIARY FOR MYSELF ALONE

1 A reference to the content of his new will (1910, Note 128) making his works freely available to all.
2 Lev was learning to sculpt.
3 By encouraging him and helping him to write his secret will which led to so much discord in the family.
4 M. F. Lodyzhensky, author of a 'mystical trilogy', discussed Indian philosophy, yoga and theosophy with Tolstoy.
5 For the text see *Letters*, II, 703.
6 Chertkov, in reply to Tolstoy's letter (see Note 5) strongly defended his position and Tolstoy acquiesced.
7 An extract from Tolstoy's diary for 29 November 1851, in which he spoke of his love for men and which Sofya Andreyevna misconstrued.

8   To please Sofya Andreyevna, Tolstoy agreed not to visit Chertkov at Telyatinki after 17 July, and Chertkov stopped visiting Yasnaya Polyana on 24 July.
9   See 1910, Note 113.
10 At this point Tolstoy includes in his diary a number of phrases which appealed to him from the speech of a peasant woman.
11 In connection with the drawing up of the secret will.
12 About the will.
13 His departure for Kochety.
14 V. M. Feokritova.
15 Chertkov offered Tolstoy advice about the treatment of neurotic patients.
16 According to Makovitsky, Tolstoy related how the French physicist and politician François Arago stopped a speaker who kept referring to him as *Monsieur* Arago and asked to be called Arago *tout court*. The context in which Tolstoy's remark was made is not clear.
17 A neuropathologist, called in to give advice about Sofya Andreyevna's apparent neurosis. He advised her not to get agitated, to take baths and to go for walks!
18 From K. Bayromov, a former Babist, who sympathised with Tolstoy's religious and philosophical views.
19 A reference to stories, inspired by Sofya Andreyevna, about an allegedly unnatural relationship between Tolstoy and Chertkov, which were spread by Zvegintseva who disliked Chertkov.
20 All right for Mavor (see 1910, Note 142) to visit Yasnaya Polyana.
21 Sofya Andreyevna had invited a priest to hold a prayer service in her bedroom and then sprinkled all the upstairs rooms, including Tolstoy's bedroom and study, with holy water to exorcise the evil spirit of Chertkov.
22 V. M. Feokritova's diary contained some abusive remarks about Tolstoy attributed to his wife.
23 See 1910, Note 156.
24 The word was used by Sofya Andreyevna, who believed that Chertkov was trying to obtain more and more of Tolstoy's manuscripts.
25 For the text of the letter in reply to Chertkov's letter of the previous day criticising Tolstoy for allowing his wife to interfere with relations between the two men see *Letters*, II, 708.
26 This last photograph of Tolstoy was taken by Bulgakov.
27 See 1910, Note 170.
28 See 1910, Note 166.
29 Chertkov came to Yasnaya Polyana on 7 October with Sofya Andreyevna's agreement.
30 See 1910, Note 113.
31 See 1910, Note 174.
32 It was rumoured that Sofya Andreyevna intended to sell the copyright of Tolstoy's works to a publishing house for a million roubles.
33 A letter to Dosev – see 1910, Note 177; the statement – a draft statement to the press that Tolstoy's works were not for sale.
34 See *Letters*, II, 711–12.

INDEX

Abbot, Lyman, 305
Adam, Paul, 459
Adler, Felix, 332
Akrshevsky, 77, 82
Aksakov, I. S., 112, 175
Aksakov, K. S., 115, 145–6
Aksakov, S. T., 129, 146, 149
Aksakovs, 129, 143–6
Alexander I, Emperor, 182–3
Alexander II, Emperor, 101, 105, 126, 164
Alexander III, Emperor, 282, 306, 323, 329–30, 340, 342
Alexeyev, N. P., 27, 38, 45–7, 49, 51, 57, 61, 67, 74, 81, 85, 148, 150
Alexeyev, P. S., 274
Alexeyev, V. I., 192, 196, 198, 239, 290
Alfieri, Vittorio, *Myrrha*, 132
Almedingen, Natalya A., 675
Alyokhin, Arkady V., 258, 267, 310, 317–8
Alyokhin, M. V., 400
Amiel, Henri-Frédéric, 320–1, 327, 484, 516, 528, 622
Andersen, Hans Christian, 128, 138, 528
Andreyev, L. N., 602, 634–5, 639–40, 654, 670
Andropov, N. P., 88, 90, 94
Annenkov, N. N., 101
Annenkov, P. V., 124–5, 128, 134, 143
Annenkova, L. F., 238, 274, 430
Arbuzov, P. P. (Pavel), 217, 303, 341
Archer, Herbert, 462
Arensky, A. S., 435, 519, 632
Aristotle, 442
Armfeldts (mother and daughter), 209–10, 216
Arnold, Gottfried, 252, 256
Arnold, Matthew, 222, 240–1, 284, 410, 442
Arsenyev, V. M., 49, 86
Arsenyeva, V. V., (Valeriya), 118–28, 130, 152
Arsenyevs, 118–9, 143
Arslan Khan, 45, 69–70, 80

Artsybashev, M. P., 602, 670
Aubrey, Charles (see Warren, Samuel), 68
Auerbach, Berthold, 126, 156–7, 161, 163
Augustine, 216
Avdeyev, M. V., 66

Baba Bharati, 564, 607
Babism, Babists, Behais, 602, 607, 659, 666
Bach, Johann Sebastian, 428, 436–7, 484
Bacon, Francis, 157;
 Novum Organum, 191
Bakhmeteva, A. N., 116
Bakunin, M. A., 618
Ballou, Adin, 253, 290, 295, 305
Balta (Isayev), 38, 49, 61
Balzac, Honoré de, 106, 134
 Honorine, 130
 La Comédie Humaine, 133
 La Cousine Bette 132–3
Bardina, S. I., 211
Barine, Arvède (Mme Vincens),
 Princesse Arabe, 240
Baryatinsky, A. I., 33, 38, 70
Battersby, H. F. P., 313
Baudelaire, Charles, 321
Baumann, Émile,
 L'immolé, 641–2
Bazykin, T., 336
Bazykina, Aksinya, 151, 154–6, 597
Beethoven, Ludwig van, 428, 430, 432, 436, 447, 484, 632
Begicheva, M. S., 117
Behrs, A. A., 166, 179, 210, 233, 622, 629
Behrs, A. Y., 165–7, 185
Behrs, Lyubov A., 116, 143, 169, 175
Behrs, Sofya A., *see* Tolstaya, S. A.
Behrs, Tatyana A., *see* Kuzminskaya, T. A.
Behrs, V. A., 223, 233, 305, 335, 567
Behrs, Yelizaveta A., 161–2, 166–8
Behrs (family), 143, 145, 152, 161, 164–6, 169, 174, 234, 453
Belinsky, V. G. 128, 426, 500, 535, 605–6

Bellamy, Edward,
  Looking Backward, 254
Béranger, Pierre-Jean de, 88
Biryukov, P. I. (Posha), 236, 243, 248, 260, 271, 276, 284, 288, 298, 323, 325, 330, 334, 340, 400, 415, 417, 420, 424, 427–8, 438, 443, 454, 459, 494, 509, 522, 534, 538–9, 573, 578, 582, 607, 633, 648, 671, 678, 680
Björnson, Björnsterne, 292, 311;
  In God's Way, 294
Blavatskaya, Y. P., 211
Bludov, D. N., 112, 114, 119, 127, 519
Bludova, A. D., 128
Boborykin, K. N., 91, 93, 95
Boborykin, P. D.,
  The Corpse, 319
Boccaccio, Giovanni, 457
Bochkaryov, I. I., 420, 483
Bodyansky, A. M., 417
Bogoyavlensky, N. Y., 234, 242, 314
Boissier, Gaston, 279
Bolotov, A. V., 192
Bondarev, T. M., 272, 404, 427, 551
Bota, 45
Botkin, V. P., 114–5, 124–8, 133, 136, 138–9
Boulanger, P. A., 266, 274, 298, 411, 435, 444, 446, 454, 459, 479, 480, 483, 485, 496, 498, 516, 572, 596, 627, 634, 643, 646, 648–9
Bourget, Paul, 267, 406, 649
Braddon, Mrs M. E., 185
Brahminism, Brahmin, etc., 228, 283, 529, 562, 650
Bremer, Frederika,
  The Neighbours, 136
Briggs, W., 521
Brimmer, E. V., 61, 67, 70–1
Broglie, A. de, 294
Bronevsky, Y. A., 101, 105
Brontë, Charlotte, 139, 141
Bryullov, K. P., 257, 268
Buddha, Buddhism, 204, 224, 243, 258, 264, 283, 297, 321, 418, 432, 488, 560, 562, 567, 599, 607, 628, 637, 648–9
Buffon, Georges-Louis Leclerc, 50
Bugayev, N. V., 206, 214
Bulgakov, S. N., 492, 562
Bulgakov, V. F., 609, 644, 648, 652, 655, 657–8, 663, 665, 669, 671, 673–4
Bulygin, M. V., 291, 292, 298, 310, 314, 322–3, 333, 342, 575, 586, 638, 648
Butkevich, A. S., 275, 298, 319, 415, 579

Buturlin, A. S., 537, 588, 622, 625
Buyemsky, N. I., 49, 52, 55, 57–8, 60, 63

Carlyle, Thomas, 528
Carpenter, Edward, 432, 448, 450–1, 455
Castellion, Sebastian,
  Traité des hérétiques, 410
Catherine II, Empress,
  Instructions, 4–10
Cervantes, Miguel de, 144
Chamberlain, Houston Stewart, 558
Chapelle (Luillier, C-E.), 149
Chekhov, A. P., 243, 415, 494, 497, 511, 631, 640
  On the Cart, 453
  Lady with the Dog, 475
  The Darling, 536
  Uncle Vanya, 476
Chelčický, P., 536, 649
  The Net of Faith, 252, 536
Chelyshev, M. D., 634–5
Chernyshevsky, N. G., 127, 234, 426, 658
Chertkov, V. G. (the Chertkovs), 204–9, 211–2, 214, 217, 220–2, 232, 234, 236, 243, 267, 274, 276, 280, 284, 286, 292, 299, 305, 309, 317, 325, 330–3, 335–7, 343, 398, 403, 417, 421–4, 428–31, 434–5, 437, 441, 443–5, 447–8, 450–4, 459–62, 490, 493–4, 517, 521, 523, 527, 531, 538, 543, 554, 557–8, 560, 569–71, 573, 578, 580, 584–8, 595–6, 598, 600–1, 604–8, 610–2, 615–7, 619, 624, 630–1, 633–4, 638–9, 644, 646, 649–50, 653, 655–6, 658–64, 666–75, 677–87
Chertkov, V. V. (Dima), 628, 631, 644, 646, 651–2, 659
Chertkova, A. K. (Galya), 331, 428, 451–2, 459, 482, 534, 609–12, 615, 671, 675, 678, 685, 687
Chicherin, B. N., 129, 146–51, 161–3, 168, 185, 492
Chicherina, A. N., 147
Chistyakov, M. N., 266, 284
Chopin, Frédéric, 435, 484, 637
Chukovsky, K. I., 675
Clarke, C. A.,
  Time and Eternity. The Eternal Question, 215
Clive, Mrs Caroline,
  Paul Ferroll, 244
Coleridge, Samuel Taylor, 293–4, 492
Comte, Auguste, 260
Confucius, Confucianism, 203–5, 207, 283, 485, 567, 607, 609, 611, 628, 634, 637

Cormon and Grangé,
    Le quadrille des lanciers, 132
Corneille, Pierre, 423
Creelman, J., 305
Crosby, Ernest H., 332, 422–3, 445, 564
Curtin, Jeremy, 479

Daniel, C. W., 564, 641
Dannenberg, P. A., 95
Dante Alighieri, 436, 484
Darwin, Charles, Darwinism, etc., 209,
    234, 240, 253, 259, 484, 486, 500, 513,
    654, 670
Das, Tarakuatta, 585, 591–2
Datt, A. K., 431
Daudet, Léon,
    Morticoles, 341
Davidson, John Morrison, 553
Davies, W. H.,
    Autobiography of a Super-tramp, 649
Davitt, Michael, 522
Davydov, A. I., 124
Davydov, N. V., 212, 305, 308, 413, 423,
    487, 522, 662
De Quincey, Thomas, 252
Denisenko, I. V., and family, 553, 621
Descartes, René, 188
Dickens, Charles, 149, 186
    David Copperfield, 60, 121
    Bleak House, 91
    Little Dorrit, 121
    Pickwick Papers, 122, 185
    Our Mutual Friend, 186, 588
Diderot, Denis, 303, 305–6
Dillon, E. J., 298, 319
Dmokhovskaya, A. V., 209, 211–2, 247–8
Dobrolyubov, A. M., 553, 567, 584
Dobrolyubov, N. A., 426, 535
Dole, Nathaniel, 234, 243
Dolgorukov, N. A., 114
Dolgorukov, P. D., 538, 648
Dolgov, S. M., 276
Donizetti, Gaetano,
    La Fille du regiment, 131
Dostoyevsky, F. M., 641, 648, 675
    Dream of a Ridiculous Man, 310
    The Brothers Karamazov, 673–5
Drozhzhin, Y. N., 330, 398, 421
Druzhinin, A. V., 114, 123–6, 128, 136–7,
    150
    Polenka Sachs, 175
Dudyshkin, S. S., 126
Dukhobors, 415, 434, 446, 454, 456–7,
    460–2, 468, 474, 476

Dumas, Alexandre (fils), 323–4
    La Dame aux Perles, 135
Dumas, Alexandre (père), 48, 85, 90, 206
Dunayev, A. N., 236, 238–9, 243, 299,
    401, 412, 420, 435, 459, 483, 545–6,
    633, 651, 674, 687
Durda, 45–6
Dyakov, D. A., 20, 39, 118–9, 185, 207,
    246, 255
Dyakova, Y. A., 115, 144

Edwards, J. 418
Eliot, George, 480
    Adam Bede, 155
Emerson, Ralph Waldo, 149, 214, 220,
    275, 599
Engelhardt, M. A.,
    Progress as the Evolution of Cruelty, 473
Engels, Friedrich, 618
Epictetus, 204, 240, 503, 552, 567, 637,
    644
Erasmus, Desiderius, 203–4
Ertel, A. I., 272, 303, 415, 423, 593, 598,
    614
    The Gardenins, 265
Evans, F. W., 270, 277, 305

Farrar, F. W., 234
Faure, Jean Baptiste, 437
Feinermann, I. B., 253, 255
Felkersam, I. Y., 70–1
Felten, N. Y., 569, 613, 648
Feokritova, V. M. (Varya), 669–72, 676,
    680–2, 685, 687
Ferzen, G. Y., 105
Fet, A. A., 113–14, 143–5, 147–9, 151,
    153–4, 169, 176, 196, 205–6, 209–10,
    233, 236, 238, 242, 246, 331, 418, 429,
    554, 655
Feuillet, Octave, 154
Figner, Vera N., 584
Filimonov, V. S., 100
Fitz James, Louise, 130–2
Fonvizina, N. D., 192
Forel, A.,
    Die Trinksitten, 296
Foyster, C. N., 338
France, Anatole,
    Opinions socialistes, 507
Franklin journal, 24, 31, 38, 85
Freidank, Bruno,
    The Horrors of Christian Civilisation, 638,
    650
Frey, William, 241

Freytag, Gustav, 138
Friede, A. Y., 93, 95
Froebel, Julius, 157-8
Fyodorov, N. F., 199, 206, 237

Gandhi, Mohandas, 633-4, 654, 667-8
Garrison, William Lloyd, 290, 512, 516
Gastev, P. N., 313, 415-7, 675
Gautier, V. I., 39
Gay, N. N. (father), 230, 233, 239, 246, 260, 263, 276, 284-5, 292, 295, 303, 332-3
Gay, N. N. (son, Kolechka), 212, 222, 277, 333, 335, 432, 468-70, 662, 680
Gaydeburov, P. A., 272, 296
George, Henry, 333, 337, 409, 428, 537, 552, 553, 556, 614, 617, 627, 629, 637, 639
Gerschenson, M. O., 598
Gide, André,
  Retour de l'enfant prodigue, 662
Gimbut, K. F., 117-8, 123, 143, 151
Gimbut, Nadezhda N., 118
Ginzburg, I. Y., 445, 621
Girardin, Emile, 133-4
Glinka, M. I., 146
Goethe, Johann Wolfgang von, 89, 91-2, 137, 149, 154, 177, 187-8, 252, 340, 428, 436, 556-7, 614, 616
  Faust, 104, 182, 557, 642
  Werther, 122
  Wilhelm Meister, 139
  Iphigenia, 187
  Egmont, 187
Gogol, N. V., 27, 143-4, 260, 500, 602, 604-5, 607, 627
  Dead Souls, 120, 142, 605
  Government Inspector, 147, 188, 276, 605
  The Carriage, 604
Goldenweiser, A. B., 435, 445, 569, 588, 615-7, 624-5, 627, 629-31, 638, 640, 653-4, 658-9, 662-4, 671, 677-8, 682
Goldsmith, Oliver,
  The Vicar of Wakefield, 10
Golokhvastov, D. D., 204
Goltsev, V. A., 236, 241, 288, 400
Goncharov, I. A., 124, 126
  A Commonplace Story, 126
  Oblomov, 265, 268
Gorbunov, I. F., 112, 114, 149
Gorbunov-Posadov, I. I., 246, 251, 313, 317, 400, 435, 441, 460, 558, 570, 600, 607-8, 611-2, 616, 628-30, 636, 640, 643, 650, 652, 657-8, 669, 677

Gorchakov, A. I., 20, 22, 68
Gorchakov, M. D., 96-7, 101
Gorchakov, N. M., 130
Gorchakov, S. D., 22, 115
Gorchakova, A. P., 20
Gorchakovs (family), 18, 23, 69, 142, 176
Gorky, Maxim (A. M. Peshkov), 475, 483, 495, 497, 503, 511, 552, 602, 610, 639, 641, 647, 670
  Philistines, 637
Gospels, 142, 192, 204, 205-6, 217, 221-2, 231, 239, 288, 296, 418, 429-30, 442, 451, 486, 560, 566, 627-8
Grabowsky, Norbert, 604
Gradovsky, G. K., 652
Granovsky, T. N., 426
Griboyedov, A. S.,
  The Misfortune of Being Clever, 100, 124, 188
Grigorovich, D. V.,
  Country Lanes, 47
  Fishermen, 74
  The Hapless Anton, 27
Grigoryev, A. A., 114, 124, 147, 185
Groman, Tsesar, 69-70, 73-4
Gronlund, Laurence,
  Our Destiny, 302, 304
Grot, N. Y., 231-3, 236, 249, 267, 314-5, 448, 450-2, 518, 668-9
Guerrazzi, F. D.,
  L'asino, 149
Guizot-Witt, Henrietta, 185
Gusarov, I. S., 628, 640
Gusev, N. N., 574-8, 581, 590, 595, 611, 615, 625-6, 633, 636, 645-6, 657, 675
Gutzkow, Karl, 140
Guyard, Auguste, 338
Guyau, Jean-Marie, 306, 644

Hackländer, Friedrich, 142
Hadji Murat, 45, 429
Haeckel, Ernst, 616-7
Haggard, H. Rider,
  She, 240
Hall, Bolton, 564
Hansen, Peter G., 272
Hapgood, Isabel, 231, 234, 254
Haydn, Franz Joseph, 484, 632
Hegel, Georg W. F., 188, 484, 500, 606, 616, 670
Heine, Heinrich, 100, 304
Helbig, Nadezhda D. (Princess Shakovskaya), 287-8
Herron, George Davis,

Christian State, 412
Herzen, A. I., 129, 157, 288, 426, 586
   From the Other Shore, 543
Hiller, H. Croft, 627
   Meta-Christianity, 603
Höffding, Harald, 477, 626
Home, Daniel Douglas, 131
Homer, 436
   The Iliad, 141–2, 185, 297
   The Odyssey, 185, 297
Hugo, Victor, 604
   Claude Gueux, 71
   Les Misérables, 176
   L'homme qui rit, 253
   Postscriptum de ma vie, 503
Hume, David,
   Histoire d'Angleterre, 51, 55

Ibsen, Henrik, 304, 411, 475, 484
   Comedy of Love, 270
   Rosmersholm, 291
   Wilde Ente, 291
Igumnova, Yuliya (Julie), 472, 568, 587
Ikonnikov, A. I., 573
Islavin, K. A. (Kostenka), 25, 39, 60, 77, 116, 150, 193, 203, 207, 213, 232, 323
Islavin, M. A., 113
Islenyev, A. M., 176, 186, 193
Istomin, B. I., 97
Ivanov, A. P., 204, 206, 448, 480
Ivantsov-Platonov, A. M., 294

James, Henry, 304
James, William, 643
Jerome, Jerome K., 527

Kaehler, G. F., 161, 163
Kalachov, A. V., 615, 631
Kalmykova, A. M., 431
Kamensky, P. P., 126
Kant, Immanuel, 188, 231, 517, 521, 529, 542, 562, 571, 599, 608, 626, 637
Karamzin, N. M., 82
   History of the Russian State, 78, 81
Karamzina, Y. N., 135–6
Karr, Alphonse, 89
Kasatkin, N. A., 242, 336, 445, 452
Katkov, M. N., 164
Kavanagh, Julia, 185
Kavelin, K. D., 112
Keats, John, 258
Kennan, George, 231, 236
Kenworthy J. C., 332, 335, 398, 402–3, 415, 417, 421–3

Khilkov, D. A., 232, 235, 329, 413, 448, 461, 549
Khilkova, T. V., 330, 339
Khilkovsky (the Captain), 27, 46–7, 57–8, 62
Khiryakov, A. M., 648, 669
Khokhlov, P. G., 270, 310, 312, 403, 406, 407, 417
Kholevinskaya, M. M., 424
Khomyakov, A. S., 115, 146
Khomyakov, D. A., 548
Kidd, Benjamin,
   Social Evolution, 413–4
Kiesewetter, Johann G. K. F., 128–9
Kingsley, Charles,
   Hypatia, 214–5
Kireyevsky, N. V., 22, 112
Klodt, K. A., 242
Knoring, F. G., 31, 33–4, 65
Kock, Charles-Paul de,
   Madeleine, 71
Kokorev, V. A., 113, 146, 149
Kolbasin, D. Y., 121, 125, 129, 140, 143, 150
Koloshin, P. V., 105
Koloshin, S. P., 20, 23, 25
Koltsov, A. V., 142–3
Koni, A. F., 443, 519, 583, 638
Konissi, Masurato, 431
Kopylov, I. R., 662
Kopylov, N. F., 56, 151, 179
Korolenko, V. G., 651, 665, 678–9
Korolyov, Y. Y., 114
Korsh, Y. F., 147–8, 152
Kovalevsky, Y. P., 105, 122, 124–5, 143
Kozlov, A. A., 304
Kozlov, I. I., 142
Kramskoy, I. N., 208–9
Krayevsky, A. A., 111, 124–5, 128
Krivenko, S. N., 206
Kropotkin, P. A., 571
Krylov, I. A., 9
Kryzhanovsky, N. A., 93, 102, 105
Kudryavtseva, M. F., 310
Kuprin, A. I.,
   Measles, 660
   The Pit, 612
Kurnosenkova, A. P., 612, 642
Kutler, F. F., 113
Kuzminskaya, T. A. (*née* Behrs), 166, 169, 174–5, 179–80, 186, 193, 197–8, 214, 216, 219, 224, 256, 310–1, 325, 406, 420, 460, 464, 467, 515, 573
Kuzminsky, A. M., 174, 196, 198, 216–7, 219, 224, 256, 296, 324–5, 434, 587

La Boétie, Étienne de, 655
La Bruyère, Jean de, 565, 664
Lachmann, F. F., 343
Lamartine, Alphonse de, 27
　Geneviève, 27
Landowska, Wanda, 600, 645–6
Lanskoy, A. S., 114, 185
Lao Tzu, 203–6, 256, 326, 333, 611–12, 628, 631, 637
La Rochefoucauld, François de, 655
Lecky, W. E. H., 251
Legge, James, 205
　The Chinese Classics, 483
Leontyev, K. N., 278
Lermontov, M. Y., 64, 89, 90
　A Hero of our Time, 91
　Izmail Bey, 91
　Masquerade, 91
Leroy-Beaulieu, Paul, 241
Leskov, N. S., 266, 270, 278, 299, 319, 403, 458, 651
　At the End of the World, 231
　Goldsmith, 236
　No Way Out, 280
　Offended Before Christmas, 299
Lessing, Gottfried E., 327, 476, 496
Levin, L. F., 64
Lichtenberg, Georg, 309, 517, 523
Liprandi, P. P., 95–6, 98
Longinov, M. N., 111
Löwenfeld, R. V., 289
Luther, Martin, 156–7, 203–4, 216
Lvov, G. V., 20, 24
Lvov, G. Y., 313
Lvova, A. V. (Lvov family), 130, 132–3, 154–5
Lyovshin, A. I., 113

Maartens, Maarten,
　The Sin of Joost Avelingh, 290
Macaulay, Thomas Babington, Lord, 150
Maistre, Joseph de, 186
Maklakov, V. I., 629, 633
Makovitsky, Dušan, 422, 451, 531, 534, 564, 587, 611–2, 614, 626, 628, 634, 637, 639, 642, 647, 649–50, 658, 662, 664, 667–70, 673–6, 678, 682, 684
Malikov, A. K., 196, 204
Mallarmé, Stéphane, 427
Mallory, Lucy A., 527
Maltsova, A. N., 113
Manson, John, 421–2
Marakuyev, V. N., 206
Marcus Aurelius, 149, 204, 521, 562, 637

Marivaux, Pierre,
　Les Fausses confidences, 130
Mark (Luka Sekhin, Lukashka), 36–8, 78
Marx, Karl, Marxism, 425, 460, 485, 618
Masaryk, Thomas, 647, 649, 651, 655
Maude, Aylmer, 450–1, 454, 633–4, 669, 670
Maupassant, Henri de, 224, 271, 295, 326, 330–1, 484, 521, 671
　Le port, 295
　Sur l'eau, 295
Maurier, George du,
　Trilby, 423
Mavor, James, 667, 682
Maximov, S.,
　Siberia and Penal Servitude, 547–8
Maykov, A. N., 125
Mayo, Mrs I. F., 668
Mazon, André, 610
Mazzini, Giuseppe, 499, 528, 618
Meadows, T. T., 221
Mechnikov, I. I., 507–8, 615–7, 620, 622
Mélesville (pseud. Anne H. J. Duveyrier)
　Un Vers de Vergile, 130
Mencius, 209, 283, 637
Mendeleyev, D. I., 555
Mendelssohn, Felix, 127, 139
Mengden, Yelizaveta I. (and family), 129, 199, 272
Menshikov, A. S., 96–8, 101
Menshikov, M. O., 415, 417, 426, 459, 554, 590, 628, 640, 643, 653
Merezhkovsky, D. S., 503, 521, 675
Mérimée, Prosper,
　Carmen, 126
　Chronique de Charles IX, 184
Meshchersky, P. I., 134
Meshchersky, Prince, 105, 113–14
Meyer, D. I., 9
Michaud, Joseph F.,
　Histoire des Croisades, 62
Michelangelo, 428, 436
Michelet, Jules, 148–9, 223–4
Mikhaylov, K. A., 503, 521
Mikhaylovsky, N. K., 214, 303
Mikhaylovsky-Danilevsky, A. I.,
　A History of the War of 1813, 60
Mille, Pierre,
　La Biche écrasée, 662
Milyukov, P. N., 504
Milyutin, D. A.,
　A History of the War between Russia and France . . . in 1799, 73–4
Milyutin, N. A., 112–3

Minsky, N. M., 274–5
Mohammed, Muslim, etc., 237, 418, 607, 637
Molière, Jean Baptiste Poquelin, 122
  L'Avare, 130
  Le Bourgeois Gentilhomme, 122, 321
  Le malade imaginaire, 130
  Précieuses ridicules, 130
Molochnikov, V. A., 577, 583, 585–6, 611, 613, 516–2
Molostvova, Y. V., 522, 531, 674
Molostvova, Z. M., 30
Monluc, Blaise de, 149
Montaigne, Michel de, 157, 185, 303, 311, 564, 655, 675
Montégut, Emile, 147
Montesquieu, Charles-Louis de S., 5, 9, 17
Morozov, V. S., 587, 596
Mortier de Fontaine, Louis, 122–3
Moureau, G. A., 70–1
Müller, Max,
  Six Systems of Indian Philosophy, 490, 669
Murillo, Bartolomé, 131, 148
Musin-Pushkin brothers, 39

Nakhimov, P. S., 96–7, 105
Napoleon, I., 131, 182–4, 220, 475
Napoleon III, 130, 134
Naville, Ernest,
  Maine de Biran, 519
Nazhivin, I. F., 580, 638
Nekrasov, N. A., 57, 60, 63, 67, 87–8, 94, 102–3, 112–4, 119, 128, 130, 136, 140, 143–4, 148, 225
Nemirovich-Danchenko, V. I., 484
Nesterov, M. V., 569
Neverezhky (Noverezhky), 92, 103
Nicholas I, Emperor (Nikolay Pavlovich), 89, 101, 508–9, 511, 518–20, 523, 526
Nicholas II, Emperor, 342, 398, 423, 444, 447, 477, 486–7, 492–3, 496, 498–9, 531, 533–4, 545, 601, 606, 628, 633–4
Nietzsche, Friedrich, 475, 480, 487, 500, 520, 641
  Zarathustra, 488
Nikiforov, L. P., 237, 305
Nikitin, D. V., 546, 643, 659–60, 677
Nikolay Mikhaylovich, Grand Duke, 499, 531
Nikolay Nikolayevich, Grand Duke, 98
Nikolayev, P. P., 568, 672, 674
Nikolayev, S. D., 521, 537, 567, 585–7, 607, 609–10, 613–5, 627, 634, 652, 662, 669

Noailles, Duc de, 241
Nobel prize, 446
Nordau, Max, 323
Novikov, A. M., 266, 268, 271–2, 295, 307
Novikov, M. P., 424, 445, 448, 486, 503, 571, 606, 674, 686–7
Novosyolov, M. A., 232, 295, 313, 318, 340
Noyes, J. H., 247

Obolenskaya, A. A. (née Dyakova), 115, 128, 144
Obolenskaya, M. L., see Tolstaya, Marya Lvovna
Obolensky, A. V., 115
Obolensky, D. A., 39, 112, 132
Obolensky, D. D., 198, 306, 314
Obolensky, L. D., 207
Obolensky, L. Y., 247, 266, 477
Obolensky, N. L. (Kolya), 463, 496, 535, 544, 567
Odakhovsky, Y. I., 100–1, 106
Ogaryov, V. I., 19, 114
Ogolin, A. P., 63, 66, 84
Okhotnitskaya, N. P., 118–20
Olifer (Staff captain), 57, 66, 77, 81
Olkhin, 88–91
Olsufyev, Adam V., 208–9, 213, 443, 447, 496
Olsufyev, Alexander V., 477
Olsufyev, D. A., 285, 398, 574, 577, 646, 653, 666
Olsufyev, M. A., 398
Olsufyeva, A. M., 409, 415
Olsufyeva, M. A., 147
Olsufyevs (family), 132, 145, 213, 238, 398, 409, 423, 440–1
Orekhov, A. S., 69, 192
Orfano, A. G., 204, 242
Orlenev, P. N., 658–60
Orlov, N. A., 130
Orlov, N. V., 494, 587
Orlov, V. F., 205, 210, 283, 317, 610
Osten-Saken, D. Y., 98
Ostrovsky, A. N., 124, 144–5, 149
  A Lucrative Post, 129
  Among Friends One Always Comes to Terms, 94
  Poverty is No Crime, 94
  Sin and Misfortune, 175
  The Poor Bride, 126
Ozmidov, N. L., 203, 208, 213, 216, 232, 247, 335

Panayev, I. I., 105–6, 124–8

Panins (family), 24
Pankratov, A. S.,
   Seekers After God, 668
Parfeny, Abbot, 192–3
Pascal, Blaise, 204, 299, 531, 535, 562, 567, 582, 637, 662–4
Pasternak, L. D., 611
Paul I, Emperor, 74
Pauthier, Jean-Pierre Guillaume, 627
Perfilyev, V. S., 113–14, 148, 165–7
Perfilyeva, P. F. (Polenka), 88
Perfilyevs (family), 19, 24, 87, 114–15, 165–7
Perovsky, V. A., 143, 183
Perper, I. I., 617, 650
Peter I, Emperor, 51, 264
Pisarev, R. A., 195, 314
Pisemsky, A. F., 125, 128
   A Hard Lot, 296
   The Wood-Demon, 81
Pistolkors, A. V., 81
Plato, 41, 188, 190, 283, 435, 670
   Laws, 307
   Phaedon, 82
   Politicus, 41, 59
   Republic, 258
   Symposium, 52
Plutarch, 562, 564
Pogodin, M. P., 113
Poiret, Y. V., 23–4
Pokrovsky, Y. A., 231, 236
Polenov, V. D., 615
Polenz, Wilhelm von, 511
   Der Büttnerbauer, 494
   Der Grabenhäger, 498
Polivanov, A. K. (Sasha), 135
Polivanov, N. A., 165, 167, 174
Polonsky, Y. P., 198, 246
Poltoratsky, V. I., 410
Popov, Y. I., 230, 239, 249–50, 315, 319, 323, 326, 330, 334, 337, 341–2, 406, 417
Posse, V. A., 483, 506, 621, 643
Pouvillon, Émile,
   Chante-Pleure, 273
Pressensé, Edmond de, 294
Prévost, Marcel,
   Les Demi-vierges, 335
Pulley, H. W.,
   Ground Ash, 222
Pushchin, M. I., 75, 147
Pushchins (family), 134–5, 140, 148
Pushkin, A. S., 90, 117, 128, 184, 511, 602
   Boris Godunov, 187
   Eugene Onegin, 117

   The Captain's Daughter, 75
   The Gipsies, 91, 117
   The Stone Guest, 116

Quental, Anthero de, 243

Rabelais, François, 155
Racine, Jean, 132
Raguse (Maréchal Marmont), 182–3
Raitz, Joseph,
   Ecce Sacerdos, 649
Ramakrishna, 607, 638
Raphael, Sanzio, 140, 436, 484
Rayevsky, I. I., 314–6
Reichel, Eugen, 564
Rembrandt, H. van Rijn, 131,
Renan, Ernest, 252, 299–300, 564
Repin, I. Y., 208–9, 246, 317, 434, 572, 594
Réville, Albert, 656
Richter, Jean Paul, 252
Riehl, W. H., 157–8
Rigault, M., 149
Rimsky-Korsakov, N. A., 454
Rimsky-Korsakov, N. S., 107, 119
Rod, Édouard, 306
   Le sens de la vie, 239
Roosevelt, Theodore, 614
Ropshin, V.,
   The Pale Horse, 636
Rosen, 107, 119
Rossini, Gioachino,
   The Barber of Seville, 131
Rousseau, Jean-Jacques, 58, 137, 203, 508, 539, 567, 637, 642
   Confessions, 55, 57
   Émile, 55, 70, 293
   La Nouvelle Héloïse, 57
Rubens, Peter Paul, 148
Rugin, I. D., 266, 291–2, 294
Rusanov, G. A., 298, 331, 435, 452
Ruskin, John, 236, 243, 404, 480, 496, 499, 547
Ryabinin, M. A., 141

St Beuve, C. A., 148, 230
St Francis of Assisi, 327, 564, 570, 591, 663
St John, Arthur, 446, 452, 475, 479
Sabatier, Charles Paul-Marie, 327, 559
   St Francis of Assisi (Vie de S. François d'Assise), 510
Sado (Miserbiyev), 38
Saint-Simon, Claude-Henri de Rouvroy, 248
Salomon, Charles, 326, 427, 481, 662

Saltykov-Shchedrin, M. Y., 140, 143, 148, 207, 225, 245
Samarin, P. F., 195, 199, 211, 275
Samarin, Y. F., 115, 510
Sand, George, 29, 129
 Consuélo, 184
 Horace, 34
Sarrut, Germain-Marie, 134–5
Scheidemann, K. F., 87
Schilder, N. K.,
 The Emperor Alexander I, 543
 The Emperor Nicholas I, 509
 The Emperor Paul I, 543
Schiller, Johann Friedrich von, 75, 80, 93, 340
 Die Raüber, 287
 Rudolf of Habsburg, 92
 Verschwörung des Fiesko, 92
Schmidt, Marya A., 232–3, 333, 335–6, 339, 418, 420, 472, 485, 579, 581, 586, 603, 611–2, 626, 629, 639, 644, 646, 648, 669–70, 675, 684, 687
Schmitt, Eugen Heinrich, 401–3, 417–8, 423, 502, 647, 669
Schopenhauer, Arthur, 188, 191, 231, 259–60, 306, 335, 420, 487, 637, 682
Semyonov, L. D., 582, 638, 645
Semyonov, S. T., 230, 238–9, 253, 274, 629, 633, 635–6, 652, 656
Seneca, 29, 562
Sergeyenko, A. P., 398, 641, 676, 687
Sergeyenko, P. A., 418, 569, 648
Serzhputovsky, A. O. (General), 88, 102
Serzhputovsky, O. A. (Oska) 88–9, 95
Seuron, Anna, 213, 221, 409
Severnaya, M.
 A Woman's Lot, 209
Shabunin, V., 582
Shakespeare, William, 68, 149, 428, 436, 447, 484, 557, 565
 Antony and Cleopatra, 144–5
 Coriolanus, 187
 Hamlet, 129, 185
 Henry IV, 125, 187
 King Lear, 126
 Midsummer Night's Dream, 147
Shakhovskoy, D. I., 223, 398
Shaw, George Bernard, 579, 649, 653
Shcherbatov, P. A., 21
Shcherbatova, P. S., 147–8
Shestov, L. I., 649
Shevich, Lydia D., 112–4, 126–8
Shishkina, M. M. (Masha), 26, 276
Shor, D. S., 327

Shostak, Yekaterina N., 113, 143
Shubin, 88, 95
Sienkiewicz, Henryk,
 Without Dogma, 279, 286
Škarvan, A. A., 400, 420–1, 427
Skowaroda, G. S., 567
Slavophiles, Slavophilism, 112, 115, 147, 152, 264, 288, 294, 504, 536, 605
Sleptsov, V. A.,
 Hard Times, 273
Sobolev, A. I., 46, 56
Socrates, 10, 82, 205, 283, 484, 562, 567, 637
Sokolov, Father Johann, 127
Sokovnin, A. N., 113
Sologub, F.,
 The White Birch Tree, 636
Solovyov, S. M., 149
Solovyov, V. S., 199, 205, 210, 242, 247, 317, 402, 406, 562
Sopotsko, M. A., 423
Spencer, Herbert, 302, 412, 484, 518
Spinoza, Benedict de, 188, 519, 531, 562
Spir, Afrikan A., 425, 428
Sri Sankara, 673, 686
Stadling, J., 317, 398
Stakhovich, A. A., 128, 207, 232, 626
Stakhovich, M. A., 274, 282, 292, 497, 553, 579, 584, 621, 649
Stakhovich, Sofya A. (Zosya), 461, 603–4, 619, 626, 638–9, 664, 682
Stakhoviches (family), 256, 292, 445, 584, 651
Stasov, V. V., 433, 454, 474
Sterne, Laurence, 29, 31, 35, 50–1
 A Sentimental Journey, 644
 Tristram Shandy, 52
Stolypin, A. A., 93–5, 101, 105–6, 125, 128, 185
Stolypin, D. A.,
 Two Philosophies, 232
Stolypin, P. A., 569, 577, 579, 594, 598, 601, 603, 606, 612, 616, 620, 629
Storozhenko, N. I., 208, 243, 275, 452
Stowe, Harriet Beecher, 136
 Uncle Tom's Cabin, 94, 337
Strakhov, F. A., 508, 534, 608, 610–1, 638, 651, 660, 665
Strakhov, N. N., 208–10, 233, 252, 256, 258, 285–8, 306, 319, 321, 326, 336, 340, 403, 409, 413, 422–3, 458, 675
Struve, P. B., 626, 635
Styka, Jan, 622
Sue, Eugène,

750　　　　　　　　　　　　　　　　Index

The Wandering Jew, 51, 204
Sukhotin, A. M., 115, 185, 195
Sukhotin, M. M., 144–6, 149, 152
Sukhotin, M. S., 212, 223, 446, 472, 485, 508, 573, 588, 607, 610, 615, 617, 627, 638, 650, 655, 682
Sukhotin, S. M., 115
Sukhotina, T. L., *see* Tolstaya, Tatyana Lvovna
Sulerzhitsky, L. A. (Suller), 421–2, 427, 461, 463, 501
Sulimovsky, M. I., 46, 60, 66, 78, 81, 85
Sultanov, P. A., 46, 80, 82
Sunderland, J. T.,
　The Bible, its Origin, Growth and Character, 592
Sutkovoy, N. G., 560, 568, 574, 662
Suttner, B. von,
　Lay Down Your Arms, 315
Suvorin, A. S., 165–6, 239, 243, 273, 301
Suvorov, I. V. (Vanyushka), 39, 61, 67
Sverbeyeva, Y. A., 146–7, 193
Swift, Jonathan, 434
Sytin, I. D., 630, 659
Sytin, S. D., 233–4
Syutayev, V. K., 199, 576, 675

Tolstoy, Lev Nikolayevich, works:
　After the Ball, 509–11
　Albert (The Lost One, The Musician), 128–9, 131, 134–7, 142, 144–5, 147–8
　Alyosha Gorshok (Alyosha the Jug), 535
　Anna Karenina, 300
　Appeal to the Russian People (To the Government, the Revolutionaries and the People), 544–8, 554
　Berries, 539
　Bethink Yourselves! (On War), 517–21, 523
　Boyhood, 63, 67–74, 77–8, 80, 82, 85–7, 94, 114, 430
　Captive in the Caucasus, A, 640
　Carthago delenda est, 434, 457
　Childhood, 22, 47–54, 57, 60, 62, 67, 69, 94, 114, 126, 161
　Christian Teaching (The Catechism), 332–3, 338, 343, 398, 400–2, 411, 420–1, 424–5, 427–9, 431, 629
　Christianity and Patriotism (Toulon), 327, 329–30, 332, 335
　Christmas Night, 65, 67
　Conversation with a Passer-by, A (A Passer-by and a Peasant), 631, 633–5, 637, 644
　Cossacks, The (The Cossack, The Fugitive), 62, 69, 71–2, 81, 111, 117–9, 129, 133–5, 137, 139, 141–2, 144, 147–54, 158, 162, 168, 175, 184–6
　Cycle of Reading, A, 204, 528–31, 534–6, 542, 546–8, 552–3, 556, 558, 561, 564, 569, 579, 610, 618, 622, 629, 636, 647, 676, 682
　Death of Ivan Ilich, The, 212, 280
　Death Penalty and Christianity, The, 594, 598, 601
　Destruction of Hell and its Rebuilding (The Devil in Hell), 401, 452, 454, 504
　Devil, The, (Friedrichs), 269–70, 283, 603, 613
　Divine and the Human, The, 514–5, 518–9, 521, 525, 543–4
　Dream, A (Conversation at Dinner), 639, 643–6
　Dream of a Young Tsar, The, 343
　End of the World, The (The Tower of Siloam), 539–44
　Esarhaddon, King of Assyria, 510
　Family Happiness, 141, 154
　Family of the Gentry, A, 111, 117, 126
　Father Sergey, 266, 276, 284, 288, 290–1, 295–6, 300, 308–10, 312, 315, 401–2, 452, 458–60
　Father Vasily (Vasily of Mozhaisk), 556–8, 560
　First Distiller, The, 249
　First Step, The (Gluttony), 284, 286, 309, 312
　For Every Day (A New Cycle of Reading), 549, 561–2, 564–8, 570–1, 573–9, 581, 585, 588, 590–3, 601, 614, 619, 622, 628, 637, 640–3, 647–8, 650, 654, 659
　Forged Coupon, The, 300, 312, 401, 449, 452, 473, 503, 513–7
　Four Periods of Growth, 33, 38, 63
　Fruits of Enlightenment, The, 244–5, 255, 272–6, 279, 282, 301, 306, 317, 340
　Great Sin, A (Defenders of the People), 537–9, 541–2
　Green Stick, The (Who am I?), 530, 535–6, 543–4
　Hadji-Murat, 429, 431–2, 443, 447–50, 452–4, 457, 492–4, 501–2, 504, 508, 510, 518
　Help! 435
　History of Yesterday, A, 25
　How to Read the Gospels, and what their Essential Nature is, 429

Index

Hunting Ground, The, 121, 129, 138, 139, 141–2, 185
I Cannot Be Silent (Thou Shalt Not Kill), 479, 484, 583–5, 588
Idyll, An, 157–8, 160
Inevitable Revolution, The (The Revolution of Consciousness), 607–9, 611, 614–5, 617
Issue of a Newspaper, An, 230, 601, 603–4
It is Time to Understand (Anarchism), 633–4, 640, 642
Journey to Mamakay Yurt, A, 61
Karma, foreword to, 342
Khodynka, 649
Kill no man, 569–70
Kingdom of God is Within You, The, 296–7, 299–300, 303–4, 306–7, 313–20, 322–5, 327, 620
Korney Vasilyev, 452, 535, 608
Kreutzer Sonata, The, 245, 251, 253–9, 261, 263–5, 267–8, 272, 274–9, 283, 287, 291, 300–1, 308, 315, 323, 487
Landowner's Morning, A (see The Novel of a Russian Landowner), 126
Law of Violence and the Law of Love, The (There's an End to Everything), 579–80, 582–3, 585–6, 588, 661
Letter to a Student about the Law, A, 609–10
Letter to an Indian, 585, 592–4, 604, 610, 633, 651
Light Shineth in Darkness, The, 312, 322, 340, 401, 421–3, 426, 432, 439, 445, 482, 486, 503, 543
Living Corpse, A, 330, 453, 476, 478–82, 484, 486–7, 489
Lucerne, 138
Master and Man, 338, 343, 398, 400–3
Meeting a Moscow Acquaintance in the Detachment (Reduced to the Ranks), 81, 124–5
Memoirs, 506, 513, 522, 526, 530–1, 544–5
Monk Iliodor, The, 598, 600–1, 606
Mother (Notes of a Mother), 306–7, 401, 452
Murderers (The Lost One), 594–5
Must it be so? 482–4
Nicholas Stick (Nikolay Palkin), 305
No one is to blame, 595
Non-action, 324–5, 327
Notes of a Billiard Marker, 72, 74, 87, 102
Notes for Officers, 496
Notes for Soldiers, 440, 493–4, 496

Notes of a Madman (Notes not of a Madman), 207, 212, 300, 438–9
Novel of a Russian Landowner, The (see A Landowner's Morning), 52, 58–61, 63–4, 71, 76, 82–4, 88, 106, 117, 124–5
On Art, 244, 253, 256, 299, 324
On Education, 609–11, 614
On Insanity, 660–1, 665, 679
On 'Landmarks', 610, 612, 614
On Life, 230, 244, 245, 268, 441, 548, 616
On Science, 619–20, 625–6, 640, 643
On Shakespeare and the Drama, 511–3, 516
On Socialism, 672–5, 677
On the Famine, 314–5
On the Meaning of the Russian Revolution (Two Ways), 549, 552–4, 556, 558–9
On the State (The Police-constable), 606, 613
On War, 626
On What People Call Art, 433
One Commandment, The (On Love), 612–3, 615–9, 625
One Good Turn Deserves Another, 651–2, 656–8
One Thing Needful, The (The Stone, The Corner-stone), 513, 516, 519, 521–2, 525, 529–31, 533–6, 541
Only Way, The (see To the Working People), 495–6, 662
Patriotism and the Government, 476–7
Patriotism or Peace? 422
Pavlusha (Pavel, Who are the Murderers?), 598, 604, 606, 608
Polikushka, 161, 174, 640
Posthumous Notes of Fyodor Kuzmich, (Alexander I), 300, 312, 401, 452, 543–6
Power of Darkness, The, 276, 419–20, 487
Practical Person, A, 111, 117, 126, 129
Prayer, 514, 537
Primer, 404, 589
Punishments in the Army, 112
Raid, The (A Letter from the Caucasus), 49–50, 52–4, 57–8, 61, 63–4, 81, 94
Religion and Morality, 326
Reply to a Polish Lady, A, 628–9, 631
Resurrection (Koni's story), 239, 272–4, 277, 285–6, 298, 300, 308, 310, 401, 407, 409–11, 413, 415–20, 423, 426–8, 432, 439, 452, 460–3, 467–70, 472–3, 479, 486–7, 524–6

Science and Art, 263
Sevastopol in August, 107–8, 124
Sevastopol in December, 103–6
Sevastopol in May (A Spring Night), 103–5, 107
Shame, 420
Slavery of Our Times, The (On the 36-hour Day), 474, 476–9
Snowstorm, The, 86, 111, 124
Strider, 116, 176–7
Summer in the Country, A, 151–2
There are no Guilty People in the World, 610, 612, 616–7, 619, 655, 669
Three Days in the Country (Poverty, The Living and the Dying), 640, 642–4, 646–7
Three Deaths, 146–7, 150–1
Three Fables, 327, 400
Three Questions, 510, 542
Thoughts of Wise People for Every Day, 515–6, 547
Time to Come to our Senses, 250
To the Clergy, 502–3
To the Working People (see The Only Way), 495, 500–1, 506, 508–9
To the Young (Have Faith in Yourselves), 560
Two Hussars (Father and Son), 111–14
Uncle's Blessing, 122
War and Peace (1805), 181–7, 594
Way of Life, The, 648–55, 657–8, 660, 662, 666, 669
What for? 548, 552
What I Believe, 204, 207, 222, 234, 242, 296–7, 424
What I Dreamed About, 560
What is Art? 426, 445–8, 451–6
What is Religion and what is its Essential Nature? 485, 494, 496–8
What is the Way Out? 482
What is to be done? 557, 560–1
What Men Live By, 250
What Then Must We Do? 206, 211–2, 216, 240, 245
Who is Right? 315, 401, 420
Why Do Men Stupefy Themselves? 253, 282, 288
Wisdom of Children, The, 602, 603–4, 606, 608, 610–1, 640, 658, 660, 683
Wood-felling, The (Notes of a Bombardier), 69, 71, 81, 83–5, 88–92, 94, 105–6
Work, Death and Sickness, 510
Yasnaya Polyana School in November and December, 163
Youth, 67, 101–4, 106–8, 111, 117, 119, 121–3, 126, 129
Taine, Hippolyte, 527
Taneyev, S. I., 246, 415, 427, 430
Taoism, 607
Thiers, Adolphe, 46
Thackeray, William Makepeace, 85
  Henry Esmond, 104
  Pendennis, 105
  The Newcomes, 119, 284
  Vanity Fair, 104
Thoreau, Henry, 507
Thousand and One Nights, The, 471
Tikhon Zadonsky, 264
Timm, V. F., 113
Tocqueville, Alexis de, 134, 540
Tokutomi, Kenjiro, 548, 553
Tolstaya, Alexandra Andreyevna (Granny), 113, 133–4, 139, 143–5, 148–50, 210, 213, 216, 251–2, 519, 650–1
Tolstaya, Alexandra Lvovna (Sasha; Tolstoy's daughter), 218, 265, 319, 332, 407, 415, 418–9, 459, 487, 495–7, 518, 522, 534, 539, 548, 555, 559, 568, 571, 579, 581, 583–4, 596–7, 606–7, 609, 611–2, 619, 625–7, 629–30, 634, 636–8, 642, 646–9, 652–5, 657–8, 660, 662, 665–7, 669–74, 676–87
Tolstaya, Marya Lvovna (Masha, Tolstoy's daughter), 194, 215, 217, 219–20, 222–3, 233, 236, 239–40, 244, 248, 250, 252, 256–8, 260, 276, 279, 284, 288, 292–3, 295–6, 298–9, 301, 307, 310, 314, 318, 322, 324–7, 329, 331–2, 336–7, 339–40, 342, 402–3, 406, 415–6, 421, 423, 425, 427, 434–5, 444, 450, 458–9, 461–4, 468–70, 472, 474, 476, 478, 481–2, 485–6, 496–8, 511, 518, 523, 535, 541–2, 544, 554–5, 560–1
Tolstaya Marya Nikolayevna (Masha; Mashenka; Tolstoy's sister), 26, 57, 67, 70–2, 82, 87, 102–3, 116, 120–2, 124, 140, 142, 144, 146–9, 152, 154–6, 158, 160, 165, 179–80, 193, 213–4, 274, 278, 415, 460, 496, 500, 624, 626, 628, 676
Tolstaya Sofya Andreyevna, *née* Behrs (Tolstoy's wife), 164–9, 174–86, 192, 196, 198, 205, 207, 211–3, 215–25, 232–4, 237–8, 240, 243–4, 246, 251, 253–8, 260–1, 263, 265–6, 270,

272–3, 276, 279–80, 284–6, 288–93, 295, 297–9, 301, 303–7, 309, 312–9, 324–7, 329–37, 339–43, 398–410, 412, 414–5, 418–23, 426, 430–3, 435, 438–42, 444, 446–53, 456–8, 460–70, 480–2, 488, 495, 516, 527, 529, 534, 537–9, 548, 555–6, 566, 571–2, 578, 581, 584, 586–7, 592–4, 596–7, 600–1, 605, 608–9, 611–5, 617, 620–2, 624–6, 629, 631–6, 638–40, 643, 648, 653, 655, 657–87
Tolstaya, Tatyana Lvovna (Tanya; Tolstoy's daughter), 196–7, 199, 204–5, 207–9, 211–2, 215, 218–24, 233–4, 238, 243, 248–9, 251, 253, 257, 263, 270–1, 274–6, 278, 282, 290, 294, 296, 301, 303, 307, 310, 312, 314, 317–9, 326–7, 329–32, 337–42, 398, 401, 403, 410, 415, 418, 424, 429–30, 434, 439, 441, 443–4, 446, 449–52, 454, 458–9, 462–4, 468–70, 472, 477–80, 482, 484, 486, 488, 491, 494, 497–8, 500, 508, 542, 544, 553, 565–6, 569, 571, 573, 584, 588, 607, 610–1, 617, 619, 621, 650, 655–6, 658, 660, 663–5, 672, 677, 680–1, 685–7
Tolstoy, Andrey Lvovich (Andryusha; Tolstoy's son), 193, 231, 284, 286, 306, 309, 313, 322, 331, 334, 336, 338, 408–10, 414–9, 421–2, 425, 432, 434, 446, 462, 468–70, 472, 476, 480–2, 513, 522, 525, 528, 548, 552, 554–5, 559, 567–9, 575–6, 578, 583, 595, 599, 606, 611, 633, 636, 642–3, 655, 664, 675–7
Tolstoy, Dmitry Nikolayevich (Mitya, Mitenka; Tolstoy's brother), 40, 87–8, 108, 111
Tolstoy Ilya Lvovich (Tolstoy's son), 192, 213, 216, 218, 220, 222, 250, 255, 274, 279, 292, 300, 306–7, 311, 320, 329–30, 402, 412, 417, 421, 431, 433, 439, 446, 458–9, 469, 488, 502, 536, 538, 544, 552, 634
Tolstoy, Ivan Lvovich (Vanechka; Tolstoy's son), 237–8, 255, 260–1, 305–6, 332, 398, 401–2, 405, 409, 418
Tolstoy, Lev Lvovich (Lyova; Tolstoy's son), 216, 218, 230–2, 234, 236, 238, 242, 252–3, 256–8, 261, 263, 265, 269, 273, 280, 282, 292, 294, 296, 299, 304, 307, 309, 313, 316–20, 322, 326–7, 329–32, 334–5, 337, 340, 342–3, 400, 408, 411, 431, 433–4, 444, 448–50, 458–9, 462, 480, 485, 487–8, 503, 534, 536, 539, 564, 566, 608, 616–7, 662–4, 677–9
Tolstoy, Mikhail Lvovich (Misha; Tolstoy's son), 209–10, 232, 236, 266, 306, 313, 322, 331, 334, 338, 412, 414–5, 419–20, 425, 444, 446, 459, 462–3, 468, 491, 509, 539, 555, 583, 592, 604, 609, 654
Tolstoy, Nikolay Nikolayevich (Nikolenka; Tolstoy's brother), 22, 24, 26, 27, 31–4, 38, 43, 45–52, 57, 59, 60, 62–5, 67, 69–71, 85–7, 103, 118, 127, 142, 145–6, 148, 150–1, 157–8, 167, 185, 401, 546
Tolstoy, N. S., 144
Tolstoy, Sergey Lvovich (Seryozha; Tolstoy's son), 182–3, 185, 192, 194, 196–7, 204, 212–3, 216–7, 219–20, 222–3, 242, 248, 278, 285, 289, 292, 300, 307, 314, 320, 331, 335, 340–2, 403, 407, 409–11, 413, 415, 421, 428, 431–2, 435, 439, 446, 457, 462–3, 469, 472, 474–5, 477–8, 480–1, 485, 496, 501, 515, 534, 538, 548, 552, 555, 576–8, 581, 585, 609, 614–5, 622, 624, 629, 638, 646, 652, 657, 659, 661–2, 664, 666, 671, 675–7
Tolstoy, Sergey Nikolayevich (Tolstoy's brother), 26, 48, 56, 67–8, 70, 75, 86–8, 120–1, 123, 131–2, 140–2, 144–7, 152, 157, 161, 167–8, 176, 179, 182, 184–5, 204–5, 207, 210–11, 213, 223, 291, 406–7, 427, 429–30, 460, 464, 470, 482, 486, 511–2, 523–4, 526–8
Tolstoy, Valeryan Petrovich (Tolstoy's brother-in-law), 26, 46, 57, 70–2, 82, 86–7, 102–3, 111, 116, 120, 122, 127, 140
Tonilov, L. V. (Lev Ryzhy), 598, 644
Torelli-Viollier, Maria, *The Beauty*, 313
Totleben, E. I., 97, 100, 133
Tregubov, I. M., 317, 407, 415, 434, 452, 454, 460, 497, 552, 612, 614
Tretyakov, P. M., 209, 243
Trollope, Anthony, *The Bertrams*, 185
Trubetskaya, Y. N., 131–3, 144
Trubetskoy, P. P., 658
Trubetskoy, S. N., 267, 452
Trusson, F. I., 114

Tsezarkhan (Groman, ensign), 60, 69
Turgenev, A. M., 113
Turgenev, I. S., 74, 102–3, 108, 111–12, 114, 116, 120–4, 126–34, 136, 139–41, 149, 151–2, 160, 162, 198–9, 213, 557, 616
  A Sportsman's Sketches, 71
  An Outing to the Woods, 225
  Asya, 146
  Breakfast with the Marshal of the Nobility, 309
  Enough, 321
  Faust, 123
  Hamlet and Don Quixote, 321, 535
  Pasynkov, 225
  The Diary of a Superfluous Man, 114
Turgenev, N. N., 122,
Turgeneva, O. A., 113, 124, 127–8, 152
Turner, C. E., 335
Tyutchev, F. I., 484
Tyutcheva, Y. F., 129, 144–7, 149, 152, 167
Tyutchevs, 165, 167

Ukhtomsky, e. E., 459
Urusov, L. D., 193–4, 205, 207, 212, 216, 219, 221, 223, 237, 244–5, 255, 257–8, 290, 296
Usov, S. A., 211–3, 406
Uspensky, N. V., 250
Ustryalov, N. G.,
  Russian History, 81

Van der Veer, J., 431, 433
Velikanov, P. V., 335, 546, 552, 558, 626
Venevitinov, M. A., 192
Vengerov, S. A., 404
Verdi, Giuseppe,
  Rigoletto, 131–2
Veresayev, V. V., 656
Vergani, Jenny, 86, 116, 118–23, 129
Verigin, P. V., 431, 503
Verne, Jules, 189
Veselitskaya, L. I., 413, 483
Viardot, Pauline, 130, 133
Vivekananda, Swami, 580, 587–8, 607
Vogué, Melchior de, 272
Volkonskaya, L. I., 42, 88, 97, 111
Voltaire, François-Marie Arouet de, 240
  Zadig, 239
Vorontsov, M. S., 30, 68
Vostorgov, I. I.,
  Signs of the Times, 612
Vyazemsky, K. A., 312

Vyazemsky, P. A., 127

Wagner, Wilhelm Richard, 259, 386, 484
Waliszewski, K., 564
Wallace, Lewis,
  Ben Hur, 239
Ward, Mrs Humphry,
  Robert Elsmere, 236, 238
Warren, Samuel, 68
Weismann, A., 414
Welsh, Hannah, 335
Westerners, Westernism, 115, 149
Whitman, Walt, 239, 252, 266
Williams, F. W.,
  True son of Liberty, 327
Williams, H.,
  Ethics of Diet, 307
Wipper, R. Y., 657
Wiseman, N., 150
Witte, S. Y., 434, 490
Wundt, Wilhelm, 477

Xenophon,
  Memorabilia, 564

Yakovleva, P. V., 20
Yanovich, (Ensign), 45–7, 65
Yanzhul, I. I., 236, 242–3, 248, 279
Yaroshenko, N. A., 243, 441
Yepishka (Yepifan Sekhin), 36–8, 62, 66, 69–70, 72, 75, 77–8, 80, 83–4, 148
Yergolskaya, Tatyana Alexandrovna (Auntie), 19, 25, 26, 48, 50, 53, 70, 82, 87–9, 101, 103, 111, 113, 116, 118, 121–4, 127, 133, 135, 141–2, 145–9, 152, 161, 164, 168–9, 176–7, 179–80, 514
Yermak, 51
Yermolov, A. P., 36, 49
Yershov, A. I., 144
  Sevastopol Memoirs, 236–7, 239, 242
Yuryev, S. A., 197, 206
Yushkova, Pelageya Ilinichna (Aunt Polina), 87–8, 108, 111, 179

Zagoskin, S. M., 115
Zdziechowski, M. E., 415, 423
Zhemchuzhnikov, A. M., 129
Zhukevich-Stosh, M. P., 67, 85
Zhukova, M. S.,
  Nadenka, 73
Zinger, A. V., 274, 629, 637
Zlatovratsky, N. N., 206, 237, 248
Zola, Émile, 323–4

Zolotaryov, V. P., 259, 314
Zotov, V. R.,
  The Old House, 50
Zschokke, Johann H. D.,
  Hours of Devotion, 54

Zuyev, V. Y., 76, 82
Zyabrev, O. N., 86, 117
Zyabrev, P. O., 218
Zyabrev, V. Y., 140, 142, 151, 168